THE REVISION REVISED.

THE REVISION REVISED.

THREE ARTICLES

REPRINTED FROM THE 'QUARTERLY REVIEW'.

I. THE NEW GREEK TEXT.
II. THE NEW ENGLISH VERSION.
III. WESTCOTT AND HORT'S NEW TEXTUAL THEORY.

TO WHICH IS ADDED A

REPLY TO BISHOP ELLICOTT'S PAMPHLET

IN DEFENCE OF

THE REVISERS AND THEIR GREEK TEXT OF THE NEW TESTAMENT:

INCLUDING A VINDICATION OF THE TRADITIONAL READING
OF 1 TIMOTHY III. 16.

BY JOHN WILLIAM BURGON, B.D.

DEAN OF CHICHESTER.

"It is happened unto them according to the true proverb, Κύων ἐπί-
στρέψας ἐπὶ τὸ ἴδιον ἐξέραμα · and, ˊΥς λουσαμένη εἰς κύλισμα βορβόρου."
—2 PETER ii. 22.
"Little children,—Keep yourselves from idols."—1 JOHN v. 21.

2nd Printing, September, 1, 2000

DEAN BURGON SOCIETY PRESS
Box 354
Collingswood, New Jersey 08108
www.DeanBurgonSociety.org
ISBN 1-888328-01-0

Foreword

The Publishers. This book, *The Revision Revised*, is published by the Dean Burgon Society, Incorporated (DBS). The Society takes its name from Dean John William Burgon (1813-1888), a conservative Anglican clergyman. The DBS is recognized by the I.R.S. as a non-profit, tax exempt organization. All contributions are tax deductible. The Society's main purpose is stated in its slogan, **"IN DEFENSE OF TRADITIONAL BIBLE TEXTS."** The DBS was founded in 1978, and, since then, has held its annual two-day conference in the United States and Canada. During this time, many excellent messages on textual issues are presented. The messages are available in three forms: (1) video cassettes; (2) audio cassettes, and (3) the printed message book. For information on receiving any of the above, plus a copy of the *"THE ARTICLES OF FAITH, AND ORGANIZATION"* of the Dean Burgon Society, please write or phone its office at **609-854-4452**. You may use your CREDIT CARD if you wish, and send your order by **FAX** at **609-854-2464** or by **E-Mail** at **DBSN@Juno.Com**.

The Dean Burgon News. The Society has a paper called *The Dean Burgon News*. Within its pages the Society proclaims:

"The DEAN BURGON SOCIETY, INCORPORATED proudly takes its name in honor of John William Burgon (1813-1888), the Dean of Chichester in England, whose tireless and accurate scholarship and contribution in the area of New Testament Textual Criticism; whose defense of the Traditional Greek Text against its many enemies; and whose firm belief in the verbal inspiration and inerrancy of the Bible, we believe, have all been unsurpassed either before or since his time!"

The Present Reprint. The DEAN BURGON SOCIETY, INCORPORATED is pleased to present, in this form, one of Dean John William Burgon's most convincing books, *The Revision Revised*. This is the second reprint of one of Dean Burgon's books, the first one being *The Last Twelve Verses of Mark*. [It is available as #1139 for a GIFT of $15 + $3 for postage and handling.] This edition of *The Revision Revised* is page for page like the original book written in 1883 by Dean Burgon. In the **APPENDIX** you will find a 36-page summarization of the main points brought out in the book. You might want to begin by reading the **APPENDIX** first.

The Importance of *The Revision Revised*. There is no one book that exposes Westcott and Hort's false Greek text and false Greek theory behind that text any more thoroughly and convincingly than *The Revision Revised*. Dean Burgon defends the traditional text of the New Testament. He also shows clearly the defects in both manuscript "B" (Vatican) and manuscript "Aleph" (Sinai). It is very important to see the arguments contained in this historic volume because virtually the same Greek text of Westcott and Hort (1881) forms the basis of almost all of the modern versions and perversions. As proof of this, you can turn to **APPENDIX pages 2-3** for seven quotes that tie the Westcott and Hort's Greek text to the Greek texts of Nestle-Aland and the United Bible Society.

The Reason Modern Revised Greek Texts Are Like Westcott and Hort's Text. It is very easy to understand why the 1881 Greek Text of Westcott and Hort is almost the same as that of the modern revised Greek texts such as Nestle-Aland, United Bible Society and others. Both groups (Westcott and Hort and modern textual revisers) draw largely, if not exclusively, on the false readings of manuscripts "B" (Vatican) and "Aleph" (Sinai). It is axiomatic that "things equal to the same thing are equal to each other."

Other Books by Dean Burgon. For those wanting to read four other excellent reprints (all but #1 are presently in xeroxed format), the following can be ordered from THE DEAN BURGON SOCIETY:

1. *The Last Twelve Verses of Mark, 400 pages* for a gift of **$15.00**.
2. *The Traditional Text of the Holy Gospels*, 350 pages for a gift of **$15.00**..
3. *Causes of Corruption of the Holy Gospels*, 316 pages for a gift of **$14.00**...
4. *Inspiration and Interpretation*, 567 pages for a gift of **$25.00**.

Please add **$5.00** for postage and handling when you order.

Future Reprints. As funds permit, the DEAN BURGON SOCIETY hopes to bring into reprint form in the same way as this present book many, if not all of the above titles.

Sincerely for God's Written Words,

D. A. Waite

DAW/w`

Rev. D. A. Waite, Th.D., Ph.D.
President, THE DEAN BURGON SOCIETY ·

**The
Dean Burgon
Society**
In Defense of Traditional Bible Texts
Box 354
Collingswood, New Jersey 08108, U.S.A.

John William Burgon (1813-1888)

The following is PREBENDARY SCRIVENER'S *recently published estimate of the System on which* DRS. WESTCOTT AND HORT *have constructed their* 'Revised Greek Text of the New Testament' (1881). — *That System, the Chairman of the Revising Body* (BISHOP ELLICOTT) *has entirely adopted* (*see below, pp.* 391 *to* 397), *and made the basis of his Defence of* THE REVISERS *and their* 'New Greek Text.'

(1.) " There is little hope for the stability of their imposing structure, if *its foundations have been laid on the sandy ground of ingenious conjecture.* And, since barely the smallest vestige of historical evidence has ever been alleged in support of the views of these accomplished Editors, their teaching must either be received as intuitively true, or *dismissed from our consideration as precarious and even visionary.*"

(2.) " DR. HORT'S System *is entirely destitute of historical foundation.*"

(3.) " We are compelled to repeat as emphatically as ever our strong conviction that the Hypothesis to whose proof he has devoted so many laborious years, *is destitute not only of historical foundation, but of all probability, resulting from the internal goodness of the Text which its adoption would force upon us.*"

(4.) " ' We cannot doubt' (says DR. HORT) 'that S. Luke xxiii. 34 comes from an extraneous source.' [*Notes,* p. 68.]—*Nor can we, on our part, doubt,*" (rejoins DR. SCRIVENER,) " *that the System which entails such consequences is hopelessly self-condemned.*"

SCRIVENER'S 'Plain Introduction,' &c. [ed. 1883]: pp. 531, 537, 542, 604.

TO THE

RIGHT HON. VISCOUNT CRANBROOK, G.C.S.I.,

&c., &c., &c.

My dear Lord Cranbrook,

Allow me the gratification of dedicating the present Volume to yourself; but for whom—(I reserve the explanation for another day)—it would never have been written.

This is not, (as you will perceive at a glance,) the Treatise which a few years ago I told you I had in hand ; and which, but for the present hindrance, might by this time have been completed. It has however grown out of that other work in the manner explained at the beginning of my Preface. Moreover it contains not a few specimens of the argumentation of which the work in question, when at last it sees the light, will be discovered to be full.

My one object has been to defeat the mischievous attempt which was made in 1881 to thrust upon this Church and Realm a Revision of the Sacred Text, which—recommended though it be by eminent names—I am thoroughly convinced, and am able to prove, is untrustworthy from beginning to end.

The reason is plain. It has been constructed throughout on an utterly erroneous hypothesis. And I inscribe this Volume to you, my friend, as a conspicuous member of that body of faithful and learned Laity by whose deliberate verdict, when the whole of the evidence has been produced and the case has been fully argued out, I shall be quite willing that my contention may stand or fall.

The English (*as well as the Greek*) *of the newly " Revised Version " is hopelessly at fault. It is to me simply unintelligible how a company of Scholars can have spent ten years in elaborating such a very unsatisfactory production. Their uncouth phraseology and their jerky sentences, their pedantic obscurity and their unidiomatic English, contrast painfully with " the happy turns of expression, the music of the cadences, the felicities of the rhythm" of our Authorized Version. The transition from one to the other, as the Bishop of Lincoln remarks, is like exchanging a well-built carriage for a vehicle without springs, in which you get jolted to death on a newly-mended and rarely-traversed road. But the " Revised Version " is inaccurate as well ; exhibits defective scholarship, I mean, in countless places.*

It is, however, the systematic depravation of the underlying Greek *which does so grievously offend me : for this is nothing else but a poisoning of the River of Life at its sacred source. Our Revisers, (with the best and purest intentions, no doubt,) stand convicted of having deliberately rejected the words of*

Inspiration in every page, and of having substituted for them fabricated Readings which the Church has long since refused to acknowledge, or else has rejected with abhorrence; and which only survive at this time in a little handful of documents of the most depraved type.

As Critics they have had abundant warning. Twelve years ago (1871) *a volume appeared on* 'the last Twelve Verses of the Gospel according to S. Mark,'—*of which the declared object was to vindicate those Verses against certain critical objectors, and to establish them by an exhaustive argumentative process. Up to this hour, for a very obvious reason, no answer to that volume has been attempted. And yet, at the end of ten years* (1881),—*not only in the Revised English but also in the volume which professes to exhibit the underlying Greek, (which at least is indefensible,)—the Revisers are observed to separate off those Twelve precious Verses from their context, in token that they are no part of the genuine Gospel. Such a deliberate preference of* 'mumpsimus' *to* 'sumpsimus' *is by no means calculated to conciliate favour, or even to win respect. The Revisers have in fact been the dupes of an ingenious Theorist, concerning whose extraordinary views you are invited to read what Dr. Scrivener has recently put forth. The words of the last-named writer (who is* facile princeps *in Textual Criticism) will be found facing the beginning of the present Dedication.*

If, therefore, any do complain that I have sometimes hit my opponents rather hard, I take leave to point out that "to every-

thing there is a season, and a time to every purpose under the sun" : *" a time to embrace, and a ti : to be far from embracing"* : *a time for speaking smoothly, and a time for speaking sharply. And that when the words of Inspiration are seriously imperilled, as now they are, it is scarcely possible for one who is determined effectually to preserve the Deposit in its integrity, to hit either too straight or too hard. In handling certain recent utterances of Bishop Ellicott, I considered throughout that it was* the ' Textual Critic,'—*not the Successor of the Apostles,—with whom I had to do.*

And thus I commend my Volume, the fruit of many years of incessant anxious toil, to your indulgence: requesting that you will receive it as a token of my sincere respect and admiration; and desiring to be remembered, my dear Lord Cranbrook, as

Your grateful and affectionate

Friend and Servant,

JOHN W. BURGON.

DEANERY, CHICHESTER,
  ALL SAINTS' DAY. 1883.

PREFACE.

THE ensuing three Articles from the 'Quarterly Review,' —(wrung out of me by the publication [May 17th, 1881] of the 'Revision' of our 'Authorized Version of the New Testament,')—appear in their present form in compliance with an amount of continuous solicitation that they should be separately published, which it would have been alike unreasonable and ungracious to disregard. I was not prepared for it. It has caused me—as letter after letter has reached my hands—mixed feelings; has revived all my original disinclination and regret. For, gratified as I cannot but feel by the reception my labours have met with,—(and only the Author of my being knows what an amount of antecedent toil is represented by the ensuing pages,)— I yet deplore more heartily than I am able to express, the injustice done to the cause of Truth by handling the subject in this fragmentary way, and by exhibiting the evidence for what is most certainly true, in such a very incomplete form. A systematic Treatise is the indispensable condition for securing cordial assent to the view for which I mainly contend. The cogency of the argument lies entirely in the cumulative character of the proof. It requires to be demonstrated by induction from a large collection of particular instances, as well as by the complex exhibition of many converging lines of evidence, that the testimony of one small group of documents, or rather, of one particular manuscript,—(namely the Vatican Codex B, which, for some unexplained reason, it is just now the fashion to regard with superstitious deference,) —is the reverse of trustworthy. Nothing in fact but a considerable Treatise will ever effectually break the yoke of that iron tyranny to which the excellent Bishop of Gloucester and Bristol and his colleagues have recently bowed their necks; and are now for imposing on all English-speaking men. In brief, if I were not, on the one hand, thoroughly convinced of the strength of my position,—(and I know it to be absolutely impregnable);—yet more, if on the other hand, I did not cherish entire confidence in the practical good sense and fairness of the English mind;—I could not have brought myself to come before the public in the unsystematic way which alone is possible in the pages of a Review. I must have waited, at all hazards, till I had finished ' my Book.'

But then, delay would have been fatal. I saw plainly that unless a sharp blow was delivered immediately, the Citadel would be in the enemy's hands. I knew also that it was just possible to condense into 60 or 70 closely-printed pages what must *logically* prove fatal to the ' Revision.' So I set to work; and during the long summer days of 1881 (June to September) the foremost of these three Articles was elaborated. When the October number of ' the Quarterly ' appeared, I comforted myself with the secret consciousness that enough was by this time on record, even had my life been suddenly brought to a close, to secure the ultimate re-jection of the ' Revision' of 1881. I knew that the ' New Greek Text,' (and therefore the ' New English Version '),

had received its death-blow. It might for a few years drag
out a maimed existence; eagerly defended by some,—timidly
pleaded for by others. But such efforts could be of no avail.
Its days were already numbered. The effect of more and
yet more learned investigation,—of more elaborate and more
extended inquiry,—*must* be to convince mankind more and
yet more thoroughly that the principles on which it had been
constructed were radically unsound. In the end, when parti-
sanship had cooled down, and passion had evaporated, and
prejudice had ceased to find an auditory, the 'Revision' of
1881 must come to be universally regarded as—what it most
certainly is,—*the most astonishing, as well as the most calamitous
literary blunder of the Age.*

I. I pointed out that 'the NEW GREEK TEXT,'—which, in
defiance of their instructions,[1] the Revisionists of 'the
Authorized English Version' had been so ill-advised as to
spend ten years in elaborating,—was a wholly untrustworthy
performance : was full of the gravest errors from beginning
to end: had been constructed throughout on an entirely
mistaken Theory. Availing myself of the published confession of one of the Revisionists,[2] I explained the nature of
the calamity which had befallen the Revision. I traced the
mischief home to its true authors,—Drs. Westcott and Hort;
a copy .of whose unpublished Text of the N. T. (the most
vicious in existence) had been confidentially, and under
pledges of the strictest secrecy, placed in the hands of every

---

[1] Any one who desires to see this charge established, is invited to read
from page 399 to page 413 of what follows.

[2] Dr. Newth. See pp. 37-9.

member of the revising Body.[1]   I called attention to the
fact that, unacquainted with the difficult and delicate science
of Textual Criticism, the Revisionists had, in an evil hour,
surrendered themselves to Dr. Hort's guidance : had preferred
his counsels to those of Prebendary Scrivener, (an infinitely
more trustworthy guide): and that the work before the
public was the piteous—but *inevitable*—result.   All this I
explained in the October number of the ' Quarterly Review '
for 1881.[2]

II. In thus demonstrating the worthlessness of the ' New
Greek Text' of the Revisionists, I considered that I had
destroyed the key of their position.   And so perforce I
had : for if the underlying Greek Text be mistaken, what
else but incorrect must the English Translation be ?   But on
examining the so-called ' Revision of the Authorized Version,' I speedily made the further discovery that the Revised
English would have been in itself intolerable, even had the
Greek been let alone.   In the first place, to my surprise and
annoyance, it proved to be *a New Translation* (rather than a
Revision of the Old) which had been attempted.   Painfully
apparent were the tokens which met me on every side
that the Revisionists had been supremely eager not so much
to correct none but " plain and clear errors,"—as to introduce
as many changes into the English of the New Testament
Scriptures as they conveniently could.[3]   A skittish impatience
of the admirable work before them, and a strange inability

---

[1] See pp. 24–9 : 97, &c.   [2] See below, pp. 1 to 110.
[3] This will be found more fully explained from pp. 127 to 130: pp. 154
to 164: also pp. 400 to 403.   See also the quotations on pp. 112 and 368.

to appreciate its manifold excellences :—a singular imagination on the part of the promiscuous Company which met in the Jerusalem Chamber that they were competent to improve the Authorized Version in every part, and an unaccountable forgetfulness that the fundamental condition under which the task of Revision had been by themselves undertaken, was that they should abstain from all but "*necessary*" changes :—*this* proved to be only part of the offence which the Revisionists had committed. It was found that they had erred through *defective Scholarship* to an extent, and with a frequency, which to me is simply inexplicable. I accordingly made it my business to demonstrate all this in a second Article which appeared in the next (the January) number of the 'Quarterly Review,' and was entitled 'THE NEW ENGLISH TRANSLATION.' [1]

III. Thereupon, a pretence was set up in many quarters, (*but only by the Revisionists and their friends,*) that all my labour hitherto had been thrown away, because I had omitted to disprove the principles on which this 'New Greek Text' is founded. I flattered myself indeed that quite enough had been said to make it logically certain that the underlying 'Textual Theory' *must be* worthless. But I was not suffered to cherish this conviction in quiet. It was again and again cast in my teeth that I had not yet grappled with Drs. Westcott and Hort's 'arguments.' " Instead of condemning *their Text*, why do you not disprove *their Theory ?*" It was tauntingly insinuated that I knew better than to cross swords

---

[1] See below, pp. 113 to 232.

with the two Cambridge Professors. This reduced me to the
necessity of either leaving it to be inferred from my silence
that I had found Drs. Westcott and Hort's 'arguments'
unanswerable; or else of coming forward with their book in
my hand, and demonstrating that in their solemn pages an
attentive reader finds himself encountered by nothing but a
series of unsupported assumptions: that their (so called)
'Theory' is in reality nothing else but a weak effort of the
Imagination: that the tissue which these accomplished
scholars have been thirty years in elaborating, proves on
inspection to be as flimsy and as worthless as any spider's
web.

I made it my business in consequence to expose, somewhat in detail, (in a third Article, which appeared in the
'Quarterly Review' for April 1882), the absolute absurdity,
—(I use the word advisedly)—of 'WESTCOTT AND HORT'S
NEW TEXTUAL THEORY;'[1] and I now respectfully commend
those 130 pages to the attention of candid and unprejudiced
readers. It were idle to expect to convince any others. We
have it on good authority (Dr. Westcott's) that "he who has
long pondered over a train of Reasoning, *becomes unable to
detect its weak points.*"[2] A yet stranger phenomenon is, that
those who have once committed themselves to an erroneous
Theory, seem to be incapable of opening their eyes to the
untrustworthiness of the fabric they have erected, even when
it comes down in their sight, like a child's house built with
playing-cards,—and presents to every eye but their own the
appearance of a shapeless ruin.

---

[1] See below, pp. 235 to 366.   [2] *Gospel of the Resurrection,* p. viii.

§ 1. Two full years have elapsed since the first of these Essays was published; and my Criticism—for the best of reasons — remains to this hour unanswered. The public has been assured indeed, (in the course of some hysterical remarks by Canon Farrar [1]), that "the 'Quarterly Reviewer' can be refuted as fully as he desires as soon as any scholar has the leisure to answer him." The 'Quarterly Reviewer' can afford to wait,—if the Revisers can. But they are reminded that it is no answer to one who has demolished their master's 'Theory,' for the pupils to keep on reproducing fragments of it; and by their mistakes and exaggerations, to make both themselves and him, ridiculous.

---

[1] Reference is made to a vulgar effusion in the '*Contemporary Review*' for March 1882: from which it chiefly appears that Canon (now Archdeacon) Farrar is unable to forgive S. Mark the Evangelist for having written the 16th verse of his concluding chapter. The Venerable writer is in consequence for ever denouncing those "*last Twelve Verses*." In March 1882, (pretending to review my Articles in the 'Quarterly,') he says:—" In spite of Dean Burgon's Essay on the subject, the minds of most scholars are *quite unalterably made up* on such questions as the authenticity of the last twelve verses of S. Mark." [*Contemporary Review*, vol. xli. p. 365.] And in the ensuing October,—" If, among *positive results*, any one should set down such facts as that ... Mark xvi. 9–20 ... *formed no part of the original apostolic autograph* ... He, I say, who should enumerate these points as being *beyond the reach of serious dispute* ... would be expressing the views which are *regarded as indisputable* by the vast majority of such recent critics as have established any claim to serious attention." [*Expositor*, p. 173.]

It may not be without use to the Venerable writer that he should be reminded that critical questions, instead of being disposed of by such language as the foregoing, are not even touched thereby. One is surprised to have to tell a " fellow of Trinity College, Cambridge," so obvious a truth as that by such writing he does but effectually put himself out of court. By proclaiming that his mind is "*quite unalterably made up*" that the end of S. Mark's Gospel is not authentic, he admits that he is impervious to argument and therefore incapable of understanding proof. It is a mere waste of time to reason with an unfortunate who announces that he is beyond the reach of conviction.

§ 2. Thus, a writer in the ' Church Quarterly ' for January
1882, (whose knowledge of the subject is entirely derived
from what Dr. Hort has taught him,)—being evidently
much exercised by the first of my three Articles in the
' Quarterly Review,'—gravely informs the public that "it is
useless to parade such an array of venerable witnesses,"
(meaning the enumerations of Fathers of the IIIrd, IVth, and
Vth centuries which are given below, at pp. 42–4: 80–1 :
84 : 133 : 212–3 : 359–60 : 421 : 423 : 486–90 :)—*"for they
have absolutely nothing to say which deserves a moment's hearing."* [1]—What a pity it is, (while he was about it), that
the learned gentleman did not go on to explain that the
moon is made of green cheese !

§ 3. Dr. Sanday,[2] in a kindred spirit, delivers it as his
opinion, that " the one thing " I lack " is a grasp on the
central condition of the problem : "—that I do " not seem to
have the faintest glimmering of the principle of ' Genealogy : ' "
—that I am " all at sea : "—that my " heaviest batteries are
discharged at random : "—and a great deal more to the same
effect. The learned Professor is quite welcome to think such
things of me, if he pleases. Οὐ φροντὶς Ἱπποκλείδῃ.

§ 4. At the end of a year, a Reviewer of quite a different
calibre made his appearance in the January number (1883)
of the ' Church Quarterly : ' in return for whose not very

---

[1] No. xxviii., page 436. If any one cares to know what the teaching
was which the writer in the ' Church Quarterly ' was intending to reproduce, he is invited to read from p. 296 to p. 300 of the present volume.
[2] *Contemporary Review*, (Dec. 1881),—p. 985 seq.

encouraging estimate of my labours, I gladly record my conviction that if he will seriously apply his powerful and accurate mind to the department of Textual Criticism, he will probably produce a work which will help materially to establish the study in which he takes such an intelligent interest, on a scientific basis. But then, he is invited to accept the friendly assurance that the indispensable condition of success in this department is, that a man should give to the subject, (which is a very intricate one and abounds in unexplored problems), his undivided attention for an extended period. I trust there is nothing unreasonable in the suggestion that one who has not done this, should be very circumspect when he sits in judgment on a neighbour of his who, for very many years past, has given to Textual Criticism the whole of his time;—has freely sacrificed health, ease, relaxation, even necessary rest, to this one object;—has made it his one business to acquire such an independent mastery of the subject as shall qualify him to do battle successfully for the imperilled letter of GOD's Word. My friend however thinks differently. He says of me,—

" In his first Article there was something amusing in the simplicity with which 'Lloyd's Greek Testament' (which is only a convenient little Oxford edition of the ordinary kind) was put forth as the final standard of appeal. It recalled to our recollection Bentley's sarcasm upon the text of Stephanus, which 'your learned Whitbyus' takes for the sacred original in every syllable." (P. 354.)

§ 5. On referring to the passage where my 'simplicity' has afforded amusement to a friend whose brilliant conversation is always a delight to *me*, I read as follows,—

"It is discovered that in the 111 (out of 320) pages of a copy of Lloyd's Greek Testament, in which alone these five manuscripts are collectively available for comparison in the Gospels, —the serious deflections of A from the *Textus Receptus* amount in all to only 842: whereas in c they amount to 1798: in B, to 2370: in ℵ, to 3392: in D, to 4697. The readings *peculiar to* A within the same limits are 133: those peculiar to c are 170. But those of B amount to 197: while ℵ exhibits 443: and the readings peculiar to D (within the same limits), are no fewer than 1829 . . . . We submit that these facts are not altogether calculated to inspire confidence in codices B ℵ C D."[1]

§ 6. But how (let me ask) does it appear from this, that I have "put forth Lloyd's Greek Testament as the *final standard of Appeal*"? True, that, in order to exhibit clearly their respective divergences, I have referred five famous codices (A B ℵ C D)—certain of which are found to have turned the brain of Critics of the new school—to *one and the same familiar exhibition of the commonly received Text of the New Testament:* but by so doing I have not by any means assumed *the Textual purity* of that common standard. In other words I have not made it "*the final standard of Appeal.*" *All* Critics,—wherever found,—at all times, have collated with the commonly received Text: but only as the most convenient *standard of Comparison ;* not, surely, as the

---

[1] Q. R. (No. 304,) p. 313.—The passage referred to will be found below (at p. 14),—slightly modified, in order to protect myself against the risk of *future* misconception. My Reviewer refers to four other places. He will find that my only object in them all was to prove that codices A B ℵ C D *yield divergent testimony ;* and therefore, so habitually *contradict* one another, as effectually to invalidate their own evidence throughout. This has never been *proved* before. It can *only* be proved, in fact, by one who has laboriously collated the codices in question, and submitted to the drudgery of exactly tabulating the result.

absolute *standard of Excellence.* The result of the experiment already referred to,—(and, I beg to say, it was an exceedingly laborious experiment,)—has been, to demonstrate that the five Manuscripts in question stand apart from one another in the following proportions :—

842 (A) : 1798 (C) : 2370 (B) : 3392 (ℵ) : 4697 (D).

But would not the same result have been obtained if the 'five old uncials' had been *referred to any other common standard which can be named ?* In the meantime, what else is the inevitable inference from this phenomenon but that four out of the five *must* be—while all the five *may* be— outrageously depraved documents ? instead of being fit to be made our exclusive guides to the Truth of Scripture,—as Critics of the school of Tischendorf and Tregelles would have us believe that they are ?

§ 7. I cited a book which is in the hands of every schoolboy, (Lloyd's 'Greek Testament,') *only* in order to facilitate reference, and to make sure that my statements would be at once understood by the least learned person who could be supposed to have access to the 'Quarterly.' I presumed every scholar to be aware that Bp. Lloyd (1827) professes to reproduce Mill's text; and that Mill (1707) reproduces the text of Stephens ;[1] and that Stephens (1550) exhibits with sufficient accuracy the Traditional text,—which is confessedly

---

[1] " Damus tibi in manus Novum Testamentum *idem profecto,* quod ad textum attinet, cum ed. Milliană,"—are the well known opening words of the 'Monitum' prefixed to Lloyd's N. T.—And Mill, according to Scrivener, [*Introduction,* p. 399,] "only aims at reproducing Stephens' text of 1550, though in a few places he departs from it, whether by accident or design." Such places are found to amount in all to *twenty-nine.*

at least 1530 years old.[1]   Now, if a tolerable approximation
to the text of A.D. 350 may *not* be accepted as *a standard of
Comparison,*—will the writer in the 'Church Quarterly' be
so obliging as to inform us *which* exhibition of the sacred
Text *may ?*

§ 8. A pamphlet by the Bishop of Gloucester and Bristol,[2]
which appeared in April 1882, remains to be considered.
Written expressly in defence of the Revisers and their New
Greek Text, this composition displays a slenderness of
acquaintance with the subject now under discussion, for
which I was little prepared.   Inasmuch however as it is the
production of the Chairman of the Revisionist body, and
professes to be a reply to my first two Articles, I have
bestowed upon it an elaborate and particular rejoinder
extending to an hundred-and-fifty pages.[3]   I shall in
consequence be very brief concerning it in this place.

§ 9. The respected writer does nothing else but reproduce
Westcott and Hort's theory *in Westcott and Hort's words.*
He contributes nothing of his own.   The singular infelicity
which attended his complaint that the 'Quarterly Reviewer'
"censures their [Westcott and Hort's] Text," but, "has not
attempted *a serious examination of the arguments which they
allege in its support,*" I have sufficiently dwelt upon elsewhere.[4]   The rest of the Bishop's contention may be summed

---

[1] See below, pp. 257–8 : also p. 390.
[2] *The Revisers and the Greek Text of the New Testament, &c.*—Macmillan, pp. 79.
[3] See below, pp. 369 to 520.   [4] Pages 371–2.

up in two propositions :—The first, (I.) That if the Revisionists are wrong in their 'New Greek Text,' then (not only
Westcott and Hort, but) Lachmann, Tischendorf and Tregelles
must be wrong also,—a statement which I hold to be incontrovertible.—The Bishop's other position is also undeniable :
viz. (II.) That in order to pass an equitable judgment on
ancient documents, they are to be carefully studied, closely
compared, and tested by a more scientific process than rough
comparison with the *Textus Receptus*.[1] . . . Thus, on both
heads, I find myself entirely at one with Bp. Ellicott.

§ 10. And yet,—as the last 150 pages of the present
volume show,—I have the misfortune to be at issue with the
learned writer on almost every particular which he proposes
for discussion.   Thus,

§ 11. At page 64 of his pamphlet, he fastens resolutely
upon the famous problem whether 'GOD' (Θεός), or 'who'
(ὅς), is to be read in 1 Timothy iii. 16.   I had upheld
the former reading in eight pages.   He contends for the
latter, with something like acrimony, in twelve.[2]   I have
been at the pains, in consequence, to write a 'DISSERTATION'
of seventy-six pages on this important subject,[3]—the prepar-
ation of which (may I be allowed to record the circumstance
in passing ?) occupied me closely for six months,[4] and taxed
me severely.   Thus, the only point which Bishop Ellicott
has condescended to discuss argumentatively with me, will
be found to enjoy full half of my letter to him in reply.

---

[1] *Pamphlet*, pp. 77 : 39, 40, 41.   [2] See below, p. 425.
[3] Pages 424–501.   [4] From January till June 1883.

The 'Dissertation' referred to, I submit with humble confidence to the judgment of educated Englishmen. It requires no learning to understand the case. And I have particularly to request that those who will be at the pains to look into this question, will remember,—(1) That the place of Scripture discussed (viz. 1 Tim. iii. 16) was deliberately selected for a trial of strength by the Bishop: (I should not have chosen it myself):—(2) That on the issue of the contention which he has thus himself invited, we have respectively staked our critical reputation. The discussion exhibits very fairly our two methods,—his and mine; and "is of great importance as an example," "illustrating in a striking manner" our respective positions,—as the Bishop himself has been careful to remind his readers.[1]

§ 12. One merely desirous of taking a general survey of this question, is invited to read from page 485 to 496 of the present volume. To understand the case thoroughly, he must submit to the labour of beginning at p. 424 and reading down to p. 501.

§ 13. A thoughtful person who has been at the pains to do this, will be apt on laying down the book to ask,—"But is it not very remarkable that so many as five of the ancient Versions should favour the reading 'which,' ($\mu\nu\sigma\tau\acute{\eta}\rho\iota o\nu\cdot$ ὃ ἐφανερώθη,) instead of 'GOD' ($\Theta\epsilon\acute{o}\varsigma$)"?—"Yes, it is very remarkable," I answer. "For though the Old Latin and the two Egyptian Versions are constantly observed to conspire

---

[1] *Pamphlet,* p. 76.

in error, they rarely find allies in the Peschito and the
Æthiopic. On the other hand, you are to remember that
besides VERSIONS, the FATHERS have to be inquired after :
while more important than either is the testimony of the
COPIES. Now, the combined witness to 'GOD' (Θεός),—so
multitudinous, so respectable, so varied, so unequivocal,—of
the Copies and of the Fathers (in addition to three of the
Versions) is simply overwhelming. It becomes undeniable
that Θεός is by far the best supported reading of the present
place."

§ 14. When, however, such an one as Tischendorf or
Tregelles,—Hort or Ellicott,—would put me down by reminding me that half-a-dozen of the oldest Versions are
against me,—" *That* argument" (I reply) "is not allowable
on *your* lips. For if the united testimony of *five* of the
Versions really be, in your account, decisive,—Why do you
deny the genuineness of the 'last Twelve Verses of S. Mark's
Gospel, *which are recognized by every one of the Versions?*
Those Verses are besides attested *by every known Copy*, except
two of bad character : *by a mighty chorus of Fathers : by the
unfaltering Tradition of the Church universal.* First remove
from S. Mark xvi. 20, your brand of suspicion, and then
come back to me in order that we may discuss together how
1 Tim. iii. 16 is to be read. And yet, when you come back,
it must not be to plead in favour of ' who' (ὅς), in place of
'GOD' (Θεός). For *not* 'who' (ὅς), remember, but 'which' (ὅ)
is the reading advocated by those five earliest Versions." . . .
In other words,—the reading of 1 Tim. iii. 16, which the
Revisers have adopted, enjoys, (as I have shown from page
428 to page 501), *the feeblest attestation of any ;* besides

being condemned by internal considerations and the universal
Tradition of the Eastern Church.

§ 15. I pass on, after modestly asking,—Is it too much to
hope, (I covet no other guerdon for my labour!) that we
shall hear no more about substituting "who" for "GOD" in
1 Tim. iii. 16 ? We may not go on disputing for ever: and
surely, until men are able to produce some more cogent
evidence than has yet come to light in support of "the
mystery of godliness, *who*" (τὸ τῆς εὐσεβείας μυστήριον·
ὅς),—all sincere inquirers after Truth are bound to accept
that reading which has been demonstrated to be by far the
best attested. Enough however on this head.

§ 16. It was said just now that I cordially concur with
Bp. Ellicott in the second of his two propositions,—viz. That
"no equitable judgment can be passed on ancient documents
until they are carefully studied, and closely compared with
each other, and tested by a more scientific process than rough
comparison with" the *Textus Receptus.* I wish to add a few
words on this subject: the rather, because what I am about
to say will be found as applicable to my Reviewer in the
'Church Quarterly' as to the Bishop. Both have misappre-
hended this matter, and in exactly the same way. Where
such accomplished Scholars have erred, what wonder if
ordinary readers should find themselves all a-field ?

§ 17. In Textual Criticism then, "rough comparison" can
seldom, if ever, be of any real use. On the other hand, the
exact *Collation* of documents whether ancient or modern with

the received Text, is the necessary foundation of all scientific
Criticism. I employ that Text,—(as Mill, Bentley, Wetstein;
Griesbach, Matthæi, Scholz; Tischendorf, Tregelles, Scrivener,
employed it before me,)—not as a criterion of *Excellence,* but
as a standard of *Comparison.* All this will be found fully
explained below, from page 383 to page 391. Whenever I
would judge of *the authenticity* of any particular reading, I
insist on bringing it, wherever found,—whether in Justin
Martyr and Irenæus, on the one hand; or in Stephens and
Elzevir, on the other;—to the test of *Catholic Antiquity.* If
that witness is consentient, or very nearly so, whether for or
against any given reading, I hold it to be decisive. To no
other system of arbitration will I submit myself. I decline
to recognise any other criterion of Truth.

§ 18. What compels me to repeat this so often, is the
impatient self-sufficiency of these last days, which is for
breaking away from the old restraints; and for erecting the
individual conscience into an authority from which there
shall be no appeal. I know but too well how laborious is
the scientific method which *I* advocate. A long summer day
disappears, while the student—with all his appliances about
him—is resolutely threshing out some minute textual problem.
Another, and yet another bright day vanishes. Comes Saturday
evening at last, and a page of illegible manuscript is all that
he has to show for a week's heavy toil. *Quousque tandem?*
And yet, it is the indispensable condition of progress in an
unexplored region, that a few should thus labour, until a
path has been cut through the forest,—a road laid down,—
huts built,—a *modus vivendi* established. In this department

of sacred Science, men have been going on too long inventing
their facts, and delivering themselves of oracular decrees, on
the sole responsibility of their own inner consciousness.
There is great convenience in such a method certainly,—a
charming simplicity which is in a high degree attractive to
flesh and blood. It dispenses with proof. It furnishes no
evidence. It asserts when it ought to argue.[1]   It reiterates
when it is called upon to explain.[2]   " I am sir Oracle." . . .
This,—which I venture to style the *unscientific* method,—
reached its culminating point when Professors Westcott and
Hort recently put forth their Recension of the Greek Text.
Their work is indeed quite a psychological curiosity.
Incomprehensible to me is it how two able men of
disciplined understandings can have seriously put forth
the volume which they call " INTRODUCTION—APPENDIX."
It is the very *Reductio ad absurdum* of the uncritical
method of the last fifty years. And it is especially in
opposition to this new method of theirs that I so strenuously
insist that *the consentient voice of Catholic Antiquity* is to be
diligently inquired after and submissively listened to ; for
that *this*, in the end, will prove our *only* safe guide.

§ 19. Let this be a sufficient reply to my Reviewer in
the 'Church Quarterly,'—who, I observe, notes, as a fundamental defect in my Articles, " the want of a consistent working Theory, such as would enable us to weigh, as well as
count, the suffrages of MSS., Versions, and Fathers." [3]   He is
reminded that it was no part of my business to propound a

---

[1] E.g. pages 252–268 : 269–277 : 305–308.   [2] E.g. pages 302–306.
[3] Page 354.

'Theory.' My *method* I have explained often and fully enough. My business was to prove that the theory of Drs. Westcott and Hort,—which (as Bp. Ellicott's pamphlet proves) has been mainly adopted by the Revisionists,—is not only a worthless, but an utterly absurd one. And I have proved it. The method I persistently advocate in every case of a supposed doubtful Reading, (I say it for the last time, and request that I may be no more misrepresented,) is, that *an appeal shall be unreservedly made to Catholic Antiquity;* and that the combined verdict of Manuscripts, Versions, Fathers, shall be regarded as decisive.

§ 20. I find myself, in the mean time, met by the scoffs, jeers, misrepresentations of the disciples of this new School ; who, instead of producing historical facts and intelligible arguments, appeal to the decrees of their teachers,—which *I* disallow, and which *they* are unable to substantiate. They delight in announcing that Textual Criticism made " *a fresh departure* " with the edition of Drs. Westcott and Hort : that the work of those scholars "*marks an era,*" and is spoken of in Germany as "*epoch-making.*" My own belief is, that the Edition in question, if it be epoch-making at all, marks *that* epoch at which the current of critical thought, reversing its wayward course, began once more to flow in its ancient healthy channel. ' Cloud-land ' having been duly sighted on the 14th September 1881,[1] " a fresh departure " was insisted upon by public opinion,—and a deliberate return was made, —to *terra firma,* and *terra cognita,* and common sense. So

---

[1] On that day appeared Dr. Hort's ' *Introduction and Appendix* ' to the N. T. as edited by himself and Dr. Westcott.

far from "its paramount claim to the respect of future generations," being "the restitution of a more ancient and a purer Text,"—I venture to predict that the edition of the two Cambridge Professors will be hereafter remembered as indicating the furthest point ever reached by the self-evolved imaginations of English disciples of the school of Lachmann, Tischendorf, Tregelles. The recoil promises to be complete. English good sense is ever observed to prevail in the long run; although for a few years a foreign fashion may acquire the ascendant, and beguile a few unstable wits.

§ 21. It only remains to state that in republishing these Essays I have availed myself of the opportunity to make several corrections and additions; as well as here and there to expand what before had been too briefly delivered. My learned friend and kind neighbour, the Rev. R. Cowley Powles, has ably helped me to correct the sheets. Much valuable assistance has been zealously rendered me throughout by my nephew, the Rev. William F. Rose, Vicar of Worle, Somersetshire. But the unwearied patience and consummate skill of my Secretary (M. W.) passes praise. Every syllable of the present volume has been transcribed by her for the press; and to her I am indebted for two of my Indices.—The obligations under which many learned men, both at home and abroad, have laid me, will be found faithfully acknowledged, in the proper place, at the foot of the page. I am sincerely grateful to them all.

§ 22. It will be readily believed that I have been sorely tempted to recast the whole and to strengthen my position

in every part: but then, the work would have no longer been,
—"Three Articles reprinted from the Quarterly Review."
Earnestly have I desired, for many years past, to produce
a systematic Treatise on this great subject. My aspiration
all along has been, and still is, in place of the absolute
Empiricism which has hitherto prevailed in Textual inquiry
to exhibit the logical outlines of what, I am persuaded, is
destined to become a truly delightful Science. But I more
than long,—I fairly *ache* to have done with Controversy, and
to be free to devote myself to the work of Interpretation.
My apology for bestowing so large a portion of my time on
Textual Criticism, is David's when he was reproached by his
brethren for appearing on the field of battle,—"Is there not
a cause?"

§ 23. For,—let it clearly be noted,—it is no longer the
case that critical doubts concerning the sacred Text are
confined to critical Editions of the Greek. So long as scholars
were content to ventilate their crotchets in a little arena of
their own,—however mistaken they might be, and even
though they changed their opinions once in every ten years,—
no great harm was likely to come of it. Students of the
Greek Testament were sure to have their attention called
to the subject,—which must always be in the highest degree
desirable; and it was to be expected that in this, as in every
other department of learning, the progress of Inquiry would
result in gradual accessions of certain Knowledge. After
many years it might be found practicable to put forth by
authority a carefully considered Revision of the commonly
received Greek Text.

§ 24. But instead of all this, a Revision of the *English Authorised Version* having been sanctioned by the Convocation of the Southern Province in 1871, the opportunity was eagerly snatched at by two irresponsible scholars of the University of Cambridge for obtaining the general sanction of the Revising body, and thus indirectly of Convocation, for a private venture of their own,—their own privately devised Revision of the *Greek Text.* On that Greek Text of theirs, (which I hold to be the most depraved which has ever appeared in print), with some slight modifications, our Authorised English Version has been silently revised: silently, I say, for in the margin of the English no record is preserved of the underlying Textual changes which have been introduced by the Revisionists. On the contrary. Use has been made of that margin to insinuate suspicion and distrust in count- less particulars as to the authenticity of the Text which has been suffered to remain unaltered. In the meantime, the country has been flooded with two editions of the New Greek Text; and thus the door has been set wide open for universal mistrust of the Truth of Scripture to enter.

§ 25. Even schoolboys, it seems, are to have these crude views thrust upon them. Witness the 'Cambridge Greek Testament for Schools,' edited by Dean Perowne,—who in- forms us at the outset that '*the Syndics of the Cambridge University Press* have not thought it desirable to reprint the text in common use.' A consensus of Drs. Tischendorf and Tregelles,—who confessedly employed *the self-same mistaken major premiss* in remodelling the Sacred Text,—seems, in a general way, to represent those Syndics' notion of Textual purity. By this means every most serious deformity in the edition of Drs. Westcott and Hort, becomes promoted to honour, and is being thrust on the unsuspecting youth of England as the genuine utterance of the HOLY GHOST. Would it not have been the fairer, the more faithful as well as the more judicious course,—seeing that in respect of this abstruse and important question *adhuc sub judice lis est*,— to wait patiently awhile? Certainly not to snatch an opportunity "while men slept," and in this way indirectly to prejudge the solemn issue! Not by such methods is the cause of GOD's Truth on earth to be promoted. Even this however is not all. Bishop Lightfoot has been informed that "the Bible Society has permitted its Translators to adopt the Text of the Revised Version *where it commends itself to their judgment.*" [1] In other words, persons wholly unacquainted with the dangers which beset this delicate and difficult problem are invited to determine, by the light of Nature and on the '*solvere ambulando*' principle, what *is* inspired Scripture, what *not :* and as a necessary consequence are encouraged to disseminate in heathen lands Readings which, a few years hence,—(so at least I venture to predict,)—will be universally recognized as worthless.

§ 26. If all this does not constitute a valid reason for descending into the arena of controversy, it would in my judgment be impossible to indicate an occasion when the Christian soldier *is* called upon to do so :—the rather, because certain of those who, from their rank and station in the

---

[1] '*Charge*,' published in the *Guardian*, Dec. 20, 1882, p. 1813.

Church, ought to be the champions of the Truth, are at this time found to be among its most vigorous assailants.

§ 27. Let me,—(and with this I conclude),—in giving the present Volume to the world, be allowed to request that it may be accepted as a sample of how Deans employ their time,—the use they make of their opportunities.   Nowhere but under the shadow of a Cathedral, (or in a College,) can such laborious endeavours as the present *pro Ecclesiâ Dei* be successfully prosecuted.

J. W. B.

Deanery, Chichester,
   All Saints' Day, 1883.

GENERAL SUMMARY OF CONTENTS.

TABLE OF CONTENTS.

ARTICLE I.—THE NEW GREEK TEXT.

ARTICLE II.—THE NEW ENGLISH VERSION.

d

ARTICLE I.

THE NEW GREEK TEXT.

"One question in connexion with the Authorized Version I have purposely neglected. It seemed useless to discuss its REVISION. *The Revision of the original Texts must precede the Revision of the Translation :* and *the time for this, even in the New Testament, has not yet fully come.*"— DR. WESTCOTT.[1]

"It is my honest conviction that for any authoritative REVISION, we are not yet mature; *either in Biblical learning or Hellenistic scholarship.* There is good scholarship in this country, ... but *it has certainly not yet been sufficiently directed to the study of the New Testament* . . . . to render any national attempt at REVISION either hopeful or lastingly profitable."—BISHOP ELLICOTT.[2]

"I am persuaded that a REVISION ought to come : I am convinced that it will come. Not however, I would trust, as yet; for *we are not as yet in any respect prepared for it.* *The Greek and the English* which should enable us to bring this to a successful end, *might, it is feared, be wanting alike.*"—ARCHBISHOP TRENCH.[3]

---

[1] Preface to *History of the English Bible* (p. ix.),—1868.
[2] Preface to *Pastoral Epistles* (p. xiv.),—1861.
[3] *The Authorized Version of the N. T.* (p. 3),—1858.

THE

REVISION REVISED.

ARTICLE I.—THE NEW GREEK TEXT.

"It is happened unto them according to the true proverb, Κύων ἐπι-
στρέψας ἐπὶ τὸ ἴδιον ἐξέραμα · and, Ὗς λουσαμένη εἰς κύλισμα βορβόρου."
—2 PETER ii. 22.

" Little children,—Keep yourselves from idols."—1 JOHN v. 21.

AT a period of extraordinary intellectual activity like the
present, it can occasion no surprise—although it may
reasonably create anxiety—if the most sacred and cherished
of our Institutions are constrained each in turn to submit to
the ordeal of hostile scrutiny; sometimes even to bear the
brunt of actual attack. When however at last the very
citadel of revealed Truth is observed to have been reached,
and to be undergoing systematic assault and battery,
lookers-on may be excused if they show themselves more
than usually solicitous, ' ne quid detrimenti Civitas DEI
capiat.' A Revision of the Authorized Version of the New
Testament,[1] purporting to have been executed by authority
of the Convocation of the Southern Province, and declaring
itself the exclusive property of our two ancient Universities,
has recently (17th May, 1881) appeared; of which the
essential feature proves to be, that it is founded on *an*

---

[1] *The New Testament of Our Lord and Saviour JESUS CHRIST translated
out of the Greek: being the Version set forth* A.D. 1611, *compared with the
most ancient Authorities, and Revised* A.D. 1881. Printed for the Universities of Oxford and Cambridge, 1881.

B

entirely New Recension of the Greek Text.[1] A claim is at
the same time set up on behalf of the last-named production
that it exhibits a closer approximation to the inspired Autographs than the world has hitherto seen.   Not unreasonable
therefore is the expectation entertained by its Authors that
the 'New English Version' founded on this 'New Greek
Text' is destined to supersede the 'Authorized Version' of
1611.   *Quæ cum ita sint,* it is clearly high time that every
faithful man among us should bestir himself: and in
particular that such as have made Greek Textual Criticism
in any degree their study should address themselves to the
investigation of the claims of this, the latest product of the
combined Biblical learning of the Church and of the sects.

For it must be plain to all, that the issue which has been
thus at last raised, is of the most serious character.   The
Authors of this new Revision of the Greek have either entitled
themselves to the Church's profound reverence and abiding
gratitude; or else they have laid themselves open to her
gravest censure, and must experience at her hands nothing
short of stern and well-merited rebuke.   No middle course
presents itself; since assuredly *to construct a new Greek Text*
formed no part of the Instructions which the Revisionists
received at the hands of the Convocation of the Southern
Province.   Rather were they warned against venturing on
such an experiment; the fundamental principle of the entire
undertaking having been declared at the outset to be—That

---

[1] *The New Testament in the Original Greek, according to the Text
followed in the Authorized Version, together with the Variations adopted
in the Revised Version.*   Edited for the Syndics of the Cambridge
University Press, by F. H. A. Scrivener, M.A., D.C.L., LL.D., Prebendary
of Exeter and Vicar of Hendon.   Cambridge, 1881.

ʼΗ ΚΑΙΝΗ ΔΙΑΘΗΚΗ.   *The Greek Testament, with the Readings
adopted by the Revisers of the Authorized Version.*   [Edited by the Ven.
Archdeacon Palmer, D.D.]   Oxford, 1881.

'a Revision of *the Authorized Version*' is desirable ; and the
terms of the original Resolution of Feb. 10th, 1870, being,
that the removal of 'PLAIN AND CLEAR ERRORS' was alone con-
templated,—'whether in the Greek Text originally adopted
by the Translators, or in the Translation made from the
same.' Such were in fact *the limits formally imposed by Convocation,* (10th Feb. and 3rd, 5th May, 1870,) *on the work of
Revision.* Only NECESSARY changes were to be made. The
first Rule of the Committee (25th May) was similar in
character : viz.—'*To introduce as few alterations as possible
into the Text of the Authorized Version,* consistently with faithfulness.'

But further, we were reconciled to the prospect of a
Revised Greek Text, by noting that a limit was prescribed to
the amount of licence which could by possibility result, by
the insertion of a proviso, which however is now discovered
to have been entirely disregarded by the Revisionists. The
condition was enjoined upon them that whenever '*decidedly
preponderating evidence*' constrained their adoption of some
change in ' the Text from which the Authorized Version was
made,' *they should indicate such alteration in the margin.*
Will it be believed that, this notwithstanding, *not one* of the
many alterations which have been introduced into the
original Text is so commemorated ? On the contrary : singular to relate, the Margin is disfigured throughout with
ominous hints that, had ' Some ancient authorities,' ' Many
ancient authorities,' ' Many very ancient authorities,' been
attended to, a vast many more changes might, could, would,
or should have been introduced into the Greek Text than
have been actually adopted. And yet, this is precisely the
kind of record which we ought to have been spared :—

(1) First,—Because it was plainly external to the province
of the Revisionists to introduce any such details into their
margin *at all :* their very function being, on the contrary, to

investigate Textual questions in conclave, and to present the ordinary Reader with *the result* of their deliberations.   Their business was to correct "*plain and clear errors;*"   not, certainly, to invent a fresh crop of unheard-of doubts and difficulties.   This first.—Now,

(2) That a diversity of opinion would sometimes be found to exist in the revising body was to have been expected , but when once two-thirds of their number had finally "settled" any question, it is plainly unreasonable that the discomfited minority should claim the privilege of evermore parading their grievance before the public ; and in effect should be allowed to represent *that* as a corporate doubt, which was in reality the result of individual idiosyncrasy.   It is not reasonable that the echoes of a forgotten strife should be thus prolonged for ever; least of all in the margin of 'the Gospel of peace.'

(3) In fact, the privilege of figuring in the margin of the N. T., (instead of standing in the Text,) is even attended by a fatal result: for, (as Bp. Ellicott remarks,) 'the judgment commonly entertained in reference to our present margin,' (*i.e.* the margin of the A. V.) is, that *its contents are* 'exegetically or critically *superior to the Text.*'[1]   It will certainly be long before this popular estimate is unconditionally abandoned.   But,

(4) Especially do we deprecate the introduction into the margin of all this strange lore, because we insist on behalf of unlearned persons that they ought not to be molested with information which cannot, by possibility, be of the slightest service to them: with vague statements about "ancient authorities,"—of the importance, or unimportance, of which they know absolutely nothing, nor indeed ever can know.   Unlearned readers on taking the Revision into their hands, (*i.e.* at least 999 readers out of 1000,) will *never* be

---

[1] *On Revision,*—pp. 215–6.

aware whether these (so-called) 'Various Readings' are to be
scornfully scouted, as nothing else but ancient perversions
of the Truth ; or else are to be lovingly cherished, as *alternative*' [see the Revisers' *Preface* (iii. 1.)] exhibitions of the
inspired Verity,—to their own abiding perplexity and infinite
distress.

Undeniable at all events it is, that the effect which these
ever-recurring announcements produce on the devout reader
of Scripture is the reverse of edifying: is never helpful: is
always bewildering.   A man of ordinary acuteness can but
exclaim,—'Yes, very likely.   But *what of it?*   My eye
happens to alight on "Bethesda" (in S. John v. 2) ; against
which I find in the margin,—"Some ancient authorities read
Bethsaida, others *Bethzatha*."   Am I then to understand that
in the judgment of the Revisionists it is uncertain *which* of
those three names is right?'.. Not so the expert, who is
overheard to moralize concerning the phenomena of the case
after a less ceremonious fashion:—'"*Bethsaida*"!   Yes, the
old Latin [1] and the Vulgate,[2] countenanced by *one* manuscript
of bad character, so reads.   "*Bethzatha*"!   Yes, the blunder
is found in *two* manuscripts, both of bad character.   Why do
you not go on to tell us that *another* manuscript exhibits
"*Belzetha*"?—another (supported by Eusebius [3] and [in one
place] by Cyril [4]), "*Bezatha*"?   Nay, why not say plainly that
there are found to exist *upwards of thirty* blundering representations of this same word; but that "*Bethesda*"—(the
reading of sixteen uncials and the whole body of the cursives,
besides the Peschito and Cureton's Syriac, the Armenian,
Georgian and Slavonic Versions,—Didymus,[5] Chrysostom,[6]
and Cyril [7]),—is the only reasonable way of exhibiting it?   To

---

[1] Tertullian, *bis.*   [2] Hieron. *Opp.* ii. 177 c (see the note).
[3] Apud Hieron. iii. 121.   [4] iv. 617 c (ed. Pusey).
[5] P. 272.   [6] i. 548 c ; viii. 207 a.   [7] iv. 205.

speak plainly, *Why encumber your margin with such a note at all ?'* . . But we are moving forward too fast.

It can never be any question among scholars, that a fatal error was committed when a body of Divines, appointed *to revise the Authorized English Version* of the New Testament Scriptures, addressed themselves to the solution of an entirely different and far more intricate problem, namely *the re-construction of the Greek Text.* We are content to pass over much that is distressing in the antecedent history of their enterprise. We forbear at this time of day to investigate, by an appeal to documents and dates, certain proceedings in and out of Convocation, on which it is known that the gravest diversity of sentiment still prevails among Churchmen.[1] This we do, not by any means as ourselves 'halting between two opinions,' but only as sincerely desirous that the work before us may stand or fall, judged by its own intrinsic merits. Whether or no Convocation,—when it 'nominated certain of its own members to undertake the work of Revision,' and authorized them 'to refer when they considered it desirable to Divines, Scholars, and Literary men, at home or abroad, *for their opinion;'*—whether Convocation intended thereby to sanction the actual *co-optation* into the Company appointed by themselves, of members of the Presbyterian, the Wesleyan, the Baptist, the Congregationalist, the Socinian body; *this* we venture to think may fairly be doubted.— Whether again Convocation can have foreseen that of the ninety-nine Scholars in all who have taken part in this work of Revision, only forty-nine would be Churchmen, while the remaining fifty would belong to the sects :[2]—*this* also we

---

[1] A reference to the *Journal of Convocation,* for a twelvemonth after the proposal for a Revision of the Authorized Version was seriously entertained, will reveal more than it would be convenient in this place even to allude to.

[2] We derive our information from the learned Congregationalist, Dr. Newth,—*Lectures on Bible Revision* (1881), p. 116.

venture to think may be reasonably called in question.— Whether lastly, the Canterbury Convocation, had it been appealed to with reference to 'the Westminster-Abbey scandal' (June 22nd, 1870), would not have cleared itself of the suspicion of complicity, by an unequivocal resolution,— we entertain no manner of doubt.—But we decline to enter upon these, or any other like matters. Our business is exclusively with *the result* at which the Revisionists of the New Testament have arrived: and it is to this that we now address ourselves; with the mere avowal of our grave anxiety at the spectacle of an assembly of scholars, appointed to revise *an English Translation,* finding themselves called upon, as every fresh difficulty emerged, to develop the skill requisite for *critically revising the original Greek Text.* What else is implied by the very endeavour, but a singular expectation that experts in one Science may, at a moment's notice, show themselves proficients in another,—and *that* one of the most difficult and delicate imaginable?

Enough has been said to make it plain why, in the ensuing pages, we propose to pursue a different course from that which has been adopted by Reviewers generally, since the memorable day (May 17th, 1881) when the work of the Revisionists was for the first time submitted to public scrutiny. The one point which, with rare exceptions, has ever since monopolized attention, has been the merits or demerits of *their English rendering* of certain Greek words and expressions. But there is clearly a question of prior interest and infinitely greater importance, which has to be settled first: namely, the merits or demerits of *the changes which the same Scholars have taken upon themselves to introduce into the Greek Text.* Until it has been ascertained that the result of their labours exhibits a decided improvement upon what before was read, it is clearly a mere waste of time to enquire into the merits of their work as *Revisers of a*

Translation. But in fact it has to be proved that the Revisionists have restricted themselves to the removal of "plain and clear *errors*" from the commonly received Text. We are distressed to discover that, on the contrary, they have done something quite different. The treatment which the N. T. has experienced at the hands of the Revisionists recals the fate of some ancient edifice which confessedly required to be painted, papered, scoured,—with a minimum of masons' and carpenters' work,—in order to be inhabited with comfort for the next hundred years : but those entrusted with the job were so ill-advised as to persuade themselves that it required to be to a great extent rebuilt. Accordingly, in an evil hour they set about removing foundations, and did so much structural mischief that in the end it became necessary to proceed against them for damages.

Without the remotest intention of imposing views of our own on the general Reader, but only to enable him to give his intelligent assent to much that is to follow, we find ourselves constrained in the first instance,—before conducting him over any part of the domain which the Revisionists have ventured uninvited to occupy,—to premise a few ordinary facts which lie on the threshold of the science of Textual Criticism. Until these have been clearly apprehended, no progress whatever is possible.

(1) The provision, then, which the Divine Author of Scripture is found to have made for the preservation in its integrity of His written Word, is of a peculiarly varied and highly complex description. First,—By causing that a vast multiplication of COPIES should be required all down the ages, —beginning at the earliest period, and continuing in an ever-increasing ratio until the actual invention of Printing,—He provided the most effectual security imaginable against fraud. True, that millions of the copies so produced have long since

perished : but it is nevertheless a plain fact that there survive of the Gospels alone upwards of one thousand copies to the present day.

(2) Next, VERSIONS. The necessity of translating the Scriptures into divers languages for the use of different branches of the early Church, procured that many an authentic record has been preserved of the New Testament as it existed in the first few centuries of the Christian era. Thus, the Peschito Syriac and the old Latin version are believed to have been executed in the IInd century. " It is no stretch of imagination" (wrote Bp. Ellicott in 1870,) " to suppose that portions of the Peschito might have been in the hands of S. John, or that the Old Latin represented the current views of the Roman Christians of the IInd century."[1] The two Egyptian translations are referred to the IIIrd and IVth. The Vulgate (or revised Latin) and the Gothic are also claimed for the IVth: the Armenian, and possibly the Æthiopic, belong to the Vth.

(3) Lastly, the requirements of assailants and apologists alike, the business of Commentators, the needs of controversialists and teachers in every age, have resulted in a vast accumulation of additional evidence, of which it is scarcely possible to over-estimate the importance. For in this way it has come to pass that every famous Doctor of the Church in turn has quoted more or less largely from the sacred writings, and thus has borne testimony to the contents of the codices with which he was individually familiar. PATRISTIC CITATIONS accordingly are a third mighty safeguard of the integrity of the deposit.

To weigh these three instruments of Criticism—COPIES, VERSIONS, FATHERS—one against another, is obviously im-

---

[1] *On Revision*, pp. 26-7.

possible on the present occasion. Such a discussion would
grow at once into a treatise.[1] Certain explanatory details,
together with a few words of caution, are as much as may be
attempted.

I. And, first of all, the reader has need to be apprised
(with reference to the first-named class of evidence) that most
of our extant COPIES of the N. T. Scriptures are comparatively
of recent date, ranging from the Xth to the XIVth century of
our era. That these are in every instance copies of yet older
manuscripts, is self-evident; and that in the main they
represent faithfully the sacred autographs themselves, no
reasonable person doubts.[2] Still, it is undeniable that

---

[1] Dr. Scrivener's *Plain Introduction to the Criticism of the New
Testament*, 2nd edition, 1874 (pp. 607), may be confidently recommended
to any one who desires to master the outlines of Textual Criticism under
the guidance of a judicious, impartial, and thoroughly competent guide. A
new and revised edition of this excellent treatise will appear shortly.

[2] Studious readers are invited to enquire for Dr. Scrivener's *Full and
exact Collation of about Twenty Greek Manuscripts of the Holy Gospels
(hitherto unexamined), deposited in the British Museum, the Archiepiscopal Library at Lambeth, &c., with a Critical Introduction.* (Pp.
lxxiv. and 178.) 1853. The introductory matter deserves very
attentive perusal.—With equal confidence we beg to recommend his
*Exact Transcript of the Codex Augiensis, a Græco-Latin Manuscript
of S. Paul's Epistles, deposited in the Library of Trinity College,
Cambridge; to which is added a full Collation of Fifty Manuscripts,
containing various portions of the Greek New Testament, in the Libraries
of Cambridge, Parham, Leicester, Oxford, Lambeth, the British Museum,
&c. With a Critical Introduction* (which must also be carefully studied).
(Pp. lxxx. and 563.) 1859.—Learned readers can scarcely require to
be told of the same learned scholar's *Novum Testamentum Textûs
Stephanici*, A.D. 1550. *Accedunt variæ Lectiones Editionum Bezæ, Elzeviri,
Lachmanni, Tischendorfii, Tregellesii.* Curante F. H. A. Scrivener,
A.M., D.C.L., LL.D. [1860.] Editio auctior et emendatior. 1877.—
Those who merely wish for a short popular Introduction to the subject
may be grateful to be told of Dr. Scrivener's *Six Lectures on the Text of
the N. T. and the Ancient MSS. which contain it, chiefly addressed to
those who do not read Greek.* 1875.

they *are* thus separated by about a thousand years from their inspired archetypes. Readers are reminded, in passing, that the little handful of copies on which we rely for the texts of Herodotus and Thucydides, of Æschylus and Sophocles, are removed from *their* originals by full 500 years more: and that, instead of a thousand, or half a thousand copies, we are dependent for the text of certain of these authors on as many copies as may be counted on the fingers of one hand. In truth, the security which the Text of the New Testament enjoys is altogether unique and extraordinary. To specify one single consideration, which has never yet attracted nearly the amount of attention it deserves,—'Lectionaries' abound, which establish the Text which has been publicly read in the churches of the East, from *at least* A.D. 400 until the time of the invention of printing.

But here an important consideration claims special attention. We allude to the result of increased acquaintance with certain of the oldest extant codices of the N. T. Two of these,—viz. a copy in the Vatican technically indicated by the letter B, and the recently-discovered Sinaitic codex, styled after the first letter of the Hebrew alphabet א,—are thought to belong to the IVth century. Two are assigned to the Vth, viz. the Alexandrian (A) in the British Museum, and the rescript codex preserved at Paris, designated c. One is probably of the VIth, viz. the codex Bezæ (D) preserved at Cambridge. Singular to relate, the first, second, fourth, and fifth of these codices (B א C D), but especially B and א, have within the last twenty years established a tyrannical ascendency over the imagination of the Critics, which can only be fitly spoken of as a blind superstition. It matters nothing that all four are discovered on careful scrutiny to differ essentially, not only from ninety-nine out of a hundred of the whole body of extant MSS. besides, but even *from one another.* This last circumstance, obviously fatal to their corporate pretensions, is unaccountably overlooked. And yet it admits of only one satisfactory explanation : viz. that *in different degrees* they all five exhibit a fabricated text. Between the first two (B and א) there subsists an amount of sinister resemblance, which proves that they must have been derived at no very remote period from the same corrupt original. Tischendorf insists that they were partly written by the same scribe. Yet do they stand asunder in every page ; as well as differ widely from the commonly received Text, with which they have been carefully collated. On being referred to this standard, in the Gospels alone, B is found to omit at least 2877 words : to add, 536 : to substitute, 935 : to transpose, 2098 : to modify, 1132 (in all 7578) : —the corresponding figures for א being severally 3455, 839, 1114, 2299, 1265 (in all 8972). And be it remembered that the omissions, additions, substitutions, ·transpositions, and modifications, *are by no means the same* in both. It is in fact *easier to find two consecutive verses in which these two MSS. differ the one from the other, than two consecutive verses in which they entirely agree.*

But by far the most depraved text is that exhibited by codex D. 'No known manuscript contains so many bold and extensive interpolations. Its variations from the sacred Text are beyond all other example.'[1] This, however, is not the result of its being the most recent of the five, but (singular to relate) is due to quite an opposite cause. It is thought (not without reason) to exhibit a IInd-century text. 'When we turn to the Acts of the

---

[1] Scrivener's *Plain Introduction,*—p. 118.

Apostles,' (says the learned editor of the codex in question, Dr. Scrivener,[1])—

' We find ourselves confronted with a text, the like to which we have no experience of elsewhere.   It is hardly an exaggeration to assert that codex D reproduces the *Textus receptus* much in the same way that one of the best Chaldee Targums does the Hebrew of the Old Testament: so wide are the variations in the diction, so constant and inveterate the practice of expounding the narrative by means of interpolations which seldom recommend themselves as genuine by even a semblance of internal probability.'

' *Vix dici potest*' (says Mill) '*quam supra omnem modum licenter se gesserit, ac plane lasciverit Interpolator.*' Though a large portion of the Gospels is missing, in what remains (tested by the same standard) we find 3704 words omitted: no less than 2213 added, and 2121 substituted.   The words transposed amount to 3471: and 1772 have been modified: the deflections from the Received Text thus amounting in all to 13,281.—Next to D, the most untrustworthy codex is ℵ, which bears on its front a memorable note of the evil repute under which it has always laboured: viz. it is found that at least *ten* revisers between the IVth and the XIIth centuries busied themselves with the task of correcting its many and extraordinary perversions of the truth of Scripture.[2]—Next in

---

[1] *Bezæ Codex Cantabrigiensis: being an exact Copy, in ordinary Type, of the celebrated Uncial Græco-Latin Manuscript of the Four Gospels and Acts of the Apostles, written early in the Sixth Century, and presented to the University of Cambridge by Theodore Beza*, A.D. 1581.   Edited, with a Critical Introduction, Annotations, and Facsimiles, by Frederick H. Scrivener, M.A., Rector of S. Gerrans, Cornwall.   (Pp. lxiv. and 453.) Cambridge, 1864.   No one who aspires to a competent acquaintance with Textual Criticism can afford to be without this book.

[2] On the subject of codex ℵ we beg (once for all) to refer scholars to Scrivener's *Full Collation of the Codex Sinaiticus with the Received Text of the New Testament.   To which is prefixed a Critical Introduction.* [1863.]   2nd Edition, revised.   (Pp. lxxii. and 163.)   1867.

impurity comes B:—then, the fragmentary codex C: our own A being, beyond all doubt, disfigured by the fewest blemishes of any.

What precedes admits to some extent of further numerical illustration. It is discovered that in the 111 (out of 320) pages of an ordinary copy of the Greek Testament, in which alone these five manuscripts are collectively available for comparison in the Gospels,—the serious deflections of A from the *Textus receptus* amount in all to only 842: whereas in C they amount to 1798: in B, to 2370: in א, to 3392: in D, to 4697. The readings *peculiar to* A within the same limits are 133: those peculiar to C are 170. But those of B amount to 197: while א exhibits 443: and the readings peculiar to D (within the same limits), are no fewer than 1829. . . . We submit that these facts—*which result from merely referring five manuscripts to one and the same common standard*—are by no means calculated to inspire confidence in codices B א C D:—codices, be it remembered, which come to us without a character, without a history, in fact without antecedents of *any* kind.

But let the learned chairman of the New Testament company of Revisionists (Bp. Ellicott) be heard on this subject. He is characterizing these same 'old uncials,' which it is just now the fashion—or rather, the *craze*—to hold up as oracular, and to which his lordship is as devotedly and blindly attached as any of his neighbours :—

'The *simplicity and dignified conciseness*' (he says) ' of the Vatican manuscript (B): the *greater expansiveness* of our own Alexandrian (A): the *partially mixed characteristics* of the Sinaitic (א): the *paraphrastic tone* of the *singular* codex Bezæ (D), are now brought home to the student.'[1]

Could ingenuity have devised severer satire than such a

---

[1] Bishop Ellicott's *Considerations on Revision*, &c. (1870), p. 40.

description of four professing *transcripts* of a book ; and *that*
book, the everlasting Gospel itself ? — transcripts, be it
observed in passing, on which it is just now the fashion to
rely implicitly for the very orthography of proper names,—
the spelling of common words,—the minutiæ of grammar.
What (we ask) would be thought of four such ' *copies* ' of
Thucydides or of Shakspeare ?   Imagine it gravely proposed,
by the aid of four such conflicting documents, to re-adjust
the text of the funeral oration of Pericles, or to re-edit
' Hamlet.'   *Risum teneatis amici?*   Why, some of the poet's
most familiar lines would cease to be recognizable : e.g. A,—
' *Toby or not Toby ; that is the question :* ' B,—' *Tob or not,
is the question :* ' א,—' *To be a tub, or not to be a tub ; the question is that :* ' C,—' *The question is, to `beat, or not to beat
Toby ?* ' : D (the ' singular codex '),—' *The only question is
this : to beat that Toby, or to be a tub ?* '

And yet—without by any means subscribing to the precise
terms in which the judicious Prelate characterizes those *ignes
fatui* which have so persistently and egregiously led his lordship and his colleagues astray—(for indeed one seems rather
to be reading a description of four styles of composition, or
of as many fashions in ladies' dress, than of four copies of
the Gospel)—we have already furnished indirect proof that
his estimate of the codices in question is in the main correct.
Further acquaintance with them does but intensify the bad
character which he has given them.   Let no one suppose
that we deny their extraordinary value,—their unrivalled
critical interest,—nay, their actual *use* in helping to settle
the truth of Scripture.   What we are just now insisting upon
is only the *depraved text* of codices א A B C D,—especially of
א B D.   And because this is a matter which lies at the root of
the whole controversy, and because we cannot afford that
there shall exist in our reader's mind the slightest doubt on

this part of the subject, we shall be constrained once and again to trouble him with detailed specimens of the contents of א B, &c., in proof of the justice of what we have been alleging. We venture to assure him, without a particle of hesitation, that א B D are *three of the most scandalously corrupt copies extant :*—exhibit *the most shamefully mutilated* texts which are anywhere to be met with :—have become, by whatever process (for their history is wholly unknown), the depositories of the largest amount of *fabricated readings,* ancient *blunders,* and *intentional perversions of Truth,*— which are discoverable in any known copies of the Word of GOD.

But in fact take a single page of any ordinary copy of the Greek Testament,—Bp. Lloyd's edition, suppose. Turn to page 184. It contains ten verses of S. Luke's Gospel, ch. viii. 35 to 44. Now, proceed to collate those ten verses. You will make the notable discovery that, within those narrow limits, by codex D alone the text has been depraved 53 times, resulting in no less than 103 corrupt readings, 93 *of which are found only in* D. The words omitted by D are 40 : the words added are 4. Twenty-five words have been substituted for others, and 14 transposed. Variations of case, tense, &c., amount to 16 ; and the phrase of the Evangelist has been departed from 11 times. Happily, the other four 'old uncials' are here available. And it is found that (within the same limits, and referred to the same test,) A exhibits 3 omissions, 2 of which are *peculiar to* A.—B omits 12 words, 6 of which are *peculiar to* B : substitutes 3 words : transposes 4 : and exhibits 6 lesser changes —2 of them being its own peculiar property.—א has 5 readings (affecting 8 words) *peculiar to itself.* Its omissions are 7 : its additions, 2 : its substitutions, 4 : 2 words are transposed ; and it exhibits 4 lesser discrepancies.—C has 7 readings (affecting 15 words) *peculiar to itself.* Its omissions are 4 :

its additions, 7 : its substitutions, 7 : its words transposed, 7. It has 2 lesser discrepancies, and it alters the Evangelist's phrase 4 times.

But (we shall be asked) what amount of *agreement*, in respect of 'Various Readings,' is discovered to subsist between these 5 codices ? for *that*, after all, is the practical question. We answer,—A has been already shown to stand alone twice : B, 6 times : ℵ, 8 times : C, 15 times ; D, 93 times.— We have further to state that A B stand together by themselves once : B ℵ, 4 times : B C, 1 : B D, 1 : ℵ C, 1 : C D, 1.— A ℵ C conspire 1 : B ℵ C, 1 : B ℵ D, 1 : A B ℵ C, *once* (viz. in reading ἐρώτησεν, which Tischendorf admits to be a corrupt reading) : B ℵ C D, also *once*.—The 5 'old uncials' therefore (A B ℵ C D) combine, and again stand apart, with singular impartiality.—Lastly, they are *never once* found to be in accord in respect of *any single 'various Reading.'*—Will any one, after a candid survey of the premises, deem us un-reasonable, if we avow that such a specimen of the *concordia discors* which everywhere prevails between the oldest uncials, but which especially characterizes ℵ B D, indisposes us greatly to suffer their unsupported authority to determine for us the Text of Scripture ?

Let no one at all events obscure the one question at issue, by asking,—'Whether we consider the *Textus Receptus* infallible ?' The merit or demerit of the Received Text has absolutely *nothing whatever to do with the question.* We care nothing about it. *Any* Text would equally suit our present purpose. *Any* Text would show the 'old uncials' per-petually at discord *among themselves.* To raise an irrelevant discussion, at the outset, concerning the *Textus Receptus :*— to describe the haste with which Erasmus produced the first published edition of the N. T. :—to make sport about the

copies which he employed :—all this kind of thing is the
proceeding of one who seeks to mislead his readers :—to throw
dust into their eyes :—to divert their attention from the problem actually before them :—*not*—(as we confidently expect
when we have to do with such writers as these)—the method
of a sincere lover of Truth.   To proceed, however.

II. and III. Nothing has been said as yet concerning the
Text exhibited by the earliest of the VERSIONS and by the
most ancient of the FATHERS.   But, for the purpose we have
just now in hand, neither are such details necessary.   We
desire to hasten forward.   A somewhat fuller review of
certain of our oldest available materials might prove even
more discouraging.   But *that* would only be because it is
impossible, within such narrow limits as the present, to give
the reader any idea at all of the wealth of our actual
resources ; and to convince him of the extent to which the
least trustworthy of our guides prove in turn invaluable
helps in correcting the exorbitances of their fellows.   The
practical result in fact of what has been hitherto offered is
after all but this, that we have to be on our guard against
pinning our faith exclusively on two or three,—least of all
on one or two ancient documents ; and of adopting *them*
exclusively for our guides.   We are shown, in other words,
that it is utterly out of the question to rely on any single
set or *group* of authorities, much less on any single document, for the determination of the Text of Scripture.
Happily, our MANUSCRIPTS are numerous : most of them are
in the main trustworthy : *all* of them represent far older
documents than themselves.   Our VERSIONS (two of which
are more ancient by a couple of centuries than any sacred
codex extant) severally correct and check one another.
Lastly, in the writings of a host of FATHERS,—the principal
being Eusebius, Athanasius, Basil, the Gregories, Didymus,

Epiphanius, Chrysostom, the Cyrils, Theodoret,—we are provided with contemporaneous evidence which, whenever it can be had, becomes an effectual safeguard against the unsupported decrees of our oldest codices, A B א C D, as well as the occasional vagaries of the Versions. In the writings of Irenæus, Clemens Alex., Origen, Dionysius Alex., Hippolytus, we meet with older evidence still. No more precarious foundation for a reading, in fact, can be named, than the unsupported advocacy of a single Manuscript, or Version, or Father; or even of two or three of these combined.

But indeed the principle involved in the foregoing remarks admits of being far more broadly stated. It even stands to reason that we may safely reject any reading which, out of the whole body of available authorities,—Manuscripts, Versions, Fathers,—finds support nowhere save in one and the same little handful of suspicious documents. For we resolutely maintain, that *external Evidence* must after all be our best, our only safe guide; and (to come to the point) we refuse to throw in our lot with those who, disregarding the witness of *every other* known Codex—*every other* Version— *every other* available Ecclesiastical Writer,—insist on following the dictates of a little group of authorities, of which nothing whatever is known with so much certainty as that often, when they concur exclusively, it is to mislead. We speak of codices B or א or D; the IXth-century codex L, and such cursives[1] as 13 or 33; a few copies of the old Latin and one of the Egyptian versions: perhaps Origen.—Not theory

---

[1] The epithet '*cursive*,' is used to denote manuscripts written in 'running-hand,' of which the oldest known specimens belong to the IXth century. '*Uncial*' manuscripts are those which are written in capital letters. A '*codex*' popularly signifies a *manuscript*. A 'version' is *a translation*. A 'recension' is *a revision*. (We have been requested to explain these terms.)

therefore :—not prejudice :—not conjecture :—not unproved
assertion :—not any single codex, and *certainly* not codex B :
—not an imaginary ' Antiochene Recension' of another
imaginary ' Pre-Syrian Text :'—not antecedent fancies about
the affinity of documents :—neither ' the [purely arbitrary]
method of genealogy,'—nor one man's notions (*which may be
reversed by another man's notions*) of ' Transcriptional Probability :'—not ' instinctive processes of Criticism,'—least of
all ' the individual mind,' with its ' supposed power of
divining the Original Text'—of which no intelligible account
can be rendered :—nothing of this sort,—(however specious
and plausible it may sound, especially when set forth in
confident language ; advocated with a great show of unintelligible learning; supported by a formidable array of
cabalistic symbols and mysterious contractions; above all
when recommended by justly respected names,)—nothing of
this sort, we say, must be allowed to determine for us the
Text of Scripture. The very proposal should set us on our
guard against the *certainty* of imposition.

We deem it even axiomatic, that, in every case of doubt
or difficulty—supposed or real — our critical method must
be the same : namely, after patiently collecting *all* the
available evidence, then, without partiality or prejudice, to
adjudicate between the conflicting authorities, and loyally to
accept that verdict for which there is clearly the preponderating evidence. *The best supported Reading*, in other words,
must always be held to be *the true Reading :* and nothing
may be rejected from the commonly received Text, except on
evidence which shall *clearly* outweigh the evidence for
retaining it. We are glad to know that, so far at least, we
once had Bp. Ellicott with us. He announced (in 1870) that
the best way of proceeding with the work of Revision is, " *to
make the Textus Receptus the standard,*—departing from it

only when critical or grammatical considerations *show that it is clearly necessary.*"[1] We ourselves mean no more. Whenever the evidence is about evenly balanced, few it is hoped will deny that the Text which has been 'in possession' for three centuries and a half, and which rests on infinitely better manuscript evidence than that of any ancient work which can be named,—should, for every reason, be let alone.[2]

But, (we shall perhaps be asked,) has any critical Editor of the N. T. seriously taught the reverse of all this? Yes indeed, we answer. Lachmann, Tregelles, Tischendorf,—the most recent and most famous of modern editors,—have all three adopted a directly opposite theory of textual revision. With the first-named, fifty years ago (1831), virtually originated the principle of recurring exclusively to a few ancient documents to the exclusion of the many. 'LACHMANN's text seldom rests on more than four Greek codices, very often on three, not unfrequently on two, *sometimes on only one.*'[3] Bishop Ellicott speaks of it as "a text composed *on the narrowest and most exclusive principles.*"[4] Of the Greek

---

[1] *Considerations on Revision*, p. 30.

[2] Once for all, we request it may be clearly understood that we do not, by any means, claim *perfection* for the Received Text. We entertain no extravagant notions on this subject. Again and again we shall have occasion to point out (*e. g.* at page 107) that the *Textus Receptus* needs correction. We do but insist, (1) That it is an incomparably better text than that which either Lachmann, or Tischendorf, or Tregelles has produced: infinitely preferable to the 'New Greek Text' of the Revisionists. And, (2) That to be improved, the *Textus Receptus* will have to be revised on entirely different 'principles' from those which are just now in fashion. Men must begin by unlearning the *German prejudices* of the last fifty years ; and address themselves, instead, to the stern logic of *facts.*

[3] Scrivener's *Introduction*, pp. 342–4.

[4] *Ut suprà*, p. 46. We prefer to quote the indictment against Lachmann, Tischendorf, Tregelles, from the pages of Revisionists.

Fathers (Lachmann says) he employed *only Origen*.[1] Paying extraordinary deference to the Latin Version, he entirely disregarded the coëval Syriac translation. The result of such a system must needs prove satisfactory to no one except its author.

Lachmann's leading fallacy has perforce proved fatal to the value of the text put forth by DR. TREGELLES. Of the scrupulous accuracy, the indefatigable industry, the pious zeal of that estimable and devoted scholar, we speak not. All honour to his memory ! As a specimen of conscientious labour, his edition of the N. T. (1857–72) passes praise, and will *never* lose its value. But it has only to be stated, that Tregelles effectually persuaded himself that ' *eighty-nine ninetieths* ' of our extant manuscripts and other authorities may safely be rejected and lost sight of when we come to amend the text and try to restore it to its primitive purity,[2] —to make it plain that in Textual Criticism he must needs be regarded as an untrustworthy teacher. *Why* he should have condescended to employ no patristic authority later than Eusebius [fl. A.D. 320], he does not explain. "His critical principles," (says Bishop Ellicott,) "especially his general principles of estimating and regarding modern manuscripts, are now perhaps justly called in question."[3]

"The case of DR. TISCHENDORF" (proceeds Bp. Ellicott) "is still more easily disposed of. *Which* of this most inconstant Critic's texts are we to select ? Surely not the last, in which an exaggerated preference for a single Manuscript which he has had the good fortune to discover, has betrayed him into

---

[1] ' Ex scriptoribus Græcis *tantisper Origene solo* usi sumus.'—*Præfatio*, p. xxi.
[2] Scrivener's *Plain Introd.* p. 397.   [3] *Ut suprà*, p. 48.

an almost child-like infirmity of critical judgment. Surely
also not his seventh edition, which . . . exhibits all the
instability which a comparatively recent recognition of the
authority of cursive manuscripts might be supposed likely to
introduce."[1]   With Dr. Tischendorf,—(whom one vastly his
superior in learning, accuracy, and judgment, has generously
styled 'the first Biblical Critic in Europe'[2])—"*the evidence
of codex* ℵ, supported or even unsupported by one or two
other authorities of any description, is sufficient to outweigh
any other witnesses,—whether Manuscripts, Versions, or
ecclesiastical Writers."[3]   We need say no more.   Until the
foregoing charge has been disproved, Dr. Tischendorf's last
edition of the N. T., however precious as a vast storehouse of
materials for criticism,—however admirable as a specimen
of unwearied labour, critical learning, and first-rate ability,
—must be admitted to be an utterly unsatisfactory exhibition of the inspired Text.   It has been ascertained that
his discovery of codex ℵ caused his 8th edition (1865–72)
to differ from his 7th in no less than 3505 places,—"to the
scandal of the science of Comparative Criticism, as well as to
his own grave discredit for discernment and consistency."[4]
But, in fact, what is to be thought of a Critic who,—because
the last verse of S. John's Gospel, in ℵ, seemed to himself to
be *written with a different pen* from the rest,—has actually
omitted that verse (xxi. 25) *entirely*, in defiance of *every
known Copy, every known Version*, and the explicit testimony
of *a host of Fathers?*   Such are Origen (in 11 places),—
Eusebius (in 3),—Gregory Nyss. (in 2),—Gregory Nazian.,—
ps.-Dionys. Alex.,[5] —Nonnus,—Chrysostom (in 6 places),—
Theodorus Mops. (in 2),—Isidorus,—Cyril Alex. (in 2),—
Victor Ant.,—Ammonius, — Severus, — Maximus,—Andreas

---

[1] *Ut suprà*, p. 47.   [2] Prebendary Scrivener, *ibid*. (ed. 1874), p. 429.
[3] *Ibid.* p. 470.   [4] *Ibid.*   [5] *Concilia*, i. 852.

Cretensis,—Ambrose,—Gaudentius,—Philastrius, — Sedulius, —Jerome,—Augustine (in 6 places). That Tischendorf was a critic of amazing research, singular shrewdness, indefatigable industry ; and that he enjoyed an unrivalled familiarity with ancient documents ; no fair person will deny. But (in the words of Bishop Ellicott,[1] whom we quote so perseveringly for a reason not hard to divine,) his 'great inconstancy,'—his 'natural want of sobriety of critical judgment,'—and his 'unreasonable deference to the readings found in his own codex Sinaiticus ; '—to which should be added '*the utter absence in him of any intelligible fixed critical principles ; '*— all this makes Tischendorf one of the worst of guides to the true Text of Scripture.

The last to enter the field are DRS. WESTCOTT and HORT, whose beautifully-printed edition of 'the New Testament in the original Greek'[2] was published *within five days* of the 'Revised Authorized Version' itself; a "confidential" copy of their work having been already entrusted to every member of the New Test. company of Revisionists to guide them in their labours,—under pledge that they should neither show nor communicate its contents to any one else.—The learned Editors candidly avow, that they 'have deliberately chosen on the whole to rely for documentary evidence on the stores accumulated by their predecessors, and to confine themselves to their proper work of editing the text itself.'[3] Nothing therefore has to be enquired after, except the critical principles on which they have proceeded. And, after assuring

---

[1] *Ut suprà*, p. 47.

[2] *The New Testament in the Original Greek.* The Text revised by Brooke Foss Westcott, D.D., and Fenton John Anthony Hort, D.D. Cambridge and London, 1881.

[3] From the Preface prefixed to the 'limited and private issue' of 1870, p. vi.

us that 'the study of Grouping is the foundation of all
enduring Criticism,'[1] they produce their secret: viz. That in
'every one of our witnesses' *except codex* B, the 'corruptions
are innumerable;'[2] and that, in the Gospels, the one 'group
of witnesses' *of* '*incomparable value*,' is codex B in 'combination with another primary Greek manuscript, as ℵ B, B L, B C,
B T, B D, B Ξ, A B, B Z, B 33, and in S. Mark B Δ.'[3] This is
'Textual Criticism made easy,' certainly. Well aware of the
preposterous results to which such a major premiss must
inevitably lead, we are not surprised to find a plea straightway put in for '*instinctive processes of Criticism*,' of which *the
foundation* '*needs perpetual correction and recorrection*.' But
our confidence fairly gives way when, in the same breath, the
accomplished Editors proceed as follows:—'But *we are
obliged to come to the individual mind* at last; and canons of
Criticism are useful only as warnings against *natural illusions*, and aids to circumspect consideration, not as absolute
rules to prescribe the final decision. It is true that no *individual mind* can ever work with perfect uniformity, or free
itself completely from *its own idiosyncrasies*. Yet a clear
sense of the danger of *unconscious caprice* may do much
towards excluding it. We trust also that the present Text
has escaped some risks of this kind by being the joint production of two Editors of different habits of mind'[4] . . . A
somewhat insecure safeguard surely! May we be permitted
without offence to point out that the 'idiosyncrasies' of an
'individual mind' (to which we learn with astonishment 'we
are obliged to come at last') are probably the very worst
foundation possible on which to build the recension of an
inspired writing? With regret we record our conviction,
that these accomplished scholars have succeeded in producing
a Text vastly more remote from the inspired autographs of

---

[1] *Ut suprà*, p. xv.   [2] *Ibid.* p. xviii.   [3] *Ibid.* p. xvi.   [4] *Ibid.* pp. xviii., xix.

the Evangelists than any which has appeared since the invention of printing. When full Prolegomena have been furnished we shall know more about the matter;[1] but to

---

[1] [*Note,—that I have thought it best, for many reasons, to retain the ensuing note as it originally appeared ; merely restoring [within brackets] those printed portions of it for which there really was no room. The third Article in the present volume will be found to supply an ample exposure of the shallowness of Drs. Westcott and Hort's Textual Theory.*]

While these sheets are passing through the press, a copy of the long-expected volume reaches us. The theory of the respected authors proves to be the shallowest imaginable. It is briefly *this* :—Fastening on the two oldest codices extant (B and ℵ, both of the IVth century), they invent the following hypothesis :—' That the ancestries of those two manuscripts *diverged from a point near the autographs, and never came into contact subsequently.*' [No reason is produced for this opinion.]

Having thus secured two independent witnesses of what was in the sacred autographs, the Editors claim that *the coincidence* of ℵ and B must ' mark those portions of text in which two primitive and entirely separate lines of transmission had not come to differ from each other through independent corruption :' and therefore that, ' in the absence of specially strong internal evidence to the contrary,' ' the readings of ℵ and B combined *may safely be accepted as genuine.*'

But what is to be done when the same two codices diverge *one from the other ?*—In all such cases (we are assured) the readings of any ' binary combination' of B are to be preferred; because ' on the closest scrutiny,' they generally ' have *the ring of genuineness ;*' hardly ever ' *look suspicious* after full consideration.' ' Even when B stands *quite alone,* its readings must never be lightly rejected.' [We are not told why.

But, (rejoins the student who, after careful collation of codex B, has arrived at a vastly different estimate of its character,)—What is to be done when internal and external evidence alike condemn a reading of B ? How is ' *mumpsimus* ' for example to be treated?—' *Mumpsimus* ' (the Editors solemnly reply) as ' the better attested reading '—(by which they mean the reading attested by B,)—we place in our margin. ' *Sumpsimus,*' apparently the *right* reading, we place in the text within ††; in token that it is probably ' *a successful ancient conjecture.*'

We smile, and resume :—But how is the fact to be accounted for that the text of Chrysostom and (in the main) of the rest of the IVth-century Fathers, to whom we are so largely indebted for our critical materials, and who must have employed codices fully as old as B and ℵ: how is it, we

judge from the Remarks (in pp. 541–62) which the learned
Editors (Revisionists themselves) have subjoined to their
elegantly-printed volume, it is to be feared that the fabric

---

ask, that the text of all these, including codex A, differs essentially from
the text exhibited by codices B and ℵ?—The editors reply,—The text of
Chrysostom and the rest, we designate 'Syrian,' and assume to have been
the result of an 'editorial Revision,' which we conjecturally assign to the
second half of the IIIrd century. It is the 'Pre-Syrian' text that we are
in search of; and we recognize the object of our search in codex B.

We stare, and smile again. But how then does it come to pass (we
rejoin) that the Peschito, or primitive *Syriac*, which is older by full a
century and a half than the last-named date, is practically still the same
text?—This fatal circumstance (not overlooked by the learned Editors)
they encounter with another conjectural assumption. 'A Revision' (say
they) 'of the Old Syriac version appears to have taken place early in the
IVth century, or sooner; and doubtless in some connexion with the
Syrian revision of the Greek text, the readings being to a very great
extent coincident.'

And pray, where *is* ' the *Old Syriac* version' of which you speak?—It
is (reply the Editors) our way of designating the fragmentary Syriac MS.
commonly known as 'Cureton's.'—Your way (we rejoin) of manipulating
facts, and disposing of evidence is certainly the most convenient, as it is
the most extraordinary, imaginable: yet is it altogether inadmissible in a
grave enquiry like the present. Syriac scholars are of a widely different
opinion from yourselves. Do you not perceive that you have been drawing upon your imagination for every one of your facts?

We decline in short on the mere conjectural *ipse dixit* of these two
respected scholars to admit either that the Peschito is a Revision of
Cureton's Syriac Version;—or that it was executed about A.D. 325;—or
that the text of Chrysostom and the other principal IVth-century Fathers
is the result of an unrecorded 'Antiochian Revision' which took place
about the year A.D. 275.

But instead of troubling ourselves with removing the upper story of
the visionary structure before us,—which reminds us painfully of a house
which we once remember building with playing-cards,—we begin by
removing the basement-story, which brings the entire superstructure in
an instant to the ground.]

For we decline to admit that the texts exhibited by B ℵ can have
'diverged from a point near the sacred autographs, and never come into
contact subsequently.' We are able to show, on the contrary, that the

will be found to rest too exclusively on vague assumption
and unproved hypothesis.   In other words, a painful appre-
hension is created that their edition of ' The New Testament
in the original Greek' will be found to partake incon-

---

readings they jointly embody afford the strongest presumption that the
MSS. which contain them are nothing else but specimens of those 'corrected,' i.e. *corrupted* copies, which are known to have abounded in the
earliest ages of the Church.   From the prevalence of identical depravations
in either, we infer that they are, on the contrary, derived from the same
not very remote depraved original : and therefore, that their coincidence,
when they differ from all (or nearly all) other MSS., so far from marking
' two primitive and entirely separate lines of transmission' of the inspired
autographs, does but mark what was derived from the same corrupt
common ancestor ; whereby the supposed two independent witnesses to the
Evangelic verity become resolved into *a single witness to a fabricated text
of the IIIrd century.*

It is impossible in the meantime to withhold from these learned and
excellent men (who are infinitely better than their theory) the tribute of
our sympathy and concern at the evident perplexity and constant distress
to which their own fatal major premiss has reduced them.   The Nemesis
of Superstition and Idolatry is ever the same.   Doubt,—unbelief,—
credulity,—general mistrust of *all* evidence, is the inevitable sequel and
penalty.   In 1870, Drs. Westcott and Hort solemnly assured their brother
Revisionists that ' the prevalent assumption, that throughout the N. T. the
true text is to be found *somewhere* among recorded readings, *does not stand
the test of experience:*' [a] and they are evidently still haunted by the same
spectral suspicion.   They see a ghost to be exorcised in every dark corner.
' The Art of *Conjectural Emendation*' (says Dr. Hort) ' depends for its
success so much on personal endowments, fertility of resource in the first
instance, and even more an appreciation of language too delicate to acquiesce
in merely plausible corrections, that it is easy to forget its true character
as a critical operation founded on knowledge and method.' [b]   Specimens of
the writer's skill in this department abound.   *One* occurs at p. 135 (*App.*)
where, *in defiance of every known document,* he seeks to evacuate S. Paul's
memorable injunction to Timothy (2 Tim. i. 13) of all its significance.
[A fuller exposure of Dr. Hort's handling of this important text will be
found later in the present volume.]   May we be allowed to assure the
accomplished writer that IN BIBLICAL TEXTUAL CRITICISM, 'CONJECTURAL
EMENDATION' HAS NO PLACE?

---

[a] P. xxi.   [b] *Introd.* p. 71.

veniently of the nature of a work of the Imagination. As codex א proved fatal to Dr. Tischendorf, so is codex B evidently the rock on which Drs. Westcott and Hort have split. Did it ever occur to those learned men to enquire how the Septuagint Version of the *Old* Testament has fared at the hands of codex B? They are respectfully invited to address themselves to this very damaging enquiry.

But surely (rejoins the intelligent Reader, coming fresh to these studies), the oldest extant Manuscripts (B א A C D) *must* exhibit the purest text! Is it not so?

It *ought* to be so, no doubt (we answer); but it certainly *need not* be the case.

We know that Origen in Palestine, Lucian at Antioch, Hesychius in Egypt, 'revised' the text of the N. T. Unfortunately, they did their work in an age when such fatal misapprehension prevailed on the subject, that each in turn will have inevitably imported a fresh assortment of *monstra* into the sacred writings. Add, the baneful influence of such spirits as Theophilus (sixth Bishop of Antioch, A.D. 168), Tatian, Ammonius, &c., of whom we know there were very many in the primitive age, — some of whose productions, we further know, were freely multiplied in every quarter of ancient Christendom:—add, the fabricated Gospels which anciently abounded; notably the *Gospel of the Hebrews*, about which Jerome is so communicative, and which (he says) he had translated into Greek and Latin:—lastly, freely grant that here and there, with well-meant assiduity, the orthodox themselves may have sought to prop up truths which the early heretics (Basilides, A.D. 134, Valentinus, A.D. 140, with his disciple Heracleon, Marcion, A.D. 150, and the rest,) most perseveringly assailed;—and we have sufficiently explained how it comes to pass that not a few of the codices of primitive Christendom must have exhibited Texts which were even scandalously corrupt. 'It is no less true to fact than paradoxical in sound,' writes the most learned of the Revisionist body,

'that the worst corruptions, to which the New Testament has ever been subjected, originated within a hundred years after it was composed : that Irenæus [A.D. 150] and the African Fathers, and the whole Western, with a portion of the Syrian Church, used far inferior manuscripts to those employed by Stunica, or Erasmus, or Stephens thirteen centuries later, when moulding the Textus Receptus.'[1]

And what else are codices אּ B C D but *specimens—in vastly different degrees—of the class thus characterized* by Prebendary Scrivener ? Nay, who will venture to deny that those codices are indebted for their preservation *solely* to the circumstance, that they were long since recognized as the depositories of Readings which rendered them utterly untrustworthy ?

Only by singling out some definite portion of the Gospels, and attending closely to the handling it has experienced at the hands of A אּ B C D,—to the last four of which it is just now the fashion to bow down as to an oracular voice from which there shall be no appeal,—can the student become aware of the hopelessness of any attempt to construct the Text of the N. T. out of the materials which those codices exclusively supply. Let us this time take S. Mark's account of the healing of 'the paralytic borne of four' (ch. ii. 1–12),— and confront their exhibition of it, with that of the commonly received Text. In the course of those 12 verses, (not reckoning 4 blunders and certain peculiarities of spelling,) there will be found to be 60 variations of reading,—of which

---

[1] Scrivener, *Introduction*, p. 453.—Stunica, it will be remembered, was the chief editor of the Complutensian, or *first printed* edition of the New Testament, (1514).

55 are nothing else but depravations of the text, the result of inattention or licentiousness. Westcott and Hort adopt 23 of these:—(18, in which ℵ B conspire to vouch for a reading: 2, where ℵ is unsupported by B: 2, where B is unsupported by ℵ: 1, where C D are supported by neither ℵ nor B). Now, in the present instance, the 'five old uncials' *cannot be* the depositories of a tradition,—whether Western or Eastern,—because they render inconsistent testimony *in every verse.* It must further be admitted, (for this is really not a question of opinion, but a plain matter of fact,) that it is unreasonable to place confidence in such documents. What would be thought in a Court of Law of five witnesses, called up 47 times for examination, who should be observed to bear contradictory testimony *every time?*

But the whole of the problem does not by any means lie on the surface. All that *appears* is that the five oldest uncials are not trustworthy witnesses; which singly, in the course of 12 verses separate themselves from their fellows 33 times: viz. A, twice;—ℵ, 5 times;—B, 6 times;—C, thrice;—D, 17 times: and which also enter into the 11 following combinations with one another in opposition to the ordinary Text:—A C, twice;—ℵ B, 10 times;—ℵ D, once;—C D, 3 times;—ℵ B C, once;—ℵ B D, 5 times;—ℵ C D, once;— B C D, once;—A ℵ C D, once;—A B C D, once;—A ℵ B C D, once. (Note, that on this last occasion, which is the *only* time when they all 5 agree, *they are certainly all 5 wrong.*) But this, as was observed before, lies on the surface. On closer critical inspection, it is further discovered that their testimony betrays the baseness of their origin by its intrinsic worthlessness. Thus, in Mk. ii. 1, the delicate precision of the announcement ἠκούσθη ὅτι ΕΙΣ ΟΙΚΟΝ ΕΣΤΙ (that '*He has gone in*'), disappears from ℵ B D:—as well as (in ver. 2) the circumstance that it became the signal for many '*immediately*' (ℵ B) to assemble about the door.—In ver. 4, S. Mark explains his predecessor's concise

statement that the paralytic was 'brought to' our SAVIOUR,[1]
by remarking that the thing was '*impossible*' by the ordinary
method of approach.   Accordingly, his account of the expedient resorted to by the bearers fills one entire verse (ver. 4)
of his Gospel.   In the mean time, א B by exhibiting (in
S. Mark ii. 3,) 'bringing unto Him one sick of the palsy'
(φέροντες πρὸς αὐτὸν παραλυτικόν,—which is but a senseless
transposition of πρὸς αὐτόν, παραλυτικὸν φέροντες), do their
best to obliterate the exquisite significance of the second
Evangelist's method.—In the next verse, the perplexity of
the bearers, who, because they could not '*come nigh* Him'
(προσεγγίσαι αὐτῷ), unroofed the house, is lost in א B,—whose
προσενέγκαι has been obtained either from Matt. ix. 2, or else
from Luke v. 18, 19 (εἰσενεγκεῖν, εἰσενέγκωσιν).   'The bed
WHERE WAS the paralytic' (τὸν κράββατον ⸰ΟΠΟΥ ⸰ΗΝ ὁ παρα-
λυτικός, in imitation of 'the roof WHERE WAS' Jesus (τὴν
στέγην ⸰ΟΠΟΥ ⸰ΗΝ [ὁ Ἰησοῦς], which had immediately preceded), is just one of those tasteless depravations, for which
א B, and especially D, are conspicuous among manuscripts.—
In the last verse, the *instantaneous rising* of the paralytic,
noticed by S. Mark (ἠγέρθη εὐθέως), and insisted upon by
S. Luke ('*and immediately he rose up* before them,'—καὶ
παραχρῆμα· ἀναστὰς ἐνώπιον αὐτῶν), is obliterated by
shifting εὐθέως in א B and C to a place where εὐθέως is not
wanted, and where its significancy disappears.

Other instances of Assimilation are conspicuous.   All must
see that, in ver. 5, καὶ ἰδών (א B C) is derived from Matt. ix. 2
and Luke v. 20: as well as that 'Son, *be of good cheer*' (C) is
imported hither from Matt. ix. 2.   '*My* son,' on the other hand
(א), is a mere effort of the imagination.   In the same verse,
σου αἱ ἁμαρτίαι (א B D) is either from Matt. ix. 5 (*sic*); or

---

[1] προσέφερον αὐτῷ,—S. Matt. ix. 2.

else from ver. 9, lower down in S. Mark's narrative. Λέγοντες, in ver. 6 (D), is from S. Luke v. 21. Ὕπαγε (א) in ver. 9, and ὕπαγε εἰς τὸν οἰκόν σου (D), are clearly importations from ver 11. The strange confusion in ver. 7,—' *Because this man thus speaketh, he blasphemeth* ' (B),—and ' *Why doth this man thus speak? He blasphemeth* ' (א D),—is due solely to Mtt. ix. 3 : —while the appendix proposed by א as a substitute for ' We never saw it on this fashion ' (οὐδέποτε οὕτως εἴδομεν), in ver 12 (viz. ' It was never so seen in Israel,' οὐδέποτε οὕτως ἐφάνη ἐν τῷ 'Ισραήλ), has been transplanted hither from S. Matt. ix. 33.

We shall perhaps be told that, scandalously corrupt as the text of א B C D hereabouts may be, no reason has been shown as yet for suspecting that *heretical* depravation ever had anything to do with such phenomena. *That* (we answer) is only because the writings of the early depravers and fabricators of Gospels have universally perished. From the slender relics of their iniquitous performances which have survived to our time, we are sometimes able to lay our finger on a foul blot and to say, ' *This* came from Tatian's Diatessaron ; and *that* from Marcion's mutilated recension of the Gospel according to S. Luke.' The piercing of our SAVIOUR'S side, transplanted by codices א B C from S. John xix. 34 into S. Matt. xxvii. 49, is an instance of the former,—which it may reasonably create astonishment to find that Drs. Westcott and Hort (*alone among Editors*) have nevertheless admitted into their text, as equally trustworthy with the last 12 verses of S. Mark's Gospel. But it occasions a stronger sentiment than surprise to discover that this, ' the gravest interpolation yet laid to the charge of B,'—this ' sentence which neither they nor any other competent scholar can possibly believe that the Evangelist ever wrote,' [1]—has been

---

[1] Scrivener, *Plain Introd.* p. 472.

actually foisted into the margin of *the Revised Version* of
S. Matthew xxvii. 49. Were not the Revisionists aware that
such a disfigurement must prove fatal to their work? *For
whose* benefit is the information volunteered that 'many
ancient authorities' are thus grossly interpolated?

An instructive specimen of depravation follows, which can
be traced to Marcion's mutilated recension of S. Luke's
Gospel. We venture to entreat the favour of the reader's
sustained attention to the license with which the LORD'S
Prayer as given in S. Luke's Gospel (xi. 2–4), is exhibited by
codices א A B C D. For every reason one would have expected
that so precious a formula would have been found enshrined
in the 'old uncials' in peculiar safety; handled by copyists
of the IVth, Vth, and VIth centuries with peculiar reverence.
Let us ascertain exactly what has befallen it :—

(*a*) D introduces the LORD'S Prayer by interpolating the
following paraphrase of S. Matt. vi. 7 :—'*Use not vain
repetitions as the rest : for some suppose that they shall be
heard by their much speaking. But when ye pray*' . . . After
which portentous exordium,

(*b*) B א omit the 5 words, '*Our*' '*which art in heaven,*' Then,

(*c*) D omits the article (τό) before 'name :' and supplements the first petition with the words 'upon us' (ἐφ' ἡμᾶς).
It must needs also transpose the words '*Thy Kingdom*' (ἡ
βασιλεία σου).

(*d*) B in turn omits the third petition,—'*Thy will be done,
as in heaven, also on the earth ;*' which 11 words א retains, but
adds '*so*' before '*also,*' and omits the article (τῆς); finding for
once an ally in A C D.

(*e*) א D for δίδου write δός (from Matt.).

(*f*) א omits the article (τό) before '*day by day.*' And,

(*g*) D, instead of the 3 last-named words, writes '*this day*'
(from Matt.) : substitutes '*debts*' (τὰ ὀφειλήματα) for '*sins*' (τὰ

ἁμαρτήματα,—also from Matt.) : and in place of '*for* [*we*]
ourselves' (καὶ γὰρ αὐτοί) writes '*as also we*' (ὡς καὶ ἡμεῖς,
again from Matt.).—But,

(*h*) ℵ shows its sympathy with D by accepting two-thirds
of this last blunder : exhibiting '*as also* [*we*] *ourselves*' (ὡς καὶ
αὐτοί).

(*i*) D consistently reads '*our debtors*' (τοῖς ὀφειλέταις ἡμῶν)
in place of '*every one that is indebted to us*' (παντὶ ὀφείλοντι
ἡμῖν).—Finally,

(*j*) B ℵ omit the last petition,—'*but deliver us from evil*'
(ἀλλὰ ῥῦσαι ἡμᾶς ἀπὸ τοῦ πονηροῦ)—unsupported by A C or D.
Of lesser discrepancies we decline to take account.

So then, these five 'first-class authorities' are found to
throw themselves into *six different combinations* in their
departures from S. Luke's way of exhibiting the LORD's
Prayer,—which, among them, they contrive to falsify in
respect of no less than 45 words; and yet *they are never able
to agree among themselves as to any single various reading* :
while *only once* are more than two of them observed to stand
together,—viz. in the unauthorized omission of the article.
In respect of 32 (out of the 45) words, *they bear in turn solitary evidence.* What need to declare that it is *certainly false*
in every instance ? Such however is the infatuation of the
Critics, that the vagaries of B are all taken for gospel. Besides
omitting the 11 words which B omits jointly with ℵ, Drs. Westcott and Hort erase from the Book of Life those other 11
precious words which are omitted by B only. And in this
way it comes to pass that the mutilated condition to which
the scalpel of Marcion the heretic reduced the LORD's Prayer
some 1730 years ago,[1] (for the mischief can all be traced back

---

[1] The words omitted are therefore the following 22 :—ἡμῶν, ὁ ἐν τοῖς
οὐρανοῖς . . . γενηθήτω τὸ θέλημά σου, ὡς ἐν οὐρανῷ, καὶ ἐπὶ τῆς γῆς . . .
ἀλλὰ ῥῦσαι ἡμᾶς ἀπὸ τοῦ πονηροῦ.

to *him !*), is palmed off on the Church of England by the Revisionists as the work of the HOLY GHOST!

(A) We may now proceed with our examination of their work, beginning—as Dr. Roberts (one of the Revisionists) does, when explaining the method and results of their labours— with what we hold to be the gravest blot of all, viz. the marks of serious suspicion which we find set against the last Twelve verses of S. Mark's Gospel. Well may the learned Presbyterian anticipate that—

'The reader will be struck by the appearance which this long paragraph presents in the Revised Version. Although inserted, it is marked off by a considerable space from the rest of the Gospel. A note is also placed in the margin containing a brief explanation of this.'[1]

A *very* brief ' explanation' certainly : for the note *explains* nothing. Allusion is made to the following words—

'The two oldest Greek manuscripts, and some other authorities, omit from ver. 9 to the end. Some other authorities have a different ending to the Gospel.'

But now,—For the use of *whom* has this piece of information been volunteered ? Not for learned readers certainly: it being familiarly known to all, that codices B and ℵ *alone of manuscripts* (to their own effectual condemnation) omit these 12 verses. But then scholars know something more about the matter. They also know that these 12 verses have been made the subject of a separate treatise extending to upwards of 300 pages,—which treatise has now been before the world for a full decade of years, and for the best of reasons has never yet been answered. Its object, stated on its title-page, was to vindicate against recent critical objectors, and to

---

[1] *Companion to the Revised Version,* p. 61.

establish 'the last Twelve Verses' of S. Mark's Gospel.[1]
Moreover, competent judges at once admitted that the author
had succeeded in doing what he undertook to do.[2] *Can* it
then be right (we respectfully enquire) still to insinuate into
unlearned minds distrust of twelve consecutive verses of the
everlasting Gospel, which yet have been demonstrated to be
as trustworthy as any other verses which can be named?

The question arises,—But how did it come to pass that
such evil counsels were allowed to prevail in the Jerusalem
Chamber?   Light has been thrown on the subject by two
of the New Test. company.   And first by the learned Congregationalist, Dr. Newth, who has been at the pains to
describe the method which was pursued on every occasion.
The practice (he informs us) was as follows.   The Bishop of
Gloucester and Bristol, as chairman, asks—

'Whether any *Textual* Changes are proposed?   The evidence
for and against is briefly stated, and the proposal considered.
The duty of stating this evidence is by tacit consent devolved
upon (*sic*) two members of the Company, who from their previous studies are specially entitled to speak with authority upon
such questions,—Dr. Scrivener and *Dr. Hort*,—and who come
prepared to enumerate particularly the authorities on either
side. Dr. Scrivener opens up the matter by stating the facts of
the case, and by giving his judgment on the bearings of the
evidence.   Dr. Hort follows, and mentions any additional
matters that may call for notice; and, if differing from Dr.
Scrivener's estimate of the weight of the evidence, gives his

---

[1] *The last Twelve Verses of the Gospel according to S. Mark, vindicated
against recent critical Objectors and established,* by the Rev. J. W. Burgon,—
pp. 334, published by Parker, Oxford, 1871.

[2] As Dr. Jacobson and Dr. Chr. Wordsworth,—the learned Bishops of
Chester and Lincoln.   It is right to state that Bp. Ellicott ' *considers the
passage doubtful.*' (*On Revision,* p. 36.) Dr. Scrivener (it is well known)
differs entirely from Bp. Ellicott on this important point.

reasons and states his own view. After discussion, the vote of
the Company is taken, and the proposed Reading accepted or
rejected. *The Text being thus settled*, the Chairman asks for
proposals on the Rendering."[1]

And thus, the men who were appointed to improve *the
English Translation* are exhibited to us remodelling *the
original Greek*. At a moment's notice, as if by intuition,—
by an act which can only be described as the exercise of
instinct,—these eminent Divines undertake to decide which
shall be deemed the genuine utterances of the HOLY GHOST,[2]
—which *not*. Each is called upon to give his vote, and he
gives it. ' *The Text being thus settled*,' they proceed to do the
only thing they were originally appointed to do; viz. to try
their hands at improving our Authorized Version. But we
venture respectfully to suggest, that by no such ' rough and
ready' process is that most delicate and difficult of all critical
problems—the truth of Scripture—to be ' settled.'

Sir Edmund Beckett remarks that if the description above
given " of the process by which the Revisionists ' settled' the
Greek alterations, is not a kind of joke, it is quite enough to
' settle' this Revised Greek Testament in a very different
sense."[3]   And so, in truth, it clearly is.—" Such a proceeding
appeared to me so strange," (writes the learned and judicious
Editor of the *Speaker's Commentary*,) " that I fully expected
that the account would be corrected, or that some explanation
would be given which might remove the very unpleasant
impression."[4]   We have since heard on the best authority,

---

[1] *Lectures on Bible Revision*, pp. 119–20.
[2] τὰς ἀληθεῖς ῥήσεις Πνεύματος τοῦ Ἁγίου.—Clemens Rom., c. 45.
[3] *Should the Revised New Testament be authorized?*—p. 42.
[4] *Revised Version of the first three Gospels, considered*,—by Canon
Cook,—pp. 221-2.

that namely of Bishop Ellicott himself,[1] that Dr. Newth's account of the method of 'settling' the text of the N. T., pursued in the Jerusalem Chamber, is correct.

But in fact, it proves to have been, from the very first, a definite part of the Programme. The chairman of the Revisionist body, Bishop Ellicott,—when he had " to consider the practical question,"—whether " (1), to construct a critical Text first: or (2), to use preferentially, though not exclusively, some current Text: or (3), *simply to proceed onward* with the work of Revision, whether of Text or Translation, making the current *Textus Receptus* the standard, and departing from it only when critical or grammatical considerations show that it is clearly necessary,—in fact, *solvere ambulando;*" announces, at the end of 19 pages,—" We are driven then to the third alternative."[2]

We naturally cast about for some evidence that the members of the New Testament company possess that mastery of the subject which alone could justify one of their number (Dr. Milligan) in asserting roundly that these 12 verses are ' *not from the pen of S. Mark himself;*'[3] and another (Dr. Roberts) in maintaining that ' the passage is *not the immediate production of S. Mark.*'[4] Dr. Roberts assures us that—

' Eusebius, Gregory of Nyssa, Victor of Antioch, Severus of Antioch, Jerome, as well as other writers, especially Greeks, testify that these verses were not written by S. Mark, or not found in the best copies.'[5]

Will the learned writer permit us to assure him in return that he is entirely mistaken? He is requested to believe that Gregory of Nyssa says nothing of the sort—*says*

---

[1] At p. 34 of his pamphlet in reply to the first two of the present Articles.

[2] *On Revision,* pp. 30 and 49.   [3] *Words of the N. T.* p. 193.

[4] *Companion to the Revised Version,* p. 63.   [5] *Ibid.* p. 62.

nothing at all concerning these verses: that Victor of Antioch vouches emphatically for their *genuineness*: that Severus does but copy, while Jerome does but translate, a few random expressions of Eusebius : and that Eusebius himself *nowhere* 'testifies that these verses were not written by S. Mark.' So far from it, Eusebius actually *quotes the verses*, quotes them as *genuine.* Dr. Roberts is further assured that there are *no* 'other writers,' whether Greek or Latin, who insinuate doubt concerning these verses. On the contrary, besides *both* the Latin and *all the* Syriac—besides the Gothic and the *two* Egyptian versions—there exist four authorities of the IInd century ;— as many of the IIIrd ;—five of the Vth ;—four of the VIth ;— as many of the VIIth ;—together with *at least ten* of the IVth[1] (*contemporaries therefore of codices* B *and* ℵ);—which actually *recognize* the verses in question.   Now, when to *every known Manuscript but two* of bad character, besides *every ancient Version, some one-and-thirty Fathers* have been added, 18 of whom must have used copies at least as old as either B or ℵ, —Dr. Roberts is assured that an amount of external authority has been accumulated which is simply overwhelming in discussions of this nature.

But the significance of a single feature of the Lectionary, of which up to this point nothing has been said, is alone sufficient to determine the controversy.   We refer to the fact that *in every part of Eastern Christendom* these same 12 verses —neither more nor less—have been from the earliest recorded period, and still are, a *proper lesson both for the Easter season and for Ascension Day.*

---

[1] Viz. Eusebius, — Macarius Magnes, — Aphraates, — Didymus, — the Syriac *Acts of the App.,* — Epiphanius, — Ambrose, — Chrysostom, — Jerome,—Augustine. It happens that the disputation of Macarius Magnes (A.D. 300–350) with a heathen philosopher, which has recently come to light, contains an elaborate discussion of S. Mark xvi. 17, 18.   Add the curious story related by the author of the *Paschal Chronicle* (A.D. 628) concerning Leontius, Bishop of Antioch (A.D. 348),—p. 289.   This has been hitherto overlooked.

We pass on.

(B) A more grievous perversion of the truth of Scripture is scarcely to be found than occurs in the proposed revised exhibition of S. Luke ii. 14, in the Greek and English alike; for indeed not only is the proposed Greek text (ἐν ἀνθρώποις εὐδοκίας) impossible, but the English of the Revisionists ('*peace among men in whom he is well pleased*') 'can be arrived at' (as one of themselves has justly remarked) 'only through some process which would make any phrase bear almost any meaning the translator might like to put upon it.'[1] More than that: the harmony of the exquisite three-part hymn, which the Angels sang on the night of the Nativity, becomes hopelessly marred, and its structural symmetry destroyed, by the welding of the second and third members of the sentence into one. Singular to relate, the addition of *a single final letter* (ς) has done all this mischief. Quite as singular is it that we should be able at the end of upwards of 1700 years to discover what occasioned its calamitous insertion. From the archetypal copy, by the aid of which the old Latin translation was made, (for the Latin copies *all* read '*pax hominibus bonæ voluntatis*,') the preposition ἐν was evidently away,—absorbed apparently by the ἀν which immediately follows. In order therefore to make a sentence of some sort out of words which, without ἐν, are simply unintelligible, εὐδοκία was turned into εὐδοκίας. It is accordingly a significant circumstance that, whereas there exists *no* Greek copy of the Gospels which *omits* the ἐν, there is scarcely a Latin exhibition of the place to be found which contains it.[2] To return however to the genuine clause,— 'Good-will towards men' (ἐν ἀνθρώποις εὐδοκία):

---

[1] Scrivener's *Introduction*, p. 515.

[2] Tisch. specifies 7 Latin copies. Origen (iii. 946 *f.*), Jerome (vii. 282), and Leo (ap. Sabatier) are the only patristic quotations discoverable.

Absolutely decisive of the true reading of the passage —irrespectively of internal considerations—ought to be the consideration that it is vouched for *by every known copy* of the Gospels of whatever sort, excepting only ℵ A B D : the first and third of which, however, were anciently corrected and brought into conformity with the Received Text; while the second (A) is observed to be so inconstant in its testimony, that in the primitive 'Morning-hymn' (given in another page of the same codex, and containing a quotation of S. Luke ii. 14), the correct reading of the place is found. D's complicity in error is the less important, because of the ascertained sympathy between that codex and the Latin. In the meantime the two Syriac Versions are a full set-off against the Latin copies; while the hostile evidence of the Gothic (which this time sides with the Latin) is more than neutralized by the unexpected desertion of the Coptic version from the opposite camp. The Armenian, Georgian, Æthiopic, Slavonic and Arabian versions, are besides all with the Received Text. It therefore comes to this :—We are invited to make our election between every other copy of the Gospels,—every known Lectionary,—and (not least of all) the ascertained ecclesiastical usage of the Eastern Church from the beginning,—on the one hand : and the testimony of four Codices without a history or a character, which concur in upholding a patent mistake, on the other. Will any one hesitate as to which of these two parties has the stronger claim on his allegiance ?

Could doubt be supposed to be entertained in any quarter, it must at all events be borne away by the torrent of Patristic authority which is available on the present occasion :—

In the IInd century,—we have the testimony of (1) Irenæus.[1]

------

[1] i. 459.

In the IIIrd,—that of (2) Origen [1] in 3 places,—and of (3) the *Apostolical Constitutions* [2] in 2.

In the IVth,—(4) Eusebius,[3]—(5) Aphraates the Persian,[4] —(6) Titus of Bostra, [5] each twice;—(7) Didymus [6] in 3 places;—(8) Gregory of Nazianzus,[7]—(9) Cyril of Jerusalem,[8] —(10) Epiphanius [9] twice ; —(11) Gregory of Nyssa [10] 4 times,—(12) Ephraem Syrus,[11]—(13) Philo bishop of Carpasus,[12]—(14) Chrysostom,[13] in 9 places,—and (15) a nameless preacher at Antioch,[14] — all these, *contemporaries (be it remembered) of* B *and* ℵ, are found to bear concurrent testimony in favour of the commonly received text.

In the Vth century,—(16) Cyril of Alexandria,[15] on no less than 14 occasions, vouches for it also;—(17) Theodoret [16] on 4;—(18) Theodotus of Ancyra [17] on 5 (once [18] in a homily preached before the Council of Ephesus on Christmas-day, A.D. 431);—(19) Proclus [19] archbishop of Constantinople;— (20) Paulus [20] bishop of Emesa (in a sermon preached before Cyril of Alexandria on Christmas-day, A.D. 431);—(21) the Eastern bishops [21] at Ephesus collectively, A.D. 431 (an unusually weighty piece of evidence);—and lastly, (22) Basil

[1] i. 374; ii. 714; iv. 15.   [2] vii. 47; viii. 13.
[3] *Dem. Ev.* pp. 163, 342.   [4] i. 180, 385.
[5] In loc.   Also *in Luc.* xix. 29 (*Cat. Ox.* 141).
[6] *De Trin.* p. 84; Cord. *Cat. in Ps.* ii. 450, 745.
[7] i. 845,—which is reproduced in the *Paschal Chronicle*, p. 374.
[8] P. 180; cf. p. 162.   [9] i. 154, 1047.   [10] i. 355, 696, 6 ; 97 iii. 346.
[11] Gr. iii. 434.   [12] Ap. Galland. ix. 754.
[13] i. 587 ; ii. 453, 454 ; vi. 393 ; vii. 311, 674 ; viii. 85 ; xi. 347.   Also *Cat. in Ps.* iii. 139.   [14] Ap. Chrys. vi. 424; cf. p. 417.
[15] *In Luc.* pp. 12, 16, 502 (= Mai, ii. 128).   Also Mai, ii. 343, *Hom. de Incarn.* p. 109.   *Opp.* ii. 593; v.¹ 681, 30, 128, 380, 402, 154; vi. 398. Maii, iii.² 286.   [16] i. 290, 1298; ii. 18; iii. 480.
[17] Ap. Galland. ix. 446, 476.   *Concil.* iii. 1001, 1023.
[18] *Concil.* iii. 1002.   [19] Ap. Galland. ix. 629.
[20] *Concil.* iii. 1095.   [21] *Concil.* iii. 829 = Cyr. *Opp.* vi. 159.

of Seleucia.[1] Now, let it be remarked that *these were contemporaries of codex* A.

In the VIth century,—the Patristic witnesses are (23) Cosmas, the voyager,[2] 5 times,—(24) Anastasius Sinaita,[3] — (25) Eulogius[4] archbishop of Alexandria: *contemporaries, be it remembered, of codex* D.

In the VIIth,—(26) Andreas of Crete [5] twice.

And in the VIIIth,—(27) Cosmas[6] bishop of Maiuma near Gaza,—and his pupil (28) John Damascene,[7] —and (29) Germanus [8] archbishop of Constantinople.

To these 29 illustrious names are to be added unknown writers of uncertain date, but *all* of considerable antiquity; and some [9] are proved by internal evidence to belong to the IVth or Vth century,—in short, to be of the date of the Fathers whose names 16 of them severally bear, but among whose genuine works their productions are probably *not* to be reckoned. One of these was anciently mistaken for (30) Gregory Thaumaturgus: [10] a second, for (31) Methodius: [11] a third, for (32) Basil.[12] Three others, with different degrees of reasonableness, have been supposed to be (33, 34, 35) Athanasius.[13] One has passed for (36) Gregory of Nyssa; [14] another for (37) Epiphanius; [15] while no less than eight (38 to 45) have been mistaken for Chrysostom,[16] some of them being certainly his contemporaries. Add (46) one anonymous Father,[17] and (47) the author of the apocryphal

---

[1] *Nov. Auctar.* i. 596.   [2] Montf. ii. 152, 160, 247, 269.
[3] *Hexaem.* ed. Migne, vol. 89, p. 899.   [4] Ap. Galland. xii. 308.
[5] Ed. Combefis, 14, 54 ; ap. Galland. xiii. 100, 123.
[6] Ap. Galland. xiii. 235.   [7] ii. 836.
[8] Ap. Galland. xiii. 212.   [9] E.g. Chrys. *Opp.* viii.; *Append.* 214.
[10] P. 6 D.   [11] Ap. Galland. iii. 809.   [12] ii. 602.
[13] ii. 101, 122, 407.   [14] iii. 447.   [15] ii. 298.
[16] ii. 804; iii. 783; v. 638, 670, 788; viii. 214, 285; x. 754, 821.
[17] Cord. *Cat. in Ps.* ii. 960.

Acta Pilati,—and it will be perceived that 18 ancient authorities have been added to the list, every whit as competent to witness what was the text of S. Luke ii. 14 at the time when A B ℵ D were written, as Basil or Athanasius, Epiphanius or Chrysostom themselves.[1] *For our present purpose* they are *Codices* of the IVth, Vth, and VIth centuries. In this way then, far more than *forty-seven* ancient witnesses have come back to testify to the men of this generation that the commonly received reading of S. Luke ii. 14 is *the true reading*, and that the text which the Revisionists are seeking to palm off upon us is *a fabrication and a blunder*. Will any one be found to maintain that the authority of B and ℵ is appreciable, when confronted by the first 15 *contemporary Ecclesiastical Writers* above enumerated? or that A can stand against the 7 which follow?

This is not all however. Survey the preceding enumeration geographically, and note that, besides 1 name from Gaul,—at least 2 stand for Constantinople,—while 5 are dotted over Asia Minor:—10 at least represent Antioch; and —6, other parts of Syria:—3 stand for Palestine, and 12 for other Churches of the East:—at least 5 are Alexandrian,— 2 are men of Cyprus, and—1 is from Crete. If the articulate voices of so many illustrious Bishops, coming back to us in this way from every part of ancient Christendom and all delivering the same unfaltering message, — if *this* be not allowed to be decisive on a point of the kind just now before us, then pray let us have it explained to us,—What amount of evidence *will* men accept as final? It is high time that this were known . . . The plain truth is, that a case has

---

[1] Of the ninety-two places above quoted, Tischendorf knew of only *eleven*, Tregelles adduces only *six*.—Neither critic seems to have been aware that 'Gregory Thaum.' is not the author of the citation they ascribe to him. And why does Tischendorf quote as Basil's what *is known* not to have been his?

been established against ℵ A B D and the Latin version, which
amounts to *proof* that those documents, even when they conspire to yield the self-same evidence, are not to be depended
on as witnesses to the text of Scripture.   The history of
the reading advocated by the Revisionists is briefly this :—*It
emerges into notice in the* II*nd century ; and in the* V*th, disappears from sight entirely.*

Enough and to spare has now been offered concerning
the true reading of S. Luke ii. 14.   But because we propose
to ourselves that *no uncertainty whatever* shall remain on
this subject, it will not be wasted labour if at parting we
pour into the ruined citadel just enough of shot and shell to
leave no dark corner standing for the ghost of a respectable
doubt hereafter to hide in.   Now, it is confessedly nothing
else but the high estimate which Critics have conceived of
the value of the testimony of the old uncials (ℵ A B C D),
which has occasioned any doubt at all to exist in this behalf.
Let the learned Reader then ascertain for himself the
character of codices ℵ A B C D hereabouts, by collating *the
context in which S. Luke* ii. 14 *is found,* viz. the 13 verses
which precede and the one verse (ver. 15) which immediately
follows.   If the old uncials are observed all to sing in tune
throughout, hereabouts, well and good : but if on the contrary, their voices prove utterly discordant, *who* sees not that
the last pretence has been taken away for placing *any confidence at all* in their testimony concerning the text of
ver. 14, turning as it does on the presence or absence of *a
single letter ?* . . . He will find, as the result of his analysis,
that within the space of those 14 verses, the old uncials are
responsible for 56 'various readings' (so-called): singly, for
41 ; in combination with one another, for 15.   So diverse,
however, is the testimony they respectively render, that they
are found severally to differ from the Text of the cursives no

less than 70 times.   Among them, besides twice varying the
phrase,—they contrive to omit 19 words:—to add 4:—to
substitute 17:—to alter 10:—to transpose 24.—Lastly, these
five codices are observed (within the same narrow limits) to
fall into *ten* different combinations: viz. B ℵ, for 5 readings;
—B D, for 2;—ℵ C, ℵ D, A C, ℵ B D, A ℵ D, A B ℵ D, B ℵ C D,
A B ℵ C D, for 1 each. A therefore, which stands alone *twice*,
is found in combination 4 times;—C, which stands alone
once, is found in combination 4 times;[1]—B, which stands
alone 5 times, is found in combination 6 times;—ℵ, which
stands alone 11 times, is found in combination 8 times;—D,
which stands alone 22 times, is found in combination 7
times. . . . And now,—for the last time we ask the question,
—With what show of reason can the unintelligible εὐδοκίας
(of ℵ A B D) be upheld as genuine, in defiance of *the whole
body of Manuscripts*, uncial and cursive,—the great bulk of
the Versions,—and the mighty array of (upwards of fifty)
Fathers exhibited above?

(c) We are at last able to proceed, with a promise that
we shall rarely prove so tedious again.   But it is absolutely
necessary to begin by clearing the ground.   We may not
go on doubting for ever.   The 'Angelic hymn,' and 'The
last 12 Verses' of S. Mark's Gospel, are convenient places
for a trial of strength.   *It has now been proved* that the commonly received text of S. Luke ii. 14 is the true text,—the
Revisionists' emendation of the place, a palpable mistake.
On behalf of the second Gospel, we claim to have also
established that an important portion of the sacred narrative
has been unjustly branded with a note of ignominy; from
which we solemnly call upon the Revisionists to set the
Evangelist free.   The pretence that no harm has been done

---

[1] But then, note that c is only available for comparison down to the end
of ver. 5.   In the 9 verses which have been lost, who shall say how many
more eccentricities would have been discoverable?

him by the mere statement of what is an undeniable fact,—
(viz. that ' the two oldest Greek manuscripts, and some other
authorities, omit from verse 9 to the end;' and that ' some
other authorities have a different ending to the Gospel,')—
will not stand examination. Pin to the shoulder of an
honourable man a hearsay libel on his character, and see
what he will have to say to you! Besides,— *Why have the
12 verses been further separated off from the rest of the Gospel*?
This at least is unjustifiable.

Those who, with Drs. Roberts and Milligan,[1] have been
taught to maintain ' that the passage *is not the immediate
production of S. Mark,*'—' *can hardly be regarded as a part
of the original Gospel ;* but is rather an addition made to
it at a very early age, whether in the lifetime of the
Evangelist or not, it is impossible to say:'—such Critics are
informed that they stultify themselves when they proceed
in the same breath to assure the offended reader that the
passage ' is nevertheless *possessed of full canonical authority.*'[2]
Men who so write show that they do not understand the
question. For if these 12 verses *are* ' canonical Scripture,'—
as much inspired as the 12 verses which precede them, and
as worthy of undoubting confidence,—then, whether they be
' the production of S. Mark,' or of some other, is a purely
irrelevant circumstance. The *Authorship* of the passage, as
every one must see, is not the question. The last 12 verses
of Deuteronomy, for instance, were probably not written by
Moses. Do we therefore separate them off from the rest of
Deuteronomy, and encumber the margin with a note expressive of our opinion ? Our Revisionists, so far from holding
what follows to be ' canonical Scripture,' are careful to state
that a rival ending to be found elsewhere merits serious
attention. S. Mark xvi. 9–20, therefore (*according to them*),

---

[1] *Companion to the Revised Version*, pp. 62, 63. *Words of the N. T.*
p. 193.   [2] *Words of the N. T.* p. 193.

is *not certainly* a genuine part of the Gospel; *may*, after all,
be nothing else but a spurious accretion to the text. And as
long as such doubts are put forth by our Revisionists, they
publish to the world that, *in their account* at all events,
these verses are *not* 'possessed of full canonical authority.'
If 'the two oldest Greek manuscripts' *justly* 'omit from
verse 9 to the end' (as stated in the margin), will any one
deny that our printed Text ought to omit them also?[1]　On
the other hand, if the circumstance is a mere literary
curiosity, will any one maintain that it is entitled to
abiding record in the margin of the *English Version* of the
everlasting page?—*affords any warrant whatever for sepa-*
rating 'the last Twelve Verses' from their context?

(D) We can probably render ordinary readers no more
effectual service, than by offering now to guide them over
a few select places, concerning the true reading of which
the Revisionists either entertain such serious doubts that
they have *recorded* their uncertainty in the margin of their
work; or else, entertaining no doubts at all, have deliberately thrust a new reading into the body of their text, and
that, without explanation, apology, or indeed record of any
kind.[2]　One remark should be premised, viz. that 'various

---

[1] Drs. Westcott and Hort (consistently enough) put them *on the self-*
same footing with the evidently spurious ending found in L.

[2] True, that a separate volume of Greek Text has been put forth, showing every change which has been either actually accepted, or else suggested
for future possible acceptance. But (in the words of the accomplished
editor), 'the *Revisers are not responsible for its publication.*' Moreover,
(and this is the chief point,) it is a sealed book to all but Scholars.

It were unhandsome, however, to take leave of the learned labours of
Prebendary Scrivener and Archdeacon Palmer, without a few words of
sympathy and admiration. Their volumes (mentioned at the beginning
of the present Article) are all that was to have been expected from the
exquisite scholarship of their respective editors, and will be of abiding
interest and value. *Both* volumes should be in the hands of every

E

Readings' as they are (often most unreasonably) called, are seldom if ever the result of conscious *fraud*. An immense number are to be ascribed to sheer accident. It was through erroneous judgment, we repeat, not with evil intent, that men took liberties with the deposit. They imported into their copies whatever readings they considered highly recommended. By some of these ancient Critics it seems to have been thought allowable *to abbreviate*, by simply leaving out whatever did not appear to themselves strictly necessary: by others, to *transpose* the words—even the members—of a sentence, almost to any extent: by others, to *substitute* easy expressions for difficult ones. In this way it comes to pass that we are often presented, and in the oldest documents of all, with Readings which stand self-condemned; are clearly fabrications. That it was held allowable to assimilate one Gospel to another, is quite certain. Add, that as early as the IInd century there abounded in the Church documents,— 'Diatessarons' they were sometimes called,—of which the avowed object was to weave one continuous and connected narrative 'out of the four;'—and we shall find that as many heads have been provided, as will suffice for the classification of almost every various reading which we are likely to encounter in our study of the Gospels.

I. To ACCIDENTAL CAUSES then we give the foremost place,

---

scholar, for neither of them supersedes the other. Dr. Scrivener has (with rare ability and immense labour) set before the Church, *for the first time, the Greek Text which was followed by the Revisers of* 1611, viz. Beza's N. T. of 1598, supplemented in above 190 places from other sources; every one of which the editor traces out in his *Appendix*, pp. 648–56. At the foot of each page, he shows what changes have been introduced into the Text by the Revisers of 1881.—Dr. Palmer, taking *the Text of Stephens* (1550) as his basis, presents us with the Readings adopted by the Revisers of the 'Authorized Version,' and relegates the displaced Readings (of 1611) to the foot of each page.—We cordially congratulate them both, and thank them for the good service they have rendered.

and of these we have already furnished the reader with two
notable and altogether dissimilar specimens.   The first (viz.
the omission of S. Mark xvi. 9–20 from certain ancient copies
of the Gospel) seems to have originated in an unique circumstance.   According to the Western order of the four, S. Mark
occupies *the last* place.   From the earliest period it had been
customary to write τέλος ("END") after the 8th verse of
his last chapter, in token that *there* a famous ecclesiastical
lection comes to a close.   *Let the last leaf of one very ancient
archetypal copy have begun at ver. 9 ; and let that last leaf
have perished ;—and all is plain.*   A faithful copyist will
have ended the Gospel perforce — as B and ℵ have done—
at S. Mark xvi. 8. . . . Our other example (S. Luke ii. 14)
will have resulted from an accident of the most ordinary
description,—as was explained at the outset.—To the foregoing, a few other specimens of erroneous readings resulting
from Accident shall now be added.

(*a*) Always instructive, it is sometimes even entertaining
to trace the history of a mistake which, dating from the IInd
or IIIrd century, has remained without a patron all down the
subsequent ages, until at last it has been suddenly taken
up in our own times by an Editor of the sacred Text, and
straightway palmed off upon an unlearned generation as
the genuine work of the HOLY GHOST.   Thus, whereas the
Church has hitherto supposed that S. Paul's company ' were
in all in the ship *two hundred threescore and sixteen souls* '
(Acts xxvii. 37), Drs. Westcott and Hort (relying on the
authority of B and the Sahidic version) insist that what S.
Luke actually wrote was ' *about seventy-six.*'   In other words,
instead of διακόσιαι ἐβδομηκονταέξ, we are invited henceforth to read ὩC ἐβδομηκονταέξ.   What can have given rise
to so formidable a discrepancy ?   Mere accident, we answer.
First, whereas S. Luke certainly wrote ἦμεν δὲ ἐν τῷ πλοίῳ

E 2

αἱ πᾶσαι ψυχαί, his last six words at some very early period underwent the familiar process of Transposition, and became, αἱ πᾶσαι ψυχαὶ ἐν τῷ πλοίῳ; whereby the *word* πλοίῳ and the *numbers* διακόσιαι ἑβδομηκοντάεξ were brought into close proximity. (It is thus that Lachmann, Tischendorf, Tregelles, &c., wrongly exhibit the place.) But since '276' when represented in Greek numerals is COS, the inevitable consequence was that the words (written in uncials) ran thus: ΨΥΧΑΙΕΝΤΩΠΛΟΙΩCOS. Behold, the secret is out! Who sees not what has happened? There has been no intentional falsification of the text. There has been no critical disinclination to believe that 'a corn-ship, presumably heavily laden, would contain so many souls,'—as an excellent judge supposes.[1] The discrepancy has been the result of sheer accident: is the merest blunder. Some IInd-century copyist connected the last letter of ΠΛΟΙΩ with the next ensuing numeral, which stands for 200 (viz. C); and made an *independent word* of it, viz. ὡς—i.e. 'about.' But when C (i.e. 200) has been taken away from COS (i.e. 276), 76 is perforce all that remains. In other words, the result of so slight a blunder has been that instead of '*two hundred* and seventy-six' (COS), some one wrote ὡς ος' — i.e. '*about* seventy-six.' His blunder would have been diverting had it been confined to the pages of a codex which is *full* of blunders. When however it is adopted by the latest Editors of the N. T. (Drs. Westcott and Hort),—and by their influence has been foisted into the margin of our revised English Version — it becomes high time that we should reclaim against such a gratuitous depravation of Scripture.

All this ought not to have required explaining: the blunder is so gross,—its history so patent. But surely, had

---

[1] The number is not excessive. There were about 600 persons aboard the ship in which Josephus traversed the same waters. (*Life*, c. III.)

its origin been ever so obscure, the most elementary critical knowledge joined to a little mother-wit ought to convince a man that the reading ὡς ἑβδομηκονταέξ *cannot* be trustworthy.   A reading discoverable only in codex B and one Egyptian version (which was evidently executed from codices of the same corrupt type as codex B) *may always be dismissed as certainly spurious.*   But further,—Although a man might of course say ' about *seventy* ' or ' about *eighty*,' (which is how Epiphanius [1] quotes the place,) *who* sees not that ' about seventy-*six* ' is an impossible expression ?   Lastly, the two false witnesses give divergent testimony even while they seem to be at one : for the Sahidic (or Thebaic) version arranges the words in an order *peculiar to itself.*

(*b*) Another corruption of the text, with which it is proposed henceforth to disfigure our Authorized Version, (originating like the last in sheer accident,) occurs in Acts xviii. 7.   It is related concerning S. Paul, at Corinth, that having forsaken the synagogue of the Jews, ' he entered into a certain man's house *named Justus* ' (ὀνόματι 'Ιούστου). That this is what S. Luke wrote, is to be inferred from the fact that it is found in almost every known copy of the Acts, beginning with A D G H L P.   Chrysostom—the only ancient Greek Father who quotes the place—*so* quotes it.   This is, in consequence, the reading of Lachmann, Tregelles, and Tischendorf in his 7th edition.   But then, the last syllable of ' name ' (ONOMATI) and the first three letters of ' Justus ' (IOYCTOY), in an uncial copy, may easily get mistaken for an independent word.   Indeed it only wants a horizontal stroke (at the summit of the second ι in TIIOY) to produce ' Titus ' (TITOY).   In the Syriac and Sahidic versions accordingly, ' Titus ' actually stands *in place of* ' Justus,'—a reading

---

[1] ii. 61 and 83.

no longer discoverable in any extant codex. As a matter of fact, the error resulted *not* in the *substitution* of 'Titus' for 'Justus,' but in the introduction of *both* names where S. Luke wrote but one. א and E, the Vulgate, and the Coptic version, exhibit '*Titus Justus.*' And that the foregoing is a true account of the birth and parentage of 'Titus' is proved by the tell-tale circumstance, that in B the letters TI and IOY are all religiously retained, and a supernumerary letter (T) has been thrust in between,—the result of which is to give us one more imaginary gentleman, viz. '*Titius* Justus;' with whose appearance,—(and he is found *nowhere* but in codex B,)—Tischendorf in his 8th ed., with Westcott and Hort in theirs, are so captivated, that they actually give him a place in their text. It was out of compassion (we presume) for the friendless stranger '*Titus* Justus' that our Revisionists have, in preference, promoted *him* to honour : in which act of humanity they stand alone. Their 'new Greek Text' is *the only one in existence* in which the imaginary foreigner has been advanced to citizenship, and assigned 'a local habitation and a name.' . . . . Those must have been wondrous drowsy days in the Jerusalem Chamber when such manipulations of the inspired text were possible !

(*c*) The two foregoing depravations grew out of the ancient practice of writing the Scriptures in uncial characters (i. e. in capital letters), no space being interposed between the words. Another striking instance is supplied by S. Matthew xi. 23 and S. Luke x. 15, where however the error is so transparent that the wonder is how it can ever have imposed upon any one. What makes the matter serious is, that it gives a turn to a certain Divine saying, of which it is incredible that either our SAVIOUR or His Evangelists knew anything. We have hitherto believed that the solemn words ran as follows :—'And thou, Capernaum, which art exalted (ἡ ... ὑψωθεῖσα) unto heaven, shalt be brought down (καταβιβασθήσῃ) to hell.' For this, our Revisionists invite us to substitute, in S. Luke as well as in S. Matthew,—'And thou, Capernaum, shalt thou be exalted (μὴ ... ὑψωθήσῃ;) unto heaven?' And then, in S. Matthew, (but not in S. Luke,)—'Thou shalt go down (καταβήσῃ) into Hades.' Now, what can have happened to occasion such a curious perversion of our LORD's true utterance, and to cause Him to ask an unmeaning *question* about the future, when He was clearly announcing a *fact*, founded on the history of the past?

A stupid blunder has been made (we answer), of which traces survive (as usual) only in the same little handful of suspicious documents. The final letter of Capernaum (M) by cleaving to the next ensuing letter (H) has made an independent word (MH); which new word necessitates a change in the construction, and causes the sentence to become interrogative. And yet, fourteen of the uncial manuscripts and the whole body of the cursives know nothing of this: neither does the Peschito—nor the Gothic version: no,—nor Chrysostom,—nor Cyril,—nor ps.-Cæsarius,—nor Theodoret,—the only Fathers who quote either place. The sole witnesses for μὴ ... ὑψωθήσῃ in *both* Gospels are ℵ B, copies of the old Latin, Cureton's Syriac, the Coptic, and the Æthiopic versions,—a consensus of authorities which ought to be held fatal to any reading. c joins the conspiracy in Matthew xi. 23, but not in Luke x. 15: D L consent in Luke, but not in Matthew. The Vulgate, which sided with ℵ B in S. Matthew, forsakes them in S. Luke. In writing *both* times καταβήσῃ ('thou shalt go down'), codex B (forsaken this time by ℵ) is supported by a single manuscript, viz. D. But because, in Matthew xi. 23, B obtains the sanction of the Latin copies, καταβήσῃ is actually introduced into the Revised Text, and we are quietly informed in the margin that 'Many ancient authorities read *be brought down :*' the truth being (as the reader has been made aware) that there are *only two manuscripts in existence which read anything else.* And (what deserves attention) those two manuscripts are convicted of having *borrowed their quotation from the Septuagint,*[1] and therefore stand self-condemned. . . . Were the occupants of the Jerusalem Chamber all—saving the two who in their published edition insist on reading (with B and D) καταβήσῃ in both places—*all* fast asleep when they became consenting parties to this sad mistake?

II. It is time to explain that, if the most serious depravations of Scripture are due to Accident, a vast number are unmistakably the result of DESIGN, and are very clumsily executed too. The enumeration of a few of these may prove instructive: and we shall begin with something which is found in S. Mark xi. 3. With nothing perhaps will each several instance so much impress the devout student of Scripture, as with the exquisite structure of a narrative in which corrupt readings stand self-revealed and self-condemned, the instant they are ordered to come to the front and show themselves. But the point to which we especially invite his attention is, the sufficiency of the *external evidence* which Divine Wisdom is observed to have invariably provided for the establishment of the truth of His written Word.

(*a*) When our LORD was about to enter His capital in lowly triumph, He is observed to have given to 'two of His disciples' directions well calculated to suggest the mysterious nature of the incident which was to follow. They were commanded to proceed to the entrance of a certain village,—to unloose a certain colt which they would find

---

[1] Isaiah xiv. 15.

tied there,—and to bring the creature straightway to JESUS.
Any obstacle which they might encounter would at once
disappear before the simple announcement that 'the LORD
hath need of him.'[1] But, singular to relate, this transaction
is found to have struck some third-rate IIIrd-century Critic
as not altogether correct. The good man was evidently of
opinion that the colt,—as soon as the purpose had been
accomplished for which it had been obtained,—ought in
common fairness to have been returned to 'the owners
thereof.' (S. Luke xix. 33.) Availing himself therefore of
there being no nominative before 'will send' (in S. Mark
xi. 3), he assumed that it was *of Himself* that our LORD was
still speaking: feigned that the sentence is to be explained
thus:—'say ye, "that the LORD hath need of him *and
will straightway send him hither."' According to this view
of the case, our SAVIOUR instructed His two Disciples to
convey to the owner of the colt an undertaking from Himself *that He would send the creature back as soon as He had
done with it:* would treat the colt, in short, *as a loan.* A
more stupid imagination one has seldom had to deal with.
But in the meantime, by way of clenching the matter, the
Critic proceeded on his own responsibility to thrust into the
text the word '*again*' (πάλιν). The fate of such an unauthorized accretion might have been confidently predicted.
After skipping about in quest of a fixed resting-place for a
few centuries (see the note at foot [2]), πάλιν has shared the
invariable fate of all such spurious adjuncts to the truth of
Scripture, viz.: It has been effectually eliminated from the
copies. Traces of it linger on only in those untrustworthy
witnesses א B C D L Δ, and about twice as many cursive

---

[1] S. Matthew xxi. 1–3. S. Mark xi. 1–6. S. Luke xix. 29–34.

[2] א D L read—αὐτὸν ἀποστελλει ΠΑΛΙΝ ὦδε : C*,—αὐτον ΠΑΛΙΝ ἀποστελλει ὦδε : B,—ἀποστελλει ΠΑΛΙΝ αὐτον ὦδε : Δ,—ἀποστελλει ΠΑΛΙΝ
ὦδε : y^cr—αὐτον ἀποστελλει ΠΑΛΙΝ.

copies, also of depraved type. So transparent a fabrication ought in fact to have been long since forgotten. Yet have our Revisionists not been afraid to revive it. In S. Mark xi. 3, they invite us henceforth to read, 'And if any one say unto you, Why do ye this? say ye, The LORD hath need of him, and straightway *He* (i.e. the LORD) *will send him* BACK *hither.'* .... Of what can they have been dreaming? They cannot pretend that they have *Antiquity* on their side: for, besides the whole mass of copies with A at their head, *both* the Syriac, *both* the Latin, and *both* the Egyptian versions, the Gothic, the Armenian,—all in fact except the Æthiopic, —are against them. Even Origen, who twice inserts πάλιν,[1] twice leaves it out.[2] *Quid plura?*

(*b*) No need to look elsewhere for our next instance. A novel statement arrests attention five verses lower down: viz. that 'Many spread their garments upon the way' [and why not '*in* the way'? εἰς does not mean 'upon']; 'and others, branches *which they had cut from the fields*' (S. Mark xi. 8). But how in the world could they have done *that?* They must have been clever people certainly if they 'cut *branches* from' anything except *trees*. Was it because our Revisionists felt this, that in the margin they volunteer the information, that the Greek for 'branches' is in strictness '*layers of leaves*'? But what *are* 'layers of leaves'? and what *proof* is there that στοιβάδες has that meaning? and how could '*layers of leaves*' have been suddenly procured from such a quarter? We turn to our Authorized Version, and are refreshed by the familiar and intelligible words: 'And others cut down branches off the trees and strawed them in the way.' Why then has this been changed? In an ordinary sentence, consisting of 12 words, we find that 2

---

[1] iii. 722, 740.   [2] iii. 737, iv. 181.

words have been substituted for other 2 ; that 1 has undergone modification; that 5 have been ejected. *Why* is all
this ? asks the unlearned Reader. He shall be told.

An instance is furnished us of the perplexity which a
difficult word sometimes occasioned the ancients, as well
as of the serious consequences which have sometimes resulted therefrom to the text of Scripture itself. S. Matthew,
after narrating that 'a very great multitude spread their
garments in the way,' adds, 'others cut branches (κλάδους)
from the trees and strawed them in the way.' [1] But would
not branches of any considerable size have impeded progress, inconveniently encumbering the road ? No doubt they
would. Accordingly, as S. Mark (with S. Matthew's Gospel
before him) is careful to explain, they were *not* 'branches
of any considerable size,' but 'leafy twigs'—'*foliage*,' in fact
it was—'cut from the trees and strawed in the way.' The
word, however, which he employs (στοιβάδας) is an unique
word—very like another of similar sound (στιβάδας), yet
distinct from it in sense, if not in origin. Unfortunately,
all this was not understood in a highly uncritical and most
licentious age. With the best intentions, (for the good man
was only seeking to reconcile two inconvenient parallel
statements,) some Revisionist of the IInd century, having
convinced himself that the latter word (στιβάδας) might with
advantage take the place of S. Mark's word (στοιβάδας),
substituted this for that. In consequence, it survives to this
day in nine uncial copies headed by ℵ B. But then, στιβάς
does not mean 'a branch' *at all ;* no, nor a 'layer of leaves'
either ; but *a pallet—a floor-bed*, in fact, of the humblest
type, constructed of grass, rushes, straw, brushwood, leaves,
or any similar substance. On the other hand, because such
materials are not obtainable *from trees* exactly, the ancient

---

[1] S. Matt. xxi. 8.

Critic judged it expedient further to change δένδρων into ἀγρῶν ('*fields*'). Even this was not altogether satisfactory. Στιβάς, as explained already, in strictness means a 'bed.' Only by a certain amount of license can it be supposed to denote the materials of which a bed is composed; whereas the Evangelist speaks of something "strawn." *The self-same copies*, therefore, which exhibit '*fields*' (in lieu of '*trees*'), by introducing a slight change in the construction (κόψαντες for ἔκοπτον), and *omitting* the words ' and strawed them in ˏthe way,' are observed—after a summary fashion of their own, (with which, however, readers of B ℵ D are only too fami-liar)—to dispose of this difficulty by putting it nearly out of sight.   The only result of all this misplaced officiousness is a miserable travestie of the sacred words :—ἄλλοι δὲ στι-βάδας, κόψαντες ἐκ τῶν ἀγρῶν : 7 words in place of 12 !

But the calamitous circumstance is that the Critics have all to a man fallen into the trap.   True, that Origen (who once writes στοιβάδας and once στιβάδας), as well as the two Egyptian versions, side with ℵ B C L Δ in reading ἐκ τῶν ἀγρῶν : but then *both versions* (with c) *decline to alter the construction* of the sentence ; and (with Origen) *decline to omit the clause* ἐστρώννυον εἰς τὴν ὁδόν : while, against this little band of disunited witnesses, are marshalled all the remaining fourteen uncials, headed by A D—the Peschito and the Philoxenian Syriac ; the Italic, the Vulgate, the Gothic, the Armenian, the Georgian, and the Æthiopic as well as the Slavonic versions, besides the whole body of the cursives. Whether therefore Antiquity, Variety, Respectability of wit-nesses, numbers, or the reason of the thing be appealed to, the case of our opponents breaks hopelessly down.   Does any one seriously suppose that, if S. Mark had written the common word στιβάδας, so vast a majority of the copies at this day would exhibit the improbable στοιβάδας ?   Had the same S. Mark expressed nothing else but ΚΟΨΑΝΤΕΣ ἐκ τῶν

'ΑΓΡ ΩΝ, will any one persuade us that *every copy in existence but five* would present us with 'ΕΚΟΠΤΟΝ ἐκ τῶν ΔΕ'ΝΔΡΩΝ, καὶ 'ΕΣΤΡΩ'ΝΝΤΟΝ ΕΙ'Σ ΤΗ'Ν 'ΟΔΟ'Ν ? And let us not be told that there has been Assimilation here.   There has been none. S. Matthew (xxi. 8) writes 'ΑΠΟ' τῶν δένδρων . . . . 'ΕΝ τῇ ὁδῷ : S. Mark (xi. 8), 'ΕΚ τῶν δένδρων . . . . . ΕΓΣ τὴν ὁδόν. The types are distinct, and have been faithfully retained all down the ages.   The common reading is certainly correct. The Critics are certainly in error.   And we exclaim (surely not without good reason) against the hardship of thus having an exploded corruption of the text of Scripture furbished up afresh and thrust upon us, after lying deservedly forgotten for upwards of a thousand years.

(*c*) Take a yet grosser specimen, which has nevertheless imposed just as completely upon our Revisionists.   It is found in S. Luke's Gospel (xxiii. 45), and belongs to the history of the Crucifixion.   All are aware that as, at the typical redemption out of Egypt, there had been a preternatural darkness over the land for three days,[1] so, preliminary to the actual Exodus of ' the Israel of GOD,' ' there was darkness over all the land' for three hours.[2] S. Luke adds the further statement,—' *And the sun was darkened* ' (καὶ ἐσκοτίσθη ὁ ἥλιος).   Now the proof that this is what S. Luke actually wrote, is the most obvious and conclusive possible.   Ἐσκοτίσθη is found in all the most ancient documents.   Marcion [3] (whose date is A.D. 130–50) so exhibits the place :—besides the old Latin [4] and the Vulgate :—the Peschito, Cureton's, and the Philoxenian Syriac versions :— the Armenian, — the Æthiopic, — the Georgian, — and the

---

[1] Exod. x. 21–23.
[2] S. Matth. xxvii. 45 ; S. Mark xv. 33 ; S. Lu. xxiii. 44.
[3] Ap. Epiphan. i. 317 and 347.
[4] *Intenebricatus est sol*—a : *obscuratus est sol*—b : *tenebricavit sol*—c.

Slavonic. — Hippolytus [1] (A.D. 190–227), — Athanasius,[2] — Ephraem Syr.,[3]—Gregory Naz.,[3*]—Theodore Mops.,[4]—Nilus the monk,[5]—Severianus, (in a homily preserved in Armenian, p. 439,)—Cyril of Alexandria,[6] — the apocryphal *Gospel of Nicodemus* — and the *Anaphora Pilati*,'[7] — are all witnesses to the same effect. Add the *Acta Pilati* [8] — and the Syriac *Acts of the Apostles*.[9] — Let it suffice of the Latins to quote Tertullian.[10] — But the most striking evidence is the consentient testimony of the manuscripts, viz. *all the uncials* but 3 and-a-half, and *every known Evangelium*.

That the darkness spoken of was a divine portent—*not* an eclipse of the sun, but an incident wholly out of the course of nature—the ancients clearly recognize. Origen,[11]—Julius Africanus [12] (A.D. 220),—Macarius Magnes[13] (A.D. 330),—are even eloquent on the subject. Chrysostom's evidence is unequivocal.[14] It is, nevertheless, well known that this place of S. Luke's Gospel was tampered with from a very early period ; and that Origen [15] (A.D. 186–253), and perhaps Eusebius,[16]

---

[1] Ap. Routh, *Opusc.* i. 79.   [2] i. 90, 913 ; ap. Epiph. i. 1006.
[3] *Syr.* ii. 48.   So also *Evan. Conc.* pp. 245, 256, 257.   [3*] i. 867.
[4] Mai, *Scriptt. Vett.* vi. 64.   [5] i. 305.
[6] Ap. Mai, ii. 436 ; iii. 395.   Also *Luc.* 722.   [7] i. 288, 417.
[8] P. 233.   [9] Ed. by Wright, p. 16.
[10] ' Sol mediâ die *tenebricavit*.'   Adv. Jud. c. xiii.
[11] iii. 922–4.   Read the whole of cap. 134.   See also ap. Galland. xiv. 82, append., which by the way deserves to be compared with Chrys. vii. 825 a.
[12] ἀλλ' ἦν σκότος θεοποίητον, διότι τὸν Κύριον συνέβη παθεῖν.—Routh, ii. 298.
[13] εἶτ' ἐξαίφνης κατενεχθὲν ψηλαφητὸν σκότος, ἡλίου τὴν οἰκείαν αὐγὴν ἀποκρύψαντος, p. 29.
[14] ὅτι γὰρ οὐκ ἦν ἔκλειψις [sc. τὸ σκότος ἐκεῖνο] οὐκ ἐντεῦθεν μόνον δῆλον ἦν, ἀλλὰ καὶ ἀπὸ τοῦ καιροῦ. τρεῖς γὰρ ὥρας παρέμεινεν· ἡ δὲ ἔκλειψις ἐν μιᾷ καιροῦ γίνεται ῥοπῇ.—vii. 825 a.
[15] i. 414, 415; iii. 56.
[16] Ap. Mai, iv. 206.   But further on he says: αὐτίκα γοῦν ἐπὶ τῷ πάθει οὐχ ἥλιος μόνον ἐσκότασεν κ. τ. λ.—Cyril of Jerusalem (pp. 57, 146, 199,

employed copies which had been depraved. In some copies, writes Origen, instead of 'and the sun was darkened' (καὶ ἐσκοτίσθη ὁ ἥλιος), is found 'the sun having become eclipsed' (τοῦ ἡλίου ἐκλιπόντος). He points out with truth that the thing spoken of is a physical impossibility, and delivers it as his opinion that the corruption of the text was due either to some friendly hand in order to *account for* the darkness; or else, (which he,[1] and Jerome [2] after him, thought more likely,) to the enemies of Revelation, who sought in this way to provide themselves with a pretext for cavil. Either way, Origen and Jerome elaborately assert that ἐσκοτίσθη is the only true reading of S. Luke xxiii. 45. Will it be believed that this gross fabrication—for no other reason but because it is found in ℵ B L, and *probably* once existed in C [3]—has been resuscitated in 1881, and foisted into the sacred Text by our Revisionists?

It would be interesting to have this proceeding of theirs explained. *Why* should the truth dwell exclusively [4] with ℵ B L? It cannot be pretended that between the IVth and Vth centuries, when the copies ℵ B were made, and the Vth and VIth centuries, when the copies A Q D R were executed, this

---

201, 202) and Cosmas (ap. Montf. ii. 177 *bis*) were apparently acquainted with the same reading, but neither of them actually quotes Luke xxiii. 45.

[1] 'In quibusdam exemplaribus non habetur *tenebræ factæ sunt, et obscuratus est sol* : sed ita, *tenebræ factæ sunt super omnem terram, sole deficiente.* Et forsitan ausus est aliquis quasi manifestius aliquid dicere volens, pro, *et obscuratus est sol*, ponere *deficiente sole*, existimans quod non aliter potuissent fieri tenebræ, nisi sole deficiente. Puto autem magis quod insidiatores ecclesiæ Christi mutaverunt hoc verbum, quoniam *tenebræ factæ sunt sole deficiente*, ut verisimiliter evangelia argui possint secundum adinventiones volentium arguere illa.' (iii. 923 f. a.)

[2] vii. 235. '*Qui scripserunt contra Evangelia*, suspicantur deliquium solis,' &c.

[3] This rests on little more than conjecture. Tisch. *Cod. Ephr. Syr.* p. 327.

[4] 'Εκλείποντος is only found besides in eleven lectionaries.

corruption of the text arose: for (as was explained at the
outset) the reading in question (καὶ ἐσκοτίσθη ὁ ἥλιος) is found
in all the oldest and most famous documents. Our Revisionists cannot take their stand on ' Antiquity,'—for as we
have seen, *all the Versions* (with the single exception of the
Coptic [1]),—and the oldest Church writers, (Marcion, Origen,
Julius Africanus, Hippolytus, Athanasius, Gregory Naz.,
Ephraem, &c.,) are *all* against them.—They cannot advance
the claim of ' clearly preponderating evidence ; ' for they have
but a single Version,—*not* a single Father,—and but three-
and-a-half Evangelia to appeal to, out of perhaps three
hundred and fifty times that number.—They cannot pretend
that essential probability is in favour of the reading of א B ;
seeing that the thing stated is astronomically impossible.—
They will not tell us that critical opinion is with them: for
their judgment is opposed to that of every Critic ancient and
modern, except Tischendorf since his discovery of codex א.—
Of what nature then will be their proof ? . . . *Nothing*
results from the discovery that א reads τοῦ ἡλίου ἐκλιπόντος,
B ἐκλείποντος,—except that those two codices are of the same
corrupt type as those which Origen deliberately condemned
1650 years ago. In the meantime, with more of ingenuity
than of ingenuousness, our Revisionists attempt to conceal
the foolishness of the text of their choice by translating it

---

[1] The Thebaic represents ' the sun *setting* ;' which, (like the mention of
' *eclipse*,') is only another *interpretation* of the darkness,—derived from Jer.
xv. 9 or Amos viii. 9 (' *occidit* sol meridie '). Compare Irenæus iv. 33. 12,
(p. 273,) who says that these two prophecies found fulfilment in ' eum
occasum solis qui, crucifixo eo, fuit ab horâ sextâ.' He alludes to the same
places in iv. 34. 3 (p. 275). So does Jerome (on Matt. xxvii. 45),—" Et
hoc factum reor, ut compleatur prophetia," and then he quotes Amos and
Jeremiah ; finely adding (from some ancient source),—" Videturque mihi
clarissimum lumen mundi, hoc est luminare majus, retraxisse radios suos,
ne aut pendentem videret Dominum; aut impii blasphemantes suâ luce
fruerentur."

unfairly. They present us with, ' *the sun's light failing.*' But
this is a gloss of their own. There is no mention of ' the
sun's *light* ' in the Greek. Nor perhaps, if the rationale of
the original expression were accurately ascertained, would
such a paraphrase of it prove correct.[1] But, in fact, the
phrase ἔκλειψις ἡλίου means ' an eclipse of the sun,' and *no
other thing.* In like manner, τοῦ ἡλίου ἐκλείποντος [2] (as our
Revisionists are perfectly well aware) means ' *the sun becoming eclipsed,*' or ' *suffering eclipse.*' It is easy for Revisionists
to " emphatically deny that there is anything in the Greek
word ἐκλείπειν, when associated with the sun, which involves
necessarily the notion of an eclipse."[3] The *fact* referred to
may not be so disposed of. It lies outside the province of
' emphatic denial.' Let them ask any Scholar in Europe what
τοῦ ἡλίου ἐκλιπόντος means ; and see if he does not tell
them that it can *only* mean, ' the sun *having become eclipsed* '!
They know this every bit as well as their Reviewer. And
they ought either to have had the manliness to render the
words faithfully, or else the good sense to let the Greek
alone,—which they are respectfully assured was their only
proper course. Καὶ ἐσκοτίσθη ὁ ἥλιος is, in fact, clearly
above suspicion. Τοῦ ἡλίου ἐκλείποντος, which these learned
men (with the best intentions) have put in its place, is, to
speak plainly, a transparent fabrication. That it enjoys
' *clearly preponderating evidence,*' is what no person, fair or
unfair, will for an instant venture to pretend.

III. Next, let us produce an instance of depravation of
Scripture resulting from the practice of ASSIMILATION, which

---

[1] Our old friend of Halicarnassus (vii. 37), speaking of an eclipse which
happened B.C. 481, remarks : ὁ ἥλιος ἐκλιπὼν τὴν ἐκ τοῦ οὐρανοῦ ἕδρην.

[2] For it will be perceived that our Revisionists have adopted the reading
vouched for *only by codex* B. What C* once read is as uncertain as it is
unimportant.   [3] Bp. Ellicott's pamphlet, p. 60.

prevailed anciently to an extent which baffles arithmetic. We choose the most famous instance that presents itself.

(a) It occurs in S. Mark vi. 20, and is more than un-suspected. The substitution (on the authority of ℵ B L and the Coptic) of ἠπόρει for ἐποίει in that verse, (i.e. the state-ment that Herod 'was much *perplexed*,'—instead of Herod '*did* many things,') is even vaunted by the Critics as the recovery of the true reading of the place—long obscured by the ' very singular expression ' ἐποίει. To ourselves the only ' very singular' thing is, how men of first-rate ability can fail to see that, on the contrary, the proposed substitute is simply fatal to the SPIRIT'S teaching in this place. "Common sense is staggered by such a rendering," (remarks the learned Bishop of Lincoln). "People are not wont to *hear gladly* those by whom they are *much perplexed*." [1] But in fact, the sacred writer's object clearly is, to record the striking cir-cumstance that Herod was so moved by the discourses of John, (whom he used to ' listen to with pleasure,') that he even '*did many things*' (πολλὰ ἐποίει) *in conformity with the Baptist's teaching*.[2] . . . And yet, if this be so, how (we shall be asked) has ' he was much perplexed' (πολλὰ ἠπόρει) contrived to effect a lodgment in *so many as three* copies of the second Gospel ?

It has resulted from nothing else, we reply, but the deter-mination to assimilate a statement of S. Mark (vi. 20) con-cerning Herod and John the Baptist, with another and a dis-tinct statement of S. Luke (ix. 7), having reference to Herod

---

[1] *On the Revised Version*, p. 14.

[2] πολλὰ κατὰ γνώμην αὐτοῦ διεπράττετο, as (probably) Victor of Antioch (*Cat.* p. 128), explains the place. He cites some one else (p. 129) who exhibits ἠπόρει ; and who explains it of Herod's difficulty *about getting rid of Herodias.*

and our LORD. S. Luke, speaking of the fame of our
SAVIOUR's miracles at a period subsequent to the Baptist's
murder, declares that when Herod 'heard *all things that were
done* BY HIM' (ἤκουσε τὰ γινόμενα ὑπ' αὐτοῦ πάντα), 'he *was
much perplexed*' (διηπόρει).—Statements so entirely distinct
and diverse from one another as *this* of S. Luke, and *that*
(given above) of S. Mark, might surely (one would think)
have been let alone. On the contrary. A glance at the
foot of the page will show that in the IInd century S. Mark's
words were solicited in all sorts of ways. A persistent determination existed to make him say that Herod having 'heard
of *many things which* THE BAPTIST *did*,' &c.[1]—a strange perversion of the Evangelist's meaning, truly, and only to be
accounted for in one way.[2]

---

[1] καὶ ἀκούσας αὐτοῦ πολλὰ ἃ ἐποίει, καὶ ἡδέως αὐτοῦ ἤκουεν, will have
been the reading of that lost venerable codex of the Gospels which is
chiefly represented at this day by Evann. 13-69-124-346,—as explained
by Professor Abbott in his Introduction to Prof. Ferrar's *Collation of four
important MSS.*, etc. (Dublin 1877). The same reading is also found in
Evann. 28 : 122 : 541 : 572, and Evst. 196.

Different must have been the reading of that other venerable exemplar
which supplied the Latin Church with its earliest Text. But of this let
the reader judge:—' *Et cum audisset illum multa facere, libenter*,' &c. (c :
also 'Codex Aureus' and γ, both at Stockholm): ' *et audito eo quod multa
faciebat, et libenter*,' &c. (g² q): ' *et audiens illum quia multa faciebat, et
libenter*,' &c. (b). The Anglo-Saxon, ('*and he heard that he many wonders
wrought, and he gladly heard him*') approaches nearest to the last two.

The Peschito Syriac (which is without variety of reading here) in strictness exhibits :—' *And many things he was hearing* [from] *him and doing ;
and gladly he was hearing him.*' But this, by competent Syriac scholars,
is considered to represent,—καὶ πολλὰ ἀκούων αὐτοῦ, ἐποίει· καὶ ἡδέως
ἤκουεν αὐτοῦ.—Cod. Δ is peculiar in exhibiting καὶ ἀκούσας αὐτοῦ πολλά,
ἡδέως αὐτοῦ ἤκουεν,—omitting ἐποίει, καί.—The Coptic also renders, ' *et
audiebat multa ab eo, et anxio erat corde*.' From all this, it becomes clear
that the actual *intention* of the blundering author of the text exhibited by
א B L was, to connect πολλά, *not* with ἠπόρει, but with ἀκούσας. So the
Arabian version : but not the Gothic, Armenian, Sclavonic, or Georgian,—
as Dr. S. C. Malan informs the Reviewer.

[2] Note, that tokens abound of a determination anciently to assimilate

F 2

Had this been *all*, however, the matter would have attracted no attention. One such fabrication more or less in the Latin version, which abounds in fabricated readings, is of little moment. But then, the Greek scribes had recourse to a more subtle device for assimilating Mark vi. 20 to Luke ix. 7. They perceived that S. Mark's ἐποίει might be almost identified with S. Luke's διηπόρει, by *merely changing two of the letters*, viz. by substituting η for ε and ρ for ι. From this, there results in S. Mk. vi. 20 : 'and having heard many things of him, *he was perplexed ;*' which is very nearly identical

---

the Gospels hereabouts. Thus, because the first half of Luke ix. 10 $\binom{\xi a}{\eta}$ and the whole of Mk. vi. 30 $\binom{\xi a}{\eta}$ are bracketed together by Eusebius, the former place in codex A is found brought into conformity with the latter by the unauthorized insertion of the clause καὶ ὅσα ἐδίδαξαν.— The parallelism of Mtt. xiv. 13 and Lu. ix. 10 is the reason why D exhibits in the latter place ἀν- (instead of ὑπ)εχώρησε.—In like manner, in Lu. ix. 10, codex A exhibits εἰς ἔρημον τόπον, instead of εἰς τόπον ἔρημον; only because ἔρημον τόπον is the order of Mtt. xiv. 13 and Mk. vi. 32.—So again, codex אּ, in the same verse of S. Luke, entirely omits the final clause πόλεως καλουμένης Βηθσαϊδά, only in order to assimilate its text to that of the two earlier Gospels.—But there is no need to look beyond the limits of S. Mark vi. 14–16, for proofs of Assimilation. Instead of ἐκ νεκρῶν ἠγέρθη (in ver. 14), B and אּ exhibit ἐγήγερται ἐκ νεκρῶν—only because those words are found in Lu. ix. 7. A substitutes ἀνέστη (for ἠγέρθη)—only because that word is found in Lu. ix. 8. For ἠγέρθη ἐκ νεκρῶν, C substitutes ἠγέρθη ἀπὸ τῶν νεκρῶν—only because S. Matth. so writes in ch. xiv. 2. D inserts καὶ ἔβαλεν εἰς φυλακήν into ver. 17—only because of Mtt. xiv. 3 and Lu. iii. 20. In אּ B L Δ, βαπτίζοντος (for βαπτιστοῦ) stands in ver. 24—only by Assimilation with ver. 14. (L is for assimilating ver. 25 likewise). K Δ Π, the Syr., and copies of the old Latin, transpose ἐνεργοῦσιν αἱ δυνάμεις (in ver. 14)—only because those words are transposed in Mtt. xiv. 2. . . . If facts like these do not open men's eyes to the danger of following the fashionable guides, it is to be feared that nothing ever will. The foulest blot of all remains to be noticed. Will it be believed that in ver. 22, codices אּ B D L Δ conspire in representing the dancer (whose name is *known* to have been ' Salome') as *another ' Herodias '—Herod's own daughter ?* This gross perversion of the truth, alike of Scripture and of history—a reading as preposterous as it is revolting, and therefore rejected hitherto by *all* the editors and *all* the critics—finds undoubting favour with Drs. Westcott and Hort. Calamitous to relate, *it also disfigures the margin of our Revised Version of S. Mark* vi. 22, *in consequence.*

with what is found in S. Lu. ix. 7. This fatal substitution (of
ἠπόρει for ἐποίει) survives happily only in codices א B L and
the Coptic version—all of bad character. But (calamitous to
relate) the Critics, having disinterred this long-since-forgotten
fabrication, are making vigorous efforts to galvanize it, at the
end of fifteen centuries, into ghastly life and activity. We
venture to assure them that they will not succeed. Herod's
'perplexity' did not begin until John had been beheaded,
and the fame reached Herod of the miracles which our
SAVIOUR wrought. The apocryphal statement, now for the
first time thrust into an English copy of the New Testament,
may be summarily dismissed. But the marvel will for ever
remain that a company of distinguished Scholars (A.D. 1881)
could so effectually persuade themselves that ἐποίει (in
S. Mark vi. 20) is. a "*plain and clear error*," and that there is
"*decidedly preponderating evidence*" in favour of ἠπόρει,—as to
venture *to substitute the latter word for the former.* This
will for ever remain a marvel, we say; seeing that *all the
uncials* except three of bad character, together with *every
known cursive without exception* ;—the old Latin and the
Vulgate, the Peschito and the Philoxenian Syriac, the Armenian, Æthiopic, Slavonian and Georgian versions,—are with
the traditional Text. (The Thebaic, the Gothic, and Cureton's
Syriac are defective here. The ancient Fathers are silent.)

IV. More serious in its consequences, however, than any
other source of mischief which can be named, is the process
of MUTILATION, to which, from the beginning, the Text of
Scripture has been subjected. By the 'Mutilation' of Scripture we do but mean the intentional Omission—*from whatever
cause proceeding*—of genuine portions. And the causes of it
have been numerous as well as diverse. Often, indeed,
there seems to have been at work nothing else but a
strange passion for getting rid of whatever portions of the

inspired Text have seemed to anybody superfluous,—or at all events have appeared capable of being removed without manifest injury to the sense.   But the estimate of the tasteless IInd-century Critic will never be that of the well-informed Reader, furnished with the ordinary instincts of piety and reverence.   This barbarous mutilation of the Gospel, by the unceremonious excision of a multitude of little words, is often attended by no worse consequence than that thereby an extraordinary baldness is imparted to the Evangelical narrative.   The removal of so many of the coupling-hooks is apt to cause the curtains of the Tabernacle to hang wondrous ungracefully ; but often *that* is all.   Some-times, however, (as might have been confidently anticipated,) the result is calamitous in a high degree.   Not only is the beauty of the narrative effectually marred, (as *e.g.* by the barbarous excision of καί — εὐθέως — μετὰ δακρύων — Κύριε, from S. Mark ix. 24):[1]—the doctrinal teaching of our SAVIOUR'S discourses in countless places, damaged, (as *e. g.* by the omission of καὶ νηστείᾳ from verse 29):—absurd ex-pressions attributed to the Holy One which He certainly never uttered, (as *e.g.* by truncating of its last word the phrase τό, Εἰ δύνασαι πιστεῦσαι in verse 23):—but (I.) The narrative is often rendered in a manner unintelligible ; or else (II.), The entire point of a precious incident is made to disappear from sight; or else (III.), An imaginary incident is fabricated: or lastly (IV.), Some precious saying of our Divine LORD is turned into absolute nonsense.   Take a

---

[1] i.e. '*And*' is omitted by B L Δ: '*immediately*' by א C: '*with tears*' by א A B C L Δ: '*Lord*' by א A B C D L.—In S. Mark vi. 16—(viz. 'But when Herod heard thereof, he said [This is] John whom I beheaded.   He is risen [from the dead],')—the five words in brackets are omitted by our Revisers on the authority of א B (D) L Δ.   But א D further omit Ἰωάννην: C D omit ὁ: א B D L omit ὅτι.   To enumerate and explain the effects of all the barbarous Mutilations which the Gospels alone have sustained at the hands of א, of B, and of D—*would fill many volumes like the present.*

single short example of what has last been offered, from each
of the Gospels in turn.

(I.) In S. Matthew xiv. 30, we are invited henceforth to
submit to the information concerning Simon Peter, that
' *when he saw the wind,* he was afraid.' The sight must have
been peculiar, certainly. So, indeed, is the expression. But
Simon Peter was as unconscious of the one as S. Matthew of
the other. Such curiosities are the peculiar property of
codices א B—the Coptic version—and the Revisionists. The
predicate of the proposition (viz. '*that it was strong,*' contained in the single word ἰσχυρόν) has been wantonly excised.
That is all !—although Dr. Hort succeeded in persuading his
colleagues to the contrary. A more solemn—a far sadder
instance, awaits us in the next Gospel.

(II.) The first three Evangelists are careful to note ' the
loud cry ' with which the Redeemer of the World expired.
But it was reserved for S. Mark (as Chrysostom pointed out
long since) to record (xv. 39) the memorable circumstance
that *this particular portent* it was, which wrought conviction
in the soul of the Roman soldier whose office it was to be
present on that terrible occasion. The man had often witnessed death by Crucifixion, and must have been well
acquainted with its ordinary phenomena. Never before had
he witnessed anything like this. He was stationed where he
could see and hear all that happened : ' standing ' (S. Mark
says) ' near ' our SAVIOUR,—' *over against Him.*' ' Now, when
the Centurion saw that it was *after so crying out* (κράξας),
that He expired ' (xv. 39) he uttered the memorable words,
' Truly this man *was* the SON OF GOD ! ' ' What chiefly
moved him to make that confession of his faith was that our
SAVIOUR evidently died *with power.*'[1] " The miracle " (says
Bp. Pearson) " was not in the death, but *in the voice.* The

---

[1] Chrysostom, vii. 825.

strangeness was not that He should die, but that at the point
of death He should *cry out so loud.* He died not by, but
with a Miracle."[1] . . . All this however is lost in ℵ B L, which
literally *stand alone*[2] in leaving out the central and only
important word, κράξας. Calamitous to relate, they are followed herein by our Revisionists: who (misled by Dr. Hort)
invite us henceforth to read,—' Now when the Centurion saw
that He so gave up the ghost.'

(iii.) In S. Luke xxiii. 42, by leaving out two little words
(τω and κε̄), the same blind guides, under the same blind
guidance, effectually misrepresent the record concerning the
repentant malefactor. Henceforth they would have us believe that ' he said, " JESUS, remember me when thou comest
:n thy Kingdom." ' (Dr. Hort was fortunately unable to persuade the Revisionists to follow him in further substituting
' *into* thy kingdom ' for ' *in* thy kingdom ; ' and so converting
what, in the A. V., is nothing worse than a palpable mistranslation,[3] into what would have been an indelible blot.
The record of his discomfiture survives in the margin).
Whereas none of the Churches of Christendom have ever yet
doubted that S. Luke's record is, that the dying man ' said
unto JESUS, LORD, remember me,' &c.

(iv.) In S. John xiv. 4, by eliminating the second καί and
the second οἴδατε, our SAVIOUR is now made to say, ' And
whither I go, *ye know the way ;* ' which is really almost nonsense. What He actually said was, ' And whither I go ye
know, and the way ye know ; ' *in consequence of which* (as we
all remember) ' Thomas saith unto Him, LORD, we know

---

[1] *On the Creed,* Art. iv. ' Dead:' about half-way through.

[2] The Coptic represents ὅτι ἐξέπνευσε.

[3] Namely, of 'EN τῇ βασ. σου, which is the reading of *every known copy
but two* ; besides Origen, Eusebius, Cyril Jer., Chrysostom, &c. Only B L
read EI'Σ,—which Westcott and Hort adopt.

not "whither" Thou goest, and how can we know "the
way"?' . . . Let these four samples suffice of a style of depravation with which, at the end of 1800 years, it is deliberately
proposed to disfigure every page of the everlasting Gospel,
and for which, were it tolerated, the Church would have
to thank no one so much as Drs. Westcott and Hort.

We cannot afford, however, so to dismiss the phenomena
already opened up to the Reader's notice. For indeed, this
astonishing taste for mutilating and maiming the Sacred
Deposit, is perhaps the strangest phenomenon in the history
of Textual Criticism.

It is in this way that a famous expression in S. Luke vi. 1
has disappeared from codices א B L. The reader may not be
displeased to listen to an anecdote which has hitherto escaped
the vigilance of the Critics :—

'I once asked my teacher, Gregory of Nazianzus,'—(the
words are Jerome's in a letter to Nepotianus),—'to explain to
me the meaning of S. Luke's expression σάββατον δευτερόπρωτον, literally the "second-first sabbath." "I will tell you
all about it in church," he replied. "The congregation
shall shout applause, and you shall have your choice,—either
to stand silent and look like a fool, or else to pretend you
understand what you do not."' But 'eleganter lusit,' says
Jerome.[1] The point of the joke was this: Gregory, being
a great rhetorician and orator, would have descanted so
elegantly on the signification of the word δευτερόπρωτον that
the congregation would have been borne away by his melli-
fluous periods, quite regardless of the sense. In other words,
Gregory of Nazianzus [A.D. 360] is found to have no more
understood the word than Jerome did [370].

Ambrose[2] of Milan [370] attempts to explain the diffi-

---

[1] i. 261.   [2] i. 936, 1363.

cult expression, but with indifferent success. Epiphanius[1] of
Cyprus [370] does the same;—and so, Isidorus[2] [400] called
'Pelusiota' after the place of his residence in Lower Egypt.—
Ps.-Cæsarius[3] also volunteers remarks on the word [A.D. 400 ?].
—It is further explained in the *Paschal Chronicle*,[4]—and by
Chrysostom[5] [370] at Antioch.—' *Sabbatum secundo-primum*' is
found in the old Latin, and is retained by the Vulgate. Earlier
evidence on the subject does not exist. We venture to assume
that a word so attested must at least be entitled to *its place in
the Gospel.* Such a body of first-rate positive IVth-century
testimony, coming from every part of ancient Christendom,
added to the significant fact that δευτερόπρωτον is found in
every codex extant except ℵ B L, and half a dozen cursives of
suspicious character, ought surely to be regarded as decisive.
That an unintelligible word should have got *omitted* from a
few copies, requires no explanation. Every one who has
attended to the matter is aware that the negative evidence of
certain of the Versions also is of little weight on such occasions as the present. They are observed constantly to leave
out what they either failed quite to understand, or else
found untranslateable. On the other hand, it would be inexplicable indeed, that an unique expression like the present
should have *established itself universally,* if it were actually
spurious. This is precisely an occasion for calling to mind
the precept *proclivi scriptioni præstat ardua.* Apart from
external evidence, it is a thousand times more likely that
such a peculiar word as this should be genuine, than the reverse. Tischendorf accordingly retains it, moved by this very
consideration.[6]   It got excised, however, here and there from
manuscripts at a very early date. And, incredible as it may
appear, it is a fact, that in consequence of its absence from

---

[1] i. 158.   [2] P. 301.   [3] Ap. Galland. vi. 53.
[4] P. 396.   [5] vii. 431.
[6] ' Ut ab additamenti ratione alienum est, ita cur omiserint in promptu
est.'

the mutilated codices above referred to, S. Luke's famous ' second-first Sabbath ' has been *thrust out of his Gospel by our Revisionists.*

But indeed, Mutilation has been practised throughout. By codex B (collated with the traditional Text), no less than 2877 words have been excised from the four Gospels alone : by codex ℵ,—3455 words : by codex D,—3704 words.[1]

As interesting a set of instances of this, as are to be anywhere met with, occurs within the compass of the last three chapters of S. Luke's Gospel, from which about 200 words have been either forcibly ejected by our Revisionists, or else served with 'notice to quit.' We proceed to specify the chief of these :—

(1) S. Luke xxii. 19, 20. (Account of the Institution of the Sacrament of the LORD'S Supper,—from " which is given for you " to the end,—32 words.)

(2) *ibid.* 43, 44. (Our SAVIOUR'S Agony in the garden,— 26 words.)

(3) xxiii. 17. (The custom of releasing one at the Passover, —8 words.)

(4) *ibid.* 34. (Our LORD'S prayer on behalf of His murderers, —12 words.)

(5) *ibid.* 38. (The record that the title on the Cross was written in Greek, Latin, and Hebrew,—7 words.)

---

[1] But then, 25 (out of 320) pages of D are lost : D's omissions in the Gospels may therefore be estimated at 4000. Codex A does not admit of comparison, the first 24 chapters of S. Matthew having perished ; but, from examining the way it exhibits the other three Gospels, it is found that 650 would about represent the number of words omitted from its text.—The discrepancy between the texts of B ℵ D, thus *for the first time brought distinctly into notice,* let it be distinctly borne in mind, is a matter wholly irrespective of the merits or demerits of the Textus Receptus,—which, for convenience only, is adopted as a standard : not, of course, of *Excellence* but only of *Comparison.*

(6) xxiv. 1. ("and certain with them,"—4 words.)

(7) *ibid.* 3. ("of the LORD JESUS,"—3 words.)

(8) *ibid.* 6. ("He is not here, but He is risen,"—5 words.)

(9) *ibid.* 9. ("from the sepulchre,"—3 words.)

(10) *ibid.* 12. (The mention of S. Peter's visit to the sepulchre,—22 words.)

(11) *ibid.* 36. ("and saith unto them, Peace be unto you !" —5 words.)

(12) *ibid.* 40. ("and when He had thus spoken, He showed them His hands and His feet,"—10 words.)

(13) *ibid.* 42. ("and of an honeycomb,"—4 words.)

(14) *ibid.* 51. ("and was carried up into Heaven,"—5.)

(15) *ibid.* 52. ("worshipped Him,"—2 words.)

(16) *ibid.* 53. ("praising and,"—2 words.)

On an attentive survey of the foregoing sixteen instances of unauthorized Omission, it will be perceived that the 1st passage (S. Luke xxii. 19, 20) must have been eliminated from the Text because the mention of *two* Cups seemed to create a difficulty.—The 2nd has been suppressed because (see p. 82) the incident was deemed derogatory to the majesty of GOD Incarnate.—The 3rd and 5th were held to be superfluous, because the information which they contain has been already conveyed by the parallel passages.—The 10th will have been omitted as apparently inconsistent with the strict letter of S. John xx. 1–10.—The 6th and 13th are certainly instances of enforced Harmony. — Most of the others (the 4th, 7th, 8th, 9th, 11th, 12th, 14th, 15th, 16th) seem to have been excised through mere wantonness,—the veriest licentiousness.—In the meantime, so far are Drs. Westcott and Hort from accepting the foregoing account of the matter, that they even style the 1st 'a *perverse interpolation :*' in which view of the subject, however, they enjoy the distinction of standing entirely alone. With the same 'moral certainty,' they further proceed to shut up within double

brackets the 2nd, 4th, 7th, 10th, 11th, 12th, 14th, 15th :
while the 3rd, 5th, 6th, 13th, and 16th, they exclude from
their Text as indisputably spurious matter.

Now, we are not about to abuse our Readers' patience by
an investigation of the several points raised by the foregoing
statement. In fact, all should have been passed by in silence,
but that unhappily the ' Revision' of our Authorized Version is touched thereby very nearly indeed. So intimate
(may we not say, *so fatal?*) proves to be the sympathy
between the labours of Drs. Westcott and Hort and those of
our Revisionists, that *whatever the former have shut up within
double brackets, the latter are discovered to have branded with a
note of suspicion,* conceived invariably in the same terms :
viz., ' Some ancient authorities omit.' And further, *whatever
those Editors have rejected from their Text, these Revisionists
have rejected also.* It becomes necessary, therefore, briefly to
enquire after the precise amount of ·manuscript authority
which underlies certain of the foregoing changes. And
happily this may be done in a few words.

The *sole* authority for just half of the places above enumerated [1] is *a single Greek codex,*—and that, the most depraved
of all,—viz. Beza's D.[2] It should further be stated that the
only allies discoverable for D are a few copies of the old
Latin. What we are saying will seem scarcely credible : but
it is a plain fact, of which any one may convince himself who
will be at the pains to inspect the critical apparatus at the
foot of the pages of Tischendorf's last (8th) edition. Our
Revisionists' notion, therefore, of what constitutes ' weighty
evidence ' is now before the Reader. If, in *his* judgment, the
testimony of *one single manuscript,* (and *that* manuscript the

---

[1] Viz. the 1st, the 7th to 12th inclusive, and the 15th.

[2] Concerning ' *the singular codex* D,'—as Bp. Ellicott phrases it,—see
back, pages 14 and 15.

Codex Bezæ (D),)—does really invalidate that of *all other Manuscripts and all other Versions* in the world,—then of course, the Greek Text of the Revisionists will in his judgment be a thing to be rejoiced over. But what if he should be of opinion that such testimony, in and by itself, is simply worthless? We shrewdly suspect that the Revisionists' view of what constitutes 'weighty Evidence' will be found to end where it began, viz. in the Jerusalem Chamber.

For, when we reach down codex D from the shelf, we are reminded that, within the space of the three chapters of S. Luke's Gospel now under consideration, there are in all no less than 354 words omitted; *of which,* 250 *are omitted by* D *alone.* May we have it explained to us why, of those 354 words, only 25 are singled out by Drs. Westcott and Hort for permanent excision from the sacred Text? Within the same compass, no less than 173 words have been *added* by D to the commonly Received Text,—146, *substituted,*—243, *transposed.* May we ask how it comes to pass that of those 562 words *not one* has been promoted to their margin by the Revisionists? . . . Return we, however, to our list of the changes which they actually *have* effected.

(1) Now, that ecclesiastical usage and the parallel places would seriously affect such precious words as are found in S. Luke xxii. 19, 20,—was to have been expected. Yet has the type been preserved all along, from the beginning, with singular exactness; except in one little handful of singularly licentious documents, viz. in D a ff[2] i l, which *leave all out;* —in b e, which substitute verses 17 and 18;—and in 'the singular and sometimes rather wild Curetonian Syriac Version,'[1] which, retaining the 10 words of ver. 19, substitutes

---

[1] Bp. Ellicott *On Revision,*—p. 42. Concerning the value of the last-named authority, it is a satisfaction to enjoy the deliberate testimony of the Chairman of the Revisionist body. See below, p. 85.

verses 17, 18 for ver. 20. Enough for the condemnation of
D survives in Justin,[1]—Basil,[2]—Epiphanius,[3]—Theodoret,[4]—
Cyril,[5]—Maximus,[6]—Jerome.[7] But why delay ourselves concerning a place vouched for *by every known copy of the Gospels
except* D?   Drs. Westcott and Hort entertain ' *no moral
doubt* that the [32] words [given at foot[8]] were absent from
the original text of S. Luke;' in which opinion, happily,
they stand alone. But why did our Revisionists suffer themselves to be led astray by such blind guidance?

The next place is entitled to far graver attention, and may
on no account be lightly dismissed, seeing that these two
verses contain the sole record of that ' Agony in the Garden'
which the universal Church has almost erected into an
article of the Faith.

(2) That the incident of the ministering Angel, the Agony
and bloody sweat of the world's Redeemer (S. Luke xxii. 43,
44), was anciently absent from certain copies of the Gospels,
is expressly recorded by Hilary,[9] by Jerome,[10] and others.
Only necessary is it to read the apologetic remarks which
Ambrose introduces when he reaches S. Luke xxii. 43,[11] to
understand what has evidently led to this serious mutilation
of Scripture,—traces of which survive at this day exclusively
in *four* codices, viz. A B R T. Singular to relate, in the
Gospel which was read on Maundy-Thursday these two
verses of S. Luke's Gospel are thrust in between the 39th

---

[1] i. 156.   [2] ii. 254.   [3] i. 344.   [4] iv. 220, 1218.
[5] *In Luc.* 664 (Mai, iv. 1105).   [6] ii. 653.
[7] 'In Lucâ legimus *duos calices*, quibus discipulis propinavit,' vii. 216.
[8] Τὸ ὑπὲρ ὑμῶν διδόμενον· τοῦτο ποιεῖτε εἰς τὴν ἐμὴν ἀνάμνησιν. ὡσαύ-
τως καὶ τὸ ποτήριον μετὰ τὸ δειπνῆσαι, λέγων, Τοῦτο τὸ ποτήριον, ἡ καινὴ
διαθήκη ἐν τῷ αἵματί μου, τὸ ὑπὲρ ὑμῶν ἐκχυνόμενον.
[9] P. 1062.   [10] ii. 747.   [11] i. 1516. See below, p. 82.

and the 40th verses of S. Matthew xxvi. Hence, 4 cursive copies, viz. 13-69-124-346—(confessedly derived from a common ancient archetype,[1] and therefore not four witnesses but only one),—actually exhibit these two Verses in that place. But will any unprejudiced person of sound mind entertain a doubt concerning the genuineness of these two verses, witnessed to as they are by *the whole body of the Manuscripts,* uncial as well as cursive, and *by every ancient Version?* . . . . If such a thing were possible, it is hoped that the following enumeration of ancient Fathers, who distinctly recognize the place under discussion, must at least be held to be decisive :—viz.

Justin M.,[2]—Irenæus[3] in the IInd century :—

Hippolytus,[4] — Dionysius Alex.,[5]—ps. Tatian,[6] in the IIIrd :—

Arius,[7] — Eusebius,[8] — Athanasius,[9] — Ephraem Syr.,[10]— Didymus,[11]—Gregory Naz.,[12]—Epiphanius,[13]—Chrysostom,[14] —ps.-Dionysius Areop.,[15] in the IVth :—

Julian the heretic,[16]—Theodorus Mops.,[17]—Nestorius,[18]— Cyril Alex.,[19]—Paulus, bishop of Emesa,[20]—Gennadius,[21]— Theodoret,[22]—and several Oriental Bishops (A.D. 431),[23] in the Vth :—besides

---

[1] Abbott's *Collation of four important Manuscripts,* &c., 1877.
[2] ii. 354.   [3] Pp. 543 and 681 (=ed. Mass. 219 and 277).
[4] *Contra Noet.* c. 18; also ap. Theodoret iv. 132-3.
[5] Ap. Galland. xix.; *Append.* 116, 117.
[6] *Evan. Conc.* pp. 55, 235.   [7] Ap. Epiph. i. 742, 785.
[8] It is § 283 in his sectional system.   [9] P. 1121.
[10] ii. 43; v. 392; vi. 604. Also *Evan. Conc.* 235. And see below, p. 82.
[11] Pp. 394, 402.   [12] i. 551.
[13] [i. 742, 785;] ii. 36, 42.   [14] v. 263; vii. 791; viii. 377.
[15] ii. 39.   [16] Ap. Theod. Mops.
[17] In loc. bis; ap. Galland. xii. 693; and Mai, *Scriptt. Vett.* vi. 306.
[18] *Concilia,* iii. 327 a.   [19] Ap. Mai, iii. 389.
[20] *Concilia,* iii. 1101 d.   [21] Schol. 34.
[22] i. 692; iv. 271, 429; v. 23. *Conc.* iii. 907 e.   [23] *Concilia,* iii. 740 d.

Ps.-Cæsarius,[1]—Theodosius Alex.,[2]—John Damascene,[3]—Maximus,[4]—Theodorus hæret.,[5]—Leontius Byz.,[6] — Anastasius Sin.,[7]—Photius :[8] and of the Latins, Hilary,[9]—Jerome,[10]—Augustine,[11]—Cassian,[12]—Paulinus,[13]—Facundus.[14]

It will be seen that we have been enumerating *upwards of forty famous personages from every part of ancient Christendom*, who recognize these verses as genuine; fourteen of them being as old,—some of them, a great deal older,—than our oldest MSS.— *Why* therefore Drs. Westcott and Hort should insist on shutting up these 26 precious words—this article of the Faith—in double brackets, in token that it is ' morally certain' that verses 43 and 44 are of spurious origin, we are at a loss to divine.[15] We can but ejaculate (in the very words they proceed to disallow),—' FATHER, forgive them; for they know not what they do.' But our especial concern is with *our Revisionists;* and we do not exceed our province when we come forward to reproach them sternly for having succumbed to such evil counsels, and deliberately branded these Verses with their own corporate expression of doubt. For unless *that* be the purpose of the marginal Note which they have set against these verses, we fail to understand the Revisers' language and are wholly at a loss to divine what purpose that note of theirs can be meant to serve.   It is pre-

---

[1] Ap. Galland. vi. 16, 17, 19.   [2] Ap. Cosmam, ii. 331.
[3] i. 544.   [4] In Dionys. ii. 18, 30.
[5] Ap. Galland. xii. 693.   [6] *Ibid.* 688.
[7] Pp. 108, 1028, 1048.   [8] *Epist.* 138.
[9] P. 1061.   [10] ii. 747.   [11] iv. 901, 902, 1013, 1564.
[12] P. 373.   [13] Ap. Galland. ix. 40.   [14] *Ibid.* xi. 693.

[15] Let their own account of the matter be heard :—' The documentary evidence clearly designates [these verses] as *an early Western interpolation*, adopted in eclectic texts.'—' They can only be *a fragment from the Traditions*, written or oral, which were for a while at least *locally current :'* —an ' evangelic Tradition,' therefore, ' *rescued from oblivion by the Scribes of the second century.*'

G

faced by a formula which, (as we learn from their own
Preface,) offers to the reader the "alternative" of *omitting* the
Verses in question: implies that "*it would not be safe*" any
longer to accept them,—as the Church has hitherto done,—
with undoubting confidence. In a word,—*it brands them with
suspicion.* . . . . We have been so full on this subject,—(not
half of our references were known to Tischendorf,)—because
of the unspeakable preciousness of the record; and because
we desire to see an end at last to expressions of doubt and
uncertainty on points which really afford not a shadow of
pretence for either. These two Verses were excised through
mistaken piety by certain of the orthodox,—jealous for the
honour of their LORD, and alarmed by the use which the
impugners of His GODhead freely made of them.[1] Hence
Ephraem [*Carmina Nisibena*, p. 145] puts the following words
into the mouth of Satan, addressing the host of Hell:—" One
thing I witnessed in Him which especially comforts me. I
saw Him praying; and I rejoiced, for His countenance
changed and He was afraid. *His sweat was drops of blood*,
for He had a presentiment that His day had come. This was
the fairest sight of all,—unless, to be sure, He was practising
deception on me. For verily if He hath deceived me, then it
is all over,—both with me, and with you, my servants!"

(4) Next in importance after the preceding, comes the
Prayer which the SAVIOUR of the World breathed from the
Cross on behalf of His murderers (S. Luke xxiii. 34). These
twelve precious words,—('Then said JESUS, FATHER, forgive
them; for they know not what they do,')—like those
twenty-six words in S. Luke xxii. 43, 44 which we have been
considering already, Drs. Westcott and Hort enclose within
double brackets in token of the 'moral certainty' they enter-

---

[1] Consider the places referred to in Epiphanius.

tain that the words are spurious.[1]   And yet these words are
found in *every known uncial* and in *every known cursive Copy,*
except four; besides being found *in every ancient Version.*   And
what,—(we ask the question with sincere simplicity,)—
what amount of evidence is calculated to inspire undoubting
confidence in any existing Reading, if not such a concurrence
of Authorities as this ? . . . We forbear to insist upon the probabilities of the case.   The Divine power and sweetness of the
incident shall not be enlarged upon.   We introduce no
considerations resulting from Internal Evidence.   True, that
" few verses of the Gospels bear in themselves a surer witness
to the Truth of what they record, than this." (It is the
admission of the very man [2] who has nevertheless dared to
brand it with suspicion.)   But we reject his loathsome patron-
age with indignation. "Internal Evidence,"—"Transcriptional
Probability,"—and all such 'chaff and draff,' with which he
fills his pages *ad nauseam,* and mystifies nobody but himself,
—shall be allowed no place in the present discussion.   Let
this verse of Scripture stand or fall as it meets with sufficient
external testimony, or is forsaken thereby.   How then about
the *Patristic* evidence,—for this is all that remains unexplored ?

   Only a fraction of it was known to Tischendorf.   We
find our SAVIOUR'S Prayer attested,—

---

   [1] The Editors shall speak for themselves concerning this, the first of the
'Seven last Words :'—'We cannot doubt that *it comes from an extraneous
source :'*—'need not have belonged originally *to the book in which it is now
included :'*—is '*a Western interpolation.*'
   Dr. Hort,—unconscious apparently that he is *at the bar,* not *on the bench,*
—passes sentence (in his usual imperial style)—"Text, Western and
Syrian" (p. 67).—But then, (1st) It happens that our LORD'S intercession
on behalf of His murderers is attested by upwards of forty Patristic
witnesses *from every part of ancient Christendom :* while, (2ndly) On the
contrary, the places in which it is *not found* are certain copies of the old
Latin, and codex D, which is supposed to be our great 'Western' witness.
   [2] Dr. Hort's *N. T.* vol. ii.   *Note,* p. 68.

In the IInd century by Hegesippus,[1]—and by Irenæus : [2]—

In the IIIrd, by Hippolytus,[3]—by Origen,[4]—by the *Apostolic Constitutions*,[5]—by the *Clementine Homilies*,[6]—by ps.-Tatian,[7]—and by the disputation of Archelaus with Manes :[8]—

In the IVth, by Eusebius,[9]—by Athanasius,[10]—by Gregory Nyss.,[11]—by Theodorus Herac.,[12]—by Basil,[13]—by Chrysostom,[14]—by Ephraem Syr.,[15]—by ps.-Ephraim,[16]—by ps.-Dionysius Areop.,[17]—by the Apocryphal *Acta Pilati*,[18]—by the *Acta Philippi*,[19]—and by the Syriac *Acts of the App.*,[20] —by ps.-Ignatius,[21]—and ps.-Justin :[22]—

In the Vth, by Theodoret,[23]—by Cyril,[24]—by Eutherius :[25]

In the VIth, by Anastasius Sin.,[26]—by Hesychius :[27]—

In the VIIth, by Antiochus mon.,[28]—by Maximus,[29]—by Andreas Cret. : [30]—

---

[1] Ap. Eus. *Hist. Eccl.* ii. 23.　　[2] P. 521 and . . . [Mass. 210 and 277.]

[3] Ed. Lagarde, p. 65 *line* 3.　　[4] ii. 188.　*Hær.* iii. 18 p. 5.

[5] Ap. Gall. iii. 38, 127.　　[6] *Ibid.* ii. 714.　(*Hom.* xi. 20.)

[7] *Evan. Conc.* 275.　　[8] Ap. Routh, v. 161.

[9] He places the verses in *Can.* x.　　[10] i. 1120.　　[11] iii. 289.

[12] *Cat. in Ps.* iii. 219.　　[13] i. 290.　　[14] 15 times.

[15] ii. 48, 321, 428 ; ii. (*syr.*) 233.　　[16] *Evan. Conc.* 117, 256.

[17] i. 607.　　[18] Pp. 232, 286.　　[19] P. 85.

[20] Pp. 11, 16.　Dr. Wright assigns them to the IVth century.

[21] *Eph.* c. x.　　[22] ii. 166, 168, 226.　　[23] 6 times.

[24] Ap. Mai, ii. 197 (= Cramer 52) ; iii. 392.—Dr. Hort's strenuous pleading for the authority of Cyril on this occasion (who however is plainly against him) is amusing.　So is his claim to have the cursive " 82 " on his side.　He is certainly reduced to terrible straits throughout his ingenious volume.　Yet are we scarcely prepared to find an upright and honourable man contending so hotly, and almost on any pretext, for the support of those very Fathers which, when they are against him, (as, 99 times out of 100, they are,) he treats with utter contumely.　He is observed to put up with any ally, however insignificant, who even *seems* to be on his side.

[25] Ap. Theod. v. 1152.　　[26] Pp. 423, 457.

[27] *Cat. in Ps.* i. 768 ; ii. 663.　　[28] Pp. 1109, 1134.

[29] i. 374.　　[30] P. 93.

In the VIIIth, by John Damascene,[1]—besides ps.-Chry-
sostom,[2]—ps. Amphilochius,[3]—and the *Opus imperf.*[4]

Add to this, (since Latin authorities have been brought to
the front),—Ambrose,[5]—Hilary,[6]—Jerome,[7]—Augustine,[8]—
and other earlier writers.[9]

We have thus again enumerated *upwards of forty* ancient
Fathers. And again we ask, With what show of reason is
the brand set upon these 12 words? Gravely to cite, as
if there were anything in it, such counter-evidence as the
following, to the foregoing torrent of Testimony from every
part of ancient Christendom:—viz: 'ʙ ᴅ, 38, 435, a b d and
one Egyptian version'—might really have been mistaken for
a *mauvaise plaisanterie*, were it not that the gravity of the
occasion effectually precludes the supposition. How could
our Revisionists *dare* to insinuate doubts into wavering
hearts and unlearned heads, where (as here) they were *bound*
to know, there exists *no manner of doubt at all?*

(5) The record of the same Evangelist (S. Luke xxiii. 38)
that the Inscription over our Sᴀᴠɪᴏᴜʀ's Cross was 'written
. . . in letters of Greek, and Latin, and Hebrew,' *disappears
entirely* from our 'Revised' version; and this, for no other
reason, but because the incident is omitted by ʙ ᴄ ʟ, the
corrupt Egyptian versions, and Cureton's depraved Syriac:
the text of which (according to Bp. Ellicott[10]) "is of a
very composite nature,—*sometimes inclining to the shortness
and simplicity of the Vatican manuscript*" (ʙ): e.g. on the
present occasion. But surely the negative testimony of this
little band of disreputable witnesses is entirely outweighed
by the positive evidence of ℵ ᴀ ᴅ Q ʀ with 13 other uncials,—

---

[1] ii. 67, 747. 　　[2] i. 814; ii. 819; v. 735. 　　[3] P. 88.
[4] Ap. Chrys. vi. 191. 　[5] 11 times. 　[6] P. 782 f. 　[7] 12 times.
[8] More than 60 times. 　[9] Ap. Cypr. (ed. Baluze), &c. &c.
[10] *On Revision,*—p. 42 *note.* See above, p. 78 *note.*

the evidence of *the entire body of the cursives,*—the sanction of the Latin,—the. Peschito and Philoxenian Syriac,—the Armenian,—Æthiopic,—and Georgian versions ; besides Eusebius—whose testimony (which is express) has been hitherto strangely overlooked,[1]—and Cyril.[2]   Against the threefold plea of Antiquity, Respectability of witnesses, Universality of testimony,—what have our Revisionists to show ?   (*a*) They cannot pretend that there has been Assimilation here ; for the type of S. John xix. 20 is essentially different, and has retained its distinctive character all down the ages.   (*b*) Nor can they pretend that the condition of the Text hereabouts bears traces of having been jealously guarded.   We ask the Reader's attention to this matter just for a moment.   There may be some of the occupants of the Jerusalem Chamber even, to whom what we are about to offer may not be altogether without the grace of novelty :—

That the Title on the Cross is diversely set down by each of the four Evangelists,—all men are aware.   But perhaps all are not aware that *S. Luke's record* of the Title (in ch. xxiii. 38) is exhibited *in four different ways* by codices A B C D :—

A exhibits—OYTOC ECTIN O BACIΛEYC TⲰN IOYΔAIⲰN

B (with ℵ L and a) exhibits—O BACIΛEYC TⲰN IOYΔAIⲰN OYTOC

C exhibits—O BACIΛEYC TⲰN IOYΔAIⲰN (which is Mk. xv. 26).

D (with e and ff[2]) exhibits—O BACIΛEYC TⲰN IOYΔAIⲰN OYTOC ECTIN (which is the words of the Evangelist transposed).

We propose to recur to the foregoing specimens of licentiousness by-and-by.[3]   For the moment, let it be added that

---

[1] *Eclog. Proph.* p. 89.   [2] *In Luc.* 435 and 718.
[3] See pages 93 to 97.

codex X and the Sahidic version conspire in a fifth variety,
viz., ΟΥΤΟϹ ΕϹΤΙΝ ΙΗϹΟΥϹ Ο ΒΑϹΙΛΕΥϹ ΤⲰΝ ΙΟΥΔΑΙⲰΝ
(which is S. Matt. xxvii. 37); while Ambrose[1] is found to
have used a Latin copy which represented ΙΗϹΟΥϹ Ο ΝΑΖⲰ-
ΡΑΙΟϹ Ο ΒΑϹΙΛΕΥϹ ΤⲰΝ ΙΟΥΔΑΙⲰΝ (which is S. John xix. 18).
We spare the reader any remarks of our own on all this.   He
is competent to draw his own painful inferences, and will not
fail to make his own damaging reflections.   He shall only be
further informed that 14 uncials and the whole body of the
cursive copies side with codex A in upholding the Traditional
Text; that the Vulgate,[2]—the Peschito,—Cureton's Syriac,—
the Philoxenian; — besides the Coptic, — Armenian, — and
Æthiopic versions—are all on the same side: lastly, that
Origen,[3]—Eusebius,—and Gregory of Nyssa[4] are in addition
consentient witnesses;—and we can hardly be mistaken if
we venture to anticipate (1st),—That the Reader will agree
with us that the Text with which we are best acquainted
(as usual) is here deserving of all confidence; and (2ndly),
—That the Revisionists who assure us ' that they did not
esteem it within their province to construct a continuous and
complete Greek Text;' (and who were never authorized to
construct *a new Greek Text at all;*) were not justified in the
course they have pursued with regard to S. Luke xxiii. 38.
' THIS IS THE KING OF THE JEWS' is the only idiomatic way
of rendering into English the title according to S. Luke,
whether the reading of A or of B be adopted; but, in order to
make it plain that they *reject the Greek of* A *in favour of* B,
the Revisionists have gone out of their way.   They have
instructed the two Editors of ' *The Greek Testament with the*

---

[1] i. 1528.

[2] So Sedulius Paschalis, ap. Galland. ix. 595.   [3] iii. 2.

[4] Euseb. *Ecl. Proph.* p. 89: Greg. Nyss. i. 570.—These last two places
have hitherto escaped observation.

Readings adopted by the Revisers of the Authorized Version'[1]
to exhibit S. Luke xxiii. 38 *as it stands in the mutilated
recension of Drs. Westcott and Hort.*[2] And if *this* procedure,
repeated many hundreds of times, be not constructing a 'new
Greek Text' of the N. T., we have yet to learn what *is*.

(6) From the first verse of the concluding chapter of
S. Luke's Gospel, is excluded the familiar clause—'*and certain
others with them*' (καί τινες σὺν αὐταῖς). And pray, why?
For no other reason but because א B C L, with some Latin
authorities, omit the clause;—and our Revisionists do the
like, on the plea that they have only been getting rid of a
'harmonistic insertion.'[3]   But it is nothing of the sort, as we
proceed to explain.

Ammonius, or some predecessor of his early in the IInd
century, saw fit (with perverse ingenuity) to seek to *force*
S. Luke xxiii. 55 into agreement with S. Matt. xxvii. 61 and
S. Mark xv. 47, by turning κατακολουθήσασαι δὲ καὶ γυναῖκες,
—into κατηκολούθησαν δὲ ΔΎΟ γυναῖκες. This done, in order
to produce 'harmonistic' agreement and to be thorough, the
same misguided individual proceeded to run his pen through
the words 'and certain with them' (καί τινες σὺν αὐταῖς) as
inopportune; and his work was ended. 1750 years have
rolled by since then, and—What traces remain of the man's
foolishness?   Of his *first* feat (we answer), Eusebius,[4] D and
Evan. 29, besides five copies of the old Latin (a b e ff² q), are

---

[1] See above, pp. 49–50, note [2].

[2] Viz., thus :—ἦν δὲ καὶ ἐπιγραφὴ ἐπ' αὐτῷ, Ὁ βασιλεὺς τῶν Ἰουδαίων
οὗτος.   [3] Dean Alford, *in loc.*

[4] ὁ Λουκᾶς μιᾷ λέγει τῶν σαββάτων ὄρθρου βαθέος φέρειν ἀρώματα γυναῖκας
ΔΎΟ τὰς ἀκολουθησάσας αὐτῷ, αἵ τινες ἦσαν ἀπὸ τῆς Γαλιλαίας συνακολου-
θήσασαι, ὅτε ἔθαπτον αὐτὸν ἐλθούσαι ἐπὶ τὸ μνῆμα· αἵτινες ΔΎΟ, κ.τ.λ.,—
ad Marinum, ap. Mai, iv. 266.

the sole surviving Witnesses. Of his *second* achievement, א B C L, 33, 124, have preserved a record; besides seven copies of the old Latin (a b c e ff[2] g[1] l), together with the Vulgate, the Coptic, and Eusebius in one place[1] though not in another.[2] The Reader is therefore invited to notice that the tables have been unexpectedly turned upon our opponents. S. Luke introduced the words 'and certain with them,' in order to prepare us for what he will have to say in xxiv. 10,—viz. 'It was Mary Magdalene, and Joanna, and Mary the mother of James, and *other women with them*, which told these things unto the Apostles.' Some stupid harmonizer in the IInd century omitted the words, because they were in his way. Calamitous however it is that a clause which the Church has long since deliberately reinstated should, in the year 1881, be as deliberately banished for the second time from the sacred page by our Revisionists; who under the plea of *amending our English Authorized Version* have (with the best intentions) *falsified the Greek Text* of the Gospels in countless places,—often, as here, without notice and without apology.

(10) We find it impossible to pass by in silence the treatment which S. Luke xxiv. 12 has experienced at their hands. They have branded with doubt S. Luke's memorable account of S. Peter's visit to the sepulchre. And why? Let the evidence *for* this precious portion of the narrative be first rehearsed. Nineteen uncials then, with א A B at their head, supported by *every known cursive* copy,—all these vouch for the genuineness of the verse in question. The Latin,—the Syriac,—and the Egyptian versions also contain it. Eusebius,[3]—Gregory of Nyssa,[4]—Cyril,[5]—Severus,[6]—Ammonius,[7]

---

[1] Ps. i. 79.   [2] *Dem.* 492.
[3] Ap. Mai, iv. 287, 293.   [4] i. 364.   [5] Ap. Mai, ii. 439.
[6] Ap. Galland. xi. 224.   [7] *Cat. in Joann.* p. 453.

and others [1] refer to it : while *no ancient writer* is found to
impugn it.   Then, *why* the double brackets of Drs. Westcott
and Hort ? and *why* the correlative marginal note of our Revisionists ?—Simply because D and 5 copies of the old Latin
(a b e l fu) leave these 22 words out.

(11) On the same sorry evidence—(viz. D and 5 copies of
the old Latin)—it is proposed henceforth to omit our
Saviour's greeting to His disciples when He appeared among
them in the upper chamber on the evening of the first Easter
Day.   And yet the precious words ('*and saith unto them,
Peace be unto you*' [Lu. xxiv. 36],) are vouched for by 18
uncials (with ℵ A B at their head), and *every known cursive
copy* of the Gospels : by all the Versions : and (as before) by
Eusebius,[2]—and Ambrose,[3]—by Chrysostom,[4]—and Cyril,[5]—
and Augustine.[6]

(12) The same remarks suggest themselves on a survey of
the evidence for S. Luke xxiv. 40 :—'*And when He had
thus spoken, He showed them His hands and His feet.*'   The
words are found in 18 uncials (beginning with ℵ A B), and in
every known cursive: in the Latin,[7] — the Syriac,—the
Egyptian,—in short, *in all the ancient Versions.*   Besides
these, ps.-Justin,[8]—Eusebius,[9]—Athanasius,[10]—Ambrose (in
Greek),[11] — Epiphanius,[12] — Chrysostom,[13] — Cyril,[14]—Theo-

---

[1] Ps.-Chrys. viii. 161–2.   Johannes Thessal. ap. Galland. xiii. 189.

[2] Ap. Mai, iv. 293 *bis* ; 294 *diserte*.   [3] i. 506, 1541.   [4] iii. 91.

[5] iv. 1108, and *Luc.* 728 (= Mai, ii. 441).   [6] iii.[2] 142 ; viii. 472.

[7] So Tertullian :—' *Manus et pedes suos inspiciendos offert*' (*Carn.* c. 5).
' *Inspectui eorum manus et pedes suos offert* ' (*Marc.* iv. c. 43).   Also
Jerome i. 712.

[8] *De Resur.* 240 (quoted by J. Damascene, ii. 762).

[9] Ap. Mai, iv. 294.   [10] i. 906, quoted by Epiph. i. 1003.

[11] Ap. Theodoret, iv. 141.   [12] i. 49.   [13] i. 510 ; ii. 408, 418 ; iii. 91.

[14] iv. 1108 ; vi. 23 (*Trin.*).   Ap. Mai, ii. 442 *ter*.

doret,[1]—Ammonius,[2]—and John Damascene [3]—quote them.
What but the veriest trifling is it, in the face of such a
body of evidence, to bring forward the fact that D and 5
copies of the old Latin, with Cureton's Syriac (of which
we have had the character already [4]), *omit* the words in
question?

The foregoing enumeration of instances of Mutilation
might be enlarged to almost any extent.   Take only three
more short but striking specimens, before we pass on:—

(*a*) Thus, the precious verse (S. Matthew xvii. 21) which
declares that ' *this kind* [of evil spirit] *goeth not out but by
prayer and fasting,*' is expunged by our Revisionists;
although it is vouched for by every known uncial *but two*
(B ℵ), every known cursive *but one* (Evan. 33); is witnessed
to by the Old Latin and the Vulgate,—the Syriac, Coptic,
Armenian, Georgian, Æthiopic, and Slavonic versions; by
Origen,[5]— Athanasius,[6]— Basil,[7]— Chrysostom,[8] — the *Opus
imperf.,*[9]—the Syriac Clement,[10]—and John Damascene;[11]—
by Tertullian,—Ambrose,—Hilary,—Juvencus,—Augustine,
—Maximus Taur.,—and by the Syriac version of the *Canons
of Eusebius:* above all by the Universal East,—having been
read in all the churches of Oriental Christendom on the 10th
Sunday after Pentecost, from the earliest period.   Why, in
the world, then (our readers will ask) have the Revisionists
left those words out?... For no other reason, we answer,
but because Drs. Westcott and Hort place them among the
interpolations which they consider unworthy of being even

---

[1] iv. 272.
[2] *Cat. in Joan.* 462, 3.
[3] i. 303.
[4] See above, pp. 78 and 85.
[5] iii. 579.
[6] ii. 114 (ed. 1698).
[7] ii. 9, 362, 622.
[8] ii. 309; iv. 30; v. 531; vii. 581.
[9] vi. 79.
[10] *Ep.* i. (ap. Gall. i. p. xii.)
[11] ii. 464.

'exceptionally retained in association with the true Text.'[1]
'Western and Syrian' is their oracular sentence.[2]

(b) The blessed declaration, '*The Son of Man is come to save that which was lost*,'—has in like manner been expunged by our Revisionists from S. Matth. xviii. 11; although it is attested by every known uncial except B ‭א‬ L, and every known cursive *except three*: by the old Latin and the Vulgate: by the Peschito, Cureton's and the Philoxenian Syriac: by the Coptic, Armenian, Æthiopic, Georgian and Slavonic versions:[3] — by Origen,[4] — Theodorus Heracl.,[5] — Chrysostom[6]—and Jovius[7] the monk ;—by Tertullian,[8]—Ambrose,[9]—Hilary,[10]—Jerome,[11]—pope Damasus[12]—and Augustine:[13]—above all, by the Universal Eastern Church,—for it has been read in all assemblies of the faithful on the morrow of Pentecost, from the beginning. Why then (the reader will again ask) have the Revisionists expunged this verse? We can only answer as before,—because Drs. Westcott and Hort consign it to the *limbus* of their *Appendix;* class it among their 'Rejected Readings' of the most hopeless type.[14] As before, *all* their sentence is 'Western and Syrian.' They add, 'Interpolated either from Lu. xix. 10, or from an independent source, written or oral.'[15] . . . Will the English Church suffer herself to be in this way defrauded of her priceless inheritance,—through the irreverent bungling of well-intentioned, but utterly misguided men?

---

[1] *Text*, pp. 565 and 571.   [2] *Append.* p. 14.
[3] We depend for our Versions on Dr. S. C. Malan: pp. 31, 44.
[4] ii. 147. *Conc.* v. 675.   [5] Cord. *Cat.* i. 376.
[6] vii. 599, 600 *diserte*.   [7] Ap. Photium, p. 644.
[8] Three times.   [9] i. 663, 1461, ii. 1137.
[10] Pp. 367, 699.   [11] vii. 139.
[12] Ap. Galland. vi. 324.   [13] iii. P. i. 760.
[14] *Text*, p. 572.   [15] *Append.* p. 14.

(c) In the same way, our LORD's important saying,—' *Ye
know not what manner of spirit ye are of: for the Son of man
is not come to destroy men's lives, but to save them* ' (S. Luke
ix. 55, 56), has disappeared from our ' Revised' Version ;
although Manuscripts, Versions, Fathers from the *second
century* downwards, (as Tischendorf admits,) witness eloquently in its favour.

V. In conclusion, we propose to advert, just for a moment,
to those five several mis-representations of S. Luke's ' Title
on the Cross,' which were rehearsed above, viz. in page 86.
At so gross an exhibition of licentiousness, it is the mere
instinct of Natural Piety to exclaim,—But then, could not
those men even set down so sacred a record as *that,* correctly ?
They could, had they been so minded, no doubt, (we answer):
but, marvellous to relate, the TRANSPOSITION of words,—no
matter how significant, sacred, solemn ;—of short clauses,—
even of whole sentences of Scripture ; — was anciently
accounted an allowable, even a graceful exercise of the critical
faculty.

The thing alluded to is incredible at first sight ; being so
often done, apparently, without any reason whatever,—or
rather in defiance of all reason.   Let *candidus lector* be the
judge whether we speak truly or not.   Whereas S. Luke
(xxiv. 41) says, ' *And while they yet believed not for joy,
and wondered,*' the scribe of codex A (by way of improving
upon the Evangelist) transposes his sentence into this, 'And
while they yet disbelieved Him, *and wondered for joy :*'[1]
which is almost nonsense, or quite.

But take a less solemn example.   Instead of,—' And His

---

[1] ἔτι δὲ ἀπιστούντων αὐτῷ, καὶ θαυμαζόντων ἀπὸ τῆς χαρᾶς.

disciples plucked *the ears of corn, and ate them,* (τοὺς
στάχυας, καὶ ἤσθιον,) rubbing them ir their hands' (S. Luke
vi. 1),—B C L R, by *transposing* four Greek words, present us
with, 'And His disciples plucked, *and ate the ears of corn,*
(καὶ ἤσθιον τοὺς στάχυας,) rubbing them,' &c. Now this
might have been an agreeable occupation for horses and for
another quadruped, no doubt; but hardly for men. This
curiosity, which (happily) proved indigestible to our Revisionists, is nevertheless swallowed whole by Drs. Westcott
and Hort as genuine and wholesome Gospel. (*O dura
Doctorum ilia!*)—But to proceed.

Then further, these preposterous Transpositions are of
such perpetual recurrence,—are so utterly useless or else so
exceedingly mischievous, *always* so tasteless,—that familiarity
with the phenomenon rather increases than lessens our
astonishment. What *does* astonish us, however, is to find
learned men in the year of grace 1881, freely resuscitating
these long-since-forgotten *bêtises* of long-since-forgotten
Critics, and seeking to palm them off upon a busy and a
careless age, as so many new revelations. That we may not
be thought to have shown undue partiality for the xxiind,
xxiiird, and xxivth chapters of S. Luke's Gospel by selecting
our instances of *Mutilation* from those three chapters, we
will now look for specimens of *Transposition* in the xixth
and xxth chapters of the same Gospel. The reader is
invited to collate the Text of the oldest uncials, throughout
these two chapters, with the commonly Received Text. He
will find that within the compass of 88 consecutive verses,[1]
codices א A B C D Q exhibit no less than 74 instances of Transposition:—for 39 of which, D is responsible :—א B, for 14:—
א and א B D, for 4 each :—A B and א A B, for 3 each :—A, for

---

2 :—B, C, Q, א A, and A D, each for 1.—In other words, he will
find that in no less than 44 of these instances of Transposition, D is implicated :—א, in 26 :—B, in 25 :—A, in 10 :—while
C and Q are concerned in only one a-piece. . . . . It should
be added that Drs. Westcott and Hort have adopted *every one
of the 25 in which codex B is concerned*—a significant indication of the superstitious reverence in which they hold that
demonstrably corrupt and most untrustworthy document.[1]
Every other case of Transposition they have rejected.   By
their own confession, therefore, 49 out of the 74 (i.e. two-
thirds of the entire number) are instances of depravation.
We turn with curiosity to the Revised Version ; and discover
that out of the 25 so retained, the Editors in question were
only able to persuade the Revisionists to adopt 8.   So that,
in the judgment of the Revisionists, 66 out of 74, or *eleven-*

---

[1] We take leave to point out that, however favourable the estimate Drs.
Westcott and Hort may have personally formed of the value and importance of the Vatican Codex (B), nothing can excuse their summary handling,
not to say their contemptuous disregard, of all evidence adverse to that of
their own favourite guide.   They *pass by* whatever makes against the
reading they adopt, with the oracular announcement that the rival reading
is ' *Syrian,*' ' *Western,*' ' *Western and Syrian,*' as the case may be.

But we respectfully submit that ' *Syrian,*' ' *Western,*' ' *Western and
Syrian,*' as Critical expressions, are absolutely without meaning, as well as
without use to a student in this difficult department of sacred Science.
They supply no information.   They are never supported by a particle of
intelligible evidence.   They are often demonstrably wrong, and *always*
unreasonable.   They are *Dictation*, not *Criticism*.   When at last it is
discovered that they do but signify that certain words *are not found in
codex* B,—they are perceived to be the veriest *foolishness* also.

Progress is impossible while this method is permitted to prevail.   If
these distinguished Professors have enjoyed a Revelation as to what the
Evangelists actually wrote, they would do well to acquaint the world with
the fact at the earliest possible moment.   If, on the contrary, they are
merely relying on their own inner consciousness for the power of divining
the truth of Scripture at a glance,—they must be prepared to find their
decrees treated with the contumely which is due to imposture, of whatever
kind.

twelfths, are instances of licentious tampering with the deposit. .... O to participate in the verifying faculty which guided the teachers to discern in 25 cases of Transposition out of 74, the genuine work of the HOLY GHOST! O, far more, to have been born with that loftier instinct which enabled the pupils (Doctors Roberts and Milligan, Newth and Moulton, Vance Smith and Brown, Angus and Eadie) to winnow out from the entire lot exactly 8, and to reject the remaining 66 as nothing worth!

According to our own best judgment, (and we have carefully examined them all,) *every one* of the 74 is worthless. But then *we* make it our fundamental rule to reason always from grounds of external Evidence,—never from postulates of the Imagination. Moreover, in the application of our rule, we begrudge no amount of labour : reckoning a long summer's day well spent if it has enabled us to ascertain the truth concerning one single controverted word of Scripture. Thus, when we find that our Revisionists, at the suggestion of Dr. Hort, have transposed the familiar Angelic utterance (in S. Luke xxiv. 7), λέγων ὅτι δεῖ τὸν υἱὸν τοῦ ἀνθρώπου παραδοθῆναι,—into this, λέγων τὸν υἱὸν τοῦ ἀνθρώπου ὅτι δεῖ, &c., we at once enquire for *the evidence.* And when we find that *no* single Father, *no* single Version, and no Codex—except the notorious ℵ B C L—advocates the proposed transposition ; but on the contrary that every Father (from A.D. 150 downwards) who quotes the place, quotes it as it stands in the Textus receptus ;[1] — we have no hesitation whatever in rejecting it. It is found in the midst of a very thicket of fabricated readings. It has nothing whatever to recommend it. It is condemned by the consentient voice of Antiquity.

---

[1] Marcion (Epiph. i. 317) ; — Eusebius (Mai, iv. 266) ; — Epiphanius (i. 348) ;—Cyril (Mai, ii. 438) ;—John Thessal. (Galland. xiii. 188).

It is advocated only by four copies,—which *never* combine exclusively, except to misrepresent the truth of Scripture and to seduce the simple.

But the foregoing, which is a fair typical sample of countless other instances of unauthorized Transposition, may not be dismissed without a few words of serious remonstrance. Our contention is that, inasmuch as the effect of such transposition *is incapable of being idiomatically represented in the English language*,—(for, in all such cases, the Revised Version retains the rendering of the Authorized,)—our Revisionists have violated the spirit as well as the letter of their instructions, in putting forth *a new Greek Text*, and silently introducing into it a countless number of these and similar depravations of Scripture. These Textual curiosities (for they are nothing more) are absolutely out of place in a *Revision of the English Version*: achieve no lawful purpose: are sure to mislead the unwary. This first.—Secondly, we submit that,—strong as, no doubt, the temptation must have been, to secure the sanction of the N. T. Revisionists for their own private Recension of the Greek, (printed long since, but published simultaneously with the ' Revised Version ')—it is to be regretted that Drs. Westcott and Hort should have yielded thereto. Man's impatience never promotes GOD'S Truth. The interests of Textual Criticism would rather have suggested, that the Recension of that accomplished pair of Professors should have been submitted to public inspection in the first instance. The astonishing Text which it advocates might have been left with comparative safety to take its chance in the Jerusalem Chamber, after it had undergone the searching ordeal of competent Criticism, and been freely ventilated at home and abroad for a decade of years. But on the contrary. It was kept close. It might be seen only by the Revisers: and even *they* were tied down to secrecy as

H

to the letter-press by which it was accompanied. . . . All this strikes us as painful in a high degree.

VI. Hitherto we have referred almost exclusively to the Gospels. In conclusion, we invite attention to our Revisionists' treatment of 1 Tim. iii. 16—the *crux criticorum*, as Prebendary Scrivener styles it.[1] We cannot act more fairly than by inviting a learned member of the revising body to speak on behalf of his brethren. We shall in this way ascertain the amount of acquaintance with the subject enjoyed by some of those who have been so obliging as to furnish the Church with a new Recension of the Greek of the New Testament. Dr. Roberts says :—

'The English reader will probably be startled to find that the familiar text,—"*And without controversy great is the mystery of godliness :* GOD *was manifest in the flesh,*" has been exchanged in the Revised Version for the following,—"*And without controversy great is the mystery of godliness ; He who was manifested in the flesh.*" A note on the margin states that "the word *GOD*, in place of *He who,* rests on no sufficient ancient evidence;" and it may be well that, in a passage of so great importance, the reader should be convinced that such is the case.

'What, then, let us enquire, is the amount of evidence which can be produced in support of the reading "GOD"? This is soon stated. Not one of the early Fathers can be certainly quoted for it. None of the very ancient versions support it. No uncial witnesses to it, with the doubtful exception of A .... But even granting that the weighty suffrage of the Alexandrian manuscript is in favour of "GOD," far more evidence can be produced in support of "who." א and probably c witness to this reading, and it has also powerful testimony from the versions and Fathers. Moreover, the relative "who" is a far more difficult reading than "GOD," and could hardly have been substituted for the latter. On every ground, therefore, we conclude that

---

[1] [The discussion of this text has been left very nearly as it originally stood,—the rather, because the reading of 1 Tim. iii. 16 will be found fully discussed at the end of the present volume. See *Index of Texts.*]

this interesting and important passage must stand as it has been given in the Revised Version.'[1]

And now, having heard the learned Presbyterian on behalf of his brother-Revisionists, we request that we may be ourselves listened to in reply.

The place of Scripture before us, the Reader is assured, presents a memorable instance of the mischief which occasionally resulted to the inspired Text from the ancient practice of executing copies of the Scriptures in uncial characters. S. Paul *certainly* wrote μέγα ἐστὶ τὸ τῆς εὐσεβείας μυστήριον· Θεὸς ἐφανερώθη ἐν σαρκί, ('*Great is the mystery of godliness:* GOD *was manifested in the flesh.*') But it requires to be explained at the outset, that the holy Name when abbreviated (which it always was), thus,—ΘC ('GOD'), is only distinguishable from the relative pronoun 'who' (OC), by two horizontal strokes,—which, in manuscripts of early date, it was often the practice to trace so faintly that at present they can scarcely be discerned.[2] Need we go on? An archetypal copy in which one or both of these slight strokes had vanished from the word ΘC ('GOD'), gave rise to the reading OC ('who'),—of which nonsensical substitute, traces survive in *only two*[3] manuscripts,—א and 17: not, for certain, in *one single* ancient Father,—no, nor for certain in *one single* ancient Version. So transparent, in fact, is the absurdity of writing τὸ μυστήριον ὅς ('the mystery *who*'), that copyists promptly substituted ὅ ('*which*'): thus furnishing another illustration of the well-known property of

---

[1] *Companion to the Revised Version,* &c., by Alex. Roberts, D.D. (2nd edit.), pp. 66–8.

[2] Of this, any one may convince himself by merely inspecting the 2 pages of codex A which are exposed to view at the British Museum.

[3] For, of the 3 cursives usually cited for the same reading (17, 73, 181), the second proves (on enquiry at Upsala) to be merely an abridgment of Œcumenius, who certainly read Θεός; and the last is non-existent.

a fabricated reading, viz. sooner or later inevitably to become
the parent of a second.   Happily, to this second mistake
the sole surviving witness is the Codex Claromontanus, of
the VIth century (D): the only Patristic evidence in its
favour being Gelasius of Cyzicus,[1] (whose date is A.D. 476):
and the unknown author of a homily in the appendix to
Chrysostom.[2]   The Versions—all but the Georgian and the
Slavonic, which agree with the Received Text—favour it
unquestionably; for they are observed invariably to make
the relative pronoun agree in gender with the word which
represents μυστήριον ('mystery') which immediately precedes it.   Thus, in the Syriac Versions, ὅς ('who') is found,
—but only because the Syriac equivalent for μυστήριον is
of the masculine gender: in the Latin, quod ('which')—but
only because mysterium in Latin (like μυστήριον in Greek)
is neuter.   Over this latter reading, however, we need not
linger; seeing that ὅ does not find a single patron at the
present day.   And yet, this was the reading which was eagerly
upheld during the last century: Wetstein and Sir Isaac
Newton being its most strenuous advocates.

It is time to pass under hasty review the direct evidence for the true reading.   A and C exhibited ΘC until
ink, thumbing, and the injurious use of chemicals, obliterated
what once was patent.   It is too late, by full 150 years, to
contend on the negative side of this question.—F and G,
which exhibit ΘC and OC respectively, were confessedly
derived from a common archetype: in which archetype, it is
evident that the horizontal stroke which distinguishes Θ
from O must have been so faintly traced as to be scarcely
discernible.   The supposition that, in this place, the stroke
in question represents the aspirate, is scarcely admissible.
There is no single example of ὅς written ΘC in any part of

---

[1] Concilia, ii. 217 c.   [2] viii. 214 b.

either Cod. F *or Cod.* G.   On the other hand, in the only place
where OC represents ΘC, it is written OC *in both.*   Prejudice herself may be safely called upon to accept the obvious
and only lawful inference.

To come to the point,—Θεός is the reading of *all the
uncial copies extant but two* (viz. ℵ which exhibits ὅς, and
D which exhibits ὅ), and of all the cursives *but one* (viz. 17).
The universal consent of the Lectionaries proves that Θεός
has been read in all the assemblies of the faithful from the
IVth or Vth century of our era.   At what earlier period of
her existence is it supposed then that the Church ('the
witness and keeper of Holy Writ,') availed herself of her
privilege to substitute Θεός for ὅς or ὅ,—whether in error
or in fraud?   Nothing short of a conspiracy, to which every
region of the Eastern Church must have been a party, would
account for the phenomenon.

We enquire next for the testimony of the Fathers; and
we discover that—(1) Gregory of Nyssa quotes Θεός *twenty-
two times*:[1]—that Θεός is also recognized by (2) his namesake of Nazianzus in two places;[2]—as well as by (3) Didymus of Alexandria;[3]—(4) by ps.-Dionysius Alex.;[4]—and (5)
by Diodorus of Tarsus.[5]—(6) Chrysostom quotes 1 Tim. iii.
16 in conformity with the received text at least three times;[6]

---

[1] A single quotation is better than many references.   Among a multitude of proofs that CHRIST is GOD, Gregory says :—Τιμοθέῳ δὲ διαρρήδην
βοᾷ· ὅτι ὁ Θεὸς ἐφανερώθη ἐν σαρκί, ἐδικαιώθη ἐν πνεύματι.   ii. 693.

[2] Τοῦτο ἡμῖν τὸ μέγα μυστήριον . . ὁ ἐνανθρωπήσας δι' ἡμᾶς καὶ
πτωχεύσας Θεός, ἵνα ἀναστήσῃ τὴν σάρκα.   (i. 215 a.)—Τί τὸ μέγα μυστήριον; . . Θεὸς ἄνθρωπος γίνεται.   (i. 685 b.)

[3] *De Trin.* p. 83—where the testimony is express.

[4] Θεὸς γὰρ ἐφανερώθη ἐν σαρκί.—*Concilia,* i. 853 d.

[5] Cramer's *Cat. in Rom.* p. 124.

[6] One quotation may suffice :—Τὸ δὲ Θεὸν ὄντα, ἄνθρωπον θελῆσαι
γενέσθαι καὶ ἀνεσχέσθαι καταβῆναι τοσοῦτον . . . τοῦτό ἐστι τὸ ἐκπλήξεως
γέμον.   ὃ δὴ καὶ Παῦλος θαυμάζων ἔλεγεν· καὶ ὁμολογουμένως μέγα ἐστὶ
τὸ τῆς εὐσεβείας μυστήριον· ποῖον μέγα; Θεὸς ἐφανερώθη ἐν σαρκί· καὶ

—and (7) Cyril Al. as often :[1]—(8) Theodoret, four times :[2]—
(9) an unknown author of the age of Nestorius (A.D. 430),
once :[3]—(10) Severus, Bp. of Antioch (A.D. 512), once.[4]—
(11) Macedonius (A.D. 506) patriarch of CP.,[5] of whom it
has been absurdly related that he *invented* the reading, is a
witness for Θεός perforce ; so is—(12) Euthalius, and—(13)
John Damascene on two occasions.[6]—(14) An unknown
writer who has been mistaken for Athanasius,[7]—(15) besides
not a few ancient scholiasts, close the list : for we pass by
the testimony of—(16) Epiphanius at the 7th Nicene Council
(A.D. 787),—of (17) Œcumenius,—of (18) Theophylact.

It will be observed that neither has anything been said
about the many indirect allusions of earlier Fathers to this
place of Scripture ; and yet some of these are too striking
to be overlooked : as when—(19) Basil, writing of our
Saviour, says αὐτὸς ἐφανερώθη ἐν σαρκί :[8]—and (20) Gregory Thaum., καὶ ἔστι Θεὸς ἀληθινὸς ὁ ἄσαρκος ἐν σαρκὶ
φανερωθείς :[9]—and before him, (21) Hippolytus, οὗτος
προελθὼν εἰς κόσμον, Θεὸς ἐν σώματι ἐφανερώθη :[10]—and
(22) Theodotus the Gnostic, ὁ Σωτὴρ ὤφθη κατιὼν τοῖς

πάλιν ἀλλαχοῦ · οὐ γὰρ ἀγγέλων ἐπιλαμβάνεται ὁ Θεός, κ. τ. λ. i. 497.
= Galland. xiv. 141.

[1] The following may suffice :—μέγα γὰρ τότε τῆς εὐσεβείας μυστήριον ·
πεφανέρωται γὰρ ἐν σαρκὶ Θεὸς ὢν καὶ ὁ Λόγος · ἐδικαιώθη δὲ καὶ ἐν πνεύματι. v. p. ii. ; p. 154 c d.—In a newly-recovered treatise of Cyril, 1 Tim.
iii. 16 is quoted at length with Θεός, followed by a remark on the ἐν αὐτῷ
φανερωθεὶς Θεός. This at least is decisive. The place has been hitherto
overlooked.   [2] i. 92 ; iii. 657 ; iv. 19, 23.

[3] Apud Athanasium, *Opp.* ii. 33, where see Garnier's prefatory note.

[4] Καθ᾿ ὃ γὰρ ὑπῆρχε Θεὸς [sc. ὁ Χριστὸς] τοῦτον ᾔτει τὸν νομοθέτην
δοθῆναι πᾶσι τοῖς ἔθνεσι . . . τοιγαροῦν καὶ δεξάμενα τὰ ἔθνη τὸν νομοθέτην,
τὸν ἐν σαρκὶ φανερωθέντα Θεόν. Cramer's *Cat.* iii. 69. The quotation
is from the lost work of Severus against Julian of Halicarnassus.

[5] Galland. xii. 152 e, 153 e, with the notes both of Garnier and
Gallandius.

[6] i. 313 ; ii. 263.   [7] Ap. Athanas. i. 706.

[8] iii. 401-2.   [9] Ap. Phot. 230.   [10] *Contra Hær. Noet.* c. 17.

ἀγγέλοις:[1]—and (23) Barnabas, Ἰησοῦς . . . . ὁ υἱὸς τοῦ Θεοῦ τύπῳ καὶ ἐν σαρκὶ φανερωθείς:[2]—and earlier still (24) Ignatius: Θεοῦ ἀνθρωπίνως φανερουμένου:—ἐν σαρκὶ γενόμενος Θεός:—εἷς Θεὸς ἔστιν ὁ φανερώσας ἑαυτὸν διὰ Ἰησοῦ Χριστοῦ τοῦ υἱοῦ αὐτοῦ.[3]—Are we to suppose that *none* of these primitive writers read the place as *we* do ?

Against this array of Testimony, the only evidence which the unwearied industry of 150 years has succeeded in eliciting, is as follows:—(1) The exploded *Latin* fable that Macedonius (A.D. 506) *invented* the reading:[4]—(2) the fact that Epiphanius,—*professing to transcribe*[5] from an earlier treatise of his own[6] (in which ἐφανερώθη stands *without a nominative*), prefixes ὅς:—(3) the statement of an unknown scholiast, that in one particular place of Cyril's writings where the Greek is lost, Cyril wrote ὅς,—(which seems to be an entire mistake ; but which, even if it were a fact, would be sufficiently explained by the discovery that in two other places of Cyril's writings the evidence *fluctuates* between ὅς and Θεός):—(4) a quotation in an epistle of Eutherius of Tyana (it exists only in Latin) where 'qui' is found:—(5) a casual reference (in Jerome's commentary on Isaiah) to our LORD, as One 'qui apparuit in carne, justificatus est in spiritu,'—which Bp. Pearson might have written.—Lastly, (6) a passage of Theodorus Mopsuest. (quoted at the Council of Constantinople, A.D. 553), where the reading is 'qui,'—which is balanced by the discovery that in another place of his writings quoted at the same Council, the original is translated 'quod.' And this closes the evidence. Will any unprejudiced person, on reviewing the premises, seriously declare that ὅς is the better sustained reading of the two ?

---

[1] Ap. Clem. Al. 973. [2] Cap. xii. [3] *Ad Eph.* c. 19, 7 ; *ad Magn.* c. 8.
[4] See Scrivener's *Plain Introd.* pp. 555-6, and Berriman's *Dissertation*, pp. 229-263. Also the end of this volume. [5] i. 887 c. [6] ii. 74 b.

For ourselves, we venture to deem it incredible that a Reading which—(*a*) Is not to be found in more than *two* copies (ℵ and 17) of S. Paul's Epistles : which—(*b*) Is not certainly supported by a single Version :—(*c*) Nor is clearly advocated by a single Father,—*can* be genuine. It does not at all events admit of question, that until *far* stronger evidence can be produced in its favour, ὅς ('who') may on no account be permitted to usurp the place of the commonly received Θεός ('GOD') of 1 Tim. iii. 16. But the present exhibits in a striking and instructive way all the characteristic tokens of a depravation of the text. (1st) At an exceedingly early period it resulted in *another* deflection. (2nd) It is without the note of *Continuity;* having died out of the Church's memory well-nigh 1400 years ago. (3rd) It is deficient in *Universality;* having been all along denied the Church's corporate sanction. As a necessary consequence, (4th) It rests at this day on wholly *insufficient Evidence:* Manuscripts, Versions, Fathers being *all* against it. (5th) It carries on its front its own refutation. For, as all must see, ΘΣ might easily be mistaken for ΟC : but in order to make ΟC into ΘΣ, *two horizontal lines must of set purpose be added to the copy.* It is therefore a vast deal *more likely* that ΘΣ became ΟC, than that ΟC became ΘΣ. (6th) Lastly, it is condemned by internal considerations. Ὅς is in truth so grossly improbable—rather, so *impossible*—a reading, that under any circumstances we must have anxiously enquired whether no escape from it was discoverable : whether there exists no way of explaining *how* so patent an absurdity as μυστή-ριον ὅς *may* have arisen ? And on being reminded that the disappearance of two faint horizontal strokes, *or even of one,* would fully account for the impossible reading,—(and thus much, at least, all admit,)—should we not have felt that it required an overwhelming consensus of authorities in favour of ὅς, to render such an alternative deserving of serious

attention? It is a mere abuse of Bengel's famous axiom
to recal it on occasions like the present. We shall be landed
in a bathos indeed if we allow *gross improbability* to become a
constraining motive with us in revising the sacred Text.

And thus much for the true reading of 1 Tim. iii. 16. We
invite the reader to refer back [1] to a Reviser's estimate of
the evidence in favour of Θεός and ὅς respectively, and to
contrast it with our own. If he is impressed with the
strength of the cause of our opponents,—their mastery of the
subject,—and the reasonableness of their contention,—we
shall be surprised. And yet *that* is not the question just
now before us. The *only* question (be it clearly remembered) which · has to be considered, is *this:*—Can it be said
with truth that the "evidence" for ὅς (as against Θεός)
in 1 Tim. iii. 16 is "*clearly preponderating*"? Can it be
maintained that Θεός is a '*plain and clear error*'? Unless
this can be affirmed—*cadit quæstio.* The traditional reading
of the place ought to have been let alone. May we be
permitted to say without offence that, in our humble judgment, if the Church of England, at the Revisers' bidding,
were to adopt this and thousands of other depravations of
the sacred page,[2]—with which the Church Universal was once
well acquainted, but which in her corporate character she has
long since unconditionally condemned and abandoned,—she
would deserve to be pointed at with scorn by the rest of
Christendom? Yes, and to have *that* openly said of her

---

[1] See above, p. 98.

[2] As, that stupid fabrication, Τί με ἐρωτᾷς περὶ τοῦ ἀγαθοῦ; (in S. Matth.
xix. 17):—the new incidents and sayings proposed for adoption, as in S.
Mark i. 27 (in the Synagogue of Capernaum): in S. John xiii. 21–6 (at the
last supper): in S. Luke xxiv. 17 (on the way to Emmaus):—the many
proposed omissions, as in S. Matth. vi. 13 (the Doxology): in xvi. 2, 3
(the signs of the weather): in S. Mark ix. 44 & 46 (the words of woe): in
S. John v. 3, 4 (the Angel troubling the pool), &c. &c. &c.

which S. Peter openly said of the false teachers of his day
who fell back into the very errors which they had already
abjured. The place will be found in 2 S. Peter ii. 22. So singularly applicable is it to the matter in hand, that we can but
invite attention to the quotation on our title-page and p. 1.

And here we make an end.

1. Those who may have taken up the present Article in
expectation of being entertained with another of those discussions (of which we suspect the public must be already
getting somewhat weary), concerning the degree of ability
which the New Testament Revisionists have displayed in
their rendering into English of the Greek, will at first experience disappointment. Readers of intelligence, however, who
have been at the pains to follow us through the foregoing
pages, will be constrained to admit that we have done more
faithful service to the cause of Sacred Truth by the course
we have been pursuing, than if we had merely multiplied
instances of incorrect and unsatisfactory *Translation.* There
is (and this we endeavoured to explain at the outset) a question of prior interest and far graver importance which has to
be settled *first,* viz. the degree of confidence which is due to
the underlying NEW GREEK TEXT which our Revisionists have
constructed. In other words, before discussing their *new
Renderings,* we have to examine their *new Readings.*[1] The
silence which Scholars have hitherto maintained on this part

---

[1] It cannot be too plainly or too often stated that learned Prebendary
Scrivener is *wholly guiltless* of the many spurious 'Readings' with which
a majority of his co-Revisionists have corrupted the Word of GOD. He
pleaded faithfully,—but he pleaded in vain.—It is right also to state
that the scholarlike Bp. of S. Andrews (Dr. Charles Wordsworth) has
fully purged himself of the suspicion of complicity, by his printed (not
published) remonstrances with his colleagues.—The excellent Bp. of
Salisbury (Dr. Moberly) attended only 121 of their 407 meetings; and
that judicious scholar, the Abp. of Dublin (Dr. Trench) only 63. The
reader will find more on this subject at the close of Art. II.,—pp. 228–30.

of the subject is to ourselves scarcely intelligible. But it makes
us the more anxious to invite attention to this neglected aspect
of the problem; the rather, because we have thoroughly convinced ourselves that the 'new Greek Text' put forth by the
Revisionists of our Authorized Version is *utterly inadmissible.* The traditional Text has been departed from by them
nearly 6000 times,—almost invariably *for the worse.*

2. Fully to dispose of *all* these multitudinous corruptions
would require a bulky Treatise. But the reader is requested
to observe that, if we are right in the few instances we
have culled out from the mass,—*then we are right in all.* If
we have succeeded in proving that the little handful of
authorities on which the 'new Greek Text' depends, are the
reverse of trustworthy,—are absolutely misleading,—then,
we have cut away from under the Revisionists the very
ground on which they have hitherto been standing. And in
that case, the structure which they have built up throughout
a decade of years, with such evident self-complacency, collapses 'like the baseless fabric of a vision.'

3. For no one may flatter himself that, by undergoing
a *further* process of 'Revision,' the 'Revised Version' may
after all be rendered trustworthy. The eloquent and excellent Bishop of Derry is 'convinced that, with all its undeniable merits, it will have to be somewhat extensively revised.'
And so perhaps are we. But (what is a far more important
circumstance) we are further convinced that a prior act of
penance to be submitted to by the Revisers would be the
restoration of the underlying Greek Text to very nearly—*not
quite*—the state in which they found it when they entered
upon their ill-advised undertaking. 'Very nearly — not
quite:' for, in not a few particulars, the 'Textus receptus'
does call for Revision, certainly; although Revision on
entirely different principles from those which are found to
have prevailed in the Jerusalem Chamber. To mention a

single instance :—When our LORD first sent forth His Twelve
Apostles, it was certainly no part of His ministerial commission to them to ' *raise the dead* ' (νεκροὺς ἐγείρετε, S.
Matthew x. 8). This is easily demonstrable. Yet is the
spurious clause retained by our Revisionists; because it is
found in those corrupt witnesses—א B C D, and the Latin
copies.[1]   When will men learn unconditionally to put away
from themselves the weak superstition which is for investing
with oracular authority the foregoing quaternion of demonstrably depraved Codices ?

4. ' It may be said '—(to quote again from Bp. Alexander's
recent Charge),—' that there is a want of modesty in dissent-
ing from the conclusions of a two-thirds majority of a body
so learned.   But the rough process of counting heads imposes
unduly on the imagination.   One could easily name *eight*
in that assembly, whose *unanimity* would be practically
almost decisive ; but we have no means of knowing that
these did not *form the minority* in resisting the changes
which we most regret.'   The Bishop is speaking of the
English Revision.   Having regard to the Greek Text exclusively, *we* also (strange to relate) had singled out *exactly eight*
from the members of the New Testament company—Divines
of undoubted orthodoxy, who for their splendid scholarship
and proficiency in the best learning, or else for their refined
taste and admirable judgment, might (as we humbly think),
under certain safeguards, have been safely entrusted even with
the responsibility of revising the Sacred Text.   Under the
guidance of Prebendary Scrivener (who among living Englishmen is *facile princeps* in these pursuits) it is scarcely to be
anticipated that, WHEN UNANIMOUS, such Divines would ever

---

[1] Eusebius,—Basil,—Chrysostom (*in loc.*),—Jerome,—Juvencus,—omit
the words. P. E. Pusey found them in *no* Syriac copy. But the conclusive
evidence is supplied by the Manuscripts ; not more than 1 out of 20 of
which contain this clause.

have materially erred.   But then, of course, a previous life-
long familiarity with the Science of *Textual Criticism*, or at
least leisure for prosecuting it now, for ten or twenty years,
with absolutely undivided attention,—would be the indispensable requisite for the success of such an undertaking; and
this, undeniably, is a qualification rather to be desiderated
than looked for at the hands of English Divines of note at
the present day.   On the other hand, (loyalty to our Master
constrains us to make the avowal,) the motley assortment of
names, twenty-eight in all, specified by Dr. Newth, at p. 125
of his interesting little volume, joined to the fact that the
average attendance *was not so many as sixteen*,—concerning
whom, moreover, the fact has transpired that some of the
most judicious of their number often *declined to give any
vote at all*,—is by no means calculated to inspire any sort of
confidence.   But, in truth, considerable familiarity with these
pursuits may easily co-exist with a natural inaptitude for
their successful cultivation, which shall prove simply fatal.
In support of this remark, one has but to refer to the
instance supplied by Dr. Hort.   The Sacred Text has none
to fear so much as those who *feel* rather than think : who
imagine rather than reason : who rely on a supposed *verifying faculty* of their own, of which they are able to render
no intelligible account; and who, (to use Bishop Ellicott's
phrase,) have the misfortune to conceive themselves possessed
of a "*power of divining the Original Text*,"—which would
be even diverting, if the practical result of their self-decep-
tion were not so exceedingly serious.

5. In a future number, we may perhaps enquire into the
measure of success which has attended the Revisers' *Revision
of the English* of our Authorized Version of 1611.   We have
occupied ourselves at this time exclusively with a survey
of the seriously mutilated and otherwise grossly depraved
NEW GREEK TEXT, on which their edifice has been reared.

And the circumstance which, in conclusion, we desire to impress upon our Readers, is this,—that the insecurity of that foundation is so alarming, that, except as a concession due to the solemnity of the undertaking just now under review, further Criticism might very well be dispensed with, as a thing superfluous. Even could it be proved concerning the superstructure, that '*it had been* [*ever so*] *well builded*,'[1] (to adopt another of our Revisionists' unhappy perversions of Scripture,) the fatal objection would remain, viz. that it is not '*founded upon the rock.*'[2] It has been the ruin of the present undertaking—as far as the Sacred Text is concerned—that the majority of the Revisionist body have been misled throughout by the oracular decrees and impetuous advocacy of Drs. Westcott and Hort ; who, with the purest intentions and most laudable industry, have constructed a Text demonstrably more remote from the Evangelic verity, than any which has ever yet seen the light. 'The old is good,'[3] say the Revisionists : but we venture solemnly to assure them that '*the old is better ;*'[4] and that this remark holds every bit as true of their Revision of the Greek throughout, as of their infelicitous exhibition of S. Luke v. 39. To attempt, as they have done, to build the Text of the New Testament on a tissue of unproved assertions and the eccentricities of a single codex of bad character, is about as hopeful a proceeding as would be the attempt to erect an Eddystone lighthouse on the Goodwin Sands.

---

[1] 'Revised Text' of S. Luke vi. 48.

[2] 'Authorized Version,' supported by A C D and 12 other uncials, the whole body of the cursives, the Syriac, Latin, and Gothic versions.

[3] 'Revised Text ' of S. Luke v. 39.

[4] 'Authorized Version,' supported by A C and 14 other uncials, the whole body of the cursives, and *all* the versions except the Peschito and the Coptic.

ARTICLE II.

THE NEW ENGLISH VERSION.

" Such is the time-honoured Version which we have been called upon to revise! We have had to study this great Version carefully and minutely, line by line; and the longer we have been engaged upon it the more we have learned to admire *its simplicity, its dignity, its power, its happy turns of expression, its general accuracy,* and we must not fail to add, *the music of its cadences, and the felicities of its rhythm.* To render a work that had reached this high standard of excellence, still more excellent; to increase its fidelity, without destroying its charm; was the task committed to us."—PREFACE TO THE REVISED VERSION.

" To pass from the one to the other, is, as it were, to alight from a well-built and well-hung carriage which glides easily over a macadamized road,—and to get into one *which has bad springs or none at all,* and in which you are *jolted in ruts with aching bones over the stones of a newly-mended and rarely traversed road,* like some of the roads in our North Lincolnshire villages."—BISHOP WORDSWORTH.[1]

" No Revision at the present day could hope to meet with an hour's acceptance if it failed to preserve the tone, rhythm, and diction of the present Authorized Version."—BISHOP ELLICOTT.[2]

---

[1] *Address at Lincoln Diocesan Conference,*—p. 16.
[2] *On Revision,*—p. 99.

REVISION REVISED.

ARTICLE II.—THE NEW ENGLISH VERSION.

"I testify unto every man that heareth the words of the prophecy of
this Book,—If any man shall add unto these things, GOD shall add unto
him the plagues that are written in this Book.

"And if any man shall take away from the words of the Book of
this prophecy, GOD shall take away his part out of the Book of Life, and
out of the holy City, and from the things which are written in this Book."
—REVELATION xxii. 18, 19.

WHATEVER may be urged in favour of Biblical Revision, it
is at least undeniable that the undertaking involves a tremendous risk. Our Authorized Version is the one religious
link which at present binds together ninety millions of
English-speaking men scattered over the earth's surface. Is
it reasonable that so unutterably precious, so sacred a bond
should be endangered, for the sake of representing certain
words more accurately,—here and there translating a tense
with greater precision,—getting rid of a few archaisms? It
may be confidently assumed that no 'Revision' of our
Authorized Version, however judiciously executed, will ever
occupy the place in public esteem which is actually enjoyed
by the work of the Translators of 1611,—the noblest literary
work in the Anglo-Saxon language. We shall in fact never
have *another* 'Authorized Version.' And this single consideration may be thought absolutely fatal to the project,
except in a greatly modified form. To be brief,—As a
companion in the study and for private edification: as a
book of reference for critical purposes, especially in respect

I

of difficult and controverted passages :—we hold that a
revised edition of the Authorized Version of our English
Bible, (if executed with consummate ability and learning,)
would at any time be a work of inestimable value.   The
method of such a performance, whether by marginal Notes
or in some other way, we forbear to determine.   But
certainly only as a handmaid is it to be desired.   As something *intended to supersede* our present English Bible, we are
thoroughly convinced that the project of a rival Translation
is not to be entertained for a moment.   For ourselves, we
deprecate it entirely.

On the other hand, *who* could have possibly foreseen what
has actually come to pass since the Convocation of the
Southern Province (in Feb. 1870) declared itself favourable
to ' a Revision of the Authorized Version,' and appointed a
Committee of Divines to undertake the work ?   *Who* was
to suppose that the Instructions given to the Revisionists
would be by them systematically disregarded ?   *Who* was
to imagine that an utterly untrustworthy ' new Greek Text,'
constructed on mistaken principles, — (say rather, on *no
principles at all*,)—would be the fatal result?   To speak
more truly,— *Who* could have anticipated that the opportunity would have been adroitly seized to inflict upon the
Church the text of Drs. Westcott and Hort, in all its
essential features,—a text which, as will be found elsewhere
largely explained, we hold to be *the most vicious Recension of
the original Greek in existence?*   Above all,— *Who* was to
foresee that instead of removing ' *plain* and *clear errors* '
from our Version, the Revisionists,—(besides systematically
removing out of sight so many of the genuine utterances of
the SPIRIT,)—would themselves introduce a countless number
of blemishes, unknown to it before ?   Lastly, how was it to
have been believed that the Revisionists would show them-

selves industrious in sowing broadcast over four continents doubts as to the Truth of Scripture, which it will never be in their power either to remove or to recal? *Nescit vox missa reverti.*

For, the ill-advised practice of recording, in the margin of an English Bible, certain of the blunders—(such things cannot by any stretch of courtesy be styled 'Various Readings')—which disfigure 'some' or 'many' 'ancient authorities,' can only result in hopelessly unsettling the faith of millions. It cannot be defended on the plea of candour,—the candour which is determined that men shall 'know the worst.' '*The worst*' has NOT *been told*: and it were dishonesty to insinuate that *it has.* If all the cases were faithfully exhibited where 'a few,' 'some,' or 'many ancient authorities' read differently from what is exhibited in the actual Text, not only would the margin prove insufficient to contain the record, but *the very page itself* would not nearly suffice. Take a single instance (the first which comes to mind), of the thing referred to. Such illustrations might be multiplied to any extent :—

In S. Luke iii. 22, (in place of 'Thou art my beloved Son; *in Thee I am well pleased,*') the following authorities of the IInd, IIIrd and IVth centuries, read,—'*this day have I begotten Thee :*' viz.—codex D and the most ancient copies of the old Latin (a, b, c, ff[2], l),—Justin Martyr in three places[1] (A.D. 140),—Clemens Alex.[2] (A.D. 190),—and Methodius[3] (A.D. 290) among the Greeks. Lactantius[4] (A.D. 300),—Hilary[5] (A.D. 350),—Juvencus[6] (A.D. 330),—Faustus[7] (A.D. 400), and—

---

[1] *Dial.* capp. 88 and 103 (pp. 306, 310, 352).
[2] P. 113.
[3] Ap. Galland. iii. 719, c d.
[4] iv. 15 (ap. Gall. iv. 296 b).
[5] 42 b, 961 e, 1094 a.
[6] Ap. Galland. iv. 605 (ver. 365–6).
[7] Ap. Aug. viii. 423 e.

Augustine[1] amongst the Latins. The reading in question was doubtless derived from the *Ebionite Gospel*[2] (IInd cent.). Now, we desire to have it explained to us *why* an exhibition of the Text supported by such an amount of first-rate primitive testimony as the preceding, obtains *no notice whatever* in our Revisionists' margin,—if indeed it was the object of their perpetually recurring marginal annotations, to put the unlearned reader on a level with the critical Scholar; to keep nothing back from him; and so forth? . . . It is the gross one-sidedness, the patent *unfairness*, in a critical point of view, of this work, (which professes to be nothing else but *a Revision of the English Version of* 1611,)—which chiefly shocks and offends us.

For, on the other hand, of what possible use can it be to encumber the margin of S. Luke x. 41, 42 (for example), with the announcement that ' A few ancient authorities read *Martha, Martha, thou art troubled : Mary hath chosen* &c.' (the fact being, that D *alone* of MSS. omits ' *careful and* ' . . . ' *about many things. But one thing is needful, and* ' . . .) ? With the record of this circumstance, is it reasonable (we ask) to choke up our English margin,—to create perplexity and to insinuate doubt? The author of the foregoing

---

[1] " Vox illa Patris, quæ super baptizatum facta est *Ego hodie genui te*," (*Enchirid.* c. 49 [*Opp.* vi. 215 a]):—

" Illud vero quod nonnulli codices habent secundum Lucam, hoc illa voce sonuisse quod in Psalmo scriptum est, *Filius meus es tu : ego hodie genui te*, quanquam in antiquioribus codicibus Græcis non inveniri perhibeatur, tamen si aliquibus fide dignis exemplaribus confirmari possit, quid aliud quam utrumque intelligendum est quolibet verborum ordine de cælo sonuisse ?" (*De Cons. Ev.* ii. c. 14 [*Opp.* iii. P. ii. 46 d e]). Augustine seems to allude to what is found to have existed in the *Ebionite Gospel*.

[2] Epiphanius (i. 138 b) quotes the passage which contains the statement.

marginal Annotation was of course aware that the same
'singular codex' (as Bp. Ellicott styles cod. D) omits, in
S. Luke's Gospel alone, no less than 1552 words : and he will
of course have ascertained (by counting) that the words in
S. Luke's Gospel amount to 19,941. Why then did he not
tell *the whole* truth ; and instead of '*&c.*,' proceed as follows ?
—' But inasmuch as cod. D is so scandalously corrupt that
about *one word in thirteen* is missing throughout, the absence
of nine words in this place is of no manner of importance or
significancy. The precious saying omitted is above suspicion, and the first half of the present Annotation might have
been spared.' . . . We submit that a Note like that, although
rather 'singular' in style, really *would* have been to some
extent helpful,—if not to the learned, at least to the unlearned reader.

In the meantime, unlearned and learned readers alike
are competent to see that the foregoing perturbation of
S. Luke x. 41, 42 rests on *the same* manuscript authority
as the perturbation of ch. iii. 22, which immediately preceded
it. The *Patristic* attestation, on the other hand, of the reading
which has been promoted to the margin, is almost *nil :*
whereas *that* of the neglected place has been shown to be
considerable, very ancient, and of high respectability.

But in fact,—(let the Truth be plainly stated ; for, when
GOD's Word is at stake, circumlocution is contemptible,
while concealment would be a crime ;) — '*Faithfulness*'
towards the public, a stern resolve that the English reader
'shall know the worst,' and all that kind of thing,—such
considerations have had nothing whatever to do with the
matter. A vastly different principle has prevailed with the
Revisionists. Themselves the dupes of an utterly mistaken
Theory of Textual Criticism, their supreme solicitude has

been *to impose that same Theory,*—(*which is Westcott and Hort's,*)—with all its bitter consequences, on the unlearned and unsuspicious public.

We shall of course be indignantly called upon to explain what we mean by so injurious—so damning—an imputation? For all reply, we are content to refer to the sample of our meaning which will be found below, in pp. 137–8. The exposure of what has there been shown to be the method of the Revisionists in respect of S. Mark vi. 11, might be repeated hundreds of times. It would in fact *fill a volume.* We shall therefore pass on, when we have asked the Revisionists in turn—*How they have dared* so effectually to blot out those many precious words from the Book of Life, that no mere English reader, depending on the Revised Version for his knowledge of the Gospels, can by possibility suspect their existence? . . . Supposing even that it *was* the calamitous result of their mistaken principles that they found themselves constrained on countless occasions, to omit from their Text precious sayings of our LORD and His Apostles,—what possible excuse will they offer for not having preserved a record of words so amply attested, *at least in their margin?*

Even so, however, the whole amount of the mischief which has been effected by our Revisionists has not been stated. For the Greek Text which they have invented proves to be so hopelessly depraved throughout, that if it were to be thrust upon the Church's acceptance, we should be a thousand times worse off than we were with the Text which Erasmus and the Complutensian,—Stephens, and Beza, and the Elzevirs,—bequeathed to us upwards of three centuries ago. On this part of the subject we have remarked at length already [pp. 1–110]: yet shall we be constrained to recur once and again to the underlying Greek Text of the Revisionists,

inasmuch as it is impòssible to stir in any direction with the
task before us, without being painfully reminded of its existence. Not only do the familiar Parables, Miracles, Discourses
of our LORD, trip us up at every step, but we cannot open
the first page of the Gospel—no, nor indeed read *the first line*
—without being brought to a standstill. Thus,

1. S. Matthew begins,—'The book of the generation of
JESUS CHRIST' (ver. 1).—Good. But here the margin volunteers two pieces of information : first,—'Or, *birth :* as in
ver. 18.' We refer to ver. 18, and read—'Now the birth of
JESUS CHRIST was on this wise.' Good again ; but the
margin says,—'Or, *generation :* as in ver. 1.' Are we then
to understand that *the same Greek word*, diversely rendered
in English, occurs in both places ? We refer to the '*new
Greek Text :*' and there it stands,—γένεσις in either verse.
But if the word be the same, why (on the Revisers' theory)
is it diversely rendered ?

In the meantime, *who* knows not that there is all the
difference in the world between S. Matthew's γένεσις, in
ver. 1,—and the same S. Matthew's γέννησις, in ver. 18 ?
The latter, the Evangelist's announcement of the circumstances of the human Nativity of CHRIST: the former, the
Evangelist's unobtrusive way of recalling the Septuagintal
rendering of Gen. ii. 4 and v. 1 :[1] the same Evangelist's
calm method of guiding the devout and thoughtful student
to discern in the Gospel the History of the ' new Creation,'—
by thus providing that when first the Gospel opens its lips, it
shall syllable the name of the first book of the elder Covenant ? We are pointing out that it more than startles—it
supremely offends—one who is even slenderly acquainted

[1] Αὕτη ἡ βίβλος γενέσεως—οὐρανοῦ καὶ γῆς : also—ἀνθρώπων.

with the treasures of wisdom hid in the very diction of the
N. T. Scriptures, to discover that a deliberate effort has been
made to get rid of the very foremost of those notes of Divine
intelligence, by confounding two words which all down the
ages have been carefully kept distinct; and that this effort
is the result of an exaggerated estimate of a few codices
which happen to be written in the uncial character, viz.
two of the IVth century (B א); one of the Vth (c); two of
the VIth (P z); one of the IXth (Δ); one of the Xth (s).

The Versions [1]—(which are our *oldest* witnesses)—are
perforce only partially helpful here. Note however, that *the
only one which favours* γένεσις is the heretical Harkleian
Syriac, executed in the VIIth century. The Peschito and
Cureton's Syriac distinguish between γένεσις in ver. 1 and
γέννησις in ver. 18: as do the Slavonic and the Arabian
Versions. The Egyptian, Armenian, Æthiopic and Georgian,
have only one word for both. Let no one suppose however
that *therefore* their testimony is ambiguous. It is γέννησις
(*not* γένεσις) which they exhibit, both in ver. 1 and in ver. 18.[2]
The Latin ('*generatio*') is an equivocal rendering certainly :
but the earliest Latin writer who quotes the two places,
(viz. Tertullian) employs the word '*genitura*' in S. Matth.
i. 1,—but '*nativitas*' in ver. 18,—which no one seems to
have noticed.[3] Now, Tertullian, (as one who sometimes

---

[1] For my information on this subject, I am entirely indebted to one
who is always liberal in communicating the lore of which he is perhaps the
sole living depositary in England,—the Rev. Dr. S. C. Malan. See his
Seven Chapters of the Revision of 1881, *revised,*—p. 3. But especially
should the reader be referred to Dr. Malan's learned dissertation on this very
subject in his *Select Readings in Westcott and Hort's Gr. Text of S.
Matth.,*—pp. 1 to 22.

[2] So Dr. Malan in his *Select Readings* (see above note [1]),—pp. 15, 17, 19.

[3] " Liber *genituræ* Jesu Christi filii David, filii Abraham " ... "Gra-
datim ordo deducitur ad Christi *nativitatem.*"—*De Carne Christi*, c. 22.

wrote in Greek,) is known to have been conversant with
the Greek copies of his day; and 'his day,' be it remembered, is A.D. 190. He evidently recognized the parallelism
between S. Matt. i. 1 and Gen. ii. 4,—where the old Latin
exhibits 'liber *creaturæ*' or '*facturæ*,' as the rendering of
βίβλος γενέσεως. And so much for the testimony of the
Versions.

But on reference to Manuscript and to Patristic authority[1]
we are encountered by an overwhelming amount of testimony for γέννησις in ver. 18 : and this, considering the
nature of the case, is an extraordinary circumstance. Quite
plain is it that the Ancients were wide awake to the difference between spelling the word with one N or with two,—
as the little dissertation of the heretic Nestorius[2] in itself
would be enough to prove. Γέννησις, in the meantime, is
the word employed by Justin M.,[3]—by Clemens Alex.,[4]—by
Athanasius,[5]—by Gregory of Nazianzus,[6]—by Cyril Alex.,[7]
—by Nestorius,[8] — by Chrysostom,[9] — by Theodorus Mop-

---

[1] A friendly critic complains that we do not specify which editions of the
Fathers we quote. Our reply is—This [was] a Review, not a Treatise. We
are *constrained* to omit such details. Briefly, we always quote *the best
Edition*. Critical readers can experience *no* difficulty in verifying our
references. A few details shall however be added : Justin (*Otto*): Irenæus
(*Stieren*): Clemens Al. (*Potter*): Tertullian (*Oehler*): Cyprian (*Baluze*):
Eusebius (*Gaisford*): Athanas. (1698): Greg. Nyss. (1638): Epiphan.
(1622): Didymus (1769): Ephraem Syr. (1732): Jerome (*Vallarsi*):
Nilus (1668–73): Chrysostom (*Montfaucon*): Cyril (*Aubert*): Isidorus
(1638): Theodoret (*Schulze*): Maximus (1675): John Damascene (*Le-
quien*): Photius (1653). Most of the others (as Origen, Greg. Nazianz.,
Basil, Cyril of Jer., Ambrose, Hilary, Augustine), are quoted from the
Benedictine editions. When we say ' Mai,' we always mean his *Nova
Biblioth. PP.* 1852-71. By ' Montfaucon,' we mean the *Nov. Coll. PP.*
1707. It is *necessity* that makes us so brief.

[2] *Concilia*, iii. 521 a to d.   [3] i.[2] 340.   [4] P. 889 line 37 (γένησιν).
[5] i. 943 c.   [6] i. 735.   [7] v.[1] 363, 676.
[8] *Concil*. iii. 325 (= Cyril v.[2] 28 a).   [9] vii. 48 ; viii. 314.

suest.,[1]—and by three other ancients.[2]   Evèn more deserving
of attention is it that Irenæus [3] (A.D. 170)—(whom Germanus [4] copies at the end of 550 years)—calls attention to
the difference between the spelling of ver. 1 and ver. 18.
So does Didymus:[5]—so does Basil:[6]—so does Epiphanius.[7]
—Origen[8] (A.D. 210) is even eloquent on the subject.—Tertullian (A.D. 190) we have heard already.—It is a significant
circumstance, that the only Patristic authorities discoverable
on the other side are Eusebius, Theodoret, and the authors
of an heretical Creed [9]—whom Athanasius holds up to scorn.[10]
... Will the Revisionists still pretend to tell us that γέννησις
in verse 18 is a 'plain and clear error'?

2. This, however, is not all.   Against the words 'of JESUS
CHRIST,' a further critical annotation is volunteered; to the
effect that 'Some ancient authorities read *of the Christ.*'   In
reply to which, we assert that *not one single known MS.*
omits the word 'JESUS:' whilst its presence is vouched for
by ps.-Tatian,[11]—Irenæus,—Origen,—Eusebius,—Didymus,—
Epiphanius, — Chrysostom, — Cyril, — in addition to *every
known Greek copy of the Gospels,* and not a few of the Versions, including the Peschito and both the Egyptian.   What else
but nugatory therefore is such a piece of information as this?

3. And so much for the first, second, and third Critical
annotations, with which the margin of the revised N. T. is

---

[1] *In Matth.* ii. 16.

[2] Ps.-Athanas. ii. 306 and 700: ps.-Chrysost. xii. 694.

[3] P. 470.   [4] Gall. ix. 215.

[5] *Trin.* 188.   [6] i. 250 b.   [7] i. 426 a (γένησις).

[8] Διαφέρει γένεσις καὶ γέννησις· γένεσις μὲν γάρ ἐστι παρὰ Θεοῦ
πρώτη πλάσις, γέννησις δὲ ἡ ἐκ καταδίκης τοῦ θανάτου διὰ τὴν παράβασιν ἐξ
ἀλλήλων διαδοχή.—Galland. xiv. *Append.* pp. 73, 74.

[9] [dated 22 May A.D. 359] ap. Athan. i. 721 d.   [10] i. 722 c.

[11] P. 20 of the newly-recovered *Diatessaron,* translated from the Armenian.
The Exposition is claimed for Ephraem Syrus.

disfigured. Hoping that the worst is now over, we read on till we reach ver. 25, where we encounter a statement which fairly trips us up : viz.,—' And knew her not *till she had brought forth a son.*' No intimation is afforded of what has been here effected; but in the meantime every one's memory supplies the epithet ('her first-born') which has been ejected. Whether something very like indignation is not excited by the discovery that these important words have been surreptitiously withdrawn from their place, let others say. For ourselves, when we find that only א B Z and two cursive copies can be produced for the omission, we are at a loss to understand of what the Revisionists can have been dreaming. Did they know[1] that,—besides the Vulgate, the Peschito and Philoxenian Syriac, the Æthiopic, Armenian, Georgian, and Slavonian Versions,[2]—a whole torrent of Fathers are at hand to vouch for the genuineness of the epithet they were so unceremoniously excising? They are invited to refer to ps.-Tatian,[3]—to Athanasius,[4]— to Didymus,[5]—to Cyril of Jer.,[6]—to Basil,[7]—to Greg. Nyss.,[8] —to Ephraem Syr.,[9]—to Epiphanius,[10]—to Chrysostom,[11]— to Proclus,[12]—to Isidorus Pelus.,[13]—to John Damasc.,[14]—to Photius,[15]—to Nicetas :[16]—besides, of the Latins, Ambrose,[17] —the *Opus imp.*,—Augustine,—and not least to Jerome[18]— eighteen Fathers in all. And how is it possible, (we ask,)

---

[1] Dr. Malan, *Seven Chapters of the Revision, revised,* p. 7.

[2] See below, note [13].   [3] See p. 122, note [11].

[4] i. 938, 952. Also ps.-Athan. ii. 409, excellently.

[5] *Trin.* 349.   [6] P. 116.   [7] i. 392; ii. 599, 600.   [8] ii. 229.

[9] See p. 122, note [11].   [10] i. 426, 1049 (5 times), 1052-3.

[11] vii. 76.   [12] Galland. ix. 636.

[13] P. 6 (τὸν υἱὸν αὐτῆς : which is also the reading of Syrᶜᵘ and of the Sahidic. The Memphitic version represents τὸν υἱόν.)

[14] i. 276.   [15] Gal. xiii. 662.   [16] *In Cat.*   [17] ii. 462.

[18] ' *Ex hoc loco quidam perversissime suspicantur et alios filios habuisse Mariam, dicentes primogenitum non dici nisi qui habeat et fratres*' (vii. 14). He refers to his treatise against Helvidius, ii. 210.

that two copies of the IVth century (B ℵ) and one of the VIth (z)—all three without a character—backed by a few copies of the old Latin, should be supposed to be any counterpoise at all for such an array of first-rate contemporary evidence as the foregoing ?

Enough has been offered by this time to prove that an authoritative Revision of the Greek Text will have to precede any future Revision of the English of the New Testament. Equally certain is it that for such an undertaking the time has not yet come. " It is my honest conviction,"— (remarks Bp. Ellicott, the Chairman of the Revisionists,)— " that for any authoritative Revision, we are not yet mature : either in Biblical learning or Hellenistic scholarship." [1] The same opinion precisely is found to have been cherished by Dr. Westcott till *within about a year-and-a-half* [2] of the first assembling of the New Testament Company in the Jerusalem Chamber, 22nd June, 1870. True, that we enjoy access to—suppose from 1000 to 2000—more MANUSCRIPTS than were available when the Textus Recept. was formed. But nineteen-twentieths of those documents, for any use which has been made of them, might just as well be still lying in the monastic libraries from which they were obtained.—True, that four out of our five oldest uncials have come to light since the year 1628 ; but, *who knows how to use them ?*—True, that we have made acquaintance with certain ancient VERSIONS, about which little or nothing was known 200 years ago : but,—(with the solitary exception of the Rev. Solomon Cæsar Malan, the learned Vicar of Broadwindsor,— who, by the way, is always ready to lend a torch to his benighted brethren,)—what living Englishman is able to tell

---

[1] Preface to *Pastoral Epistles*,—more fully quoted facing p. 1.
[2] The Preface (quoted above facing p. 1,) is dated 3rd Nov. 1868.

us what they all contain ?   A smattering acquaintance with
the languages of ancient Egypt,—the Gothic, Æthiopic, Armenian, Georgian and Slavonian Versions,—is of no manner
of avail.   In no department, probably, is 'a little learning'
more sure to prove 'a dangerous thing.'—True, lastly, that
the FATHERS have been better edited within the last 250
years: during which period some fresh Patristic writings
have also come to light.   But, with the exception of Theodoret among the Greeks and Tertullian among the Latins,
which of the Fathers has been satisfactorily indexed ?

Even what precedes is not nearly all.   *The fundamental
Principles* of the Science of Textual Criticism are not yet
apprehended.   In proof of this assertion, we appeal to the
new Greek Text of Drs. Westcott and Hort,—which, beyond
all controversy, is more hopelessly remote from the inspired
Original than any which has yet appeared.   Let a generation
of Students give themselves entirely up to this neglected
branch of sacred Science.   Let 500 more COPIES of the
Gospels, Acts, and Epistles, be diligently collated.   Let at
least 100 of the ancient *Lectionaries* be very exactly collated
also.   Let the most important of the ancient VERSIONS be
edited afresh, and let the languages in which these are
written be for the first time really *mastered* by Englishmen.
*Above all, let the FATHERS be called upon to give up their
precious secrets.*   Let their writings be ransacked and indexed,
and (where needful) let the MSS. of their works be diligently inspected, in order that we may know what actually
is the evidence which they afford.   Only so will it ever be
possible to obtain a Greek Text on which absolute reliance
may be placed, and which may serve as the basis for a
satisfactory Revision of our Authorized Version.   Nay, let
whatever unpublished works of the ancient Greek Fathers are
anywhere known to exist,—(and not a few precious remains

of theirs are lying hid in great national libraries, both at
home and abroad,)—let these be printed.   The men could
easily be found : the money, far more easily.—When all this
has been done,—*not before*—then in GOD's Name, let *the
Church* address herself to the great undertaking.   Do but
revive the arrangements which were adopted in King James's
days : and we venture to predict that less than a third part
of ten years will be found abundantly to suffice for the work.
How the coming men will smile at the picture Dr. Newth[1]
has drawn of what was the method of procedure in the reign
of Queen Victoria!   Will they not peruse with downright
merriment Bp. Ellicott's jaunty proposal " *simply to proceed
onward with the work*,"—[to wit, of constructing a new Greek
Text,]—" in fact, *solvere ambulando*," [*necnon in laqueum
cadendo*] ?[2]

I. We cannot, it is presumed, act more fairly by the
Revisers' work,[3] than by following them over some of the
ground which they claim to have made their own, and
which, at the conclusion of their labours, their Right

---

[1] *Lectures on Biblical Revision*, (1881) pp. 116 seqq. See above, pp. 37-9.

[2] *On Revision*, pp. 30 and 49.

[3] *The New Testament of Our Lord and Saviour JESUS CHRIST, translated
out of the Greek: being the Version set forth* A.D. 1611, *compared with
the most ancient Authorities, and Revised* A.D. 1881.   Printed for the
Universities of Oxford and Cambridge, 1881.

*The New Testament in the Original Greek, according to the Text
followed in the Authorized Version, together with the Variations adopted in
the Revised Version.*   Edited for the Syndics of the Cambridge University
Press, by F. H. A. Scrivener, M.A., D.C.L., LL.D., Prebendary of Exeter
and Vicar of Hendon.   Cambridge, 1881.

'Η ΚΑΙΝΗ ΔΙΑΘΗΚΗ.   *The Greek Testament, with the Readings
adopted by the Revisers of the Authorized Version.*   [Edited by the Ven.
Archdeacon Palmer, D.D.]   Oxford, 1881.

The New Testament in the Original Greek.   The Text revised by
Brooke Foss Westcott, D.D., and Fenton John Anthony Hort, D.D.
Cambridge and London, 1881.

Reverend Chairman evidently surveys with self-complacency. First, he invites attention to the Principle and Rule for their guidance agreed to by the Committee of Convocation (25th May, 1870), viz. 'To INTRODUCE AS FEW ALTERATIONS AS POSSIBLE INTO THE TEXT OF THE AUTHORIZED VERSION, CONSISTENTLY WITH FAITHFULNESS.' Words could not be more emphatic. ' PLAIN AND CLEAR ERRORS ' were to be corrected. ' NECESSARY emendations' were to be made. But (in the words of the Southern Convocation) 'We do not contemplate any new Translation, *or any alteration of the language,* EXCEPT WHERE, in the judgment of the most competent Scholars, SUCH CHANGE IS NECESSARY.' The watchword, therefore, given to the company of Revisionists was,— ' NECESSITY.' *Necessity* was to determine whether they were to depart from the language of the Authorized Version, or not ; for the alterations were to be AS FEW AS POSSIBLE.

(*a*) Now it is idle to deny that this fundamental Principle has been utterly set at defiance. To such an extent is this the case, that even an unlettered Reader is competent to judge them. When we find ' *to* ' substituted for ' unto ' (*passim*) :—' *hereby* ' for ' by this ' (1 Jo. v. 2) :—' all that *are,*' for ' all that be ' (Rom. i. 7) :—' *alway* ' for ' always ' (2 Thess. i. 3) :—' we *that,*' ' them *that,*' for ' we *which,*' ' them *which* ' (1 Thess. iv. 15) ; and yet ' every spirit *which,*' for ' every spirit that ' (1 Jo. iv. 3), and ' he *who* is not of GOD,' for ' he that is not of GOD ' (ver. 6,—although ' he *that* knoweth GOD ' had preceded, in the same verse) :—' *my* host ' for ' mine host ' (Rom. xvi. 23) ; and ' *underneath* ' for ' under ' (Rev. vi. 9) : —it becomes clear that the Revisers' notion of NECESSITY is not that of the rest of mankind. But let the plain Truth be stated. Certain of them, when remonstrated with by their fellows for the manifest disregard they were showing to the Instructions subject to which they had undertaken the work of Revision, are reported to have even gloried in their shame. The majority, it is clear, have even ostentatiously set those Instructions at defiance.

Was the course they pursued,—(we ask the question respectfully,)—strictly *honest* ? To decline the work entirely under the prescribed Conditions, was always in their power. But, first to accept the Conditions, and straightway to act in defiance of them,—*this* strikes us as a method of proceeding which it is difficult to reconcile with the high character of the occupants of the Jerusalem Chamber. To proceed however.

'Nevertheless' and 'notwithstanding' have had a sad time of it. One or other of them has been turned out in favour of '*howbeit*' (S. Lu. x. 11, 20),—of '*only*' (Phil. iii. 16), —of '*only that*' (i. 18),—of '*yet*' (S. Matth. xi. 11),—of '*but*' (xvii. 27),—of '*and yet*' (James ii. 16). . . . We find '*take heed*' substituted for 'beware' (Col. ii. 8) :—'*custom*' for 'manner' (S. Jo. xix. 40) :—'he was *amazed*,' for 'he was astonished :' (S. Lu. v. 9) :—'*Is it I, LORD?*' for 'LORD, is it I?' (S. Matth. xxvi. 22) :—'*straightway* the cock crew,' for 'immediately the cock crew' (S. Jo. xviii. 27) :—'Then *therefore he delivered Him*,' for 'Then delivered he Him therefore' (xix. 16) :— '*brought* it to His mouth,' for 'put it to His mouth' (ver. 29) : —'*He manifested Himself on this wise*,' for 'on this wise shewed He Himself' (xxi. 1) :—'*So when they got out upon the land*,' for 'As soon then as they were come to land' (ver. 9) : —'the things *concerning*,' for 'the things pertaining to the kingdom of GOD' (Acts i. 3) :—'as *GOD's steward*,' for 'as the steward of GOD' (Tit. i. 7) : but 'the *belly of the whale*' for 'the whale's belly' (S. Matth. xii. 40), and '*device of man*' for 'man's device' in Acts xvii. 29.—These, and hundreds of similar alterations have been evidently made out of the

merest wantonness. After substituting '*therefore*' for 'then'
(as the rendering of οὖν) a score of times,—the Revisionists
quite needlessly substitute '*then*' for 'therefore' in S. Jo. xix.
42.—And why has the singularly beautiful greeting of 'the
elder unto the well-beloved Gaius,' been exchanged for 'unto
Gaius the beloved'? (3 John, ver. 1).

(*b*) We turn a few pages, and find 'he that *doeth* sin,'
substituted for 'he that committeth sin;' and '*To this end*' put
in the place of 'For this purpose' (1 Jo. iii. 8):—'*have beheld*
and *bear witness*,' for 'have seen and do testify' (iv. 14):—
'*hereby*' for 'by this' (v. 2):—'*Judas*' for 'Jude' (Jude
ver. 1), although '*Mark*' was substituted for 'Marcus' (in
1 Pet. v. 13), and '*Timothy*' for 'Timotheus' (in Phil. i. 1):
—'how that they *said to* you,' for 'how that they told you'
(Jude ver. 18).—But why go on? The substitution of '*exceedingly*' for 'greatly' in Acts vi. 7:—'*the birds*' for 'the fowls,'
in Rev. xix. 21:—'*Almighty*' for 'Omnipotent' in ver. 6:
—'*throw down*' for 'cast down,' in S. Luke iv. 29:—'*inner
chamber*' for 'closet,' in vi. 6:—these are *not* 'necessary'
changes. . . . . We will give but three instances more:—In
1 S. Pet. v. 9, 'whom *resist*, stedfast in the faith,' has been
altered into 'whom *withstand*.' But how is 'withstand' a
better rendering for ἀντίστητε, than 'resist'? 'Resist,' at
all events, *was the Revisionists' word in S. Matth.* v. 39
and S. James iv. 7.—Why also substitute 'the *race*' (for 'the
kindred') 'of Joseph' in Acts vii. 13, although γένος was
rendered 'kindred' in iv. 6?—Do the Revisionists think
that '*fastening their eyes* on him' is a better rendering of
ἀτενίσαντες εἰς αὐτόν (Acts vi. 15) than '*looking stedfastly* on
him'? They certainly did not think so when they got to
xxiii. 1. There, because they found '*earnestly beholding* the
council,' they must needs alter the phrase into '*looking
stedfastly*.' It is clear therefore that *Caprice*, not *Necessity*,—

K

an *itching impatience* to introduce changes into the A.V., not
the discovery of '*plain and clear errors,*'—has determined
the great bulk of the alterations which molest us in every
part of the present unlearned and tasteless performance.

II. The next point to which the Revisionists direct our
attention is their NEW GREEK TEXT,—' the necessary foundation
of' their work.   And here we must renew our protest against
the wrong which has been done to English readers by the
Revisionists' disregard of the IVth Rule laid down for their
guidance, viz. that, whenever they adopted a new Textual
reading, such alteration was to be '*indicated in the margin.*'
This 'proved inconvenient,' say the Revisionists.   Yes, we
reply: but only because you saw fit, in preference, to choke
up your margin with a record of the preposterous readings
you did *not* admit.   Even so, however, the thing might to
some extent have been done, if only by a system of signs
in the margin wherever a change in the Text had been by
yourselves effected.   And, at whatever ' inconvenience,' you
were bound to do this,—partly because the Rule before you
was express: but chiefly in fairness to the English Reader.
How comes it to pass that you have *never* furnished him
with the information you stood pledged to furnish ; but have
instead, volunteered in every page information, worthless
in itself, which can only serve to unsettle the faith of unlettered millions, and to suggest unreasonable as well as
miserable doubts to the minds of all ?

For no one may for an instant imagine that the marginal
statements of which we speak are a kind of equivalent for
the *Apparatus Criticus* which is found in every principal
edition of the Greek Testament—excepting always that of
Drs. Westcott and Hort.   So far are we from deprecating
(with Daniel Whitby) the multiplication of ' Various Read-

ings,' that we rejoice in them exceedingly; knowing that they are the very foundation of our confidence and the secret of our strength. For this reason we consider Dr. Tischendorf's last (8th) edition to be furnished with not nearly enough of them, though he left all his predecessors (and himself in his 7th edition) far behind. Our quarrel with the Revisionists is *not* by any means that they have commemorated *actual* 'alternative Readings' in their margin: but that, while they have given prominence throughout to *patent Errors*, they have *unfairly excluded all mention of,—have not made the slightest allusion to,—hundreds of Readings which ought in fact rather to have stood in the Text.*

The marginal readings, which our Revisers have been so ill-advised as to put prominently forward, and to introduce to the Reader's notice with the vague statement that they are sanctioned by 'Some' (or by 'Many') 'ancient authorities,'—are specimens *arbitrarily selected* out of an immense mass; are magisterially recommended to public attention and favour; *seem* to be invested with the sanction and authority of Convocation itself. And this becomes a very serious matter indeed. No hint is given *which be* the 'ancient Authorities' so referred to:—nor what proportion they bear to the 'ancient Authorities' producible on the opposite side: —nor whether they are the *most* 'ancient Authorities' obtainable:—nor what amount of attention their testimony may reasonably claim. But in the meantime a fatal assertion is hazarded in the Preface (iii. 1.), to the effect that *in cases where 'it would not be safe to accept one Reading to the absolute exclusion of others,' 'alternative Readings'* have been given 'in the margin.' So that the 'Agony and bloody sweat' of the World's REDEEMER (Lu. xxii. 43, 44),—and His Prayer for His murderers (xxiii. 34),—and much beside of transcendent importance and inestimable value, may, *according to our Revisionists*, prove to rest upon no foundation whatever.

K 2

At all events, '*it would not be safe,*' (i.e. *it is not safe*) to place
absolute reliance on them.   Alas, how many a deadly blow
at Revealed Truth hath been in this way aimed with fatal
adroitness, which no amount of orthodox learning will ever
be able hereafter to heal, much less to undo!   Thus,—

(*a*) From the first verse of S. Mark's Gospel we are
informed that 'Some ancient authorities omit *the Son of
God.*'   Why are we *not* informed that every known uncial
Copy *except one of bad character,*—every cursive *but two,*—
every Version,—and the following Fathers,—all *contain* the
precious clause :   viz. Irenæus,—Porphyry,—Severianus of
Gabala,—Cyril Alex.,—Victor Ant.,—and others,—besides
Ambrose and Augustine among the Latins :—while the supposed adverse testimony of Serapion and Titus, Basil and
Victorinus, Cyril of Jer. and Epiphanius, proves to be all
a mistake ?   To speak plainly, since the clause is above
suspicion, *Why are we not rather told so ?*

(*b*) In the 3rd verse of the first chapter of S. John's
Gospel, we are left to take our choice between,—' without
Him was not anything made that hath been made.   In him
was life ; and the life,' &c.,—and the following absurd alternative,—' Without him was not anything made.   *That which
hath been made was life in him ;* and the life,' &c.   But we
are *not* informed that this latter monstrous figment is known
to have been the importation of the Gnostic heretics in the
IInd century, and to be as destitute of authority as it is of
sense.   *Why is prominence given only to the lie ?*

(*c*) At S. John iii. 13, we are informed that the last clause
of that famous verse ('No man hath ascended up to heaven,
but He that came down from heaven, even the Son of Man—
which is in heaven'), is not found in ' many ancient autho-

rities.' But why, in the name of common fairness, are we not *also* reminded that this, (as will be found more fully explained in the note overleaf,) is *a circumstance of no Textual significancy whatever?*

Why, above all, are we not assured that the precious clause in question (ὁ ὢν ἐν τῷ οὐρανῷ) *is* found in every MS. in the world, except five of bad character?—is recognized by *all* the Latin and *all* the Syriac versions; as well as by the Coptic,—Æthiopic,—Georgian,—and Armenian?[1]—is either quoted or insisted upon by Origen,[2]—Hippolytus,[3]—Athanasius,[4]— Didymus,[5]— Aphraates the Persian,[6]— Basil the Great,[7]— Epiphanius,[8]— Nonnus, — ps.-Dionysius Alex.,[9]— Eustathius;[10]—by Chrysostom,[11]—Theodoret,[12]—and Cyril,[13] each 4 times;—by Paulus, Bishop of Emesa[14] (in a sermon on Christmas Day, A.D. 431);—by Theodorus Mops.,[15]— Amphilochius,[16]—Severus,[17]—Theodorus Heracl.,[18]—Basilius Cil.,[19]—Cosmas,[20]—John Damascene, in 3 places,[21]—and 4 other ancient Greek writers;[22] — besides Ambrose,[23] — Novatian,[24] — Hilary,[25] — Lucifer,[26] — Victorinus,—Jerome,[27] — Cassian, — Vigilius,[28] — Zeno,[29] — Marius,[30] — Maximus Taur.,[31]—Capreolus,[32]—Augustine, &c. :—is acknowledged by Lachmann, Tregelles, Tischendorf: in short, is *quite above suspicion:* why are we not told *that?* Those 10 Versions,

---

[1] Malan's *Gospel of S. John translated from the Eleven oldest Versions.*
[2] Int. ii. 72; iv. 622 dis.   [3] *C. Noet.* § 4.   [4] i. 1275.   [5] *Trin.* 363.
[6] Ap. Gall. v. 67.   [7] i. 282.   [8] i. 486.
[9] *Ep. ad Paul. Sam. Concil.* i. 872 e; 889 e.   [10] Ap. Galland. iv. 563.
[11] vii. 546; viii. 153, 154, 277.   [12] iii. 570; iv. 226, 1049, 1153.
[13] iv. 150 (text); vi. 30, 169. Mai, ii. 69.   [14] *Concilia,* iii. 1102 d.
[15] Quoted by Leontius (Gall. xii. 693).   [16] *In Cat.* Cord. 96.
[17] *Ibid.* p. 94.   [18] *Cat. in Ps.* ii. 323 and 343.   [19] Ap. Photium, p. 281.
[20] Montf. ii. 286.   [21] i. 288, 559, 567.
[22] Ps.-Athan. ii. 464. Another, 625. Another, 630. Ps.-Epiphan. ii. 287.
[23] i. 863, 903, 1428.   [24] Gall. iii. 296.   [25] 32 dis.; 514; 1045 dis.
[26] Gall. vi. 192.   [27] iv. 679.   [28] Ap. Athan. ii. 646.   [29] Gall. v. 124.
[30] *Ibid.* iii. 628, 675.   [31] *Ibid.* ix. 367.   [32] *Ibid.* ix. 493.

those 38 Fathers, that host of Copies in the proportion of
995 to 5,—*why*, concerning all these is there not so much
as a hint let fall that such a mass of counter-evidence
exists ? [1] . . . Shame,—yes, *shame* on the learning which
comes abroad only to perplex the weak, and to unsettle the

---

[1] Let the Reader, with a map spread before him, survey the whereabouts
of the several Versions above enumerated, and mentally assign each
Father to his own approximate locality : then let him bear in mind that
995 out of 1000 of the extant Manuscripts agree with those Fathers and
Versions ; and let him further recognize that those MSS. (executed at
different dates in different countries) must severally represent independent
remote originals, inasmuch as *no two of them are found to be quite alike.*
—Next, let him consider that, *in all the Churches of the East*, these words
from the earliest period were read as *part of the Gospel for the Thursday
in Easter week.*—This done, let him decide whether it is reasonable that
two worshippers of codex B—A.D. 1881—should attempt to thrust all this
mass of ancient evidence clean out of sight by their peremptory sentence
of exclusion,—' Western and Syrian.'

Drs. Westcott and Hort inform us that '*the character of the attestation
marks*' the clause (ὁ ὢν ἐν τῷ οὐρανῷ), ' as a Western gloss.' But the
'attestation ' for retaining that clause—(*a*) Comes demonstrably from
every quarter of ancient Christendom :—(*b*) Is more ancient (by 200 years)
than the evidence for omitting it :—(*c*) Is more numerous, in the proportion of 99 to 1 :—(*d*) In point of respectability, stands absolutely alone.
For since we have *proved* that Origen and Didymus, Epiphanius and Cyril,
Ambrose and Jerome, *recognize* the words in dispute, of what possible
Textual significancy can it be if presently (*because it is sufficient for their
purpose*) the same Fathers are observed to quote S. John iii. 13 *no further
than down to the words ' Son of Man '*? No person, (least of all a professed Critic,) who adds to his learning a few grains of common sense and a
little candour, can be misled by such a circumstance. Origen, Eusebius,
Proclus, Ephraim Syrus, Jerome, Marius, when they are only insisting
on the doctrinal significancy of the earlier words, naturally end their
quotation at this place. The two Gregories (Naz. [ii. 87, 168] : Nyss,
[Galland. vi. 522]), writing against the Apolinarian heresy, of course
quoted the verse no further than Apolinaris himself was accustomed (for
his heresy) to adduce it. . . . About the *internal* evidence for the clause,
nothing has been said ; but *this* is simply overwhelming. We make our
appeal to *Catholic Antiquity* ; and are content to rest our cause on
External Evidence ;—on Copies, on Versions, on Fathers.

doubting, and to mislead the blind! Shame,—yes, *shame* on that two-thirds majority of well-intentioned but most incompetent men, who,—finding themselves (in an evil hour) appointed to correct "*plain and clear errors*" in the *English* 'Authorized Version,'—occupied themselves instead with *falsifying the inspired Greek Text* in countless places, and branding with suspicion some of the most precious utterances of the SPIRIT! Shame,—yes, *shame* upon them!

Why then, (it will of course be asked,) is the margin— (*a*) of S. Mark i. 1 and—(*b*) of S. John i. 3, and—(*c*) of S. John iii. 13, encumbered after this discreditable fashion? It is (we answer) only because *the Text of Drs. Westcott and Hort* is thus depraved in all three places. Those Scholars enjoy the unenviable distinction of having dared to expel from S. John iii. 13 the words ὁ ὢν ἐν τῷ οὐρανῷ, which Lachmann, Tregelles and Tischendorf were afraid to touch. Well may Dean Stanley have bestowed upon Dr. Hort the epithet of "*fearless*"! . . . If report speaks truly, it is by the merest accident that the clause in question still retains its place in *the Revised Text*.

(*d*) Only once more. And this time we will turn to the very end of the blessed volume. Against Rev. xiii. 18—

"Here is wisdom. He that hath understanding, let him "count the number of the Beast; for it is the number of a "Man: and his number is six hundred and sixty and six."

Against this, we find noted,—'Some ancient authorities read *six hundred and sixteen.*'

But why is not the *whole* Truth told? viz. why are we not informed that *only one* corrupt uncial (c):—*only one* cursive copy (11):—*only one* Father (Tichonius): and *not one* ancient Version—advocates this reading?—which, on the contrary,

Irenæus (A.D. 170) knew, but rejected; remarking that 666, which is 'found in all the best and oldest copies and is attested by men who saw John face to face,' is unquestionably the true reading.[1]   Why is not the ordinary Reader further informed that the same number (666) is expressly vouched for by Origen,[2]—by Hippolytus,[3]—by Eusebius:[4]— as well as by Victorinus—and Primasius,—not to mention Andreas and Arethas?   To come to the moderns, as a matter of fact the established reading is accepted by Lachmann, Tischendorf, Tregelles,—even by Westcott and Hort.   *Why* therefore—for what possible reason—at the end of 1700 years and upwards, is this, which is so clearly nothing else but an ancient slip of the pen, to be forced upon the attention of 90 millions of English-speaking people?

Will Bishop Ellicott and his friends venture to tell us that it has been done because " it would not be safe to accept " 666, "to the absolute exclusion of " 616? . . . "We have given *alternative Readings* in the margin," (say they,) " wherever they seem to be of sufficient importance or interest to deserve notice."   Will they venture to claim either 'interest' or 'importance' for *this?* or pretend that it is an 'alternative Reading' *at all?*   Has it been rescued from oblivion and paraded before universal· Christendom in order to perplex, mystify, and discourage 'those that have understanding,' and would fain 'count the number of the Beast,' if they were able?   Or was the intention only to insinuate one more wretched doubt—one more miserable suspicion— into minds which have been taught (*and rightly*) to place absolute reliance in the textual accuracy of all the gravest utterances of the SPIRIT : minds which are utterly incapable

---

[1] Pp. 798, 799.   iii. 414.
[3] *Ant.* c. 50; *Consum.* c. 28.   [4] *Hist. Eccl.* v. 8.

of dealing with the subtleties of Textual Criticism; and, from a one-sided statement like the present, will carry away none but entirely mistaken inferences, and the most unreasonable distrust? . . . Or, lastly, was it only because, in their opinion, the margin of every Englishman's N. T. is the fittest place for reviving the memory of obsolete blunders, and ventilating forgotten perversions of the Truth? . . . We really pause for an answer.

(e) But serious as this is, *more* serious (if possible) is the unfair *Suppression systematically practised* throughout the work before us. "We have given alternative Readings in the margin,"—(says Bishop Ellicott on behalf of his brother-Revisionists,)—"*wherever they seem to be of sufficient importance or interest to deserve notice.*" [iii. 1.]   From which statement, readers have a right to infer that whenever "alternative Readings" are *not* "given in the margin," it is because such Readings do *not* "seem to be of *sufficient importance or interest to deserve notice.*"   Will the Revisionists venture to tell us that,—(to take the first instance of unfair Suppression which presents itself,)—our LORD's saying in S. Mark vi. 11 is not "of sufficient importance or interest to deserve notice"?   We allude to the famous words,—"Verily I say unto you, It shall be more tolerable for Sodom and Gomorrah in the day of judgment, than for that city:"—words which are not only omitted from the "New English Version," but *are not suffered to leave so much as a trace of themselves in the margin.*   And yet, the saying in question is attested by the Peschito and the Philoxenian Syriac Versions : by the Old Latin : by the Coptic, Æthiopic and Gothic Versions :— by 11 uncials and by the whole bulk of the cursives :—by Irenæus and by Victor of Antioch.   So that whether Antiquity, or Variety of Attestation is considered,—whether we look for Numbers or for Respectability,—the genuineness

of the passage may be regarded as *certain.* Our complaint,
however is *not* that the Revisionists entertain a different
opinion on this head from ourselves : but that they give
the reader to understand that the state of the Evidence is
such, that it is quite "safe to accept" the shorter reading,
—" to the *absolute exclusion* of the other." — So vast is
the field before us, that this single specimen of what we
venture to call 'unfair Suppression,' must suffice. (Some
will not hesitate to bestow upon it a harsher epithet.) It
is in truth by far the most damaging feature of the work
before us, that its Authors should have so largely and so
seriously *falsified the Deposit ;* and yet, (in clear violation
of the IVth Principle or Rule laid down for their guidance
at the outset,) have suffered no trace to survive in the margin
of the deadly mischief which they have effected.

III. From the Text, the Revisionists pass on to the
TRANSLATION ; and surprise us by the avowal, that 'the
character of the Revision was determined for us from the
outset by the first Rule,—"to introduce as few alterations
as possible, consistently with faithfulness." Our task was
Revision, not Retranslation.' (This is *naïve* certainly.) They
proceed,—

' If the meaning was fairly expressed by the word or phrase
that was before us in the Authorized Version, we made no
change, even where rigid adherence to *the rule of Translating, as
far as possible, the same Greek word by the same English word* might
have prescribed some modification.'—[iii. 2 *init.*] (The italics
are our own.)

To the '*rule*' thus introduced to our notice, we shall recur
by and by [pp. 152–4 : also pp. 187–202]. We proceed
to remark on each of the five principal Classes of alterations indicated by the Revisionists : and first,—' Alterations

positively required by change of reading in the Greek Text'
(*Ibid.*).

(1) Thus, in S. John xii. 7, we find '*Suffer her to keep it*
against the day of my burying;' and in the margin (as an
alternative), 'Let her alone : *it was that she might keep it.*'—
Instead of ' as soon as JESUS heard the word,'—we are invited
to choose between '*not heeding*,' and '*overhearing* the word'
(S. Mk. v. 36) : these being intended for renderings of παρ-
ακούσας,—an expression which S. Mark certainly never employed.—'On earth, peace among men *in whom he is well
pleased*' (S. Lu. ii. 14): where the margin informs us that
'many ancient authorities read, *good pleasure among men.*'
(And why not '*good will*,'—the rendering adopted in Phil. i.
15 ?) . . . Take some more of the alterations which have
resulted from the adoption of a corrupt Text :—'Why *askest
thou me concerning that which is good ?* ' (Matth. xix. 17,—an
absurd fabrication).—'He would fain *have been filled* with the
husks,' &c. . . . 'and I perish *here* with hunger !' (χορτασ-
θῆναι, borrowed from Lu. xvi. 21 : and εγωΔΕωδε, a transparent error : S. Luke xv. 16, 17).—'When *it shall fail*, they
may receive you into the eternal tabernacles' (xvi. 9).—
—Elizabeth 'lifted up her voice *with a loud cry*' (κραυγή—
the private property of three bad MSS. and Origen: Lu. i.
42).—'And *they stood still looking sad*' (xxiv. 17,—a foolish
transcriptional blunder).—'The multitude *went up* and began
to ask him,' &c. (ἀναβάς for ἀναβοήσας, Mk. xv. 8).—'But is
guilty of *an eternal sin*' (iii. 29).—'And the officers *received
Him* with blows of their hands,'—marg. 'or *strokes of rods :*'
ΕΛΑΒΟΝ for ΕΒΑΛΟΝ (xiv. 65).—'Else, that which should fill
it up taketh from it, *the new from the old*' (ii. 21) : and 'No
man *rendeth a piece from a new garment* and putteth it upon
an old garment; else *he will rend the new*,' &c. (Lu. v. 36).—
'What is this ? *a new teaching !*' (Mk. i. 27).—'JESUS saith
unto him, *If thou canst !*' (Mk. ix. 23).—'Because of your *little*

faith' (Matth. xvii. 20).—' *We must* work the works of Him that sent Me, while it is day ' (Jo. ix. 4).—' *The man that is called* JESUS made clay ' (ver. 11).—' If ye shall ask *Me anything in My name*' (xiv. 14).—' The Father abiding in Me doeth *His works* ' (xiv. 10).—' If ye shall ask anything of the Father, *He will give it you in My name*' (xvi. 23).—' I glorified Thee on the earth, *having accomplished the work* which Thou hast given Me to do ' (xvii. 4).—' Holy Father, keep them *in Thy Name which* Thou hast given Me . . . I kept them *in Thy Name which* Thou hast given me ' (ver. 11, 12).—' She . . . saith unto Him *in Hebrew*, Rabboni ' (xx. 16).—' These things said Isaiah, *because* he saw his glory ' (xii. 41,—οτι for οτε, a common itacism).—' In tables *that are hearts of flesh* ' (ἐν πλαξὶ καρδίαις σαρκίναις, a ' perfectly absurd reading,' as Scrivener remarks, p. 442 : 2 Cor. iii. 3).—'*Now if* we put the horses' bridles [and pray, why not ' the horses' *bits* '?] into their mouths' (ειδε, an ordinary itacism for ιδε, James iii. 3). —' Unto the sick were *carried away from his body* handkerchiefs,' &c. (Acts xix. 12).—'*Ye know all things once for all* ' (Jude ver. 5).—' *We love* because he first loved us ' (1 Jo. iv. 19). —'I have found *no work of thine fulfilled* before my GOD ' (Rev. iii. 2).—' Seven Angels *arrayed with* [*precious*] *stone* ' (xv. 6), instead of ' clothed in linen,' λίθον for λίνον. (Fancy the Angels ' *clothed in stone* '! ' Precious ' is an interpolation of the Revisers).—'*.Dwelling in* the things which he hath seen : ' for which the margin offers as an alternative, ' *taking his stand upon* ' (Colossians ii. 18). But ἐμβατεύων (the word here employed) clearly means neither the one nor the other. S. Paul is delivering a warning against unduly '*prying into* the things *not* seen.' [1] A few MSS. of bad character omit the ' *not*.' That is all ! . . . These then are a handful of the less

---

[1] 'Εμβατεῦσαι ·—'Επιβῆναι τὰ ἔνδον ἐξερευνῆσαι ἢ σκοπῆσαι. Phavorinus, quoted by Brüder.

II.] REMEDYING 'INCORRECTNESS' AND 'OBSCURITY.' 141

conspicuous instances of a change in the English 'positively
required by a change of reading in the Greek Text:' every
one of them being either a pitiful blunder or else a gross
fabrication.—Take only two more: 'I neither know, nor
understand: *thou, what sayest thou?*' (Mk. xiv. 68 margin):—
'And *whither I go, ye know the way*' (Jo. xiv. 4). . . . The
A. V. is better in every instance.

(2) and (3) Next, alterations made because the A. V.
'appeared to be incorrect' or else 'obscure.' They must
needs be such as the following :—'He that *is bathed* needeth
not save to wash his feet' (S. John xiii. 10).—'LORD, if he is
fallen asleep *he will recover*' (σωθήσεται, xi. 12).—'Go ye
therefore into *the partings of the highways*' (Matth. xxii. 9).—
'Being grieved at *the hardening* of their heart' (Mk. iii. 5).—
'Light *a lamp* and put it *on the stand*' (Matt. v. 15).—'Sitting
at *the place of toll*' (ix. 9).—'The supplication of a righteous
man availeth much *in its working*' (James v. 16).—'Awake
up *righteously*' (1 Cor. xv. 34).—'*Guarded* through faith unto
a salvation' (1 Pet. i. 5).—'Wandering in . . . *the holes of
the earth*' (Heb. xi. 38—very queer places certainly to be
'wandering' in).—'*She that is in Babylon,* elect together
with you, saluteth you' (1 Pet. v. 13).—'Therefore do *these
powers work in Him*' (Matth. xiv. 2).—'In danger of the
hell of fire' (v. 22).—'*Put out* into the deep' (Luke v. 4).—
'The tomb that Abraham bought for *a price in silver*' (Acts
vii. 16).

With reference to every one of these places, (and they are
but samples of what is to be met with in every page,) we venture to assert that they are either *less* intelligible, or else *more*
inaccurate, than the expressions which they are severally intended to supersede; while, in some instances, they are *both*.
Will any one seriously contend that '*the hire of wrong-doing*'

is better than '*the wages of unrighteousness*' (2 Pet. ii. 15)?
or, will he venture to deny that, 'Come and *dine*,'—'so when
they *had dined*,'—is a hundred times better than 'Come and
break your fast,'—'so when they *had broken their fast*' (Jo.
xxi. 12, 15)?—expressions which are only introduced because
the Revisionists were ashamed (as well they might be) to
write 'breakfast' and 'breakfasted.' The seven had not been
'*fasting*.' Then, why introduce so incongruous a notion here,
—any more than into S. Luke xi. 37, 38, and xiv. 12?

Has the reader any appetite for more specimens of 'incorrectness' *remedied* and 'obscurity' *removed?* Rather, as
it seems, have *both* been largely imported into a Translation
which was singularly intelligible before. Why darken Rom.
vii. 1 and xi. 2 by introducing the interrogative particle,
and then, by mistranslating it '*Or*'?—Also, why translate
γένος '*race*'? ('a man of Cyprus *by race*,' 'a man of Pontus
by race,' 'an Alexandrian *by race*,' Acts iv. 36: xviii. 2, 24).
—'*If* there is a natural body, there is also a spiritual body,'
say the Revisionists : 'O death, where is thy victory? O *death*
where is thy sting?' (Could they not let even 1 Cor. xv. 44
and 55 alone?)—Why alter 'For the bread of GOD is *He*,' into
'For the bread of GOD is *that* which cometh down from
Heaven'? (Jo. vi. 33).—'*As long as I am* in the world,' was
surely better than '*When I am* in the world, I am the light
of the world' (ix. 5).—Is '*He went forth out of* their hand'
supposed to be an improvement upon '*He escaped out of* their
hand'? (x. 39): and is 'They loved *the glory* of men more
than *the glory* of GOD' an improvement upon '*the praise*'?
(xii. 43).—'Judas saith unto Him, LORD, *what is come to pass*
that Thou wilt manifest Thyself to us'? Is *that* supposed to
be an improvement upon xiv. 22?—How is '*If then*' an
improvement on 'Forasmuch then' in Acts xi. 17?—or how
is this endurable in Rom. vii. 15,—'For that which I do, I

know not : for *not what I would, that do I practise :* '—or this, in xvi. 25, ' The mystery which hath been *kept in silence through times eternal,* but now is manifested,' &c.—' Thou therefore, *my child,*'—addressing the Bishop of Ephesus (2 Tim. ii. 1): and ' Titus, *my true child,*'—addressing the Bishop of Crete (Tit. i. 4).

Are the following deemed improvements ?   ' Every one that *doeth* sin doeth also *lawlessness : and sin is lawlessness* ' (1 Jo. iii. 4): ' I will *move* thy candlestick out of its place ' (Rev. ii. 5) :—' a *glassy* sea ' (iv. 6) :—' a *great* voice ' (v. 12): —' Verily; not of Angels *doth He take hold,* but *He taketh hold* of the seed of Abraham : '—' He *took hold of* the blind man by *the hand :* '—' They *took hold of him* and brought him unto the Areopagus ' (Heb. ii. 16 : S. Mk. viii. 23 : Acts xvii. 19) :— ' wherefore GOD is not *ashamed of them,* to be called their GOD ' (Acts xi. 16):—' *Counted it not a prize* to be on an equality with GOD ' (Phil. ii. 6).—Why are we to substitute ' *court* ' for ' palace ' in Matth. xxvi. 3 and Lu. xi. 21 ? (Consider Matth. xii. 29 and Mk. iii. 27).—' Women received their dead *by a resurrection* ' (Heb. xi. 35) :—' If ye forgive not every one *his brother from their hearts* ' (Matth. xviii. 35) : —' If *because of meat* thy brother is grieved, thou walkest *no longer in love* ' (Rom. xiv. 15) :—' which GOD, who cannot lie, promised *before times eternal; but in his own seasons* manifested *his word in the message* ' (Tit. i. 2, 3) :—' Your *pleasures* [and why not ' lusts ' ?] that war in your members ' (James iv. 1) :—' Behold *how much wood* is kindled by *how small a fire!* ' (iii. 5).—Are these really supposed to be less ' obscure ' than the passages they are intended to supersede ?

(*a*) Not a few of the mistaken renderings of the Revisionists can only be established by an amount of illustration which is at once inconvenient to the Reviewer and unwelcome pro-

bably to the general Reader. Thus, we take leave to point out
that,—'And *coming up* at that very hour' (in Lu. ii. 38),—
as well as 'she *came up* to Him' (in Lu. x. 40), are inexact
renderings of the original. The verb ἐφιστάναι, which
etymologically signifies "to stand upon," or "over," or "by,"—
(but which retains its literal signification on only four out of
the eighteen occasions[1] when the word occurs in the Gospels
and Acts,)—is found almost invariably to denote the "*coming
suddenly upon*" a person. Hence, it is observed to be used
five times to denote the sudden appearance of friendly
visitants from the unseen world :[2] and seven times, the
sudden hostile approach of what is formidable.[3] On the
two remaining occasions, which are those before us,—
(namely, the sudden coming of Anna into the Temple[4] and
of Martha into the presence of our LORD,[5])—"*coming suddenly in*" would probably represent S. Luke's ἐπιστᾶσα
exactly. And yet, one would hesitate to import the word
"suddenly" into the narrative. So that "*coming in*" would
after all have to stand in the text, although the attentive
student of Scripture would enjoy the knowledge that something more is *implied*. In other words,—the Revisionists
would have done better if they had left both places alone. . .
These are many words ; yet is it impossible to explain
such matters at once satisfactorily and briefly.

(*b*) But more painful by far it is to discover that a
morbid striving after etymological accuracy,—added to a

---

[1] Viz. S. Luke iv. 39: Acts x. 17: xi. 11: xxii. 20.

[2] S. Luke ii. 9 (where '*came upon*' is better than '*stood by* them,' and
should have been left): xxiv. 4 : Acts xii. 7 : xxii. 13 : xxiii. 11.

[3] S. Luke xx. 1: xxi. 34 (last Day): Acts iv. 1 : vi. 12 : xvii. 5
("assault"): xxiii. 27 : xxviii. 2 (a rain-storm,—which, by the way,
suggests for τὸν ἐφεστῶτα a different rendering from '*the present*').

[4] S. Luke ii. 38.   [5] S. Luke x. 40.

calamitous preference for a depraved Text,—has proved the
ruin of one of the most affecting scenes in S. John's Gospel.
'Simon Peter beckoneth to him, *and saith unto him, Tell us
who it is of whom He speaketh*,' [a fabulous statement evidently ; for Peter beckoned, because he might *not* speak].
'He *leaning back, as he was*,'—[a very bad rendering of οὗτως,
by the way; and sure to recal inopportunely the rendering
of ὡς ἦν in S. Mark iv. 36, instead of suggesting (as it
obviously ought) the original of S. John iv. 6 :]—' on JESUS'
breast, saith unto Him, LORD who is it ?' (S. John xiii. 24–5).
Now, S. John's word concerning himself in this place is
certainly ἐπιπεσών. He '*just sank*,'—let his head '*fall*'—on
his Master's breast, and whispered his question. For this, a
few corrupt copies substitute ἀναπεσών. But ἀναπεσών *never*
means '*leaning back*.' It is descriptive of the posture of one
reclining at a meal (S. Jo. xiii. 12). Accordingly, it is 10 times
rendered by the Revisionists to '*sit down*.' Why, in this
place, and in chapter xxi. 20, *a new meaning* is thrust upon
the word, it is for the Revisionists to explain. But they
must explain the matter a vast deal better than Bp. Lightfoot
has done in his interesting little work on Revision (pp. 72–3),
or they will fail to persuade any,—except one another.

(*c*) Thus it happens that we never spend half-an-hour
over the unfortunate production before us without exclaiming
(with one in the Gospel), '*The old is better*.' Changes of *any*
sort are unwelcome in such a book as the Bible; but the
discovery that changes have been made *for the worse*, offends
greatly. To take instances at random :—Ὁ πλεῖστος ὄχλος
(in Matth. xxi. 8) is rightly rendered in our A.V. '*a very great
multitude*.'[1] Why then has it been altered by the R. V. into

---

[1] Cf. ch. xi. 20. So in Latin, *Illa plurima sacrificia*. (Cic. *De Fin.* 2.
20. 63.)

L

' *the most part of* the multitude ' ?—' Ο πολὺς ὄχλος (Mk. xii.
37), in like manner, is rightly rendered ' *the common people,*'
and ought not to have been glossed in the margin ' *the great
multitude.*'—In the R. V. of Acts x. 15, we find ' *Make* thou
not common,' introduced as an improvement on, ' *That call*
not thou common.' But ' the old is better : ' for, besides its
idiomatic and helpful ' *That,*'—the old alone states the case
truly. Peter did not ' *make,*' he only ' *called,*' something
' common.'—' All the *male* children,' as a translation of πάντας
τοὺς παῖδας (in Matth. ii. 16) is an unauthorized statement.
There is no reason for supposing that the female infants of
Bethlehem were spared in the general massacre : and the
Greek certainly conveys no such information.—' When he
came into the house, JESUS *spake first* to him '—is really an
incorrect rendering of Matth. xvii. 25 : at least, it imports
into the narrative a notion which is not found in the Greek,
and does not exhibit faithfully what the Evangelist actually
says. ' *Anticipated,*' in modern English,—' *prevented,*' in
ancient phraseology,—' *was beforehand with him* ' in language
neither new nor old,—conveys the sense of the original
exactly.—In S. Lu. vi. 35, ' Love your enemies, . . . and lend,
never despairing,' is simply a mistaken translation of ἀπελπί-
ζοντες, as the context sufficiently proves. The old rendering
is the true one.[1] And so, learnedly, the Vulgate,—*nihil inde
sperantes.* (Consider the use of ἀποβλέπειν [Heb. xi. 26] :
ἀφορᾶν [Phil. ii. 23 : Heb. xii. 2] : *abutor,* as used by Jerome
for *utor,* &c.)—' Go with them *making no distinction,*' is not the
meaning of Acts xi. 12 : which, however, was correctly translated before, viz. ' nothing doubting.'—The mischievous change
(' *save*' in place of ' *but*') in Gal. ii. 16 has been ably and
faithfully exposed by Bp. Ollivant. In the words of the

---

[1] " The context " (says learned Dr. Field) " is too strong for philological
quibbles." The words " *can by no possibility bear any other meaning.*"—
Otium Norvicense, p. 40.

learned and pious Bp. of Lincoln, 'it is illogical and erroneous, and *contradicts the whole drift of S. Paul's Argument* in that Epistle, and in the Epistle to the Romans.'

(d) We should be dealing insincerely with our Readers were we to conceal our grave dissatisfaction at not a few of the novel *expressions* which the Revisionists have sought to introduce into the English New Testament. That the malefactors between whom 'the LORD of glory' was crucified were not ordinary '*thieves*,' is obvious; yet would it have been wiser, we think, to leave the old designation undisturbed. We shall never learn to call them '*robbers*.'—'The king sent forth *a soldier of his guard*' is a gloss—not a translation of S. Mark vi. 27. '*An executioner*' surely is far preferable as the equivalent for σπεκουλάτωρ![1]—'*Assassins*' (as the rendering of σικάριοι) is an objectionable substitute for 'murderers.' A word which "belongs probably to a romantic chapter in the history of the Crusades"[2] has no business in the N. T.—And what did these learned men suppose they should gain by substituting '*the twin brothers*' for '*Castor and Pollux*' in Acts xxviii. 11? The Greek (Διόσκουροι) is neither the one nor the other.—In the same spirit, instead of, 'they that received *tribute-money*' (in S. Matth. xvii. 24), we are now presented with 'they that received *the half-shekel*:' and in verse 27,—instead of 'when thou hast opened his mouth, thou shalt find *a piece of money*,' we are favoured with 'thou shalt find *a shekel*.' But *why* the change has been made, we fail to see. The margin is *still* obliged to explain that not one of these four words is found in the original: the Greek in the former place being τὰ δίδραχμα,—in the latter, στατήρ.—'*Flute-*

---

[1] Στρατιώτης ὃς πρὸς τὸ φονεύειν τέτακται,—Theophylact, i. 201 e. Boys quotes Seneca *De Irá*:—*Tunc centurio supplicio præpositus condere gladium* speculatorem *jussit*.   [2] Trench, *Study of Words*, p. 106.

players' (for 'minstrels') in S. Matthew ix. 23, is a mistake. An αὐλητής played *the pipe* (αὐλός, 1 Cor. xiv. 7),— hence 'pipers' in Rev. xviii. 22; (where by the way μουσικοί ['musicians'] is perversely and less accurately rendered '*minstrels*').— Once more. '*Undressed* cloth' (Mk. ii. 21), because it is an expression popularly understood only in certain districts of England, and a *vox artis*, ought not to have been introduced into the Gospels. '*New*' is preferable.—'*Wineskins*' (Mtt. ix. 17: Mk. ii. 22: Lu. v. 37) is a term unintelligible to the generality; as the Revisionists confess, for they explain it by a note,—'That is, *skins used as bottles*.' What else is this but substituting a new difficulty for an old one ?—'*Silver*,' now for the first time thrust into Acts viii. 20, is unreasonable. Like 'argent,' in French, ἀργύριον as much means 'money,' here as in S. Matthew xxv. 18, 27, &c.—In S. James ii. 19, we should like to know what is gained by the introduction of the '*shuddering*' devils.—To take an example from a different class of words,—Who will say that 'Thou *mindest* not the things of God' is a better rendering of οὐ φρονεῖς, than the old 'Thou *savourest* not,' —which at least had no ambiguity about it ? ... A friend points out that Dr. Field (a 'master in Israel') has examined 104 of the changes *made* in the Revised Version; and finds 8 questionable : 13 unnecessary : 19 faulty (i.e. cases in which the A. V. required amendment, but which the R. V. has not succeeded in amending): 64 *changes for the worse*.[1] . . . This is surely a terrible indictment for such an one as Dr. Field to bring against the Revisers,—*who were directed only to correct* 'PLAIN AND CLEAR ERRORS.'

(*e*) We really fail to understand how it has come to pass that, notwithstanding the amount of scholarship which

---

[1] *Otium Norvicense*, pars tertia, 1881, pp. 155.

sometimes sat in the Jerusalem Chamber, so many novelties
are found in the present Revision which betoken a want
of familiarity with the refinements of the Greek language
on the one hand; and (what is even more inexcusable) only
a slender acquaintance with the resources and proprieties
of English speech, on the other. A fair average instance
of this occurs in Acts xxi. 37, where (instead of 'Canst
thou *speak* Greek?') Ἑλληνιστὶ γινώσκεις; is rendered 'Dost
thou *know* Greek?' That γινώσκειν means 'to know' (and
not 'to speak') is undeniable: and yet, in the account of
all, except the driest and stupidest of pedagogues, Ἑλληνιστὶ
γινώσκεις; must be translated 'Canst thou *speak* Greek?'
For (as every schoolboy is aware) Ἑλληνιστί is an adverb,
and signifies '*in Greek fashion*:' so that something has to be
supplied: and the full expression, if it must needs be given,
would be, 'Dost thou know [how to talk] in Greek?' But
then, this condensation of phrase proves to be the established
idiom of the language:[1] so that the rejection of the learned
rendering of Tyndale, Cranmer, the Geneva, the Rheims,
and the Translators of 1611 ('*Canst thou speak* Greek?')—
the rejection of this, at the end of 270 years, in favour of
'*Dost thou know* Greek?' really betrays ignorance. It is worse
than bad Taste. It is a stupid and deliberate *blunder*.

(*f*) The substitution of '*they weighed unto him*' (in place
of '*they covenanted with him for*') 'thirty pieces of silver'
(S. Matth. xxvi. 15) is another of those plausible mistakes,
into which a little learning (proverbially 'a dangerous thing')
is for ever conducting its unfortunate possessor; but from
which it was to have been expected that the undoubted

---

[1] Compare Xenophon (*Cyrop.* vii. 6. 8), τοὺς Συριστὶ ἐπισταμένους. The
plena locutio is found in Nehem. xiii. 24,—οἱ υἱοὶ αὐτῶν ἥμισυ λαλοῦντες
Ἀζωτιστί, καὶ οὐκ εἰσὶν ἐπιγινώσκοντες λαλεῖν Ἰουδαϊστί (quoted by
Wetstein).

attainments of some who frequented the Jerusalem Chamber would have effectually preserved the Revisionists. That ἔστησαν is intended to recal Zech. xi. 12, is obvious; as well as that *there* it refers to the ancient practice of *weighing* uncoined money. It does not, however, by any means follow, that it was customary to *weigh* shekels in the days of the Gospel. Coined money, in fact, was never weighed, but always counted; and these were shekels, i.e. *didrachms* (Matth. xvii. 24). The truth (it lies on the surface) is, that there exists a happy ambiguity about the word ἔστησαν, of which the Evangelist has not been slow to avail himself. In the particular case before us, it is expressly recorded that in the first instance money did *not* pass,—only a bargain was made, and a certain sum promised. S. Mark's record is that the chief priests were glad at the proposal of Judas, '*and promised* to give him money' (xiv. 11): S. Luke's, that '*they covenanted*' to do so (xxii. 5, 6). And with this, the statement of the first Evangelist is found to be in strictest agreement. The chief Priests ' set ' or ' appointed ' [1] him a certain sum. The perfectly accurate rendering of S. Matth. xxvi. 15, therefore, exhibited by our Authorized Version, has been set aside to make way for *a misrepresentation of the Evangelist's meaning.* ' In the judgment of the most competent scholars,' was ' such change NECESSARY ' ?

(*g*) We respectfully think that it would have been more becoming in such a company as that which assembled in the Jerusalem Chamber, as well as more consistent with their Instructions, if *in doubtful cases* they had abstained from touching the Authorized Version, but had recorded their own conjectural emendations *in the margin.* How rash and in-

---

[1] Cf. Acts i. 23; xvii. 31. The Latin is ' *statuerunt* ' or ' *constituerunt*.' The Revisionists give ' appointed ' in the second of these places, and ' put forward ' in the first. In both,—What becomes of their uniformity ?

felicitous, for example, is the following rendering of the
famous words in Acts xxvi. 28, 29, which we find thrust
upon us without apology or explanation; without, in fact,
any marginal note at all:—'And Agrippa said unto Paul,
With but little persuasion thou wouldest fain make me a
Christian. And Paul said, I would to GOD, that whether
with little or with much,' &c. Now this is indefensible. For,
in the first place, to get any such meaning out of the words,
our Revisionists have been obliged to substitute the fabricated ποιῆσαι (the peculiar property of א A B and a few
cursives) for γενέσθαι in ver. 28. Moreover, even so, the
words do not yield the required sense. We venture to point
out, that this is precisely one of the occasions where the
opinion of a first-rate Greek Father is of paramount importance. The moderns confess themselves unable to discover
a single instance of the phrase ἐν ὀλίγῳ in the sense of '*within
a little.*' Cyril of Jerusalem (A.D. 350) and Chrysostom
(A.D. 400), on the contrary, evidently considered that here
the expression can mean nothing else; and they were competent judges, seeing that Greek was their native language:
far better judges (be it remarked in passing) on a point of
this kind than the whole body of Revisionists put together.
'Such an amount of victorious grace and wisdom did Paul
derive from the HOLY SPIRIT' (says Cyril), 'that even King
Agrippa at last exclaimed,'[1] &c. From which it is evident
that Cyril regarded Agrippa's words as an avowal that he
was well-nigh overcome by the Apostle's argument. And so
Chrysostom,[2] who says plainly that ἐν ὀλίγῳ means 'within
a little,'[3] and assumes that 'within a little' S. Paul had

---

[1] P. 279.

[2] καὶ τὸν δικαστὴν εἶλεν ὁ τέως κατάδικος εἶναι νομιζόμενος καὶ τὴν νίκην
αὐτὸς ὁ χειρωθεὶς ὁμολογεῖ λαμπρᾷ τῇ φωνῇ παρόντων ἁπάντων λέγων, ἐν
ὀλίγῳ κ. τ. λ. x. 307 b. (= xii. 433 a).

[3] ἐν ὀλίγῳ · τουτέστι παρὰ μικρόν. ix. 391 a.

persuaded his judge.[1] He even puts παρ' ὀλίγον into Agrippa's mouth.[2] So also, in effect, Theodoret.[3] From all which it is reasonable, in the absence of any evidence to the contrary, to infer that our A. V. reflects faithfully what was the Church's traditionary interpretation of Acts xxvi. 28 in the first half of the fourth century. Let it only be added that a better judge of such matters than any who frequented the Jerusalem Chamber—the late President of Magdalen, Dr. Routh,— writes: '*Vertendum esse sequentia suadent, Me fere Christianum fieri suades. Interp. Vulgata habet, In modico suades me Christianum fieri.*'[4] Yes, the Apostle's rejoinder fixes the meaning of what Agrippa had said before.—And this shall suffice. We pass on, only repeating our devout wish that what the Revisionists failed to understand, or were unable *materially and certainly* to improve, they would have been so obliging as to let alone. In the present instance the A. V. is probably right; the R. V., probably wrong. No one, at all events, can pretend that the rendering with which we are all familiar is "*a plain and clear error.*" And confessedly, unless it was, it should have been left unmolested. But to proceed.

(4) and (5) There can be no question as to the absolute duty of rendering identical expressions *in strictly parallel places of the Gospels* by strictly identical language. So far we are wholly at one with the Revisionists. But 'alterations [supposed to be] rendered necessary *by consequence*' (*Preface*, iii. 2.), are quite a different matter: and we venture to think that it is precisely in their pursuit of a mechanical uniformity of rendering, that our Revisionists have most often as well as most grievously lost their way. We differ from them in fact *in limine.* 'When a particular word' (say they) 'is found to

---

[1] καὶ τὸν δικάζοντα μικροῦ μεταπεῖσαι, ὡς καὶ αὐτὸν ἐκεῖνον λέγειν, ἐν ὀλίγῳ κ. τ. λ. ii. 516 d.   [2] iii. 399 d.

[3] v. 930 (παρ' ὀλίγον).   [4] MS. Note in his copy of the N. T.

recur with characteristic frequency in any one of the Sacred
Writers, it is obviously desirable to adopt for it some uniform
rendering' (iii. 2). 'Desirable'! Yes, but in what sense?
It is much to be desired, no doubt, that the English language
always contained *the exact counterparts* of Greek words : and
of course, if it did, it would be in the highest degree 'desirable'
that a Translator should always employ those words and
no other. But then it happens unfortunately that *precisely
equivalent words do not exist.* Τέκνον, nine times out of ten
signifies nothing else but '*child.*' On the tenth occasion,
however, (e.g. where Abraham is addressing the rich man
in Hades,) it would be absurd so to render it. We translate
'*Son.*' We are in fact without choice.—Take another ordinary
Greek term, σπλάγχνα, which occurs 11 times in the N. T.,
and which the A. V. uniformly renders 'bowels.' Well, and
'bowels' confessedly σπλάγχνα are. Yet have our Revisionists felt themselves under the 'necessity' of rendering the
word '*heart,*' in Col. iii. 12,—'*very heart,*' in Philemon,
ver. 12,—'*affections,*' in 2 Cor. vi. 12,—'*inward affection,*'
in vii. 15,—'*tender mercies*' in Phil. i. 8,—'*compassion*' in
1 Jo. iii. 17,—'*bowels*' only in Acts i. 18.—These learned
men, however, put forward in illustration of their own principle
of translation, the word εὐθέως,—which occurs about 80
times in the N. T.: nearly half the instances being found in
S. Mark's Gospel. We accept their challenge; and assert
that it is tasteless barbarism to seek to impose upon εὐθέως,—
no matter *what* the context in which it stands,—the sense of
'*straightway,*'—only because εὐθύς, the adjective, generally
(not always) means 'straight.' Where a miracle of healing
is described (as in S. Matth. viii. 3 : xx. 34. S. Lu. v. 13), since
the benefit was no doubt instantaneous, it is surely the mere
instinct of 'faithfulness' to translate εὐθέως '*immediately.*'
So, in respect of the sudden act which saved Peter from
sinking (S. Matth. xiv. 31); and that punctual cock-crow

(xxvi. 74), which (S. Luke says) did not so much follow, as *accompany* his denial (xxii. 60). But surely not so, when *the growth of a seed* is the thing spoken of (Matth. xiii. 5)! Acts again, which must needs have occupied some little time in the doing, reasonably suggest some such rendering as '*forthwith*' or '*straightway*,'—(e.g. S. Matth. xiv. 22 : xxi. 2 : and S. John vi. 21) : while, in 3 John ver. 14, the meaning (as the Revisionists confess) can only be '*shortly*.' ... So plain a matter really ought not to require so many words. We repeat, that the Revisionists set out with a mistaken Principle. They clearly *do not understand their Trade.*

They invite our attention to their rendering of certain of the Greek Tenses, and of the definite Article. We regret to discover that, in both respects, their work is disfigured throughout by changes which convict a majority of their body alike of an imperfect acquaintance with the genius of the Greek language, and of scarcely a moderate appreciation of the idiomatic proprieties of their own. Such a charge must of necessity, when it has been substantiated, press heavily upon such a work as the present; for it is not as when a solitary error has been detected, which may be rectified. A vicious *system* of rendering Tenses, and representing the Greek Article, is sure to crop up in every part of the undertaking, and must occasionally be attended by consequences of a serious nature.

1. Now, that we may not be misunderstood, we admit at once that, in teaching *boys* how to turn Greek into English, we insist that every tense shall be marked by its own appropriate sign. There is no telling how helpful it will prove in the end, that every word shall at first have been rendered with painful accuracy. Let the Article be [mis-]represented —the Prepositions caricatured—the Particles magnified,—

let the very order of the words at first, (however impossible,) be religiously retained. Merciless accuracy having been in this way acquired, a youth has to be *un*taught these servile habits. He has to be reminded of the requirements of the *English idiom*, and speedily becomes aware that the idiomatic rendering of a Greek author into English, is a higher achievement by far, than his former slavish endeavour always to render the same word and tense in the same slavish way.

2. But what supremely annoys us in the work just now under review is, that the schoolboy method of translation already noticed is therein exhibited in constant operation throughout. It becomes oppressive. We are never permitted to believe that we are in the company of Scholars who are altogether masters of their own language. Their solicitude ever seems to be twofold :—(1) To exhibit a singular indifference to the proprieties of English speech, while they maintain a servile adherence (etymological or idiomatic, as the case may be) to the Greek :—(2) Right or wrong, to part company from William Tyndale and the giants who gave us our ' Authorized Version.'

Take a few illustrations of what precedes from the second chapter of S. Matthew's Gospel :—

(1.) Thus, in ver. 2, the correct English rendering ' *we have seen* ' is made to give place to the incorrect ' *we saw* his star in the east.'—In ver. 9, the idiomatic ' *when they had heard the king*, they departed,' is rejected for the unidiomatic ' And they, *having heard the king*, went their way.' —In ver. 15, we are treated to ' that it might be fulfilled which was spoken by the LORD *through* the prophet, saying, Out of Egypt *did I call* my son.' And yet who sees not, that in both instances the old rendering is better ? Important as it may be, *in the lecture-room,* to insist on what is implied by τὸ ῥηθὲν ῾ΥΠΟ᾽ τοῦ κυρίου ΔΙΑ᾽ τοῦ προφήτου, it is simply preposterous to *come abroad* with such refinements. It is to stultify oneself and to render one's author unintelligible. Moreover, the attempt to be so wondrous literal is safe to break down at the end of a few verses. Thus, if διά is '*through*' in verse 15,—why not in verse 17 and in verse 23 ?

(2.) Note how infelicitously, in S. Matth. ii. 1, 'there came wise men from the east' is changed into '*wise men from the east came.*'—In ver. 4, the accurate, 'And when [Herod] had gathered together' (συναγαγών) &c., is displaced for the inaccurate, 'And *gathering together*' &c.—In ver. 6, we are presented with the unintelligible, ' And thou *Bethlehem, land of Judah :*' while in ver. 7, 'Then Herod *privily called* the wise men, and *learned of them carefully,*' is improperly put in the place of 'Then Herod, when he had privily called the wise men, enquired of them diligently' (ἠκρίβωσε παρ᾽ αὐτῶν).—In ver. 11, the familiar ' And when they were come into the house, they saw' &c., is needlessly changed into ' They *came into the house,* and saw :' while 'and when they had opened (ἀνοίξαντες) their treasures,' is also needlessly altered into 'and *opening* their treasures.'—In ver. 12, the R. V. is careful to print '*of* Goᴅ' in italics, where italics are not necessary : seeing that χρηματισθέντες *implies* 'being warned of Goᴅ' (as the translators of 1611 were well aware [1]) : whereas in countless other places the same Revisionists reject the use of italics where italics are absolutely required.—Their 'until I *tell thee*' (in ver. 13) is a most unworthy substitute for ' until I *bring thee word.*'—And will they pretend that they have improved the rendering of the

---

[1] And the Revisionists : for see Rom. xi. 4.

concluding words of the chapter? If Ναζωραῖος κληθήσεται
does not mean 'He shall be called a Nazarene,' what in the
world *does* it mean? The ὅτι of quotation they elsewhere
omit. Then why, here,—' *That* it might be fulfilled . . . *that*'?
—Surely, every one of these is an alteration made for alteration's sake, and in every instance *for the worse.*

We began by surveying *the Greek* of the first chapter of
S. Matthew's Gospel. We have now surveyed *the English* of
the second chapter. What does the Reader think of the result?

IV. Next, the Revisionists invite attention to certain
points of detail: and first, to their rendering of THE TENSES
OF THE VERB. They begin with the Greek Aorist,—(in
their account) 'perhaps the most important' detail of all:—

'We have not attempted to violate the idiom of our language
by forms of expression which it would not bear. But we have
often ventured to represent the Greek aorist by the English
preterite, even when the reader may find some passing difficulty
in such a rendering, because we have felt convinced that the
true meaning of the original was obscured by the presence of
the familiar auxiliary. A remarkable illustration may be
found in the seventeenth chapter of S. John's Gospel.'—
Preface, iii. 2,—(*latter part*).

(*a*) We turn to the place indicated, and are constrained
to assure these well-intentioned men, that the phenomenon
we there witness is absolutely fatal to their pretensions
as '*Revisers*' of our Authorized Version. Were it only 'some
passing difficulty' which their method occasions us, we
might have hoped that time would enable us to overcome
it. But since it is *the genius of the English language* to
which we find they have offered violence; the fixed and
universally-understood idiom of our native tongue which
they have systematically set at defiance; the matter is
absolutely without remedy. The difference between the
A. V. and the R. V. seems to ourselves to be simply this,—

that the renderings in the former are the idiomatic English representations of certain well-understood Greek tenses: while the proposed substitutes are nothing else but the pedantic efforts of mere grammarians to reproduce in another language idioms which it abhors. But the Reader shall judge for himself: for *this* at least is a point on which every educated Englishman is fully competent to pass sentence.

When our Divine Lord, at the close of His Ministry,— (He had in fact reached the very last night of His earthly life, and it wanted but a few hours of His Passion,)—when He, at such a moment, addressing the Eternal Father, says, ἐγώ σε ἐδόξασα ἐπὶ τῆς γῆς· τὸ ἔργον ἐτελείωσα . . . . ἐφανέρωσά σου τὸ ὄνομα τοῖς ἀνθρώποις, &c. [Jo. xvii. 4, 6], there can be no doubt whatever that, had He pronounced those words in English, He would have said (with our A. V.) 'I *have glorified* Thee on the earth: I *have finished* the work:' 'I *have manifested* Thy Name.' The pedantry which (on the plea that the Evangelist employs the aorist, not the perfect tense,) would twist all this into the indefinite past,—'I glorified' . . . 'I finished' . . . 'I manifested,'—we pronounce altogether insufferable. We absolutely refuse it a hearing. Presently (in ver. 14) He says,—'I have given them Thy word; and the world *hath hated them.*' And in ver. 25,— 'O righteous Father, the world *hath not known* Thee; but I *have known* Thee, and these *have known* that Thou *hast sent* Me.' *Who* would consent to substitute for these expressions,—'the world hated them:' and 'the world knew Thee not, but I knew Thee; and these knew that Thou didst send Me'?—Or turn to another Gospel. *Which* is better,— 'Some one hath touched Me: for I perceive that virtue is gone out of Me,' (S. Lu. viii. 46):—or,—'Some one *did touch* Me: for *I perceived* that power *had gone forth* from Me'?

When the reference is to an act so extremely recent, *who* is
not aware that the second of these renderings is abhorrent to
the genius of the English language? As for ἔγνων, it is
(like *novi* in Latin) present in *sense* though past in *form,*—
here as in S. Lu. xvi. 3.—But turn to yet another Gospel.
Which is better in S. Matth. xvi. 7 :—' *we took* no bread,' or
' It is because *we have taken* no bread' ?—Again. When Simon
Peter (in reply to the command that he should thrust out
into deep water and let down his net for a draught,) is heard
to exclaim,—' Master, we have toiled all the night, and have
taken nothing: nevertheless at Thy word I will let down
the net ' (Lu. v. 5),—*who* would tolerate the proposal to put
in the place of it,—' Master, *we toiled all night,* and *took*
nothing: but at Thy word,' &c. It is not too much to
declare that the idiom of the English language refuses
peremptorily to submit to such handling. Quite in vain
is it to encounter us with reminder that κοπιάσαντες and
ἐλάβομεν are aorists. The answer is,—We know it: but we
deny that it follows that the words are to be rendered ' we
toiled all night, and *took* nothing.' There are laws of
English Idiom as well as laws of Greek Grammar : and when
these clash in what is meant to be a translation into English
out of Greek, the latter must perforce give way to the former,
—or we make ourselves ridiculous, and misrepresent what we
propose to translate.

All this is so undeniable that it ought not to require to be
insisted upon. But in fact our Revisionists by their occasional practice show that they fully admit *the Principle* we
are contending for. Thus, ἦραν (in S. Jo. xx. 2 and 13) is
by them translated ' *they have taken :* '—ἱνατί με ἐγκατέλιπες ;
(S. Matt. xxvii. 46) ' Why *hast Thou forsaken* Me ? '[1] :—ἔδειξα

---

[1] Yet even here they cannot abstain from putting in the margin the
peculiarly infelicitous alternative,—' *Why didst thou forsake Me ?* '

(S. Jo. x. 32) '*have I showed :*'—ἀπέστειλε (vi. 29) '*He hath sent :*' — ἠτιμάσατε (James ii. 6) '*ye have dishonoured :*'— ἐκαθάρισε (Acts x. 15) '*hath cleansed :*'—ἔστησεν (xvii. 31) '*He hath appointed.*' But indeed instances abound every-where. In fact, the requirements of the case are often observed to *force* them to be idiomatic. Τί ἐποίησας; (in Jo. xviii. 35), they rightly render "What *hast* thou done?":—and ἔγραψα (in 1 Jo. ii. 14, 21), "I *have* written;"—and ἤκουσα (in Acts ix. 13), "I *have* heard."—On the other hand, by translating οὐκ εἴασεν (in Acts xxviii. 4), "*hath not* suffered," they may be thought to have overshot the mark. They seem to have overlooked the fact that, when once S. Paul had been bitten by the viper, "the barbarians" looked upon him as *a dead man;* and therefore discoursed about what Justice "*did not* suffer," as about an entirely past transaction.

But now, *Who* sees not that the admission, once and again deliberately made, that sometimes it is not only lawful, but even *necessary*, to accommodate the Greek aorist (when translated into English) with the sign of the perfect,— reduces the whole matter (of the signs of the tenses) to a mere question of *Taste?* In view of such instances as the foregoing, where severe logical necessity has compelled the Revisionists to abandon their position and fly, it is plain that their contention is at an end,—so far as *right* and *wrong* are concerned. They virtually admit that they have been all along unjustly forcing on an independent language an alien yoke.[1] Henceforth, it simply becomes a question to be repeated, as every fresh emergency arises,—Which then is *the more idiomatic* of these two English renderings? . . . . Conversely, twice at least (Heb. xi. 17 and 28), the Revi-

---

[1] As in Rom. vi. 2: ix. 13. 1 Cor. i. 27: vi. 20: ix. 11. Ephes. iv. 20, &c. &c.

sionists have represented the *Greek perfect* by the English indefinite preterite.

(*b*) Besides this offensive pedantry in respect of the Aorist, we are often annoyed by an *unidiomatic* rendering of the Imperfect. True enough it is that 'the servants and the officers *were standing* . . . . and *were warming* themselves : ' Peter also '*was standing* with them and *was warming* himself' (S. Jo. xviii. 18). But we do not so express ourselves in English, unless we are about to add something which shall *account for* our particularity and precision. Any one, for example, desirous of stating what had been for years his daily practice, would say—'*I left* my house.' Only when he wanted to explain that, on leaving it for the 1000th time, he met a friend coming up the steps to pay him a visit, would an Englishman think of saying, '*I was leaving* the house.' A Greek writer, on the other hand, would not *trust* this to the imperfect. He would use the present participle in the dative case, ('*To me, leaving my house,*'[1] &c.). One is astonished to have to explain such things . . . . 'If therefore thou *art offering* thy gift at the altar' (Matt. v. 23), may seem to some a clever translation. To ourselves, it reads like a senseless exaggeration of the original.[2] It sounds (and *is*) as unnatural as to say (in S. Lu. ii. 33) 'And His father [a depravation of the text] and His mother *were marvelling* at the things which were spoken concerning Him : '— or (in Heb. xi. 17) 'yea, he that had received the promises *was offering up* his only-begotten son : '—or, of the cripple at Lystra (Acts xiv. 9), 'the same heard Paul *speaking*.'

(*c*) On the other hand, there are occasions confessedly when the Greek Aorist absolutely demands to be rendered

---

[1] Comp. S. Matth. viii. 1, 5, 23, 28; ix. 27, 28; xxi. 23.
Ἐὰν οὖν προσφέρῃς.

into English by the sign of the *Pluperfect.* An instance
meets us while we write : ὡς δὲ ἐπαύσατο λαλῶν (S. Lu. v. 4),
—where our Revisionists are found to retain the idiomatic
rendering of our Authorized Version,—'When He *had left*
speaking.' Of what possible avail could it be, on such an
occasion, to insist that, because ἐπαύσατο is not in the
pluperfect tense, it may not be accommodated with *the sign*
of the pluperfect when it is being translated into English ?—
The R. V. has shown less consideration in S. Jo. xviii. 24,—
where ' Now Annas *had sent* Him bound unto Caiaphas the
high priest,' is right, and wanted no revision.—Such places as
Matth. xxvii. 60, Jo. xxi. 15, Acts xii. 17, and Heb. iv. 8,
on the other hand, simply defy the Revisionists. For perforce Joseph ' *had hewn* out' (ἐλατόμησε) the new tomb
which became our LORD'S : and the seven Apostles, confessedly,
'*had dined*' (ἠρίστησαν): and S. Peter, of course, 'declared
unto them how the LORD *had brought him out* of the prison '
(ἐξήγαγεν): and it is impossible to substitute anything for
' If Jesus [Joshua] *had given* them rest' (κατέπαυσεν).—
Then of course there are occasions, (not a few,) where the
Aorist (often an indefinite present in Greek) claims to be
Englished by the sign of the present tense : as where S. John
says (Rev.· xix. 6), 'The LORD GOD Omnipotent reigneth'
(ἐβασίλευσε). There is no striving against such instances.
They *insist* on being rendered according to the genius of the
language into which it is proposed to render them :—as when
ἔκειτο (in S. Jo. xx. 12) exacts for its rendering ' *had lain.*'

(*d*) It shall only be pointed out here in addition, for the
student's benefit, that there is one highly interesting place
(viz. S. Matth. xxviii. 2), which in every age has misled
Critics and Divines (as Origen and Eusebius); Poets (as
Rogers); Painters (as West);—yes, and will continue to mislead readers for many a year to come :—and all because men

II.] THROUGHOUT BY THE REVISIONISTS. 163

have failed to perceive that the aorist is used there for the pluperfect. Translate,—'There *had been* a great earthquake:' [and so (1611–1881) our margin,—until in short 'the Revisionists' interfered:] 'for the Angel of the LORD *had* descended from heaven, and *come and rolled away* (ἀπεκύλισε) the stone from the door, and sat upon it.' Strange, that for 1800 years Commentators should have failed to perceive that the Evangelist is describing what terrified '*the keepers.*' '*The women*' saw no Angel sitting upon the stone! — though Origen,[1] — Dionysius of Alexandria,[2] — Eusebius,[3] — ps.-Gregory Naz.,[4]—Cyril Alex.,[5]—Hesychius,[6]—and so many others—have taken it for granted that they *did.*

(*e*) Then further, (to dismiss the subject and pass on,)— There are occasions where the Greek *perfect* exacts the sign of the *present* at the hands of the English translator : as when Martha says,—' Yea LORD, *I believe* that Thou art the CHRIST ' (S. Jo. xi. 27).[7] What else but the veriest pedantry is it to thrust in there '*I have believed,*' as the English equivalent for πεπίστευκα?—Just as intolerable is the officiousness which would thrust into the LORD's prayer (Matt. vi. 12), "as we also *have forgiven* (ἀφήκαμεν) our debtors."[8]—On the other hand, there are Greek *presents* (whatever the Revisionists may think) which are just as peremptory in requiring *the sign of the future,* at the hands of the idiomatic translator into English. Three such cases are found in S. Jo. xvi. 16, 17, 19. Surely, the future is *inherent* in the present ἔρχομαι! In Jo. xiv. 18 (and many similar places), *who* can endure, ' I will not leave you desolate : *I come unto you* ' ?

---

[1] ii. 155.   [2] Routh, *Rell.* iii. 226 *ad calc.*   [3] Ap. Mai, iv. 266.
[4] ii. 1324.   [5] ii. 380.   [6] Ap. Greg. Nyss. iii. 403.
[7] So also Heb. xi. 17, 28. And see the Revision of S. James i. 11.

[8] Comp. ἀφίεμεν in S. Lu. xi. 4. In the case of certain Greek verbs, the *preterite* in form is invariably *present* in signification. See Dr. Field's delightful *Otium Norvicense,* p. 65.

(*f*) But instances abound. How does it happen that the inaccurate rendering of ἐκκόπτεται—ἐκβάλλεται—has been retained in S. Matth. iii. 10, S. Lu. iii. 9 ?

V. Next, concerning the DEFINITE ARTICLE ; in the case of which, (say the Revisionists,)

'many changes have been made.' 'We have been careful to observe the use of the Article wherever it seemed to be idiomatically possible: where it did not seem to be possible, we have yielded to necessity.'—(*Preface*, iii. 2,—*ad fin.*)

In reply, instead of offering counter-statements of our own we content ourselves with submitting a few specimens to the Reader's judgment; and invite him to decide between the Reviewer and the Reviewed . . . ' *The* sower went forth to sow ' (Matth. xiii. 3).—' It is greater than *the* herbs ' (ver. 32).— ' Let him be to thee as *the* Gentile and *the* publican ' (xviii. 17).—'The unclean spirit, when he is gone out of *the* man ' (xii. 43).—' Did I not choose you *the* twelve ? ' (Jo. vi. 70). —' If I then, *the* Lord and *the* master ' (xiii. 14).—' For *the* joy that a man is born into the world ' (xvi. 21).—' But as touching Apollos *the* brother ' (1 Cor. xvi. 12).—' *The* Bishop must be blameless . . . able to exhort in *the* sound doctrine ' (Titus i. 7, 9).—' *The* lust when it hath conceived, beareth sin : and *the* sin, when it is full grown ' &c.   (James i. 15).— ' Doth *the* fountain send forth from the same opening sweet water and bitter ? ' (iii. 11).—' Speak thou the things which befit *the* sound doctrine ' (Titus ii. 1).—' The time will come when they will not endure *the* sound doctrine ' (2 Tim. iv. 3).—' We had *the* fathers of our flesh to chasten us ' (Heb. xii. 9).—' Follow after peace with all men, and *the* sanctification ' (ver. 14).—' Who is *the* liar but he that denieth that JESUS is the CHRIST ? ' (1 Jo. ii. 22).—' Not with *the* water only, but with *the* water and with *the* blood ' (v. 6).—' He that hath the SON, hath *the* life : he that hath not the SON of GOD hath not *the* life ' (ver. 12).

To rejoin, as if it were a sufficient answer, that the definite Article is found in all these places in the original Greek,— is preposterous.   In French also we say 'Telle est *la* vie:' but, in translating from the French, we do not *therefore* say ' Such is *the* life.'   May we, without offence, suggest the study of Middleton *On the Doctrine of the Greek Article* to those members of the Revisionists' body who have favoured us with the foregoing crop of mistaken renderings ?

So, in respect of the indefinite article, we are presented with,—'*An* eternal' (for '*the* everlasting') 'gospel to proclaim' (Rev. xiv. 6):—and 'one like unto *a* son of man,' for ' one like unto *the* Son of Man' in ver. 14.—Why '*a* SAVIOUR' in Phil. iii. 20?   There is but one! (Acts iv. 12).—On the other hand, Kρανίον is rendered ' *The* skull' in S. Lu. xxiii. 33.   It is hard to see why.—These instances taken at random must suffice.   They might be multiplied to any extent.   If the Reader considers that the idiomatic use of the English Article is understood by the authors of these specimen cases, we shall be surprised, and sorry—*for him.*

VI. The Revisionists announce that they ' have been particularly careful' as to THE PRONOUNS [iii. 2 *ad fin.*]. We recal with regret that this is also a particular wherein we have been specially annoyed and offended.   Annoyed—at their practice of *repeating the nominative* (e.g. in Mk. i. 13 : Jo. xx. 12) to an extent unknown, abhorrent even, to our language, except indeed when a fresh substantive statement is made : offended —at their license of translation, *when it suits them* to be licentious.—Thus, (as the Bp. of S. Andrews has well pointed out,) ' *it is He that*' is an incorrect translation of αὐτός in S. Matth. i. 21,—a famous passage.   Even worse, because it is unfair, is ' *He who*' as the rendering of ὅς in 1 Tim. iii. 16,—another famous passage, which we have discussed elsewhere.[1]

---

[1] See above, pp. 98–106. Also *infra*, towards the end.

VII. 'In the case of the PARTICLES' (say the Revisionists),

'we have been able to maintain a reasonable amount of *consistency.* The Particles in the Greek Testament are, as is well known, comparatively few, and they are commonly used with precision. It has therefore been the more necessary here to preserve a general *uniformity of rendering.*'—(iii. 2 *ad fin.*)

Such an announcement, we submit, is calculated to occasion nothing so much as uneasiness and astonishment. Of all the parts of speech, the Greek Particles,—(especially throughout the period when the Language was in its decadence,)—are the least capable of being drilled into 'a general uniformity of rendering;' and he who tries the experiment ought to be the first to be aware of the fact. The refinement and delicacy which they impart to a narrative or a sentiment, are not to be told. But then, from the very nature of the case, '*uniformity of rendering*' is precisely the thing they will not submit to. They take their colour from their context: often mean two quite different things in the course of two successive verses: sometimes are best rendered by a long and formidable word;[1] sometimes cannot (without a certain amount of impropriety or inconvenience) be rendered *at all.*[2] Let us illustrate what we have been saying by actual appeals to Scripture.

(1) And first, we will derive our proofs from the use which the sacred Writers make of the particle of most

---

[1] As in S. Matth. xi. 11 and 2 Tim. iv. 17, where δέ is rendered "notwithstanding:"—Phil. i. 24 and Heb. xii. 11, where it is "nevertheless."

[2] *Eight* times in succession in 1 Cor. xii. 8–10, δέ is not represented in the A. V. The ancients *felt* so keenly what Tyndale, Cranmer, the Geneva, the Rheims, and the A. V. ventured to exhibit, that as often as not they leave out the δέ,—in which our Revisionists twice follow them. The reader of taste is invited to note the precious result of inserting 'and,' as the Revisionists have done six times, where according to the genius of the English language it is not wanted at all.

frequent recurrence—δέ. It is said to be employed in the N. T. 3115 times. As for its meaning, we have the unimpeachable authority of the Revisionists themselves for saying that it may be represented by any of the following words :— 'but,'—'and,'[1]—'yea,'[2]—'what,'[3]—'now,'[4]—'and that,'[5]— 'howbeit,'[6]—'even,'[7]—'therefore,'[8]—'I say,'[9]—'also,'[10]— 'yet,'[11]—'for.'[12] To which 12 renderings, King James's translators (mostly following Tyndale) are observed to add at least these other 12 :—'wherefore,'[13]—'so,'[14]—'moreover,'[15] —'yea and,'[16]—'furthermore,'[17]—'nevertheless,'[18]—'notwithstanding,'[19]—'yet but,'[20]—'truly,'[21]—'or,'[22]—'as for,'[23] —'then,'[24]—'and yet.'[25] It shall suffice to add that, by the pitiful substitution of 'but' or 'and' on *most* of the foregoing occasions, the freshness and freedom of almost every passage has been made to disappear: the plain fact being that the men of 1611—above all, that William Tyndale 77 years before them—produced a work of real genius; seizing with generous warmth the meaning and intention of the sacred Writers, and perpetually varying the phrase, as they felt or fancied that Evangelists and Apostles would have varied it, had they had to express themselves in English: whereas the men of 1881 have fulfilled their task in what can only be described as *a spirit of servile pedantry.* The Grammarian (pure and simple) crops up everywhere. We seem never to rise above the atmosphere of the lecture-room, —the startling fact that μέν means 'indeed,' and δέ 'but.'

---

[1] 38 times in the Genealogy, S. Matth. i.   [2] Rom. xiv. 4 : xv. 20.
[3] Rom. ix. 22.   [4] 1 Cor. xii. 27.   [5] Gal. ii. 4.
[6] Acts xxvii. 26.   [7] Rom. iii. 22.   [8] Ephes. iv. 1.
[9] 2 Cor. v. 8.   [10] S. Mark xv. 31.   [11] S. Mark vi. 29.
[12] 1 Cor. x. 1.   [13] S. Matth. vi. 30.   [14] S. John xx. 4.
[15] 2 Cor. i. 23.   [16] 2 Cor. vii. 13.   [17] 2 Cor. ii. 12.
[18] 2 Pet. iii. 13.   [19] S. Matth. ii. 22.   [20] 1 Cor. xii. 20.
[21] 1 S. John i. 3.   [22] S. Matth. xxv. 39.   [23] Acts viii. 3.
[24] Rom. xii. 6.   [25] S. Matth. vi. 29.

We subjoin a single specimen of the countless changes introduced in the rendering of Particles, and then hasten on. In 1 Cor. xii. 20, for three centuries and a half, Englishmen have been contented to read (with William Tyndale), ' But now are they many members, YET BUT one body.'   Our Revisionists, (overcome by the knowledge that δέ means ' but,' and yielding to the supposed ' necessity for preserving a general uniformity of rendering,') substitute,—'_But_ now they are many members, _but_ one body.'   Comment ought to be superfluous.   We neither overlook the fact that δέ occurs here twice, nor deny that it is fairly represented by ' but ' in the first instance.   We assert nevertheless that, on the second occasion, ' YET BUT ' ought to have been let alone. And this is a fair sample of the changes which have been effected _many times in every page._   To proceed however.

(2) The interrogative particle ἤ occurs at the beginning of a sentence at least 8 or 10 times in the N. T.; first, in S. Matth. vii. 9.   It is often scarcely translateable,—being apparently invested with no more emphasis than belongs to our colloquial interrogative ' _Eh ?_ '   But sometimes it would evidently bear to be represented by ' Pray,' [1]—being at least equivalent to φέρε in Greek or _age_ in Latin.   Once only (viz. in 1 Cor. xiv. 36) does this interrogative particle so eloquently plead for recognition in the text, that both our A. V. and the R. V. have rendered it ' What ? '—by which word, by the way, it might very fairly have been represented in S. Matth. xxvi. 53 and Rom. vi. 3 : vii. 1.   In five of the places where the particle occurs, King James's Translators are observed to have given it up in despair.[2]   But what is to be thought of the adventurous dulness which (with the single exception already indicated) has _invariably_ rendered ἤ by

---

[1] As in S. Matth. vii. 9 : xii. 29 : xx. 15.   Rom. iii. 29.

[2] S. Matth. xx. 15 : xxvi. 53.   Rom. iii. 29 : vi. 3 : vii. 1.

the conjunction '*or*'? The blunder is the more inexcusable, because the intrusion of such an irrelevant conjunction into places where it is without either use or meaning cannot have failed to attract the notice of every member of the Revising body.

(3) At the risk of being wearisome, we must add a few words.—Καί, though no particle but a conjunction, may for our present purpose be reasonably spoken of under the same head; being diversely rendered 'and,'—'and yet,'[1]—'then,'[2] —'or,'[3]—'neither,'[4]—'though,'[5]—'so,'[6]—'but,'[7]—'for,'[8]— 'that,'[9]—in conformity with what may be called the genius of the English language. The last six of these renderings, however, our Revisionists disallow ; everywhere thrusting out the word which the argument seems rather to require, and with mechanical precision thrusting into its place every time the (perfectly safe, but often palpably inappropriate) word, 'and.' With what amount of benefit this has been effected, one or two samples will sufficiently illustrate :—

(*a*) The Revisionists inform us that when " the high priest Ananias commanded them that stood by him to smite him on the mouth,"—S. Paul exclaimed, "GOD shall smite thee, thou whited wall : AND sittest thou to judge me after the law, and commandest me to be smitten contrary to the law ? " [10] . . . Do these learned men really imagine that they have improved upon the A. V. by their officiousness in altering 'FOR' into 'AND'?

(*b*) The same Apostle, having ended his argument to the Hebrews, remarks,—' *So* we see that they could not enter in because of unbelief' (Heb. iii. 19) : for which, our Revisionists

---

[1] S. John xvi. 32.   [2] S. Luke xix. 23.   [3] 2 Cor. xiii. 1.
[4] S. Luke xii. 2.   [5] S. Luke xviii. 7.   [6] S. Luke xiv. 21.
[7] 1 S. John ii. 27.   [8] 1 S. John i. 2.   [9] S. Mark ix. 39.
[10] Acts xxiii. 3.

again substitute 'And.' Begin the sentence with 'AND,' (instead of 'So,') and, in compensation for what you have clearly *lost*, what have you *gained?* . . . Once more :—

(c) Consider what S. Paul writes concerning Apollos (in 1 Cor. xvi. 12), and then say what possible advantage is obtained by writing 'AND' (instead of 'BUT') his will was not at all to come at this time'. . . . Yet once more ; and on *this* occasion, scholarship is to some extent involved :—

(d) When S. James (i. 11) says ἀνέτειλε γὰρ ὁ ἥλιος . . . καὶ ἐξήρανε τὸν χόρτον,—*who* knows not that what his language strictly means in idiomatic English, is,—' *No sooner* does the sun arise,' '*than* it withereth the grass'? And so in effect our Translators of 1611. What possible improvement on this can it be to substitute, 'For the sun ariseth . . . AND withereth the grass'?—Only once more :—

(e) Though καί undeniably means 'and,' and πῶς, 'how,' —*who* knows not that καὶ πῶς means '*How then?*' And yet, (as if a stupid little boy had been at work,) in two places,—(namely, in S. Mark iv. 13 and S. Luke xx. 44,)— 'AND HOW' is found mercilessly thrust in, to the great detriment of the discourse ; while in other two,—(namely, in S. John xiv. 5 and 9,)—the text itself has been mercilessly deprived of its characteristic καί by the Revisionists.—Let this suffice. One might fill many quires of paper with such instances of tasteless, senseless, vexatious, and *most unscholarlike* innovation.

VIII. 'Many changes' (we are informed) 'have been introduced in the rendering of the PREPOSITIONS.' [*Preface*, iii. 2, *ad fin.*] :—and we are speedily reminded of the truth of the statement, for (as was shown above [pp. 155–6]) the second chapter of S. Matthew's Gospel exhibits the Revisionists 'all a-field' in respect of διά. 'We have rarely made any change' (they add) 'where the true meaning of the original would be apparent to *a Reader of ordinary intelligence.*' It

would of course ill become such an one as the present
Reviewer to lay claim to the foregoing flattering designation :
but really, when he now for the first time reads (in Acts
ix. 25) that the disciples of Damascus let S. Paul down
'*through the wall*,' he must be pardoned for regretting the
absence of a marginal reference to the history of Pyramus
and Thisbe in order to suggest *how* the operation was effected :
for, as it stands, the R. V. is to him simply unintelligible.
Inasmuch as the basket (σπυρίς) in which the Apostle
effected his escape was of considerable size, do but think
what an extravagantly large hole it must have been to enable
them *both* to get through ! . . . But let us look further.

Was it then in order to bring Scripture within the *captus*
of ' a Reader of ordinary intelligence' that the Revisers have
introduced no less than *thirty changes* into *eight-and-thirty
words* of S. Peter's 2nd Epistle ?   Particular attention is
invited to the following interesting specimen of ' *Revision.*'
It is the only one we shall offer of the many *contrasts* we
had marked for insertion.   We venture also to enquire,
whether the Revisers will consent to abide by it as a
specimen of their skill in dealing with the Preposition ἐν ?

A.V.	R.V.
' And beside all this, giving all diligence, add to your faith virtue ; and to virtue knowledge ; and to knowledge temperance ; and to temperance patience ; and to patience godliness ; and to godliness brotherly kindness ; and to brotherly kindness charity.'—[2 Pet. i. 5–7.]	' Yea, and for this very cause adding on your part all diligence, in your faith supply virtue ; and in your virtue knowledge ; and in your knowledge temperance ; and in your temperance patience ; and in your patience godliness ; and in your godliness love of the brethren ; and in your love of the brethren love.'

The foregoing strikes us as a singular illustration of the Revisionists' statement (*Preface*, iii. 2),—'We made *no* change *if the meaning was fairly exprèssed* by the word or phrase that was before us in the Authorized Version.' To ourselves it appears that *every one of those* 30 *changes is a change for the worse;* and that one of the most exquisite passages in the N. T. has been hopelessly spoiled,—rendered in fact well-nigh unintelligible,—by the pedantic officiousness of the Revisers. Were they—(if the question be allowable)—bent on removing none but '*plain and clear errors,*' when they substituted those 30 words? Was it in token of their stern resolve ' to introduce into the Text *as few alterations as possible,*' that they spared the eight words which remain out of the eight-and-thirty?

As for their *wooden* rendering of ἐν, it ought to suffice to refer them to S. Mk. i. 23, S. Lu. xiv. 31, to prove that sometimes ἐν can only be rendered ' *with :*'—and to S. Luke vii. 17, to show them that ἐν sometimes means ' *throughout :*'—and to Col. i. 16, and Heb. i. 1, 2, in proof that sometimes it means ' *by.*'—On the other hand, their suggestion that ἐν may be rendered ' *by* ' in S. Luke i. 51, convicts them of not being aware that ' the proud-in-the-imagination-of-their-hearts' is *a phrase*—in which perforce ' *by* ' has no business whatever. One is surprised to have to teach professed Critics and Scholars an elementary fact like this.

In brief, these learned men are respectfully assured that there is not one of the ' Parts of Speech' which will consent to be handled after the inhumane fashion which seems to be to themselves congenial. Whatever they may think of the matter, it is nothing else but absurd to speak of an Angel ' casting his sickle *into the earth*' (Rev. xiv. 19).—As for his ' pouring out his bowl *upon the air*' (xvi. 17),—we really fail to understand the nature of the operation.—And pray,

What is supposed to be the meaning of 'the things *upon the heavens*'—in Ephesians i. 10 ?

Returning to the preposition διά followed by the genitive, —(in respect of which the Revisionists challenge Criticism by complaining in their Preface [iii. 3 *ad fin.*] that in the A. V. 'ideas of instrumentality or of mediate agency, distinctly marked in the original, have been *confused or obscured in the Translation,*')—we have to point out :—

(1st) That these distinguished individuals seem not to be aware that the proprieties of English speech forbid the use of '*through*' (as a substitute for '*by*') in certain expressions where instrumentality is concerned.   Thus, 'the Son of man' was not betrayed '*through*' Judas, but '*by*' him (Matt. xxvi. 24 : Luke xxii. 22).—Still less is it allowable to say that a prophecy was 'spoken,' nay '*written,*' '*through* the Prophet' (Matth. i. 22 and margin of ii. 5).   'Who spake *by the Prophets,*' is even an article of the Faith.

And (2ndly),—That these scholars have in consequence adopted a see-saw method of rendering διά,—sometimes in one way, sometimes in the other. First, they give us 'wonders and signs done *by* the Apostles' (Acts ii. 43 ; but in the margin, 'Or, *through*'): presently, 'a notable miracle hath been wrought *through* them' (iv. 16 : and this time, the margin withholds the alternative, 'Or, *by*').   Is then 'the true meaning' of '*by,*' in the former place, 'apparent to a Reader of ordinary intelligence '? but so obscure in the latter as to render *necessary* the alteration to '*through*'?   Or (*sit venia verbo*),—Was it a mere 'toss-up' with the Revisionists *what* is the proper rendering of διά ?

(3rdly), In an earlier place (ii. 22), we read of 'miracles, wonders, and signs' which 'GOD did *by*' JESUS of Nazareth. Was it reverence, which, on that occasion, forbad the use of '*through*'—even in the margin ? We hope so : but the preposition is still the same—διά not ὑπό.

Lastly (4thly),—The doctrine that Creation is the work of the Divine WORD, all Scripture attests. ' All things were made *by* Him ' (S. Jo. i. 3) :—'the world was made *by* Him ' (ver. 10).—Why then, in Col. i. 16, where the same statement is repeated,—(' all things were created *by* Him and for Him,')—do we find ' *through*' substituted for ' *by* '? And why is the same offence repeated in 1 Cor. viii. 6,—(where we *ought* to read, — ' one GOD, the FATHER, of whom are all things . . . and one LORD JESUS CHRIST, *by* whom are all things ') ?—Why, especially, in Heb. i. 2, in place of ' *by* whom also [viz. by THE SON] He made the worlds,' do we find substituted ' *through* whom' ? . . . . And why add to this glaring inconsistency the wretched vacillation of giving us the choice of ' *through*' (in place of ' *by* ') in the margin of S. John i. 3 and 10, and not even offering us the alternative of ' *by* ' (in place of ' *through*') in any of the other places,—although the preposition is διά on every occasion ?

And thus much for the Revisers' handling of the Prepositions. We shall have said all that we can find room for, when we have further directed attention to the uncritical and unscholarlike Note with which they have disfigured the margin of S. Mark i. 9. We are there informed that, according to the Greek, our SAVIOUR ' was baptized *into the Jordan*,'—an unintelligible statement to English readers, as well as a misleading one. Especially on their guard should the Revisers have been hereabouts,—seeing that, in a place of vital importance on the opposite side of the open page (viz. in S. Matth. xxviii. 19), they had already substituted ' *into* ' for ' *in*.' This latter alteration, one of the Revisers (Dr. Vance Smith) rejoices over, because it obliterates (in his account) the evidence for Trinitarian doctrine. That the

Revisionists, as a body, intended nothing less, — *who* can doubt? But then, if they really deemed it necessary to append a note to S. Mark i. 9 in order to explain to the public that the preposition εἰς signifies '*into*' rather than '*in*,'— why did they not at least go on to record the elementary fact that εἰς has here (what grammarians call) a 'pregnant signification'? that it implies—(every schoolboy knows it!)— *and that it is used in order to imply*—that the Holy One '*went down* INTO,' and so, '*was baptized* IN the Jordan'?[1] . . . But *why*, in the name of common sense, *did not the Revisionists let the Preposition alone?*

IX. The MARGIN of the Revision is the last point to which our attention is invited, and in the following terms:—

'The subject of the Marginal Notes deserves special attention. They represent the results of *a large amount of careful and elaborate discussion*, and will, perhaps, by their very presence, indicate to some extent the intricacy of many of the questions that have almost daily come before us for decision. These Notes fall into four main groups:—*First*, Notes specifying such differences of reading as were judged to be of sufficient import- ance to require a particular notice;—*Secondly*, Notes indicating the exact rendering of words to which, for the sake of English idiom, we were obliged to give a less exact rendering in the text;—*Thirdly*, Notes, very few in number, affording some ex- planation which the original appeared to require;—*Fourthly*, Alternative Renderings in difficult or debateable passages. The Notes of this last group are numerous, and largely in excess of those which were admitted by our predecessors. In the 270 years that have passed away since their labours were concluded, the Sacred Text has been minutely examined, discussed in every detail, and analysed with a grammatical precision unknown in the days of the last Revision. There has thus been accumu-

---

[1] Consider S. Matth. iii. 16,—ἀνέβη ἀπὸ τοῦ ὕδατος : and ver. 6,—ἐβαπ- τίζοντο ἐν τῷ Ἰορδάνῃ.

lated a large amount of materials that have prepared the way
for different renderings, which necessarily came under discussion.'—(*Preface*, iii. 4.)

When a body of distinguished Scholars bespeak attention
to a certain part of their work in such terms as these, it is
painful for a Critic to be obliged to declare that he has
surveyed this department of their undertaking with even less
satisfaction than any other. So long, however, as he assigns
the grounds of his dissatisfaction, the Reviewed cannot complain. The Reviewer puts himself into their power. If he is
mistaken in his censure, his credit is gone. Let us take the
groups in order :—

(1) Having already stated our objections against the many
Notes which specify *Textual errors* which the Revisionists
declined to adopt,—we shall here furnish only two instances
of the mischief we deplore :—

(*a*) Against the words, ' And while they *abode* in Galilee '
(S. Matthew xvii. 22), we find it stated,—' Some ancient
authorities read *were gathering themselves together*.' The plain
English of which queer piece of information is that א and B
exhibit in this place an impossible and untranslatable Reading,—the substitution of which for ἀναστρεφομένων δὲ αὐτῶν
can only have proceeded from some Western critic, who was
sufficiently unacquainted with the Greek language to suppose
that ΣΥΝ-στρεφομένων δὲ αὐτῶν, might possibly be the exact
equivalent for *Con-versantibus autem illis*. This is not the
place for discussing a kind of hallucination which prevailed
largely in the earliest age, especially in regions where Greek
was habitually read through Latin spectacles. (Thus it was,
obviously, that the preposterous substitution of EURAQUILO
for 'Euroclydon,' in Acts xxvii. 14, took its rise.) Such
blunders would be laughable if encountered anywhere except
on holy ground. Apart, however, from the lamentable lack

of critical judgment which a marginal note like the present displays, what is to be thought of the scholarship which elicits ' *While they were gathering themselves together*' out of συστρεφομένων δὲ αὐτῶν? Are we to suppose that the clue to the Revisers' rendering is to be found in (συστρέψαντος) Acts xxviii. 3 ? We should be sorry to think it. They are assured that the source of the *Textual* blunder which they mistranslate is to be found, instead, in Baruch iii. 38.[1]

(*b*) For what conceivable reason is the world now informed that, instead of *Melita*,—' some ancient authorities read *Melitene*,' in Acts xxviii. 1 ? Is every pitiful blunder of cod. B to live on in the margin of every Englishman's copy of the New Testament, for ever ? Why, *all* other MSS.—the Syriac and the Latin versions,—Pamphilus of Cæsarea [2] (A.D. 294), the friend of Eusebius,—Cyril of Jerusalem,[3]—Chrysostom,[4]—John Damascene,[5]— all the Fathers in short who quote the place ; — the coins, the ancient geographers ;— *all* read Μελίτη; which has also been acquiesced in by every critical Editor of the N. T.—(*excepting always Drs. Westcott and Hort*), from the invention of Printing till now. But because these two misguided men, without apology, explanation, note or comment of any kind, have adopted ' *Melitene*' into their text, is the Church of England to be dragged through the mire also, and made ridiculous in the eyes of Christendom ? This blunder moreover is 'gross as a mountain, open, palpable.' One glance at the place, written in uncials, explains how it arose :—ΜελιτηΗΝΗσοσκαλειται. Some stupid scribe (as the reader sees) has connected the first syllable of νῆσος with the last syllable of Μελίτη.[6] *That*

---

[1] ἐν τοῖς ἀνθρώποις συναναεστράφη.   [2] Galland. iv. 6 b *bis*.
[3] P. 279.   [4] ix. 400.   [5] ii. 707.
[6] The circumstance is noticed and explained in the same way by Dr. Field in his delightful *Otium Norvicense*.

is all! The blunder—(for a blunder it most certainly is)—belongs to the age and country in which '*Melitene*' was by far the more familiar word, being the name of the metropolitan see of Armenia;[1] mention of which crops up in the *Concilia* repeatedly.[2]

(2) and (4) The second and the fourth group may be considered together. The former comprises those words of which the *less exact* rendering finds place in the Text:—the latter, '*Alternative renderings* in difficult and debateable passages.'

We presume that here our attention is specially invited to such notes as the following. Against 1 Cor. xv. 34,—'*Awake out of drunkenness righteously:*'—against S. John i. 14,—'*an only begotten from a father:*'—against 1 Pet. iii. 20,—'*into which few, that is, eight souls, were brought safely through water:*'—against 2 Pet. iii. 7,—'*stored with fire:*'—against S. John xviii. 37,—'*Thou sayest it, because I am a king:*'—against Ephes. iii. 21,—'*All the generations of the age of the ages:*'—against Jude ver. 14,—'*His holy myriads:*'—against Heb. xii. 18,—'*a palpable and kindled fire:*'—against Lu. xv. 31,—'*Child,* thou art ever with me:'—against Matth. xxi. 28, —'*Child,* go work to-day in my vineyard:'—against xxiv. 3,—'What shall be the sign of Thy *presence,* and of *the consummation of the age?*' — against Tit. i. 2, — '*before times eternal:*' against Mk. iv. 29,—'When the fruit *alloweth* [and why not '*yieldeth* itself'?], straightway *he sendeth forth* the sickle:'—against Ephes. iv. 17,—'*through every joint of the supply:*'—against ver. 29,—'*the building up of the need:*'—against Lu. ii. 29,—'*Master,* now lettest thou Thy *bondservant* depart in peace:'—against Acts iv. 24,—'*O Master,* thou that didst make the heaven and the earth:'—against

---

[1] *Concilia,* iv. 79 e.

[2] Thus Cyril addresses one of his Epistles to Acacius Bp. of Melitene,—*Concilia,* iii. 1111.

Lu. i. 78,—'Because of *the heart of mercy* of our GOD.' Concerning all such renderings we will but say, that although they are unquestionably better in the Margin than in the Text; it also admits no manner of doubt that they would have been best of all in neither. Were the Revisionists serious when they suggested as the more 'exact' rendering of 2 Pet. i. 20,—'No prophecy of Scripture is of *special* interpretation'? And what did they mean (1 Pet. ii. 2) by '*the spiritual milk which is without guile*'?

Not a few marginal glosses might have been dispensed with. Thus, against διδάσκαλος, upwards of 50 times stands the Annotation, 'Or, *teacher.*'—Ἄρτος, (another word of perpetual recurrence,) is every time explained to mean '*a loaf.*' But is this reasonable? seeing that φαγεῖν ἄρτον (Luke xiv. 1) can mean nothing else but 'to eat *bread*:' not to mention the petition for '*daily bread*' in the LORD's prayer. These learned men, however, do not spare us even when mention is made of 'taking the children's *bread* and casting it to the dogs' (Mk. vii. 27): while in the enquiry,—'If a son shall ask *bread* of any of you that is a father' (Lu. xi. 11), '*loaf*' is actually thrust into the text.—We cannot understand why such marked favour has been shown to similar easy words. Δοῦλος, occurring upwards of 100 times in the New Testament, is invariably honoured (sometimes [as in Jo. xv. 15] *twice in the course of the same verse*) with 2 lines to itself, to explain that in Greek it is '*bondservant.*'—About 60 times, δαιμόνιον is explained in the margin to be '*demon*' in the Greek.—It has been deemed necessary 15 times to devote *three lines* to explain the value of 'a penny.'—Whenever τέκνον is rendered '*Son,*' we are molested with a marginal annotation, to the effect that the Greek word means '*child.*' Had the Revisionists been consistent, the margins would not nearly have sufficed for the many interesting details of this nature with which their knowledge of Greek would have furnished them.

May we be allowed to suggest, that it would have been better worth while to explain to the unlearned that ἀρχαί in S. Peter's vision (Acts x. 11; xi. 5) in strictness means not 'corners,' but '*beginnings*' [cf. Gen. ii. 10] :—that τὴν πρώτην (in Lu. xv. 22) is literally '*the first*' [cf. Gen. iii. 7] (not 'the best') 'robe :'—that ἀληθινός (e.g. in Lu. xvi. 11 : Jo. i. 9 : vi. 32; and especially in xv. 1 and Heb. viii. 2 and ix. 24) means '*very*' or '*real*,' rather than 'true'?—And when two different words are employed in Greek (as in S. Jo. xxi. 15, 16, 17 :—S. Mk. vii. 33, 35, &c. &c.), would it not have been as well to try to *represent* them in English? For want of such assistance, no unlearned reader of S. Matth. iv. 18, 20, 21 : S. Mk. i. 16, 18, 19 : S. Lu. v. 2,—will ever be able to understand the precise circumstances under which the first four Apostles left their '*nets*.'

(3) The third group consists of *Explanatory Notes* required by the obscurity of the original. Such must be the annotation against S. Luke i. 15 (explanatory of 'strong drink'),— 'Gr. *sikera*.' And yet, the word (σίκερα) happens to be *not* Greek, but Hebrew.—On the other hand, such must be the annotation against μωρέ, in S. Matth. v. 22 :—'Or, *Moreh*, a Hebrew expression of condemnation;' which statement is incorrect. The word proves to be *not* Hebrew, but Greek.— And this, against 'Maran atha' in 1 Cor. xvi. 22,—'That is, *Our Lord cometh:*' which also proves to be a mistake. The phrase means '*Our Lord is come*,'—which represents a widely different notion.[1]—Surely a room-full of learned men, volunteering to put the N. T. to-rights, ought to have made more

---

[1] See Dr. Field's delightful *Otium Norvicense* (Pars tertia), 1881, pp. 1–4 and 110, 111. This masterly contribution to Sacred Criticism ought to be in the hands of every student of Scripture.

sure of their elementary *facts* before they ventured to compromise the Church of England after this fashion !—Against
' *the husks* which the swine did eat' (Lu. xv. 16), we find, ' Gr.
the pods of the carob tree,'—which is really not true. The Greek
word is κεράτια,—which only signifies ' the pods of the carob
tree,' as ' French beans' signifies ' the pods of the *Phaseolus
vulgaris.*'—By the way, is it *quite* certain that μύλος ὀνικός
[in Matth. xviii. 6 and Lu. xvii. 2 (not Mk. ix. 42)] signifies
' *a mill-stone turned by an ass* ' ? Hilary certainly thought so :
but is the thing at all likely ? What if it should appear that
μύλος ὀνικός merely denotes the *upper* mill-stone (λίθος
μυλικός, as S. Mark calls it,—*the stone that grinds*), and which
we know was called ὄνος by the ancients ?[1]—Why is ' the
brook Cedron' (Jo. xviii. 1) first spelt ' Kidron,' and then
explained to mean ' *ravine of the cedars* '? which ' *Kidron* ' no
more means than ' *Kishon* ' means ' *of the ivies,*'—(though the
Septuagintal usage [Judges iv. 13 : Ps. lxxxiii. 9] shows that
τῶν κισσῶν was its common Hellenistic designation). As
for calling the Kidron ' *a ravine,*' you might as well call
' Mercury ' in ' Tom quad ' ' *a lake.*' ' Infelicitous' is the
mildest epithet we can bestow upon marginal annotations
crude, questionable,—even *inaccurate* as these.

Then further, ' Simon, the son of *Jona* ' (in S. John i. 42
and xxi. 15), is for the first time introduced to our notice
by the Revisionists as ' the son of *John :*' with an officious
marginal annotation that in Greek the name is written
' *Ioanes.*' But is it fair in the Revisers (we modestly ask)
to thrust in this way the *bétises* of their favourite codex B
upon us ? *In no codex in the world except the Vatican codex*
B, is ' Ioannes ' spelt ' *Ioanes* ' in this place. Besides, the
name of Simon Peter's father was *not* ' John ' at all, but
' *Jona,*'—as appears from S. Matth. xvi. 17, and the present

---

[1] See Hesychius, and the notes on the place.

two places in S. John's Gospel; where the evidence *against*
' Ioannes' is overwhelming. This is in fact the handy-work of
Dr. Hort. But surely the office of marginal notes ought to be
to assist, not to mislead plain readers : honestly, to state *facts*,
—not, by a side-wind, to commit the Church of England to *a
new (and absurd) Textual theory !* The *actual Truth*, we insist,
should be stated in the margin, whenever unnecessary information is gratuitously thrust upon unlearned and unsuspicious
readers. . . . Thus, we avow that we are offended at reading
(against S. John i. 18)—' Many very ancient authorities read
' *God only begotten:*' whereas the 'authorities' alluded to
read μονογενὴς Θεός,—(whether with or without the article
[ὁ] prefixed,)—which (as the Revisionists are perfectly well
aware) means '*the only-begotten God*,' and no other thing.
Why then did they not say so ? *Because* (we answer)—*they
were ashamed of the expression.* But to proceed.—The information is volunteered (against Matth. xxvi. 36 and Mk.
xiv. 32) that χωρίον means ' *an enclosed piece of ground*,'—
which is not true. The statement seems to have proceeded
from the individual who translated ἄμφοδον (in Mk. xi. 4)
the ' *open street:* ' whereas the word merely denotes the ' high-
way,'—literally the ' *thoroughfare.*'

A very little real familiarity with the Septuagint would
have secured these Revisers against the perpetual exposure
which they make of themselves in their marginal Notes.—
(*a*) Πάσας τὰς ἡμέρας, for instance, is quite an ordinary
expression for ' always,' and therefore should not be exhibited
(in the margin of S. Matth. xxviii. 20) as a curiosity,—' Gr.
all the days.'—So (*b*) with respect to the word αἰών, which
seems to have greatly exercised the Revisionists. What need,
every time it occurs, to explain that εἰς τοὺς αἰῶνας τῶν
αἰώνων means literally ' *unto the ages of the ages* ' ? Surely
(as in Ps. xlv. 6, quoted Heb. i. 8,) the established rendering

('for ever and ever') is plain enough and needs no gloss!—
Again, (c) the numeral εἷς, representing the Hebrew substitute
for the indefinite article, prevails throughout the Septuagint.
Examples of its use occur in the N. T. in S. Matth. viii. 19
and ix. 18;—xxvi. 69 (μία παιδίσκη), Mk. xii. 42 : and in
Rev. viii. 13: ix. 13: xviii. 21 and xix. 17;—where 'one
scribe,' 'one ruler,' 'one widow,' 'one eagle,' 'one voice,' 'one
angel,' are really nothing else but mistranslations.   True, that
εἷς is found in the original Greek: but what then?   Because
'une' means 'one,' will it be pretended that 'Tu es une bête'
would be properly rendered 'Thou art one beast'?

(d) Far more serious is the substitution of 'having a great
priest over the house of GOD' (Heb. x. 21), for 'having an
high priest:' inasmuch as this obscures 'the pointed reference
to our LORD as the antitype of the Jewish high priest,'—who
(except in Lev. iv. 3) is designated, not ἀρχιερεύς, but either
ὁ ἱερεὺς ὁ μέγας, or else ὁ ἱερεύς only,—as in Acts v. 24 [1]. . .
And (e) why are we presented with 'For no word from GOD
shall be void of power' (in S. Luke i. 37)?   Seeing that the
Greek of that place has been fashioned on the Septuagintal
rendering of Gen. xviii. 14 ('Is anything too hard for the
LORD?' [2]), we venture to think that the A. V. ('for with GOD
nothing shall be impossible' [3]) ought to have been let alone.
It cannot be mended.   One is surprised to discover that
among so many respectable Divines there seems not to have
been one sufficiently familiar with the Septuagint to preserve
his brethren from perpetually falling into such mistakes as
the foregoing.   We really had no idea that the Hellenistic

---

[1] *Notes designed to illustrate some expressions in the Gk. Test. by a
reference to the* LXX., &c.   By C. F. B. Wood, Præcentor of Llandaff,—
Rivingtons, 1882, (pp. 21,)—p. 17 :—an admirable performance, only far too
brief.

[2] Μὴ ἀδυνατήσει παρὰ τῷ θεῷ ῥῆμα;

[3] Οὐκ ἀδυνατήσει παρὰ τῷ θεῷ πᾶν ῥῆμα.

scholarship of those who represented the Church and the
Sects in the Jerusalem Chamber, was so inconsiderable.

Two or three of the foregoing examples refer to matters of
a recondite nature. Not so the majority of the Annotations
which belong to this third group; which we have examined
with real astonishment—and in fact have remarked upon
already. Shall we be thought hard to please if we avow
that we rather desiderate 'Explanatory Notes' on matters
which really *do* call for explanation? as, to be reminded of
what kind was the 'net' (ἀμφίβληστρον) mentioned in Matth.
iv. 18 (*not* 20), and Mk. i. 16 (*not* 18):—to see it explained
(against Matth. ii. 23) that *netser* (the root of 'Nazareth')
denotes 'Branch:'—and against Matth. iii. 5; Lu. iii. 3, that
ἡ περίχωρος τοῦ Ἰορδάνου, signifies 'the *depressed valley of
the Jordan*,' as the usage of the LXX. proves.[1] We should
have been glad to see, against S. Lu. ix. 31,—'Gr. *Exodus*.'—
At least in the margin, we might have been told that '*Olivet*'
is the true rendering of Lu. xix. 29 and xxi. 37: (or were the
Revisionists not aware of the fact? They are respectfully referred to the Bp. of Lincoln's note on the place last quoted.)
—Nay, why not tell us (against Matth. i. 21) that 'JESUS'
means [not '*Saviour*,' but] '*JEHOVAH is Salvation*'?

But above all, surely so many learned men ought to have
spared us the absurd Annotation set against '*ointment of
spikenard*' (νάρδου πιστικῆς,) in S. Mark xiv. 3 and in S. John
xii. 3. Their marginal Note is as follows:—

'Gr. *pistic nard*, pistic being perhaps a local name. Others
take it to mean *genuine*; others *liquid*.'

Can Scholars require to be told that '*liquid*' is an *impossible*

---

[1] [Pointed out to me by Professor Gandell,—whose exquisite familiarity
with Scripture is only equalled by his readiness to communicate his
knowledge to others.]

sense of πιστική in this place? The epithet so interpreted must be derived (like πιστός [*Prom. V.* v. 489]) from πίνω, and would mean *drinkable:* but since ointment *cannot* be drunk, it is certain that we must seek the etymology of the word elsewhere. And why should the weak ancient conjecture be retained that it is 'perhaps a *local* name'? Do Divines require to have it explained to them that the one 'locality' which effectually fixes the word's meaning, is *its place in the everlasting Gospel?* ... Be silent on such lofty matters if you will, by all means; but 'who are these that darken counsel by words without knowledge?' S. Mark and S. John (whose narratives by the way never touch exclusively except in this place [1]) are observed here to employ an ordinary word with lofty spiritual purpose. The *pure faith* (πίστις) in which that offering of the ointment was made, determines the choice of an unusual epithet (πιστικός) which shall signify 'faithful' rather than 'genuine,'—shall suggest a *moral* rather than a *commercial* quality : just as, presently, Mary's 'breaking' the box (συντρίψασα) is designated by a word which has reference to a broken heart.[2] She '*contrited*' it, S. Mark says; and S. John adds a statement which implies that the Church has been rendered fragrant by her act for ever.[3] (We trust to be forgiven for having said a little more than the occasion absolutely requires.)

(5) Under which of the four previous 'groups' certain Annotations which disfigure the margin of the first chapter of

---

[1] μύρου νάρδου πιστικῆς and ἐνταφιασμός,—S. Mark xiv. 3 and 8 : S. John xii. 3 and 7. Hear Origen (apud Hieron. iii. 517):—' Non de nardo propositum est nunc Spiritui Sancto dicere, neque de hoc quod oculis intuemur, Evangelista scribit, unguento; sed *de nardo spirituali.*' And so Jerome himself, vii. 212.

[2] Ps. xxxiii. 18 (ἐγγὺς Κύριος τοῖς συντετριμμένοις τὴν καρδίαν): Is. lvii. 15.

[3] Consider Ignatius, *ad Ephes.* c. xvii. Also, the exquisite remark of Theod. Heracl. in Cramer's *Cat.*

S. Matthew's Gospel, should fall,—we know not. Let them
be briefly considered by themselves.

So dull of comprehension are we, that we fail to see
on what principle it is stated that—'Ram,' 'Asa,' 'Amon,'
'Shealtiel,' are in Greek ('Gr.') '*Aram*,' '*Asaph*,' '*Amos*,'
'*Salathiel*.' For (1),—Surely it was just as needful (or just
as needless) to explain that 'Perez,' 'Zarah,' 'Hezron,'
'Nahson,' are in Greek '*Phares*,' '*Zara*,' '*Esrom*,' '*Naasson*.'—
But (2), Through what 'necessity' are the names, which we
have been hitherto contented to read as the Evangelist wrote
them, now exhibited on the first page of the Gospel in any
other way ?[1]—(3) Assuming, however, the O. T. spelling
is to be adopted, then *let us have it explained to us why* '*Jeconiah*' *in ver.* 11 *is not written* 'Jehoiakim'?   (As for 'Jeconiah' in ver. 12,—it was for the Revisionists to settle whether
they would call him 'Jehoiachin,' 'Jeconiah,' or 'Coniah.'
[By the way,—Is it lawful to suppose that *they did not know*
that 'Jechonias' here represents two different persons ?])—
On the other hand, (4) '*Amos*' probably,—'*Asaph*' certainly,—
are corrupt exhibitions of 'Amon' and 'Asa :' and, if noticed
at all, should have been introduced to the reader's notice
with the customary formula, 'some ancient authorities,' &c.—
To proceed—(5), Why substitute 'Immanuel' (for 'Emmanuel') in ver. 23,—only to have to state in the margin that
S. Matthew writes it '*Emmanuel*'?   By strict parity of
reasoning, against 'Naphtali' (in ch. iv. 13, 15), the Revisionists ought to have written 'Gr. *Nephthaleim*.'—And
(6), If this is to be the rule, then why are we not told that

---

[1] We prefer that readers should be reminded, by the varied form, of the
Greek original.   In the extreme case (Acts vii. 45 : Hebr. iv. 8), is it not
far more edifying that attention should be in this way directed to the
identity of the names '*Joshua*' and '*Jesus*,' than that the latter word
should be entirely obliterated by the former ;—and this, only for the sake
of unmistakeably proclaiming, (what yet must needs be perfectly manifest,
viz.) that '*Joshua*' is the personage spoken of?

'Mary is in "Gr. *Mariam*"'? and why is not Zacharias written '*Zachariah*'? . . . But (to conclude),—What is the object of all this officiousness? and (its unavoidable adjunct) all this inconsistency? Has the spelling of the 42 names been revolutionized, in order to sever with the Past and to make 'a fresh departure'? Or were the four marginal notes added *only for the sake of obtaining, by a side-wind, the (apparent) sanction of the Church* to the preposterous notion that 'Asa' was written '*Asaph*' by the Evangelist—in conformity with six MSS. of bad character, but in defiance of History, documentary Evidence, and internal Probability? Canon Cook [pp. 23–24] has some important remarks on this.

X. We must needs advert again to the ominous admission made in the Revisionists' *Preface* (iii. 2 *init.*), that to some extent they recognized the duty of a '*rigid adherence to the rule of translating,* as far as possible, *the same Greek word by the same English word.*' This mistaken principle of theirs lies at the root of so much of the mischief which has befallen the Authorized Version, that it calls for fuller consideration at our hands than it has hitherto (viz. at pp. 138 and 152) received.

The 'Translators' of 1611, towards the close of their long and quaint Address 'to the Reader,' offer the following statement concerning what had been their own practice:—
'We have not *tied ourselves*' (say they) '*to an uniformity of phrasing, or to an identity of words,* as some peradventure would wish that we had done.' On this, they presently enlarge. We have been 'especially careful,' have even 'made a conscience,' 'not to vary from the sense of that which we had translated before, if the word signified the same thing in both places.' But then, (as they shrewdly point out in passing,) '*there be some words that be not of the*

same sense everywhere.'   And had this been the sum of their avowal, no one with a spark of Taste, or with the least appreciation of what constitutes real Scholarship, would have been found to differ from them.   Nay, even when they go on to explain that they have not thought it desirable to insist on invariably expressing 'the same notion' by employing 'the same particular word;'—(which they illustrate by instancing terms which, in their account, may with advantage be diversely rendered in different places;)—we are still disposed to avow ourselves of their mind.   'If' (say they,) 'we translate the Hebrew or Greek word once *purpose,* never to call it *intent;* if one where *journeying,* never *travelling;* if one where *think,* never *suppose;* if one where *pain,* never *ache;* if one where *joy,* never *gladness;*—thus to mince the matter, we thought to savour more of curiosity than of wisdom.'   And yet it is plain that a different principle is here indicated from that which went before.   The remark 'that niceness in words was always counted the next step to trifling,' suggests that, in the Translators' opinion, it matters little *which* word, in the several pairs of words they instance, is employed; and that, for their own parts, they rather rejoice in the ease and freedom which an ample vocabulary supplies to a Translator of Holy Scripture.   Here also however, as already hinted, we are disposed to go along with them.   Rhythm, subtle associations of thought, proprieties of diction which are rather to be felt than analysed,—any of such causes may reasonably determine a Translator to reject 'purpose,' 'journey,' 'think,' 'pain,' 'joy,'—in favour of 'intent,' 'travel,' 'suppose,' 'ache,' 'gladness.'

But then it speedily becomes evident that, at the bottom of all this, there existed in the minds of the Revisionists of 1611 a profound (shall we not rather say a *prophetic ?*) consciousness, that the fate of the English

Language itself was bound up with the fate of their Translation. *Hence* their reluctance to incur the responsibility of
tying themselves 'to an uniformity of phrasing, or to an
identity of words.' We should be liable to censure (such is
their plain avowal), 'if we should say, as it were, unto certain
words, Stand up higher, have a place in the Bible always;
and to others of like quality, Get you hence, be banished for
ever.' But this, to say the least, is to introduce a distinct and
a somewhat novel consideration. We would not be thought
to deny that there is some—perhaps a great deal—of truth
in it : but by this time we seem to have entirely shifted our
ground. And we more than suspect that, if a jury of English
scholars of the highest mark could be impanelled to declare
their mind on the subject thus submitted to their judgment,
there would be practical unanimity among them in declaring,
that these learned men,—with whom all would avow hearty
sympathy, and whose taste and skill all would eagerly
acknowledge,—have occasionally pushed the license they
enunciate so vigorously, a little—perhaps a great deal—too
far. For ourselves, we are glad to be able to subscribe
cordially to the sentiment on this head expressed by the
author of the *Preface* of 1881 :

'They seem '—(he says, speaking of the Revisionists of 1611)
—'to have been guided by the feeling that their Version would
secure for the words they used a lasting place in the language;
and they express a fear lest they should "be charged (by scoffers)
with some unequal dealing towards a great number of good
English words," which, without this liberty on their part, would
not have a place in the pages of the English Bible. Still it cannot be doubted that their studied avoidance of uniformity in the
rendering of the same words, even when occurring in the same
context, is one of the blemishes in their work.'—*Preface*, (i. 2).

Yes, it cannot be doubted. When S. Paul, in a long and
familiar passage (2 Cor. i. 3–7), is observed studiously to

linger over the same word (παράκλησις namely, which is generally rendered ' *comfort* ') ;—to harp upon it ;—to reproduce it *ten times* in the course of those five verses ;—it seems unreasonable that a Translator, as if in defiance of the Apostle, should on four occasions (viz. when the word comes back for the 6th, 7th, 9th, and 10th times), for ' *comfort* ' substitute ' *consolation.*' And this one example may serve as well as a hundred. It would really seem as if the Revisionists of 1611 had considered it a graceful achievement to vary the English phrase even on occasions where a marked identity of expression characterizes the original Greek. When we find them turning ' goodly apparel,' (in S. James ii. 2,) into ' gay clothing,' (in ver. 3,)—we can but conjecture that they conceived themselves at liberty to act exactly as S. James himself would (possibly) have acted had he been writing English.

But if the learned men who gave us our A. V. may be thought to have erred on the side of excess, there can be no doubt whatever, (at least among competent judges,) that our Revisionists have sinned far more grievously and with greater injury to the Deposit, by their slavish proclivity to the opposite form of error. We must needs speak out plainly : for the question before us is not, What defects are discoverable in our Authorized Version ?—but, What amount of gain would be likely to accrue to the Church if the present Revision were accepted as a substitute ? And we assert without hesitation, that the amount of certain loss would so largely outweigh the amount of possible gain, that the proposal may not be seriously entertained for a moment. As well on grounds of Scholarship and Taste, as of Textual Criticism (as explained at large in our former Article), the work before us is immensely inferior. To speak plainly, it is an utter failure.

XI. For the respected Authors of it practically deny the truth of the principle enunciated by their predecessors of 1611, viz. that *there be some words that be not of the same sense everywhere.'* On such a fundamental truism we are ashamed to enlarge: but it becomes necessary that we should do so. We proceed to illustrate, by two familiar instances,— the first which come to hand,—the mischievous result which is inevitable to an enforced uniformity of rendering.

(*a*) The verb *αἰτεῖν* confessedly means 'to ask.' And perhaps no better general English equivalent could be suggested for it. But then, *in a certain context,* ' ask ' would be an inadequate rendering: in another, it would be improper: in a third, it would be simply intolerable. Of all this, the great Scholars of 1611 showed themselves profoundly conscious. Accordingly, when this same verb (in the middle voice) is employed to describe how the clamorous rabble, besieging Pilate, claimed their accustomed privilege, (viz. to have the prisoner of their choice released unto them,) those ancient men, with a fine instinct, retain Tyndale's rendering *'desired'* [1] in S. Mark (xv. 8),—and his *'required'* in S. Luke (xxiii. 23).—When, however, the humble entreaty, which Joseph of Arimathea addressed to the same Pilate (viz. that he might be allowed to take away the Body of JESUS), is in question, then the same Scholars (following Tyndale and Cranmer), with the same propriety exhibit *'begged.'*—King David, inasmuch as he only *'desired* to find a habitation for the GOD of Jacob,' of course may not be said to have *'asked'* to do so ; and yet S. Stephen (Acts vii. 46) does not hesitate to employ the verb *ᾐτήσατο.*—So again, when they of Tyre and Sidon approached Herod whom they had offended: they

---

[1] So, in S. Luke xxiii. 25, and Acts iii. 14: xiii. 28,—still following Tyndale.

did but ' *desire* ' peace.[1]—S. Paul, in like manner, addressing the Ephesians : ' I *desire* that ye faint not at my tribulations for you.' [2]

But our Revisionists,—possessed with the single idea that αἰτεῖν means ' to *ask* ' and αἰτεῖσθαι ' to *ask for*,'—have proceeded mechanically to inflict that rendering on every one of the foregoing passages.   In defiance of propriety,—of reason,—even (in David's case) of historical truth,[3]—they have thrust in ' *asked* ' everywhere.   At last, however, they are encountered by two places which absolutely refuse to submit to such iron bondage.   The terror-stricken jailer of Philippi, when *he* ' asked ' for lights, must needs have done so after a truly imperious fashion.   Accordingly, the ' *called for* '[4] of Tyndale and all subsequent translators, is *pro hâc vice* allowed by our Revisionists to stand.   And to conclude, —When S. Paul, speaking of his supplications on behalf of the Christians at Colosse, uses this same verb (αἰτούμενοι) in a context where ' *to ask* ' would be intolerable, our Revisionists render the word ' *to make request ;* '[5]—though they might just as well have let alone the rendering of *all* their predecessors,—viz. ' *to desire*.'

These are many words, but we know not how to make them fewer.   Let this one example, (only because it is the first which presented itself,) stand for a thousand others. Apart from the grievous lack of Taste (not to say of Scholarship) which such a method betrays,—*who* sees not that the only excuse which could have been invented for it has

---

[1] Acts xii. 20.   [2] Eph. iii. 13.

[3] For, as the story plainly shows (2 Sam. vii. 2, 3 ; 1 Chron. xvii. 1, 2), it was only ' *in his heart* ' to build GOD an house (1 Kings viii. 17, 18). Hence Cranmer's ' *he would fain* ' have done so.

[4] Acts xvi. 29.   [5] Col. i. 9.

disappeared by the time we reach the end of our investigation ? If *αἰτέω, αἰτοῦμαι* had been *invariably* translated 'ask,'
'ask for,' it might at least have been pretended that ' the
English Reader is in this way put entirely on a level with the
Greek Scholar ; '—though it would have been a vain pretence,
as all must admit who understand the power of language.
Once make it apparent that just in a single place, perhaps in
two, the Translator found himself forced to break through
his rigid uniformity of rendering,—and *what* remains but an
uneasy suspicion that then there must have been a strain
put on the Evangelists' meaning in a vast proportion of the
other seventy places where *αἰτεῖν* occurs ?   An unlearned
reader's confidence in his guide vanishes ; and he finds that
he has had not a few deflections from the Authorized Version
thrust upon him, of which he reasonably questions alike the
taste and the necessity,—e.g. at S. Matth. xx. 20.

(*b*) But take a more interesting example.   In S. Mark
i. 18, the A. V. has, 'and straightway they *forsook* ' (which
the Revisionists alter into '*left*') 'their nets.'   Why ?
Because in verse 20, the same word *ἀφέντες* will recur ; and
because the Revisionists propose to let the statement ('they
left their father Zebedee') stand.   They 'level up' accordingly ; and plume themselves on their consistency.

We venture to point out, however, that the verb
ἀφιέναι is one of a large family of verbs which,—always
retaining their own essential signification,—yet depend for
their English rendering entirely on the context in which
they occur.   Thus, *ἀφιέναι* is rightly rendered '*to suffer*,' in
S. Matth. iii. 15 ;—'*to leave*,' in iv. 11 ;—'*to let have*,' in v. 40 ;
—'*to forgive*,' in vi. 12, 14, 15 ;—'*to let*,' in vii. 4 ;—'*to yield
up*,' in xxvii. 50 ;—'*to let go*,' in S. Mark xi. 6 ;—'*to let alone*,'
in xiv. 6.   Here then, by the admission of the Revisionists,

o

are eight diversities of meaning in the same word.   But they make the admission grudgingly; and, in order to render ἀφιέναι as often as possible '*leave*,' they do violence to many a place of Scripture where some other word would have been more appropriate.   Thus '*laying aside*' might have stood in S. Mark vii. 8.   '*Suffered*' (or 'let') was preferable in S. Luke xii. 39.   And, (to return to the place from which we started,) in S. Mark i. 18, 'forsook' was better than 'left.' And why?   Because men '*leave* their father,' (as the Collect for S. James's Day bears witness); but '*forsake* all covetous desires' (as the Collect for S. Matthew's Day aptly attests). For which reason,—'And they all *forsook* Him' was infinitely preferable to 'and they all *left* Him, and fled,' in S. Mark xiv. 50.   We insist that a vast deal more is lost by this perpetual disregard of the idiomatic proprieties of the English language, than is gained by a pedantic striving after uniformity of rendering, only because the Greek word happens to be the same.

For it is sure sometimes to happen that what seems mere licentiousness proves on closer inspection to be unobtrusive Scholarship of the best kind.   An illustration presents itself in connection with the word just now before us.   It is found to have been our SAVIOUR'S practice to '*send away*' the multitude whom He had been feeding or teaching, in some formal manner,—whether with an act of solemn benediction, or words of commendatory prayer, or both.   Accordingly, on the memorable occasion when, at the close of a long day of superhuman exertion, His bodily powers succumbed, and the Disciples were fain to take Him 'as He was' in the ship, and at once He 'fell asleep;'—on that solitary occasion, *the Disciples* are related to have '*sent away* the multitudes,'—i.e. to have formally dismissed them on His behalf, as they had often seen their Master do.   The word employed to designate this practice on two memorable occasions is ἀπολύειν:[1] on the other two, ἀφιέναι.[2] This proves to have been perfectly well understood as well by the learned authors of the Latin Version of the N. T., as by the scholars who translated the Gospels into the vernacular of Palestine. It has been reserved for the boasted learning of the XIXth century to misunderstand this little circumstance entirely. The R. V. renders S. Matth. xiii. 36,—not 'Then JESUS *sent the multitude away*,' ('*dimissis turbis*' in every Latin copy,) but—'Then He *left* the multitudes.' Also S. Mark iv. 36,—not 'And when they had *sent away the multitude*,' (which the Latin always renders '*et dimittentes turbam*,') but—'And *leaving* the multitude.' Would it be altogether creditable, we respectfully ask, if at the end of 1800 years the Church of England were to put forth with authority such specimens of 'Revision' as these?

(*c*) We will trouble our Readers with yet another illustration of the principle for which we are contending.—We are soon made conscious that there has been a fidgetty anxiety on the part of the Revisionists, everywhere to substitute '*maid*' for '*damsel*' as the rendering of παιδίσκη. It offends us. 'A damsel named Rhoda,'[3]—and the 'damsel possessed with a spirit of divination,'[4]—might (we think) have been let alone. But out of curiosity we look further, to see what these gentlemen will do when they come to S. Luke xii. 45. Here, because παῖδας has been (properly) rendered 'menservants,' παιδίσκας, they (not unreasonably) render '*maid-servants*,'—whereby *they break their rule*. The crucial

---

[1] S. Matth. xiv. 15, 22, 23 (= S. Mark vi. 36, 45, [and note the substitution of ἀποταξάμενος in ver. 46]: S. Luke ix. 12): and xv. 32, 39 (=S. Mark viii. 9).   [2] S. Matt. xiii. 36: and S. Mark iv. 36.
[3] Acts xii. 13.   [4] Acts xvi. 16.

place is behind.   What will they do with the Divine
' Allegory ' in Galatians, (iv. 21 to 31,)—where all turns on
the contrast [1] between the παιδίσκη and the ἐλευθέρα,—the
fact that Hagar was a ' bondmaid,' whereas Sarah was a 'free
woman' ?   ' Maid ' clearly could not. stand here.   ' Maid-
servant ' would be intolerable.   What is to be done ?   The
Revisionists adopt a third variety of reading,—thus surren-
dering their principle entirely.   And what reader with a
spark of taste, (we confidently ask the question,) does not
resent their substitution of ' handmaid ' for ' bondmaid '
throughout these verses ?   Who will deny that the mention
of ' bondage ' in verses 24 and 25 claims, at the hands of an
intelligent English translator, that he shall avail himself of
the admirable and helpful equivalent for παιδίσκη which, as
it happens, the English language possesses ?   More than
that.   Who—(except one who is himself ' in bondage—with
his children ')—who does not respond gratefully to the exquisite taste and tact with which ' bondmaid ' itself has been
exchanged for ' bondwoman ' by our translators of 1611, in
verses 23, 30 and 31 ? . . . Verily, those men understood
their craft !   ' There were giants in those days.'   As little
would they submit to be bound by the new cords of the
Philistines as by their green withes.   Upon occasion, they
could shake themselves free from either.   And why ?   For
the selfsame reason: viz. because the SPIRIT of their GOD
was mightily upon them.

Our contention, so far, has been but this,—that it does
not by any means follow that identical Greek words and
expressions, wherever occurring, are to be rendered by identical words and expressions in English.   We desire to pass on
to something of more importance.

---

[1] Verses 22, 23, 24, 25, 26, 30, 31.

Let it not be supposed that we make light of the difficulties which our Revisionists have had to encounter; or are wanting in generous appreciation of the conscientious toil of many men for many years; or that we overlook the perils of the enterprise in which they have seen fit to adventure their reputation. If ever a severe expression escapes us, it is because our Revisionists themselves seem to have so very imperfectly realized the responsibility of their undertaking, and the peculiar difficulties by which it is unavoidably beset. The truth is,—as all who have given real thought to the subject must be aware,—the phenomena of Language are. among the most subtle and delicate imaginable : the problem of Translation, one of the most manysided and difficult that can be named. And if this holds universally, in how much greater a degree when the book to be translated is THE BIBLE! Here, anything like a mechanical *levelling up* of terms, every attempt to impose a pre-arranged system of uniform rendering on words,—every one of which has a history and (so to speak) *a will* of its own,—is inevitably destined to result in discomfiture and disappointment. But what makes this so very serious a matter is that, because *HOLY SCRIPTURE* is the Book experimented upon, the loftiest interests that can be named become imperilled; and it will constantly happen that what is not perhaps in itself a very serious mistake may yet inflict irreparable injury. We subjoin an humble illustration of our meaning—the rather, because it will afford us an opportunity for penetrating a little deeper into the proprieties of Scriptural Translation :—

(*d*) The place of our LORD'S Burial, which is mentioned upwards of 30 times in the Gospels, is styled in the original, μνημεῖον. This appellation is applied to it three times by S. Matthew;— six times by S. Mark ; — eight times by

S. Luke ;[1]—eleven times by S. John. Only on four occasions, in close succession, does the first Evangelist call it by
another name, viz. τάφος.[2] King James's translators (following Tyndale and Cranmer) decline to notice this diversity,
and uniformly style it the ' sepulchre.' So long as it belonged
to Joseph of Arimathea, they call it a ' tomb ' (Matth. xxvii.
60): when once it has been appropriated by ' the LORD of
Glory,' *in the same verse* they give it a different English
appellation. But our Revisionists of 1881, as if bent on
' making a fresh departure,' *everywhere* substitute ' *tomb* ' for
' sepulchre ' as the rendering of μνημεῖον.

Does any one ask,—And why should they *not ?* We
answer, Because, in connection with ' *the Sepulchre* ' of our
LORD, there has grown up such an ample literature and such
a famous history, that we are no longer *able* to sever ourselves
from those environments of the problem, even if we desired
to do so. In all such cases as the present, we have to
balance the Loss against the Gain. Quite idle is it for the
pedant of 1881 to insist that τάφος and μνημεῖον are two
different words. We do not dispute the fact. (Then, if he
must, let him represent τάφος in some other way.) It
remains true, notwithstanding, that the receptacle of our
SAVIOUR'S Body after His dissolution will have to be spoken
of as ' *the Holy Sepulchre* ' till the end of time ; and it is
altogether to be desired that its familiar designation should
be suffered to survive unmolested on the eternal page, in
consequence. There are, after all, mightier laws in the
Universe than those of grammar. In the quaint language of
our Translators of 1611 : ' For is the Kingdom of GOD become
words or syllables ? Why should we be in bondage to them

---

¹ Twice he calls it μνῆμα.   ² Ch. xxvii. 61, 64, 66 ; xxviii. 1.

if we may be free ? ' . . . As for considerations of etymological propriety, the nearest English equivalent for μνημεῖον
(be it remembered) is *not* ' tomb,' but ' *monument*.'

(*e*) Our Revisionists seem not to be aware that 270 years
of undisturbed possession have given to certain words rights
to which they could not else have pretended, but of which
it is impossible any more to dispossess them.   It savours of
folly as well as of pedantry even to make the attempt.
Διδαχή occurs 30,—διδασκαλία 21 times,—in the N. T.
Etymologically, both words alike mean " *teaching ;* " and are
therefore indifferently rendered ' *doctrina* ' in the Vulgate,[1]—
for which reason, ' *doctrine* ' represents both words indifferently
in our A. V.[2]   But the Revisers have well-nigh extirpated
' *DOCTRINE* ' from the N. T. : (1st), By making ' *teaching*,' the
rendering of διδαχή,[3]—(reserving ' *doctrine* ' for διδασκαλία[4]) :
and (2ndly), By 6 times substituting ' *teaching* ' (once, ' *learning* ') for ' *doctrine*,' in places where διδασκαλία occurs.[5]   This
is to be lamented every way.   The word cannot be spared so
often.   The ' *teachings* ' of our LORD and of His Apostles were
the ' doctrines' of Christianity.   When S. Paul speaks of ' the
doctrine of baptisms ' (Heb. vi. 2), it is simply incomprehensible to us why ' the *teaching* of baptisms ' should be deemed
a preferable expression.   And if the warning against being
' carried about with every wind of *doctrine*,' may stand in
Ephes. iv. 14, why may it not be left standing in Heb. xiii. 9 ? '

---

[1] Except in 2 Tim. iii. 16,—where πρὸς διδασκαλίαν is rendered *ad
docendum*.

[2] Except in Rom. xii. 7,—where ἐν τῇ διδασκαλίᾳ is rendered ' *on*
teaching.'

[3] Except in Rom. xvi. 17, where they render it ' *doctrine*.'

[4] And yet, since upwards of 50 times we are molested with a marginal
note to inform us that διδάσκαλος means ' *Teacher*,'—διδασκαλία (rather
than διδαχή) might have claimed to be rendered ' *teaching*.'

[5] Viz. Rom. xii. 7 : 1 Tim. iv. 13, 16 : v. 17 : 2 Tim. iii. 10, 16.—
Rom. xv. 4.

(*f*) In the same spirit, we can but wonder at the extravagant bad taste which, at the end of 500 years, has ventured to substitute ' *bowls* ' for ' vials ' in the Book of Revelation.[1] As a matter of fact, we venture to point out that φιάλη no more means ' *a bowl* ' than ' saucer ' means ' a cup.' But, waiving this, we are confident that our Revisers would have shown more wisdom if they had *let alone* a word which, having no English equivalent, has passed into the sacred vocabulary of the language, and has acquired a conventional signification which will cleave to it for ever. ' *Vials of wrath* ' are understood to signify the outpouring of GOD's wrathful visitations on mankind : whereas ' bowls ' really conveys no meaning at all, except a mean and unworthy, not to say an inconveniently ambiguous one. What must be the impression made on persons of very humble station,—labouring-men,—when they hear of ' the seven Angels that had *the seven bowls* ' ? (Rev. xvii. 1.) The φιάλη,—if we must needs talk like Antiquaries—is a circular, almost flat and very shallow vessel,—of which the contents can be discharged in an instant. It was used in pouring out libations. There is, at the back of it, in the centre, a hollow for the first joint of the forefinger to rest in. *Patera* the Latins called it. Specimens are to be seen in abundance.

The same Revisionists have also fallen foul of the ' alabaster *box* of ointment,'—for which they have substituted ' an alabaster *cruse* of ointment.'[2] But what *is* a ' cruse ' ? Their marginal note says, ' Or, ' *a flask :* ' but once more, what *is* ' a flask ' ? Certainly, the receptacles to which that name is now commonly applied, (e.g. a powder-flask, a Florence flask, a flask of wine, &c.) bear no resemblance whatever to the vase called ἀλάβαστρον. The probability is

---

[1] Eight times in Rev. xvi.
[2] S. Matth. xxvi. 7. S. Mark xiv. 3. S. Luke vii. 37.

that the receptacle for the precious ointment with which the
sister of Lazarus provided herself, was likest of all to a small
medicine-bottle (*lecythus* the ancients called it), made however of alabaster. Specimens of it abound. But why not
let such words alone ? The same Critics have had the good
sense to leave standing 'the bag,' for what was confessedly
a box[1] (S. John xii. 6 : xiii. 29); and 'your purses' for what
in the Greek is unmistakably 'your *girdles*'[2] (S. Matth. x. 9).
We can but repeat that possession for *five centuries* conveys
rights which it is always useless, and sometimes dangerous,
to dispute. 'Vials' will certainly have to be put back into
the Apocalypse.

(*g*) Having said so much about the proposed rendering
of such unpromising vocables as μνημεῖον—διδαχή—φιάλη,
it is time to invite the Reader's attention to the calamitous
fate which has befallen certain other words of infinitely
greater importance.

And first for 'Ἀγάπη—a substantive noun unknown to
the heathen, even as the sentiment which the word expresses
proves to be a grace of purely Christian growth. What else
but a real calamity would be the sentence of perpetual
banishment passed by our Revisionists on·'that most excellent gift, the gift of *Charity*,' and the general substitution
of 'Love' in its place ? Do not these learned men perceive
that 'Love' is not an equivalent term ? Can they require
to be told that, because of S. Paul's exquisite and life-like
portrait of 'CHARITY,' and the use which has been made of
the word in sacred literature in consequence, it has come to
pass that the word '*Charity*' connotes many ideas to which
the word 'Love' is an entire stranger ? that 'Love,' on the
contrary, has come to connote many unworthy notions
which in '*Charity*' find no place at all ? And if this be

---

[1] γλωσσόκομον. Consider the LXX. of 2 Chron. xxiv. 8, 10, 11.
[2] ζώνας.

so, how can our Revisionists expect that we shall endure the loss of the name of the very choicest of the Christian graces,—and which, if it is nowhere to be found in Scripture, will presently come to be only traditionally known among mankind, and will in the end cease to be a term clearly understood?   Have the Revisionists of 1881 considered how firmly this word '*Charity*' has established itself in the phraseology of the Church,—ancient, mediæval, modern,— as well as in our Book of Common Prayer? how thoroughly it has vindicated for itself the right of citizenship in the English language? how it has entered into our common vocabulary, and become one of the best understood of 'household words'?   Of what can they have been thinking when they deliberately obliterated from the thirteenth chapter of S. Paul's 1st Epistle to the Corinthians the nine-fold recurrence of the name of 'that most excellent gift, the gift of CHARITY'?

(*h*) With equal displeasure, but with even sadder feel-ings, we recognize in the present Revision a resolute elimination of 'MIRACLES' from the N. T.—Not so, (we shall be eagerly reminded,) but only of their *Name*.   True, but the two perforce go together, as every thoughtful man knows. At all events, the getting rid of *the Name*,—(except in the few instances which are enumerated below,)—will in the account of millions be regarded as the getting rid of *the thing*.   And in the esteem of all, learned and unlearned alike, the systematic obliteration of the signifying word from the pages of that Book to which we refer exclusively for our knowledge of the remarkable thing signified,—cannot but be looked upon as a memorable and momentous circum-stance.   Some, it may be, will be chiefly struck by the foolishness of the proceeding: for at the end of centuries of familiarity with such a word, we are no longer *able* to part company with it, even if we were inclined.   The term

has struck root firmly in our Literature : has established
itself in the terminology of Divines: has grown into our
common speech. But further, even were it possible to get
rid of the words 'Miracle' and 'Miraculous,' what else but
abiding inconvenience would be the result? for we must
still desire to speak about *the things ;* and it is a truism to
remark that there are no other words in the language which
connote the same ideas. What therefore has been gained
by substituting '*sign*' for '*miracle*' on some 19 or 20 occasions—('this beginning of *his signs* did JESUS,'—'this is
again the *second sign* that JESUS did')—we really fail to see.

That the word in the original is σημεῖον, and that σημεῖον
means 'a sign,' we are aware. But what then? Because
ἄγγελος, in strictness, means 'a messenger,'—γραφή, 'a
writing,'—ὑποκριτής, 'an actor,'—ἐκκλησία, 'an assembly,'
—εὐαγγέλιον, 'good tidings,'—ἐπίσκοπος, 'an overseer,'—
βαπτιστής, 'one that dips,'— παράδεισος, 'a garden,'—
μαθητής, 'a learner,'—χάρις, 'favour:'—are we to forego
the established English equivalents for these words, and
never more to hear of 'grace,' 'disciple,' 'Paradise,' 'Baptist,' 'Bishop,' 'Gospel,' 'Church,' 'hypocrite,' 'Scripture,'
'Angel'? Is it then desired to revolutionize our sacred
terminology? or at all events to sever with the Past, and
to translate the Scriptures into English on etymological
principles? We are amazed that the first proposal to
resort to such a preposterous method was not instantly
scouted by a large majority of those who frequented the
Jerusalem Chamber.

The words under consideration are not only not equivalent, but they are quite dissimilar. All '*signs*' are not
'*Miracles*,'[1] though all '*Miracles*' are undeniably '*signs*.'

---

[1] E.g. S. Matth. xxvi. 48. S. Luke ii. 12.

Would not a marginal annotation concerning the original word, as at S. Luke xxiii. 8, have sufficed ? And *why* was the term ' *Miracle*' as the rendering of σημεῖον [1] spared only on *that* occasion in the Gospels ; and *only* in connection with S. Peter's miracle of healing the impotent man, in the Acts ?[2] We ask the question not caring for an answer. We are merely bent on submitting to our Readers, whether,—especially in an age like the present of wide-spread unbelief in the Miraculous,—it was a judicious proceeding in our Revisionists almost everywhere to substitute ' Sign ' for ' Miracle ' as the rendering of σημεῖον.

(*i*) Every bit as offensive, in its way, is a marginal note respecting the Third Person in the Trinity, which does duty at S. Matth. i. 18 : S. Mark i. 8 : S. Luke i. 15 : Acts i. 2 : Rom. v. 5 : Heb. ii. 4.   As a rule, in short, against every fresh first mention of ' the HOLY GHOST,' five lines are punctually devoted to the remark,—' *Or*, Holy Spirit : *and so throughout this book.*'   Now, as Canon Cook very fairly puts the case,—

" Does this imply that the marginists object to the word ' GHOST '?   If so, it must be asked, On what grounds?   Certainly not as an archaism.   The word is in every Churchman's mouth continually.   For the sake of consistency ?   But Dr. Vance Smith complains bitterly of the *inconsistency* of his colleagues in reference to this very question,—see his *Texts and Margins*, pp. 7, 8, 45.   I would not suggest a doctrinal bias : but to prove that it had no influence, a strong, if not unanimous, declaration on the part of the Revisers is called for. Dr. Vance Smith alleges this notice as one of the clearest proofs

---

[1] Δύναμις is rendered 'miracle' in the R. V. about half-a-dozen times.

[2] Acts iv. 16, 22.— On the other hand, ' sign ' was allowed to represent σημεῖον repeatedly in the A. V., as in S. Matth. xii. 38, &c., and the parallel places : S. Mark xvi. 17, 20 : S. John xx. 30.

that the Revisers ought in consistency to discard the word as
'*a poor and almost obsolete* equivalent for Spirit.'"[1]

But in fact when one of the Revisionists openly claims,
on behalf of the Revision, that "in the most substantial
sense," (whatever *that* may happen to mean,) it is "contrary
to fact" "that the doctrines of popular Theology remain
unaffected, untouched by the results of the Revision,"[2]—
Charity itself is constrained to use language which by a
certain school will be deemed uncharitable. If doctrinal
prepossession had no share in the production under review,
—why is no protest publicly put forth against such language
as the foregoing, when employed by a conspicuous Member
of the Revisionist body ?

(*j*) In a similar spirit to that which dictated our remarks
on the attempted elimination of '*Miracles*' from the N. T. of
the future,—we altogether disapprove of the attempt to
introduce '*is Epileptic*,' as the rendering of σεληνιάζεται, in
S. Matth. xvii. 15. The miracle performed on '*the lunatic
child*' may never more come abroad under a different name.
In a matter like this, 500 years of occupation, (or rather
1700, for '*lunaticus*' is the reading of all the Latin copies,)
constitute a title which may not be disputed. '*EPILEPTIC*'
is a sorry *gloss*—not a translation. Even were it demonstrable that Epilepsy exclusively exhibits every feature related in connection with the present case ;[3] and that sufferers
from Epilepsy are specially affected by the moon's changes,
(neither of which things are *certainly* true): even so, the
Revisionists would be wholly unwarranted in doing violence
to the Evangelist's language, in order to bring into promi-

---

[1] Canon Cook's *Revised Version of the first three Gospels considered*, &c.
—p. 26 : an admirable performance,—unanswered, because *unanswerable.*
[2] Dr. Vance Smith's *Revised Texts and Margins*,—p. 45.
[3] S. Matth. xvii. 15: S. Mk. ix. 18, 20, 22, 26 : S. Lu. ix. 39, 42.

nence their own private opinion that what is called ' *Lunacy* ' here (and in ch. iv. 24) is to be identified with the ordinary malady called ' Epilepsy.' This was confessedly an extraordinary case of *demoniacal possession* [1] besides. The Revisionists have in fact gone out of their way in order to introduce us to a set of difficulties with which before we had no acquaintance. And after all, the English reader desires to know—*not*, by any means, what two-thirds of the Revisionists *conjecture* was the matter with the child, but— *what the child's Father actually said* was the matter with him. Now, the Father undeniably did *not* say that the child was ' Epileptic,' but that he was ' *Lunatic.*' The man employed a term which (singular to relate) has its own precise English equivalent;—a term which embodies to this hour (as it did anciently) the popular belief that the moon influences certain forms of disease. With the advance of Science, civilized nations surrender such Beliefs; but they do not *therefore* revolutionize their Terminology. ' The advance of Science,' however, has nothing whatever to do with *the Translation of the word* before us. The Author of this particular rendering (begging his pardon) is open to a process ' de *lunatico inquirendo* ' for having imagined the contrary.

(*k*) The foregoing instances suggest the remark, that the Ecclesiastical Historian of future years will point with concern

---

[1] Consider our LORD's solemn words in Mtt. xvii. 21,—' *But this kind goeth not out save by prayer and fasting,*'—12 words left out by the R. V., though witnessed to by *all the Copies but* 3 : by the Latin, Syriac, Coptic, and Armenian Versions: and by the following Fathers :—(1) Origen, (2) Tertullian, (3) the Syriac Clement, (4) the Syriac *Canons of Eusebius*, (5) Athanasius, (6) Basil, (7) Ambrose, (8) Juvencus, (9) Chrysostom, (10) *Opus imp.*, (11) Hilary, (12) Augustine, (13) J. Damascene, and others. Then (it will be asked), why have the Revisionists left them out ? Because (we answer) they have been misled by B and א, Cureton's Syriac and the Sahidic,—as untrustworthy a quaternion of witnesses to the text of Scripture as could be named.

to the sad evidences that the Church had fallen on evil days
when the present Revision was undertaken.   With fatal
fidelity does it, every here and there, reflect the sickly hues
of 'modern Thought,' which is too often but another name
for the latest phase of Unfaithfulness.   Thus, in view of
the present controversy about the Eternity of Future Punish-
ment, which has brought into prominence a supposed distinction between the import of the epithets 'ETERNAL' and
'EVERLASTING,'—how painful is it to discover that the latter
epithet, (which is the one objected to by the unbelieving
school,) has been by our Revisionists diligently excluded[1]
every time it occurs as the translation of αἰώνιος, in favour of
the more palatable epithet 'eternal'!   King James's Translators showed themselves impartial to a fault.   As if to mark
that, in their account, the words are of identical import, they
even introduced *both words into the same verse*[2] of Scripture.
Is it fair that such a body of men as the Revisionists of
1881, claiming the sanction of the Convocation of the
Southern Province, should, in a matter like the present,
throw all their weight into the scale of Misbelief?   They
were authorized only to remove 'plain and clear *errors.*'
They were instructed to introduce 'as few changes as possible.'   Why have they needlessly gone out of their way,
on the contrary, indirectly to show their sympathy with
those who deny what has been the Church's teaching for
1800 years?   Our Creeds, Te Deum, Litany, Offices, Articles,
—our whole Prayer Book, breathes a different spirit and
speaks a different language. . . . Have our Revisionists persuaded the Old Testament company to follow their example?
It will be calamitous if they *have.*   There will be serious

---

[1] The word is only not banished entirely from the N. T.   It occurs
twice (viz. in Rom. i. 20, and Jude ver. 6), but only as the rendering of
ἀΐδιος.   [2] S. Matth. xxv. 46.

discrepancy of teaching between the Old and the New
Testament if they have *not*.

(*l*) What means also the fidgetty anxiety manifested
throughout these pages to explain away, or at least to
evacuate, expressions which have to do with ETERNITY?
Why, for example, is 'the *world* (αἰών) to come,' invariably
glossed 'the *age* to come'? and εἰς τοὺς αἰῶνας so persistently
explained in the margin to mean, '*unto the ages*'? (See the
margin of Rom. ix. 5. Are we to read 'GOD blessed *unto the
ages*'?) Also εἰς τοὺς αἰῶνας τῶν αἰώνων, '*unto the ages of
the ages*'? Surely we, whose language furnishes expressions
of precisely similar character (viz. 'for ever,' and 'for ever
and ever'), might dispense with information hazy and unprofitable as this!

(*m*) Again. At a period of prevailing unbelief in the
INSPIRATION of Scripture, nothing but real necessity could
warrant any meddling with such a testimony on the subject
as is found in 2 Tim. iii. 16. We have hitherto been taught
to believe that '*All Scripture is given by inspiration of GOD*
and is profitable,' &c. The ancients[1] clearly so understood
S. Paul's words: and so do the most learned and thoughtful
of the moderns. Πᾶσα γραφή, even if it be interpreted
'every Scripture,' can only mean every portion of those
ἱερὰ γράμματα of which the Apostle had been speaking in
the previous verse; and therefore must needs signify *the
whole of Scripture*.[2] So that the expression '*all Scripture*'

---

[1] Clemens Al. (p. 71) says:—τὰς γραφὰς ὁ Ἀπόστολος θεοπνεύστους
καλεῖ, ὠφελίμους οὔσας. Tertullian,—*Legimus omnem Scripturam
ædificationi habilem, divinitus inspirari.* Origen (ii. 443),—πᾶσα γραφὴ
θεόπνευστος οὖσα ὠφέλιμός ἐστι. Gregory Nyss. (ii. 605),—πᾶσα γραφὴ
θεόπνευστος λέγεται. Dial. (ap. Orig. i. 808),—πᾶσα γραφὴ θεόπνευστος
λέγεται παρὰ τοῦ Ἀποστόλου. So Basil, Chrysostom, Cyril, Theodoret, &c.

[2] See Archdeacon Lee *on Inspiration*, pp. 261-3, reading his notes.

expresses S. Paul's meaning exactly, and should not have been disturbed.

But—'It is very difficult' (so at least thinks the Right Rev. Chairman of the Revisers) 'to decide whether θεόπνευστος is a part of the predicate, καί being the simple copula; or whether it is a part of the subject. Lexicography and grammar contribute but little towards a decision.' Not so thought Bishop Middleton. 'I do not recollect' (he says) 'any passage in the N. T. in which two Adjectives, apparently connected by the copulative, were intended by the writer to be so unnaturally disjoined. He who can produce such an instance, will do much towards establishing the plausibility of a translation, which otherwise must appear, to say the least of it, to be forced and improbable.'— And yet it is proposed to thrust this 'forced and improbable' translation on the acceptance of all English-speaking people, wherever found, on the plea of *necessity!* Our Revisionists translate, 'Every Scripture inspired of GOD *is also profitable*,' &c.,— which of course may be plausibly declared to imply that a distinction is drawn by the Apostle himself between inspired and uninspired Scripture. And pray, (we should be presently asked,) is not many a Scripture (or writing) 'profitable for teaching,' &c. which is *not* commonly held to be 'inspired of GOD'? . . . But in fact the proposed rendering is inadmissible, being without logical coherence and consistency. The utmost that could be pretended would be that S. Paul's assertion is that 'every portion of Scripture *being inspired*' (i.e. inasmuch as it is—because it is—inspired); 'is *also* profitable,' &c. Else there would be no meaning in the καί. But, in the name of common sense, if this be so, *why* have the blessed words been meddled with?

(*n*) All are unhappily familiar with the avidity with which the disciples of a certain School fasten upon a myste-

rious expression in S. Mark's Gospel (xiii. 32), which *seems*
to predicate concerning the Eternal SON, limitation in respect
of Knowledge. This is not the place for vindicating the
Catholic Doctrine of the SON's 'equality with the FATHER as
touching His GoDhead;' or for explaining that, in consequence, all things that the FATHER hath, (*the knowledge of
'that Day and Hour' included,*) the SON hath likewise.[1] But
this *is* the place for calling attention to the deplorable
circumstance that the clause '*neither the* SON,' which has an
indisputable right to its place in S. Mark's Gospel, has on
insufficient authority by our Revisionists been thrust into
S. Matth. xxvi. 36, where it has no business whatever, and
from which the word 'only' effectually excludes it.[2] We
call attention to this circumstance with sincere sorrow : but
it is sorrow largely mixed with indignation. What else but
the betrayal of a sacred trust is it when Divines appointed
to correct manifest errors in *the English* of the N. T. go out
of their way to introduce an error like this into the *Greek*
Text which Catholic Antiquity would have repudiated with
indignation, and for which certainly the plea of 'necessity'
cannot be pretended ?

(*o*) A MARGINAL ANNOTATION set over against Romans ix. 5
is the last thing of this kind to which we shall invite attention. S. Paul declares it to be Israel's highest boast and
glory that of them, 'as concerning the flesh [came] CHRIST,

---

[1] S. John xvi. 15.

[2] Study by all means Basil's letter to Amphilochius, (vol. iii. p. 360 to
362.)—Ἔστιν οὖν ὁ νοῦς ὁ παρὰ τῷ Μάρκῳ τοιοῦτος · Περὶ δὲ τῆς ἡμέρας
ἐκείνης ἢ ὥρας, οὐδεὶς οἶδεν, οὔτε οἱ ἄγγελοι τοῦ Θεοῦ, ἀλλ' οὐδ' ἂν ὁ Υἱὸς
ἔγνω, εἰ μὴ ὁ Πατήρ · ἐκ γὰρ τοῦ Πατρὸς αὐτῷ ὑπῆρχε δεδομένη ἡ γνῶσις . . ·
τουτέστιν, ἡ αἰτία τοῦ εἰδέναι τὸν Υἱὸν παρὰ τοῦ Πατρός · καὶ ἀβίαστός ἐστι
τῷ εὐγνωμόνως ἀκούοντι ἡ ἐξήγησις αὕτη.   ἐπειδὴ οὐ πρόσκειται τὸ μόνος ·
ὡς καὶ παρὰ τῷ Ματθαίῳ.— (p. 362 c.)   Basil says of this interpretation—
ἃ τοίνυν ἐκ παιδὸς παρὰ τῶν πατέρων ἠκούσαμεν.

who is over all [things], GOD *blessed for ever !* Amen.' A grander or more unequivocal testimony to our LORD'S eternal GODhead is nowhere to be found in Scripture. Accordingly, these words have been as confidently appealed to by faithful Doctors of the Church in every age, as they have been unsparingly assailed by unbelievers. The dishonest shifts by which the latter seek to evacuate the record which they are powerless to refute or deny, are paraded by our ill-starred Revisionists in the following terms :—

'Some modern Interpreters place a full stop after *flesh,* and translate, *He who is God over all be* (*is*) *blessed for ever :* or, *He who is over all is God, blessed for ever.* Others punctuate, *flesh, who is over all. God be* (*is*) *blessed for ever.*'

Now this is a matter,—let it be clearly observed,—which, (as Dr. Hort is aware,) "belongs to *Interpretation,*—and *not to Textual Criticism.*" [1] What business then has it in these pages at all ? Is it then the function of Divines appointed *to revise the Authorized Version,* to give information to the 90 millions of English-speaking Christians scattered throughout the world as to the unfaithfulness of '*some modern Interpreters*' ? [2] We have hitherto supposed that it was '*Ancient* authorities' exclusively, — (whether 'a few,' or 'some,' or 'many,')—to which we are invited to submit our judgment. How does it come to pass that *the Socinian gloss* on this grand text (Rom. ix. 5) has been brought into such extraordinary prominence ? Did our Revisionists consider that their marginal note would travel to earth's remotest verge,—give universal currency to the view of 'some modern Interpreters,'—and in the end 'tell it out among the heathen' also ? We refer to Manuscripts,—Versions,—Fathers : and what do we find ? (1) It is demonstrable that *the oldest*

---

[1] *Notes,* p. 109.

[2] *Celebre effugium,* (as Dr. Routh calls it,) *quod ex falsâ verborum constructione Critici quidam hæreticis pararunt. Reliqq.* iii. 322–3.

Codices, besides the whole body of the ,cursives, know nothing
about the method of 'some modern Interpreters.'[1]— (2)
' There is absolutely not a shadow, *not a tittle of evidence, in
any of the ancient Versions,* to warrant what they do.'[2]—(3)
How then, about the old Fathers? for the sentiments of our
best modern Divines, as Pearson and Bull, we know by
heart.   We find that the expression '*who is over all* [things],
God blessed for ever' is expressly acknowledged to refer to
our SAVIOUR by the following 60 illustrious names:—

Irenæus,[3]—Hippolytus in 3 places,[4]—Origen,[5]—Malchion,
in the name of six of the Bishops at the Council of Antioch,
A.D. 269,[6]—ps.-Dionysius Alex., twice,[7]—the Constt. App.,[8]—
Athanasius in 6 places,[9] —Basil in 2 places,[10]— Didymus in
5 places,[11]—Greg. Nyssen. in 5 places,[12]—Epiphanius in 5
places,[13]—Theodorus Mops.,[14]—Methodius,[15]—Eustathius,[16]—
Eulogius, twice,[17]—Cæsarius, 3 times,[18]—Theophilus Alex.,
twice,[19] — Nestorius, [20]— Theodotus of Ancyra,[21] — Proclus,
twice,[22]—Severianus Bp. of Gabala,[23]—Chrysostom, 8 times,[24]

---

[1] c alone has a point between ὁ ὢν ἐπὶ πάντων and Θεὸς εὐλογητὸς εἰς
τοὺς αἰῶνας.   But this is an entirely different thing from what is noted in
the margin.   [2] MS. communication from the Rev. S. C. Malan.
[3] i. 506.   [4] *Opusc.* i. 52, 58; *Phil.* 339.   [5] iv. 612.
[6] Routh, *Reliqq. Sac.* iii. 292, and 287.   (*Concil.* i. 845 b. c.)
[7] *Concilia,* i. 873 d: 876 a.   [8] vi. c. 26.
[9] i. 414, 415, 429, 617, 684, 908.   [10] i. 282.   And *in Cat.* 317.
[11] *Trin.* 21, 29, 327, 392.   Mai, vii. 303.
[12] ii. 596 a, (quoted by the Emp. Justinian [*Concil.* v. 697] and the
Chronicon Paschale, 355), 693, 697; iii. 287.   Galland. vi. 575.
[13] i. 481, 487, 894, 978; ii. 74.   [14] Ap. Cyril (ed. Pusey), v. 534.
[15] Ap. Gall. iii. 805.   [16] Ap. Gall. iv. 576.
[17] Ap. Phot. col. 761, 853.   [18] Ap. Gall. vi. 8, 9, 80.
[19] Ap. Gall. vii. 618, and ap. Hieron. i. 560.
[20] *Concilia,* iii. 522 e (= iv. 297 d = ap. Gall. viii. 667).   Also, *Concilia* (Harduin), i. 1413 a.   [21] Ap. Gall. ix. 474.
[22] Ap. Gall. ix. 690, 691 (= *Concil.* iii. 1230, 1231).
[23] *Homilia (Arm.),* p. 165 and 249.
[24] i. 464, 483; vi. 534; vii. 51; viii. 191; ix. 604, 653; x. 172.

—Cyril Alex., 15 times,[1]—Paulus Bp. of Emesa,[2]—Theodoret, 12 times,[3]—Gennadius, Abp. of C. P.,[4]—Severus, Abp. of Antioch,[5] — Amphilochius,[6] — Gelasius Cyz.,[7] — Anastasius Ant.,[8] — Leontius Byz., 3 times,[9]— Maximus,[10] — J. Damascene, 3 times.[11] Besides of the Latins, Tertullian, twice,[12]— Cyprian,[13]—Novatian, twice,[14]—Ambrose, 5 times,[15]—Palladius the Arian at the Council of Aquileia,[16]—Hilary, 7 times,[17]—Jerome, twice,[18]—Augustine, about 30 times,— Victorinus,[19]—the *Breviarium*, twice,[20]—Marius Mercator,[21] —Cassian, twice,[22]—Alcimus Avit.,[23]—Fulgentius, twice,[24]— Leo, Bp. of Rome, twice,[25]—Ferrandus, twice,[26]—Facundus : [27] —to whom must be added 6 ancient writers, of whom 3 [28] have been mistaken for Athanasius,—and 3 [29] for Chrysostom. All these see in Rom. ix. 5, a glorious assertion of the eternal GODhead of CHRIST.

Against such an overwhelming torrent of Patristic testimony,—for we have enumerated *upwards of sixty* ancient Fathers—it will not surely be pretended that the Socinian interpretation, to which our Revisionists give such promi-

---

[1] v.[1] 20, 503, 765, 792 ; v.[2] 58, 105, 118, 148; vi. 328. Ap. Mai, ii. 70, 86, 96, 104 ; iii. 84 *in Luc.* 26.

[2] *Concilia*, iii. 1099 b.

[3] i. 103; ii. 1355; iii. 215, 470; iv. 17, 433, 1148, 1264, 1295, 1309 ; v. 67, 1093.   [4] Cramer's *Cat.* 160.   [5] *Ibid. in Act.* 40.

[6] P. 166.   [7] *Concilia*, ii. 195.   [8] Ap. Gall. xii. 251.

[9] Ap. Gall. xii. 682.   [10] ii. 64.   [11] i. 557 ; ii. 35, 88.

[12] Prax. 13, 15—'Christum autem et ipse Deum cognominavit, *Quorum patres, et ex quibus Christus secundum carnem, qui est super omnia Deus benedictus in ævum.'*   [13] P. 287.   [14] Ap. Gall. iii. 296, 313.

[15] i. 1470; ii. 457, 546, 609, 790.   [16] *Concilia*, ii. 982 c.

[17] 78, 155, 393, 850, 970, 1125, 1232.   [18] i. 870, 872.

[19] Ap. Gall. viii. 157.   [20] Ap. Gall. vii. 589, 590.

[21] Ap. Gall. viii. 627.   [22] 709, 711.   [23] Ap. Gall. x. 722.

[24] Ap. Gall. xi. 233, 237.   [25] *Concilia*, iii. 1364, 1382.

[26] Ap. Gall. 352, 357.   [27] *Ibid.* 674.

[28] ii. 16, 215, 413.   [29] i. 839; v. 769; xii. 421.

nence, can stand. But why has it been introduced *at all* ? We shall have every Christian reader with us in our contention, that such perverse imaginations of ' modern Interpreters' are not entitled to a place in the margin of the N. T. For our Revisionists to have even given them currency, and thereby a species of sanction, constitutes in our view a very grave offence.[1] A public retractation and a very humble Apology we claim at their hands. Indifferent Scholarship, and mistaken views of Textual Criticism, are at least venial matters. But *a Socinian gloss gratuitously thrust into the margin of every Englishman's N. T.* admits of no excuse—is not to be tolerated on *any* terms. It would by itself, in our account, have been sufficient to determine the fate of the present Revision.

XII. Are we to regard it as a kind of *set-off* against all that goes before, that in an age when the personality of Satan is freely called in question, ' THE EVIL ONE' has been actually *thrust into the Lord's Prayer* ? A more injudicious and unwarrantable innovation it would be impossible to indicate in any part of the present unhappy volume. The case has been argued out with much learning and ability by two eminent Divines, Bp. Lightfoot and Canon Cook. The Canon remains master of the field. That *the change ought never to have been made* is demonstrable. The grounds of this assertion are soon stated. To begin, (1) It is admitted on all hands that it must for ever remain a matter of opinion only whether in the expression ἀπὸ τοῦ πονηροῦ, the nominative case is τὸ πονηρόν (as in S. Matth. v. 37, 39: Rom. xii. 9), or ὁ πονηρός (as in S. Matth. xiii. 19, 38: Eph. vi.

---

[1] Those of our readers who wish to pursue this subject further may consult with advantage Dr. Gifford's learned note on the passage in the *Speaker's Commentary*. Dr. Gifford justly remarks that ' it is the natural and simple construction, which every Greek scholar would adopt without hesitation, if no question of doctrine were involved.'

16),—either of which yields a good sense. But then—(2)
The Church of England in her formularies having emphatically declared that, for her part, she adheres to the former
alternative, it was in a very high degree unbecoming for the
Revisionists to pretend to the enjoyment of *certain* knowledge that the Church of England in so doing was mistaken :
and unless ' from evil ' be " *a clear and plain error*," the Revisionists were bound to let it alone. Next—(3), It can
never be right to impose the narrower interpretation on
words which have always been understood to bear the larger
sense : especially when (as in the present instance) the
larger meaning distinctly includes and covers the lesser :
witness the paraphrase in our Church Catechism,—' and that
He will keep us (*a*) from all sin and wickedness, and (*b*)
from our ghostly enemy, and (*c*) from everlasting death.'—(4)
But indeed Catholic Tradition claims to be heard in this
behalf. Every Christian at his Baptism renounces not only
' the Devil,' but also ' *all his works*, the vain pomp and glory
of the world, with all covetous desires of the same, and the
carnal desires of the flesh.' [1]   And at this point—(5), The
voice of an inspired Apostle interposes in attestation that
this is indeed the true acceptation of the last petition in the
LORD's Prayer : for when S. Paul says—' the LORD will
deliver me *from every evil work* and will preserve me unto
His heavenly kingdom ; to whom be glory for ever and ever.
Amen,' [2]—what else is he referring to but to the words just

---

[1] Note, that this has been the language of the Church from the
beginning. Thus Tertullian,—'Aquam adituri . . . contestamur nos re-
nuntiare diabolo, *et pompæ et angelis ejus* ' (i. 421) : and Ambrose,—
' Quando te interrogavit, Abrenuntias diabolo *et operibus ejus*, quid respondisti ? Abrenuntio. Abrenuntias *sæculo et voluptatibus ejus*, quid
respondisti ? Abrenuntio ' (ii. 350 c) : and Ephraem Syrus,—'Ἀποτάσσομαι
τῷ Σατανᾷ καὶ πᾶσιν τοῖς ἔργοις αὐτοῦ (ii. 195 and iii. 399). And Cæsarius
of Arles,—' Abrenuntias diabolo, *pompis et operibus ejus* . . . Abrenuntio '
(Galland. xi. 18 e).   [2] 2 Tim. iv. 18.

now under consideration ? He explains that in the LORD'S
Prayer it is '*from every evil work*' that we pray to be
'delivered.' (Note also, that he retains *the Doxology*.) Compare the places :—

S. Matth. vi. 13.—ἀλλὰ ῥῦσαι ἡμᾶς ἀπὸ τοῦ πονηροῦ. ὅτι
σοῦ ἐστιν ἡ βασιλεία . . . καὶ ἡ δόξα εἰς τοὺς αἰῶνας. ἀμήν.

2 Tim. iv. 18.—καὶ ῥύσεταί με ὁ Κύριος ἀπὸ παντὸς ἔργου
πονηροῦ· καὶ σώσει εἰς τὴν βασιλείαν αὐτοῦ· . . . . ᾧ ἡ δόξα εἰς
τοὺς αἰῶνας . . . . ἀμήν.

Then further—(6), What more unlikely than that our
LORD would end with giving such prominence to that rebel
Angel whom by dying He is declared to have 'destroyed'?
(Heb. ii. 14 : 1 John iii. 8.) For, take away the Doxology
(as our Revisionists propose), and we shall begin the LORD'S
Prayer with 'OUR FATHER,' and literally end it with—*the
Devil !*—But above all,—(7) Let it never be forgotten that
this is *the pattern Prayer*, a portion of every Christian
child's daily utterance,—the most sacred of all our formularies, and by far the most often repeated,—into which it is
attempted in this way to introduce a startling novelty.
Lastly—(8), When it is called to mind that nothing short of
necessity has warranted the Revisionists in introducing a
single change into the A. V.,—"*clear and plain errors*"—and
that no such plea can be feigned on the present occasion, the
liberty which they have taken in this place must be admitted
to be absolutely without excuse. . . . Such at least are the
grounds on which, for our own part, we refuse to entertain
the proposed introduction of the Devil into the LORD'S
Prayer. From the position we have taken up, it will be
found utterly impossible to dislodge us.

XIII. It is often urged on behalf of the Revisionists
that over not a few dark places of S. Paul's Epistles their
labours have thrown important light. Let it not be supposed

that we deny this. Many a Scriptural difficulty vanishes
the instant a place is accurately translated : a far greater
number, when the rendering is idiomatic.   It would be
strange indeed if, at the end of ten years, the combined
labours of upwards of twenty Scholars, whose *raison d'être* as
Revisionists was to do this very thing, had not resulted in
the removal of many an obscurity in the A. V. of Gospels
and Epistles alike.   What offends us is the discovery that,
for every obscurity which has been removed, at least half a
dozen others have been introduced : in other words, that the
result of this Revision has been the planting in of a *fresh
crop of difficulties*, before undreamed of ; so that a perpetual
wrestling with *these* is what hereafter awaits the diligent
student of the New Testament.

We speak not now of passages which have been merely
altered for the worse : as when, (in S. James i. 17, 18,) we
are invited to read,—'Every good gift and every *perfect boon*
is from above, coming down from the Father of lights, with
whom *can be no variation*, neither *shadow that is cast by
turning*.   Of his own will *he brought us forth*.'   Grievous as
such blemishes are, it is seen at a glance that they must be
set down to nothing worse than tasteless assiduity.   What we
complain of is that, misled by a depraved Text, our Revisers
have often made nonsense of what before was perfectly clear :
and have not only thrust many of our LORD'S precious utterances out of sight, (e.g. Matt. xvii. 21 : Mark x. 21 and xi. 26 :
Luke ix. 55, 56) ; but have attributed to Him absurd sayings
which He certainly never uttered, (e.g. Matt. xix. 17) ; or else,
given such a twist to what He actually said, that His
blessed words are no longer recognizable, (as in S. Matt. xi. 23 :
S. Mark ix. 23 : xi. 3).   Take a sample :—

(1.) The Church has always understood her LORD to say,
—'FATHER, I will that they also, whom Thou hast given Me,

be with Me where I am; that they may behold My glory.'[1]
We reject with downright indignation the proposal henceforth to read instead,—' *Father, that which Thou hast given
Me I will that, where I am, they also may be with Me,*' &c.
We suspect a misprint. The passage reads like nonsense.
Yes, and nonsense it is,—in Greek as well as in English:
(ὅ has been written for οὕς—one of the countless *bétises* for
which ℵ B D are exclusively responsible; and which the
weak superstition of these last days is for erecting into a
new Revelation). We appeal to the old Latin and to the
Vulgate, — to the better Egyptian and to all the Syriac
versions: to *every known Lectionary*: to Clemens Alex.,[2]—
to Eusebius,[3]—to Nonnus,[4]—to Basil,[5]—to Chrysostom,[6]—to
Cyril,[7]—to Cælestinus,[8]—to Theodoret:[9] not to mention
Cyprian,[10]—Ambrose,[11]—Hilary,[12] &c.:[13] and above all, 16
uncials, beginning with A and C,—and the whole body of
the cursives. So many words ought not to be required. If
men prefer *their* 'mumpsimus' to *our* 'sumpsimus,' let them
by all means have it: but pray let them keep their rubbish to
themselves,—and at least leave our Saviour's words alone.

(2.) We shall be told that the foregoing is an outrageous
instance. It is. Then take a few milder cases. They abound,
turn whichever way we will. Thus, we are invited to believe
that S. Luke relates concerning our Saviour that He '*was
led by the Spirit in the wilderness during forty days*' (iv. 1).
We stare at this new revelation, and refer to the familiar
Greek. It proves to be the Greek of *all the copies in the*

---

[1] S. John xvii. 24.   [2] P. 140.   [3] Marcell. p. 192.
[4] *In loc. diserte.*   [5] *Eth.* ii. 297.   [6] viii. 485.
[7] *Text,* iv. 1003; *Comm.* 1007, which are *two distinct authorities,* as
learned readers of Cyril are aware.   [8] *Concilia,* iii. 356 d.
[9] iv. 450.   [10] Pp. 235, 321.   [11] i. 412; ii. 566, 649.
[12] Pp. 1017, 1033.
[13] Victricius ap. Gall. viii. 230. Also ps.-Chrys. v. 680.

world but four; the Greek which supplied the Latin, the
Syrian, the Coptic Churches, with the text of their respective Versions ; the Greek which was familiar to
Origen,[1] — to Eusebius,[2] — to Basil,[3] — to Didymus, [4] — to
Theodoret,[5] — to Maximus,[6] — and to two other ancient
writers, one of whom has been mistaken for Chrysostom,[7] the
other for Basil.[8]   It is therefore quite above suspicion.   And
it informs us that JESUS 'was led by the Spirit *into the
wilderness;'* and there was *'forty days tempted of the Devil.'*
What then has happened to obscure so plain a statement ?
Nothing more serious than that—(1) Four copies of bad
character (א B D L) exhibit 'in' instead of 'into:' and that
—(2) Our Revisionists have been persuaded to believe that
therefore S. Luke must needs have done the same.   Accordingly they invite us to share their conviction that it was the
leading about of our LORD, (and not His *Temptation*,) which
lasted for 40 days.   And this sorry misconception is to be
thrust upon the 90 millions of English-speaking Christians
throughout the world,—under the plea of 'necessity'! . . . .
But let us turn to a more interesting specimen of the mischievous consequences which would ensue from the acceptance
of the present so-called 'Revision.'

(3.) What is to be thought of *this*, as a substitute for the
familiar language of 2 Cor. xii. 7 ?—*'And by reason of the
exceeding greatness of the revelations—wherefore, that I should
not be exalted overmuch*, there was given to me a thorn in the
flesh.'   The word 'wherefore' (διό), which occasions all the
difficulty—(breaking the back of the sentence and neces-
sitating the hypothesis of a change of construction)—is due
solely to the influence of א A B.   The ordinary Text is recog-

---

[1] iii. 966 *dis.*   [2] *Dem.* 92.   [3] i. 319.   [4] *Trin.* 190.
[5] v. 1039, 1069.   [6] ii. 460.   [7] v. 615.
[8] ii. 584.   Cyril read the place both ways:—v.[2] 156, and *in Luc.* p. 52.

nized by almost every other copy; by the Latin,—Syriac,—
Gothic,—Armenian Versions;—as well as by Irenæus,[1]—
Origen,[2]— Macarius,[3] — Athanasius,[4] — Chrysostom,[5]—Theodoret,[6]—John Damascene.[7] Even Tischendorf here makes
a stand and refuses to follow his accustomed guides.[8] In
plain terms, the text of 2 Cor. xii. 7 is beyond the reach of
suspicion. Scarcely intelligible is the infatuation of which
our Revisers have been the dupes.—*Quousque tandem ?*

(4.) Now this is the method of the Revising body throughout : viz. so seriously to maim the Text of many a familiar
passage of Holy Writ as effectually to mar it. Even where
they remedy an inaccuracy in the rendering of the A. V.,
they often inflict a more grievous injury than mistranslation
on the inspired Text. An instance occurs at S. John x. 14,
where the good Shepherd says,—'I know Mine own *and am
known of Mine,* even as the FATHER knoweth Me and I know
the Father.' By thrusting in here the Manichæan depravation ('*and Mine own know Me*'), our Revisionists have
obliterated the exquisite diversity of expression in the
original,—which implies that whereas the knowledge which
subsists between the FATHER and the SON is identical on
either side, not such is the knowledge which subsists between
the creature and the Creator. The refinement in question
has been faithfully retained all down the ages by every copy
in existence except four of bad character,—א B D L. It is
witnessed to by the Syriac,—by Macarius,[9]—Gregory Naz.,[10]
— Chrysostom,[11]—Cyril Alex.,[12]—Theodoret,[13]—Maximus.[14]

---

[1] i. 720.   [2] ii. 381 ; iii. 962 ; iv. 601.   [3] Ap. Galland. vii. 183.
[4] Ap. Montf. ii. 67.   [5] iii. 333 ; v. 444 ; x. 498, 620 ; xii. 329.
[6] ii. 77 ; iii. 349.   [7] ii. 252.
[8] 'Deseruimus fere quos sequi solemus codices.'
[9] P. 38 (= Gall. vii. 26).   [10] i. 298, 613.
[11] viii. 351, 352.   [12] iv. 652 c, 653 a, 654 d.
[13] i. 748 ; iv. 274, 550.   [14] *In Dionys. Ar.* ii. 192.

But why go on ? Does any one in his sober senses suppose
that if S. John had written '*Mine own know Me,*' 996 manuscripts out of 1000, at the end of 1800 years, would be found
to exhibit '*I am known of Mine* '?

(5.) The foregoing instances must suffice. A brief enumeration of many more has been given already, at pp. 144(*b*)–
152.

Now, in view of the phenomenon just discovered to us,
—(viz. for one crop of deformities weeded out, an infinitely
larger crop of far grosser deformities as industriously
planted in,)—we confess to a feeling of distress and annoyance which altogether indisposes us to accord to the
Revisionists that language of congratulation with which it
would have been so agreeable to receive their well-meant
endeavours. The serious question at once arises,—Is it to
be thought that upon the whole we are gainers, or losers, by
the Revised Version ? And there seems to be no certain
way of resolving this doubt, but by opening a 'Profit and
Loss account' with the Revisers,—crediting them with every
item of *gain*, and debiting them with every item of *loss*.
But then,—(and we ask the question with sanguine simplicity,)—Why should it not be *all* gain and *no* loss, when,
at the end of 270 years, a confessedly noble work, a truly
unique specimen of genius, taste and learning, is submitted
to a body of Scholars, equipped with every external advantage, *only* in order that they may improve upon it—*if they
are able ?* These learned individuals have had upwards of
ten years wherein to do their work. They have enjoyed the
benefit of the tentative labours of a host of predecessors,—
some for their warning, some for their help and guidance.
They have all along had before their eyes the solemn injunction that, whatever they were not able *certainly* to
improve, they were to be *supremely careful to let alone.*

They were warned at the outset against any but '*necessary*' changes. Their sole business was to remove '*plain and clear errors.*' They had pledged themselves to introduce '*as few alterations as possible.*' Why then, we again ask,—*Why* should not every single innovation which they introduced into the grand old exemplar before them, prove to be a manifest, an undeniable change for the better?[1]

XIV. The more we ponder over this unfortunate production, the more cordially do we regret that it was ever undertaken. Verily, the Northern Convocation displayed a far-sighted wisdom when it pronounced against the project from the first. We are constrained to declare that could we have conceived it possible that the persons originally appointed by the Southern Province would have co-opted into their body persons capable of executing their work with such extravagant licentiousness as well as such conspicuous bad taste, we should never have entertained one hopeful thought on the subject. For indeed every characteristic feature of the work of the Revisionists offends us,—as well

---

[1] As these sheets are passing through the press, we have received a book by Sir Edmund Beckett, entitled, *Should the Revised New Testament be Authorized?* In four Chapters, the author discusses with characteristic vigour, first, the principles and method of the Revisers, and then the Gospel of S. Matthew, the Epistle to the Hebrews, and the Apocalypse, as fair samples of their work, with a union of sound sense, forensic skill, and scholarship more skilful than to deserve his cautious disclaimer. Amidst details open, of course, to discussion, abundant proofs are set forth, in a most telling style, that the plea of 'necessity' and 'faithfulness' utterly fails, in justification of a mass of alterations, which, in point of English composition, carry their condemnation on their face, and, to sum up the great distinction between the two Versions, illustrate 'the difference between working by *discretion* and by *rules*—by which no great thing was ever done or ever will be.' Sir Edmund Beckett is very happy in his exposure of the abuse of the famous canon of preferring the stranger reading to the more obvious, as if copyists never made stupid blunders or perpetrated wilful absurdities. The work deserves the notice of all English readers.

in respect of what they have left undone, as of what they have been the first to venture to do:—

(*a*) Charged ' to introduce *as few* alterations as possible into the Text of the Authorized Version,' they have on the contrary evidently acted throughout on the principle of making *as many* changes in it as they conveniently could.

(*b*) Directed ' to limit, *as far as possible*, the expression of such alterations to the language of the Authorized and earlier English Versions,'—they have introduced such terms as ' assassin,' ' apparition,' ' boon,' ' disparagement,' ' divinity,' ' effulgence,' ' epileptic,' ' fickleness,' ' gratulation,' ' irksome,' ' interpose,' ' pitiable,' ' sluggish,' ' stupor,' ' surpass,' ' tranquil :' such compounds as ' self-control,' ' world-ruler :' such phrases as '*draw up* a narrative :' ' *the impulse* of the steersman :' ' *in lack* of daily food :' ' *exercising* oversight.' These are but a very few samples of the offence committed by our Revisionists, of which we complain.

(*c*) Whereas they were required ' to *revise* the Headings of the Chapters,' they have not even *retained* them. We demand at least to have our excellent ' Headings ' back.

(*d*) And what has become of our time-honoured ' Marginal References,'—*the very best Commentary* on the Bible, as we believe,—certainly the very best help for the right understanding of Scripture,—which the wit of man hath ever yet devised ? The ' Marginal References ' would be lost to the Church for ever, if the work of the Revisionists were allowed to stand: the space required for their insertion having been completely swallowed up by the senseless, and worse than senseless, Textual Annotations which at present infest the margin of every sacred page. We are beyond measure amazed that the Revisionists have even deprived the reader of the *essential aid* of references to the places of the Old Testament which are quoted in the New.

(*e*) Let the remark be added in passing, that we greatly

dislike the affectation of printing certain quotations from the Old Testament after the strange method adopted by our Revisers from Drs. Westcott and Hort.

(*f*) The further external *assimilation of the Sacred Volume to an ordinary book* by getting rid of the division into Verses, we also hold to be a great mistake. In the Greek, by all means let the verses be merely noted in the margin : but, for more than one weighty reason, in the *English* Bible let the established and peculiar method of printing the Word of GOD, tide what tide, be scrupulously retained.

(*g*) But incomparably the gravest offence is behind. By far the most serious of all is *that* Error to the consideration of which we devoted our former Article. THE NEW GREEK TEXT which, in defiance of their Instructions,[1] our Revisionists have constructed, has been proved to be utterly undeserving of confidence. Built up on a fallacy which since

---

[1] It has been objected by certain of the Revisionists that it is not fair to say that 'they were appointed to do one thing, and have done another.' We are glad of this opportunity to explain.

That *some* corrections of the Text were necessary, we are well aware : and had those *necessary* changes been made, we should only have had words of commendation and thanks to offer. But it is found that by Dr. Hort's eager advocacy two-thirds of the Revisionists have made a vast number of *perfectly needless changes* :—(1) Changes which *are incapable of being represented in a Translation* : as ἐμοῦ for μου,—πάντες for ἅπαντες,—ὅτε for ὁπότε. Again, since γέννησις, at least as much as γένεσις, means ' birth,' why γένεσις in S. Matth. i. 18 ? Why, also, inform us that instead of ἐν τῷ ἀμπελῶνι αὐτοῦ πεφυτευμένην, they prefer πεφυτευμένην ἐν τῷ ἀμπελῶνι αὐτοῦ? and instead of καρπὸν ζητῶν,—ζητῶν καρπόν? Now this they have done *throughout*,—at least 341 times in S. Luke alone. But (what is far worse), (2) They suggest in the margin changes which yet they *do not adopt*. These numerous changes are, *by their own confession*, not ' necessary :' and yet they are of a most serious character. In fact, it is of these we chiefly complain.—But, indeed (3), *How many* of their *other* alterations of the Text will the Revisionists undertake to defend publicly on the plea of ' *Necessity* ' ?

[A vast deal more will be found on this subject towards the close of the present volume. In the meantime, see above, pages 87–88.]

1831 has been dominant in Germany, and which has lately found but too much favour among ourselves, it is in the main a reproduction of the recent labours of Doctors Westcott and Hort. But we have already recorded our conviction, that the results at which those eminent Scholars have arrived are wholly inadmissible. It follows that, in our account, the 'New English Version,' has been all along a foredoomed thing. If the 'New Greek Text' be indeed a tissue of fabricated Readings, the translation of these into English must needs prove lost labour. It is superfluous to enquire into the merits of the English rendering of words which Evangelists and Apostles demonstrably never wrote.

(*h*) Even this, however, is not nearly all. As Translators, full two-thirds of the Revisionists have shown themselves singularly deficient,—alike in their critical acquaintance with the language out of which they had to translate, and in their familiarity with the idiomatic requirements of their own tongue. They had a noble Version before them, which they have contrived to spoil in every part. Its dignified simplicity and essential faithfulness, its manly grace and its delightful rhythm, they have shown themselves alike unable to imitate and unwilling to retain. Their queer uncouth phraseology and their jerky sentences :—their pedantic obscurity and their stiff, constrained manner :— their fidgetty affectation of accuracy,—and their habitual achievement of English which fails to exhibit the spirit of the original Greek ;—are sorry substitutes for the living freshness, and elastic freedom, and habitual fidelity of the grand old Version which we inherited from our Fathers, and which has sustained the spiritual life of the Church of England, and of all English-speaking Christians, for 350 years. Linked with all our holiest, happiest memories, and bound up with all our purest aspirations : part and parcel of

Q

whatever there is of good about us : fraught with men's hopes of a blessed Eternity and many a bright vision of the never-ending Life;—the Authorized Version, wherever it was possible, *should have been jealously retained.* But on the contrary. Every familiar cadence has been dislocated : the congenial flow of almost every verse of Scripture has been hopelessly marred : so many of those little connecting words, which give life and continuity to a narrative, have been vexatiously displaced, that a perpetual sense of annoyance is created. The countless minute alterations which have been needlessly introduced into every familiar page prove at last as tormenting as a swarm of flies to the weary traveller on a summer's day.[1] To speak plainly, the book has been made *unreadable.*

But in fact the distinguished Chairman of the New Testament Company (Bishop Ellicott,) has delivered himself on this subject in language which leaves nothing to be desired, and which we willingly make our own. "No Revision " (he says) "in the present day *could hope to meet with an hour's acceptance* if it failed to preserve the tone, rhythm, and diction of the present Authorized Version."[2]—What else is this but a vaticination,—of which the uninspired Author, by his own act and deed, has ensured the punctual fulfilment ?

We lay the Revisers' volume down convinced that the case of their work is simply hopeless. *Non ego paucis offendar maculis.* Had the blemishes been capable of being reckoned up, it might have been worth while to try to remedy some of them. But when, instead of being disfigured

---

[1] " We meet in every page " (says Dr. Wordsworth, the learned Bishop of Lincoln,) " with small changes which are vexatious, teasing, and irritating ; even the more so because they are small (as small insects sting most sharply), *which seem almost to be made merely for the sake of change.*"—p. 25.

[2] *On the Revision of the English Version,* &c. (1870), p. 99.

by a few weeds scattered here and there, the whole field
proves to be sown over in every direction with thorns and
briars ; above all when, deep beneath the surface, roots of
bitterness to be counted by thousands, are found to have
been silently planted in, which are sure to produce poisonous
fruit after many days :—under *such* circumstances only one
course can be prescribed.   Let the entire area be ploughed
up,—ploughed deep ; and let the ground be left for a decent
space of time without cultivation.   It is idle—worse than
idle—to dream of revising, *with a view to retaining*, this
Revision.   Another generation of students must be suffered
to arise.   Time must be given for Passion and Prejudice
to cool effectually down.   Partizanship, (which at present
prevails to an extraordinary extent, but which is wondrously
out of place in *this* department of Sacred Learning,)—
Partizanship must be completely outlived, — before the
Church can venture, with the remotest prospect of a successful issue, to organize another attempt at revising the
Authorized Version of the New Testament Scriptures.

Yes, and in the meantime—(let it in all faithfulness be
added)—the Science of Textual Criticism will have to be
prosecuted, *for the first time*, in a scholarlike manner.   Fundamental Principles, — sufficiently axiomatic to ensure
general acceptance,—will have to be laid down for men's
guidance.   The time has quite gone by for vaunting ' *the
now established Principles of Textual Criticism*,'[1]—as if they
had an actual existence.   Let us be shown, instead, *which
those Principles be*.   As for the weak superstition of these
last days, which—*without proof of any kind*—would erect two
IVth-century Copies of the New Testament, (demonstrably
derived from one and the same utterly depraved archetype,)

---

[1] Bp. Ellicott, *Diocesan Progress*, Jan. 1882,—p. 19.

into an authority from which there shall be no appeal,—it cannot be too soon or too unconditionally abandoned. And, perhaps beyond all things, men must be invited to disabuse their minds of the singular imagination that it is in their power, when addressing themselves to that most difficult and delicate of problems,—*the improvement of the Traditional Text*,—' solvere ambulando.'[1]   They are assured that they may not take to Textual Criticism as ducks take to the water. They will be drowned inevitably if they are so ill-advised as to make the attempt.

Then further, those who would interpret the New Testament Scriptures, are reminded that a thorough acquaintance with the Septuagintal Version of the Old Testament is one indispensable condition of success.[2]   And finally, the Revisionists of the future (if they desire that their labours should be crowned), will find it their wisdom to practise a severe self-denial ; to confine themselves to the correction of *"plain and clear errors;"* and in fact to "introduce into the Text *as few alterations as possible.*"

On a review of all that has happened, from first to last, we can but feel greatly concerned : greatly surprised : most of all, disappointed. We had expected a vastly different result. It is partly (not quite) accounted for, by the rare attendance in the Jerusalem Chamber of some of the names on which we had chiefly relied.   Bishop Moberly (of Salisbury) was

---

[1] Bp. Ellicott, *On Revision,*—p. 49.

[2] ' *Qui* LXX *interpretes non legit, aut minus legit accurate, is sciat se non adeo idoneum, qui Scripta Evangelica Apostolica de Græco in Latinum, aut alium aliquem sermonem transferat, ut ut in aliis Græcis scriptoribus multum diuque fuerit versatus.*' (John Bois, 1619.)—' *Græcum N. T. contextum rite intellecturo nihil est utilius quam diligenter versasse Alexandrinàm antiqui Fœderis interpretationem,* E QUÀ UNÂ PLUS PETI POTERIT AUXILII, QUAM EX VETERIBUS SCRIPTORIBUS GRÆCIS SIMUL SUMTIS. *Centena reperientur in N. T. nusquam obvia in scriptis Græcorum veterum, sed frequentata in Alexandrinâ versione.*' (Valcknaer, 1715–85.)

present on only 121 occasions: Bishop Wordsworth (of S. Andrews) on only 109 : Archbishop Trench (of Dublin) on only 63 : Bishop Wilberforce on only *one*. The Archbishop, in his Charge, adverts to ' the not unfrequent sacrifice of grace and ease to the rigorous requirements of a literal accuracy ; ' and regards them ' as pushed to a faulty excess ' (p. 22).   Eleven years before the scheme for the present ' Revision ' had been matured, the same distinguished and judicious Prelate, (then Dean of Westminster,) persuaded as he was that a Revision *ought* to come, and convinced that in time it *would* come, deprecated its being attempted *yet*.   His words were,—" Not however, I would trust, as yet : for we are not as yet *in any respect prepared for it. The Greek, and the English* which should enable us to bring this to a successful end might, it is to be feared, be wanting alike." [1]   Archbishop Trench, with wise after-thought, in a second edition, explained himself to mean " *that special Hellenistic Greek, here required.*"

The Bp. of S. Andrews has long since, in the fullest manner, cleared himself from the suspicion of complicity in the errors of the work before us,—as well in respect of the ' New Greek Text ' as of the ' New English Version.'   In the Charge which he delivered at his Diocesan Synod, (22nd Sept. 1880,) he openly stated that two years before the work was finally completed, he had felt obliged to address a printed circular to each member of the Company, in which he strongly remonstrated against the excess to which changes had been carried ; and that the remonstrance had been, for the most part, unheeded.   Had this been otherwise, there is good reason to believe that the reception which the Revision has met with would have been far less unfavour-able, and that many a controversy which it has stirred up, would have been avoided.   We have been assured that the

---

[1] *On the Authorized Version,*—p. 3.

Bp. of S. Andrews would have actually resigned his place in the Company at that time, if he had not been led to expect that some opportunity would have been taken by the Minority, when the work was finished, to express their formal dissent from the course which had been followed, and many of the conclusions which had been adopted.

Were certain other excellent personages, (Scholars and Divines of the best type) who were often present, disposed at this late hour to come forward, they too would doubtless tell us that they heartily regretted what was done, but were powerless to prevent it. It is no secret that Dr. Lee,— the learned Archdeacon of Dublin,—(one of the few really competent members of the Revising body,)—found himself perpetually in the minority.

The same is to be recorded concerning Dr. Roberts, whose work on the Gospels (published in 1864) shows that he is not by any means so entirely a novice in the mysteries of Textual Criticism as certain of his colleagues.—One famous Scholar and excellent Divine,—a Dean whom we forbear to name,—with the modesty of real learning, often withheld what (had he given it) would have been an adverse vote.— Another learned and accomplished Dean (Dr. Merivale), after attending 19 meetings of the Revising body, withdrew in disgust from them entirely. He disapproved *the method* of his colleagues, and was determined to incur no share of responsibility for the probable result of their deliberations.— By the way,—What about a certain solemn Protest, by means of which the Minority had resolved *liberare animas suas* concerning the open disregard shown by the Majority for the conditions under which they had been entrusted with the work of Revision, but which was withheld at the last moment? Inasmuch as their reasons for the course they eventually adopted seemed sufficient to those high-minded and honourable men, we forbear to challenge it. Nothing however shall deter us from plainly avowing our own opinion that human regards scarcely deserve a hearing when GOD'S Truth is imperilled. And that the Truth of GOD'S Word in countless instances *has been* ignorantly sacrificed by a majority of the Revisionists—(out of deference to a worthless Theory, newly invented and passionately advocated by two of their body),—has been already demonstrated; as far, that is, as demonstration is *possible* in this subject matter.

As for Prebendary Scrivener,—*the only really competent Textual Critic of the whole party,*—it is well known that he found himself perpetually outvoted by two-thirds of those present. We look forward to the forthcoming new edition of his *Plain Introduction,* in the confident belief that he will there make it abundantly plain that he is in no degree responsible for the monstrous Text which it became his painful duty to conduct through the Press on behalf of the entire body, of which he continued to the last to be a member. It is no secret that, throughout, Dr. Scrivener pleaded in vain for the general view we have ourselves advocated in this and the preceding Article.

All alike may at least enjoy the real satisfaction of knowing that, besides having stimulated, to an extraordinary extent, public attention to the contents of the Book of Life, they have been instrumental in awakening a living interest in one important but neglected department of Sacred Science, which will not easily be again put to sleep. It may reasonably prove a solace to them to reflect that they have besides, although perhaps in ways they did not anticipate, rendered excellent service to mankind. A monument they have certainly erected to themselves,—though neither of their Taste nor yet of their Learning. Their well-meant endeavours have provided an admirable text-book for

Teachers of Divinity,—who will henceforth instruct their pupils to beware of the Textual errors of the Revisionists of 1881, as well as of their tasteless, injudicious, and unsatisfactory essays in Translation. This work of theirs will discharge the office of a warning beacon to as many as shall hereafter embark on the same perilous enterprise with themselves. It will convince men of the danger of pursuing the same ill-omened course: trusting to the same unskilful guidance: venturing too near the same wreck-strewn shore.

Its effect will be to open men's eyes, as nothing else could possibly have done, to the dangers which beset the Revision of Scripture. It will teach faithful hearts to cling the closer to the priceless treasure which was bequeathed to them by the piety and wisdom of their fathers. It will dispel for ever the dream of those who have secretly imagined that a more exact Version, undertaken with the boasted helps of this nineteenth century of ours, would bring to light something which has been hitherto unfairly kept concealed or else misrepresented. Not the least service which the Revisionists have rendered has been the proof their work affords, how very seldom our Authorized Version is materially wrong: how faithful and trustworthy, on the contrary, it is throughout. Let it be also candidly admitted that, even where (in our judgment) the Revisionists have erred, they have never had the misfortune *seriously* to obscure a single feature of Divine Truth; nor have they in any quarter (as we hope) inflicted wounds which will be attended with worse results than to leave a hideous scar behind them. It is but fair to add that their work bears marks of an amount of conscientious (though misdirected) labour, which those only can fully appreciate who have made the same province of study to some extent their own.

ARTICLE III.

WESTCOTT AND HORT'S NEW TEXTUAL THEORY.

" In the determination of disputed readings, these Critics avail themselves of so small a portion of existing materials, or allow so little weight
to others, that the Student who follows them has positively *less ground
for his convictions than former Scholars had at any period in the history
of modern Criticism.*"—CANON COOK, p. 16.

" We have no right, doubtless, to assume that our Principles are infallible : but we *have* a right to claim that any one who rejects them . . . .
should confute the Arguments and rebut the Evidence on which the
opposite conclusion has been founded. *Strong expressions of Individual
Opinion are not Arguments.*"—BP. ELLICOTT's Pamphlet, (1882,) p. 40.

Our " method involves vast research, unwearied patience . . . It will
therefore find but little favour with *those who adopt the easy method* . . . . .
*of using some favourite Manuscript, or some supposed power of divining
the Original Text.*"—BP. ELLICOTT, *Ibid.* p. 19.

" Non enim sumus sicut plurimi, adulterantes (καπηλεύοντες) verbum
DEI."—2 Cor. ii. 17.

REVISION REVISED.

ARTICLE III.—WESTCOTT AND HORT'S NEW TEXTUAL THEORY.

"Who is this that darkeneth counsel by words without knowledge?"
—Job xxxviii. 2.

"Can the blind lead the blind? shall they not both fall into the ditch?"—S. Luke vi. 39.

PROPOSING to ourselves (May 17th, 1881) to enquire into the merits of the recent Revision of the Authorized Version of the New Testament Scriptures, we speedily became aware that an entirely different problem awaited us and demanded preliminary investigation. We made the distressing discovery, that the underlying Greek Text had been completely re-fashioned throughout. It was accordingly not so much a 'Revised English Version' as a 'New Greek Text,' which was challenging public acceptance. Premature therefore,—not to say preposterous,—would have been any enquiry into the degree of ability with which the original Greek had been rendered into English by our Revisionists, until we had first satisfied ourselves that it was still 'the original Greek' with which we had to deal: or whether it had been the supreme infelicity of a body of Scholars claiming to act by the authority of the sacred Synod of Canterbury, to put themselves into the hands of some ingenious theory-monger, and to become the dupes of any of the strange delusions which are found unhappily still to prevail in certain quarters, on the subject of Textual Criticism.

The correction of known Textual errors of course we eagerly expected: and on every occasion when the Traditional Text was altered, we as confidently depended on finding a record of the circumstance inserted with religious fidelity into the margin,—as agreed upon by the Revisionists at the outset.   In both of these expectations however we found ourselves sadly disappointed.   The Revisionists have *not* corrected the 'known Textual errors.'   On the other hand, besides silently adopting most of those wretched fabrications which are just now in favour with the German school, they have encumbered their margin with those other Readings which, after due examination, *they had themselves deliberately rejected.*   For why?   Because, in their collective judgment, ' for the present, it would not be safe to accept one Reading to the absolute exclusion of others.' [1]   A fatal admission truly!   What are found in the margin are therefore ' *alternative Readings*,'—in the opinion of these self-constituted representatives of the Church and of the Sects.

It becomes evident that, by this ill-advised proceeding, our Revisionists would convert every Englishman's copy of the New Testament into a one-sided Introduction to the Critical difficulties of the Greek Text; a labyrinth, out of which they have not been at the pains to supply him with a single hint as to how he may find his way. On the contrary.   By candidly avowing that they find themselves enveloped in the same Stygian darkness with the ordinary English Reader, they give him to understand that

---

[1] *Preface*, p. xiv.

there is absolutely no escape from the difficulty. What else must be the result of all this but general uncertainty, confusion, distress? A hazy mistrust of all Scripture has been insinuated into the hearts and minds of countless millions, who in this way have been *forced* to become doubters,—yes, doubters in the Truth of Revelation itself. One recals sorrowfully the terrible woe denounced by the Author of Scripture on those who minister occasions of falling to others:—'It must needs be that offences come; but woe to that man by whom the offence cometh!'

For ourselves, shocked and offended at the unfaithfulness which could so deal with the sacred Deposit, we made it our business to expose, somewhat in detail, what had been the method of our Revisionists. In our October number[1] we demonstrated, (as far as was possible within such narrow limits,) the utterly untrustworthy character of not a few of the results at which, after ten years of careful study, these distinguished Scholars proclaim to the civilized world that they have deliberately arrived. In our January number[2] also, we found it impossible to avoid extending our enumeration of Textual errors and multiplying our proofs, while we were making it our business to show that, even had their *Text* been faultless, their *Translation* must needs be rejected as intolerable, on grounds of defective Scholarship and egregious bad Taste. The popular verdict has in the meantime been pronounced unmistakably. It is already admitted on all hands that the Revision has been a prodigious blunder. How it came about that, with such a first-rate textual Critic among them as Prebendary Scrivener,[3] the Revisers of 1881

---

[1] *Quarterly Review*, No. 304.   [2] *Quarterly Review*, No. 305.

[3] At the head of the present Article, as it originally appeared, will be found enumerated Dr. Scrivener's principal works. It shall but be said of

should have deliberately gone back to those vile fabrications from which the good Providence of GOD preserved Erasmus and Stunica,—Stephens and Beza and the Elzevirs,—three centuries ago :—how it happened that, with so many splendid Scholars sitting round their table, they should have produced a Translation which, for the most part, reads like a first-rate school-boy's *crib*,—tasteless, unlovely, harsh, unidiomatic ;—servile without being really faithful,—pedantic without being really learned ;—an unreadable Translation, in short ; the result of a vast amount of labour indeed, but of wondrous little skill :—how all this has come about, it were utterly useless at this time of day to enquire.

---

them, that they are wholly unrivalled, or rather unapproached, in their particular department. Himself an exact and elegant Scholar,—a most patient and accurate observer of Textual phenomena, as well as an interesting and judicious expositor of their significance and value ;—guarded in his statements, temperate in his language, fair and impartial (even kind) to all who come in his way :—Dr. Scrivener is the very best teacher and guide to whom a beginner can resort, who desires to be led by the hand, as it were, through the intricate mazes of Textual Criticism. His *Plain Introduction to the Criticism of the New Testament for the use of Biblical Students*, (of which a third edition is now in the press,) is perforce the most generally useful, because the most comprehensive, of his works ; but we strenuously recommend the three prefatory chapters of his *Full and Exact Collation of about twenty Greek Manuscripts of the Gospels* [pp. lxxiv. and 178,—1853], and the two prefatory chapters of his *Exact Transcript of the Codex Augiensis*, &c., to which is added a full Collation of Fifty Manuscripts, [pp. lxxx. and 563,—1859,] to the attention of students. His Collation of *Codex Bezæ* (D) is perhaps the greatest of his works : but whatever he has done, he has done best. It is instructive to compare his collation of Cod. ℵ with Tischendorf's. No reader of the Greek Testament can afford to be without his reprint of Stephens' ed. of 1550 : and English readers are reminded that Dr. Scrivener's is the only *classical* edition of the English Bible,—*The Cambridge Paragraph Bible*, &c., 1870-3. His Preface or 'Introduction' (pp. ix.-cxx.) passes praise. Ordinary English readers should enquire for his *Six Lectures on the Text of the N. T.*, &c., 1875,—which is in fact an attempt to popularize the *Plain Introduction*. The reader is referred to note (¹) at the foot of page 243.

Unable to disprove the correctness of our Criticism on the Revised Greek Text, even in a single instance, certain partizans of the Revision,—singular to relate,—have been ever since industriously promulgating the notion, that the Reviewer's great misfortune and fatal disadvantage all along has been, that he wrote his first Article before the publication of Drs. Westcott and Hort's Critical '*Introduction*.' Had he but been so happy as to have been made aware by those eminent Scholars of the critical principles which have guided them in the construction of their Text, how differently must he have expressed himself throughout, and to what widely different conclusions must he have inevitably arrived! This is what has been once and again either openly declared, or else privately intimated, in many quarters.   Some, in the warmth of their partizanship, have been so ill-advised as to insinuate that it argues either a deficiency of moral courage, or else of intellectual perception, in the Reviewer, that he has not long since grappled definitely with the Theory of Drs. Westcott and Hort,—and either published an Answer to it, or else frankly admitted that he finds it unanswerable.

(*a*) All of which strikes us as queer in a high degree. First, because as a matter of fact we were careful to make it plain that the *Introduction* in question had duly reached us *before the first sheet* of our earlier Article had left our hands. To be brief,—we made it our business to procure a copy and read it through, the instant we heard of its publication : and on our fourteenth page (see above, pp. 26–8) we endeavoured to compress into a long foot-note some account of a Theory which (we take leave to say) can appear formidable only to one who either lacks the patience to study it, or else the knowledge requisite to understand it.   We found that, from a diligent perusal of the *Preface* prefixed to the 'limited and private issue' of 1870, we had formed a perfectly correct estimate of the contents of the *Introduction ;* and had already characterized it with entire accuracy at pp. 24 to 29 of our first Article. Drs. Westcott and Hort's *New Testament in the original Greek* was discovered to 'partake inconveniently of the nature of a work of the Imagination,'—as we had anticipated. We became easily convinced that 'those accomplished Scholars had succeeded in producing a Text vastly more remote from the inspired autographs of the Evangelists and Apostles of our LORD, than any which has appeared since the invention of Printing.'

(*b*) But the queerest circumstance is behind. How is it supposed that any amount of study of *the last new Theory* of Textual Revision can seriously affect a Reviewer's estimate of the evidential value of the historical *facts* on which he relies for his proof that a certain exhibition of the Greek Text is untrustworthy ? The *onus probandi* rests clearly not with *him*, but with those who call those proofs of his in question. More of this, however, by and by. We are impatient to get on.

(*c*) And then, lastly,—What have *we* to do with *the Theory* of Drs. Westcott and Hort ? or indeed with the Theory of *any other person who can be named ?* We have been examining the new Greek Text *of the Revisionists*. We have condemned, after furnishing detailed proof, *the results* at which— by whatever means—that distinguished body of Scholars has arrived. Surely it is competent to us to upset their *conclusion*, without being constrained also to investigate in detail the illicit logical processes by which two of their number in a separate publication have arrived at far graver results, and often even stand hopelessly apart, the one from the other ! We say it in no boastful spirit, but we have an undoubted right to assume, that unless the Revisionists are able by a stronger array of authorities to set aside the evidence we have already brought forward, the calamitous destiny of their ' Revision,' so far as the New Testament is concerned, is simply a thing inevitable.

Let it not be imagined, however, from what goes before, that we desire to shirk the proposed encounter with the advocates of this last new Text, or that we entertain the slightest intention of doing so. We willingly accept the assurance, that it is only because Drs. Westcott and Hort are virtually responsible for the Revisers' Greek Text, that it is so imperiously demanded by the Revisers and their partizans, that the Theory of the two Cambridge Professors may be critically examined. We can sympathize also with the secret distress of certain of the body, who now, when it is all too late to remedy the mischief, begin to suspect that they have been led away by the hardihood of self-assertion;— overpowered by the *facundia præceps* of one who is at least a thorough believer in his own self-evolved opinions;—imposed upon by the seemingly consentient pages of Tischendorf and Tregelles, Westcott and Hort.—Without further preface we begin.

It is presumed that we shall be rendering acceptable service in certain quarters if,—before investigating the particular Theory which has been proposed for consideration,—we endeavour to give the unlearned English Reader some general notion, (it must perforce be a very imperfect one,) of the nature of the controversy to which the Theory now to be considered belongs, and out of which it has sprung. Claiming to be an attempt to determine the Truth of Scripture on scientific principles, the work before us may be regarded as the latest outcome of that violent recoil from the Traditional Greek Text,—that strange impatience of its authority, or

R

rather denial that it possesses any authority at all,—which began with Lachmann just 50 years ago (viz. in 1831), and has prevailed ever since; its most conspicuous promoters being Tregelles (1857–72) and Tischendorf (1865–72).

The true nature of the Principles which respectively animate the two parties in this controversy is at this time as much as ever,—perhaps *more* than ever,—popularly misunderstood. The common view of the contention in which they are engaged, is certainly the reverse of complimentary to the school of which Dr. Scrivener is the most accomplished living exponent. We hear it confidently asserted that the contention is nothing else but an irrational endeavour on the one part to set up the many modern against the few ancient Witnesses ;—the later cursive copies against the 'old Uncials ;' —inveterate traditional Error against undoubted primitive Truth. The disciples of the new popular school, on the contrary, are represented as relying exclusively *on Antiquity.* We respectfully assure as many as require the assurance, that the actual contention is of an entirely different nature. But, before we offer a single word in the way of explanation, let the position of our assailants at least be correctly ascertained and clearly established. We have already been constrained to some extent to go over this ground : but we will not repeat ourselves. The Reader is referred back, in the meantime, to pp. 21–24.

LACHMANN's ruling principle then, was exclusive reliance on a very few ancient authorities—*because* they are 'ancient.' He constructed his Text on three or four,—not unfrequently on *one or two,*—Greek codices. Of the Greek Fathers, he relied on Origen. Of the oldest Versions, he cared only for the Latin. To the Syriac (concerning which, see above, p. 9), he paid no attention. We venture to think his method *irrational.* But this is really a point on which the thoughtful reader is competent to judge for himself. He is invited to read the note at foot of the page.[1]

TREGELLES adopted the same strange method. He resorted to a very few out of the entire mass of ' ancient Authorities ' for the construction of his Text. His proceeding is exactly that of a man, who—in order that he may the better explore a comparatively unknown region—begins by putting out both his eyes ; and resolutely refuses the help of the natives to show him the way. *Why* he rejected the testimony of *every Father of the IVth century, except Eusebius,*—it were unprofitable to enquire.

TISCHENDORF, the last and by far the ablest Critic of the three, knew better than to reject ' *eighty-nine ninetieths* ' of the extant witnesses. He had recourse to the ingenious expedient of *adducing* all the available evidence, but *adopting* just as little of it as he chose : and he *chose* to adopt those readings only, which are vouched for by the same little band of authorities whose partial testimony had already proved fatal to the decrees of Lachmann and Tregelles. Happy in having discovered (in 1859) an uncial codex (א) second in antiquity only to the oldest before known (B), and strongly

---

[1] 'Agmen ducit Carolus Lachmannus (*N. T. Berolini* 1842–50), ingenii viribus et elegantiâ doctrinæ haud pluribus impar ; editor N. T. audacior quam limatior : cujus textum, a recepto longè decedentem, tantopere judicibus quibusdam subtilioribus placuisse jamdudum miramur : quippe qui, abjectâ tot cæterorum codicum Græcorum ope, perpaucis antiquissimis (nec iis integris, nec per eum satis accuratè collatis) innixus, libros sacros ad sæculi post Christum quarti normam restituisse sibi videatur ; versionum porrò (cujuslibet codicis ætatem facilè superantium) Syriacæ atque Ægyptiacarum contemptor, neutrius linguæ peritus ; Latinarum contrà nimius fautor, præ Bentleio ipso Bentleianus.'—Scrivener's Preface to *Nov. Test. textûs Stephanici*, &c. See above, p. 238, *note.*

resembling that famous IVth-century codex in the character of its contents, he suffered his judgment to be overpowered by the circumstance. He at once (1865–72) remodelled his 7th edition (1856–9) in 3505 places,—' to the scandal of the science of Comparative Criticism, as well as to his own grave discredit for discernment and consistency.'[1] And yet he knew concerning Cod. ℵ, that at least ten different Revisers from the Vth century downwards had laboured to remedy the scandalously corrupt condition of a text which, ' as it proceeded from the first scribe,' even Tregelles describes as ' *very rough.*'[2] But in fact the infatuation which prevails to this hour in this department of sacred Science can only be spoken of as incredible. Enough has been said to show— (the only point we are bent on establishing)—that the one distinctive tenet of the three most famous Critics since 1831 has been a superstitious reverence for whatever is found in the *same little handful* of early,—but *not* the earliest,—*nor yet of necessity the purest*,—documents.

Against this arbitrary method of theirs we solemnly, stiffly remonstrate. ' Strange,' we venture to exclaim, (addressing the living representatives of the school of Lachmann, and Tregelles, and Tischendorf) :—' Strange, that you should not perceive that you are the dupes of a fallacy which is even transparent. You *talk* of " Antiquity." But you must know very well that you actually *mean* something different. You fasten upon three, or perhaps four,—on two, or perhaps three,—on *one, or perhaps two*,—documents of the IVth or Vth century. But then, confessedly, these are one, two, three, or four *specimens only* of Antiquity,—not " Antiquity " itself. And what if they should even prove to be *unfair samples* of Antiquity ? Thus, you are observed always to

---

[1] Scrivener's *Introduction*, p. 429. [2] N. T. Part II. p. 2

quote cod. B or at least cod. ℵ. Pray, why may not the Truth
reside instead with A, or C, or D ?—You quote the old Latin
or the Coptic. Why may not the Peschito or the Sahidic
be right rather ?—You quote either Origen or else Eusebius,
—but why not Didymus and Athanasius, Epiphanius and
Basil, Chrysostom and Theodoret, the Gregories and the
Cyrils ? . . . . It will appear therefore that we are every bit
as strongly convinced as you can be of the paramount claims
of 'Antiquity :' but that, eschewing prejudice and partiality,
we differ from you only in *this*, viz. that we absolutely refuse
to bow down before the *particular specimens of Antiquity*
which you have arbitrarily selected as the objects of your
superstition.   You are illogical enough to propose to include
within your list of "ancient Authorities," codd. 1, 33 and 69,
—which are severally MSS. of the Xth, XIth, and XIVth
centuries. And why ? Only because the Text of those 3
copies is observed to bear a sinister resemblance to that of
codex B. But then why, in the name of common sense, do you
not show corresponding favour to the remaining 997 cursive
Copies of the N.T.,—seeing that these are observed to bear
the same general resemblance to codex A ? . . . You are for ever
talking about " old Readings." Have you not yet discovered
that ALL " Readings " are " OLD " ? '

The last contribution to this department of sacred Science
is a critical edition of the New Testament by Drs. WESTCOTT
and HORT. About this, we proceed to offer a few remarks.

I. The first thing here which unfavourably arrests attention is the circumstance that this proves to be the only
Critical Edition of the New Testament since the days of Mill,
which does not even pretend to contribute something to our
previous critical knowledge of the subject. Mill it was
(1707) who gave us the great bulk of our various Readings ;

which Bengel (1734) slightly, and Wetstein (1751–2) very considerably, enlarged.—The accurate Matthæi (1782–8) acquainted us with the contents of about 100 codices more ; and was followed by Griesbach (1796–1806) with important additional materials.—Birch had in the meantime (1788) culled from the principal libraries of Europe a large assortment of new Readings : while truly marvellous was the accession of evidence which Scholz brought to light in 1830.—And though Lachmann (1842–50) did wondrous little in this department, he yet furnished the critical authority (such as it is) for his own unsatisfactory Text.—Tregelles (1857–72), by his exact collations of MSS. and examination of the earliest Fathers, has laid the Church under an abiding obligation : and what is to be said of Tischendorf (1856–72), who has contributed more to our knowledge than any other editor of the N. T. since the days of Mill ?—Dr. Scrivener, though he has not independently edited the original Text, is clearly to be reckoned among those who *have,* by reason of his large, important, and accurate contributions to our knowledge of ancient documents. Transfer his collections of various Readings to the foot of the page of a copy of the commonly Received Text,—and ' *Scrivener's New Testament* '[1] might stand between the editions of Mill and of Wetstein. Let the truth be told. C. F. Matthæi and he are *the only two Scholars who have collated any considerable number of sacred Codices with the needful amount of accuracy.*[2]

---

[1] No one who attends ever so little to the subject can require to be assured that ' *The New Testament in the Original Greek, according to the text followed in the Authorized Version, together with the variations adopted in the Revised Version,*' edited by Dr. Scrivener for the Syndics of the Cambridge University Press, 1881, does not by any means represent his own views. The learned Prebendary merely edited the decisions of the two-thirds majority of the Revisionists,—*which were not his own.*

[2] Those who have never tried the experiment, can have no idea of the strain on the attention which such works as those enumerated in p. 238

Now, we trust we shall be forgiven if, at the close of the preceding enumeration, we confess to something like displeasure at the oracular tone assumed by Drs. Westcott and Hort in dealing with the Text of Scripture, though they admit (page 90) that they 'rely for documentary evidence on the stores accumulated by their predecessors.' Confident as those distinguished Professors may reasonably feel of their ability to dispense with the ordinary appliances of Textual Criticism ; and proud (as they must naturally be) of a verifying faculty which (although they are able to give no account of it) yet enables them infallibly to discriminate between the false and the true, as well as to assign 'a local habitation and a name' to every word,—inspired or uninspired,—which purports to belong to the N. T. :—they must not be offended with us if we freely assure them at the outset that we shall decline to accept a single argumentative assertion of theirs for which they fail to offer sufficient proof. Their wholly unsupported decrees, at the risk of being thought uncivil, we shall unceremoniously reject, as soon as we have allowed them a hearing.

This resolve bodes ill, we freely admit, to harmonious progress. But it is inevitable. For, to speak plainly, we never before met with such a singular tissue of magisterial statements, unsupported by a particle of rational evidence, as we meet with here. The abstruse gravity, the long-winded earnestness of the writer's manner, contrast whimsically with the utterly inconsequential character of his antecedents

---

(*note*) occasion. At the same time, it cannot be too clearly understood that it is chiefly by the multiplication of *exact* collations of MSS. that an abiding foundation will some day be laid on which to build up the *Science* of Textual Criticism. We may safely keep our ' *Theories* ' back till we have collated our MSS.,—re-edited our Versions,—indexed our Fathers. They will be abundantly in time *then*.

and his consequents throughout. Professor Hort—(for 'the writing of the volume and the other accompaniments of the Text devolved' on *him*,[1])—Dr. Hort seems to mistake his Opinions for facts,—his Assertions for arguments,—and a Reiteration of either for an accession of evidence. There is throughout the volume, apparently, a dread of *Facts* which is even extraordinary. An actual illustration of the learned Author's meaning,—a concrete case,—seems as if it were *never* forthcoming. At last it comes: but the phenomenon is straightway discovered to admit of at least two interpretations, and therefore never to prove the thing intended. In a person of high education,—in one accustomed to exact reasoning,—we should have supposed all this impossible. . . . . But it is high time to unfold the *Introduction* at the first page, and to begin to read.

II. It opens (p. 1–11) with some unsatisfactory Remarks on 'Transmission by Writing ;' vague and inaccurate,—unsupported by one single Textual reference,—and labouring under the grave defect of leaving the most instructive phenomena of the problem wholly untouched. For, inasmuch as ' Transmission by writing' involves two distinct classes of errors, (1st) Those which are the result of *Accident*,—and (2ndly) Those which are the result of *Design*,—it is to use a Reader badly not to take the earliest opportunity of explaining to him that what makes codd. B ℵ D such utterly untrustworthy guides, (except when supported by a large amount of extraneous evidence,) is the circumstance that *Design* had evidently so much to do with a vast proportion of the peculiar errors in which they severally abound. In other words, each of those codices clearly exhibits a fabricated Text,— is the result of arbitrary and reckless *Recension*.

---

[1] *Introduction*, p. 18.

Now, this is not a matter of opinion, but of fact. In
S. Luke's Gospel alone (collated with the traditional Text)
the *transpositions* in codex B amount to 228,—affecting 654
words : in codex D, to 464,—affecting 1401 words. Proceeding with our examination of the same Gospel according to
S. Luke, we find that the words *omitted* in B are 757,—in D,
1552. The words *substituted* in B amount to 309,—in D, to
1006. The readings *peculiar* to B are 138, and affect 215
words ; — those peculiar to D, are 1731, and affect 4090
words. Wondrous few of these *can* have been due to accidental causes. The Text of one or of both codices must
needs be depraved. (As for ℵ, it is so frequently found in
accord with B, that out of consideration for our Readers, we
omit the corresponding figures.)

We turn to codd. A and C—(executed, suppose, a hundred
years *after* B, and a hundred years *before* D)—and the figures
are found to be as follows :—

	In A.	In C.
The transpositions are	75	67
affecting	199 words ...	197
The words omitted are	208	175
The words substituted	111	115
The peculiar readings	90	87
affecting	131 words ...	127

Now, (as we had occasion to explain in a previous page,[1])
it is entirely to misunderstand the question, to object that
the preceding Collation has been made with the Text of
Stephanus open before us. Robert Etienne in the XVIth
century was not *the cause* why cod. B in the IVth, and cod. D
in the VIth, are so widely discordant from one another ;
A and C, so utterly at variance with both. The simplest

---

[1] See lower part of page 17.   Also note at p. 75 and middle of p. 262.

explanation of the phenomena is the truest; namely, that B and D exhibit grossly depraved Texts;—a circumstance of which it is impossible that the ordinary Reader should be too soon or too often reminded.   But to proceed.

III. Some remarks follow, on what is strangely styled ' Transmission by printed Editions : ' in the course of which Dr. Hort informs us that Lachmann's Text of 1831 was ' the first founded on documentary authority.'[1] .... On *what* then, pray, does the learned Professor imagine that the Texts of Erasmus (1516) and of Stunica (1522) were founded ?   His statement is incorrect.   The actual difference between Lachmann's Text and those of the earlier Editors is, that *his* ' documentary authority' is partial, narrow, self-contradictory ; and is proved to be untrustworthy by a free appeal to Antiquity.   *Their* documentary authority, derived from independent sources,—though partial and narrow as that on which Lachmann relied,—exhibits (*under the good Providence of GOD,*) a Traditional Text, the general purity of which is demonstrated by all the evidence which 350 years of subsequent research have succeeded in accumu-lating ; and which is confessedly the Text of A.D. 375.

IV. We are favoured, in the third place, with the ' History of this Edition:' in which the point that chiefly arrests attention is the explanation afforded of the many and serious occasions on which Dr. Westcott (' W.') and Dr. Hort (' H.'), finding it impossible to agree, have set down their respective notions separately and subscribed them with their respective initial.   We are reminded of what was wittily said con-cerning Richard Baxter : viz. that even if no one but himself existed in the Church, ' Richard ' would still be found to

---

[1] P. 13, cf. p. viii.

disagree with 'Baxter,'—and 'Baxter' with 'Richard' . . . .
We read with uneasiness that

'no individual mind can ever act with perfect uniformity, or
free itself completely from *its own Idiosyncrasies ;*' and that
'the danger of *unconscious Caprice* is inseparable from personal
judgment.'—(p. 17.)

All this reminds us painfully of certain statements made
by the same Editors in 1870 :—

'We are obliged to come to the *individual mind* at last ; and
Canons of Criticism are useful only as warnings against *natural
illusions*, and aids to circumspect consideration, not as absolute
rules to prescribe the final decision.'—(pp. xviii., xix.)

May we be permitted without offence to point out (not for
the first time) that 'idiosyncrasies' and 'unconscious caprice,'
and the fancies of the 'individual mind,' can be allowed *no
place whatever* in a problem of such gravity and importance
as the present ? Once admit such elements, and we are
safe to find ourselves in cloud-land to-morrow. A weaker
foundation on which to build, is not to be named. And
when we find that the learned Professors 'venture to hope
that the present Text has escaped some risks of this kind by
being the production of two Editors of different habits of
mind, working independently and to a great extent on
different plans,'—we can but avow our conviction that the
safeguard is altogether inadequate. When two men, devoted
to the same pursuit, are in daily confidential intercourse on
such a subject, the '*natural illusions*' of either have a,
marvellous tendency to communicate themselves. Their
Reader's only protection is rigidly to *insist* on the production
of *Proof* for everything which these authors say.

V. The dissertation on 'Intrinsic' and 'Transcriptional
Probability' which follows (pp. 20–30),—being *unsupported
by one single instance or illustration*,—we pass by. It ignores

throughout the fact, that the most serious corruptions of
MSS. are due, *not* to 'Scribes' or 'Copyists,' (of whom, by
the way, we find perpetual mention every time we open the
page ;) but to the persons who employed them.   So far from
thinking with Dr. Hort that 'the value of the evidence
obtained from Transcriptional Probability is incontestable,'
—for that, 'without its aid, Textual Criticism could rarely
obtain a high degree of security,' (p. 24,)—we venture to
declare that inasmuch as one expert's notions of what is
'transcriptionally probable' prove to be the diametrical
reverse of another expert's notions, the supposed evidence
to be derived from this source may, with advantage, be
neglected altogether.   Let the study of *Documentary Evidence*
be allowed to take its place.   Notions of 'Probability' are
the very pest of those departments of Science which admit
of an appeal to *Fact*.

VI. A signal proof of the justice of our last remark is
furnished by the plea which is straightway put in (pp. 30–1)
for the superior necessity of attending to 'the relative antecedent credibility of Witnesses.'   In other words, 'The comparative trustworthiness of documentary Authorities' is
proposed as a far weightier consideration than 'Intrinsic'
and 'Transcriptional Probability.'   Accordingly we are
assured (in capital letters) that 'Knowledge of Documents
should precede final judgment upon readings' (p. 31).

'Knowledge'! Yes, but how acquired? Suppose two
rival documents,—cod. A and cod. B.   May we be informed
how you would proceed with respect to them ?

'Where one of the documents is found habitually to contain
morally certain, or at least strongly preferred, Readings,—and the
other habitually to contain their rejected rivals,—we [i.e. *Dr.
Hort*] can have no doubt that the Text of the first has been

transmitted in comparative purity ; and that the Text of the second has suffered comparatively large corruption.'—(p. 32.)

But can such words have been written seriously ? Is it gravely pretended that Readings become *'morally certain,'* because they are *'strongly preferred'* ? Are we (in other words) seriously invited to admit that the 'STRONG PREFE- RENCE' of 'the individual mind' is to be the ultimate standard of appeal ? If so, though *you* (Dr. Hort) may *'have no doubt'* as to which is the purer manuscript,—see you not plainly that a man of different 'idiosyncrasy' from yourself, may just as reasonably claim to 'have no doubt' —*that you are mistaken ?* . . . One is reminded of a passage in p. 61 : viz.—

'If we find in any group of documents a succession of Readings exhibiting an exceptional purity of text, that is,— *Readings which the fullest consideration of Internal Evidence pronounces to be right, in opposition to formidable arrays of Documentary Evidence;* the cause must be that, as far at least as these Readings are concerned, some one exceptionally pure MS. was the common ancestor of all the members of the group.'

But how does *that* appear ? 'The cause' *may* be *the erro- neous judgment of the Critic,*—may it not ? . . . Dr. Hort is for setting up what his own inner consciousness 'pronounces to be right,' against 'Documentary Evidence,' however mul- titudinous. He claims that his own verifying faculty shall be supreme,—shall settle every question. Can he be in earnest ?

VII. We are next introduced to the subject of 'Genea- logical Evidence' (p. 39); and are made attentive : for we speedily find ourselves challenged to admit that a 'total change in the bearing of the evidence' is 'made by the intro- duction of the factor of Genealogy' (p. 43). Presuming that the *meaning* of the learned Writer must rather be that *if we did but know* the genealogy of MSS., we should be in a position to reason more confidently concerning their Texts,—

we read on: and speedily come to a second axiom (which is again printed in capital letters), viz. that 'All trustworthy restoration of corrupted Texts is founded on the study of their History' (p. 40). We really read and wonder. Are we then engaged in *the 'restoration of corrupted Texts'*? If so,—which be they? We require—(1) To be shown the '*corrupted Texts*' referred to : and then—(2) To be convinced that 'the study of *their History*'—(as distinguished from an examination of the evidence for or against *their Readings*)— is a thing feasible.

'A simple instance' (says Dr. Hort) 'will show at once the practical bearing' of ' the principle here laid down.'—(p. 40.)

But (as usual) Dr. Hort produces *no* instance. He merely proceeds to 'suppose' a case (§ 50), which he confesses (§ 53) does not exist. So that we are moving in a land of shadows. And this, he straightway follows up by the assertion that

'it would be difficult to insist too strongly on the transforma- tion of the superficial aspects of numerical authority effected by recognition of Genealogy.'—(p. 43.)

Presently, he assures us that

'a few documents are not, by reason of their mere paucity, appreciably less likely to be right than a multitude opposed to them.' (p. 45.)

On this head, we take leave to entertain a somewhat different opinion. *Apart from the character of the Witnesses,* when 5 men say one thing, and 995 say the exact contra- dictory, we are apt to regard it even as axiomatic that, 'by reason of their mere paucity,' the few 'are appreciably far less likely to be right than the multitude opposed to them.' Dr. Hort seems to share our opinion ; for he remarks,—

'A presumption indeed remains that a majority of extant documents is more likely to represent a majority of ancestral documents, than *vice versá.*'

Exactly so! We meant, and we mean *that*, and no other thing. But then, we venture to point out, that the learned Professor considerably understates the case: seeing that the ' *vice versâ presumption* ' is absolutely non-existent. On the other hand, apart from *Proof to the contrary*, we are disposed to maintain that 'a majority of extant documents' in the proportion of 995 to 5,—and sometimes of 1999 to 1,—creates more than 'a presumption.' It amounts to *Proof of ' a majority of ancestral documents.'*

Not so thinks Dr. Hort. 'This presumption,' (he seems to have persuaded himself,) may be disposed of by his mere assertion that it 'is too minute to weigh against the smallest tangible evidence of other kinds' (*Ibid.*). As usual, how-ever, he furnishes us with *no evidence at all*,—'tangible' or 'intangible.' Can he wonder if we smile at his unsupported *dictum*, and pass on? . . . The argumentative import of his twenty weary pages on 'Genealogical Evidence' (pp. 39–59), appears to be resolvable into the following barren truism: viz. That if, out of 10 copies of Scripture, 9 *could be proved* to have been executed from one and the same common original (p. 41), those 9 would cease to be regarded as 9 independent witnesses. But does the learned Critic really require to be told that we want no diagram of an imaginary case (p. 54) to convince us of *that?*

The one thing here which moves our astonishment, is, that Dr. Hort does not seem to reflect that *therefore* (indeed *by his own showing*) codices B and ℵ, having been *demonstrably* " executed from one and the same common original," are not to be reckoned as *two* independent witnesses to the Text of the New Testament, but as little more than *one*. (See p. 257.)

High time however is it to declare that, in strictness, all this talk about 'Genealogical evidence,' when applied to

Manuscripts, is—*moonshine*. The expression is metaphorical, and assumes that it has fared with MSS. as it fares with the successive generations of a family ; and so, to a remarkable extent, no doubt, it *has*. But then, it happens, unfortunately, that we are unacquainted with *one single instance* of a known MS. copied from another known MS. And perforce all talk about ' Genealogical evidence,' where *no single step in the descent* can be produced,—in other words, *where no Genealogical evidence exists,*—is absurd. The living inhabitants of a village, congregated in the churchyard where the bodies of their forgotten progenitors for 1000 years repose without memorials of any kind,—is a faint image of the relation which subsists between extant copies of the Gospels and the sources from which they were derived. That, in either case, there has been repeated mixture, is undeniable ; but since the Parish-register is lost, and not a vestige of Tradition survives, it is idle to pretend to argue on *that* part of the subject. It may be reasonably assumed however that those 50 yeomen, bearing as many Saxon surnames, indicate as many remote *ancestors* of some sort. That they represent as many *families*, is at least a *fact*. Further we cannot go.

But the illustration is misleading, because inadequate. Assemble rather an Englishman, an Irishman, a Scot; a Frenchman, a German, a Spaniard ; a Russian, a Pole, an Hungarian ; an Italian, a Greek, a Turk. From Noah these 12 are all confessedly descended; but if *they* are silent, and *you* know nothing whatever about their antecedents,—your remarks about their respective ' genealogies ' must needs prove as barren—as Dr. Hort's about the ' genealogies ' of copies of Scripture. ' *The factor of Genealogy,*' in short, in this discussion, represents a mere phantom of the brain : is the name of an imagination—not of a fact.

The nearest approximation to the phenomenon about which
Dr. Hort writes so glibly, is supplied—(1) by Codd. F and G
of S. Paul, which are found to be independent transcripts of
the same venerable lost original :—(2) by Codd. 13, 69, 124
and 346, which were confessedly derived from one and the
same queer archetype : *and especially*—(3) by Codd. B *and* א.
These two famous manuscripts, because they are disfigured
exclusively by the self-same mistakes, are convicted of being
descended (and not very remotely) from the self-same very
corrupt original.   By consequence, the combined evidence
of F and G is but that of a single codex.   Evan. 13, 69, 124,
346, when they agree, would be conveniently designated by
a symbol, or a single capital letter.   Codd. B and א, as already
hinted (p. 255), are not to be reckoned as two witnesses.
Certainly, they have not nearly the Textual significancy and
importance of B in conjunction with A, or of A in conjunction
with C.   At best, they do but equal $1\frac{1}{2}$ copies.   Nothing of
this kind however is what Drs. Westcott and Hort intend
to convey,—or indeed seem to understand.

VIII. It is not until we reach p. 94, that these learned men
favour us with a single actual appeal to Scripture.   At p. 90,
Dr. Hort,—who has hitherto -been skirmishing over the
ground, and leaving us to wonder what in the world it can
be that he is driving at,—announces a chapter on the
' Results of Genealogical evidence proper ; ' and proposes to
' determine the Genealogical relations of the chief ancient
Texts.'   Impatient for argument, (at page 92,) we read as
follows :—

' The fundamental Text of *late extant Greek MSS.* generally
is *beyond all question identical* with the dominant Antiochian
or Græco-Syrian Text of the *second half of the fourth century.*'

We request, in passing, that the foregoing statement may
be carefully noted.   The Traditional Greek Text of the New

Testament,—the TEXTUS RECEPTUS, in short,—is, according to
Dr. Hort, 'BEYOND ALL QUESTION' the 'TEXT OF THE SECOND
HALF OF THE FOURTH CENTURY.' We shall gratefully avail
ourselves of his candid admission, by and by.

Having thus *assumed* a 'dominant Antiochian or Græco-
Syrian text of the second half of the IVth century,' Dr. H.
attempts, by an analysis of what he is pleased to call '*conflate* Readings,' to prove the 'posteriority of "Syrian" to
"Western" and other "Neutral" readings.' . . . Strange
method of procedure! seeing that, of those second and third
classes of readings, we have not as yet so much as heard
the names. Let us however without more delay be shown
those specimens of 'Conflation' which, in Dr. Hort's judgment, supply 'the clearest evidence' (p. 94) that 'Syrian'
are posterior alike to 'Western' and to 'Neutral readings.'
Of these, after 30 years of laborious research, Dr. Westcott
and he flatter themselves that they have succeeded in de-
tecting *eight*.

IX. Now because, on the one hand, it would be unreasonable to fill up the space at our disposal with details which
none but professed students will care to read;—and because,
on the other, we cannot afford to pass by anything in these
pages which pretends to be of the nature of proof;—we have
consigned our account of Dr. Hort's 8 instances of *Conflation* (which prove to be less than 7) to the foot of the page.[1]

---

[1] They are as follows:—

[1st] S. Mark (vi. 33) relates that on a certain occasion the multitude,
when they beheld our SAVIOUR and His Disciples departing in order to
cross over unto the other side of the lake, ran on foot thither,—(a) '*and
outwent them*—(β) *and came together unto Him*' (*i.e.* on His stepping out
of the boat : not, as Dr. Hort strangely imagines [p. 99], on His emerging
from the scene of His 'retirement' in ' some sequestered nook ').

Now here, A substitutes συνέδραμον [*sic*] for συνῆλθον.—א B with the
Coptic and the Vulg. omit clause (β).—D omits clause (a). but substitutes
'*there*' (αὐτοῦ) for '*unto Him*' in clause (β),—exhibits therefore a

And, after an attentive survey of the Textual phenomena connected with these 7 specimens, we are constrained to

---

fabricated text.—The Syriac condenses the two clauses thus :—'*got there before Him.*'—L, Δ, 69, and 4 or 5 of the old Latin copies, read diversely from all the rest and from one another. The present is, in fact, one of those many places in S. Mark's Gospel where all is contradiction in those depraved witnesses which Lachmann made it his business to bring into fashion. Of *Confusion* there is plenty. 'Conflation'—as the Reader sees—there is none.

[2nd] In S. Mark viii. 26, our SAVIOUR (after restoring sight to the blind man of Bethsaida) is related to have said, — (a) ' *Neither enter into the village* '—(β) ' *nor tell it to any one*—(γ) *in the village.*' (And let it be noted that the trustworthiness of this way of exhibiting the text is vouched for by A C N Δ and 12 other uncials : by the whole body of the cursives : by the Peschito and Harklensian, the Gothic, Armenian, and Æthiopic Versions : and by the only Father who quotes the place—Victor of Antioch.*)

But it is found that the ' two false witnesses ' (א B) omit clauses (β) and (γ), retaining only clause (a). One of these two however (א), aware that under such circumstances μηδέ is intolerable,† substitutes μή. As for D and the Vulg., they substitute and paraphrase, importing from Matt. ix. 6 (or Mk. ii. 11), ' *Depart unto thine house.*' D proceeds,—' *and tell it to no one* [μηδενὶ εἴπῃς, from Matth. viii. 4,] *in the village.*' Six copies of the old Latin (b f ff⁻² g⁻¹⁻² l), with the Vulgate, exhibit the following paraphrase of the entire place:—' *Depart unto thine house, and if thou enterest into the village, tell it to no one.*' The same reading exactly is found in Evan. 13–69–346 : 28, 61, 473, and i, (except that 28, 61, 346 exhibit ' *say nothing* [from Mk. i. 44] *to no one.*') All six however add at the end,—' *not even in the village.*' Evan. 124 and a stand alone in exhibiting,—' *Depart unto thine house ; and enter not into the village ; neither tell it to any one,*'—to which 124 [not a] adds,—' *in the village.*' . . . *Why* all this contradiction and confusion is now to be called 'Conflation,'—and what ' clear evidence ' is to be elicited therefrom that ' Syrian ' are posterior alike to ' Western ' and to ' neutral ' readings,—passes our powers of comprehension.

We shall be content to hasten forward when we have further informed our Readers that while Lachmann and Tregelles abide by the Received Text in this place ; Tischendorf, *alone of Editors,* adopts the reading of א (μη εις την κωμην εισελθης): while Westcott and Hort, *alone of Editors,*

---

* Cramer's *Cat.* p. 345, lines 3 and 8.

† Dr. Hort, on the contrary, (only because he finds it in B,) considers μηδέ ' *simple and vigorous* ' as well as ' unique' and ' peculiar ' (p. 100).

assert that the interpretation put upon them by Drs. Westcott and Hort, is purely arbitrary : a baseless imagination,—

---

adopt the reading of B ($\mu\eta\delta\epsilon$ $\epsilon\iota s$ $\tau\eta\nu$ $\kappa\omega\mu\eta\nu$ $\epsilon\iota\sigma\epsilon\lambda\theta\eta s$),—so ending the
sentence.   What else however but calamitous is it to find that Westcott
and Hort have persuaded their fellow Revisers to adopt the same mutilated
exhibition of the Sacred Text?   The consequence is, that henceforth,—
instead of ' *Neither go into the town, nor tell it to any in the town,*'—
we are invited to read, ' *Do not even enter into the village.*'

[3rd] In S. Mk. ix. 38,—S. John, speaking of one who cast out devils in
Christ's Name, says—(a) ' *who followeth not us, and we forbad him—*(β)
because he followeth not us.'

Here, ℵ B C L Δ the Syriac, Coptic, and Æthiopic, omit clause (a), retaining (β).   D with the old Latin and the Vulg. omit clause (β), but retain
(a).—Both clauses are found in A N with 11 other uncials and the whole
body of the cursives, besides the Gothic, and the only Father who quotes
the place,—Basil [ii. 252].—Why should the pretence be set up that there
has been ' Conflation' here ?   Two Omissions do not make one Conflation.

[4th] In Mk. ix. 49,—our Saviour says,—' *For* (a) *every one shall be
salted with fire—and* (β) *every sacrifice shall be salted with salt.*'

Here, clause (a) is omitted by D and a few copies of the old Latin ;
clause (β) by ℵ B L Δ.

But such an ordinary circumstance as the omission of half-a-dozen
words by Cod. D is so nearly without textual significancy, as scarcely to
merit commemoration.   And do Drs. Westcott and Hort really propose
to build their huge and unwieldy hypothesis on so flimsy a circumstance
as the concurrence in error of ℵ B L Δ,—especially in S. Mark's Gospel,
which those codices exhibit more unfaithfully than any other codices that
can be named?   Against them, are to be set on the present occasion A C D N
with 12 other uncials and the whole body of the cursives: the Ital. and
Vulgate;   both Syriac;   the Coptic, Gothic, Armenian, and Æthiopic
Versions;   besides the only Father who quotes the place,—Victor of
Antioch.   [Also ' Anon.' p. 206 : and see Cramer's *Cat.* p. 368.]

[5th] S. Luke (ix. 10) relates how, on a certain occasion, our Saviour
' *withdrew to a desert place belonging to the city called Bethsaida :*' which
S. Luke expresses in six words: viz. [1] $\epsilon\iota s$ [2] $\tau\acute{o}\pi o\nu$ [3] $\check{\epsilon}\rho\eta\mu o\nu$ [4] $\pi\acute{o}\lambda\epsilon\omega s$
[5] $\kappa\alpha\lambda o\nu\mu\acute{\epsilon}\nu\eta s$ [6] $B\eta\theta\sigma\alpha\ddot{\iota}\delta\acute{a}$: of which six words,—

    (a)—ℵ and Syrᵒⁿ retain but three,—1, 2, 3.

    (b)—The Peschito retains but four,—1, 2, 3, 6.

    (c)—B L X Ξ D and the 2 Egyptian versions retain other four,—1, 4,
        5, 6 : but for $\pi\acute{o}\lambda\epsilon\omega s$ $\kappa\alpha\lambda o\nu\mu\acute{\epsilon}\nu\eta s$ D exhibits $\kappa\acute{\omega}\mu\eta\nu$ $\lambda\epsilon\gamma o\mu\acute{\epsilon}\nu\eta\nu$.

    (d)—The old Latin and Vulg. retain five,—1, 2, 3, 5, 6 : but for
        ' *qui* (or *quod*) *vocabatur,*' the Vulg. *b* and *c* exhibit ' *qui* (or
        quod) *est.*'

a dream and nothing more.   Something has been attempted
analogous to the familiar fallacy, in Divinity, of building a

---

(e)—3 cursives retain other five, viz. 1, 2, 4, 5, 6: while,

(f)—A C Δ E, with 9 more uncials and the great bulk of the cursives,
—the Harklensian, Gothic, Armenian, and Æthiopic
Versions,—retain *all the six words.*

In view of which facts, it probably never occurred to any one before to
suggest that the best attested reading of all is the result of 'conflation,'
i.e. of *spurious mixture.*   Note, that ℵ and D have, this time, changed
sides.

[6th] S. Luke (xi. 54) speaks of the Scribes and Pharisees as (a) ' *lying
in wait for Him,*' (β) *seeking* (γ) *to catch something out of His mouth* (δ)
that they might accuse Him.'   This is the reading of 14 uncials headed by
A C, and of the whole body of the cursives: the reading of the Vulgate also
and of the Syriac.   What is to be said against it?

It is found that ℵ B L with the Coptic and Æthiopic Versions omit
clauses (β) and (δ), but retain clauses (a) and (γ).—Cod. D, in conjunction
with Cureton's Syriac and the old Latin, retains clause (β), and *paraphrases
all the rest of the sentence.*   How then can it be pretended that there has
been any 'Conflation' here?

In the meantime, how unreasonable is the excision from the Revised Text
of clauses (β) and (δ)—(ζητοῦντες ... ἵνα κατηγορήσωσιν αὐτόν)—which are
attested by A C D and 12 other uncials, together with the whole body of
the cursives; by all the Syriac and by all the Latin copies! . . . Are we
then to understand that ℵ B, and the Coptic Version, outweigh every other
authority which can be named?

[7th] The 'rich fool' in the parable (S. Lu. xii. 18), speaks of (a) πάντα
τὰ γενήματά μου, καὶ (β) τὰ ἀγαθά μου.   (So A Q and 13 other uncials,
besides the whole body of the cursives; the Vulgate, Basil, and Cyril.)

But ℵ D (with the old Latin and Cureton's Syriac [which however drops
the πάντα]), retaining clause (a), omit clause (β).—On the other hand, B T,
(with the Egyptian Versions, the Syriac, the Armenian, and Æthiopic,)
retaining clause (β), substitute τὸν σῖτον (a gloss) for τὰ γενήματα in clause
(a).   Lachmann, Tisch., and Alford, accordingly retain the traditional
text in this place.   So does Tregelles, and so do Westcott and Hort,—
only substituting τὸν σῖτον for τὰ γενήματα.   Confessedly therefore there
has been no ' Syrian conflation' *here :* for all that has happened has been
the substitution by B of τὸν σῖτον for τὰ γενήματα ; and the omission of 4
words by ℵ D.   This instance must therefore have been an oversight.—
Only once more.

[8th] S. Luke's Gospel ends (xxiv. 53) with the record that the Apostles
were continually in the Temple, ' (a) *praising and* (β) *blessing God.*'   Such

false and hitherto unheard-of doctrine on a few isolated places of Scripture, divorced from their context. The actual *facts* of the case shall be submitted to the judgment of learned and unlearned Readers alike : and we promise beforehand to abide by the unprejudiced verdict of either :—

(*a*) S. Mark's Gospel is found to contain in all 11,646 words : of which (collated with the Traditional Text) A omits 138 : B, 762 : ℵ, 870 : D, 900.—S. Luke contains 19,941 words : of which A omits 208 : B, 757 ; ℵ, 816 : D, no less than 1552. (Let us not be told that the traditional Text is itself not altogether trustworthy. *That* is a matter entirely beside the question just now before the Reader,—as we have already, over and again, had occasion to explain.[1] Codices must needs all alike be compared *with something*,—must perforce all alike be referred to *some one common standard :* and we, for our part, are content to employ (as every Critic has been content before us) the traditional Text, as the most convenient standard that can be named. So employed, (viz. as a standard of *comparison*, not of *excellence*,) the commonly Received Text, more conveniently than any other, *reveals* — certainly does not *occasion* — different degrees of discrepancy. And now, to proceed.)

---

is the reading of 13 uncials headed by A and every known cursive : a few copies of the old Lat., the Vulg., Syriac, Philox., Æthiopic, and Armenian Versions. But it is found that ℵ B C omit clause (*a*) : while D and seven copies of the old Latin omit clause (*β*).

And this completes the evidence for ' Conflation.' We have displayed it thus minutely, lest we should be suspected of unfairness towards the esteemed writers on *the only occasion* on which they have attempted argumentative proof. Their theory has at last *forced them* to make an appeal to Scripture, and to produce some actual specimens of their meaning. After ransacking the Gospels for 30 years, they have at last fastened upon *eight :* of which (as we have seen), several have really no business to be cited,—as not fulfilling the necessary conditions of the problem. To prevent cavil however, let *all but one*, the [7th], pass unchallenged.

[1] The Reader is referred to pp. 17, 75, 249.

(b) Dr. Hort has detected *four* instances in S. Mark's Gospel, only *three* in S. Luke's—*seven* in all—where Codices B ℵ and D happen to concur in making an omission *at the same place,* but not *of the same words.* We shall probably be best understood if we produce an instance of the thing spoken of: and no fairer example can be imagined than the last of the eight, of which Dr. Hort says,—' This simple instance needs no explanation ' (p. 104).   Instead of αἰνοῦντες καὶ εὐλογοῦντες,—(which is the reading of *every known copy* of the Gospels *except five,*)—ℵ B C L exhibit only εὐλογοῦντες: D, only αἰνοῦντες.   (To speak quite accurately, ℵ B C L omit αἰνοῦντες καί and are followed by Westcott and Hort: D omits καὶ εὐλογοῦντες, and is followed by Tischendorf. Lachmann declines to follow either.   Tregelles doubts.)

(c) Now, upon this (and the six other instances, which however prove to be a vast deal less apt for their purpose than the present), these learned men have gratuitously built up the following extravagant and astonishing theory:—

(d) They assume,—(they do not attempt to *prove:* in fact they *never* prove *anything:*)—(1) That αἰνοῦντες καί—and καὶ εὐλογοῦντες—are respectively fragments of two independent Primitive Texts, which they arbitrarily designate as ' Western ' and ' Neutral,' respectively:—(2) That the latter of the two, [*only* however because it is vouched for by B and ℵ,] must needs exhibit what the Evangelist actually wrote: [though *why* it must, these learned men forget to explain:]—(3) That in the middle of the IIIrd and of the IVth century the two Texts referred to were with design and by authority welded together, and became (what the same irresponsible Critics are pleased to call) the ' Syrian text.'—(4) That αἰνοῦντες καὶ εὐλογοῦντες, being thus shown [?] to be ' a Syrian *Conflation,*' may be rejected at once.   (*Notes,* p. 73.)

X. But we demur to this weak imagination, (which only by courtesy can be called 'a Theory,') on every ground, and are constrained to remonstrate with our would-be Guides at every step. They assume everything. They prove nothing. And the facts of the case lend them no favour at all. For first,—We only find εὐλογοῦντες standing alone, in two documents of the IVth century, in two of the Vth, and in one of the VIIIth: while, for αἰνοῦντες standing alone, the only Greek voucher producible is a notoriously corrupt copy of the VIth century. True, that here a few copies of the old Latin side with D: but then a few copies also side with the traditional Text: and Jerome is found to have adjudicated between their rival claims in favour of the latter. The probabilities of the case are in fact simply overwhelming; for, since D omits 1552 words out of 19,941 (i.e. about one word in 13), why may not καὶ εὐλογοῦντες be two of the words it omits,—in which case there has been no 'Conflation'?

Nay, look into the matter a little more closely :—(for surely, before we put up with this queer illusion, it is our duty to look it very steadily in the face:)—and note, that in this last chapter of S. Luke's Gospel, which consists of 837 words, no less than 121 are omitted by cod. D. To state the case differently,—D is observed to leave out one word in seven in the very chapter of S. Luke which supplies the instance of 'Conflation' under review. What possible significance therefore can be supposed to attach to its omission of the clause καὶ εὐλογοῦντες? And since, mutatis mutandis, the same remarks apply to the 6 remaining cases,—(for one, viz. the [7th], is clearly an oversight,)—will any Reader of ordinary fairness and intelligence be surprised to hear that we reject the assumed 'Conflation' unconditionally, as a silly dream? It is founded entirely upon the omission of 21 (or at most 42) words out of a total of 31,587 from Codd. B א D. And yet it is demonstrable that out of that total, B omits 1519 : ℵ, 1686 : D, 2452. The occasional *coincidence in Omission* of B + ℵ and D, was in a manner inevitable, and is undeserving of notice. If,—(which is as likely as not,)—on *six* occasions, B + ℵ and D have but omitted *different words in the same sentence,* then *there has been no ' Conflation ; '* and the (so-called) ' Theory,' which was to have revolutionized the Text of the N. T., is discovered to rest absolutely *upon nothing.* It bursts, like a very thin bubble : floats away like a film of gossamer, and disappears from sight.

But further, as a matter of fact, *at least five* out of the eight instances cited,—viz. the [1st], [2nd], [5th], [6th], [7th], —*fail to exhibit the alleged phenomena :* conspicuously ought never to have been adduced. For, in the [1st], D merely *abridges* the sentence : in the [2nd], it *paraphrases* 11 words by 11 ; and in the [6th], it *paraphrases* 12 words by 9. In the [5th], B D merely *abridge.* The utmost *residuum* of fact which survives, is therefore as follows :—

[3rd]. In a sentence of 11 words, B ℵ omit 4 : D other 4.

[4th].   „   „   9 words, B ℵ omit 5 : D other 5.

[8th].   „   „   5 words, B ℵ omit 2 : D other 2.

But if *this* be ' the clearest Evidence ' (p. 94) producible for ' the Theory of Conflation,'—then, the less said about the ' Theory,' the better for the credit of its distinguished Inventors. How *any* rational Textual Theory is to be constructed out of the foregoing Omissions, we fail to divine. But indeed the whole matter is demonstrably a weak imagination,—*a dream,* and nothing more.

XI. In the meantime, Drs. Westcott and Hort, instead of realizing the insecurity of the ground under their feet, proceed gravely to build upon it, and to treat their hypothetical assumptions as well-ascertained facts. They imagine that they have already been led by 'independent Evidence' to regard 'the longer readings as conflate each from the two earlier readings:'—whereas, up to p. 105 (where the statement occurs), they have really failed to produce a single particle of evidence, direct or indirect, for their opinion. 'We have found reason to believe' the Readings of א B L, (say they,) 'to be the original Readings.'—But why, if this is the case, have they kept their 'finding' so entirely to themselves?— *No reason whatever* have they assigned for their belief. The Reader is presently assured (p. 106) that '*it is certain*' that the Readings exhibited by the traditional Text in the eight ·supposed cases of 'Conflation' are all posterior in date to the fragmentary readings exhibited by B and D. But, once more, What is *the ground* of this 'certainty'?—Presently (viz. in p. 107), the Reader meets with the further assurance that

'*the proved* actual use of [shorter] documents in the conflate Readings renders their use elsewhere a *vera causa* in the New-tonian sense.'

But, once more,—*Where* and *what* is the 'proof' referred to? May a plain man, sincerely in search of Truth,—after wasting many precious hours over these barren pages—be permitted to declare that he resents such solemn trifling? (He craves to be forgiven if he avows that '*Pickwickian*' —not 'Newtonian'—was the epithet which solicited him, when he had to transcribe for the Printer the passage which immediately precedes.)

XII. Next come 8 pages (pp. 107–15) headed—'Posteriority of "Syrian" to "Western" and other (neutral and "Alexandrian") Readings, shown by Ante-Nicene Patristic evidence.'

In which however we are really 'shown' nothing of the sort. *Bold Assertions* abound, (as usual with this respected

writer,) but *Proof* he never attempts any. ·Not a particle of
' Evidence ' is adduced.—Next come 5 pages headed,—' Posteriority of Syrian to Western, Alexandrian, and other
(neutral) Readings, shown by Internal evidence of Syrian
readings ' (p. 115).

But again we are ' *shown* ' absolutely nothing : although
we are treated to the assurance that we have been shown
many wonders. Thus, ' the Syrian conflate Readings *have
shown* the Syrian text to be posterior to at least two ancient
forms still extant ' (p. 115) : which is the very thing they
have signally failed to do. Next,

' Patristic evidence *has shown* that these two ancient Texts,
and also a third, must have already existed early in the third
century, and suggested very strong grounds for believing that
in the middle of the century the Syrian Text had not yet been
formed.'

Whereas *no single appeal* has been made to the evidence
supplied by *one single ancient Father !*—

' Another step is gained by a close examination of all Readings
distinctively Syrian.'—(*Ibid.*)

And yet we are never told which the ' Readings distinctively
Syrian ' *are*,—although they are henceforth referred to in
every page. Neither are we instructed how to recognize
them when we see them ; which is unfortunate, since ' it
follows,'—(though we entirely fail to see from *what*,)—' that
all distinctively Syrian Readings may be set aside at once as
certainly originating after the middle of the third century.'
(p. 117) . . . Let us hear a little more on the subject :—

' The same *Facts* '—(though Dr. Hort has not hitherto favoured
us with *any*)—' lead to another conclusion of equal or even
greater importance respecting non-distinctive Syrian Readings
. . . Since the Syrian Text is only a modified eclectic combination of earlier Texts independently attested,'—

(for it is in this confident style that these eminent Scholars

handle the problem they undertook to solve, but as yet
have failed even *to touch*),—

' existing documents descended from it can attest nothing but
itself.'—(p. 118.)

Presently, we are informed that ' it follows from what has
been said above,'—(though *how* it follows, we fail to see,)—
' that all Readings in which the Pre-Syrian texts concur, *must
be accepted at once as the Apostolic Readings:*' and that ' all
distinctively Syrian Readings *must be at once rejected.*'—
(p. 119.)

Trenchant decrees of this kind at last arrest attention.
It becomes apparent that we have to do with a Writer who
has discovered a summary way of dealing with the Text of
Scripture, and who is prepared to impart his secret to any
who care to accept—without questioning—his views. We
look back to see where this accession of confidence began,
and are reminded that at p. 108 Dr. Hort announced that for
convenience he should henceforth speak of certain 'groups of
documents,' by the conventional names ' Western '—' Pre-
Syrian '—' Alexandrian '—and so forth. Accordingly, ever
since, (sometimes eight or ten times in the course of a single
page,[1]) we have encountered this arbitrary terminology : have
been required to accept it as the expression of ascertained
facts in Textual Science. Not till we find ourselves flounder-
ing in the deep mire, do we become fully aware of the
absurdity of our position. Then at last, (and high time too !),
we insist on knowing what on earth our Guide is about,
and whither he is proposing to lead us ? . . . . More con-
siderate to our Readers than he has been to us, we propose
before going any further, (instead of mystifying the subject
as Dr. Hort has done,) to state in a few plain words what

---

[1] *E.g.* pp. 115, 116, 117, 118, &c.

the present Theory, divested of pedantry and circumlocution, proves to be ; and what is Dr. Hort's actual contention.

XIII. The one great Fact, which especially troubles him and his joint Editor,[1]—(as well it may)—is *The Traditional Greek Text* of the New Testament Scriptures. Call this Text Erasmian or Complutensian,—the Text of Stephens, or of Beza, or of the Elzevirs,—call it the ' Received,' or the *Traditional Greek Text*, or whatever other name you please; —the fact remains, that a Text *has* come down to us which is attested by a general consensus of ancient Copies, ancient Fathers, ancient Versions. This, at all events, is a point on which, (happily,) there exists entire conformity of opinion between Dr. Hort and ourselves. Our Readers cannot have yet forgotten his virtual admission that,—*Beyond all question* the *Textus Receptus* is *the dominant Græco-Syrian Text of* A.D. 350 *to* A.D. 400.[2]

Obtained from a variety of sources, this Text proves to be essentially *the same* in all. That it requires Revision in respect of many of its lesser details, is undeniable: but it is at least as certain that it is an excellent Text as it stands, and that the use of it will never lead critical students of Scripture seriously astray,—which is what no one will venture to predicate concerning any single Critical Edition of the N. T. which has been published since the days of Griesbach, by the disciples of Griesbach's school.

XIV. In marked contrast to the Text we speak of,—(which is identical with the Text of every extant Lectionary of the Greek Church, and may therefore reasonably claim to be spoken of as the *Traditional* Text,)—is *that* contained in a

---

[1] Referred to below, p. 296.
[2] See above, pages 257 (bottom) and 258 (top).

little handful of documents of which the most famous are codices B א, and the Coptic Version (as far as it is known), on the one hand,—cod. D and the old Latin copies, on the other. To magnify the merits of these, as helps and guides, and to ignore their many patent and scandalous defects and blemishes :—*per fas et nefas* to vindicate their paramount authority wherever it is in any way possible to do so ; and when *that* is clearly impossible, then to treat their errors as the ancient Egyptians treated their cats, dogs, monkeys, and other vermin,—namely, to embalm them, and pay them Divine honours :—*such* for the last 50 years has been the practice of the dominant school of Textual Criticism among ourselves.   The natural and even necessary correlative of this, has been the disparagement of the merits of the commonly Received Text : which has come to be spoken of, (we know not why,) as contemptuously, almost as bitterly, as if it had been at last ascertained to be untrustworthy in every respect : a thing undeserving alike of a place and of a name among the monuments of the Past.   Even to have ' used the Received Text *as a basis for correction* ' (p. 184) is stigmatized by Dr. Hort as one ' great cause ' why Griesbach went astray.

XV. Drs. Westcott and Hort have in fact outstripped their predecessors in this singular race. Their absolute contempt for the Traditional Text,—their superstitious veneration for a few ancient documents ; (which documents however they freely confess *are not more ancient* than the ' Traditional Text ' which they despise ;)—knows no bounds. But the thing just now to be attended to is the argumentative process whereby they seek to justify their preference.—LACHMANN avowedly took his stand on a very few of the oldest known documents : and though TREGELLES slightly enlarged the area of his predecessor's observations, his method was practically identical with that of Lachmann.—TISCHENDORF, appealing to every

known authority, invariably shows himself regardless of the
evidence he has himself accumulated.   Where certain of the
uncials are,—*there* his verdict is sure also to be . . . .   Anything more unscientific, more unphilosophical, more trans-
parently *foolish* than such a method, can scarcely be conceived : but it has prevailed for 50 years, and is now at last
more hotly than ever advocated by Drs. WESTCOTT and HORT.
Only, (to their credit be it recorded,) they have had the sense
to perceive that it must needs be recommended by *Arguments*
of some sort, or else it will inevitably fall to pieces the
first fine day any one is found to charge it, with the necessary knowledge of the subject, and with sufficient resoluteness
of purpose, to make him a formidable foe.

XVI. Their expedient has been as follows.—Aware that
the Received or Traditional Greek Text (to quote their own
words,) ' *is virtually identical with that used by Chrysostom and
other Antiochian Fathers in the latter part of the IVth century :* ' and fully alive to the fact that it ' *must therefore have
been represented by Manuscripts as old as any which are
now surviving* ' (*Text*, p. 547),—they have invented an extraordinary Hypothesis in order to account for its existence :—

They assume that the writings of Origen ' establish the prior
existence of at least three types of Text : '—the most clearly
marked of which, they call the ' Western : '—another, less
prominent, they designate as ' Alexandrian : '—the third holds
(they say) a middle or ' Neutral ' position.   (That all this is
mere *moonshine*,—a day-dream and no more,—we shall insist,
until some proofs have been produced that the respected
Authors are moving amid material forms,—not discoursing
with the creations of their own brain.)   ' The priority of two
at least of these three Texts just noticed to the Syrian Text,'
they are confident has been established by the eight ' *conflate* '

Syrian Readings which they flatter themselves they have already resolved into their ' Western ' and ' Neutral ' elements (*Text*, p. 547). This, however, is a part of the subject on which we venture to hope that our Readers by this time have formed a tolerably clear opinion for themselves. The ground has been cleared of the flimsy superstructure which these Critics have been 30 years in raising, ever since we blew away (pp. 258–65) the airy foundation on which it rested.

At the end of some confident yet singularly hazy statements concerning the characteristics of ' Western ' (pp. 120–6), of ' Neutral ' (126–30), and of ' Alexandrian ' Readings (130–2), Dr. Hort favours us with the assurance that—

'The Syrian Text, to which the order of time now brings us,' ' is the chief monument of a new period of textual history.'— (p. 132.)

' Now, the three great lines were brought together, and made to contribute to the formation of a new Text different from all.'—(p. 133.)

Let it only be carefully remembered that it is of something virtually identical with the *Textus Receptus* that we are just now reading an imaginary history, and it is presumed that the most careless will be made attentive.

'The Syrian Text must in fact be the result of a "*Recension*," ... performed deliberately by Editors, and not merely by Scribes.'—(*Ibid.*)

But *why* ' must' it? Instead of ' *must in fact*,' we are disposed to read ' *may—in fiction*.' The learned Critic can but mean that, on comparing the Text of Fathers of the IVth century with the Text of cod. B, it becomes to himself self-evident that *one of the two* has been fabricated. Granted. Then,—Why should not *the solitary Codex* be the offending party? For what imaginable reason should cod. B,—which comes to us without a character, and which, when tried by the test of primitive Antiquity, stands convicted of '*universa vitiositas*,' (to use Tischendorf's expression) ;—*why* (we ask) should *codex* B be upheld 'contra mundum' ? . . . Dr. Hort proceeds—(still speaking of '*the* [imaginary] *Syrian Text*'),—

'It was probably initiated by the distracting and inconvenient currency of at least three conflicting Texts in the same region.'—(p. 133.)

Well but,—Would it not have been more methodical if 'the currency of at least three conflicting Texts in the same region,' had been first *demonstrated?* or, at least, shown to be a thing probable ? Till this 'distracting' phenomenon has been to some extent proved to have any existence in *fact*, what possible 'probability' can be claimed for the history of a 'Recension,'—which very Recension, up to this point, *has not been proved to have ever taken place at all !*

'Each Text may perhaps have found a Patron in some leading personage or see, and thus have seemed to call for a conciliation of rival claims.'—(p. 134.)

Why yes, to be sure,—'each Text [*if it existed*] may perhaps [*or perhaps may not*] have found a Patron in some leading personage [as Dr. Hort or Dr. Scrivener in our own days]:' but then, be it remembered, this will only have been possible, —(*a*) If the Recension *ever took place :* and—(*b*) If it was conducted after the extraordinary fashion which prevailed in the Jerusalem Chamber from 1870 to 1881 : for which we have the unimpeachable testimony of an eye-witness ;[1] confirmed by the Chairman of the Revisionist body,—by whom in fact it was deliberately invented.[2]

But then, since not a shadow of proof is forthcoming that *any such Recension as Dr. Hort imagines ever took place at all*,—what else but a purely gratuitous exercise of

---

[1] See above, pp. 37 to 38.   [2] *Ibid.* p. 39.

T

the imaginative faculty is it, that Dr. Hort should proceed further to invent the method which might, or could, or would, or should have been pursued, if it *had* taken place ?

Having however in this way (1) Assumed a ' Syrian Recension,'—(2) Invented the cause of it,—and (3) Dreamed the process by which it was carried into execution,—the Critic hastens, *more suo*, to characterize *the historical result* in the following terms :—

' The qualities which THE AUTHORS OF THE SYRIAN TEXT seem to have most desired to impress on it are lucidity and completeness.   They were evidently anxious to remove all stumbling-blocks out of the way of the ordinary reader, so far as this could be done without recourse to violent measures. They were apparently equally desirous that he should have the benefit of instructive matter contained in all the existing Texts, provided it did not confuse the context or introduce seeming contradictions.   New Omissions accordingly are rare, and where they occur are usually found to contribute to apparent simplicity.   New Interpolations, on the other hand, are abundant, most of them being due to harmonistic or other assimilation, fortunately capricious and incomplete.   Both in matter and in diction THE SYRIAN TEXT is conspicuously a full Text.   It delights in Pronouns, Conjunctions, and Expletives and supplied links of all kinds, as well as in more considerable Additions.   As distinguished from the *bold vigour* of the " Western " scribes, and *the refined scholarship* of the " Alexandrians," the spirit of its own corrections is at once sensible and feeble.   Entirely blameless, on either literary or religious grounds, as regards vulgarized or unworthy diction, yet *shewing no marks of either Critical or Spiritual insight, it presents the New Testament in a form smooth and attractive, but appreciably impoverished in sense and force ; more fitted for cursory perusal or recitation than for repeated and diligent study.*'—(pp. 134–5.)

XVII. We forbear to offer any remarks on this.   We should be thought uncivil were we to declare our own candid estimate of ˙ the critical and spiritual ' perception of the man who could permit himself so to write.   We prefer to proceed with our sketch of the Theory, (of *the Dream* rather,) which is intended to account for the existence of the Traditional Text of the N.T. : only venturing again to submit that surely it would have been. high time to discuss the characteristics which 'the Authors of the Syrian Text' impressed upon their work, when it had been first established—or at least rendered probable—that the supposed Operators and that the assumed Operation have any existence except in the fertile brain of this distinguished and highly imaginative writer.

XVIII. Now, the first consideration which strikes us as fatal to Dr. Hort's unsupported conjecture concerning the date of the Text he calls ' Syrian ' or ' Antiochian,' is the fact that what he so designates bears a most inconvenient resemblance to the Peschito or ancient Syriac Version ; which, like the old Latin, is (by consent of the Critics) generally assigned to the second century of our era. ' It is at any rate no stretch of imagination,' (according to Bp. Ellicott,) ' to suppose that portions of it might have been in the hands of S. John.' [p. 26.] Accordingly, these Editors assure us that—

' the only way of explaining the whole body of facts is *to suppose* that the Syriac, like the Latin Version, underwent Revision long after its origin ; and that our ordinary Syriac MSS. represent not the primitive but the altered Syriac Text.'—(p. 136.)

' A Revision of the old Syriac Version *appears* to have taken place in the IVth century, or sooner ; and *doubtless in some connexion with the Syrian Revision of the Greek Text,* the readings being to a very great extent coincident.'—(*Text*, 552.)

' Till recently, the Peschito has been known only in the form which it finally received by *an evidently authoritative Revision,'—a Syriac 'Vulgate' answering to the Latin 'Vulgate.'*—(p. 84.)

' Historical antecedents render it *tolerably certain* that the locality of such an authoritative Revision '—(which Revision however, be it observed, still rests wholly on unsupported conjecture)—' would be either Edessa or Nisibis.'—(p. 136.)

In the meantime, the abominably corrupt document known as ' Cureton's Syriac,' is, by another bold hypothesis, assumed to be the only surviving specimen of the unrevised Version, and is henceforth *invariably* designated by these authors as ' the old Syriac ; ' and referred to, as ' syr. vt.,'—(in imitation of the Latin ' *vetus* ') : the venerable Peschito being referred to as the ' Vulgate Syriac,'—' syr. vg.'

' When therefore we find large and peculiar coincidences between the *revised Syriac Text* and the Text of the Antiochian Fathers of the latter part of the IVth century,'—[of which coincidences, (be it remarked in passing,) the obvious explanation is, that the Texts referred to are faithful traditional representations of the inspired autographs ;]—' and *strong indications* that the Revision *was deliberate and in some way authoritative* in both cases,—*it becomes natural to suppose* that the two operations had some historical connexion.'—(pp. 136–7.)

XIX. But how does it happen—(let the question be asked without offence)—that a man of good abilities, bred in a University which is supposed to cultivate especially the Science of exact reasoning, should habitually allow himself in such slipshod writing as this ?   The very *fact* of a ' Revision ' of the Syriac has all to be proved ; and until it has been *demonstrated*, cannot of course be reasoned upon as a fact.   Instead of demonstration, we find ourselves invited (1) —' *To suppose* ' that such a Revision took place : and (2)—' *To suppose* ' that all our existing Manuscripts represent it.   But (as we have said) not a shadow of reason is produced *why* we should be so complaisant as ' to suppose ' either the one thing or the other.   In the meantime, the accomplished Critic hastens to assure us that there exist ' strong indications '— (why are we not *shown* them ?)—that the Revision he speaks of was ' deliberate, and in some way authoritative.'

Out of this grows a ' natural supposition ' that " two [purely imaginary] operations," " had some *historical con-*

nexion." Already therefore has the shadow thickened into a substance. "The *Revised* Syriac Text" has by this time come to be spoken of as an admitted fact. The process whereby it came into being is even assumed to have been "deliberate and authoritative." These Editors henceforth style the Peschito the '*Syriac* Vulgate,'—as confidently as Jerome's Revision of the old Latin is styled the '*Latin* Vulgate.' They even assure us that ' Cureton's Syriac' ' renders the comparatively late and "revised" character of the Syriac Vulgate *a matter of certainty*' (p. 84). The very city in which the latter underwent Revision, can, it seems, be fixed with '*tolerable certainty*' (p. 136). . . . Can Dr. Hort be serious?

At the end of a series of conjectures, (the foundation of which is the hypothesis of an Antiochian Recension of the Greek,) the learned writer announces that—' The textual elements of each principal document *having been thus ascertained*, it now becomes possible *to determine the Genealogy of a much larger number of individual readings than before*' (*Text*, p. 552).—We read and marvel.

So then, in brief, the Theory of Drs. Westcott and Hort is this :—that, somewhere between A.D. 250 and A.D. 350,

'(1) The growing diversity and confusion of Greek Texts led to an authoritative Revision at Antioch :—which (2) was then taken as a standard for a similar authoritative Revision of the Syriac text :—and (3) was itself at a later time subjected to a second authoritative Revision '—this ' final process ' having been ' apparently completed by [A.D.] 350 or thereabouts.'—(p. 137.)

XX. Now, instead of insisting that this entire Theory is made up of a series of purely gratuitous assumptions,— destitute alike of attestation and of probability : and that, as a mere effort of the Imagination, it is entitled to no manner of consideration or respect at our hands :—instead of dealing *thus* with what precedes, we propose to be most kind and accommodating to Dr. Hort. We proceed *to accept his Theory in its entirety.* We will, with the Reader's permission, assume that *all* he tells us is historically true : is an authentic narrative of what actually did take place. We shall in the end invite the same Reader to recognize the inevitable consequences of our admission : to which we shall inexorably pin the learned Editors—bind them hand and foot;—of course reserving to ourselves the right of disallowing *for ourselves* as much of the matter as we please.

Somewhere between A.D. 250 and 350 therefore,—('it is impossible to say with confidence' [p. 137] what was the actual date, but these Editors evidently incline to the latter half of the IIIrd century, i.e. *circa* A.D. 275);—we are to believe that the Ecclesiastical heads of the four great Patriarchates of Eastern Christendom,—Alexandria, Antioch, Jerusalem, Constantinople,—had become so troubled at witnessing the prevalence of depraved copies of Holy Scripture in their respective churches, that they resolved by common consent on achieving an authoritative Revision which should henceforth become the standard Text of all the Patriarchates of the East. The same sentiment of distress— (by the hypothesis) penetrated into Syria proper ; and the Bishops of Edessa or Nisibis, ('great centres of life and culture to the Churches whose language was Syriac,' [p. 136,]) lent themselves so effectually to the project, that a single fragmentary document is, at the present day, the only vestige remaining of the Text which before had been universally prevalent in the Syriac-speaking Churches of antiquity. 'The *almost total extinction of Old Syriac MSS.,* contrasted with the great number of extant *Vulgate Syriac MSS.*,'—(for it is thus that Dr. Hort habitually exhibits evidence !),—is to be attributed, it seems, to the power and influence of the Authors of the imaginary Syriac Revision. [*ibid.*] Bp. Ellicott, by the way (an unexceptionable witness), characterizes Cureton's Syriac as ' *singular and sometimes rather wild.*' ' *The text, of a very composite nature ;* sometimes *inclining to the shortness and simplicity of the Vatican manuscript, but more commonly presenting the same paraphrastic character of text as the Codex Bezæ.*' [p. 42.]   (It is, in fact, an *utterly depraved* and *fabricated* document.)

We venture to remark in passing that Textual matters must have everywhere reached a very alarming pass indeed to render intelligible the resort to so extraordinary a step as a representative Conference of the ' leading Personages or Sees ' (p. 134) of Eastern Christendom.   The inference is at least inevitable, that men in high place at that time deemed themselves competent to grapple with the problem.   Enough was familiarly known about the character and the sources of these corrupt Texts to make it certain that they would be recognizable when produced ; and that, when condemned by authority, they would no longer be propagated, and in the end would cease to molest the Church.   Thus much, at all events, is legitimately to be inferred from the hypothesis.

XXI. Behold then from every principal Diocese of ancient Christendom, and in the Church's palmiest days, the most famous of the ante-Nicene Fathers repair to Antioch.   They go up by authority,' and are attended by skilled Ecclesiastics of the highest theological attainment.   Bearers are they perforce of a vast number of Copies of the Scriptures : and (by the hypothesis) *the latest possible dates* of any of these Copies must range between A.D. 250 and 350.   But the Delegates of so many ancient Sees will have been supremely careful, before starting on so important and solemn an errand, to make diligent search for the oldest Copies anywhere discoverable : and when they reach the scene of their deliberations, we may be certain that they are able to appeal to not a few codices *written within a hundred years of the* date of the *inspired Autographs* themselves.   Copies of the Scriptures authenticated as having belonged to the most famous of their predecessors,—and held by them in high repute for the presumed purity of their Texts—will have been freely produced: while, in select receptacles, will have been stowed away—for purposes of comparison and avoidance— specimens of those dreaded Texts whose existence has been the sole cause why (by the hypothesis) this extraordinary concourse of learned Ecclesiastics has taken place.

After solemnly invoking the Divine blessing, these men address themselves assiduously to their task; and (by the hypothesis) they proceed to condemn every codex which exhibits a 'strictly Western,' or a 'strictly Alexandrian,' or a 'strictly Neutral' type.   In plain English, if codices B, ℵ, and D had been before them, they would have unceremoniously rejected all three ; but then, (by the hypothesis) neither of the two first-named had yet come into being : while 200 years at least must roll out before Cod. D would see the light.   In the meantime, the *immediate ancestors* of B ℵ and D will perforce have come under judicial scrutiny ; and, (by the hypothesis,) they will have been scornfully rejected by the general consent of the Judges.

XXII.   Pass an interval—(are we to suppose of fifty years ?)—and the work referred to is '*subjected to a second authoritative Revision.*'   *Again*, therefore, behold the piety and learning of the four great Patriarchates of the East, formally represented at Antioch !   The Church is now in her palmiest days.   Some of her greatest men belong to the period of which we are speaking.   Eusebius (A.D. 308– 340) is in his glory.   One whole generation has come and gone since the last Textual Conference was held, at Antioch.

Yet is no inclination manifested to reverse the decrees of the earlier Conference. This second Recension of the Text of Scripture does but 'carry out more completely the purposes of the first;' and 'the final process was apparently completed by A.D. 350' (p. 137).—So far the Cambridge Professor.

XXIII. But the one important fact implied by this august deliberation concerning the Text of Scripture has been conveniently passed over by Dr. Hort in profound silence. We take leave to repair his omission by inviting the Reader's particular attention to it.

We request him to note that, *by the hypothesis*, there will have been submitted to the scrutiny of these many ancient Ecclesiastics *not a few codices of exactly the same type as codices* B *and* ℵ: especially as codex B. We are able even to specify with precision certain features which the codices in question will have all concurred in exhibiting. Thus,—

(1) From S. Mark's Gospel, those depraved copies will have omitted THE LAST TWELVE VERSES (xvi. 9–20).

(2) From S. Luke's Gospel the same corrupt copies will have omitted our SAVIOUR'S AGONY IN THE GARDEN (xxii. 43, 44).

(3) His PRAYER ON BEHALF OF HIS MURDERERS (xxiii. 34), will have also been away.

(4) The INSCRIPTION ON THE CROSS, in GREEK, LATIN, AND HEBREW (xxiii. 38), will have been partly, misrepresented,—partly, away.

(5) And there will have been no account discoverable of S. PETER'S VISIT TO THE SEPULCHRE (xxiv. 12).

(6) Absent will have been also the record of our LORD'S ASCENSION INTO HEAVEN (*ibid.* 51).

(7) Also, from S. John's Gospel, the codices in question

will have omitted the incident of THE TROUBLING OF THE
POOL OF BETHESDA (v. 3, 4).

Now, we request that it may be clearly noted that,
according to Dr. Hort, against every copy of the Gospels so
maimed and mutilated, (i.e. *against every copy of the Gospels
of the same type as codices* B *and* ℵ,)—the many illustrious
Bishops who, (*still* according to Dr. Hort,) assembled at
Antioch, first in A.D. 250 and then in A.D. 350,—by common
consent set a mark of *condemnation*. We are assured that
those famous men,—those Fathers of the Church,—were
emphatic in their sanction, instead, of codices of the type
of Cod. A,—in which all these seven omitted passages (and
many hundreds besides) are duly found in their proper
places.

When, therefore, at the end of a thousand and half a
thousand years, Dr. Hort (guided by his inner consciousness,
and depending on an intellectual illumination of which he is
able to give no intelligible account) proposes to reverse the
deliberate sentence of Antiquity,—his position strikes us as
bordering on the ludicrous. Concerning the seven places above
referred to, which the assembled Fathers pronounce to be
genuine Scripture, and declare to be worthy of all acceptation,—Dr. Hort expresses himself in terms which—could
they have been heard at Antioch—must, it is thought, have
brought down upon his head tokens of displeasure which
might have even proved inconvenient. But let the respected
gentleman by all means be allowed to speak for himself :—

(1) THE LAST TWELVE VERSES of S. Mark (he would have
been heard to say) are a 'very early interpolation.' 'Its
authorship and precise date must remain unknown.' 'It
manifestly cannot claim any Apostolic authority.' 'It is

doubtless founded on some tradition of the Apostolic age.'—
(*Notes*, pp. 46 and 51.)

(2) THE AGONY IN THE GARDEN (he would have told them)
is 'an early Western interpolation,' and 'can only be a
fragment from traditions, written or oral,'—'rescued from
oblivion by the scribes of the second century.'—(pp. 66–7.)

(3) THE PRAYER OF OUR LORD FOR HIS MURDERERS (Dr.
Hort would have said),—' I cannot doubt comes from an
extraneous source.' It is ' a Western interpolation.'—(p.68.)

(4) TO THE INSCRIPTION ON THE CROSS, IN GREEK, LATIN,
AND HEBREW [S. Luke xxiii. 38], he would not have allowed
so much as a hearing.

(5) The spuriousness of the narrative of S. PETER'S VISIT
TO THE SEPULCHRE [S. Luke xxiv. 12] (the same Ante-Nicene
Fathers would have learned) he regards as a 'moral certainty.'
He would have assured them that it is ' a Western non-in-
terpolation.'—(p. 71.)

(6) They would have learned that, in the account of the
same Critic, S. Luke xxiv. 51 is another spurious addition to
the inspired Text : another 'Western non-interpolation.'
Dr. Hort would have tried to persuade them that OUR LORD'S
ASCENSION INTO HEAVEN '*was evidently inserted from an
assumption* that a separation from the disciples at the close
of a Gospel *must be the Ascension*,' (*Notes*, p. 73). . . . (What
the Ante-Nicene Fathers would have thought of their teacher
we forbear to conjecture.)—(p. 71.)

(7) THE TROUBLING OF THE POOL OF BETHESDA [S. John v.
3, 4] is not even allowed a bracketed place in Dr. Hort's
Text. How the accomplished Critic would have set about
persuading the Ante-Nicene Fathers that they were in error
for holding it to be genuine Scripture, it is hard to imagine.

XXIV. It is plain therefore that Dr. Hort is in direct
antagonism with the collective mind of Patristic Antiquity.

Why, when it suits him, he should appeal to the same
Ancients for support,—we fail to understand. 'If Baal be
GOD, then follow *him !'* Dr. Hort has his codex B and his
codex א to guide him. He informs us (p. 276) that 'the fullest
consideration does but increase the conviction that the *pre-
eminent relative purity'* of those two codices 'is approximately
*absolute,—a true approximate reproduction of the Text of the
Autographs.'* On the other hand, he has discovered that
the Received Text is virtually the production of the Fathers
of the Nicene Age (A.D. 250–A.D. 350),—exhibits a Text
fabricated throughout by the united efforts of those well-
intentioned but thoroughly misguided men. What is it to
him, henceforth, how Athanasius, or Didymus, or Cyril exhibits a place ?

Yes, we repeat it,—Dr. Hort is in direct antagonism with
the Fathers of the IIIrd and the IVth Century. His own
fantastic hypothesis of a 'Syrian Text,'—the solemn expression of the collective wisdom and deliberate judgment
of the Fathers of the Nicene Age (A.D. 250–A.D. 350),—is the
best answer which can by possibility be invented to his own
pages,—is, in our account, the one sufficient and conclusive
refutation of his own Text.

Thus, his prolix and perverse discussion of S. Mark xvi.
9–20 (viz. from p. 28 to p. 51 of his *Notes*),—which, carefully
analysed, is found merely to amount to 'Thank you for showing us our mistake; but we mean to stick to our *Mumpsimus !'* : — those many inferences as well from what the
Fathers do *not* say, as from what they *do ;*—are all effectually
disposed of by his own theory of a 'Syrian text.' A mighty
array of forgotten Bishops, Fathers, Doctors of the Nicene
period, come back and calmly assure the accomplished Professor that the evidence on which he relies is but an insigni-

ficant fraction of the evidence which was before themselves
when they delivered their judgment. 'Had you known but
the thousandth part of what we knew familiarly,' say they,
'you would have spared yourself this exposure. You seem
to have forgotten that Eusebius was one of the chief persons
in our assembly; that Cyril of Jerusalem and Athanasius,
Basil and Gregory of Nazianzus, as well as his namesake
of Nyssa,—were all living when we held our Textual Conference, and some of them, though young men, were even
parties to our decree.' . . . Now, as an *argumentum ad
hominem*, this, be it observed, is decisive and admits of no
rejoinder.

XXV. How then about those 'Syrian *Conflations*' concerning which a few pages back we heard so much, and for
which Dr. Hort considers the august tribunal of which we
are now speaking to be responsible ? He is convinced that
the (so-called) Syrian Text (which he regards as the product
of their deliberations), is 'an eclectic text *combining Readings
from the three principal Texts*' (p. 145): which Readings in
consequence he calls '*conflate*.' How then is it to be supposed that these 'Conflations' arose ? The answer is obvious.
As 'Conflations,' *they have no existence*,—save in the fertile
brain of Dr. Hort. Could the ante-Nicene fathers who
never met at Antioch have been interrogated by him concerning this matter, — (let the Hibernian supposition be
allowed for argument sake !)—they would perforce have made
answer,—' You quite mistake the purpose for which we came
together, learned sir ! You are evidently thinking of your
Jerusalem Chamber and of the unheard-of method devised by
your Bishop' [see pp. 37 to 39: also p. 273] 'for ascertaining
the Truth of Scripture. Well may the resuscitation of so many
forgotten blunders have occupied you and your colleagues
for as long a period as was expended on the Siege of Troy !

Our business was not to *invent* readings whether by " Conflation" or otherwise, but only to distinguish between
spurious Texts and genuine,—families of fabricated MSS.,
and those which we knew to be trustworthy,—mutilated and
unmutilated Copies.   Every one of what *you* are pleased to
call " Conflate Readings," learned sir, we found—just as *you*
find them—in 99 out of 100 of our copies : and we gave
them our deliberate approval, and left them standing in the
Text in consequence.   We believed them to be,—we are
confident that they *are*,—the very words of the Evangelists
and Apostles of the LORD : the *ipsissima verba* of the SPIRIT :
" *the true sayings of the* HOLY GHOST." '   [See p. 38, note [2].]

All this however by the way.   The essential thing to be
borne in mind is that, according to Dr. Hort,—*on two distinct
occasions between* A.D. 250 *and* 350—the whole Eastern Church,
meeting by representation in her palmiest days, deliberately
put forth *that* Traditional Text of the N.T. with which we at
this day are chiefly familiar.   That this is indeed his view of
the matter, there can at least be no doubt.   He says :—

‘ *An authoritative Revision* at Antioch .... was itself subjected
to *a second authoritative Revision* carrying out more completely
the purposes of the first.’ ‘ At what date between A.D. 250 and
350 *the first process* took place, it is impossible to say with confidence.’ ‘ *The final process* was apparently completed by A.D. 350
or thereabouts.’—(p. 137.)

‘ The fundamental text of late extant Greek MSS. generally
is beyond all question identical with the dominant Antiochian or
Græco-Syrian text of *the second half of the IVth century.*’—(p. 92.)

Be it so.   It follows that the Text exhibited by such
codices as B and ℵ *was deliberately condemned* by the assembled
piety, learning, and judgment of the four great Patriarchates
of Eastern Christendom.   At a period when there existed
nothing more modern than Codices B and ℵ, — nothing *so*
modern as A and C,—all specimens of the former class were

rejected : while such codices as bore a general resemblance to
A were by common consent pointed out as deserving of
confidence and *recommended for repeated Transcription.*

XXVI. Pass *fifteen hundred* years, and the Reader is invited
to note attentively what has come to pass.   Time has made
a clean sweep, it may be, of every Greek codex belonging to
either of the two dates above indicated.   Every tradition
belonging to the period has also long since utterly perished.
When lo, in A.D. 1831, under the auspices of Dr. Lachmann,
'a new departure' is made.   Up springs what may be called
the new German school of Textual Criticism,—of which the
fundamental principle is a superstitious deference to the
decrees of cod. B.   The heresy prevails for fifty years (1831–
81) and obtains many adherents.   The practical result is,
that its chief promoters make it their business to throw discredit on the result of the two great Antiochian Revisions
already spoken of!   The (so-called) 'Syrian Text'—although
assumed by Drs. Westcott and Hort to be the product of the
combined wisdom, piety, and learning of the great Patriarchates of the East from A.D. 250 to A.D. 350; 'a "Recension"
in the proper sense of the word ; a work of attempted Criticism, performed deliberately by Editors and not merely by
Scribes' (p. 133) :—this 'Syrian Text,' Doctors Westcott and
Hort denounce as ' *showing no marks of either critical or spiritual insight :*'—

It 'presents' (say they) 'the New Testament in a form
smooth and attractive, but *appreciably impoverished in sense and
force ;* more fitted for cursory perusal or recitation than for
repeated and diligent study.'—(p. 135.)

XXVII. We are content to leave this matter to the
Reader's judgment.   For ourselves, we make no secret of
the grotesqueness of the contrast thus, for the second time,
presented to the imagination.   On *that* side, by the hypo-

thesis, sit the greatest Doctors of primitive Christendom, assembled in solemn conclave. Every most illustrious name is there. By ingeniously drawing a purely arbitrary hard-and-fast line at the year A.D. 350, and so anticipating many a '*floruit*' by something between five and five-and-twenty years, Dr. Hort's intention is plain: but the expedient will not serve his turn. Quite content are we with the names secured to us within the proposed limits of time. On *that* side then, we behold congregated choice representatives of the wisdom, the piety, the learning of the Eastern Church, from A.D. 250 to A.D. 350.—On this side sits—Dr. Hort! . . . An interval of 1532 years separates these two parties.

XXVIII. And first,—How may the former assemblage be supposed to have been occupying themselves? The object with which those distinguished personages came together was the loftiest, the purest, the holiest imaginable: viz. to purge out from the sacred Text the many corruptions by which, in their judgments, it had become depraved during the 250 (or at the utmost 300) years which have elapsed since it first came into existence; to detect the counterfeit and to eliminate the spurious. Not unaware by any means are they of the carelessness of Scribes, nor yet of the corruptions which have been brought in through the officiousness of critical ' Correctors' of the Text. To what has resulted from the misdirected piety of the Orthodox, they are every bit as fully alive as to what has crept in through the malignity of Heretical Teachers. Moreover, while the memory survives in all its freshness of the depravations which the inspired Text has experienced from these and other similar corrupting influences, the *means abound* and *are at hand* of *testing* every suspected place of Scripture. Well, and next,—How have these holy men prospered in their holy enterprise?

XXIX. According to Dr. Hort, by a strange fatality,—a most unaccountable and truly disastrous proclivity to error, —these illustrious Fathers of the Church have been at every instant substituting the spurious for the genuine,—a fabricated Text in place of the Evangelical Verity. Miserable men! In the Gospels alone they have interpolated about 3,100 words: have omitted about 700: have substituted about 1000; have transposed about 2200: have altered (in respect of number, case, mood, tense, person, &c.) about 1200.[1] This done, they have amused themselves with the give-and-take process of mutual accommodation which we are taught to call ' *Conflation:*' in plain terms, *they have been manufacturing Scripture.* The Text, as it comes forth from their hands,—

(*a*) "*Shews no marks of either critical or spiritual insight:*"—

(*b*) "Presents the New Testament in a form smooth and attractive, but *appreciably impoverished in sense and force:*"—

(*c*) "*Is more fitted for cursory perusal or recitation, than for repeated and diligent study.*"

Moreover, the mischief has proved infectious,—has spread. In Syria also, at Edessa or Nisibis,—(for it is as well to be circumstantial in such matters,)—the self-same iniquity is about to be perpetrated; of which the Peschito will be the abiding monument: *one* solitary witness only to the pure Text being suffered to escape. Cureton's fragmentary Syriac will

---

[1] To speak with entire accuracy, Drs. Westcott and Hort require us to believe that the Authors of the [imaginary] Syrian Revisions of A.D. 250 and A.D. 350, interpolated the genuine Text of the Gospels, with between 2877 (B) and 3455 (ℵ) spurious words; mutilated the genuine Text in respect of between 536 (B) and 839 (ℵ) words :—substituted for as many genuine words, between 935 (B) and 1114 (ℵ) uninspired words :—licentiously transposed between 2098 (B) and 2299 (ℵ) :—and in respect of number, case, mood, tense, person, &c., altered without authority between 1132 (B) and 1265 (ℵ) words.

U

alone remain to exhibit to mankind the outlines of primitive Truth. (The reader is reminded of the character already given of the document in question at the summit of page 279. Its extravagance can only be fully appreciated by one who will be at the pains to read it steadily through.)

XXX. And pray, (we ask,)—*Who* says all this? *Who* is it who gravely puts forth all this egregious nonsense? . . . It is Dr. Hort, (we answer,) at pp. 134–5 of the volume now under review. In fact, according to *him*, those primitive Fathers have been the great falsifiers of Scripture; have proved the worst enemies of the pure Word of GOD; have shamefully betrayed their sacred trust; have done the diametrical reverse of what (by the hypothesis) they came together for the sole purpose of doing. They have depraved and corrupted that sacred Text which it was their aim, their duty, and their professed object to purge from its errors. And (by the hypothesis) Dr. Hort, at the end of 1532 years,—aided by codex B and his own self-evolved powers of divination,—has found them out, and now holds them up to the contempt and scorn of the British public.

XXXI. In the meantime the illustrious Professor invites us to believe that the mistaken textual judgment pronounced at Antioch in A.D. 350 had an immediate effect on the Text of Scripture throughout the world. We are requested to suppose that it resulted in the instantaneous extinction of codices the like of B ℵ, wherever found; and caused codices of the A type to spring up like mushrooms in their place, and *that*, in every library of ancient Christendom. We are further required to assume that this extraordinary substitution of new evidence for old—the false for the true—fully explains why Irenæus and Hippolytus, Athanasius and Didymus, Gregory of

Nazianzus and Gregory of Nyssa, Basil and Ephraem, Epiphanius and Chrysostom, Theodore of Mopsuestia and Isidore
of Pelusium, Nilus and Nonnus, Proclus and Severianus,
the two Cyrils and Theodoret—*one and all*—show themselves strangers to the text of B and ℵ. . . . We read and
marvel.

XXXII. For, (it is time to enquire,)—Does not the learned
Professor see that, by thus getting rid of the testimony of
the whole body of the Fathers, he leaves the Science which he is
so good as to patronize in a most destitute condition,—besides
placing himself in a most inconvenient state of isolation? If
clear and consentient Patristic testimony to the Text of Scripture is not to be deemed forcible witness to its Truth,—
whither shall a man betake himself for constraining Evidence?
Dr. Hort has already set aside the Traditional Text as a thing
of no manner of importance. The venerable Syriac Version
he has also insisted on reducing very nearly to the level of
the despised cursives. As for the copies of the old Latin,
they had confessedly become so untrustworthy, at the time of
which he speaks, that a modest Revision of the Text they
embody, (the '*Vulgate*' namely,) became at last a measure
of necessity. What remains to him therefore? Can he
seriously suppose that the world will put up with the 'idiosyncrasy' of a living Doctor—his 'personal instincts' (p. xi.)—
his 'personal discernment' (p. 65),—his 'instinctive processes
of Criticism' (p. 66),—his 'individual mind,'—in preference
to articulate voices coming to us across the gulf of Time from
every part of ancient Christendom? How—with the faintest
chance of success—does Dr. Hort propose to remedy the
absence of External Testimony? If mankind can afford to
do without either consent of Copies or of Fathers, why does
mankind any longer adhere to the ancient methods of proof?
Why do Critics of every school *still* accumulate references to

MSS., explore the ancient Versions, and ransack the Patristic writings in search of neglected citations of Scripture? That the ancients were indifferent Textual Critics, is true enough. The mischief done by Origen in this department,—through his fondness for a branch of Learning in which his remarks show that he was all unskilled,—is not to be told. But then, these men lived within a very few hundred years of the Apostles of the LORD JESUS CHRIST : and when they witness to the reading of their own copies, their testimony on the point, to say the least, is worthy of our most respectful attention. *Dated codices*, in fact are they, *to all intents and purposes*, as often as they bear clear witness to the Text of Scripture : —a fact, (we take leave to throw out the remark in passing,) which has not yet nearly attracted the degree of attention which it deserves.

XXXIII. For ourselves, having said so much on this subject, it is fair that we should add,—We devoutly wish that Dr. Hort's hypothesis of an authoritative and deliberate Recension of the Text of the New Testament achieved at Antioch first, about A.D. 250, and next, about A.D. 350, were indeed an historical fact. We desire no firmer basis on which to rest our confidence in the Traditional Text of Scripture than the deliberate verdict of Antiquity,—the ascertained sanction of the collective Church, in the Nicene age.   The *Latin* 'Vulgate' [A.D. 385] is the work of a single man—Jerome. The *Syriac* 'Vulgate' [A.D. 616] was also the work of a single man—Thomas of Harkel.   But this *Greek* 'Vulgate' was (by the hypothesis) the product of the Church Catholic, [A.D. 250– A.D. 350,] in her corporate capacity. Not only should we hail such a monument of the collective piety and learning of the Church in her best days with unmingled reverence and joy, were it introduced to our notice ; but we should insist that no important deviation from such a ' *Textus Receptus* ' as *that*

would deserve to be listened to.   In other words, if Dr.
Hort's theory about the origin of the *Textus Receptus* have
any foundation at all in fact, it is 'all up' with Dr. Hort.
He is absolutely *nowhere.*   He has most ingeniously placed
himself on the horns of a fatal dilemma.

For,—(let it be carefully noted,)—the entire discussion
becomes, in this way, brought (so to speak) within the compass of a nutshell.   To state the case briefly,—We are invited
to make our election between the Fathers of the Church,
A.D. 250 and A.D. 350,—and Dr. Hort, A.D. 1881.   The issue is
really reduced to *that.*   The general question of THE TEXT OF
SCRIPTURE being the matter at stake; (not any particular
passage, remember, but *the Text of Scripture as a whole* ;)—and
the *conflicting parties* being but *two* ;— *Which* are we to
believe ? *the consentient Voice of Antiquity,*—or the solitary
modern Professor ?   Shall we accept the august Testimony
of the whole body of the Fathers ? or shall we prefer to be
guided by the self-evolved imaginations of one who confessedly has nothing to offer but conjecture ?   The question
before us is reduced to that single issue.   But in fact the
alternative admits of being yet more concisely stated.   We are
invited to make our election between FACT and—FICTION . . .
All this, of course, on the supposition that there is *any truth
at all* in Dr. Hort's ' New Textual Theory.'

XXXIV. Apart however from the gross intrinsic improbability of the supposed Recension,—the utter absence of
one particle of evidence, traditional or otherwise, that it ever
did take place, must be held to be fatal to the hypothesis
that it *did.*   It is simply incredible that an incident of such
magnitude and interest would leave no trace of itself in history.   As a conjecture—(and it only professes to be a conjecture)—Dr. Hort's notion of how the Text of the Fathers of

the IIIrd, IVth, and Vth centuries,—which, as he truly
remarks, is in the main identical with our own *Received Text*,
—came into being, must be unconditionally abandoned. In the
words of a learned living Prelate,—" *the supposition* " on which
Drs. Westcott and Hort have staked their critical reputation,
" *is a manifest absurdity.*" [1]

XXXV. We have been so full on the subject of this imaginary ' Antiochian ' or ' Syrian text,' not (the reader may be
sure) without sufficient reason. Scant satisfaction truly is
there in scattering to the winds an airy tissue which its
ingenious authors have been industriously weaving for
30 years. But it is clear that with this hypothesis of a
' Syrian ' text,—the immediate source and actual prototype of
the commonly received Text of the N. T.,—*stands or falls
their entire Textual theory.* Reject it, and the entire fabric is
observed to collapse, and subside into a shapeless ruin. And
with it, of necessity, goes the ' New Greek Text,'—and therefore the ' *New English Version* ' of our Revisionists, which in
the main has been founded on it.

XXXVI. In the meantime the phenomena upon which this
phantom has been based, remain unchanged; and fairly interpreted, will be found to conduct us to the diametrically
opposite result to that which has been arrived at by Drs.
Westcott and Hort. With perfect truth has the latter
remarked on the practical ' identity of the Text, more especially in the Gospels and Pauline Epistles, in all the known
cursive MSS., except a few ' (p. 143). We fully admit the
truth of his statement that—

' *Before the close of the IVth century*, a Greek Text not materially
differing from the almost universal Text of the IXth,'—[and

---

[1] Quoted by Canon Cook, *Revised Version Considered*,—p. 202.

why not of the VIth? of the VIIth? of the VIIIth? or again
of the Xth? of the XIth? of the XIIth?]—'century, was
dominant at Antioch.'—(p. 142.)

And why not throughout the whole of Eastern Christendom?
Why this continual mention of '*Antioch*,'—this perpetual
introduction of the epithet '*Syrian*'? Neither designation
applies to Irenæus or to Hippolytus,—to Athanasius or to
Didymus,—to Gregory of Nazianzus or to his namesake of
Nyssa,—to Basil or to Epiphanius,—to Nonnus or to Macarius,—to Proclus or to Theodorus Mops.,—to the earlier or
to the later Cyril.—In brief,

'The fundamental text of the late extant Greek MSS. generally is, beyond all question, identical with [what Dr. Hort
chooses to call] the dominant Antiochian or Græco-Syrian text
of the second half of the IVth century. . . . The Antiochian [and
other] Fathers, and the bulk of extant MSS. written from
about three or four, to ten or eleven centuries later, must
have had, in the greater number of extant variations, a common
original *either contemporary with, or older than, our oldest extant
MSS.*'—(p. 92.)

XXXVII. So far then, happily, we are entirely agreed. The
only question is,—How is this resemblance to be accounted
for? *Not*, we answer,—*not*, certainly, by putting forward so
violent and improbable—so *irrational* a conjecture as that,
first, about A.D. 250,—and then again about A.D. 350,—
an authoritative standard Text was fabricated at Antioch; of
which all other known MSS. (except a very little handful)
are nothing else but transcripts:—but rather, by loyally
recognizing, in the practical identity of the Text exhibited
by 99 out of 100 of our extant MSS., the probable general
fidelity of those many transcripts *to the inspired exemplars
themselves from which remotely they are confessedly descended.*
And surely, if it be allowable to assume (with Dr. Hort)
that for 1532 years, (viz. from A.D. 350 to A.D. 1882) the

Antiochian standard has been faithfully retained and transmitted,—it will be impossible to assign any valid reason why the inspired Original itself, the *Apostolic* standard, should not have been as faithfully transmitted and retained from the Apostolic age to the Antiochian,[1]—i.e. throughout an interval of less than 250 years, or *one-sixth* of the period.

XXXVIII. Here, it will obviously occur to enquire,—But what has been Drs. Westcott and Hort's *motive* for inventing such an improbable hypothesis? and why is Dr. Hort so strenuous in maintaining it? . . . . . We reply by reminding the Reader of certain remarks which we made at the outset.[2] The *Traditional Text* of the N. T. is a phenomenon which sorely exercises Critics of the new school. To depreciate it, is easy : to deny its critical authority, is easier still : to cast ridicule on the circumstances under which Erasmus produced his first (very faulty) edition of it (1516), is easiest of all. But *to ignore* the 'Traditional Text,' is impossible. Equally impossible is it to overlook its practical identity with the Text of Chrysostom, who lived and taught *at Antioch* till A.D. 398, when he became Abp. of *Constantinople*. Now this is a very awkward circumstance, and must in some way be got over; for it transports us, at a bound, from the stifling atmosphere of Basle and Alcala,—from Erasmus and Stunica, Stephens and Beza and the Elzevirs,—to Antioch and Constantinople in the latter part of the IVth century. What is to be done?

XXXIX. Drs. Westcott and Hort assume that this 'Antiochian text'—found in the later cursives and the Fathers of the latter half of the IVth century—must be an *artificial*, an *arbitrarily invented* standard ; a text *fabricated* between

---

[1] *i.e.* say from A.D. 90 to A.D. 250–350.   [2] See above, p. 269.

A.D. 250 and A.D. 350.   And if they may but be so fortunate
as to persuade the world to adopt their hypothesis, then all
will be easy ; for they will have reduced the supposed 'consent of Fathers' to the reproduction of one and the same
single 'primary documentary witness:'[1]—and 'it is hardly
necessary to point out the total change in the bearing
of the evidence by the introduction of *the factor of Genealogy*' (p. 43) at this particular juncture.   *Upset* the
hypothesis on the other hand, and all is reversed in a
moment.   Every attesting Father is perceived to be a dated
MS. and an independent authority; and the combined evidence of several of these becomes simply unmanageable.
In like manner, "the approximate consent of the cursives"
(see the foot-note), is perceived to be equivalent *not* to "A
PRIMARY DOCUMENTARY WITNESS,"—*not* to "ONE ANTIOCHIAN
ORIGINAL,"—but to be tantamount to the articulate speech of
many witnesses *of high character,.* coming to us *from every
quarter* of primitive Christendom.

XL. But—(the further enquiry is sure to be made)—
In favour of which document, or set of documents, have all
these fantastic efforts been made to disparage the commonly
received standards of excellence ?   The ordinary English
Reader may require to be reminded that, prior to the IVth
century, our Textual helps are few, fragmentary, and—to
speak plainly—insufficient.   As for sacred Codices of that
date, we possess NOT ONE.   Of our two primitive Versions,

---

[1] 'If,' says Dr. Hort, 'an editor were for any purpose to make it his aim
to restore as completely as possible the New Testament of Antioch in A.D.
350, he could not help taking the approximate consent of the cursives as
equivalent to *a primary documentary witness.*   And he would not be the
less justified in so doing for being unable to say precisely by what historical
agencies THE ONE ANTIOCHIAN ORIGINAL'—[note the fallacy!]—'*was multiplied into the cursive hosts of the later ages.*'—Pp. 143–4.

'the Syriac and the old Latin,' the second is grossly corrupt; owing (says Dr. Hort) 'to a perilous confusion between transcription and *reproduction;*' 'the preservation of a record and *its supposed improvement*' (p. 121). 'Further acquaintance with it only increases our distrust' (*ibid.*). In plainer English, 'the earliest readings which can be fixed chronologically' (p. 120) belong to a Version which is licentious and corrupt to an incredible extent. And though 'there is no reason to doubt that the Peschito [or ancient Syriac] is at least as old as the Latin Version' (p. 84), yet (according to Dr. Hort) it is 'impossible'—(he is nowhere so good as to explain to us wherein this supposed 'impossibility' consists),—to regard '*the present form* of the Version as a true representation of the original Syriac text.' The date of it (according to *him*) *may* be as late as A.D. 350. Anyhow, we are assured (but only by Dr. Hort) that important 'evidence for the Greek text is hardly to be looked for from *this* source' (p. 85).—The Fathers of the IIIrd century who have left behind them considerable remains in Greek are but two,—Clemens Alex. and Origen : and there are considerations attending the citations of either, which greatly detract from their value.

XLI. The question therefore recurs with redoubled emphasis,—In favour of *which* document, or set of documents, does Dr. Hort disparage the more considerable portion of that early evidence,—so much of it, namely, as belongs to the IVth century,—on which the Church has been hitherto accustomed confidently to rely ?   He asserts that,—

'Almost all Greek Fathers after Eusebius have texts so deeply affected by mixture that' they 'cannot at most count for more than so many secondary Greek uncial MSS., *inferior in most cases to the better sort of secondary uncial MSS. now existing.*'—(p. 202.)

And thus, at a stroke, behold, 'almost *all Greek Fathers after Eusebius*' — (who died A.D. 340) — are disposed of! washed overboard! put clean out of sight! Athanasius and Didymus—the 2 Basils and the 2 Gregories—the 2 Cyrils and the 2 Theodores — Epiphanius and Macarius and Ephraem—Chrysostom and Severianus and Proclus—Nilus and Nonnus—Isidore of Pelusium and Theodoret: not to mention at least as many more who have left scanty, yet most precious, remains behind them :—all these are pronounced *inferior* in authority to as many IXth- or Xth-century copies! . . . We commend, in passing, the foregoing *dictum* of these accomplished Editors to the critical judgment of all candid and intelligent Readers. *Not* as dated manuscripts, therefore, at least equal in Antiquity to the oldest which we now possess :—*not* as the authentic utterances of famous Doctors and Fathers of the Church, (instead of being the work of unknown and irresponsible Scribes):—*not* as sure witnesses of what was accounted Scripture in a known region, by a famous personage, at a well-ascertained period, (instead of coming to us, as our codices *universally* do, without a history and without a character) :—in no such light are we henceforth to regard Patristic citations of Scripture:—but only 'as so many secondary MSS., *inferior to the better sort of secondary uncials now existing.*'

XLII. That the Testimony of the Fathers, in the lump, must perforce in some such way either be ignored or else flouted, if the Text of Drs. Westcott and Hort is to stand,—we were perfectly well aware. It is simply fatal to them: *and they know it.* But we were hardly prepared for such a demonstration as *this.* Let it all pass however. The question we propose is only the following,—If the Text 'used by *great Antiochian theologians* not long after the middle of the

IVth century' (p. 146) is undeserving of our confidence:—
if we are to believe that a systematic depravation of Scripture was universally going on till about the end of the IIIrd
century; and if at that time, an authoritative and deliberate
recension of it—conducted on utterly erroneous principles—
took place at Antioch, and resulted in the vicious 'traditional Constantinopolitan' (p. 143), or (as Dr. Hort prefers
to call it) the 'eclectic Syrian Text:'—*What remains to us?*
Are we henceforth to rely on our own 'inner consciousness'
for illumination? Or is it seriously expected that for the
restoration of the inspired Verity we shall be content to
surrender ourselves blindfold to the *ipse dixit* of an unknown
and irresponsible nineteenth-century guide? If neither of
these courses is expected of us, will these Editors be so good
as to give us the names of the documents on which, in their
judgment, we *may* rely?

XLIII. We are not suffered to remain long in a state
of suspense. The assurance awaits us (at p. 150), that the
Vatican codex,

'B—is found to hold a unique position. Its text is throughout *Pre-Syrian*, perhaps *purely Pre-Syrian.* . . . From distinctively *Western* readings it seems to be all but entirely free.
. . . We have not been able to recognize as *Alexandrian* any
readings of B in any book of the New Testament. . . . . So
that . . . neither of the early streams of innovation has touched
it to any appreciable extent.'—(p. 150.)

'The text of the Sinaitic codex (א)' also 'seems to be entirely,
or all but entirely, *Pre-Syrian.* A very large part of the
text is in like manner free from *Western* or *Alexandrian* elements.'—(p. 151.)

'*Every other* known Greek manuscript has either a mixed or a
Syrian text.'—(p. 151.)

Thus then, at last, at the end of exactly 150 weary pages,
the secret comes out! The one point which the respected

Editors are found to have been all along driving at :—the one aim of those many hazy disquisitions of theirs about 'Intrinsic and Transcriptional Probability,'—'Genealogical evidence, simple and divergent,'—and 'the study of Groups:' —the one reason of all their vague terminology,—and of their baseless theory of 'Conflation,'—and of their disparagement of the Fathers :—the one *raison d'être* of their fiction of a 'Syrian' and a 'Pre-Syrian' and a 'Neutral' text :— the secret of it all comes out at last! A delightful, a truly Newtonian simplicity characterizes the final announcement. All is summed up in the curt formula—*Codex* B !

Behold then the altar at which Copies, Fathers, Versions, are all to be ruthlessly sacrificed :—the tribunal from which there shall be absolutely no appeal :—the Oracle which is to silence every doubt, resolve every riddle, smooth away every difficulty. All has been stated, where the name has been pronounced of—codex B. One is reminded of an enigmatical epitaph on the floor of the Chapel of S. John's College, ' *Verbum non amplius—Fisher*' ! To codex B all the Greek Fathers after Eusebius must give way. Even Patristic evidence *of the ante-Nicene period* 'requires critical sifting' (p. 202),—must be distrusted, may be denied (pp. 202–5), —if it shall be found to contradict Cod. B! 'B very far exceeds all other documents in neutrality of Text.'—(p. 171.)

XLIV. 'At a long interval after B, but hardly a less interval before all other MSS., stands ℵ' (p. 171).—Such is the sum of the matter! . . . . A coarser,—a clumsier,—a more unscientific,—a more *stupid* expedient for settling the true Text of Scripture was surely never invented! *But* for the many foggy, or rather unreadable disquisitions with which the *Introduction* is encumbered, "Textual Criticism made easy," might very well have been the title of the little volume now under Review; of which at last it is discovered that *the general Infallibility of Codex* B is the fundamental principle. Let us however hear these learned men out.

XLV. They begin by offering us a chapter on the ' General relations of B and א to other documents : ' wherein we are assured that,—

'*Two striking facts* successively come out with especial clearness. Every group containing both א and B, *is found* . . . to have *an apparently more original Text* than every opposed group containing neither; and every group containing B . . . *is found* in a large preponderance of cases . . . to have *an apparently more original Text* than every opposed group containing א.'— (p. 210.)

'*Is found*'! but pray,—*By whom?* And '*apparently*'! but pray,—*To whom?* and *On what grounds of Evidence?* For unless it be on *certain* grounds of Evidence, how can it be pretended that we have before us ' two striking *facts*' ?

Again, with what show of reason can it possibly be asserted that these " two striking facts " " come out with *especial clearness*"? so long as their very existence remains *in nubibus*,— has never been established, and is in fact emphatically denied? Expressions like the foregoing *then* only begin to be tolerable when it has been made plain that the Teacher has some solid foundation on which to build. Else, he occasions nothing but impatience and displeasure. Readers at first are simply annoyed at being trifled with : presently they grow restive: at last they become clamorous for demonstration, and will accept of nothing less. Let us go on however. We are still at p. 210 :—

' *We found* א and B to stand alone in their almost complete immunity from distinctive Syriac readings . . . . and B to stand far above א in its *apparent* freedom from either Western or Alexandrian readings.'—(p. 210.)

But pray, gentlemen,—*Where* and *when* did 'we find' either of these two things? We have 'found' nothing of the sort hitherto. The Reviewer is disposed to reproduce the Duke of Wellington's courteous reply to the Prince Regent, when the latter claimed the arrangements which resulted in the victory of Waterloo :—'*I have heard your Royal Highness say so.*' . . . . At the end of a few pages,

'*Having found* א B the constant element in groups of every size, distinguished by internal excellence of readings, *we found* no less excellence in the readings in which they concur without other attestations of Greek MSS., or even of Versions or Fathers.'—(p. 219.)

What! again? Why, we '*have found*' nothing as yet but Reiteration. Up to this point we have not been favoured with one particle of Evidence! . . . In the meantime, the convictions of these accomplished Critics,—(but not, unfortunately, those of their Readers,)—are observed to strengthen as they proceed. On reaching p. 224, we are assured that,

' The independence [of B and א] can be carried back so far,'—(not a hint is given *how*,)—' that their concordant testimony may be treated as equivalent to that of a MS. older than א and B themselves by at least two centuries,—*probably* by a generation or two more.'

How *that* 'independence' was established, and how *this* 'probability' has been arrived at, we cannot even imagine. The point to be attended to however, is, that by the process indicated, some such early epoch as A.D. 100 has been reached. So that now we are not surprised to hear that,

' The respective ancestries of א and B must have diverged from a common parent *extremely near the Apostolic autographs.*'—(p. 220. See top of p. 221.)
Or that,—' *The close approach to the time of the autographs* raises the presumption of purity to an unusual strength.'—(p. 224.)

And lo, before we turn the leaf, this 'presumption' is found to have ripened into certainty :—

' This general immunity from substantive error . . . . in the common original of ℵ B, in conjunction with its very high antiquity, provides in a multitude of cases *a safe criterion of genuineness, not to be distrusted* except on very clear internal evidence.   Accordingly . . . it is our belief, (1) That Readings of ℵ B *should be accepted as the true Readings* until strong internal evidence is found to the contrary ; and (2), That *no Readings of ℵ B can be safely rejected absolutely.*'—(p. 225.)

XLVI. And thus, by an unscrupulous use of the process of Reiteration, accompanied by a boundless exercise of the Imaginative faculty, we have reached the goal to which all that went before has been steadily tending : viz. the absolute supremacy of codices B and ℵ above all other codices,—and, when they differ, then of codex B.

And yet, the 'immunity from substantive error' of a *lost* Codex of *imaginary* date and *unknown* history, cannot but be a pure imagination,—(a mistaken one, as we shall presently show,)—of these respected Critics: while their proposed practical inference from it,—(viz. to regard two remote and confessedly depraved Copies of that original, as ' *a safe criterion of genuineness,*')—this, at all events, is the reverse of logical.   In the meantime, the presumed proximity of the Text of ℵ and B to the Apostolic age is henceforth discoursed of as if it were no longer matter of conjecture :—

' The ancestries of both MSS. having started from a common source *not much later than the Autographs,*' &c.—(p. 247.)

And again :—

' *Near as the divergence* of the respective ancestries of B and ℵ *must have been to the Autographs,*' &c.—(p. 273.)

Until at last, we find it announced as a 'moral certainty : '—

'*It is morally certain* that the ancestries of B and א *diverged from a point near the Autographs,* and never came into contact subsequently.'—(*Text*, p. 556.)

After which, of course, we have no right to complain if we are assured that :—

'The fullest comparison does but increase the conviction that their pre-eminent relative *purity* is approximately *absolute,—a true approximate reproduction of the Text of the Autographs.*'— (p. 296.)

XLVII. But how does it happen—(we must needs repeat the enquiry, which however we make with unfeigned astonishment,)—How does it come to pass that a man of practised intellect, addressing persons as cultivated and perhaps as acute as himself, can handle a confessedly obscure problem like the present after this strangely incoherent, this foolish and wholly inconclusive fashion ? One would have supposed that Dr. Hort's mathematical training would have made him an exact reasoner. But he writes as if he had no idea at all of the nature of demonstration, and of the process necessary in order to carry conviction home to a Reader's mind. Surely, (one tells oneself,) a minimum of 'pass' Logic would have effectually protected so accomplished a gentleman from making such a damaging exhibition of himself! For surely he must be aware that, as yet, he has produced *not one particle of evidence* that his opinion concerning B and א is well founded. And yet, how can he possibly overlook the circumstance that, unless he is able to *demonstrate* that those two codices, and especially the former of them, has 'preserved not only a very ancient Text, but *a very pure line of ancient Text*' also (p. 251), his entire work, (inasmuch as it reposes on that one assumption,) on being critically handled, crumbles to its base ; or rather melts into thin air before the

x

first puff of wind ?   He cannot, surely, require telling that those who look for Demonstration will refuse to put up with Rhetoric :—that, with no thoughtful person will Assertion pass for Argument :—nor mere Reiteration, however long persevered in, ever be mistaken for accumulated Proof.

"When I am taking a ride with Rouser,"—(quietly re-marked Professor Saville to Bodley Coxe,)—" I observe that, if I ever demur to any of his views, Rouser's practice always is, to repeat the same thing over again in the same words,— *only in a louder tone of voice*" . . . The delicate rhetorical device thus indicated proves to be not peculiar to Professors of the University of Oxford; but to be familiarly recognized as an instrument of conviction by the learned men who dwell on the banks of the Cam.   To be serious however.—Dr. Hort has evidently failed to see that nothing short of a careful induction of particular instances,—a system of laborious footnotes, or an 'Appendix' bristling with impregnable facts, —could sustain the portentous weight of his fundamental position, viz. that Codex B is so exceptionally pure a docu-ment as to deserve to be taken as a chief guide in deter-mining the Truth of Scripture.

It is related of the illustrious architect, Sir Gilbert Scott, —when he had to rebuild the massive central tower of a southern Cathedral, and to rear up thereon a lofty spire of stone,—that he made preparations for the work which astonished the Dean and Chapter of the day.   He caused the entire area to be excavated to what seemed a most unnecessary depth, and proceeded to lay a bed of concrete of fabulous solidity.   The 'wise master-builder' was determined that his work should last for ever.   Not so Drs. Westcott and Hort.   They are either troubled with no similar anxieties, or else too clear-sighted to cherish any similar hope.   They are evidently of opinion that a cloud or a quagmire will serve their turn every bit as well as granite or Portland-stone. Dr. Hort (as we have seen already, namely in p. 252,) considers that his individual 'STRONG PREFERENCE' of one set of Readings above another, is sufficient to determine whether the Manuscript which contains those Readings is pure or the contrary. '*Formidable arrays of* [hostile] *Documentary evidence*,' he disregards and sets at defiance, when once his own '*fullest consideration of Internal Evidence*' has 'pronounced certain Readings to be right' [p. 61].

The only indication we anywhere meet with of the actual *ground* of Dr. Hort's certainty, and reason of his preference, is contained in his claim that,—

'Every binary group [of MSS.] *containing* B is found to offer a large proportion of Readings, which, on the closest scrutiny, have THE RING OF GENUINENESS : while it is difficult to find any Readings so attested which LOOK SUSPICIOUS after full consideration.'—(p. 227. Also vol. i. 557—where the dictum is repeated.)

XLVIII. And thus we have, at last, an honest confession of the ultimate principle which has determined the Text of the present edition of the N. T. ' *The ring of genuineness* '! *This* it must be which was referred to when '*instinctive processes of Criticism*' were vaunted ; and the candid avowal made that 'the experience which is their foundation needs perpetual correction and recorrection.'[1]

'We are obliged' (say these accomplished writers) 'to *come to the individual mind at last*.'[2]

And thus, behold, ' at last' we *have* reached the goal ! . . . *Individual idiosyncrasy*,—*not* external Evidence :—Readings '*strongly preferred*,'—*not* Readings *strongly attested* :—'personal discernment' (self ! still self !) *conscientiously exercising*

---

[1] Preface to the ' limited and private issue ' of 1870, p. xviii. : reprinted in the *Introduction* (1881), p. 66.   [2] *Ibid.*

itself upon Codex B;—this is a true account of the Critical
method pursued by these accomplished Scholars. They
deliberately claim '*personal discernment*' as 'the surest
ground for confidence.'[1] Accordingly, they judge of Readings
by their *looks* and by their *sound.* When, in *their* opinion,
words 'look suspicious,' words are to be rejected. If a word
has ' the ring of genuineness,'—(i.e. *if it seems to them* to have
it,)—they claim that the word shall pass unchallenged.

XLIX. But it must be obvious that such a method is
wholly inadmissible. It practically dispenses with Critical
aids altogether ; substituting individual caprice for external
guidance. It can lead to no tangible result: for Readings
which 'look suspicious' to one expert, may easily *not* 'look'
so to another. A man's 'inner consciousness' cannot possibly
furnish trustworthy guidance in this subject matter. Justly
does Bp. Ellicott ridicule 'the easy method of . . . . *using a
favourite Manuscript,*' combined with '*some supposed power of
divining the Original Text ;*'[2]—unconscious apparently that he
is thereby aiming a cruel blow at certain of his friends.

As for the proposed test of Truth,—(the enquiry, namely,
whether or no a reading has ' the ring of genuineness ')—it is
founded on a transparent mistake. The coarse operation
alluded to may be described as a 'rough and ready'
expedient practised by *receivers of money* in the way of self-
defence, and *only* for their own protection, lest base metal
should be palmed off upon them unawares. But Dr. Hort
is proposing an analogous test for the exclusive satisfaction
of *him who utters* the suspected article. We therefore disallow the proposal entirely: not, of course, because we
suppose that so excellent and honourable a man as Dr. Hort

---

[1] P. 65 (§ 84). In the Table of Contents (p. xi.), ' *Personal instincts*'
are substituted for ' *Personal discernment.*'

[2] *The Revisers and the Greek Text,*—p. 19.

would attempt to pass off as genuine what he suspects to
be fabricated; but because we are fully convinced—(for
reasons 'plenty as blackberries')—that through some natural
defect, or constitutional inaptitude, he is not a competent
judge.   The man who finds '*no marks of either Critical or
Spiritual insight*' (p. 135) in the only Greek Text which was
known to scholars till A.D. 1831,—(although he confesses
that 'the text of Chrysostom and other Syrian Fathers of
the IVth century is substantially identical with it'[1]); and
vaunts in preference '*the bold vigour*' and '*refined scholarship*' which is exclusively met with in certain depraved
uncials of the same or later date :—the man who thinks it not
unlikely that the incident of the piercing of our SAVIOUR'S
side (ἄλλος δὲ λαβὼν λόγχην κ. τ. λ.) was actually found in
the genuine Text of S. Matt. xxvii. 49, *as well as* in S. John
xix. 34 :[2]—the man who is of opinion that the incident of
the Woman taken in Adultery (filling 12 verses), 'presents
serious differences from the diction of S. John's Gospel,'—
treats it as 'an insertion in a comparatively late Western
text'[3] and declines to retain it even within brackets, on the
ground that it 'would fatally interrupt' the course of the
narrative if suffered to stand :—the man who can deliberately
separate off from the end of S. Mark's Gospel, and print
separately, S. Mark's last 12 verses, (on the plea that they
'manifestly cannot claim any apostolic authority; but are
doubtless founded on some tradition of the Apostolic age;'[4])—
yet who straightway proceeds to annex, *as an alternative
Conclusion* (ἄλλως), 'the wretched supplement derived from
codex L :'[5]—the man (lastly) who, in defiance of 'solid reason
and pure taste,' finds music in the 'utterly marred' 'rhyth-
mical arrangement' of the Angels' Hymn on the night of the

---

[1] *Introduction*,—p. xiii.   [2] *Notes*, p. 22.   [3] *Notes*, p. 88.
[4] *Notes*,—p. 51.   [5] Scrivener's *Plain Introduction*,—pp. 507-8.

Nativity :[1]—such an one is not entitled to a hearing when he talks about '*the ring of genuineness.*' He has already effectually put himself out of Court. He has convicted himself of a natural infirmity of judgment,—has given proof that he labours under a peculiar Critical inaptitude for this department of enquiry,—which renders his decrees nugatory, and his opinions worthless.

L. But apart from all this, the Reader's attention is invited to a little circumstance which Dr. Hort has unaccountably overlooked: but which, the instant it has been stated, is observed to cause his picturesque theory to melt away—like a snow-wreath in the sunshine.

On reflexion, it will be perceived that the most signal deformities of codices B א D L are *instances of Omission.* In the Gospels alone, B omits 2877 words.

How,—(we beg to enquire,)—How will you apply your proposed test to a *Non-entity?* How will you ascertain whether something which *does not exist in the Text* has 'the ring of genuineness' or not? There can be *no* 'ring of genuineness,' clearly, where there is nothing to ring with! Will any one pretend that *the omission* of the incident of the troubling of the pool has in it any 'ring of genuineness'?— or dare to assert that 'the ring of genuineness' is imparted to the history of our SAVIOUR'S Passion, by *the omission* of His Agony in the Garden?—or that the narrative of His Crucifixion becomes more musical, when our Lord's Prayer for His murderers has been *omitted?*—or that ἐφοβοῦντο γάρ ('for they were afraid'), has 'the ring of genuineness' as the conclusion of the last chapter of the Gospel according to S. Mark?

But the strangest circumstance is behind. It is notorious

---

[1] Scrivener's '*Introduction,*' pp. 513–4.

that, on the contrary, Dr. Hort is frequently constrained
to admit that *the omitted words* actually *have* 'the ring of
genuineness.' The words which he insists on thrusting out
of the Text are often conspicuous *for the very quality* which
(by the hypothesis) was the warrant for their exclusion. Of
this, the Reader may convince himself by referring to the
note at foot of the present page.[1] In the meantime, the

---

[1] In S. MATTH. i. 25,—the omission of ' *her first-born :*'—in vi. 13, the
omission of the *Doxology :*—in xii. 47, the omission of *the whole verse :*—
in xvi. 2, 3, the omission of our LORD'S memorable words concerning the
signs of the weather :—in xvii. 21, the omission of the mysterious statement, ' *But this kind goeth not out save by prayer and fasting :*'—in xviii.
11, the omission of the precious words ' *For the Son of man came to save
that which was lost.'*

In S. MARK xvi. 9–20, the omission of the ' *last Twelve Verses,*'—(' the
contents of which are *not such as could have been invented* by any scribe
or editor of the Gospel,'—W. and H. p. 57). All admit that ἐφοβοῦντο
γάρ is an impossible ending.

In S. LUKE vi. 1, the suppression of the unique δευτεροπρώτῳ; (' the
very obscurity of the expression attesting strongly to its genuineness,'—
Scrivener, p. 516, and so W. and H. p. 58) :—ix. 54–56, the omitted
rebuke to the ' disciples James and John :'—in x. 41, 42, the omitted
words concerning Martha and Mary :—in xxii. 43, 44, the omission of the
Agony in the Garden,—(which nevertheless, ' *it would be impossible to
regard* as a product of the inventiveness of scribes,'—W. and H. p. 67) :—
in xxiii. 17, a memorable clause omitted :—in xxiii. 34, the omission of
our Lord's *prayer for His murderers,*—(concerning which Westcott and
Hort remark that ' *few verses of the Gospels bear in themselves a surer
witness to the truth of what they record than this*'—p. 68) :—in xxiii. 38,
the statement that the Inscription on the Cross was ' *in letters of Greek, and
Latin, and Hebrew :*'—in xxiv. 12, *the visit of S. Peter to the Sepulchre.*
Bishop Lightfoot remarks concerning S. Luke ix. 56 : xxii. 43, 44 : and
xxiii. 34,—' *It seems impossible to believe that these incidents are other
than authentic,*'—(p. 28.)

In S. JOHN iii. 13, the solemn clause ' *which is in heaven :*'—in v. 3, 4,
the omitted incident of *the troubling of the pool :*—in vii. 53 to viii. 11,
the narrative concerning the woman taken in adultery omitted,—concerning which Drs. W. and H. remark that ' *the argument which has always
told most in its favour in modern times is its own internal character.* The
story itself has justly seemed *to vouch for its own substantial truth,* and

matter discoursed of may be conveniently illustrated by a short apologue :—

Somewhere in the fens of Ely diocese, stood a crazy old church (dedicated to S. Bee, of course,) the bells of which— according to a learned Cambridge Doctor—were the most musical in the world. " I have listened to those bells," (he was accustomed to say,) " for 30 years. All other bells are cracked, harsh, out of tune. Commend me, for music, to the bells of S. Bee's ! *They* alone have *the ring of genuineness*." . . . . Accordingly, he published a treatise on Campanology, founding his theory on the musical properties of the bells of S. Bee's.—At this juncture, provokingly enough, some one directed attention to the singular fact that S. Bee's is one of the few churches in that district *without* bells : a discovery which, it is needless to add, pressed inconveniently on the learned Doctor's theory.

LI. But enough of this. We really have at last, (be it observed,) reached the end of our enquiry. Nothing comes after Dr. Hort's extravagant and unsupported estimate of Codices B and ℵ. On the contrary. Those two documents are caused to cast their sombre shadows a long way ahead, and to darken all our future. Dr. Hort takes leave of the subject with the announcement that, whatever uncertainty may attach to the evidence for particular readings,

' *The general course of future Criticism must be shaped by the happy circumstance that the fourth century has bequeathed to us two MSS.* [B and ℵ], *of which even the less incorrupt* [ℵ] *must have been of exceptional purity among its contemporaries : and which rise into greater pre-eminence of character the better the early history of the Text becomes known.*'—(p. 287.)

---

the words in which it is clothed to harmonize with those of other Gospel narratives '—(p. 87). Bishop Lightfoot remarks that ' *the narrative bears on its face the highest credentials of authentic history* '—(p. 28).

In other words, our guide assures us that in a dutiful submission to codices B and א,—(which, he naïvely remarks,
'*happen likewise to be the oldest extant* Greek MSS. of the New
Testament' [p. 212],)—lies all our hope of future progress.
(Just as if we should ever have *heard* of these two codices,
had their contents come down to us written in the ordinary
cursive character,—in a dated MS. (suppose) of the XVth
century!) . . . Moreover, Dr. Hort 'must not hesitate to
express' his own robust conviction,

'That no trustworthy improvement can be effected, *except in
accordance with the leading Principles of method which we have
endeavoured to explain.*'—(p. 285.)

LII. And this is the end of the matter.   Behold our fate
therefore :—(1) Codices B and א, with—(2) Drs. Westcott
and Hort's *Introduction* and *Notes on Select Readings* in
vindication of their contents!   It is proposed to shut us
up within those limits! . . . An uneasy suspicion however
secretly suggests itself that perhaps, as the years roll out,
something may come to light which will effectually dispel
every dream of the new School, and reduce even prejudice
itself to silence.   So Dr. Hort hastens to frown it down :—

'It would be an illusion to anticipate important changes of
Text [i.e. of the Text advocated by Drs. Westcott and Hort]
from any acquisition of new Evidence.'—(p. 285.)

And yet, *why* the anticipation of important help from the
acquisition of fresh documentary Evidence 'would be an
illusion,'—does not appear.   That the recovery of certain of
the exegetical works of Origen,—better still, of Tatian's
Diatessaron,—best of all, of a couple of MSS. of the date of
Codices B and א; but not, (like those two corrupt documents) derived from one and the same depraved archetype ;—
That any such windfall, (and it will come, some of these
days,) would infallibly disturb Drs. Westcott and Hort's

equanimity, as well as scatter to the winds not a few of their most confident conclusions,—we are well aware. *So indeed are they.* Hence, what those Critics earnestly deprecate, *we* as earnestly desire. We are therefore by no means inclined to admit, that

' Greater possibilities of improvement lie in a more exact study of the relations between the documents that we already possess ; '—(*Ibid.*)

knowing well that ' *the documents*' referred to are chiefly, (if not solely,) *Codices* B *and* ℵ: knowing also, that it is further meant, that in estimating other evidence, of whatever kind, the only thing to be enquired after is whether or no the attesting document *is generally in agreement with codex* B.

For, according to these writers,—tide what tide,—codex B is to be the standard : itself not absolutely requiring confirmation from *any* extraneous quarter. Dr. Hort asserts, (but it is, as usual, *mere* assertion,) that,

' *Even when* B *stands quite alone,* its readings must never be lightly rejected.'—(p. 557.)

And yet,—*Why* a reading found *only in codex* B should experience greater indulgence than another reading found *only in codex* A, we entirely fail to see.

On the other hand, ' *an unique criterion* is supplied by the concord of the independent attestation of B and ℵ.'—(*Notes,* p. 46.)

But pray, how does *that* appear ? Since B and ℵ are derived from one and the same original—Why should not ' the concord' spoken of be rather ' *an unique criterion*' of the *utter depravity of the archetype ?*

LIII. To conclude. We have already listened to Dr. Hort long enough. And now, since confessedly, a chain is no

stronger than it is at its weakest link; nor an edifice more
secure than the basis whereon it stands;—we must be allowed
to point out that we have been dealing throughout with a
dream, pure and simple; from which it is high time that we
should wake up, now that we have been plainly shown on
what an unsubstantial foundation these Editors have been all
along building. A child's house, several stories high, constructed out of playing-cards,—is no unapt image of the
frail erection before us. We began by carefully lifting off
the topmost story; and then, the next: but we might as well
have saved ourselves the trouble. The basement-story has
to be removed bodily, which must bring the whole edifice
down with a rush. In reply to the fantastic tissue of unproved assertions which go before, we assert as follows :—

(1) The impurity of the Texts exhibited by Codices B and
א is not a matter of opinion, but a matter of fact.[1] These are

---

[1] To some extent, even the unlearned Reader may easily convince himself of this, by examining the rejected 'alternative' Readings in the margin
of the 'Revised Version.' The 'Many' and the 'Some ancient authorities,'
there spoken of, *almost invariably include*—sometimes *denote*—codd.
B א, one or both of them. These constitute the merest fraction of the
entire amount of corrupt readings exhibited by B א; but they will give
English readers some notion of the problem just now under consideration.

Besides the details already supplied [see above, pages 16 and 17 :—30
and 31 :—46 and 47 :—75 :—249 :—262 :—289 :—316 to 319] concerning B
and א,—(the result of laborious collation,)—some particulars shall now be
added. The piercing of our SAVIOUR's side, thrust in after Matt. xxvii.
49 :—the eclipse of the sun when the moon was full, in Lu. xxiii. 45 :—
the monstrous figment concerning Herod's daughter, thrust into Mk.
vi. 22 :—the precious clauses omitted in Matt. i. 25 and xviii. 11 :—in
Lu. ix. 54-6, and in Jo. iii. 13 :—the wretched glosses in Lu. vi. 48 :
x. 42 : xv. 21 : Jo. x. 14 and Mk. vi. 20 :—the substitution of οινον (for
οξος) in Matt. xxvii. 34,—of Θεος (for υιος) in Jo. i. 18,—of ανθρωπον (for
Θεου) in ix. 35,—of οἱ οὐ (for ᾧ) in Rom. iv. 8 :—the geographical blunder in
Mk. vii. 31 : in Lu. iv. 44 :—the omission in Matt. xii. 47,—and of two

two of the least trustworthy documents in existence. So far
from allowing Dr. Hort's position that—'A Text formed' by
'taking Codex B as the sole authority,' 'would be incomparably nearer the Truth than a Text similarly taken from
any other Greek or other single document' (p. 251),—we
venture to assert that it would be, on the contrary, *by far
the foulest Text that had ever seen the light:* worse, that is
to say, even than the Text of Drs. Westcott and Hort. And
that is saying a great deal. In the brave and faithful words

---

important verses in Matt. xvi. 2, 3 :—of ιδια in Acts i. 19 :—of εγειραι και
in iii. 6 ;—and of δευτεροπρωτω in Lu. vi. 1 :—the two spurious clauses
in Mk. iii. 14, 16 :—the obvious blunders in Jo. ix. 4 and 11 :—in Acts
xii. 25—besides the impossible reading in 1 Cor. xiii. 3,—make up a
heavy indictment against B and ℵ jointly—which are here found in
company with just a very few disreputable allies. Add, the plain error at
Lu. ii. 14 :—the gloss at Mk. v. 36 :—the mere fabrication at Matt. xix.
17 :—the omissions at Matt. vi. 13 : Jo. v. 3, 4.

B (in company with others, but apart from ℵ) by exhibiting βαπτισαν-
τες in Matt. xxviii. 19 :—ωδε των in Mk. ix. 1 :—'seventy-*two*,' in Lu. x.
1 :—the blunder in Lu. xvi. 12 :—and the grievous omissions in Lu. xxii.
43, 44 (CHRIST's Agony in the Garden),—and xxiii. 34 (His prayer for His
murderers),—enjoys unenviable distinction.—B, singly, is remarkable for
an obvious blunder in Matt. xxi. 31 :—Lu. xxi. 24 :—Jo. xviii. 5 :—Acts
x. 19—and xvii. 28 :—xxvii. 37 :—not to mention the insertion of
δεδομενον in Jo. vii. 39.

ℵ (in company with others, but apart from B) is conspicuous for its
sorry interpolation of Matt. viii. 13 :—its substitution of εστιν (for ην) in
S. John i. 4 :—its geographical blunder in S. Luke xxiv. 13 :—its textual blunder at 1 Pet. i. 23.— ℵ, singly, is remarkable for its sorry paraphrase in Jo. ii. 3 :—its addition to i. 34 :—its omissions in Matt. xxiii.
35 :—Mk. i. 1 :—Jo. ix. 38 :—its insertion of Ησαιου in Matt. xiii. 35 :—
its geographical blunders in Mk. i. 28 :—Lu. i. 26 :—Acts viii. 5 :—besides
the blunders in Jo. vi. 51—and xiii. 10 :—1 Tim. iii. 16 :—Acts xxv. 13 :—
and the clearly fabricated narrative of Jo. xiii. 24. Add the fabricated
text at Mk. xiv. 30, 68, 72 ; of which the object was 'so far to assimilate
the narrative of Peter's denials with those of the other Evangelists, as
to suppress the fact, vouched for by S. Mark only, that the cock crowed
twice.'

of Prebendary Scrivener (*Introduction*, p. 453),—words which'
deserve to become famous,—

   'It is no less true to fact than paradoxical in sound, that the
worst corruptions to which the New Testament has ever been
subjected, originated within a hundred years after it was composed : that Irenæus [A.D. 150], and the African Fathers, and
the whole Western, with a portion of the Syrian Church, used
far inferior manuscripts to those employed by Stunica, or
Erasmus, or Stephens thirteen centuries later, when moulding
the Textus Receptus.'

And Codices B and ℵ are, demonstrably, nothing else but
specimens of the depraved class thus characterized.

Next—(2), We assert that, so manifest are the disfigure-
ments jointly and *exclusively* exhibited by codices B and ℵ,[1]

---

[1] Characteristic, and fatal beyond anything that can be named are, (1)
The *exclusive* omission by B and ℵ of Mark xvi. 9–20 :—(2) The omission
of εν Εφεσῳ, from Ephes. i. 1 :—(3) The blunder, αποσκιασματος, in
James i. 17 :—(4) The nonsensical συστρεφομενων in Matt. xvii. 22 :—
(5) That 'vile error,' (as Scrivener calls it,) περιελοντες, in Acts xxviii. 13 :
—(6) The impossible order of words in Lu. xxiii. 32; and (7) The extraordinary order in Acts i. 5 :—(8) The omission of the last clause of the
LORD'S prayer, in Lu. xi. 4 ; and (9) Of that solemn verse, Matt. xvii. 21;
and (10) Of ισχυρον in Matt. xiv. 30 :—(11) The substitution of εργων (for
τεκνων) in Matt. xi. 29 :—(12) Of ελιγμα (for μιγμα) in Jo. xix. 39,—and
(13) of ην τεθειμενος (for ετεθη) in John xix. 41. Then, (14) The thrusting of
Χριστος into Matt. xvi. 21,—and (15) Of ὁ Θεος into vi. 8 :—besides (16) So
minute a peculiarity as Βεεζεβουλ in Matt. x. 35 : xii. 24, 27 : Lu. xi. 15,
18, 19.   (17) Add, the gloss at Matt. xvii. 20, and (18) The omissions at
Matt. v. 22 : xvii. 21.—It must be admitted that such peculiar blemishes,
taken collectively, constitute a proof of affinity of origin,—community of
descent from one and the same disreputable ancestor.   But space fails us.

The Reader will be interested to learn that although, in the Gospels, B
combines exclusively with A, but 11 times; and with c, but 38 times :
with D, it combines exclusively 141 times, and with ℵ, 239 times : (viz.
in Matt. 121,—in Mk. 26,—in Lu. 51,—in Jo. 41 times).

Contrast it with A :—which combines exclusively with D, 21 times:
with ℵ 13 times : with B, 11 times : with c, 4 times.

that instead of accepting these codices as two ʻindependentʼ Witnesses to the inspired Original, we are constrained to regard them as little more than a single reproduction of one and the same scandalously corrupt and (*comparatively*) late Copy. By consequence, we consider their joint and exclusive attestation of any particular reading, ʻ *an unique criterion* ʼ of its worthlessness; a sufficient reason—*not* for adopting, but—for unceremoniously rejecting it.

Then—(3), As for the origin of these two curiosities, it can perforce only be divined from their contents. That they exhibit fabricated Texts is demonstrable. No amount of honest *copying*,—persevered in for any number of centuries, —could by possibility have resulted in two such documents. Separated from one another in actual date by 50, perhaps by 100 years,[1] they must needs have branched off from a common corrupt ancestor, and straightway become exposed continuously to fresh depraving influences. The result is, that codex ℵ, (which evidently has gone through more adventures and fallen into worse company than his rival,) has been corrupted to a far graver extent than codex B, and is

---

[1] The Reviewer speaks from actual inspection of both documents. They are essentially dissimilar. The learned Ceriani assured the Reviewer (in 1872) that whereas the Vatican Codex must certainly have been written *in Italy*,—the birthplace of the Sinaitic was [*not* Egypt, but] *either Palestine or Syria*. Thus, considerations of time and place effectually dispose of Tischendorf's preposterous notion that the Scribe of Codex B wrote *six leaves* of ℵ : an imagination which solely resulted from the anxiety of the Critic to secure for his own cod. ℵ the same antiquity which is claimed for the vaunted cod. B.

This opinion of Dr. Tischendorf's rests on the same fanciful basis as his notion that *the last verse* of S. John's Gospel in ℵ was not written by the same hand which wrote the rest of the Gospel. There is *no manner of difference*: though of course it is possible that the scribe took a new pen, preliminary to writing that last verse, and executing the curious and delicate ornament which follows. Concerning S. Jo. xxi. 25, see above, pp. 23–4.

even more untrustworthy.   Thus, whereas (in the Gospels alone) B has 589 Readings *quite peculiar to itself,* affecting 858 words,—ℵ has 1460 such Readings, affecting 2640 words.

One *solid fact* like the preceding, (let it be pointed out in passing,) is more helpful by far to one who would form a correct estimate of the value of a Codex, than any number of such ' reckless and unverified assertions,' not to say peremptory and baseless decrees, as abound in the highly imaginative pages of Drs. Westcott and Hort.

(4) Lastly,—We suspect that these two Manuscripts are indebted for their preservation, *solely to their ascertained evil character ;* which has occasioned that the one eventually found its way, four centuries ago, to a forgotten shelf in the Vatican library : while the other, after exercising the ingenuity of several generations of critical Correctors, eventually (viz. in A.D. 1844[1]) got deposited in the waste-paper basket of the Convent at the foot of Mount Sinai.   Had B and ℵ been copies of average purity, they must long since have shared the inevitable fate of books which are freely *used* and highly prized ; namely, they would have fallen into decadence and disappeared from sight.   But in the meantime, behold, their very Antiquity has come to be reckoned to their advantage ; and (strange to relate) is even considered to constitute a sufficient reason why they should enjoy not merely extraordinary consideration, but the actual surrender of the critical judgment.   Since 1831, Editors have vied with one another in the fulsomeness of the homage they have paid to these ' two false Witnesses,'—for such B and ℵ *are,* as the concurrent testimony of Copies, Fathers and Versions abundantly proves.   Even superstitious reverence has been claimed

---

[1] Tischendorf's narrative of the discovery of the Sinaitic manuscript (' *When were our Gospels written ?* '), [1866,] p. 23.

for these two codices : and Drs. Westcott and Hort are so far
in advance of their predecessors in the servility of their
blind adulation, that they must be allowed to have easily
won the race.

LIV. With this,—so far as the Greek Text under review is
concerned,—we might, were we so minded, reasonably make
an end.   We undertook to show that Drs. Westcott and
Hort, in the volumes before us, have built up an utterly
worthless Textual fabric ; and we consider that we have
already sufficiently shown it.   The Theory,—the Hypothesis
rather, on which their Text is founded, we have *demonstrated*
to be *simply absurd.*   Remove that hypothesis, and a heap
of unsightly ruins is all that is left behind,—except indeed
astonishment (not unmingled with concern) at the simplicity of its accomplished Authors.

Here then, we might leave off.   But we are unwilling
so to leave the matter.   Large consideration is due to
ordinary English Readers ; who must perforce look on with
utter perplexity—not to say distress—at the strange spectacle
presented by *that* Text (which is in the main *the Text of the
Revised English Version*) on the one hand,—and *this* Review
of it, on the other :—

(1) "And pray, which of you am I to believe ? "—will
inevitably be, in homely English, the exclamation with which
not a few will lay down the present number of the ' *Quarterly.*'   " I pretend to no learning.   I am not prepared to
argue the question with you.   But surely, the oldest Manuscript *must* be the purest !   It even stands to reason : does
it not ?—Then further, I admit that you *seem* to have the
best of the argument so far ; yet, since the three most famous
Editors of modern times are against you, — Lachmann,

Tregelles, Tischendorf,—excuse me if I suspect that you *must* be in the wrong, after all."

LV. With unfeigned humility, the Reviewer [*Q. R.*] proceeds to explain the matter to his supposed Objector [*S. O.*], in briefest outline, as follows:—

Q. R. "You are perfectly right. The oldest Manuscript *must* exhibit the purest text : *must* be the most trustworthy. But then, unfortunately, it happens that *we do not possess it*. 'The oldest Manuscript' is lost. You speak, of course, of the inspired Autographs. These, I say, have long since disappeared."

(2) *S. O.* "No, I meant to say that the *oldest Manuscript we possess*, if it be but a very ancient one, must needs be the purest."

Q. R. " O, but *that* is an entirely different proposition. Well, *apart from experience*, the probability that the oldest copy extant will prove the purest is, if you please, considerable. Reflection will convince you however that it is *but* a probability, at the utmost : a probability based upon more than one false assumption,—with which nevertheless you shall not be troubled. But in fact it clearly does not by any means follow that, *because* a MS. is very ancient, *therefore* the Text, which it exhibits will be very pure. That you may be thoroughly convinced of this,—(and it is really impossible for your mind to be too effectually disabused of a prepossession which has fatally misled so many,)—you are invited to enquire for a recent contribution to the learned French publication indicated at the foot of this page,[1] in which is

---

[1] 'Papyrus Inédit de la Bibliothèque de M. Ambroise Firmin-Didot. Nouveaux fragments d'Euripide et d'autres Poètes Grecs, publiés par M. Henri Weil. (Extrait des *Monumens Grecs publiés par l'Association pour l'encouragement des Etudes Grecques en France.* Année 1879.)' Pp. 36.

exhibited a fac-simile of 8 lines of the *Medea* of Euripides
(ver. 5–12), written about B.C. 200 in small uncials (at
Alexandria probably,) on papyrus. Collated with any printed
copy, the verses, you will find, have been penned with
scandalous, with incredible inaccuracy. But on this head let
the learned Editor of the document in question be listened to,
rather than the present Reviewer :—

' On voit que le texte du papyrus est hérissé des fautes les
plus graves. *Le plus récent et le plus mauvais de nos manuscrits
d'Euripide vaut infiniment mieux que cette copie,—faite, il y a deux
mille ans, dans le pays où florissaient l'érudition hellénique et la
Critique des textes.*'[1]—(p. 17.)

---

[1] The rest of the passage may not be without interest to classical
readers :—' Ce n'est pas à dire qu'elle soit tout à fait sans intérêt, sans importance pour la constitution du texte. Elle nous apprend que, au vers 5,
ἀρίστων, pour ἀριστέων (correction de Wakefield) était déjà l'ancienne
vulgate ; et que les vers 11 et 12, s'ils sont altérés, comme l'assurent
quelques éditeurs d'Euripide, l'étaient déjà dans l'antiquité.
' L'homme . . . était aussi ignorant que négligent. Je le prends pour
un Egyptien n'ayant qu'une connoissance très imparfaite de la langue
grecque, et ne possédant aucune notion ni sur l'orthographe, ni sur les
règles les plus élémentaires du trimètre iambique. Le plus singulier est
qu'il commence sa copie au milieu d'un vers et qu'il la finisse de même. Il
oublie des lettres nécessaires, il en ajoute de parasites, il les met les unes
pour les autres, il tronque les mots ou il les altère, au point de détruire
quelquefois la suite de la construction et le sens du passage.' A faithful
copy of the verses in minuscule characters is subjoined for the gratification of Scholars. We have but divided the words and inserted capital
letters :—

' ανδρων αριστων οι δε πανχρυσον δερος   5
Πελεια μετηλθον ου γαρ τον δεσποτα εμην
Μηδια πυργους γης επλευσε Ειολκιας
ερωτι θυμωδ εγπλαγις Ιανοσονος
οτ αν κτανει πισας Πελειαδας κουρας
πατερα κατοικη τηνδε γην Κορινθιαν   10
συν ανδρι και τεκνοισιν ανδανοισα μεν
φυγη πολιτων ων αφηκετο χθονος.'

An excellent scholar (R. C. P.) remarks,—' The fragment must have
been written from dictation (of small parts, as it seems to me); and by an
illiterate scribe. It is just such a result as one might expect from a half-
educated reader enunciating Milton for a half-educated writer.'

"Why, the author of the foregoing remarks might have been writing concerning Codex B !"

(3) *S. O.* "Yes: but I want *Christian* evidence. The author of that scrap of papyrus *may* have been an illiterate slave. What if it should be a *school-boy's exercise* which has come down to us? The thing is not impossible."

Q. R. "Not 'impossible' certainly: but surely highly improbable. However, let it drop. You insist on Christian evidence. You shall have it. What think you then of the following statement of a very ancient Father (Caius[1]) writing against the heresy of Theodotus and others who denied the Divinity of CHRIST? He is bearing his testimony to the liberties which had been freely taken with the Text of the New Testament in his own time, viz. about A.D. 175–200:—

'The Divine Scriptures,' he says, 'these heretics have audaciously *corrupted*: . . . laying violent hands upon them under pretence of *correcting* them. That I bring no false accusation, any one who is disposed may easily convince himself. He has but to collect the copies belonging to these persons severally; then, to compare one with another; and he will discover that their discrepancy is extraordinary. Those of Asclepiades, at all events, will be found discordant from those of Theodotus. Now, plenty of specimens of either sort are obtainable, inasmuch as these men's disciples have industriously multiplied the (so-called) "*corrected*" copies of their respective teachers, which are in reality nothing else but "*corrupted*" copies. With the foregoing copies again, those of Hermophilus will be found entirely at variance. As for the copies of Apollonides, they even contradict one another. Nay, let any one compare the fabricated text which these persons put forth in the first instance, with that which exhibits their *latest* perversions of the Truth, and he will discover that the disagreement between them is even excessive.

---

[1] See p. 324 *note* ([1]).—Photius [cod. 48] says that 'Gaius' was a presbyter of Rome, and ἐθνῶν ἐπίσκοπος. See Routh's *Reliqq.* ii. 125.

'Of the enormity of the offence of which these men have been guilty, they must needs themselves be fully aware. Either they do not believe that the Divine Scriptures are the utterance of the HOLY GHOST,—in which case they are to be regarded as unbelievers : or else, they account themselves wiser than the HOLY GHOST,—and what is that, but to have the faith of devils ? As for their denying their guilt, the thing is impossible, seeing that the copies under discussion are their own actual handywork ; and they know full well that not such as these are the Scriptures which they received at the hands of their catechetical teachers. Else, let them produce the originals from which they made their transcripts.   Certain of them indeed have not even condescended to falsify Scripture, but entirely reject Law and Prophets alike.'[1]

"Now, the foregoing statement is in a high decree suggestive. For here is an orthodox Father *of the IInd century* inviting attention to four well-known families of falsified manuscripts of the Sacred Writings ;—complaining of the hopeless divergences which they exhibit (being not only inconsistent with one another, but *with themselves*) ;—and insisting that such *corrected,* are nothing else but shamefully *corrupted* copies. He speaks of the phenomenon as being in his day notorious : and appeals to Recensions, the very names of whose authors—Theodotus, Asclepiades, Hermophilus, Apollonides—have (all but the first) long since died out of the Church's memory. You will allow therefore, (will you not ?), that by this time the claim of the *oldest existing copies* of Scripture to be the purest, has been effectually disposed of. For since there once prevailed such a multitude of corrupted copies, we have no security whatever that the oldest of our extant MSS. are not derived—remotely if not directly—from some of *them.*"

(4) *S. O.* "But at all events the chances are even. Are they not ?"

---

[1] Eusebius, *Hist. Eccl.* v. 28 (ap. Routh's *Reliqq.* ii. 132–4).

Q. R. " By no means. A copy like codex B, once *recognized* as belonging to a corrupt family,—once *known* to contain a depraved exhibition of the Sacred Text,—was more likely by far to remain unused, and so to escape destruction, than a copy highly prized and in daily use.—As for Codex א, it carries on its face its own effectual condemnation ; aptly illustrating the precept *fiat experimentum in corpore vili*. It exhibits the efforts of many generations of men to restore its Text,—(which, ' as proceeding from the first scribe,' is admitted by one of its chief admirers to be ' *very rough*,[1] ')— to something like purity. ' *At least ten different Revisers*,' from the IVth to the XIIth century, are found to have tried their hands upon it.[2]—Codex C, after having had ' at least three correctors very busily at work upon it '[3] (in the VIth and IXth centuries), finally (in the XIIth) was fairly *obliterated*, — literally *scraped out*, — to make room for the writings of a Syrian Father.—I am therefore led by *à priori* considerations to augur ill of the contents of B א C. But when I find them hopelessly at variance *among themselves:* above all, when I find (1) *all other Manuscripts* of whatever date,—(2) the *most ancient Versions*,—and (3), *the whole body of the primitive Fathers*, decidedly opposed to them,—I am (to speak plainly) at a loss to understand how any man of sound understanding, acquainted with all the facts of the case and accustomed to exact reasoning, can hesitate to regard the unsupported (or the *slenderly* supported) testimony of one or other of them as *simply worthless*. The craven homage which the foremost of the three habitually receives at the hands of Drs. Westcott and Hort, I can only describe as a weak superstition. It is something more than unreasonable. It becomes even ridiculous.—Tischendorf's preference (in his last edition) for the *bêtises* of his own codex א,

---

[1] Tregelles, Part ii. p. 2.
[2] Scrivener's prefatory *Introduction*,—p. xix.   [3] *Ibid.* p. iii.

can only be defended on the plea of parental partiality. But it is not on that account the less foolish. His 'exaggerated preference for the single manuscript which he had the good fortune to discover, *has betrayed him*'—(in the opinion of Bishop Ellicott) — '*into an almost child-like infirmity of critical judgment.*'" [1]

(5) *O. S.* "Well but,—be all *that* as it may,—Caius, remember, is speaking of *heretical* writers. When I said 'I want Christian evidence,' I meant *orthodox* evidence, of course. You would not assert (would you?) that B and ℵ exhibit traces of *heretical* depravation?"

Q. R. "Reserving my opinion on that last head, good Sir, and determined to enjoy the pleasure of your company on any reasonable terms,—(for convince you, I both can and will, though you prolong the present discussion till to-morrow morning,)—I have to ask a little favour of you: viz. that you will bear me company in an imaginary expedition.

"I request that the clock of history may be put back seventeen hundred years. This is A.D. 183, if you please: and—(indulge me in the supposition!)—you and I are walking in Alexandria. We have reached the house of one Clemens, —a learned Athenian, who has long been a resident here. Let us step into his library,—he is from home. What a queer place! See, he has been reading his Bible, which is open at S. Mark x. Is it not a well-used copy? It must be at least 50 or 60 years old. Well, but suppose only 30 or 40. It was executed therefore *within fifty years of the death of S. John the Evangelist.* Come, let us transcribe two of the

---

[1] *On Revision,*—p. 47.

columns [1] (σελίδες) as faithfully as we possibly can, and be off. . . . We are back in England again, and the clock has been put right. Now let us sit down and examine our curiosity at leisure.[2] . . . It proves on inspection to be a transcript of the 15 verses (ver. 17 to ver. 31 [1]) which relate to the coming of the rich young Ruler to our LORD.

"We make a surprising discovery. There are but 297 words in those 15 verses,—according to the traditional Text : of which, in the copy which belonged to Clemens Alexandrinus, 39 prove to have been left out : 11 words are added : 22, substituted : 27, transposed : 13, varied ; and the phrase has been altered at least 8 times. Now, 112 words out of a total of 297, is 38 per cent. What do you think of *that ?*"

(6) *S. O.* "Think ? O but, I disallow your entire proceeding ! You have no business to collate with ' a text of late and degenerate type, such as is the Received Text of the New Testament.' When *this* 'is taken as a standard, any document belonging to a purer stage of the Text must by the nature of the case have the appearance of being guilty of omissions : and the nearer the document stands to the autograph, the more numerous must be the omissions laid to its charge.' I learnt that from Westcott and Hort. See page 235 of their luminous *Introduction.*"

Q. R. "Be it so ! Collate the passage then for yourself with the Text of Drs. Westcott and Hort : which, (remember !) aspires to reproduce ' the autographs themselves ' ' with the utmost exactness which the evidence permits '

---

[1] Singular to relate, S. Mark x. 17 to 31 *exactly* fills two columns of cod. א. (See Tischendorf's reprint, 4to, p. 24*.)

[2] Clemens Al. (ed. Potter),—pp. 937-8. . . . Note, how Clemens begins § v. (p. 938, line 30). This will be found noticed below, viz. at p. 336, note [3].

(pp. 288 and 289).[1] You will find that *this* time the words
omitted amount to 44. The words added are 13 : the words
substituted, 23 : the words transposed, 34 : the words varied
16. And the phrase has been altered 9 times at least. But,
130 on a total of 297, is 44 per cent. You will also bear in
mind that Clement of Alexandria is one of our principal
authorities for the Text of the Ante-Nicene period.[2]

"And thus, I venture to presume, the imagination has been
at last effectually disposed of, that *because* Codices B and ℵ
are the two oldest Greek copies in existence, the Text
exhibited by either must *therefore* be the purest Text which
is anywhere to be met with. *It is impossible to produce a
fouler exhibition of S. Mark* x. 17–31 *than is contained in
a document full two centuries older than either* B *or* ℵ,—*itself
the property of one of the most famous of the ante-Nicene
Fathers.*"

LVI.—(7) At this stage of the argument, the Reviewer
finds himself taken aside by a friendly Critic [*F. C.*], and
privately remonstrated with somewhat as follows :—

F. C. "Do you consider, Sir, what it is you are about ?
Surely, you have been proving a vast deal too much! If
the foregoing be a fair sample of the Text of the N. T. with
which Clemens Alex. was best acquainted, it is plain that
the testimony to the Truth of Scripture borne by one of the
most ancient and most famous of the Fathers, is absolutely
worthless. Is *that* your own deliberate conviction or not ?"

Q. R. "Finish what you have to say, Sir. After that, you
shall have a full reply."

---

[1] 'This Text' (say the Editors) 'is *an attempt to reproduce at once the
autograph Text.*'—*Introduction*, p. xxviii.
[2] Westcott and Hort's *Introduction*, pp. 112–3.

(8) *F. C.* "Well then. Pray understand, I nothing doubt that in your main contention you are right; but I yet cannot help thinking that this bringing in of a famous ancient Father — *obiter* — is a very damaging proceeding. What else is such an elaborate exposure of the badness of the Text which Clemens (A.D. 150) employed, but the hopeless perplexing of a question which was already sufficiently thorny and difficult? You have, as it seems to me, imported into these 15 verses an entirely fresh crop of 'Various Readings.' Do you seriously propose them as a contribution towards ascertaining the *ipsissima verba* of the Evangelist,—the true text of S. Mark x. 17–31?"

Q. R. "Come back, if you please, Sir, to the company. Fully appreciating the friendly spirit in which you just now drew me aside, I yet insist on so making my reply that all the world shall hear it. Forgive my plainness: but you are evidently profoundly unacquainted with the problem before you,—in which however you do not by any means enjoy the distinction of standing alone.

"The foulness of a Text which must have been penned within 70 or 80 years of the death of the last of the Evangelists, is a matter of fact—which must be loyally accepted, and made the best of. The phenomenon is surprising certainly; and may well be a warning to all who (like Dr. Tregelles) regard as oracular the solitary unsupported dicta of a Writer,—provided only he can claim to have lived in the IInd or IIIrd century. To myself it occasions no sort of inconvenience. You are to be told that the exorbitances of a *single* Father,—as Clemens: a *single* Version,—as the Egyptian: a *single* Copy,—as cod. B, are of no manner of significancy or use, except as warnings: are of no manner of interest, except as illustrating the depravation which systematically assailed the written Word in the age which immediately succeeded the Apostolic: *are, in fact, of no importance whatever.* To make them the basis of an induction is preposterous. It is not allowable to infer the universal from the particular. If the bones of Goliath were to be discovered to-morrow, would you propose as an induction therefrom that it was the fashion to wear four-and-twenty fingers and toes on one's hands and feet in the days of the giant of Gath? All the wild readings of the lost Codex before us may be unceremoniously dismissed. The critical importance and value of this stray leaf from a long-since-vanished Copy is entirely different, and remains to be explained.

" You are to remember then,—perhaps you have yet to learn,—that there are but 25 occasions in the course of these 15 verses, on which either Lachmann (L.), or Tischendorf (T.), or Tregelles (Tr.), or Westcott and Hort (W. H.), or our Revisionists (R. T.), advocate a departure from the Traditional Text. To those 25 places therefore our attention is now to be directed,—on them, our eyes are to be riveted,—exclusively. And the first thing which strikes us as worthy of notice is, that the 5 authorities above specified fall into no fewer than *twelve* distinct combinations in their advocacy of certain of those 25 readings: holding all 5 together *only* 4 times.[1] The one question of interest therefore which arises,

---

[1] Besides,—All but L.   conspire   5 times.

	All but T.	„	3	„
	All but Tr.	„	1	„
Then,—	T. Tr. WH.	combine	2	„
	T. WH. RT.	„	1	„
	Tr. WH. RT.	„	1	„
	L. Tr. WH.	„	1	„
Then,—	L. T. stand by themselves		1	„
	L. Tr.	„	1	„
	T. WH. „	„	1	„
Lastly,—	L. stands alone . . .		4	„

21

is this,—What amount of sanction do any of them experience at the hands of Clemens Alexandrinus ?

"I answer,—*Only on 3 occasions does he agree with any of them.*[1] The result of a careful analysis shows further that *he sides with the Traditional Text* 17 *times :*—witnessing against Lachmann, 9 times : against Tischendorf, 10 times : against Tregelles, 11 times : against Westcott and Hort, 12 times.[2]

"So far therefore from admitting that 'the Testimony of Clemens Al.—one of the most ancient and most famous of the Fathers—is absolutely worthless,'—I have proved it to be *of very great value.* Instead of 'hopelessly perplexing the question,' his Evidence is found to have *simplified matters considerably.* So far from 'importing into these 15 verses a fresh crop of Various Readings,' he has *helped us to get rid of no less than* 17 of the existing ones. . . . 'Damaging' his evidence has certainly proved : but *only to Lachmann, Tischendorf, Tregelles, Westcott and Hort and our ill-starred Revisionists.* And yet it remains undeniably true, that 'it is impossible to produce a fouler exhibition of S. Mark x. 17–31 than is met with in a document full two centuries older than either B or א,—the property of one of the most famous of the Fathers.'[3] . . . . Have you anything further to ask ? "

(9) *F. C.* "I should certainly like, in conclusion, to be informed whether we are to infer that the nearer we approach to the date of the sacred Autographs, the more corrupt we

---

[1] *Twice* he agrees with all 5 : viz. omitting ἄρας τὸν σταυρόν in ver. 21; and in omitting ἢ γυναῖκα (in ver. 29):—*Once* he agrees with only Lachmann : viz. in transposing ταῦτα πάντα (in ver. 20).

[2] On the remaining 5 occasions (17 + 3 + 5 = 25), Clemens exhibits peculiar readings of his own,—sides with *no one.*

[3] *Q. R.* p. 360.

shall find the copies. For, if so, pray—Where and when did purity of Text begin ? "

Q. R. " You are not at liberty, logically, to draw any such inference from the premises. The purest documents of all existed perforce in the first century : *must* have then existed. The spring is perforce purest at its source. My whole contention has been, and is,—That there is nothing at all unreasonable in the supposition that two stray copies of the IVth century,—coming down to our own times without a history and without a character,—*may* exhibit a thoroughly depraved text. *More* than this does not follow lawfully from the premises. At the outset, remember, you delivered it as your opinion that ' *the oldest Manuscript we possess, if it be but a very ancient one, must needs be the purest.*' I asserted, in reply, that ' it does not by any means follow, *because* a manuscript is very ancient, that *therefore* its text will be very pure ' (p. 321) ; and all that I have been since saying, has but had for its object to prove the truth of my assertion. Facts have been incidentally elicited, I admit, calculated to inspire distrust, rather than confidence, in very ancient documents generally. But I am neither responsible for these facts ; nor for the inferences suggested by them.

" At all events, I have to request that you will not carry away so entirely erroneous a notion as that I am the advocate for *Recent*, in preference to *Ancient*, Evidence concerning the Text of Scripture. Be so obliging as not to say concerning me that I ' *count* ' instead of ' *weighing* ' my witnesses. If you have attended to the foregoing pages, and have understood them, you must by this time be aware that *in every instance* it is to ANTIQUITY that I persistently make my appeal. I abide by its sentence, and I require that you shall do the same.

"You and your friends, on the contrary, *reject the Testimony of Antiquity*. You set up, instead, some idol of your own. Thus, Tregelles worshipped 'codex B.' But 'codex B' is not 'Antiquity'!—Tischendorf assigned the place of honour to 'codex ℵ.' But once more, 'codex ℵ' is not 'Antiquity'!—You rejoice in the decrees of the VIth-century-codex D,—and of the VIIIth-century-codex L,—and of the Xth, XIth, and XIVth century codices, 1, 33, 69. But will you venture to tell me that any of these are 'Antiquity'? *Samples* of Antiquity, at best, are any of these. No more! But then, it is demonstrable that they are *unfair* samples. Why are you regardless of *all other* COPIES?—So, with respect to VERSIONS, and FATHERS. You single out one or two,—the one or two which suit your purpose; and you are for rejecting all the rest. But, once more,—The *Coptic* version is not 'Antiquity,'—neither is *Origen* 'Antiquity.' The *Syriac* Version is a full set-off against the former,—*Irenæus* more than counterbalances the latter. Whatever is found in one of these ancient authorities must confessedly be AN 'ancient Reading:' but it does not therefore follow that it is THE ancient Reading of the place. Now, it is THE *ancient Reading*, of which we are always in search. And he who sincerely desires to ascertain what actually is *the Witness of Antiquity*,—(*i.e.*, what is the prevailing testimony of all the oldest documents,)—will begin by casting his prejudices and his predilections to the winds, and will devote himself conscientiously to an impartial survey of the whole field of Evidence."

F. C. "Well but,—you have once and again admitted that the phenomena before us are extraordinary. Are you able to explain how it comes to pass that such an one as Clemens Alexandrinus employed such a scandalously corrupt copy of the Gospels as we have been considering?"

Q. R. "You are quite at liberty to ask me any question you choose. And I, for my own part, am willing to return you the best answer I am able. You will please to remember however, that the phenomena will remain,—however infelicitous my attempts to explain them may seem to yourself. My view of the matter then—(think what you will about it!)—is as follows :—

LVII. "Vanquished by *THE WORD Incarnate*, Satan next directed his subtle malice against *the Word written*. Hence, as I think,—*hence* the extraordinary fate which befel certain early transcripts of the Gospel. First, heretical assailants of Christianity,—then, orthodox defenders of the Truth,—lastly and above all, self-constituted Critics, who (like Dr. Hort) imagined themselves at liberty to resort to 'instinctive processes' of Criticism; and who, at first as well as 'at last,' freely made their appeal 'to the individual mind:'—*such* were the corrupting influences which were actively at work throughout the first hundred and fifty years after the death of S. John the Divine. Profane literature has never known anything approaching to it,—can show nothing at all like it. Satan's arts were defeated indeed through the Church's faithfulness, because,—(the good Providence of GOD had so willed it,)—the perpetual multiplication, in every quarter, of copies required for Ecclesiastical use,—not to say the solicitude of faithful men in diverse regions of ancient Christendom to retain for themselves unadulterated specimens of the inspired Text,—proved a sufficient safeguard against the grosser forms of corruption. But this was not all.

"The Church, remember, hath been from the beginning the 'Witness and Keeper of Holy Writ.'[1] Did not her Divine Author pour out upon her, in largest measure, 'the

---

[1] Article xx. § 1.

SPIRIT of Truth;' and pledge Himself that it should be that
SPIRIT's special function to '*guide*' her children '*into all the
Truth*'[1]?... That by a perpetual miracle, Sacred Manuscripts
would be protected all down the ages against depraving
influences of whatever sort,—was not to have been expected;
certainly, was never promised. But the Church, in her
collective capacity, hath nevertheless—as a matter of fact—
been perpetually purging herself of those shamefully depraved copies which once everywhere abounded within her
pale: retaining only such an amount of discrepancy in her
Text as might serve to remind her children that they carry
their 'treasure in earthen vessels,'—as well as to stimulate
them to perpetual watchfulness and solicitude for the purity
and integrity of the Deposit. Never, however, up to the
present hour, hath there been any complete eradication of
all traces of the attempted mischief,—any absolute getting
rid of every depraved copy extant. These are found to have
lingered on anciently in many quarters. *A few such copies
linger on to the present day.* The wounds were healed, but
the scars remained,—nay, the scars are discernible still.

"What, in the meantime, is to be thought of those blind
guides—those deluded ones—who would now, if they could,
persuade us to go back to those same codices of which the
Church hath already purged herself? to go back in quest of
those very Readings which, 15 or 1600 years ago, the Church
in all lands is found to have rejected with loathing? Verily,
it is 'happening unto them according to the true proverb'—
which S. Peter sets down in his 2nd Epistle,—chapter ii.
verse 22. To proceed however.

"As for Clemens,—he lived at the very time and in the
very country where the mischief referred to was most rife.
For full two centuries after his era, heretical works were so

---

[1] Εἰς πᾶσαν τὴν ἀλήθειαν.—S. John xvi. 13.

industriously multiplied, that in a diocese consisting of 800 parishes (viz. Cyrus in Syria), the Bishop (viz. Theodoret, who was appointed in A.D. 423,) complains that he found no less than 200 copies of the *Diatessaron* of Tatian the heretic,—(Tatian's date being A.D. 173,)—honourably preserved in the Churches of his (Theodoret's) diocese, and mistaken by the orthodox for an authentic performance.[1] Clemens moreover would seem to have been a trifle too familiar with the works of Basilides, Marcion, Valentinus, Heracleon, and the rest of the Gnostic crew. He habitually mistakes apocryphal writings for inspired Scripture:[2] and —with corrupted copies always at hand and before him—he is just the man to present us with a quotation like the present, and straightway to volunteer the assurance that he found it 'so written in the Gospel according to S. Mark.'[3] The archetype of Codices B and ℵ,—especially the archetype from which Cod. D was copied,—is discovered to have experienced adulteration largely from the same pestilential source which must have corrupted the copies with which Clement (and his pupil Origen after him) were most familiar.—And thus you have explained to you the reason of the disgust and indignation with which I behold in these last days a resolute attempt made to revive and to palm off upon an unlearned generation the old exploded errors, under the pretence that they are the inspired Verity itself,—providentially recovered from a neglected shelf in the Vatican,—rescued from destruction by a chance visitor to Mount Sinai."

F. C. "Will you then, in conclusion, tell us how *you* would have us proceed in order to ascertain the Truth of Scripture?"

---

[1] Theodoret, *Opp.* iv. 208.—Comp. Clinton, *F. R.* ii. *Appendix,* p. 473.

[2] The reader is invited to enquire for Bp. Kaye (of Lincoln)'s *Account of the writings of Clement of Alexandria,*—and to read the vith and viiith chapters.

[3] Ταῦτα μὲν ἐν τῷ κατὰ Μάρκον εὐαγγελίῳ γέγραπται. (§ v.),—p. 938.

Q. R. "To answer that question fully would require a considerable Treatise. I will not, however, withhold a slight outline of what I conceive to be the only safe method of procedure. I could but *fill up* that outline, and *illustrate* that method, even if I had 500 pages at my disposal.

LVIII. " On first seriously applying ourselves to these studies, many years ago, we found it wondrous difficult to divest ourselves of prepossessions very like your own. Turn which way we would, we were encountered by the same confident terminology :— ' the best documents,' — ' primary manuscripts,'—' first-rate authorities,'—' primitive evidence,' —' ancient readings,'—and so forth : and we found that thereby cod. A or B,—cod. C or D—*were invariably and exclusively meant.* It was not until we had laboriously collated these documents (including ‎א‎) for ourselves, that we became aware of their true character. Long before coming to the end of our task (and it occupied us, off and on, for eight years) we had become convinced that the supposed ' best documents ' and ' first-rate authorities ' are in reality among *the worst :*—that these Copies deserve to be called ' primary,' only because in any enumeration of manuscripts, they stand foremost ;—and that their ' Evidence,' whether ' primitive ' or not, is *contradictory* throughout.—*All* Readings, lastly, we discovered are ' ancient.'

"A diligent inspection of a vast number of later Copies scattered throughout the principal libraries of Europe, and the exact Collation of a few, further convinced us that the deference generally claimed for B, ‎א‎, C, D is nothing else but a weak superstition and a vulgar error :—that the date of a MS. is not of its essence, but is a mere accident of the problem :—and that later Copies, so far from ' crumbling down salient points, softening irregularities, conforming

z

differences,'[1] and so forth,—on countless occasions, *and as a rule*,—preserve those delicate lineaments and minute refinements which the 'old uncials' are constantly observed to obliterate.   And so, rising to a systematic survey of the entire field of Evidence, we found reason to suspect more and more the soundness of the conclusions at which Lachmann, Tregelles, and Tischendorf had arrived: while we seemed led, as if by the hand, to discern plain indications of the existence for ourselves of a far 'more excellent way.'

LIX. "For, let the ample and highly complex provision which Divine Wisdom hath made for the effectual conservation of that crowning master-piece of His own creative skill,— THE WRITTEN WORD,—be duly considered; and surely a recoil is inevitable from the strange perversity which in these last days would shut us up within the limits of a very few documents to the neglect of all the rest,—as though a revelation from Heaven had proclaimed that the Truth is to be found exclusively in *them*.   The good Providence of the Author of Scripture is discovered to have furnished His household, the Church, with (speaking roughly) 1000 copies of the Gospels :—with twenty Versions—two of which go back to the beginning of Christianity : and with the writings of a host of ancient Fathers.   *Why* out of those 1000 MSS. *two* should be singled out by Drs. Westcott and Hort for special favour,—to the practical disregard of all the rest: *why* Versions and Fathers should by them be similarly dealt with,—should be practically set aside in fact in the lump,— we fail to discover.   Certainly the pleas urged by the learned Editors[2] can appear satisfactory to no one but to themselves.

LX. "For our method then,—It is the direct contradictory to that adopted by the two Cambridge Professors.   Moreover,

[1] Alford's N. T. vol. i. *proleg.* p. 92.
[2] See p. 197 (§ 269): and p. 201 (§ 275-9) :—and p. 205 (§ 280).

it conducts us throughout to directly opposite results. We hold it to be even axiomatic that a Reading which is supported by only one document,—out of the 1100 (more or less) already specified, — whether that solitary unit be a FATHER, a VERSION, or a COPY, — stands self-condemned; may be dismissed at once, without concern or enquiry.

" Nor is the case materially altered if (as generally happens) a few colleagues of bad character are observed to side with the else solitary document.   Associated with the corrupt B, is often found the more corrupt א.   Nay, six leaves of א are confidently declared by Tischendorf to have been written by the scribe of B.   The sympathy between these two, and the Version of Lower Egypt, is even notorious.   That Origen should sometimes join the conspiracy,—and that the same Reading should find allies in certain copies of the unrevised Latin, or perhaps in Cureton's Syriac:—all *this* we deem the reverse of encouraging.   The attesting witnesses are, in our account, of so suspicious a character, that the Reading cannot be allowed.   On such occasions, we are reminded that there is truth in Dr. Hort's dictum concerning the importance of noting the tendency of certain documents to fall into ' groups:' though his assertion that ' it cannot be too often repeated that the study of grouping is *the foundation of all enduring Criticism,*' [1] we hold to be as absurd as it is untrue.

LXI. " So far negatively.—A safer, the *only* trustworthy method, in fact, of ascertaining the Truth of Scripture, we hold to be the method which,—without prejudice or partiality,— simply ascertains WHICH FORM OF THE TEXT ENJOYS THE EARLIEST, THE FULLEST, THE WIDEST, THE MOST RESPECTABLE, AND—above all things—THE MOST VARIED ATTESTATION.   That a Reading should be freely recognized alike by the earliest

---

[1] *Preface* (1870), p. xv.

and by the latest available evidence,—we hold to be a prime circumstance in its favour. That Copies, Versions, and Fathers, should all three concur in sanctioning it,—we hold to be even more conclusive. If several Fathers, living in different parts of ancient Christendom, are all observed to recognize the words, or to quote them in the same way,—we have met with all the additional confirmation we ordinarily require. Let it only be further discoverable *how* or *why* the rival Reading came into existence, and our confidence becomes absolute.

LXII. "An instance which we furnished in detail in a former article,[1] may be conveniently appealed to in illustration of what goes before. Our LORD'S 'Agony and bloody sweat,'—first mentioned by Justin Martyr (A.D. 150), is found *set down in every MS. in the world except four*. It is duly exhibited *by every known Version*. It is recognized by *upwards of forty famous Fathers* writing without concert in remote parts of ancient Christendom. Whether therefore Antiquity, — Variety of testimony, — Respectability of witnesses, — or Number, — is considered, the evidence in favour of S. Luke xxii. 43, 44 is simply overwhelming. And yet out of superstitious deference to *two* Copies of bad character, Drs. Westcott and Hort (followed by the Revisionists) set the brand of spuriousness on those 26 precious words ; professing themselves 'morally certain' that this is nothing else but a 'Western Interpolation :' whereas, mistaken zeal for the honour of Incarnate JEHOVAH alone occasioned the suppression of these two verses in a few early manuscripts. This has been explained already,— namely, in the middle of page 82.

LXIII. "Only one other instance shall be cited. The traditional reading of S. Luke ii. 14 is vouched for by *ever*

---

[1] See above, pp. 79 to 85.

known copy of the Gospels but four—3 of which are of extremely bad character, viz. ℵ B D.   The Versions are divided : but *not* the Fathers : of whom *more than forty-seven* from every part of ancient Christendom,—(Syria, Palestine, Alexandria, Asia Minor, Cyprus, Crete, Gaul,)—come back to attest that the traditional reading (as usual) is the true one.   Yet such is the infatuation of the new school, that Drs. Westcott and Hort are content to make *nonsense* of the Angelic Hymn on the night of the Nativity, rather than admit the possibility of complicity in error in ℵ B D : error in respect of *a single letter !* . . . . The Reader is invited to refer to what has already been offered on this subject, from p. 41 to p. 47.

LXIV. "It will be perceived therefore that the method we plead for consists merely in a loyal recognition of the whole of the Evidence : setting off one authority against another, laboriously and impartially; and adjudicating fairly between them *all*.   Even so hopelessly corrupt a document as Clement of Alexandria's copy of the Gospels proves to have been—(described at pp. 326–31)—is by no means without critical value.   Servilely followed, it would confessedly land us in hopeless error : but, judiciously employed, as a set-off against *other* evidence; regarded rather as a check upon the exorbitances of *other* foul documents, (*e.g.* B ℵ C and especially D) ; resorted to as a protection against the prejudice and caprice of modern Critics ;—that venerable document, with all its faults, proves invaluable.   Thus, in spite of its own aberrations, it witnesses to *the truth of the Traditional Text* of S. Mark x. 17–31—(the place of Scripture above referred to[1])—in several important particulars; siding with it against Lachmann, 9 times ;—against Tischendorf, 10 times ;—against Tregelles, 11 times ;—against Westcott and Hort, 12 times.

---

[1] Pp. 359–60.

" We deem this laborious method the only true method, in our present state of imperfect knowledge : the method, namely, of *adopting that Reading which has the fullest, the widest, and the most varied attestation. Antiquity, and Respectability of Witnesses,* are thus secured. How men can persuade themselves that 19 Copies out of every 20 may be safely disregarded, if they be but written in minuscule characters,—we fail to understand. To ourselves it seems simply an irrational proceeding. But indeed we hold this to be no *seeming* truth. The fact is absolutely demonstrable. As for building up a Text, (as Drs. Westcott and Hort have done,) with special superstitious deference to *a single codex,*— we deem it about as reasonable as would be the attempt to build up a pyramid from its apex ; in the expectation that it would stand firm on its extremity, and remain horizontal for ever."

And thus much in reply to our supposed Questioner. We have now reached the end of a prolonged discussion, which began at page 320 ; more immediately, at page 337.

LXV. In the meantime, *a pyramid balanced on its apex* proves to be no unapt image of the Textual theory of Drs.Westcott and Hort. When we reach the end of their *Introduction* we find we have reached the point to which all that went before has been evidently converging : but we make the further awkward discovery that it is the point on which all that went before absolutely *depends* also. *Apart from* codex B, the present theory could have no existence. *But for* codex B, it would never have been excogitated. *On* codex B, it entirely rests. *Out of* codex B, it has *entirely sprung.*

Take away this one codex, and Dr. Hort's volume becomes absolutely without coherence, purpose, meaning. *One-fifth*

of it[1] is devoted to remarks on B and ℵ. The fable of 'the
Syrian text' is invented solely for the glorification of B and
ℵ,—which are claimed, of course, to be '*Pre*-Syrian.' This
fills 40 pages more.[2]   And thus it would appear that the
Truth of Scripture has run a very narrow risk of being lost
for ever to mankind.   Dr. Hort contends that it more than
half lay *perdu* on a forgotten shelf in the Vatican Library ;—.
Dr. Tischendorf, that it had been deposited in a waste-paper
basket[3] in the convent of S. Catharine at the foot of Mount
Sinai,—from which he rescued it on the 4th February, 1859 :
—neither, we venture to think, a very likely circumstance.
We incline to believe that the Author of Scripture hath not
by any means shown Himself so unmindful of the safety of
the Deposit, as these distinguished gentlemen imagine.

Are we asked for the ground of our opinion ? We point
without hesitation to the 998 COPIES which remain : to the
many ancient VERSIONS : to the many venerable FATHERS,—
any one of whom we hold to be *a more trustworthy authority*
for the Text of Scripture, *when he speaks out plainly*, than
either Codex B or Codex ℵ,—aye, or than both of them put
together.   Behold, (we say,) the abundant provision which
the All-wise One hath made for the safety of the Deposit:
the 'threefold cord' which 'is not quickly broken' ! We hope
to be forgiven if we add, (not without a little warmth,) that
we altogether wonder at the perversity, the infatuation, the
blindness,—which is prepared to make light of all these precious helps, in order to magnify two of the most corrupt

---

[1] P. 210 to p. 287.   See the Contents, pp. xxiii.–xxviii.
[2] Pp. 91–119 and pp. 133–146.
[3] "I perceived *a large and wide basket* full of old parchments ; and the
librarian told me that two heaps like this had been already *committed to
the flames.*   What was my surprise to find amid this heap of papers," &c.—
(*Narrative of the discovery of the Sinaitic Manuscript,* p. 23.)

codices in existence ; and *that,* for no other reason but because, (as Dr. Hort expresses it,) they '*happen* likewise to be the oldest extant Greek MSS. of the New Testament.' (p. 212.)

LXVI. And yet, had what precedes been the sum of the matter, we should for our own parts have been perfectly well content to pass it by without a syllable of comment. So long as nothing more is endangered than the personal reputation of a couple of Scholars—at home or abroad—we can afford to look on with indifference. Their private ventures are their private concern. What excites our indignation is the spectacle of the *Church of England* becoming to some extent involved in their discomfiture, because implicated in their mistakes: dragged through the mire, to speak plainly, at the chariot-wheels of these two infelicitous Doctors, and exposed with them to the ridicule of educated Christendom. Our Church has boasted till now of learned sons in abundance within her pale, ready at a moment's notice to do her right : to expose shallow sciolism, and to vindicate that precious thing which hath been committed to her trust.[1] Where are the men *now ?* What has come to her, that, on the contrary, certain of her own Bishops and Doctors have not scrupled to enter into an irregular alliance with Sectarians,—yes, have even taken into partnership with themselves one who openly denies the eternal Godhead of our LORD JESUS CHRIST,—in order, as it would seem, to give proof to the world of the low ebb to which Taste, Scholarship, and Sacred Learning have sunk among us ?

LXVII. Worse yet. We are so distressed, because the true sufferers after all by this ill-advised proceeding, are the 90 millions of English-speaking Christian folk scattered over

---

[1] τὴν παρακαταθήκην.—1 Tim. vi. 20.

the surface of the globe.   These have had the title-deeds by
which they hold their priceless birthright, shamefully tampered with.   *Who* will venture to predict the amount of
mischief which must follow, if the '*New Greek Text*' which
has been put forth by the men who were appointed *to revise
the English Authorized Version,* should become used in our
Schools and in our Colleges,—should impose largely on the
Clergy of the Church of England? . . . But to return from
this, which however will scarcely be called a digression.

A pyramid poised on its apex then, we hold to be a fair
emblem of the Theory just now under review.   Only, unfortunately, its apex is found to be constructed of brick without
straw : say rather *of straw—without brick.*

LXVIII. *Why* such partiality has been evinced latterly
for Cod. B, none of the Critics have yet been so good as to
explain ; nor is it to be expected that, satisfactorily, any of
them ever will.   *Why* again Tischendorf should have suddenly transferred his allegiance from Cod. B to Cod. ℵ,—
unless, to be sure, he was the sport of parental partiality,—
must also remain a riddle.   If *one* of the ' old uncials ' must
needs be taken as a guide,—(though we see no sufficient
reason why *one* should be appointed to lord it over the rest,)
—we should rather have expected that Cod. A would have been
selected,[1]—the text of which

' Stands in broad contrast to those of either B or ℵ, though the
interval of years [between it and them] is probably small.'

---

[1] [While this sheet is passing through the press, I find among my
papers a note (written in 1876) by the learned, loved, and lamented
Editor of Cyril,—Philip E. Pusey,—with whom I used to be in constant
communication :—"It is not obvious to me, looking at the subject from
outside, why B C L, constituting a class of MSS. allied to each other, and
therefore nearly = 1½ MSS., are to be held to be superior to A.   It is
still less obvious to me why ***, showing up (as he does) very many grave
faults of B, should yet consider B superior in character to A."]

(p. 152.) 'By a curious and apparently unnoticed coincidence,' (proceeds Dr. Hort,) 'its Text in several books agrees with the Latin Vulgate in so many peculiar readings devoid of old Latin attestation, as to leave little doubt that a Greek MS. largely employed by Jerome'—[and why not ' THE *Greek copies* employed by Jerome'?]—' in his Revision of the Latin version must have had to a great extent a common original with A.' (*Ibid.*)

Behold a further claim of this copy on the respectful consideration of the Critics! What would be thought of the Alexandrian Codex, if some attestation were discoverable in its pages that it actually *had belonged* to the learned Palestinian father? According to Dr. Hort,

'Apart from this individual affinity, A—both in the Gospels and elsewhere—may serve as *a fair example of the Manuscripts that,* to judge by Patristic quotations, *were commonest in the IVth century.*'—(p. 152.)

O but, the evidence in favour of Codex A thickens apace! Suppose then,—(for, after this admission, the supposition is at least allowable,)—suppose the discovery were made to-morrow of half-à-score of codices of the *same date as Cod.* B, but exhibiting the *same Text as Cod.* A. What a complete revolution would be thereby effected in men's minds on Textual matters! How impossible would it be, henceforth, for B and its henchman א, to obtain so much as a hearing! Such 'an eleven' would safely defy the world! And yet, according to Dr. Hort, the supposition may any day become a fact; for he informs us,—(and we are glad to be able for once to declare that what he says is perfectly correct,)— that such manuscripts once abounded or rather *prevailed;*— ' *were commonest* in the IVth century,' when codices B and א were written. We presume that then, as now, such codices prevailed universally, in the proportion of 99 to 1.

LXIX. But—what need to say it?—we entirely disallow any such narrowing of the platform which Divine Wisdom

hath willed should be at once very varied and very ample.
Cod. A is sometimes in error: sometimes even *conspires in
error exclusively with Cod.* B.   An instance occurs in 1 S. John
v. 18,—a difficult passage, which we the more willingly proceed to remark upon, because the fact has transpired that it
is one of the few places in which *entire unanimity* prevailed
among the Revisionists,—who yet (as we shall show) have
been, one and all, mistaken in substituting '*him*' (αὐτόν) for
'*himself*' (ἑαυτόν) . . . We venture to bespeak the Reader's
attention while we produce the passage in question, and briefly
examine it.   He is assured that it exhibits a fair average
specimen of what has been the Revisionists' fatal method
in every page:—

LXX. S. John in his first Epistle (v. 18) is distinguishing
between the mere recipient of the new birth (ὁ ΓΕΝΝΗΘΕῚΣ
ἐκ τοῦ Θεοῦ),—and the man who retains the sanctifying
influences of the HOLY SPIRIT which he received when he
became regenerate (ὁ ΓΕΓΕΝΝΗΜΕΝΟΣ ἐκ τοῦ Θεοῦ).   The
latter (he says) '*sinneth not :*' the former, (he says,) '*keepeth
himself, and the Evil One toucheth him not.*'   So far, all is
intelligible.   The nominative is the same in both cases.
Substitute however ' keepeth *him* (αὐτόν),' for ' keepeth *himself* (ἑαυτόν),' and (as Dr. Scrivener admits [1]), ὁ γεννηθεὶς ἐκ
τοῦ Θεοῦ can be none other than the Only Begotten SON of
GOD.   And yet our LORD is *nowhere* in the New Testament
designated as ὁ γεννηθεὶς ἐκ τοῦ Θεοῦ.[2]   Alford accordingly
prefers to make nonsense of the place; which he translates,—
' he that hath been begotten of GOD, *it keepeth him.*'

---

[1] *Introduction*, p. 567.

[2] Let the following places be considered : S. Jo. i. 13 ; iii. 3, 5, 6, 7, 8 ;
1 Jo. ii. 29 ; iii. 9 *bis*, iv. 7 ; v. 1 *bis*, 4, 18 *bis*.   *Why* is it to be supposed
that on this last occasion THE ETERNAL SON should be intended ?

LXXI. Now, on every occasion like the present,—(instead of tampering with the text, *as Dr. Hort and our Revisionists have done without explanation or apology,*)—our safety will be found to consist in enquiring,—But (1) What have the Copies to say to this? (2) What have the Versions? and (3) What, the Fathers? . . . The answer proves to be—(1) *All the copies except three,*[1] read 'himself.'—(2) So do the Syriac and the Latin;[2]—so do the Coptic, Sahidic, Georgian, Armenian, and Æthiopic versions.[3]—(3) So, Origen clearly thrice,[4]—Didymus clearly 4 times,[5]—Ephraem Syrus clearly twice,[6]—Severus also twice,[7]—Theophylact expressly,[8]—and Œcumenius.[9]—So, indeed, Cod. A; for *the original Scribe* is found to have *corrected himself.*[10] The sum of the adverse attestation therefore which prevailed with the Revisionists, is found to have been—*Codex B and a single cursive copy* at Moscow.

This does not certainly seem to the Reviewer, (as it seemed to the Revisionists,) 'decidedly preponderating evidence.' In his account, '*plain and clear error*' dwells with *their Revision.* But this may be because,—(to quote words recently addressed by the President of the Revising body to the Clergy

---

[1] A*, B, 105.

[2] The paraphrase is interesting. The Vulgate, Jerome [ii. 321, 691], Cassian [p. 409],—'*Sed generatio Dei conservat eum:*' Chromatius [Gall. viii. 347], and Vigilius Taps. [ap. Athanas. ii. 646],—'*Quia (quoniam) nativitas Dei custodit (servat) illum.*' In a letter of 5 Bishops to Innocentius I. (A.D. 410) [Galland. viii. 598 b], it is,—'*Nativitas quæ ex Deo est.*' Such a rendering (viz. '*his having been born of* GOD') amounts to an *interpretation* of the place.

[3] From the Rev. S. C. Malan, D.D.   [4] iv. 326 b c.

[5] Gall. viii. 347,—of which the Greek is to be seen in Cramer's *Cat.* pp. 143-4. Many portions of the lost Text of this Father, (the present passage included [p. 231]) are to be found in the Scholia published by C. F. Matthæi [N. T. xi. 181 to 245-7].

[6] i. 94, 97.   [7] In *Cat.* p. 124, repeated p. 144.   [8] iii. 433 c.

[9] ii. 601 d.   [10] By putting a small uncial ∊ above the A.

and Laity of the Diocese of Gloucester and Bristol,)—
the 'Quarterly Reviewer' is '*innocently ignorant of the now
established principles of Textual Criticism.*' [1]

LXXII. 'It is easy,'—(says the learned Prelate, speaking
on his own behalf and that of his co-Revisionists,)—'to put
forth to the world a sweeping condemnation of many of
our changes of reading ; and yet all the while to be *innocently
ignorant of the now established principles of Textual Criticism.*'

May we venture to point out, that it is easier still to
denounce adverse Criticism in the lump, instead of trying to
refute it in any one particular:—to refer vaguely to 'established principles of Textual Criticism,' instead of stating
which they be :—to sneer contemptuously at endeavours,
(which, even if unsuccessful, one is apt to suppose are
entitled to sympathy at the hands of a successor of the
Apostles,) instead of showing *wherein* such efforts are repre-
hensible ?   We are content to put the following question to
any fair-minded man :—Whether of these two is the more
facile and culpable proceeding ;—(1) *Lightly to blot out an
inspired word from the Book of Life, and to impose a wrong
sense on Scripture,* as in this place the Bishop and his colleagues are found to have done :—or, (2) To fetch the same
word industriously back : to establish its meaning by
diligent and laborious enquiry : to restore both to their
rightful honours : and to set them on a basis of (*hitherto
unobserved*) evidence, from which (*faxit DEUS !*) it will be
found impossible henceforth to dislodge them ?

This only will the Reviewer add,—That if it be indeed
one of the ' now established principles of Textual Criticism,'

---

[1] *Diocesan Progress,* Jan. 1882.—[pp. 20] p. 19.

that the evidence of *two manuscripts and-a-half* outweighs the evidence of (1) All *the remainir* 997½,—(2) The whole body of the Versions,—(3) *Every Father who quotes the place, from* A.D. 210 to A.D. 1070,—and (4) *The strongest possible internal Evidence :*—if all this *indeed* be so,—he devoutly trusts that he may be permitted to retain his 'Innocence' to the last; and in his 'Ignorance,' when the days of his warfare are ended, to close his eyes in death.—And now to proceed.

LXXIII. The Nemesis of Superstition and Idolatry is ever the same. Phantoms of the imagination henceforth usurp the place of substantial forms. Interminable doubt,—wretched misbelief,—childish credulity,—judicial blindness,—are the inevitable sequel and penalty. The mind that has long allowed itself in a systematic trifling with Evidence, is observed to fall the easiest prey to Imposture. It has doubted what is *demonstrably* true : has rejected what is *indubitably* Divine. Henceforth, it is observed to mistake its own fantastic creations for historical facts : to believe things which rest on insufficient evidence, or on no evidence at all. Thus, these learned Professors,—who condemn the 'last Twelve Verses of the Gospel according to S. Mark ;' which have been accounted veritable Scripture by the Church Universal for more than 1800 years;—nevertheless accept as the genuine '*Diatessaron of Tatian*' [A.D. 170], a production which was discovered yesterday, and which *does not even claim to be* the work of that primitive writer.[1]

Yes, the Nemesis of Superstition and Idolatry is ever the same. General mistrust of *all* evidence is the sure result. In 1870, Drs. Westcott and Hort solemnly assured their

---

[1] *Introduction*, p. 283. *Notes*, pp. 3, 22, and *passim*.

brother-Revisionists that 'the prevalent assumption that throughout the N. T. the true Text is to be found *somewhere* among recorded Readings, *does not stand the test of experience.*' They are evidently still haunted by the same spectral suspicion. They invent a ghost to be exorcised in every dark corner. Accordingly, Dr. Hort favours us with a chapter on the Art of 'removing Corruptions of the sacred Text *antecedent to extant documents*' (p. 71). We are not surprised (though we *are* a little amused) to hear that,—

'The *Art of Conjectural Emendation* depends for its success so much on personal endowments, fertility of resource in the first instance, and even more an appreciation of language too delicate to acquiesce in merely plausible corrections, that it is easy to forget its true character as a critical operation founded on knowledge and method.'—(p. 71.)

LXXIV. *Very* 'easy,' certainly. One sample of Dr. Hort's skill in this department, (it occurs at page 135 of his *Notes on Select Readings*,) shall be cited in illustration. We venture to commend it to the attention of our Readers :—

(*a*) S. Paul [2 Tim. i. 13] exhorts Timothy, (whom he had set as Bp. over the Church of Ephesus,) to '*hold fast*' a certain '*form*' or '*pattern*' (ὑποτύπωσιν) '*of sound words, which*' (said he) '*thou hast heard of me.*' The flexibility and delicate precision of the Greek language enables the Apostle to indicate exactly what was the prime object of his solicitude. It proves to have been the safety of *the very words* which he had syllabled, (ὑγιαινόντων λόγων ῾ΩΝ παρ᾽ ἐμοῦ ἤκουσας). As learned Bp. Beveridge well points out,—'*which words*, not *which form*, thou hast heard of me. So that it is not so much the *form*, as the *words* themselves, which the Apostle would have him to hold fast.'[1]

---

[1] Sermons, vol. i. 132,—('*A form of sound words to be used by Ministers.*')

All this however proves abhorrent to Dr. Hort. 'This sense' (says the learned Professor) 'cannot be obtained from the text except by treating ὧν as put in the genitive by *an unusual and inexplicable attraction.* It seems more probable that ὧν is a *primitive corruption* of ὄν after πάντων.'

Now, this is quite impossible, since neither ὄν nor πάντων occurs anywhere in the neighbourhood. And as for the supposed 'unusual and inexplicable attraction,' it happens to be one of even common occurrence,—as every attentive reader of the New Testament is aware. Examples of it may be seen at 2 Cor. i. 4 and Ephes. iv. 1,—also (in Dr. Hort's text of) Ephes. i. 6 (ἧς in all 3 places). Again, in S. Luke v. 9 (whether ῇ or ὧν is read): and vi. 38 (ᾧ) :—in S. Jo. xv. 20 (οὗ) :—and xvii. 11 (ᾧ): in Acts ii. 22 (οἷς): vii. 17 (ἧς) and 45 (ὧν): in xxii. 15 (ὧν), &c. . . . But why entertain the question ? There is absolutely *no room* for such Criticism in respect of a reading which is found *in every known MS.,—in every known Version,—in every Father who quotes the place :* a reading which Divines, and Scholars who were not Divines,— Critics of the Text, and grammarians who were without prepossessions concerning Scripture,—Editors of the Greek and Translators of the Greek into other languages,—all alike have acquiesced in, from the beginning until now.

We venture to assert that it is absolutely unlawful, in the entire absence of evidence, to call such a reading as the present in question. There is absolutely no safeguard for Scripture—no limit to Controversy—if a place like this may be solicited at the mere suggestion of individual caprice. (For it is worth observing that *on this, and similar occasions, Dr. Hort is forsaken by Dr. Westcott.* Such notes are enclosed in brackets, and subscribed ' H.') In the meantime, who can forbear smiling at the self-complacency of a Critic who

puts forth remarks like those which precede ; and yet congra-
tulates himself on '*personal endowments, fertility of resource,
and a too delicate appreciation of language* '?

(*b*) Another specimen of conjectural extravagance occurs
at S. John vi. 4, where Dr. Hort labours to throw suspicion
on 'the Passover' (τὸ πάσχα),—in defiance of *every known
Manuscript,—every known Version,—*and *every Father who
quotes or recognizes the place.*[1]   We find *nine columns* devoted
to his vindication of this weak imagination ; although so
partial are his *Notes,* that countless 'various Readings' of
great interest and importance are left wholly undiscussed.
Nay, sometimes entire Epistles are dismissed with a single
weak annotation (e.g. 1 and 2 Thessalonians),—*or with none,*
as in the case of the Epistle to the Philippians.

(*c*) We charitably presume that it is in order to make
amends for having conjecturally thrust out τὸ πάσχα from S.
John vi. 4,—that Dr. Hort is for conjecturally thrusting into
Acts xx. 28, Υἱοῦ (after τοῦ ἰδίου),—an imagination to which
he devotes a column and-a-half, but *for which he is not able to
produce a particle of evidence.*   It would result in our reading, 'to feed the Church of GOD, which He purchased'—(*not*
'with *His own* blood,' but)—'with the *blood of His own*
SON:' which has evidently been suggested by nothing so
much as by the supposed necessity of getting rid of a text
which unequivocally asserts that CHRIST is GOD.[2]

---

[1] Quoted by ps.-Ephraem *Evan. Conc.* p. 135 l. 2 :—Nonnus :—Chrys.
viii. 248 :—Cyril iv. 269 e, 270 a, 273 :—Cramer's *Cat.* p. 242 l. 25 (which
is *not* from Chrys.) :—*Chron. Paschale* 217 a (*diserte*).—Recognized by
Melito (A.D. 170) :—Irenæus (A.D. 177) :—Hippolytus (A.D. 190) :—
Origen :—Eusebius :—Apollinarius Laod., &c.

[2] This is the *true* reason of the eagerness which has been displayed in
certain quarters to find ὅς, (not Θεός) in 1 Tim. iii. 16 :—just as nothing

LXXV. Some will be chiefly struck by the conceit and presumption of such suggestions as the foregoing. A yet larger number, as we believe, will be astonished by their essential foolishness. For ourselves, what surprises us most is the fatal misapprehension they evince of the true office of Textual Criticism as applied to the New Testament. It *never is to invent new Readings*, but only to adjudicate between existing and conflicting ones. He who seeks to thrust out 'THE PASSOVER' from S. John vi. 4, (where it may on no account be dispensed with [1]); and to thrust 'THE SON' into Acts xx. 28, (where His Name cannot stand without evacuating a grand Theological statement);—will do well to consider whether he does not bring himself directly under the awful malediction with which the beloved Disciple concludes and seals up the Canon of Scripture :—" I testify unto every man that heareth the words of the prophecy of this Book,—If any man shall *add unto* these things, GOD shall add unto him the plagues that are written in this Book. And if any man shall *take away from* the words of the Book of this prophecy, GOD shall take away his part out of the Book of Life, and out of the holy City, and from the things which are written in this Book."[2]

May we be allowed to assure Dr. Hort that 'CONJECTURAL EMENDATION' CAN BE ALLOWED NO PLACE WHATEVER IN THE TEXTUAL CRITICISM OF THE NEW TESTAMENT? He will no doubt disregard our counsel. May Dr. Scrivener then

---

else but a determination that CHRIST shall not be spoken of as ὁ ὢν ἐπὶ πάντων Θεός, has occasioned the supposed doubt as to the construction of Rom. ix. 5,—in which we rejoice to find that Dr. Westcott refuses to concur with Dr. Hort.

[1] See Dr. W. H. Mill's *University Sermons* (1845),—pp. 301-2 and 305 :—a volume which should be found in every clergyman's library.

[2] Rev. xxii. 18, 19.

[p. 433] be permitted to remind him that " it is now agreed among competent judges that *Conjectural emendation* must *never* be resorted to,—even in passages of acknowledged difficulty " ?

There is in fact no need for it,—nor can be : so very ample, as well as so very varied, is the evidence for the words of the New Testament.

LXXVI. Here however we regret to find we have *both* Editors against us.   They propose ' the definite question,'—

' " Are there, as a matter of fact, places in which we are *constrained by overwhelming evidence* to recognize the existence of Textual error in *all* extant documents ? "   To this question we have no hesitation in replying in the affirmative.'—(p. 279.)

Behold then the deliberate sentence of Drs. Westcott and Hort.   They flatter themselves that they are able to produce ' *overwhelming evidence* ' in proof that there are places where *every extant document* is in error.   The instance on which they both rely, is S. Peter's prophetic announcement (2 Pet. iii. 10), that in ' the day of the LORD,' ' the earth and the works that are therein *shall be burned up* ' (κατακαήσεται).

This statement is found to have been glossed or paraphrased in an age when men knew no better.   Thus, Cod. C substitutes — ' *shall vanish away:* ' [1] the Syriac and one Egyptian version,—' *shall not be found*,' (apparently in imitation of Rev. xvi. 20).   But, either because the ' not ' was accidentally omitted [2] in some very ancient exemplar ;—

---

[1] ἀφανισθήσονται.

[2] This happens not unfrequently in codices of the type of ℵ and B.   A famous instance occurs at Col. ii. 18, (ἃ μὴ ἑώρακεν ἐμβατεύων,—'*prying into the things he hath not seen* '); where ℵ * A B D * and a little handful of suspicious documents leave out the ' *not*.'   Our Editors, rather than re-

or else because it was deemed a superfluity by some Occidental critic who in his simplicity supposed that εὑρεθήσεται might well represent the Latin *urerentur*,—(somewhat as Mrs. Quickly warranted ' *hang hog* ' to be Latin for ' bacon,')—codices א and B (with four others of later date) exhibit ' *shall be found*,'[1]—which obviously makes utter nonsense of the place. (Εὑρεθήσεται appears, nevertheless, in Dr. Hort's text: *in consequence of which*, the margin of our ' Revised Version ' is disfigured with the statement that ' The most ancient manuscripts read *discovered*.') But what is there in all this to make one distrust the Traditional reading ?—supported as it is by the whole mass of Copies : by the Latin,[2]—the Coptic,—the Harkleian,—and the Æthiopic Versions :—besides the only Fathers who quote the place; viz. Cyril seven times,[3] and John Damascene [4] once ? . . . As for pretending, at the end of the foregoing enquiry, that ' we are *constrained by overwhelming evidence* to recognize the existence of textual error *in all extant documents*,'—it is evidently a mistake. Nothing else is it but a misstatement of facts.

---

cognize this blunder (so obvious and ordinary !), are for conjecturing A ΕΟΡΑΚΕΝ ΕΜΒΑΤΕΥΩΝ into ΑΕΡΑ ΚΕΝΕΜΒΑΤΕΥΩΝ; which (if it means anything at all) may as well mean,—' proceeding on an airy foundation to offer an empty conjecture.' Dismissing that conjecture as worthless, we have to set off the whole mass of the copies—against some 6 or 7 :—Irenæus (i. 847), Theodorus Mops. (in *loc.*), Chrys. (xi. 372), Theodoret (iii. 489, 490), John Damascene (ii. 211)—against no Fathers at all (for Origen once has μή [iv. 665]; once, has it not [iii. 63]; and once is doubtful [i. 583]). Jerome and Augustine both take notice of the diversity of reading, *but only to reject it.*—The Syriac versions, the Vulgate, Gothic, Georgian, Sclavonic, Æthiopic, Arabic and Armenian—(we owe the information, as usual, to Dr. Malan)—are to be set against the suspicious Coptic. All these then are with the Traditional Text: which cannot seriously be suspected of error.

[1] εὑρεθήσεται.   [2] Augustin. vii. 595.
[3] ii. 467 : iii. 865 :—ii. 707 : iii. 800 :—ii. 901. *In Luc.* pp. 428, 654.
[4] ii. 347.

LXXVII. And thus, in the entire absence of proof, Dr. Hort's view of 'the existence of corruptions' of the Text 'antecedent to all existing authority,'[1]—falls to the ground. His confident prediction, that such corruptions 'will sooner or later have to be acknowledged,' may be dismissed with a smile. So indifferent an interpreter of the Past may not presume to forecast the Future.

The one 'matter of fact,' which at every step more and more impresses an attentive student of the Text of Scripture, is,—(1st), The utterly depraved character of Codices B and א: and (2nd), The singular infatuation of Drs. Westcott and Hort in insisting that those 2 Codices '*stand alone in their almost complete immunity from error :* '[2]—that 'the fullest comparison does but increase the conviction that *their pre-eminent relative purity is approximately absolute.*'[3]

LXXVIII. Whence is it,—(we have often asked ourselves the question, while studying these laborious pages,)—How does it happen that a scholar like Dr. Hort, evidently accomplished and able, should habitually mistake the creations of his own brain for material forms? the echoes of his own voice while holding colloquy with himself, for oracular responses? We have not hitherto expressed our astonishment,—but must do so now before we make an end, —that a writer who desires to convince, can suppose that his own arbitrary use of such expressions as ' Pre-Syrian ' and ' Neutral,' — ' Western ' and ' Alexandrian,' — ' Non-Western ' and ' Non-Alexandrian,'—' Non-Alexandrian Pre-Syrian ' and ' Pre-Syrian Non-Western,'—will produce any (except an irritating) effect on the mind of an intelligent reader.

The delusion of supposing that by the free use of such a vocabulary a Critic may dispense with the ordinary processes

---

[1] Preface to ' Provisional issue,' p. xxi.
[2] *Introduction* p. 210.   [3] *Ibid.* p. 276.

of logical proof, might possibly have its beginning in the
retirement of the cloister, where there are few to listen and
none to contradict: but it can only prove abiding if there
has been no free ventilation of the individual fancy. Greatly
is it to be regretted that instead of keeping his Text a
profound secret for 30 years, Dr. Hort did not freely impart
it to the public, and solicit the favour of candid criticism.

Has no friend ever reminded him that assertions concerning the presence or absence of a 'Syrian' or a 'Pre-Syrian,'
a 'Western' or a 'Non-Western *element*,' are but wind,—
the merest chaff and draff,—*apart from proof?* Repeated *ad
nauseam*, and employed with as much peremptory precision
as if they were recognized terms connoting distinct classes
of Readings,—(whereas they are absolutely without significancy, except, let us charitably hope, to him who employs
them);—such expressions would only be allowable on the
part of the Critic, if he had first been at the pains *to index
every principal Father*,—and *to reduce Texts to families* by a
laborious process of Induction. Else, they are worse than
foolish. More than an impertinence are they. They bewilder,
and mislead, and for a while encumber and block the way.

LXXIX. This is not all however. Even when these
Editors notice hostile evidence, they do so after a fashion
which can satisfy no one but themselves. Take for example
their note on the word εἰκῆ ('*without a cause*') in S. Matthew
v. 22 ('But I say untó you, that whosoever is angry with his
brother *without a cause*'). The Reader's attention is specially
invited to the treatment which this place has experienced at
the hands of Drs. Westcott and Hort :—

(*a*) They unceremoniously eject the word from S. Mat-
thew's Gospel with their oràcular sentence, '*Western and
Syrian.*'—Aware that εἰκῆ is recognized by 'Iren. lat[3]; Eus.
D. E. Cyp.,' they yet claim for omitting it the authority of

'Just. Ptolem. (? Iren. 242 *fin.*), Tert.; and certainly' (they proceed) ' Orig. on Eph. iv. 31, noticing both readings, and similarly Hier. *loc.*, who probably follows Origen: also Ath. *Pasch.* Syr. 11 : Ps.-Ath. *Cast.* ii. 4; and others' . . . . Such is their '*Note*' on S. Matthew v. 22. It is found at p. 8 of their volume. In consequence, εἰκῇ ('*without a cause*') disappears from their Text entirely.

(*b*) But these learned men are respectfully imformed that neither Justin Martyr, nor Ptolemæus the Gnostic, nor Irenæus, no, nor Tertullian either,—that *not one of these four writers,*—supplies the wished-for evidence. As for Origen,— they are assured that *he*—*not* 'probably' but *certainly*—is the cause of all the trouble. They are reminded that Athanasius [1] quotes (*not* S. Matt. v. 22, but) 1 Jo. iii. 15. They are shown that what they call 'ps.-Ath. *Cast.*' is nothing else but a paraphrastic translation (by *Græculus quidam*) of John Cassian's *Institutes,*—' ii. 4' in the Greek representing viii. 20 in the Latin. . . . And now, how much of the adverse Evidence remains ?

(*c*) Only this :—Jerome's three books of Commentary on the Ephesians, are, in the main, a translation of Origen's lost 3 books on the same Epistle.[2] Commenting on iv. 31, Origen says that εἰκῇ has been improperly added to the Text,[3]—*which shows that in Origen's copy* εἰκῇ *was found there.* A few ancient writers in consequence (but *only* in consequence) of what Jerome (or rather Origen) thus delivers, are observed to omit εἰκῇ.[4] That is all !

(*d*) May we however respectfully ask these learned Editors why, besides Irenæus,[5]—Eusebius,[6]—and Cyprian,[7]—

---

[1] Apud Mai, vi. 105.   [2] *Opp.* vii. 543. Comp. 369.
[3] Ap. Cramer, *Cat.* vi. 187.   [4] So, Nilus, i. 270.
[5] *Interp.* 595: 607.   [6] *Dem. Evan.* p. 444.   [7] P. 306.

they do not mention that εἰκῆ is *also* the reading of Justin
Martyr,[1]—of Origen himself,[2]—of the *Constitutiones App.*,[3]—
of Basil three times,[4]—of Gregory of Nyssa,[5]—of Epiphanius,[6]—of Ephraem Syrus twice,[7]—of Isidorus twice,[8]—
of Theodore of Mops., — of Chrysostom 18 times,—of the
Opus imp. twice,[9]—of Cyril[10]—and of Theodoret[11]—(each in
3 places). It was also the reading of Severus, Abp. of
Antioch : [12]—as well as of Hilary,[13]—Lucifer,[14]—Salvian,[15]—
Philastrius,[16]—Augustine, and—Jerome,[17]—(although, when
translating from Origen, he pronounces against εἰκῆ [18]) :—not
to mention Antiochus mon.,[19]—J. Damascene,[20]—Maximus,[21]
—Photius,[22]—Euthymius,—Theophylact,—and others ? [23] . . . .
We have adduced no less than *thirty* ancient witnesses.

(*e*) Our present contention however is but this,—that a
Reading which is attested by *every uncial Copy of the Gospels
except* B *and* א; by *a* whole *torrent of Fathers;* by *every
known copy* of the old Latin,—by · *all* the Syriac, (for the
Peschito inserts [not translates] the word εἰκῆ,)—by the

---

[1] *Epist. ad Zen.* iii. 1. 78. Note, that our learned Cave considered this
to be a *genuine* work of Justin M. (A.D. 150).

[2] *Cantic.* (an early work) *interp.* iii. 39,—though elsewhere (i. 112, 181
[?] : ii. 305 *int.* [but *not* ii. 419]) he is for leaving out εἰκῆ.

[3] Gall. iii. 72 and 161.

[4] ii. 89 b and e (partly quoted in the *Cat.* of Nicetas) *expressly* : 265.

[5] i. 818 *expressly.*

[6] ii. 312 (preserved in Jerome's Latin translation, i. 240).

[7] i. 132 ; iii. 442.   [8] 472, 634.   [9] Ap. Chrys.

[10] iii. 768 : *apud Mai,* ii. 6 and iii. 268.

[11] i. 48, 664 ; iv. 946.   [12] Cramer's *Cat.* viii. 12, line 14.

[13] 128, 625.   [14] Gall. vi. 181.   [15] Gall. x. 14.   [16] Gall. vii. 509.

[17] i. 27, written when he was 42; and ii. 733, 739, written when he
was 84.

[18] vii. 26,—' *Radendum est ergo* sine causâ.' And so, at p. 636.

[19] 1064.   [20] ii. 261.   [21] ii. 592.

[22] *Amphilochia,* (Athens, 1858,)—p. 317. Also in *Cat.*

[23] *Apophthegm. PP.* [ap. Cotel. *Eccl. Gr. Mon.* i. 622].

Coptic,—as well as by the Gothic—and Armenian versions ;
—that such a reading is not to be set aside by the stupid
dictum, ' *WESTERN AND SYRIAN.*'   By no such methods will the
study of Textual Criticism be promoted, or any progress ever
be made in determining the Truth of Scripture.   There really
can be no doubt whatever,—(that is to say, if we are to be
guided by *ancient Evidence*,)—that εἰκῆ (' *without a cause* ') was
our SAVIOUR's actual word ; and that our Revisers have been
here, as in so many hundred other places, led astray by Dr.
Hort.   So true is that saying of the ancient poet,—' Evil
company doth corrupt good manners.'   'And if the blind
lead the blind,'—(a greater than Menander hath said it,)—
' *both shall fall into the ditch.*' [1]

(*f*) In the meantime, we have exhibited somewhat in detail, Drs. Westcott and Hort's Annotation on εἰκῆ, [S. Matth.
v. 22,] in order to furnish our Readers with at least *one definite specimen* of the Editorial skill and Critical ability of
these two accomplished Professors.   Their general practice,
as exhibited in the case of 1 Jo. v. 18, [see above, pp. 347–9,]
is to tamper with the sacred Text, without assigning their
authority,—indeed, without offering apology of any kind.

(*g*) The *sum* of the matter proves to be as follows: Codd.
B *and* ℵ (the ' two false Witnesses '),—B and ℵ, *alone of MSS.*
—omit εἰκῆ.   On the strength of this, Dr. Hort persuaded
his fellow Revisers to omit ' *without a cause*' from their
Revised Version: and it is proposed, in consequence, that
every Englishman's copy of S. Matthew v. 22 shall be mutilated in the same way for ever. . . . *Delirant reges, plec-
tuntur Achivi.*

(*h*) But the question arises—Will the Church of England
submit to have her immemorial heritage thus filched from

---

[1] S. Matth. xv. 14.

her? We shall be astonished indeed if she proves so regardless of her birthright.

LXXX. Lastly, the intellectual habits of these Editors have led them so to handle evidence, that the sense of proportion seems to have forsaken them. "He who has long pondered over a train of Reasoning,"—(remarks the elder Critic,)—"*becomes unable to detect its weak points.*"[1] Yes, the 'idols of the den' exercise at last a terrible ascendency over the Critical judgment. It argues an utter want of mental perspective, when we find 'the Man working on the Sabbath,' put on the same footing with 'the Woman taken in Adultery,' and conjectured to have '*come from the same source:*'—the incident of 'the Angel troubling the pool of Bethesda' dismissed, as having '*no claim to any kind of association with the true Text:*'[2]—and 'the *two* Supplements' to S. Mark's Gospel declared to '*stand on equal terms* as independent attempts to fill up a gap;' and allowed to be possibly '*of equal antiquity.*'[3] How can we wonder, after this, to find *anything* omitted,—*anything* inserted,—*anything* branded with suspicion? And the brand is very freely applied by Drs. Westcott and Hort. Their notion of the Text of the New Testament, is certainly the most extraordinary ever ventilated. It has at least the merit of entire originality. While they eagerly insist that many a passage is but 'a Western interpolation' after all; is but an 'Evangelic Tradition,' 'rescued from oblivion by the Scribes of the second century;' — they yet *incorporate those passages with the Gospel.* Careful enough to clap them into fetters first, they then, (to use their own queer phrase,) — '*provisionally associate them with the Text.*'

---

[1] *Gospel of the Resurrection,*—p. vii.   [2] *Introduction*, pp. 300–2.
[3] *Ibid.* p. 299.

LXXXI. We submit, on the contrary, that Editors who 'cannot doubt' that a certain verse 'comes from an extraneous source,'—'do not believe that it belonged originally to the Book in which it is now included,'—are unreasonable if they proceed to assign to it any actual place there at all. When men have once thoroughly convinced themselves that two Verses of S. Luke's Gospel are not Scripture, but 'only a fragment from the Traditions, written or oral, which were for a while locally current;'[1]—what else is it but the merest trifling with sacred Truth, to promote those two verses to a place in the inspired context? Is it not to be feared, that the conscious introduction of human Tradition into GOD's written Word will in the end destroy the soul's confidence in Scripture itself? opening the door for perplexity, and doubt, and presently for Unbelief itself to enter.

LXXXII. And let us not be told that the Verses stand there 'provisionally' only; and for that reason are 'enclosed within double brackets.' Suspected felons are 'provisionally' locked up, it is true: but after trial, they are either convicted and removed out of sight; or else they are acquitted and suffered to come abroad like other men. Drs. Westcott and Hort have no right at the end of thirty years of investigation, still to encumber the Evangelists with 'provisional' fetters. Those fetters either signify that the Judge is afraid to carry out his own righteous sentence : or else, that he entertains a secret suspicion that he has made a terrible mistake after all,—has condemned the innocent. Let these esteemed Scholars at least have 'the courage of their own convictions,' and be throughout as consistent as, in two famous instances (viz. at pages 113 and 241), they have been. Else, in GOD's Name, let them have the manliness to avow themselves in

---

[1] Appendix, p. 66.

error : abjure their πρῶτον ψεῦδος ; and cast the fantastic
Theory, which they have so industriously reared upon it,
unreservedly, to the winds !

LXXXIII. To conclude.—It will be the abiding distinction
of the Revised Version (*thanks to Dr. Hort,*) that it brought
to the front a question which has slept for about 100 years ;
but which may not be suffered now to rest undisturbed any
longer.   It might have slumbered on for another half-
century,—a subject of deep interest to a very little band of
Divines and Scholars ; of perplexity and distrust to all the
World besides ;—*but* for the incident which will make the
17th of May, 1881, for ever memorable in the Annals of the
Church of England.

LXXXIV. The Publication on that day of the ' Revised
English Version of the New Testament' instantly concen-
trated public attention on the neglected problem : for men
saw at a glance that the Traditional Text of 1530 years'
standing,—(the exact number is Dr. Hort's, not ours,)—had
been unceremoniously set aside in favour of *an entirely different
Recension.*   The true Authors of the mischief were not far to
seek.   Just five days before,—under the editorship of Drs.
Westcott and Hort, (Revisionists themselves,)—had appeared
the most extravagant Text which has seen the light since the
invention of Printing.   No secret was made of the fact that,
under pledges of strictest secrecy,[1] a copy of this wild performance (marked ' Confidential ') had been entrusted to
every member of the Revising body : and it has since transpired that Dr. Hort advocated his own peculiar views in the
Jerusalem Chamber with so much volubility, eagerness, pertinacity, and plausibility, that in the end—notwithstanding

---

[1] See Scrivener's *Introduction,* p. 432.

the warnings, remonstrances, entreaties of Dr. Scrivener,—his counsels prevailed; and—the utter shipwreck of the 'Revised Version' has been, (as might have been confidently predicted,) the disastrous consequence. Dr. Hort is calculated to have *talked for three years* out of the ten.

But in the meantime there has arisen *this* good out of the calamity,—namely, that men will at last require that the Textual problem shall be fairly threshed out. They will insist on having it proved to their satisfaction,—(1) That Codices B and ℵ are indeed the oracular documents which their admirers pretend; and—(2) That a narrow selection of ancient documents is a secure foundation on which to build the Text of Scripture. Failing this,—(and the *onus probandi* rests wholly with those who are for setting aside the Traditional Text in favour of another, *entirely dissimilar in character*,)—failing this, we say, it is reasonable to hope that the counsels of the '*Quarterly Review*' will be suffered to prevail. In the meantime, we repeat that this question has now to be fought out: for to ignore it any longer is impossible. Compromise of any sort between the two conflicting parties, is impossible also; for they simply contradict one another. Codd. B and ℵ are either among the purest of manuscripts,—or else they are among the very foulest. The Text of Drs. Westcott and Hort is either the very best which has ever appeared,—or else it is the very worst; the nearest to the sacred Autographs,—or the furthest from them. There is no room for *both* opinions; and there cannot exist any middle view.

The question will have to be fought out; and it must be fought out fairly. It may not be magisterially settled; but must be advocated, on either side, by the old logical method. If Continental Scholars join in the fray, England,—which in the last century took the lead in these studies,—will, it is to be hoped, maintain her ancient reputation and again occupy the front rank. The combatants may be sure that, in consequence of all that has happened, the public will be no longer indifferent spectators of the fray; for the issue concerns the inner life of the whole community,—touches men's very heart of hearts. Certain it is that—' GOD defend *the Right !*' will be the one aspiration of every faithful spirit among us. THE TRUTH,—(we avow it on behalf of Drs. Westcott and Hort as eagerly as on our own behalf,)—GOD'S TRUTH will be, as it has been throughout, the one object of all our striving. Αἴλινον αἴλινον εἰπέ, τὸ δ' εὖ νικάτω.

I HAVE BEEN VERY JEALOUS FOR THE LORD GOD OF HOSTS.

LETTER TO

BISHOP ELLICOTT,

IN REPLY TO HIS PAMPHLET.

" Nothing is more satisfactory at the present time than the evident feelings of veneration for our Authorized Version, and the very generally-felt desire for *as little change as possible.*"—BISHOP ELLICOTT.[1]

" We may be satisfied with the attempt to correct *plain and clear errors*, but *there it is our duty to stop.*"—BISHOP ELLICOTT.[2]

" We have now, at all events, no fear of *an over-corrected Version.*"—BISHOP ELLICOTT.[3]

" I fear we must say in candour that in the Revised Version we meet in every page with small *changes, which are vexatious, teasing, and irritating, even the more so because they are small ; which seem almost to be made for the sake of change.*"—BISHOP WORDSWORTH.[4]

[The question arises,]—" Whether the Church of England,—which in her Synod, so far as this Province is concerned, sanctioned a Revision of her Authorized Version *under the express condition,* which she most wisely imposed, that *no Changes should be made in it except what were absolutely necessary,*—could consistently accept a Version in which 36,000 changes have been made ; *not a fiftieth of which can be shown to be needed, or even desirable.*"—BISHOP WORDSWORTH.[5]

---

[1] *On Revision,*—p. 99.
[2] *Speech in Convocation,* Feb. 1870, (p. 83.)
[3] *On Revision,*—p. 205.
[4] *Address to Lincoln Diocesan Conference,*—p. 25.
[5] *Ibid.,*—p. 27.

LETTER TO

THE RIGHT REV. CHARLES JOHN ELLICOTT, D.D.,

BISHOP OF GLOUCESTER AND BRISTOL,

IN REPLY TO HIS PAMPHLET IN DEFENCE OF

THE REVISERS AND THEIR GREEK TEXT OF THE NEW TESTAMENT.

"WHAT COURSE WOULD REVISERS HAVE US TO FOLLOW? . . . WOULD IT BE WELL FOR THEM TO AGREE ON A CRITICAL GREEK TEXT? *TO THIS QUESTION WE VENTURE TO ANSWER VERY UNHESITATINGLY IN THE NEGATIVE.*

"THOUGH WE HAVE MUCH CRITICAL MATERIAL, AND A VERY FAIR AMOUNT OF CRITICAL KNOWLEDGE, *WE HAVE CERTAINLY NOT YET ACQUIRED SUFFICIENT CRITICAL JUDGMENT* FOR ANY BODY OF REVISERS HOPEFULLY TO UNDERTAKE SUCH A WORK AS THIS."

BISHOP ELLICOTT.[1]

MY LORD BISHOP,

Last May, you published a pamphlet of seventy-nine pages[2] in vindication of the Greek Text recently put forth by

---

[1] *Considerations on Revision,*—p. 44. The Preface is dated 23rd May, 1870. The Revisers met on the 22nd of June.

We learn from Dr. Newth's *Lectures on Bible Revision* (1881), that,—"As the general Rules under which the Revision was to be carried out had been carefully prepared, no need existed for any lengthened discussion of preliminary arrangements, and the Company upon its first meeting was able to enter at once upon its work" (p. 118) . . . "The portion prescribed for the first session was Matt. i. to iv." (p. 119). . . "The question of the spelling of proper names . . . being settled, the Company proceeded to the actual details of the Revision, and in a surprisingly short time settled down to an established method of procedure."—"All proposals made at the first Revision were decided by simple majorities" (p. 122) . . . "*The questions which concerned the Greek Text were decided for the most part at the First Revision.*" (Bp. Ellicott's *Pamphlet,* p. 34.)

[2] *The Revisers and the Greek Text of the New Testament, by two*

2 B

the New Testament Company of Revisers. It was (you said) your Answer to the first and second of my Articles in the *Quarterly Review:* [1] — all three of which, corrected and enlarged, are now submitted to the public for the second time. See above, from page 1 to page 367.

[1] *Preliminary Statement.*

You may be quite sure that I examined your pamphlet as soon as it appeared, with attention. I have since read it through several times: and—I must add—with ever-increasing astonishment. First, because it is so evidently the production of one who has never made Textual Criticism seriously his study. Next, because your pamphlet is no refutation whatever of my two Articles. You flout me : you scold me : you lecture me. But I do not find that you ever *answer* me. You re-produce the theory of Drs. Westcott and Hort,—which I claim to have demolished.[2] You seek to put me down by flourishing in my face the decrees of Lachmann, Tischendorf and Tregelles,—which, as you are well aware, I entirely dis-allow. Denunciation, my lord Bishop, is not Argument ; neither is Reiteration, Proof. And then,—Why do you impute to me opinions which I do not hold ? and charge me with a method of procedure of which I have never been guilty ? Above all, why do you seek to prejudice the question at issue between us by importing irrelevant matter which can only impose upon the ignorant and mislead the unwary ? Forgive my plainness, but really you are so conspicuously unfair,—and at the same time so manifestly unacquainted,

---

Members of the New Testament Company,—1882.   Macmillan, pp. 79, price two shillings and sixpence.

[1] " To these two articles—so far, at least, as they are concerned with the Greek Text adopted by the Revisers—our Essay is intended for an answer."—p. 79.

[2] See above, pages 235 to 366.

(except at second-hand and only in an elementary way,) with the points actually under discussion,—that, were it not for the adventitious importance attaching to any utterance of yours, deliberately put forth at this time as Chairman of the New Testament body of Revisers, I should have taken no notice of your pamphlet.

[2] *The Bishop's pamphlet was anticipated and effectually disposed of, three weeks before it appeared, by the Reviewer's Third Article.*

I am bound, at the same time, to acknowledge that you have been singularly unlucky.   While *you* were penning your Defence, (namely, throughout the first four months of 1882,) *I* was making a fatal inroad into your position, by showing how utterly without foundation is the "Textual Theory" to which you and your co-Revisers have been so rash as to commit yourselves.[1]   This fact I find duly recognized in your 'Postscript.'   "Since the foregoing pages were in print" (you say,) "a third article has appeared in the *Quarterly Review*, entitled 'Westcott and Hort's Textual Theory.'"[2]   Yes.   *I* came before the public on the 16th of April; *you* on the 4th of May, 1882.   In this way, your pamphlet was anticipated,—had in fact been fully disposed of, three weeks before it appeared.   "The Reviewer," (you complain at page 4,) " censures their [Westcott and Hort's] Text : *in neither Article has he attempted a serious examination of the arguments which they allege in its support.*"   But, (as explained,) the "serious examination" which you reproach me with having hitherto failed to produce,—had been already three weeks in the hands of readers of the *Quarterly* before your pamphlet saw the light.   You would, in consequence,

---

[1] Article III.,—see last note.   [2] *Pamphlet*, p. 79.

2 B 2

have best consulted your own reputation, I am persuaded, had you instantly recalled and suppressed your printed sheets. *What*, at all events, you can have possibly meant, while publishing them, by adding (in your 'Postscript' at page 79,)—"*In this controversy it is not for us to interpose:*" and again,—"*We find nothing in the Reviewer's third article to require further answer from us:*"—passes my comprehension; seeing that your pamphlet (page 11 to page 29) is an elaborate avowal that you have made Westcott and Hort's theory entirely your own. The Editor of the *Speaker's Commentary*, I observe, takes precisely the same view of your position. "The two Revisers" (says Canon Cook) "actually add a Postscript to their pamphlet of a single short page noticing their unexpected anticipation by the third *Quarterly Review* article; with the remark that 'in this controversy (between Westcott and Hort and the Reviewer) it is not for us to interfere:'—as if Westcott and Hort's theory of Greek Revision could be refuted, or seriously damaged, without *cutting the ground from under the Committee of Revisers on the whole of this subject.*" [1]

[3] *Bp. Ellicott remonstrated with for his unfair method of procedure.*

I should enter at once on an examination of your Reply, but that I am constrained at the outset to remonstrate with you on the exceeding unfairness of your entire method of procedure. Your business was to make it plain to the public that you have dealt faithfully with the Deposit: have strictly fulfilled the covenant into which you entered twelve years ago with

---

[1] *The Revised Version of the first three Gospels, considered in its bearings upon the record of our Lord's Words and of incidents in His Life,*— (1882. pp. 250. Murray,)—p. 232. Canon Cook's temperate and very interesting volume will be found simply unanswerable.

the Convocation of the Southern Province: have corrected
only "*plain and clear errors.*"   Instead of this, you labour to
enlist vulgar prejudice against me :—partly, by insisting that
I am for determining disputed Readings by an appeal to the
'Textus Receptus,'—which (according to you) I look upon as
faultless :—partly, by exhibiting me in disagreement with
Lachmann, Tischendorf and Tregelles.   The irrelevancy of
this latter contention,—the groundlessness of the former,—
may not be passed over without a few words of serious remonstrance.   For I claim that, in discussing the Greek Text,
I have invariably filled my pages as full of *Authorities*
for the opinions I advocate, as the limits of the page would
allow.   I may have been tediously demonstrative sometimes :
but no one can fairly tax me with having shrunk from the
severest method of evidential proof.   To find myself therefore charged with " mere denunciation,"[1]—with substituting
"strong expressions of individual opinion" for "arguments,"[2]
—and with "attempting to cut the cord by reckless and unverified assertions," (p. 25,)—astonishes me.   Such language
is in fact even ridiculously unfair.

The misrepresentation of which I complain is not only
conspicuous, but systematic.   It runs through your whole
pamphlet : is admitted by yourself at the close,—(viz. at
p. 77,)—to be *half the sum of your entire contention.*   Besides
cropping up repeatedly,[3] it finds deliberate and detailed
expression when you reach the middle of your essay,—viz. at
p. 41 : where, with reference to certain charges which I not
only bring against codices א B C L, but laboriously substantiate
by a free appeal to the contemporary evidence of Copies,
Versions, and Fathers,—you venture to express yourself concerning me as follows :—

---

[1] P. 40.   [2] *Ibid.*
[3] As at p. 4, and p. 12, and p. 13, and p. 19, and p. 40.

"To attempt to sustain such charges by a rough comparison of these ancient authorities with the Textus Receptus, and to measure the degree of their depravation by *the amount of their divergence from such a text as we have shown this Received Text really to be*, is to trifle with the subject of sacred Criticism."— p. 41.

You add :—

" Until the depravation of these ancient Manuscripts has been demonstrated in a manner more consistent with *the recognized principles of Criticism*, such charges as those to which we allude must be regarded as expressions of passion, or prejudice, and set aside by every impartial reader as assertions for which no adequate evidence has yet been produced."—pp. 41–2.

[4] (*Which be ' the recognized principles of Textual Criticism' ? —a question asked in passing.*)

But give me leave to ask in passing,— *Which*, pray, *are* " the recognized principles of Criticism " to which you refer ? I profess I have never met with them yet; and I am sure it has not been for want of diligent enquiry. You have publicly charged me before your Diocese with being " innocently ignorant of the *now established principles* of Textual Criticism."[1] But why do you not state which those principles *are ?* I am surprised. You are for ever vaunting "*principles*" which have been established by the investigations and reasonings " of Lachmann, Tischendorf and Tregelles :[2]—" the *principles* of Textual Criticism which are accepted and recognized by the great majority of modern Textual Critics : "[3]—" the *principles* on which the Textual Criticism of the last fifty years has been based : "[4]—but you never condescend to explain *which be* the ' principles' you refer to. For the last time,— *Who* established those " Principles " ? and, *Where* are they to be seen " established " ?

---

[1] See above, pp. 348–350.   [2] P. 40.   [3] P. 40.   [4] P. 77.

I will be so candid with you as frankly to avow that the
only two "principles" with which I am acquainted as held,
with anything like consent, by "the modern Textual Critics "
to whom you have surrendered your judgment, are—(1st)
A robust confidence in the revelations of their own inner
consciousness : and (2ndly) A superstitious partiality for
two codices written in the uncial character,—for which partiality they are able to assign no intelligible reason. You put
the matter as neatly as I could desire at page 19 of your
Essay,—where you condemn, with excusable warmth, "those
who adopt the easy method of *using some favourite Manuscript*,"—or of exercising "*some supposed power of divining the
original Text;*" — as if those were "the only necessary
agents for correcting the Received Text." *Why* the evidence
of codices B and א, — and perhaps the evidence of the
VIth-century codex D,—('the singular codex' as you call it;
and it is certainly a very singular codex indeed :)—*why*, I
say, the evidence of these two or three codices should be
thought to outweigh the evidence of all other documents in
existence,—whether Copies, Versions, or Fathers,—I have
never been able to discover, nor have their admirers ever
been able to tell me.

[5] *Bp. Ellicott's and the Reviewer's respective methods, contrasted.*

Waiving this however, (for it is beside the point,) I venture to ask,—With what show of reason can you pretend
that I "*sustain my charges*" against codices א B C L, "*by a
rough comparison of these ancient authorities with the* Textus
Receptus " ?[1] . . . Will you deny that it is a mere misrepresentation of the plain facts of the case, to say so ? Have I
not, on the contrary, *on every occasion* referred Readings in

---

[1] P. 41, and so at p. 77.

dispute,—the reading of א B C L on the one hand, the reading of the *Textus Receptus* on the other,—simultaneously to one and the same external standard ? Have I not persistently enquired for the verdict—so far as it has been obtainable—of CONSENTIENT ANTIQUITY ? If I have sometimes spoken of certain famous manuscripts (א B C D namely,) as exhibiting fabricated Texts, have I not been at the pains to establish the reasonableness of my assertion by showing that they yield divergent,—that is *contradictory*, testimony ?

The task of laboriously collating the five 'old uncials' throughout the Gospels, occupied me for five-and-a-half years, and taxed me severely. But I was rewarded. I rose from the investigation profoundly convinced that, however important they may be as instruments of Criticism, codices א B C D are among the most corrupt documents extant. It was a conviction derived from exact *Knowledge* and based on solid grounds of *Reason*. You, my lord Bishop, who have never gone deeply into the subject, repose simply on *Prejudice*. Never having at any time collated codices א A B C D for yourself, you are unable to gainsay a single statement of mine by a counter-appeal to *facts*. Your textual learning proves to have been all obtained at second-hand,—taken on trust. And so, instead of marshalling against me a corresponding array of ANCIENT AUTHORITIES,—you invariably attempt to put me down by an appeal to MODERN OPINION. "The *majority of modern Critics*" (you say) have declared the manuscripts in question "not only to be wholly undeserving of such charges, but, on the contrary, to exhibit a text of comparative purity." [1]

The sum of the difference therefore between our respective methods, my lord Bishop, proves to be this:—that

---

[1] P. 41.

whereas *I* endeavour by a laborious accumulation of *ancient Evidence* to demonstrate that the decrees of Lachmann, of Tischendorf and of Tregelles, *are untrustworthy ;* *your* way of reducing me to silence, is to cast Lachmann, Tregelles and Tischendorf at every instant in my teeth. You make your appeal exclusively to *them.* "It would be difficult" (you say) "to find a recent English Commentator of any considerable reputation who has not been influenced, more or less consistently, by *one or the other of these three Editors :* " [1] (as if *that* were any reason why I should do the same!) Because I pronounce the Revised reading of S. Luke ii. 14, " a grievous perversion of the truth of Scripture," you bid me consider "that in so speaking I am *censuring Lachmann, Tischendorf and Tregelles.*" You seem in fact to have utterly missed the point of my contention : which is, that the ancient Fathers collectively (A.D. 150 to A.D. 450),—inasmuch as they must needs have known far better than Lachmann, Tregelles, or Tischendorf, (A.D. 1830 to A.D. 1880,) what was the Text of the New Testament in the earliest ages,—are perforce far more trustworthy guides than they. And further, that whenever it can be clearly shown that the Ancients as a body say one thing, and the Moderns another, the opinion of the Moderns may be safely disregarded.

When therefore I open your pamphlet at the first page, and read as follows:—" A bold assault has been made in recent numbers of the *Quarterly Review* upon the whole fabric of Criticism which has been built up *during the last fifty years* by the patient labour of successive editors of the New Testament," [2]—I fail to discover that any practical inconvenience results to myself from your announcement. The same plaintive strain reappears at p. 39 ; where, having

---

[1] P. 5. [2] P. 3.

pointed out " that the text of the Revisers is, in all essential features, the same as that text in which the best critical editors, *during the past fifty years*, are generally agreed,"— you insist " that thus, any attack made on the text of the Revisers is really an attack on the critical principles that have been carefully and laboriously established *during the last half-century.*" With the self-same pathetic remonstrance you conclude your labours. "If," (you say) "the Revisers are wrong in the principles which they have applied to the determination of the Text, *the principles* on which the Textual Criticism of *the last fifty years* has been based, are wrong also."[1]...Are you then not yet aware that the alternative which seems to you so alarming is in fact my whole contention ? What else do you imagine it is that I am proposing to myself throughout, but effectually to dispel the vulgar prejudice,—say rather, to plant my heel upon the weak superstition,—which *"for the last fifty years"* has proved fatal to progress in this department of learning; and which, if it be suffered to prevail, will make *a science* of Textual Criticism impossible ? A shallow empiricism has been the prevailing result, up to this hour, of the teaching of Lachmann, and Tischendorf, and Tregelles.

[6] *Bp. Ellicott in May* 1870, *and in May* 1882.

A word in your private ear, (by your leave) in passing. You seem to have forgotten that, at the time when you entered on the work of Revision, *your own* estimate of the Texts put forth by these Editors was the reverse of favourable; *i.e.* was scarcely distinguishable from that of your present correspondent. Lachmann's you described as "a text composed on *the narrowest and most exclusive* principles,"—" really based on *little more than four manuscripts.*"

---

[1] P. 77.

—" The case of Tischendorf" (you said) " is still more easily
disposed of.   Which of this most inconstant Critic's texts are
we to select ?   Surely not the last, in which an exaggerated
preference for a single manuscript has betrayed him into *an
almost childlike infirmity of judgment.*   Surely also not the
seventh edition, which exhibits all the instability which a
comparatively recent recognition of the authority of cursive
manuscripts might be supposed likely to introduce."—As for
poor Tregelles, you said :—" His critical principles . . . . are
now, perhaps justly, called in question." His text " is rigid and
mechanical, and sometimes fails to disclose *that critical instinct
and peculiar scholarly sagacity which* "[1] have since evidently
disclosed themselves in perfection in those Members of the
Revising body who, with Bp. Ellicott at their head, systematically outvoted Prebendary Scrivener in the Jerusalem
Chamber.   But with what consistency, my lord Bishop, do
you to-day vaunt " the principles" of the very men whom
yesterday you vilipended precisely because *their " principles "*
then seemed to yourself so utterly unsatisfactory ?

[7] " *The fabric of modern Textual Criticism* " (1831–81)
          rests on an insecure basis.

I have been guilty of little else than sacrilege, it seems,
because I have ventured to send a shower of shot and shell
into the flimsy decrees of these three Critics which now you
are pleased grandiloquently to designate and describe as
" *the whole fabric of Criticism which has been built up within
the last fifty years.*"   Permit me to remind you that the
" fabric " you speak of,—(confessedly a creation of yesterday,)
—rests upon a foundation of sand ; and has been already so
formidably assailed, or else so gravely condemned by a succession of famous Critics, that as " *a fabric,*" its very

---

[1] *On Revision,* pp. 47–8.

existence may be reasonably called in question.   Tischendorf
insists on the general depravity ("*universa vitiositas*") of
codex B; on which codex nevertheless Drs. Westcott and
Hort chiefly rely,—regarding it as unique in its pre-eminent
purity.   The same pair of Critics depreciate the Traditional
Text as "beyond all question identical with the dominant
[Greek] Text *of the second half of the fourth century:*"—
whereas, "*to bring the sacred text back to the condition in which
it existed during the fourth century,*" [1] was Lachmann's one
object; the sum and substance of his striving.   "The fancy
of a Constantinopolitan text, and every inference that has
been grounded on its presumed existence," [2] Tregelles
declares to have been "swept away at once and for ever," by
Scrivener's published Collations.   And yet, what else but
this is "the fancy," (as already explained,) on which Drs.
Westcott and Hort have been for thirty years building
up their visionary Theory of Textual Criticism?—What
Griesbach attempted [1774–1805], was denounced [1782–
1805] by C. F. Matthæi; — disapproved by Scholz; —
demonstrated to be untenable by Abp. Laurence.   Finally,
in 1847, the learned J. G. Reiche, in some Observations
prefixed to his Collations of MSS. in the Paris Library,
eloquently and ably exposed the unreasonableness of *any*
theory of 'Recension,'—properly so called; [3] thereby effectu-

---

[1] Scrivener's *Introduction,*—p. 423.   [2] *Ibid.* p. 421.

[3] "Non tantum totius Antiquitatis altum de tali opere suscepto si-
lentium,—sed etiam frequentes Patrum, usque ad quartum seculum
viventium, de textu N. T. liberius tractato, impuneque corrupto, deque
summâ Codicum dissonantiâ querelæ, nec non ipsæ corruptiones inde a
primis temporibus continuo propagatæ,—satis sunt documento, neminem
opus tam arduum, scrupulorum plenum, atque invidiæ et calumniis
obnoxium, aggressum fuisse; etiamsi doctiorum Patrum de singulis locis
disputationes ostendant, eos non prorsus rudes in rebus criticis fuisse."—
*Codd. MSS. N. T. Græcorum &c. nova descriptio, et cum textu vulgo
recepto Collatio,* &c.   4to. Gottingæ, 1847.   (p. 4.)

ally anticipating Westcott and Hort's weak imagination
of a 'Syrian Text,' while he was demolishing the airy
speculations of Griesbach and Hug. 'There is no royal
road' (he said) 'to the Criticism of the N. T.: no plain and
easy method, at once reposing on a firm foundation, and
conducting securely to the wished for goal.'[1] .... Scarcely
therefore in Germany had the basement-story been laid
of that 'fabric of Criticism which has been built up during
the last fifty years,' and which *you* superstitiously admire,—
when a famous German scholar was heard denouncing the
fabric as insecure. He foretold that the '*regia via*' of
codices B and ℵ would prove a deceit and a snare : which
thing, at the end of four-and-thirty years, has punctually
come to pass.

Seven years after, Lachmann's method was solemnly
appealed from by the same J. G. Reiche :[2] whose words of
warning to his countrymen deserve the attention of every
thoughtful scholar among ourselves at this day. Of the
same general tenor and purport as Reiche's, are the utterances of those giants in Textual Criticism, Vercellone of
Rome and Ceriani of Milan. Quite unmistakable is the
verdict of our own Scrivener concerning the views of
Lachmann, Tischendorf and Tregelles, and the results to
which their system has severally conducted them.—If Alford
adopted the prejudices of his three immediate predecessors,

---

[1] He proceeds:—" Hucusque nemini contigit, nec in posterum, puto,
continget, monumentorum nostrorum, tanquam totidem testium singu-
lorum, ingens agmen ad tres quatuorve, e quibus omnium testimonium
pendeat, testes referre ; aut e testium grege innumero aliquot duces
auctoresque secernere, quorum testimonium tam plenum, certum firmum-
que sit, ut sine damno ceterorum testimonio careamus."—*Ibid.* (p. 19.)

[2] *Commentarius Criticus in N. T.* (in his Preface to the Ep. to the
Hebrews). We are indebted to Canon Cook for calling attention to this.
See by all means his *Revised Text of the first three Gospels*,—pp. 4–8.

his authority has been neutralized by the far different teaching of one infinitely his superior in judgment and learning, —the present illustrious Bishop of Lincoln.—On the same side with the last named are found the late Philip E. Pusey and Archd. Lee,—Canon Cook and Dr. Field,—the Bishop of S. Andrews and Dr. S. C. Malan. Lastly, at the end of fifty-one years, (viz. in 1881,) Drs. Westcott and Hort have revived Lachmann's unsatisfactory method,—superadding thereto not a few extravagances of their own. That their views have been received with expressions of the gravest disapprobation, no one will deny. Indispensable to their contention is the grossly improbable hypothesis that the Peschito is to be regarded as the 'Vulgate' (*i.e.* the *Revised*) Syriac; Cureton's, as the 'Vetus' or *original* Syriac version. And yet, while I write, the Abbé Martin at Paris is giving it as the result of his labours on this subject, that Cureton's Version cannot be anything of the sort.[1] Whether Westcott and Hort's theory of a '*Syrian*' Text has not received an effectual quietus, let posterity decide. Ἀμέραι δ' ἐπίλοιποι μάρτυρες σοφώτατοι.

From which it becomes apparent that, at all events, "the fabric of Criticism which has been built up within the last fifty years " has not arisen without solemn and repeated protest,—as well from within as from without. It may not therefore be spoken of by you as something which men are bound to maintain inviolate,—like an Article of the Creed. It is quite competent, I mean, for any one to denounce the entire system of Lachmann, Tischendorf and Tregelles,—*as I do now*,—as an egregious blunder; if he will but be at the

---

[1] It requires to be stated, that, (as explained by the Abbé to the present writer,) the 'Post-scriptum' of his Fascic. IV., (viz. from p. 234 to p. 236,) is a *jeu d'esprit* only,—intended to enliven a dry subject, and to entertain his pupils.

pains to establish on a severe logical basis the contradictory
of not a few of their most important decrees. And you, my
lord Bishop, are respectfully reminded that your defence of
their system, — if you must needs defend what I deem
worthless,—must be conducted, not by sneers and an affectation of superior enlightenment ; still less by intimidation,
scornful language, and all those other bad methods whereby
it has been the way of Superstition in every age to rivet the
fetters of intellectual bondage : but by severe reasoning, and
calm discussion, and a free appeal to ancient Authority, and
a patient investigation of all the external evidence accessible.
I request therefore that we may hear no more of *this* form
of argument. The Text of Lachmann and Tischendorf and
Tregelles,—of Westcott and Hort and Ellicott, (*i.e. of the
Revisers,*)—is just now on its trial before the world.[1]

[8] *Bp. Ellicott's strange notions about the ' Textus Receptus.'*

Your strangest mistakes and misrepresentations however
are connected with the 'Textus Receptus.' It evidently
exercises you sorely that " with the Quarterly Reviewer, the
Received Text is a standard, by comparison with which all
extant documents, *however indisputable their antiquity,* are
measured."[2] But pray,—

(1) By comparison with what *other* standard, if not by
the Received Text, would you yourself obtain the measure

---

[1] It seems to have escaped Bishop Ellicott's notice, (and yet the fact
well deserves commemoration) that the claims of Tischendorf and
Tregelles on the Church's gratitude, are not by any means founded on
the Texts which they severally put forth. As in the case of Mill,
Wetstein and Birch, their merit is that *they patiently accumulated
evidence.* " Tischendorf's reputation as a Biblical scholar rests less on
his critical editions of the N. T., than on the texts of the chief uncial
authorities which in rapid succession he gave to the world." (Scrivener's
Introduction,—p. 427.)   [2] P. 12.

of " all extant documents," however ancient ? . . . . This
first. And next,

(2) Why should the " *indisputable antiquity* " of a document be supposed to disqualify it from being measured by
the same standard to which (*but only for convenience*) documents of whatever date,—by common consent of scholars, at
home and abroad,—are invariably referred ? And next,

(3) Surely, you cannot require to have it explained to
you that a standard *of* COMPARISON, is not *therefore* of necessity
a standard *of* EXCELLENCE. Did you ever take the trouble to
collate a sacred manuscript ? If you ever did, pray with
what did you make your collation ? In other words, what
' standard ' did you employ ? ... Like Walton and Ussher,—like
Fell and Mill,—like Bentley, and Bengel, and Wetstein,—like
Birch, and Matthæi, and Griesbach, and Scholz,—like Lachmann, and Tregelles, and Tischendorf, and Scrivener,—I
venture to assume that you collated your manuscript,—
whether it was of "disputable" or of "indisputable antiquity,"
—with *an ordinary copy of the Received Text.* If you did not,
your collation is of no manner of use. But, above all,

(4) How does it come to pass that you speak so scornfully
of the Received Text, seeing that (at p. 12 of your pamphlet)
you assure your readers that *its pedigree may be traced back to
a period perhaps antecedent to the oldest of our extant manuscripts ?* Surely, a traditional Text which (*according to you*)
dates from about A.D. 300, is good enough for the purpose of
Collation !

(5) At last you say,—

"If there were reason to suppose that the Received Text
represented *verbatim et literatim* the text which was current at
Antioch in the days of Chrysostom, it would still be impossible
to regard it as a standard from which there was no appeal."[1]

---

[1] P. 13.

Really, my lord Bishop, you must excuse me if I declare plainly that the more I attend to your critical utterances, the more I am astonished. From the confident style in which you deliver yourself upon such matters, and especially from your having undertaken to preside over a Revision of the Sacred Text, one would suppose that at some period of your life you must have given the subject a considerable amount of time and attention. But indeed the foregoing sentence virtually contains two propositions neither of which could possibly have been penned by one even moderately acquainted with the facts of Textual Criticism. For first,

(*a*) You speak of "representing *verbatim et literatim* THE Text which was current at Antioch in the days of Chrysostom." Do you then really suppose that there existed at Antioch, at any period between A.D. 354 and A.D. 407, *some one definite Text of the N. T. CAPABLE of being so represented?*— If you do, pray will you indulge us with the grounds for such an extraordinary supposition? Your "acquaintance" (Dr. Tregelles) will tell you that such a fancy has long since been swept away "at once and for ever." And secondly,

(*b*) You say that, even if there were reason to suppose that the "Received Text" were such-and-such a thing,—"it would still be impossible to regard it as *a standard from which there was no appeal.*"

But pray, who in his senses,—what sane man in Great Britain,—ever dreamed of regarding the "Received,"—aye, *or any other known* " *Text*,"—as " a standard *from which there shall be no appeal*"? Have *I* ever done so? Have I ever *implied* as much? If I have, show me *where*. You refer your readers to the following passage in my first Article :—

"What precedes admits to some extent of further numerical illustration. It is discovered that, in 111 pages, . . . the serious

2 c

deflections of A from the *Textus Receptus* amount in all to only
842 : whereas in c they amount to 1798 : in B, to 2370 : in ℵ, to
3392 : in D, to 4697. The readings *peculiar to* A within the same
limits are 133 : those peculiar to c are 170. But those of B
amount to 197 : while ℵ exhibits 443 : and the readings peculiar
to D (within the same limits), are no fewer than 1829 . . . . We
submit that these facts are not altogether calculated to inspire
confidence in codices B ℵ c D."—p. 14.

But, do you really require to have it explained to you that
it is entirely to misunderstand the question to object to such
a comparison of·codices as is found above, (viz. in pages 14
and 17,) on the ground that it was made with the text of
Stephanus lying open before me ? Would not *the self-same
phenomenon* have been evolved by collation with *any other*
text ? If you doubt it, sit down and try the experiment for
yourself. Believe me, Robert Etienne in the XVIth century
was not *the cause* why cod. B in the IVth and cod. D in the
VIth are so widely discordant and divergent from one another :
A and c so utterly at variance with both.[1] We *must* have *some*
standard whereby to test,—wherewith to compare,—Manuscripts. What is more, (give me leave to assure you,) *to the
end of time* it will probably be the practice of scholars to compare MSS. of the N. T. with the ' Received Text.' The hopeless
discrepancies between our five " old uncials," can in no more
convenient way be exhibited, than by referring each of them in
turn to one and the same common standard. And,— *What*
standard more reasonable and more convenient than the Text
which, by the good Providence of GOD, was universally
employed throughout Europe for the first 300 years after the
invention of printing ? being practically *identical* with the
Text which (as you yourself admit) was in popular use at the
end of three centuries from the date of the sacred autographs
themselves : in other words, being more than 1500 years old.

---

[1] See above, pp. 12 : 30–3 : 34–5 : 46–7 : 75 : 94–6 : 249 : 262 : 289 : 319.

[9] *The Reviewer vindicates himself against Bp. Ellicott's misconceptions.*

But you are quite determined that I shall mean something essentially different. The Quarterly Reviewer, (you say,) is one who "contends that the Received Text needs but little emendation; and *may be used without emendation as a standard.*"[1] I am, (you say,) one of "those who adopt the easy method of making the Received Text a standard."[2] My "Criticism," (it seems,) "often rests ultimately upon the notion that it is little else but sacrilege to impugn the tradition of the last three hundred years."[3] ("*The last three hundred years:*" as if the Traditional Text of the N. Testament dated from the 25th of Queen Elizabeth!)—I regard the 'Textus Receptus' therefore, according to you, as the Ephesians regarded the image of the great goddess Diana; namely, as a thing which, one fine morning, "fell down from Jupiter."[4] I mistake the Received Text, (you imply,) for the Divine Original, the Sacred Autographs,—and erect it into "a standard from which there shall be no appeal,"—"a tradition which it is little else but sacrilege to impugn." That is how *you* state my case and condition: hopelessly *confusing* the standard of *Comparison* with the standard of *Excellence*.

By this time, however, enough has been said to convince any fair person that you are without warrant in your present contention. Let *any* candid scholar cast an impartial eye over the preceding three hundred and fifty pages,—open the volume where he will, and read steadily on to the end of any textual discussion,—and then say whether, on the contrary, my criticism does not invariably rest on the principle that the Truth of Scripture is to be sought in that form of the Sacred Text which has *the fullest, the widest, and the most varied attestation.*[5] Do I not invariably make *the consentient*

---

[1] P. 40.   [2] P. 19.   [3] P. 4.   [4] Acts xix. 35.   [5] *Suprà*, pp. 339–41.

voice of Antiquity my standard? If I do *not*,—if, on the contrary, I have ever once appealed to the 'Received Text,' and made *it* my standard,—why do you not prove the truth of your allegation by adducing in evidence that one particular instance? instead of bringing against me a charge which is utterly without foundation, and which can have no other effect but to impose upon the ignorant; to mislead the unwary; and to prejudice the great Textual question which hopelessly divides you and me? . . . I trust that at least you will not again confound the standard *of Comparison* with the standard *of Truth.*

[10] *Analysis of contents of Bp. Ellicott's pamphlet.*

You state at page 6, that what you propose to yourself by your pamphlet, is,—

" *First,* to supply accurate information, in a popular form, concerning the Greek text of the New Testament:

" *Secondly,* to establish, by means of the information so supplied, the soundness of the principles on which the Revisers have acted in their choice of readings; and by consequence, the importance of the ' New Greek Text : ' "—[or, as you phrase it at p. 29,]—" to enable the reader to form a fair judgment on the question of *the trustworthiness of the readings adopted by the Revisers.*"

To the former of these endeavours you devote twenty-three pages : (viz. p. 7 to p. 29) :—to the latter, you devote forty-two ; (viz. p. 37 to p. 78). The intervening eight pages are dedicated,—(*a*) To the constitution of the Revisionist body : and next, (*b*) To the amount of good faith with which you and your colleagues observed the conditions imposed upon you by the Southern Houses of Convocation. I propose to follow you over the ground in which you have thus entrenched yourself, and to drive you out of every position in turn.

[11] *Bp. Ellicott's account of the* ' TEXTUS RECEPTUS.'

First then, for your strenuous endeavour (pp. 7–10) to

prejudice the question by pouring contempt on the humblest ancestor of the *Textus Receptus*—namely, the first edition of Erasmus. You know very well that the 'Textus Receptus' is *not* the first edition of Erasmus. Why then do you so describe its origin as to imply that *it is?* You ridicule the circumstances under which a certain ancestor of the family first saw the light. You reproduce with evident satisfaction a silly witticism of Michaelis, viz. that, in his judgment, the Evangelium on which Erasmus chiefly relied was not worth the two florins which the monks of Basle gave for it. Equally contemptible (according to you) were the copies of the Acts, the Epistles, and the Apocalypse which the same scholar employed for the rest of his first edition. Having in this way done your best to blacken a noble house by dilating on the low ebb to which its fortunes were reduced at a critical period of its history, some three centuries and a half ago,—you pause to make your own comment on the spectacle thus exhibited to the eyes of unlearned readers, lest any should fail to draw therefrom the injurious inference which is indispensable for your argument :—

" We have entered into these details, because we desire that the general reader should know fully the true pedigree of that printed text of the Greek Testament which has been in common use for the last three centuries. It will be observed that its documentary origin is not calculated to inspire any great confidence. Its parents, as we have seen, were two or three late manuscripts of little critical value, which accident seems to have brought into the hands of their first editor."—p. 10.

Now, your account of the origin of the 'Textus Receptus' shall be suffered to stand uncontradicted. But the important *inference* which you intend that inattentive or incompetent readers should draw therefrom, shall be scattered to the winds by the unequivocal testimony of no less distinguished a witness than yourself. Notwithstanding all that has gone

before, you are constrained to confess *in the very next page*
that :—

  " The manuscripts which Erasmus used differ, for the most
part, *only in small and insignificant details from the bulk of the
cursive manuscripts.* The general character of their text is the
same. By this observation the pedigree of the Received Text
is carried up beyond the individual manuscripts used by
Erasmus . . . . *That* pedigree stretches back to a remote antiquity. *The first ancestor of the Received Text was at least
contemporary with the oldest of our extant manuscripts, if not older
than any one of them.*"—pp. 11, 12.

By your own showing therefore, the Textus Receptus is, ' *at
least,*' 1550 years old. Nay, we will have the fact over again,
in words which you adopt from p. 92 of Westcott and
Hort's *Introduction* [see above, p. 257], and clearly make
your own :—

  " The fundamental text of late extant Greek MSS. generally
is *beyond all question identical* with the dominant Antiochian or
Græco-Syrian *Text of the second half of the fourth century.*"
—p. 12.

But, if this be so,—(and I am not concerned to dispute
your statement in a single particular,)—of what possible
significancy can it be to your present contention, that the
ancestry of the WRITTEN WORD (like the ancestors of the
WORD INCARNATE) had at one time declined to the wondrous
low estate on which you enlarged at first with such evident
satisfaction ? Though the fact be admitted that Joseph " the
carpenter " was " the husband of Mary, of whom was born
JESUS, who is called CHRIST,"—what possible inconvenience
results from that circumstance so long as the only thing contended for be loyally conceded,—namely, that the descent of
MESSIAH is lineally traceable back to the patriarch Abraham,
through David the King ? And the genealogy of the
written, no less than the genealogy of the Incarnate WORD,

is traceable back by *two distinct lines of descent*, remember :
for the 'Complutensian,' which was printed in 1514, exhibits
the 'Traditional Text' with the same general fidelity as the
'Erasmian,' which did not see the light till two years later.

[12] *Bp. Ellicott derives his estimate of the* 'Textus Receptus'
from Westcott and Hort's fable of a 'Syrian Text.'

Let us hear what comes next :—

" At this point a question suggests itself which we cannot
refuse to consider. If the pedigree of the Received Text may
be traced back to so early a period, does it not deserve the
honour which is given to it by the Quarterly Reviewer ? "
—p. 12.

A very pertinent question truly. We are made attentive :
the more so, because you announce that your reply to this
question shall " go to the bottom of the controversy with
which we are concerned." [1] That reply is as follows :—

" If there were reason to suppose that the Received Text
represented *verbatim et literatim* the text which was current at
Antioch in the days of Chrysostom, it would still be impossible
to regard it as a standard *from which there was no appeal.* The
reason why this would be impossible may be stated briefly as
follows. In the ancient documents which have come down to
us,—amongst which, as is well known, are manuscripts written
in the fourth century,—we possess evidence that other texts of
the Greek Testament existed in the age of Chrysostom, materially
different from the text which he and the Antiochian writers
generally employed. Moreover, a rigorous examination of
extant documents shows that the Antiochian or (as we shall
henceforth call it with Dr. Hort) the Syrian text did not
represent an earlier tradition than those other texts, but was
in fact of later origin than the rest. We cannot accept it
therefore as *a final standard.*"—pp. 13, 14.

---

[1] P. 13.

" A *final* standard "! . . . Nay but, why do you suddenly
introduce this unheard-of characteristic ?   *Who*, pray, since
the invention of Printing was ever known to put forward *any*
existing Text as " a final standard " ?   Not the Quarterly
Reviewer certainly.   " The honour which is given to the
Textus Receptus by the Quarterly Reviewer " is no other than
the honour which it has enjoyed at the hands of scholars, by
universal consent, for the last three centuries.   That is to say,
he uses it as a standard of comparison, and employs it for
nabitual reference.   *So do you.*   You did so, at least, in the
year 1870.   You did more ; for you proposed " to proceed
with the work of Revision, whether of text or translation,
making the current ' Textus Receptus' the standard." [1]   We
are perfectly agreed therefore.   For my own part, being fully
convinced, like yourself, that essentially the Received Text is
full 1550 years old,—(yes, and a vast deal older,)—I esteem it
quite good enough for all ordinary purposes.   And yet, so
far am I from pinning my faith to it, that I eagerly make my
appeal *from* it to the threefold witness of Copies, Versions,
Fathers, whenever I find its testimony challenged.—And
with this renewed explanation of my sentiments,—(which one
would have thought that no competent person could require,)
—I proceed to consider the reply which you promise shall " go
to the bottom of the controversy with which we are concerned."   I beg that you will not again seek to divert attention from that which is the real matter of dispute betwixt
you and me.

What kind of argumentation then is this before us ?   You
assure us that,—

(*a*) " A rigorous examination of extant documents,"—
" shows " Dr. Hort—" that the Syrian text"—[which for all

---

[1] Bp. Ellicott, *On Revision*, &c.—p. 30.

practical purposes may be considered as only another name
for the " Textus Receptus "]—was of later origin than " other
texts of the Greek Testament" which " existed in the age of
Chrysostom."

(b) " We cannot accept it therefore as a final standard."

But,—Of what nature is the logical process by which you
have succeeded in convincing yourself that *this* consequent
can be got out of *that* antecedent ?   Put a parallel case :—" A
careful analysis of herbs 'shows' Dr. Short that the only safe
diet for Man is a particular kind of rank grass which grows
in the Ely fens. We must therefore leave off eating butcher's
meat."—Does *that* seem to you altogether a satisfactory
argument ?   To me, it is a mere *non sequitur.* Do but consider the matter for a moment.   " A rigorous examination of
extant documents shows " Dr. Hort—such and such things.
" A rigorous examination of the " same " documents shows "
me—that Dr. Hort *is mistaken.*   A careful study of his book
convinces *me* that his theory of a Syrian Recension, manufactured between A.D. 250 and A.D. 350, is a dream, pure and
simple—*a mere phantom of the brain.*   Dr. Hort's course is
obvious. Let him *first* make his processes of proof intelligible,
and *then* public. You cannot possibly suppose that the fable
of " a Syrian text," though it has evidently satisfied *you,*
will be accepted by thoughtful Englishmen without proof.
What prospect do you suppose you have of convincing the
world that Dr. Hort is competent to assign *a date* to this
creature of his own imagination ; of which he has hitherto
failed to demonstrate so much as the probable existence ?

I have, for my own part, established by abundant references to his writings that he is one of those who, (through
some intellectual peculiarity,) are for ever mistaking
conjectures for facts,—assertions for arguments,—-and reite-

rated asseveration for accumulated proof. He deserves sympathy, certainly: for,—(like the man who passed his life in trying to count how many grains of sand will exactly fill a quart pot;—or like his unfortunate brother, who made it his business to prove that nothing, multiplied by a sufficient number of figures, amounts to something;)—he has evidently taken a prodigious deal of useless trouble. The spectacle of an able and estimable man exhibiting such singular inaptitude for a province of study which, beyond all others, demands a clear head and a calm, dispassionate judgment,— creates distress.

[13] *Bp. Ellicott has completely adopted Westcott and Hort's Theory.*

But in the meantime, so confident are *you* of the existence of a 'Syrian text,'—(*only however because Dr. Hort is,*)—that you inflict upon your readers all the consequences which 'the Syrian text' is supposed to carry with it. Your method is certainly characterized by humility: for it consists in merely serving up to the British public a *réchauffé* of Westcott and Hort's Textual Theory. I cannot discover that you contribute anything of your own to the meagre outline you furnish of it. Everything is assumed—as before. Nothing is proved—as before. And we are referred to Dr. Hort for the resolution of every difficulty which Dr. Hort has created. "According to Dr. Hort,"—"as Dr. Hort observes,"—"to use Dr. Hort's language,"—"stated by Dr. Hort,"—"as Dr. Hort notices,"—"says Dr. Hort:" yes, from p. 14 of your pamphlet to p. 29 you do nothing else but reproduce—Dr. Hort!

First comes the fabulous account of the contents of the bulk of the cursives:[1]—then, the imaginary history of the

---

[1] P. 15.

'Syriac Vulgate;' which (it seems) bears 'indisputable traces' of being a revision, of which you have learned *from Dr. Hort* the date:[1]—then comes the same disparagement of the ancient Greek Fathers,—"for reasons which have been *stated by Dr. Hort* with great clearness and cogency:"[2]— then, the same depreciatory estimate of writers subsequent to Eusebius,—whose evidence is declared to "stand at best on no higher level than the evidence of inferior manuscripts in the uncial class:"[3] but *only* because it is discovered to be destructive of the theory *of Dr. Hort.*

Next comes "the Method of Genealogy,"—which you declare is the result of "vast research, unwearied patience, great critical sagacity;"[4] but which I am prepared to prove is, on the contrary, a shallow expedient for dispensing with scientific Induction and the laborious accumulation of evidence. This same "Method of Genealogy," you are not ashamed to announce as "the great contribution of our own times to a mastery over materials." "For the full explanation of it, you *must refer your reader to Dr. Hort's Introduction.*"[5] Can you be serious?

Then come the results to which "the application of this method *has conducted Drs. Westcott and Hort.*"[6] And first, the fable of the 'Syrian Text'—which '*Dr. Hort considers* to have been the result of a deliberate Recension,' conducted on erroneous principles. This fabricated product of the IIIrd and IVth centuries, (you say,) rose to supremacy,—became dominant at Antioch,—passed thence to Constantinople,— and once established there, soon vindicated its claim to be the N. T. of the East: whence it overran the West, and for 300 years as the 'Textus Receptus,' has held undisputed

---

[1] P. 16.   [2] P. 17.   [3] P. 18.

[4] P. 19.   [5] P. 19.   [6] P. 20.

sway.¹ Really, my lord Bishop, you describe imaginary
events in truly Oriental style. One seems to be reading not
so much of the "Syrian Text" as of the Syrian Impostor.
One expects every moment to hear of some feat of this
fabulous Recension corresponding with the surrender of
the British troops and Arabi's triumphant entry into Cairo
with the head of Sir Beauchamp Seymour in his hand!

All this is followed, of course, by the weak fable of the
'Neutral' Text, and of the absolute supremacy of Codex B,
—which is "stated *in Dr. Hort's own words:*"² —viz. "B very
far exceeds all other documents in neutrality of text, being
in fact always, or nearly always, neutral." (The *fact* being
that codex B is demonstrably one of the most corrupt documents in existence.) The posteriority of the (imaginary)
"Syrian," to the (imaginary) "Neutral," is insisted upon
next in order, as a matter of course : and declared to rest
upon three other considerations,—each one of which is found
to be pure fable : viz. (1) On the fable of 'Conflation,' which
"*seems* to supply a proof" that Syrian readings are posterior
both to Western and to Neutral readings—but, (as I have
elsewhere ³ shown, at considerable length,) most certainly *does*
not :—(2) On Ante-Nicene Patristic evidence,—of which
however not a syllable is produced :—(3) On ' *Transcriptional probability* '—which is about as useful a substitute for
proof as a sweet-pea for a walking-stick.

Widely dissimilar of course is your own view of the
importance of the foregoing instruments of conviction. To
you, "these three reasons taken together seem to make up
an argument for the posteriority of the Syrian Text, which it
is impossible to resist. They form" (you say) "a threefold
cord of evidence which [you] believe will bear any amount

¹ P. 21.   ² Pp. 23-4.   ³ *Supra*, pp. 258-266.

of argumentative strain." You rise with your subject, and at last break out into eloquence and vituperation :—'Writers like the Reviewer may attempt to cut the cord *by reckless and unverified assertions :* but *the knife has not yet been fabricated that can equitably separate any one of its strands.*' [1] ... So effectually, as well as so deliberately, have you lashed yourself—for better or for worse—to Westcott and Hort's New Textual Theory, that you must now of necessity either share its future triumphs, or else be a partaker in its coming humiliation. Am I to congratulate you on your prospects ?

For my part, I make no secret of the fact that I look upon the entire speculation about which you are so enthusiastic, as an excursion into cloud-land : a *dream* and nothing more. My contention is,—*not* that the Theory of Drs. Westcott and Hort rests on an *insecure* foundation, but, that it rests on *no foundation at all.* Moreover, I am greatly mistaken if this has not been *demonstrated* in the foregoing pages.[2] On one point, at all events, there cannot exist a particle of doubt; namely, that so far from its "*not being for you to interpose in this controversy,*"—you are without alternative. You must either come forward at once, and bring it to a successful issue : or else, you must submit to be told that you have suffered defeat, inasmuch as you are inextricably involved in Westcott and Hort's discomfiture. You are simply without remedy. *You* may "*find nothing in the Reviewer's third article to require a further . answer :* " but readers of intelligence will tell you that your finding, since it does not proceed from stupidity, can only result from your consciousness that you have made a serious blunder : and that now, the less you say about "Westcott and Hort's new textual Theory," the better.

---

[1] Pp. 25–7.   [2] See *Art.* III.,—viz. from p. 235 to 1   3.

[14] *The Question modestly proposed,— Whether Bp. Ellicott's adoption of Westcott and Hort's ' new Textual Theory ' does not amount to (what lawyers call) ' CONSPIRACY ' ?*

But, my lord Bishop, when I reach the end of your laborious avowal that you entirely accept " Westcott and Hort's new Textual Theory,"—I find it impossible to withhold the respectful enquiry,—Is such a proceeding on your part altogether allowable ? I frankly confess that to *me* the wholesale adoption by the Chairman of the Revising body, of the theory of two of the Revisers,—and then, his exclusive reproduction and vindication of *that theory,* when he undertakes,

" to supply the reader with a few broad outlines of Textual Criticism, so as to enable him to form *a fair judgment* on the question of the trustworthiness of *the readings adopted by the Revisers,*"—p. 29,

all this, my lord Bishop, I frankly avow, to *me,* looks very much indeed like what, in the language of lawyers, is called " Conspiracy." It appears then that instead of presiding over the deliberations of the Revisionists as an impartial arbiter, you have been throughout, heart and soul, an eager partizan. You have learned to employ freely Drs. Westcott and Hort's peculiar terminology. You adopt their scarcely-intelligible phrases: their wild hypotheses: their arbitrary notions about ' Intrinsic ' and ' Transcriptional Probability :' their baseless theory of ' Conflation :' their shallow ' Method of Genealogy.' You have, in short, evidently swallowed their novel invention whole. I can no longer wonder at the result arrived at by the body of Revisionists. Well may Dr. Scrivener have pleaded in vain ! He found Drs. Ellicott and Westcott and Hort too many for him ... But it is high time that I should pass on.

[15] *Proofs that the Revisers have outrageously exceeded the Instructions they received from the Convocation of the Southern Province.*

It follows next to enquire whether your work as Revisers was conducted in conformity with the conditions imposed upon you by the Southern House of Convocation, or not. " *Nothing* " (you say)—

"*can be more unjust* on the part of the Reviewer than to suggest, as he has suggested in more than one passage,[1] that the Revisers *exceeded their Instructions* in the course which they adopted with regard to the Greek Text.   On the contrary, as we shall show, they adhered most closely to their Instructions ; and did neither more nor less than they were required to do."—(p. 32.)

' The Reviewer,' my lord Bishop, proceeds to *demonstrate* that you 'exceeded your Instructions,' even to an extraordinary extent.   But it will be convenient first to hear you out.   You proceed,—

" Let us turn to the Rule.   It is simply as follows :—' That the text to be adopted be that for which the Evidence *is decidedly preponderating :* and that when the text so adopted differs from that from which the Authorized Version was made, the alteration be indicated in the margin.' "—(*Ibid.*)

But you seem to have forgotten that the ' Rule ' which you quote formed no part of the ' *Instructions* ' which were imposed upon you by Convocation.   It was one of the ' Principles *agreed to by the Committee* ' (25 May, 1870),—a Rule *of your own making* therefore,—for which Convocation neither was nor is responsible.   The ' fundamental Resolutions adopted by the Convocation of Canterbury ' (3rd and 5th May, 1870), five in number, contain no authorization whatever for making changes in the Greek Text.   They have

---

[1] You refer to such places as pp. 87–8 and 224, where see the Notes.

reference only to the work of revising '*the Authorized Version:*' an undertaking which the first Resolution declares to be 'desirable.' In order to ascertain what were the Revisers' '*Instructions* with regard to the Greek Text,' we must refer to the original Resolution of Feb. 10th, 1870 : in which the removal of '*plain and clear errors*, whether in the Greek Text originally adopted by the Translators, or in the Translation made from the same,'—is for the first and last time mentioned. That you yourself accepted this as the limit of your authority, is proved by your Speech in Convocation. "We may be satisfied" (you said) "with the attempt to correct *plain and clear errors*: but *there, it is our duty to stop.*" [1]

Now I venture to assert that not one in a hundred of the alterations you have actually made, 'whether in the Greek Text originally adopted by the Translators, or in the Translation made from the same,' are corrections of '*plain and clear errors.*' Rather,—(to adopt the words of the learned Bishop of Lincoln,)—"I fear we must say in candour that in the Revised Version we meet in every page with changes *which seem almost to be made for the sake of change.*"[2] May I trouble you to refer back to p. 112 of the present volume for a few words more on this subject from the pen of the same judicious Prelate ?

(a) *And first,—In respect of the New English Version.*

For my own part, (see above, pp. 171-2,) I thought the best thing I could do would be to illustrate the nature of my complaint, by citing and commenting on an actual instance of your method. I showed how, in revising eight-and-thirty words (2 Pet. i. 5-7), you had contrived to introduce no fewer than *thirty changes,*—every one of them being clearly

---

[1] *Chronicle of Convocation*, Feb. 1870, p. 83.   [2] See above, p. 368.

a change for the worse. You will perhaps say,—Find me
another such case! I find it, my lord Bishop, in S. Luke viii.
45, 46,—where you have made *nineteen changes* in revising
the translation of four-and-thirty words. I proceed to
transcribe the passage ; requesting you to bear in mind your
own emphatic protestation,—"We made *no* change *if the
meaning was fairly expressed* by the word or phrase before
us."

A.V.	R.V.
'Peter and they that were with him said, Master, the multitude throng thee and press thee, and sayest thou, Who touched me? And Jesus said, Somebody hath touched me : for I perceive that virtue is gone out of me.'	'Peter said, and they that were with him, Master the multitudes press thee and crush thee [5, 6, 7, 8, 9, 10.] But Jesus said, Some one did touch me : for I perceived that power had gone forth from me.'

Now pray,—Was not " the meaning *fairly expressed* " before ?
Will you tell me that in revising S. Luke viii. 45–6, you
" *made as few alterations as possible* " ? or will you venture to assert that you have removed none but " *plain and
clear errors* " ? On the contrary. I challenge any competent
scholar in Great Britain to say *whether every one of these
changes* be not either absolutely useless, or else *decidedly a
change for the worse :* six of them being downright *errors*.

The transposition in the opening sentence is infelicitous,
to say the least. (The English language will not bear such
handling. Literally, no doubt, the words mean, " said Peter,
and they that were with him." But you may not so *translate*.)—The omission of the six interesting words, indicated
within square brackets, is a serious blunder.[1] The words are

---

[1] The clause ('and sayest thou, Who touched me?') is witnessed to
by A C D P R X Γ Δ Λ Ξ Π and *every other known uncial except three of*

2 D

undoubtedly genuine. I wonder how you can have ventured thus to mutilate the Book of Life. And why did you not, out of common decency and reverence, *at least in the margin*, preserve a record of the striking clause which you thus, — with well-meant assiduity, but certainly with deplorable rashness, — forcibly ejected from the text? To proceed however.—' Multitudes,'—' but,'—' one,'—' did,'—' power,'—' forth,'—' from:'—are all seven either needless changes, or improper, or undesirable. *' Did touch,'*—*' perceived,'*—*' had gone forth,'*—are unidiomatic and incorrect expressions. I have already explained this elsewhere.[1] The aorist (ἥψατο) has here a perfect signification, as in countless other places:—ἔγνων, (like *' novi,'*) is frequently (as here) to be Englished by the present (*' I perceive'*): and *' is gone out of me'* is the nearest rendering of ἐξελθοῦσαν[2] ἀπ' ἐμοῦ

---

bad character: by every known cursive but four:—by the Old Latin and Vulgate: by all the four Syriac: by the Gothic and the Æthiopic Versions; as well as by ps.-Tatian (*Evan. Concord.* p. 77) and Chrysostom (vii. 359 a). It cannot be pretended that the words are derived from S. Mark's Gospel (as Tischendorf coarsely imagined);—for the sufficient reason that *the words are not found there.* In S. Mark (v. 31) it is,—καὶ λέγεις, Τίς μου ἥψατο; in S. Luke (viii. 45), καὶ λέγεις, Τίς ὁ ἁψάμενός μου. Moreover, this delicate distinction has been maintained all down the ages.

[1] Page 154 to p. 164.

[2] You will perhaps remind me that you do not read ἐξελθοῦσαν. I am aware that you have tacitly substituted ἐξεληλυθυῖαν,—which is only supported by *four* manuscripts of bad character: being disallowed by *eighteen uncials,* (with A C D at their head,) and *every known cursive but one;* besides the following Fathers:—Marcion[1] (A.D. 150),—Origen,[2]—the author of *the Dialogus*[3] (A.D. 325),—Epiphanius,[4]—Didymus,[5] in two places,—Basil,[6]—Chrysostom,[7]—Cyril[8] in two places,—ps.-Athanasius[9] (A.D. 400),—ps.-Chrysostom[10] ... Is it tolerable that the Sacred Text should be put to wrongs after this fashion, by a body of men who are avowedly (for see page 369) unskilled in Textual Criticism, and who were appointed only to revise the authorized *English Version?*

---

[1] Epiph. i. 313 a, 327 a.   [2] iii. 466 e.   [3] Orig. i. 853 d.   [4] i. 327 b.   [5] pp. 124, 413.
[6] iii. 8 c.   [7] vii. 532 a.   [8] Opp. vi. 99 e. Mai, ii. 226.   [9] ii. 14 c.   [10] xiii. 212 e f.

which our language will bear.—Lastly, '*press*' and '*crush*,'
as renderings of συνέχουσι and ἀποθλίβουσι, are inexact and
unscholarlike. Συνέχειν, (literally ' to encompass ' or ' hem
in,') is here to ' throng ' or ' crowd :' ἀποθλίβειν, (literally
' to squeeze,') is here to 'press.' But in fact the words were
perfectly well rendered by our Translators of 1611, and
ought to have been let alone.—This specimen may suffice,
(and it is a very fair specimen,) of what has been your
calamitous method of revising the A. V. throughout.

So much then for the Revised *English*. The fate of the
Revised *Greek* is even more extraordinary. I proceed to
explain myself by instancing what has happened in respect
of the GOSPEL ACCORDING TO S. LUKE.

(*b*) *Next,—In respect of the New Greek Text.*

On examining the 836[1] Greek Textual corrections which
you have introduced into those 1151 verses, I find that at least
356 of them *do not affect the English rendering at all*. I mean
to say that those 356 (supposed) emendations are either
incapable of being represented in a Translation, or at least
are *not* represented. Thus, in S. Luke iv. 3, whether εἶπε
δέ or καὶ εἶπεν is read :—in ver. 7, whether ἐμοῦ or μου :—in
ver. 8, whether Κύριον τὸν Θεόν σου προσκυνήσεις, or Προσκυνήσεις Κ. τὸν Θ. σου ; whether ἤγαγε δέ or καὶ ἤγαγεν ;
whether υἱός or ὁ υἱός :—in ver. 17, whether τοῦ προφήτου
Ἡσαίου or Ἡ. τοῦ προφήτου ; whether ἀνοίξας or ἀναπτύξας :
—in ver. 18, whether εὐαγγελίσασθαι or εὐαγγελίζεσθαι :—in
ver. 20, whether οἱ ὀφθαλμοὶ ἐν τῇ συναγωγῇ or ἐν τῇ συναγωγῇ
οἱ ὀφθαλμοί :—in ver. 23, whether εἰς τήν or ἐν τῇ :—in ver. 27,
whether ἐν τῷ Ἰσραὴλ ἐπὶ Ἐλισσαίου τοῦ προφήτου or ἐπὶ
Ἐλισσ., τοῦ π. ἐν τῷ Ἰ. :—in ver. 29, whether ὀφρύος or τῆς
ὀφρύος ; whether ὥστε or εἰς τό :—in ver. 35, whether ἀπ' or

---

[1] This I make the actual sum, after deducting for marginal notes and
variations in stops.

ἐξ:—in ver. 38, whether ἀπό or ἐκ; whether πενθερά or ἡ πενθερά:— in ver. 43, whether ἐπί or εἰς; whether ἀπεστάλην or ἀπέσταλμαι:—in ver. 44, whether εἰς τὰς συναγωγάς or ἐν ταῖς συναγωγαῖς:—in every one of these cases, *the English remains the same,* whichever of the alternative readings is adopted. At least 19 therefore out of the 33 changes which you introduced into the Greek Text of S. Luke iv. are plainly gratuitous.

Thirteen of those 19, (or about two-thirds,) are also in my opinion changes *for the worse:* are nothing else, I mean, but substitutions of *wrong* for *right* Readings. But *that* is not my present contention. The point I am just now contending for is this:—That, since it certainly was no part of your 'Instructions,' 'Rules,' or 'Principles' *to invent a new Greek Text,*—or indeed to meddle with the original Greek at all, *except so far as was absolutely necessary for the Revision of the English Version,*—it is surely a very grave form of inaccuracy to assert (as you now do) that you "adhered most closely to your Instructions, and did neither more nor less than you were required."—You *know* that you did a vast deal more than you had any authority or right to do: a vast deal more than you had the shadow of a pretext for doing. Worse than that. You deliberately forsook the province to which you had been exclusively appointed by the Southern Convocation,—and you ostentatiously invaded another and a distinct province; viz. *That* of the critical Editorship of the Greek Text: for which, *by your own confession,*—(I take leave to remind you of your own honest avowal, quoted above at page 369,)—you and your colleagues *knew* yourselves to be incompetent.

For, when those 356 wholly gratuitous and uncalled-for changes in the Greek of S. Luke's Gospel come to be examined in detail, they are found to affect far more than

356 words. By the result, 92 words have been omitted; and 33 added. No less than 129 words have been substituted for others which stood in the text before; and there are 66 instances of Transposition, involving the dislocation of 185 words. The changes of case, mood, tense, &c., amount in addition to 123.[1] The sum of the words which you have *needlesly* meddled with in the Greek Text of the third Gospel proves therefore to be 562.

At this rate, — (since, [excluding marginal notes and variations in stops,] Scrivener[2] counts 5337 various readings in his Notes,)—the number of alterations *gratuitously and uselessly introduced by you into the Greek Text of the entire N. T.*, is to be estimated at 3590.

And if,—(as seems probable,)—the same general proportion prevails throughout your entire work,—it will appear that the words which, without a shadow of excuse, you have *omitted* from the Greek Text of the N. T., must amount to about 590: while you have *added* in the same gratuitous way about 210; and have needlessly *substituted* about 820. Your instances of uncalled-for *transposition*, (about 420 in number,) will have involved the gratuitous dislocation of full 1190 words:—while the occasions on which, at the bidding of Drs. Westcott and Hort, you have altered case, mood, tense, &c., must amount to about 780. In this way, the sum of the changes you have effected in the Greek Text of the N. T. *in clear defiance of your Instructions,*—would amount, as already stated, to 3590.

Now, when it is considered that *not one* of those 3590

---

[1] I mean such changes as ἠγέρθη for ἐγήγερται (ix. 7),—φέρετε for ἐνέγκαντες (xv. 23), &c. These are generally the result of a change of construction.

[2] MS. communication from my friend, the Editor.

changes *in the least degree affects the English Revision,*—it is undeniable, not only that you and your friends did what you were without authority for doing :—but also that you violated as well the spirit as the letter of your Instructions. As for your present assertion (at p. 32) that you "adhered *most closely* to the Instructions you received, and *did neither more nor less than you were required to do,"*—you must submit to be reminded that it savours strongly of the nature of pure fable. The history of the new Greek Text is briefly *this :*— A majority of the Revisers—*including yourself, their Chairman,*—are found to have put yourselves almost unreservedly into the hands of Drs. Westcott and Hort. The result was obvious. When the minority, headed by Dr. Scrivener, appealed to the chair, they found themselves confronted by a prejudiced Advocate. They ought to have been listened to by an impartial Judge. *You*, my lord Bishop, are in consequence (I regret to say) responsible for all the mischief which has occurred. The blame of it rests at *your* door.

And pray disabuse yourself of the imagination that in what precedes I have been *stretching* the numbers in order to make out a case against you. It would be easy to show that in estimating the amount of needless changes at 356 out of 836, I am greatly under the mark. I have not included such cases, for instance, as your substitution of ἡ μνᾶ σου, Κύριε for Κύριε, ἡ μνᾶ σου (in xix. 18), and of Τοίνυν ἀπόδοτε for ᾿Απόδοτε τοίνυν (in xx. 25)[1],—only lest you should pretend that the transposition affects the English, and therefore *was* necessary. Had I desired to swell the number I could have easily shown that fully *half* the

---

[1] I desire to keep out of sight the *critical impropriety* of such corrections of the text. And yet, it is worth stating that ℵ B L are *the only witnesses discoverable* for the former, and *almost the only* witnesses to be found for the latter of these two utterly unmeaning changes.

changes you effected in the Greek Text were wholly superfluous for the Revision of the English Translation, and therefore were entirely without excuse.

This, in fact,—(give me leave to remind you in passing,)—
is the *true* reason why, at an early stage of your proceedings,
you resolved that *none* of the changes you introduced into
the Greek Text should find a record in your English margin.
Had *any* been recorded, *all* must have appeared. And had
this been done, you would have stood openly convicted of
having utterly disregarded the 'Instructions' you had received
from Convocation. With what face, for example, *could* you,
(in the margin of S. Luke xv. 17,) against the words " he
said,"—have printed " ἔφη not εἶπε " ? or, (at xxiv. 44,) against
the words "unto them,"—must you not have been ashamed
to encumber the already overcrowded margin with such an
irrelevant statement as,—" πρὸς αὐτούς *not* αὐτοῖς " ?

Now, if this were all, you might reply that by my own
showing the Textual changes complained of, if they do
no good, at least do no harm. But then, unhappily, you
and your friends have not confined yourselves to colourless
readings, when silently up and down every part of the N. T.
you have introduced innovations. I open your New English
Version at random (S. John iv. 15), and invite your attention to the first instance which catches my eye.

You have made the Woman of Samaria *complain of the
length of the walk* from Sychar to Jacob's well:—" Sir, give
me this water, that I thirst not, neither *come all the way*
hither to draw."—What has happened ? For ἔρχωμαι, I
discover that you have silently substituted ΔΙέρχωμαι.
(Even διέρχωμαι has no such meaning : but let *that* pass.)
What then was your authority for thrusting διέρχωμαι (which
by the way is a patent absurdity) into the Text ? The word

is found (I discover) *in only two Greek MSS. of bad character* [1]
(B ℵ), which, being derived from a common corrupt original,
can only reckon for *one :* and the *reasoning* which is supposed
to justify this change is thus supplied by Tischendorf:—" If
the Evangelist had written ἔρχ-, who would ever have
dreamed of turning it into δι-έρχωμαι?" . . . No one,
of course, (is the obvious answer,) except the inveterate
blunderer who, some 1700 years ago, seeing ΜΗΔΕΕΡΧѠΜΑΙ
before him, *reduplicated the antecedent* ΔΕ. The sum of the
matter is *that !* . . . Pass 1700 years, and the long-since-
forgotten blunder is furbished up afresh by Drs. Westcott and
Hort,—is urged upon the wondering body of Revisers as the
undoubted utterance of THE SPIRIT,—is accepted by yourself;
—finally, (in spite of many a remonstrance from Dr. Scrivener
and his friends,) is thrust upon the acceptance of 90 millions
of English-speaking men throughout the world, as the long-
lost-sight-of, but at last happily recovered, utterance of the
' Woman of Samaria !' . . . Ἄπαγε.

Ordinary readers, in the meantime, will of course assume
that the change results from the Revisers' skill in translating,
—the advances which have been made in the study of Greek ;
for no trace of the textual vagary before us survives in the
English margin.

And thus I am reminded of what I hold to be your gravest
fault of all. The rule of Committee subject to which you
commenced operations, — the Rule which re-assured the
public and reconciled the Church to the prospect of a Revised

---

[1] Characteristic of these two false-witnesses is it, that they are not able
to convey even *this* short message correctly. In reporting the two words
ἔρχωμαι ἐνθάδε, they contrive to make two blunders. B substitutes
διέρχομαι for διέρχωμαι : ℵ, ὧδε for ἐνθάδε,—which latter eccentricity
Tischendorf (characteristically) does not allude to in his note . : . " These
be thy gods, O Israel ! "

New Testament, — expressly provided that, whenever the underlying Greek Text was altered, *such alteration should be indicated in the margin.* This provision you entirely set at defiance from the very first. You have *never* indicated in the margin the alterations you introduced into the Greek Text. In fact, you made so many changes,—in other words, you seem to have so entirely lost sight of your pledge and your compact,—that compliance with this condition would have been simply impossible. I see not how your body is to be acquitted of a deliberate breach of faith.

(c) *Fatal consequences of this mistaken officiousness.*

How serious, in the meantime, *the consequences* have been, *they* only know who have been at the pains to examine your work with close attention. Not only have you, on countless occasions, thrust out words, clauses, entire sentences of genuine Scripture,—but you have been careful that no trace shall survive of the fatal injury which you have inflicted. I wonder you were not afraid. Can I be wrong in deeming such a proceeding in a high degree sinful? Has not the Spirit pronounced a tremendous doom[1] against those who do such things? Were you not afraid, for instance, to leave out (from S. Mark vi. 11) those solemn words of our Saviour,— " Verily I say unto you, It shall be more tolerable for Sodom and Gomorrha in the day of judgment, than for that city " ? Surely you will not pretend to tell me that those fifteen precious words, witnessed to as they are by *all the known copies but nine,*—by the Old Latin, the Peschito and the Philoxenian Syriac, the Coptic, the Gothic and the Æthiopic Versions,—besides Irenæus[2] and Victor[3] of Antioch:—you will not venture to say (will you?) that words so attested are

---

[1] Rev. xxii. 19.
[2] iv. 28, c. 1 (p. 655 = Mass. 265). Note that the reference is *not* to S. Matt. x. 15. [3] P. 123.

so evidently a "plain and clear error," as not to deserve even
a marginal note to attest to posterity 'that such things
were'! I say nothing of the witness of the Liturgical usage
of the Eastern Church,—which appointed these verses to be
read on S. Mark's Day :[1] nor of Theophylact,[2] nor of
Euthymius.[3] I appeal to *the consentient testimony of Catholic
antiquity.* Find me older witnesses, if you can, than the
'Elders' with whom Irenæus held converse,—men who must
have been contemporaries of S. John the Divine: or again,
than the old Latin, the Peschito, and the Coptic Versions.
Then, for the MSS.,—Have you studied S. Mark's Text to so
little purpose as not to have discovered that the six uncials
on which you rely are the depositories of an abominably
corrupt Recension of the second Gospel?

But you committed a yet more deplorable error when,—
without leaving behind either note or comment of any sort,
—you obliterated from S. Matth. v. 44, the solemn words
which I proceed to underline:—"*Bless them that curse you,
do good to them that hate you,* and pray for them which *despite-
fully use you and* persecute you." You relied almost exclusively on those two false witnesses, of which you are so
superstitiously fond, B and ℵ: regardless of the testimony of
almost all the other COPIES besides:—of almost all the
VERSIONS : — and of a host of primitive FATHERS : for the
missing clauses are more or less recognized by Justin Mart.
(A.D. 140),—by Theophilus Ant. (A.D. 168),—by Athenagoras
(A.D. 177),—by Clemens Alexan. (A.D. 192),—by Origen
(A.D. 210),—by the Apostolic Constt. (IIIrd cent.),—by
Eusebius,—by Gregory Nyss.,—by Chrysostom,—by Isidorus,
—by Nilus,—by Cyril,—by Theodoret, and certain others.
Besides, of the Latins, by Tertullian, — by Lucifer, — by

---

[1] Viz. vi. 7–13.   [2] i. 199 and 200.   [3] *In loc.*

Ambrose, — by Hilary, — by Pacian,—by Augustine, — by
Cassian, and many more . . . . Verily, my lord Bishop, your
notion of what constitutes " *clearly preponderating Evidence* "
must be freely admitted to be at once original and peculiar.
I will but respectfully declare that if it be indeed one of " *the
now established Principles of Textual Criticism* " that a bishop
is at liberty to blot out from the Gospel such precepts of
the Incarnate WORD, as these : to reject, on the plea that they
are ' plain and clear errors,' sayings attested by twelve primitive Fathers,—half of whom lived and died before our two
oldest manuscripts (B and א) came into being :—If all this be
so indeed, permit me to declare that I would not exchange
MY " *innocent ignorance* " [1] of those ' Principles ' for YOUR *guilty
knowledge* of them,—no, not for anything in the wide world
which yonder sun shines down upon.

As if what goes before had not been injury enough, you
are found to have adopted the extraordinary practice of encumbering your margin with doubts as to the Readings
which after due deliberation you had, as a body, *retained.*
Strange perversity! You could not find room to retain a
record in your margin of the many genuine words of our
Divine LORD,—His Evangelists and Apostles,—to which
Copies, Versions, Fathers lend the fullest attestation ; but
you *could* find room for an insinuation that His ' Agony and
bloody sweat,'—together with His ' Prayer on behalf of His
murderers,'—*may* after all prove to be nothing else but
spurious accretions to the Text. And yet, the pretence for
so regarding either S. Luke xxii. 43, 44, or xxiii. 34, is confessedly founded on a minimum of documentary evidence :
while, as has been already shown elsewhere,[2] an overwhelming amount of ancient testimony renders it *certain* that not a

---

[1] See above, pp. 347–9.   [2] See above, pp. 79–85.

particle of doubt attaches to the Divine record of either of those stupendous incidents . . . . Room could not be found, it seems, for a *hint* in the margin that such ghastly wounds as those above specified had been inflicted on S. Mark vi. 11 and S. Matth. v. 44;[1] but *twenty-two lines* could be spared against Rom. ix. 5 for the free ventilation of the vile Socinian gloss with which unbelievers in every age have sought to evacuate one of the grandest assertions of our SAVIOUR'S GODHEAD. May I be permitted, without offence, to avow myself utterly astonished ?

Even this however is not all. The 7th of the Rules under which you undertook the work of Revision, was, that '*the Headings of Chapters should be revised.*' This Rule you have not only failed to comply with; but you have actually deprived us of those headings entirely. You have thereby done us a grievous wrong. We demand to have the headings of our chapters back.

You have further, without warrant of any sort, deprived us of our *Marginal References.* These we cannot afford to be without. We claim that *they* also may be restored. The very best Commentary on Holy Scripture are they, with which I am acquainted. They call for learned and judicious Revision, certainly; and they might be profitably enlarged. But they may never be taken away.

And now, my lord Bishop, if I have not succeeded in convincing you that the Revisers not only " *exceeded their Instructions* in the course which they adopted with regard to the Greek Text," but even acted in open defiance of their Instructions; did both a vast deal *more* than they were authorized to do, and also a vast deal *less ;*—it has certainly been no fault of mine. As for your original contention[2] that

---

[1] See above, pp. 409-411.   [2] See above, p. 399.

"nothing can be more unjust" than THE CHARGE brought
against the Revisers of having exceeded their Instructions,
—I venture to ask, on the contrary, whether anything can
be more unreasonable (to give it no harsher name) than THE
DENIAL ?

[16] *The calamity of the 'New Greek Text' traced to its
source.*

There is no difficulty in accounting for the most serious
of the foregoing phenomena. They are the inevitable consequence of your having so far succumbed at the outset to
Drs. Westcott and Hort as to permit them to communicate
bit by bit, under promise of secrecy, their own outrageous
Revised Text of the N. T. to their colleagues, accompanied
by a printed disquisition in advocacy of their own peculiar
critical views. One would have expected in the Chairman
of the Revising body, that the instant he became aware of
any such *manœuvre* on the part of two of the society, he
would have remonstrated with them somewhat as follows, or
at least to this effect :—

"This cannot be permitted, Gentlemen, on any terms. We
have not been appointed to revise the *Greek Text* of the N. T.
Our one business is to revise the *Authorized English Version,*
—introducing such changes only as are absolutely necessary.
The Resolutions of Convocation are express on this head :
and it is my duty to see that they are faithfully carried out.
True, that we shall be obliged to avail ourselves of our skill
in Textual Criticism—(such as it is)—to correct '*plain and
clear errors*' in the Greek : but *there* we shall be obliged to
stop. I stand pledged to Convocation on this point by my
own recent utterances. That two of our members should be
solicitous (by a side-wind) to obtain for their own singular
Revision of the Greek Text the sanction of our united body,

—is intelligible enough : but I should consider myself guilty of a breach of Trust were I to lend myself to the promotion of their object. Let me hope that I have you all with me when I point out that on every occasion when Dr. Scrivener, on the one hand, (who in matters of Textual Criticism is *facile princeps* among us,) and Drs. Westcott and Hort on the other, prove to be irreconcileably opposed in their views,— *there* the Received Greek Text must by all means be let alone. We have agreed, you will remember, to 'make *the current Textus Receptus the standard ; departing from it only when critical or grammatical considerations show that it is clearly necessary.*'[1] It would be unreasonable, in my judgment, that anything in the Received Text should be claimed to be ' a clear and plain error,' on which those who represent the two antagonistic schools of Criticism find themselves utterly unable to come to any accord. In the meantime, Drs. Westcott and Hort are earnestly recommended to submit to public inspection that Text which they have been for twenty years elaborating, and which for some time past has been in print. Their labours cannot be too freely ventilated, too searchingly examined, too generally known : but I strongly deprecate their furtive production *here.* All too eager advocacy of the novel Theory of the two accomplished Professors, I shall think it my duty to discourage, and if need be to repress. A printed volume, enforced by the suasive rhetoric of its *two* producers, gives to one side an unfair advantage. But indeed I must end as I began, by respectfully inviting Drs. Westcott and Hort to remember that we meet here, *not* in order *to fabricate a new Greek Text,* but in order to *revise our ' Authorized English Version.*' " . . . . Such, in substance, is the kind of Allocution which it was to have been expected that the Episcopal Chairman of a Revising body would address to

---

[1] Bp. Ellicott *on Revision*, p. 30.

his fellow-labourers the first time he saw them enter the
Jerusalem chamber furnished with the sheets of Westcott
and Hort's N. T. ; especially if he was aware that those
Revisers had been individually talked over by the Editors of
the work in question, (themselves Revisionists); and perceived that the result of the deliberations of the entire body
was in consequence, in a fair way of becoming a foregone
conclusion, — unless indeed, by earnest remonstrance, he
might be yet in time to stave off the threatened danger.

But instead of saying anything of this kind, my lord
Bishop, it is clear from your pamphlet that you made the
Theory of Drs.Westcott and Hort *your own Theory;* and their
Text, by necessary consequence, in the main *your own Text.*
You lost sight of all the pledges you had given in Convocation. You suddenly became a partizan. Having secured the
precious advocacy of Bp. Wilberforce,—whose sentiments on
the subject you had before adopted,—you at once threw him
and them overboard.[1] . . . . I can scarcely imagine, in a good
man like yourself, conduct more reckless,—more disappoint-
ing,—more unintelligible. But I must hasten on.

[17] *Bp. Ellicott's defence of the ' New Greek Text,' in sixteen
particulars, examined.*

It follows to consider the strangest feature of your
pamphlet : viz. those two-and-thirty pages (p. 43 to p. 75) in
which, descending from generals, you venture to dispute in
sixteen particulars the sentence passed upon your new Greek
Text by the *Quarterly Review.* I call this part of your
pamphlet " strange," because it displays such singular inaptitude to appreciate the force of Evidence. But in fact,
(*sit venia verbo*) your entire method is quite unworthy of you.
Whereas *I* appeal throughout to *Ancient Testimony,* you seek

---

[1] The Bp. attended *only one meeting* of the Revisers. (Newth, p. 125.)

to put me down by flaunting in my face *Modern Opinion.* This, with a great deal of Reiteration, proves to be literally the sum of your contention.   Thus, concerning S. Matth. i. 25, the Quarterly Reviewer pointed out (*suprà* pp. 123–4) that the testimony of B ℵ, together with that of the VIth-century fragment z, and two cursive copies of bad character,—cannot possibly stand against the testimony of ALL OTHER copies. You plead in reply that on "those two oldest manuscripts *the vast majority of Critics set a high value.*"   Very likely : but for all *that,* you are I suppose aware that B and ℵ are two of the most corrupt documents in existence ?   And, inasmuch as they are confessedly derived from one and the same depraved original, you will I presume allow that they may not be adduced as two independent authorities ?   At all events, when I further show you that almost all the Versions, and literally *every one* of the Fathers who quote the place, (they are *eighteen* in number,) are against you,—how can you possibly think there is any force or relevancy whatever in your self-complacent announcement,—"We cannot hesitate to express *our agreement with Tischendorf and Tregelles* who see in these words an interpolation derived from S. Luke.   *The same appears to have been the judgment of Lachmann.*"   Do you desire that *that* should pass for argument ?

To prolong a discussion of this nature with you, were plainly futile.   Instead of repeating what I have already delivered—briefly indeed, yet sufficiently in detail,—I will content myself with humbly imitating what, if I remember rightly, was Nelson's plan when he fought the battle of the Nile.   He brought his frigates, one by one, alongside those of the enemy ;—lashed himself to the foe ;—and poured in his broadsides.   We remember with what result.   The sixteen instances which you have yourself selected, shall now be indicated.   First, on every occasion, reference shall be made to the place in the present volume where my own Criticism on your Greek Text is to be found in detail. Readers of your pamphlet are invited next to refer to your own several attempts at refutation, which shall also be indicated by a reference to your pages. I am quite contented to abide by the verdict of any unprejudiced person of average understanding and fair education :—

(1) *Four words omitted in* S. Matth. i. 25,—complained of, above, pp. 122–4.—You defend the omission in your pamphlet at pages 43–4,—falling back on Tischendorf, Tregelles and Lachmann, as explained on the opposite page. (p. 416.)

(2) *The omission of* S. Matth. xvii. 21,—proved to be indefensible, above, pp. 91–2.—The omission is defended by you at pp. 44–5,—on the ground, that although Lachmann retains the verse, and Tregelles only places it in brackets, (Tischendorf alone of the three omitting it entirely,)—" it must be remembered that here Lachmann and Tregelles were not acquainted with א."

(3) *The omission of* S. Matth. xviii. 11,—shown to be unreasonable, above, p. 92.—You defend the omission in your pp. 45–7,—remarking that " here there is even less room for doubt than in the preceding cases. The three critical editors are all agreed in rejecting this verse."

(4) *The substitution of ἠπόρει for ἐποίει,* in S. Mark vi. 20, —strongly complained of, above, pp. 66–9.—Your defence is at pp. 47–8. You urge that " in this case again the Revisers have Tischendorf only on their side, and not Lachmann nor Tregelles: but it must be remembered that these critics had not the reading of א before them."

(5) *The thrusting of πάλιν* (after ἀποστελεῖ) into S. Mark xi. 3,—objected against, above, pp. 56–8.—You defend your-

self at pp. 48–9,—and "cannot doubt that the Revisers were perfectly justified" in doing "as Tischendorf and Tregelles had done before them,"—viz. *inventing* a new Gospel incident.

(6) *The mess you have made* of S. Mark xi. 8,—exposed by the Quarterly Reviewer, above, pp. 58–61,—you defend at pp. 49–52. You have "preferred to read with Tischendorf and Tregelles." About,

(7) S. Mark xvi. 9–20,—and (8) S. Luke ii. 14,—I shall have a few serious words to say immediately. About,

(9) the 20 *certainly genuine* words you have omitted from S. Luke ix. 55, 56,—I promise to give you at no distant date an elaborate lecture. "Are we to understand" (you ask) "that the Reviewer honestly believes the added words to have formed part of the Sacred Autograph?" ('The *omitted* words,' you mean.) To be sure you are!—I answer.

(10) *The amazing blunder* endorsed by the Revisers in S. Luke x. 15; which I have exposed above, at pp. 54–6.— You defend the blunder (as usual) at pp. 55–6, remarking that the Revisers, "*with Lachmann, Tischendorf, and Tregelles,* adopt the interrogative form." (This seems to be a part of your style.)

(11) *The depraved exhibition of the Lord's Prayer* (S. Luke xi. 2–4) which I have commented on above, at pp. 34–6,— you applaud (as usual) at pp. 56–8 of your pamphlet, "with Tischendorf and Tregelles."

(12) *The omission* of 7 important words in S. Luke xxiii. 38, I have commented on, above, at pp. 85–8.—You defend the omission, and "the texts of Tischendorf and Tregelles," at pp. 58–9.

(13) *The gross fabrication* in S. Luke xxiii. 45, I have exposed, above, at pp. 61–5.—You defend it, at pp. 59–61.

(14) *A plain omission* in S. John xiv. 4, I have pointed out, above, at pp. 72–3.—You defend it, at pp. 61–2 of your pamphlet.

(15) ' *Titus Justus,*' thrust by the Revisers into Acts xviii. 7, I have shown to be an imaginary personage, above, at pp. 53–4.—You stand up for the interesting stranger at pp. 62–4 of your pamphlet.   Lastly,

(16) My discussion of 1 Tim. iii. 16 (*suprà* pp. 98–106),— you contend against from p. 64 to p. 76.—The true reading of this important place, (which is not *your* reading,) you will find fully discussed from p. 424 to p. 501.

I have already stated why I dismiss *thirteen* out of your sixteen instances in this summary manner.   The remaining *three* I have reserved for further discussion for a reason I proceed to explain.

[18] *Bp. Ellicott's claim that the Revisers were guided by ' the consentient testimony of the most ancient Authorities,'—disproved by an appeal to their handling of* S. Luke ii. 14 *and of* S. Mark xvi. 9–20.   *The self-same claim,—(namely, of abiding by the verdict of Catholic Antiquity,)—vindicated, on the contrary, for the ' Quarterly Reviewer.'*

You labour hard throughout your pamphlet to make it appear that the point at which our methods, (yours and mine,) respectively diverge,—is, that *I* insist on making my appeal to the ' *Textus Receptus ;* ' you, to *Ancient Authority.*   But happily, my lord Bishop, this is a point which admits of being brought to issue by an appeal to fact.   *You* shall first

2 E 2

be heard : and you are observed to express yourself on behalf of the Revising body, as follows :

" It was impossible to mistake the conviction upon which its Textual decisions were based.

" It was a conviction that (1) THE TRUE TEXT WAS NOT TO BE SOUGHT IN THE TEXTUS RECEPTUS ; or (2) In the bulk of the Cursive Manuscripts ; or (3) In the Uncials (with or without the support of the *Codex Alexandrinus ;*) or (4) In the Fathers who lived after Chrysostom ; or (5) In Chrysostom himself and his contemporaries ; BUT (6) IN THE CONSENTIENT TESTIMONY OF THE MOST ANCIENT AUTHORITIES."—(p. 28.)

In such terms you venture to contrast our respective methods. You want the public to believe that *I* make the ' Textus Receptus ' " *a standard from which there shall be no appeal,*"—entertain " the notion that it is *little else than sacrilege to impugn the tradition of the last* 300 *years,*" [1]—and so forth ;—while *you* and your colleagues act upon the conviction that the Truth is rather to be sought " *in the consentient testimony of the most ancient Authorities.*" I proceed to show you, by appealing to an actual instance, that neither of these statements is correct.

(*a*) And first, permit me to speak for myself. Finding that you challenge the Received reading of S. LUKE ii. 14, (' *good will towards men* ') ;—and that, (on the authority of 4 Greek Codices [א A B D], all *Latin* documents, and the Gothic Version,) you contend that ' *peace among men in whom he is well pleased* ' ought to be read, instead ;—I make my appeal unreservedly to ANTIQUITY.[2] I request *the Ancients* to adjudicate between you and me by favouring us with their verdict. Accordingly, I find as follows :

That, in the IInd century, — the Syriac Versions and Irenæus *support the Received Text :*

---

[1] Page 4.   [2] See above, pp. 41 to 47.

That, in the IIIrd century,—the Coptic Version,—Origen in 3 places, and—the Apostolical Constitutions in 2, *do the same:*

That, in the IVth century, (*to which century,* you are invited to remember, *codices* B *and* א *belong,*)—Eusebius,— Aphraates the Persian,—Titus of Bostra,—each in 2 places:— Didymus in 3:—Gregory of Nazianzus,—Cyril of Jer.,— Epiphanius 2—and Gregory of Nyssa—4 times: Ephraem Syr.,—Philo bp. of Carpasus,—Chrysostom 9 times,—and an unknown Antiochian contemporary of his:—these eleven, I once more find, are *every one against you:*

That, in the Vth century,—besides the Armenian Version, Cyril of Alex. in 14 places:—Theodoret in 4:—Theodotus of Ancyra in 5:—Proclus:—Paulus of Emesa:—the Eastern bishops of Ephesus collectively, A.D. 431;—and Basil of Seleucia:—*these contemporaries of cod.* A I find are *all eight against you:*

That, in the VIth century,—besides the Georgian—and Æthiopic Versions,—Cosmas, 5 times:—Anastasius Sinait. and Eulogius, (*contemporaries of cod.* D,) are *all three with the Traditional Text:*

That, in the VIIth and VIIIth centuries,—Andreas of Crete, 2:—pope Martinus at the Lat. Council:—Cosmas, bp. of Maiume near Gaza,—and his pupil John Damascene;— together with Germanus, abp. of Constantinople:—are again *all five with the Traditional Text.*

To these 35, must be added 18 other ancient authorities with which the reader has been already made acquainted (viz. at pp. 44–5): all of which bear the self-same evidence.

Thus I have enumerated *fifty-three* ancient Greek authorities,—of which *sixteen* belong to the IInd, IIIrd, and IVth centuries: and *thirty-seven* to the Vth, VIth, VIIth, and VIIIth.

And now, which of us two is found to have made the fairer and the fuller appeal to 'the consentient testimony of the most ancient authorities:' *you* or *I?* . . . This first.

And next, since the foregoing 53 names belong to some of the most famous personages in Ecclesiastical antiquity : are dotted over every region of ancient Christendom : in many instances are *far more ancient than codices* B *and* א :— with what show of reason will you pretend that the evidence concerning S. Luke ii. 14 " *clearly preponderates* " in favour of the reading which you and your friends prefer ?

I claim at all events to have demonstrated that *both* your statements are unfounded : viz. (1) That *I* seek for the truth of Scripture in the 'Textus Receptus:' and (2) That *you* seek it in 'the consentient testimony of the *most ancient authorities.*'—(Why not frankly avow that you believe the Truth of Scripture is to be sought for, and found, in " *the consentient testimony of codices* א *and* B " ?)

(*b*) Similarly, concerning THE LAST 12 VERSES OF S. MARK, which you brand with suspicion and separate off from the rest of the Gospel, in token that, in your opinion, there is " a breach of continuity " (p. 53), (whatever *that* may mean,) between verses 8 and 9. *Your* ground for thus disallowing the last 12 Verses of the second Gospel, is, that B and א omit them:—that a few late MSS. exhibit a wretched alternative for them:—and that Eusebius says they were often away. Now, *my* method on the contrary is to refer all such questions to " *the consentient testimony of the most ancient authorities.*" And I invite you to note the result of such an appeal in the present instance. The Verses in question I find are recognized,

In the IInd century,—By the Old Latin—and Syriac Verss. : —by Papias ;—Justin M. ;—Irenæus ;—Tertullian.

In the IIIrd century,—By the Coptic—and the Sahidic Versions :—by Hippolytus ;—by Vincentius at the seventh Council of Carthage ;—by the ' Acta Pilati ;'—and by the ' Apostolical Constitutions' in two places.

In the IVth century,—By Cureton's Syr. and the Gothic Verss. :—besides the Syriac Table of Canons ;—Eusebius ;—Macarius Magnes ;—Aphraates ; — Didymus ; — the Syriac ' Acts of the Ap. ;'—Epiphanius ;—Leontius ;—ps.-Ephraem ; —Ambrose ;—Chrysostom ;—Jerome ;—Augustine.

In the Vth century,—Besides the Armenian Vers.,—by codices A and C ;—by Leo ;—Nestorius ;—Cyril of Alexandria ;—Victor of Antioch ;—Patricius ;—Marius Mercator.

In the VIth and VIIth centuries,—Besides cod. D,—the Georgian and Æthiopic Verss. :—by Hesychius ;—Gregentius ; —Prosper ; — John, abp. of Thessalonica ; — and Modestus, bishop of Jerusalem. . . . (See above, pages 36–40.)

And now, once more, my lord Bishop,—Pray which of us is it,—*you* or *I*,—who seeks for the truth of Scripture " in *the consentient testimony of the most ancient authorities* " ? On *my* side there have been adduced in evidence *six* witnesses of the IInd century :—*six* of the IIIrd :—*fifteen* of the IVth : —*nine* of the Vth :—*eight* of the VIth and VIIth,—(44 in all) : while *you* are found to rely on codices B and ℵ (as before), supported by a single *obiter dictum* of Eusebius. I have said nothing as yet about *the whole body of the Copies* : nothing about *universal, immemorial, Liturgical use.* Do you seriously imagine that the testimony on your side is ' decidedly preponderating ' ? Above all, will you venture again to exhibit our respective methods as in your pamphlet you have done ? I protest solemnly that, in your pages, I recognize neither myself nor you.

Permit me to declare that I hold your disallowance of S. Mark xvi. 9–20 to be the gravest and most damaging of all the many mistakes which you and your friends have committed. " The textual facts," (say you, speaking of the last 12 Verses,)—" have been placed before the reader, because Truth itself demanded it." This (with Canon Cook[1]) I entirely deny. It is because " the textual facts have " NOT " been placed before the reader," that I am offended. As usual, you present your readers with a one-sided statement, —a partial, and therefore inadmissible, exhibition of the facts, —facts which, fully stated and fairly explained, would, (as you cannot fail to be aware,) be fatal to your contention.

But, I forbear to state so much as *one* of them. The evidence has already filled a volume.[2] Even if I were to allow that in your marginal note, " the textual facts *have been* [fully and fairly] *placed before the reader*,"—what possible pretence do you suppose they afford for severing the last 12 Verses from the rest of S. Mark, in token that they form no part of the genuine Gospel ? . . . This, however, is only by the way. I have proved to you that it is *I*—not *you*—who rest my case on an appeal to CATHOLIC ANTIQUITY : and this is the only thing I am concerned just now to establish.

I proceed to contribute something to the Textual Criticism of a famous place in S. Paul's first Epistle to Timothy,—on which you have challenged me to a trial of strength.

[19] "𝕲𝕺𝕯 was manifested in the flesh"

SHOWN TO BE THE TRUE READING OF 1 TIMOTHY III. 16.
A DISSERTATION.

In conclusion, you insist on ripping up the discussion concerning 1 Tim. iii. 16. I had already devoted eight pages

---

[1] Pages 17, 18.　　　[2] See above, p. 37, note (1).

to this subject.[1]   You reply in twelve.[2]   That I may not be
thought wanting in courtesy, the present rejoinder shall
extend to seventy-six.   I propose, without repeating myself,
to follow you over the ground you have re-opened.   But it
will be convenient that I should define at the outset what is
precisely the point in dispute between you and me.   I presume
it to be undeniably *this*:—That whereas the Easterns from
time immemorial, (and we with them, since Tyndale in 1534
gave us our English Version of the N. T.,) have read the
place thus :—(I set the words down in plain English, because
the issue admits of being every bit as clearly exhibited in
the vernacular, as in Greek : and because I am determined
that all who are at the pains to read the present DISSERTATION
shall understand it also :)—Whereas, I say, we have hitherto
read the place thus,

" GREAT IS THE MYSTERY OF GODLINESS :—GOD WAS MANI-
FEST IN THE FLESH, JUSTIFIED IN THE SPIRIT, SEEN OF ANGELS,
PREACHED UNTO THE GENTILES, BELIEVED ON IN THE WORLD,
RECEIVED UP INTO GLORY :"

You insist that this is a "*plain and clear error.*"   You
contend that there is "*decidedly preponderating evidence*" for
reading instead,

" GREAT IS THE MYSTERY OF GODLINESS, WHO WAS MANI-
FESTED IN THE FLESH, JUSTIFIED IN THE SPIRIT," &c. :

Which contention of yours I hold to be demonstrably incorrect, and proceed to prove is a complete misconception.

(*A*) *Preliminary explanations and cautions.*

But English readers will require to have it explained to
them at the outset, that inasmuch as ΘΕΟC (GOD) is invariably

---

[1] Pages 98–106.   [2] Pages 64–76.

written Ө͞C in manuscripts, the only difference between the
word ' GOD ' and the word ' *who* ' (OC) consists of two horizontal strokes,—one, which distinguishes Ө from O; and
another similar stroke (above the letters ӨC) which indicates
that a word has been contracted. And further, that it was
the custom to trace these two horizontal lines so wondrous
faintly that they sometimes actually elude observation.
Throughout cod. A, in fact, the letter Ө is often scarcely
distinguishable from the letter O.

It requires also to be explained for the benefit of the same
English reader,—(and it will do learned readers no harm to
be reminded,)—that " *mystery* " (μυστήριον) being a neuter
noun, *cannot* be followed by the masculine pronoun (ὅς),—
" *who.*" Such an expression is abhorrent alike to Grammar
and to Logic,—is intolerable, in Greek as in English. By
consequence, ὅς ("*who*") is found to have been early exchanged for ὅ ("*which*"). From a copy so depraved, the
Latin Version was executed in the second century. Accordingly, every known copy or quotation [1] of *the Latin* exhibits
"quod." *Greek* authorities for this reading (ὅ) are few
enough. They have been specified already, viz. at page 100.
And with this brief statement, the reading in question might
have been dismissed, seeing that it has found no patron since
Griesbach declared against it. It was however very hotly
contended for during the last century,—Sir Isaac Newton
and Wetstein being its most strenuous advocates; and it
would be unfair entirely to lose sight of it now.

The two rival readings, however, in 1 Tim. iii. 16, are,—
Θεὸς ἐφανερώθη (' GOD *was manifested* '), on the one hand;
and τὸ τῆς εὐσεβείας μυστήριον, ὅς (" *the mystery of godliness,
who*"), on the other. *These* are the two readings, I say,

---

[1] The exceptions are not worth noticing *here.*

between whose conflicting claims we are to adjudicate. For
I request that it may be loyally admitted at the outset,—
(though it has been conveniently overlooked by the Critics
whom *you* follow,)—that the expression ὃς ἐφανερώθη in
Patristic quotations, *unless it be immediately preceded by* the
word μυστήριον, is nothing to the purpose; at all events, does
not prove the thing which *you* are bent on proving. English
readers will see this at a glance. An Anglican divine,—
with reference to 1 Timothy iii. 16,—may surely speak of our
SAVIOUR as One " *who* was manifested in the flesh,"—without
risk of being straightway suspected of employing a copy of
the English Version which exhibits " *the mystery of godliness
who.*" " Ex hujusmodi locis " (as Matthæi truly remarks)
" nemo, nisi mente captus, in contextu sacro probabit ὅς." [1]

When Epiphanius therefore,—*professing to transcribe*[2] from
an earlier treatise of his own[3] where ἐφανερώθη stands
without a nominative,[4] writes (if he really does write) ὃς
ἐφανερώθη,[5]—we are not at liberty to infer therefrom that
Epiphanius is opposed to the reading Θεός.—Still less is it
lawful to draw the same inference from the Latin Version of
a letter of Eutherius [A.D. 431] in which the expression ' *qui
manifestatus est in carne,*'[6] occurs.—Least of all should we be
warranted in citing Jerome as a witness for reading ὅς in

---

[1] N. T. ed. 2da. 1807, iii. 442–3.　　　　[2] i. 887 c.
[3] Called *Ancoratus*, written in Pamphylia, A.D. 373. The extract in
Adv. Hær. extends from p. 887 to p. 899 (= *Ancor.* ii. 67–79).
[4] ii. 74 b. Note, that to begin the quotation at the word ἐφανερώθη was
a frequent practice with the ancients, especially when enough had been
said already to make it plain that it was of the SON they were speaking,
or when it would have been nothing to the purpose to begin with Θεός.
Thus Origen, iv. 465 c:—Didymus on 1 John *apud* Galland. vi. 301 a :
—Nestorius, *apud* Cyril, vi. 103 e :—ps-Chrysost. x. 763 c, 764 c:—and
the Latin of Cyril v.[1] 785. So indeed ps-Epiphanius, ii. 307 c.
[5] i. 894 c.　　　　　　　　　　[6] *Apud* Theodoret, v. 719.

this place, because (in his Commentary on Isaiah) he speaks of our SAVIOUR as One who 'was manifested in the flesh, justified in the Spirit.'[1]

As for reasoning thus concerning Cyril of Alexandria, it is demonstrably inadmissible : seeing that at the least on two distinct occasions, this Father exhibits Θεὸς ἐφανερώθη. I am not unaware that in a certain place, apostrophizing the Docetæ, he says,—" Ye do err, not knowing the Scriptures, nor indeed the *great mystery of godliness,* that is CHRIST, who (ὅς) *was manifested in the flesh, justified in the Spirit,*" [2] &c. &c. And presently, " I consider *the mystery of godliness* to be no other thing but the Word of GOD the FATHER, who (ὅς) Himself *was manifested in the flesh."* [3] But there is nothing whatever in this to invalidate the testimony of those other places in which Θεός actually occurs. It is logically inadmissible, I mean, to set aside the places where Cyril is found actually to write Θεὸς ἐφανερώθη, because in other places he employs 1 Tim. iii. 16 less precisely ; leaving it to be inferred —(which indeed is abundantly plain)—that Θεός is always his reading, from the course of his argument and from the nature of the matter in hand. But to proceed.

(*B*) *Bp. Ellicott invited to state the evidence for reading* ὅς *in* 1 Tim. iii. 16.

[a] ' *The state of the evidence,'* as declared by Bp. Ellicott.

When last the evidence for this question came before us, I introduced it by inviting a member of the Revising body (Dr. Roberts) to be spokesman on behalf of his brethren.[4] This time, I shall call upon a more distinguished, a wholly unexceptionable witness, viz. *yourself,*—who are, of course,

---

[1] iv. 622 a,—*qui apparuit in carne, justificatus est in spiritu.*
[2] *De incarn. Unig.* v. part i. 680 d e = *De rectâ fide,* v. part ii. b c.
[3] *Ibid.* 681 a = *ibid.* 6 d e.   [4] Page 98.

greatly in advance of your fellow-Revisers in respect of
critical attainments. The extent of your individual familiarity with the subject when (in 1870 namely) you proposed
to revise the Greek Text of the N. T. for the Church of
England on the *solvere-ambulando* principle,—may I presume
be lawfully inferred from the following annotation in your
"*Critical and Grammatical Commentary on the Pastoral
Epistles.*" I quote from the last Edition of 1869; only
taking the liberty—(1) To break it up into short paragraphs :
and—(2) To give *in extenso* the proper names which you
abbreviate. Thus, instead of "Theod." (which I take leave to
point out to you might mean either Theodore of Heraclea or
his namesake of Mopsuestia,—either Theodotus the Gnostic
or his namesake of Ancyra,) "Euthal.," I write "Theodoret,
Euthalius." And now for the external testimony, as *you* give
it, concerning 1 Timothy iii. 16. You inform your readers
that,—

" The state of the evidence is briefly as follows :—

(1) Ὅς is read with A¹ [*indisputably;* after minute personal
inspection ; see note, p. 104.] C¹ [Tischendorf *Prol. Cod.
Ephraemi*, § 7, p. 39.] F G ℵ (see below) ; 17, 73, 181 ; Syr.-
Philoxenian, Coptic, Sahidic, Gothic ; also (ὅς or ὅ) Syriac,
Arabic (Erpenius), Æthiopic, Armenian ; Cyril, Theodorus
Mopsuest., Epiphanius, Gelasius, Hieronymus *in Esaiam* liii. 11.

(2) ὅ, with D¹ (Claromontanus), Vulgate ; nearly all Latin
Fathers.

(3) Θεός, with D³ K L ; nearly all MSS. ; Arabic (Polyglott),
Slavonic ; Didymus, Chrysostom (? see Tregelles, p. 227 note),
Theodoret, Euthalius, Damascene, Theophylact, Œcumenius,—
Ignatius *Ephes.* 29, (but very doubtful). A hand of the 12th
century has prefixed θε to ος, the reading of ℵ ; see Tischendorf
edit. major, Plate xvii. of Scrivener's Collation of ℵ, fac-
simile (13).

On reviewing this evidence, as not only the most important
uncial MSS., but *all* the Versions older than the 7th century
are distinctly in favour of a *relative*,—as ὅ seems only a Latin-

izing variation of ὅς,—and lastly, as ὅς is the more difficult, though really the more intelligible, reading (Hofmann, *Schriftb.* Vol. I. p. 143), and on every reason more likely to have been changed into Θεός (Macedonius is actually said to have been expelled for making the change, *Liberati Diaconi Breviarium* cap. 19) than *vice versâ*, we unhesitatingly decide in favour of ὅς." —(*Pastoral Epistles*, ed. 1869, pp. 51-2.)

Such then is your own statement of the evidence on this subject. I proceed to demonstrate to you that you are completely mistaken : — mistaken as to what you say about ὅς, — mistaken as to ὅ, — mistaken as to Θεός :— mistaken in respect of Codices,—mistaken in respect of Versions,—mistaken in respect of Fathers. Your slipshod, inaccurate statements, (*all* obtained at second-hand,) will occasion me, I foresee, a vast deal of trouble; but I am determined, now at last, if the thing be possible, to set this question at rest. And that I may not be misunderstood, I beg to repeat that all I propose to myself is to *prove*— beyond the possibility of denial—that the evidence for Θεός (in 1 Timothy iii. 16) *vastly preponderates over the evidence for either ὅς or ὅ.* It will be for *you*, afterwards, to come forward and prove that, on the contrary, Θεός is a '*plain and clear error:*' *so* plain and *so* clear that you and your fellow-Revisers felt yourselves constrained to thrust it out from the place it has confessedly occupied in the New Testament for at least 1530 years.

You are further reminded, my lord Bishop, that unless you do this, you will be considered by the whole Church to have dealt unfaithfully with the Word of GOD. For, (as I shall remind you in the sequel,) it is yourself who have invited and provoked this enquiry. You devote twelve pages to it (pp. 64 to 76),—"compelled to do so by the Reviewer." "Moreover" (you announce) "this case is of great importance as an example. It illustrates in a striking manner the complete isolation of the Reviewer's position. If he is right all other Critics are wrong," &c., &c., &c.—Permit me to remind you of the warning—" Let not him that girdeth on his harness boast himself as he that putteth it off."

[b] *Testimony of the MANUSCRIPTS concerning* 1 Tim. iii. 16: *and first as to the testimony of CODEX A.*

You begin then with the *Manuscript* evidence; and you venture to assert that ΟC is "indisputably" the reading of Codex A. I am at a loss to understand how a "professed Critic,"—(who must be presumed to be acquainted with the facts of the case, and who is a lover of Truth,)—can permit himself to make such an assertion. Your certainty is based, you say, on "minute personal inspection." In other words, you are so good as to explain that you once tried a coarse experiment,[1] by which you succeeded in convincing yourself that the suspected diameter of the Ο is exactly coincident with the sagitta of an *epsilon* (ε) which happens to stand *on the back of the page.* But do you not see that unless you start with *this* for your major premiss,—' *Theta* cannot exist on one side of a page if *epsilon* stands immediately behind it on the other side,'—your experiment is *nihil ad rem*, and proves absolutely nothing?

Your "inspection" happens however to be *inaccurate* besides. You performed your experiment unskilfully. A man need only hold up the leaf to the light on a very brilliant day,—as Tregelles, Scrivener, and many besides (including your present correspondent) have done,—to be aware that the sagitta of the *epsilon* on fol. 145*b* does not cover much more than a third of the area of the *theta* on fol. 145*a*. Dr. Scrivener further points out that it cuts the circle *too*

---

[1] Note at the end of Bishop Ellicott's Commentary on 1 Timothy.

high to have been reasonably mistaken by a careful observer for the diameter of the *theta* (Θ). The experiment which you describe with such circumstantial gravity was simply nugatory therefore.

How is it, my lord Bishop, that you do not perceive that the way to ascertain the reading of Codex A at 1 Tim. iii. 16, is,—(1) To investigate *not* what is found at *the back* of the leaf, but what is written on *the front* of it? and (2), Not so much to enquire what can be deciphered of the original writing by the aid of a powerful lens *now*, as to ascertain what was apparent to the eye of competent observers when the Codex was first brought into this country, viz. 250 years ago? That Patrick Young, the first custodian and collator of the Codex [1628–1652], read ΘC, is certain.—Young communicated the 'various Readings' of A to Abp. Ussher:—and the latter, prior to 1653, communicated them to Hammond, who clearly knew nothing of OC.—It is plain that ΘC was the reading seen by Huish—when he sent his collation of the Codex (made, according to Bentley, with great exactness,[1]) to Brian Walton, who published the fifth volume of his Polyglott in 1657.—Bp. Pearson, who was very curious in such matters, says "we find not ὅς *in any copy*,"—a sufficient proof how *he* read the place in 1659.—Bp. Fell, who published an edition of the N. T. in 1675, certainly considered ΘC the reading of Cod. A.—Mill, who was at work on the Text of the N. T. from 1677 to 1707, expressly declares that he saw the remains of ΘC in this place.[2] Bentley, who had himself

---

[1] Berriman's MS. Note in the British Museum copy of his *Dissertation*, —p. 154. Another annotated copy is in the Bodleian.

[2] "Certe quidem in exemplari Alexandrino nostro, linea illa transversa quam loquor, adeo exilis ac plane evanida est, ut primo intuitu haud dubitarim ipse scriptum OC, quod proinde in variantes lectiones conjeceram .... Verum postea perlustrato attentius loco, lineolæ, quæ primam aciem fugerat, ductus quosdam ac vestigia satis certa deprehendi, præsertim ad partem sinistram, quæ peripheriam literæ pertingit," &c.—*In loco.*

(1716) collated the MS. with the utmost accuracy (" *accuratissime ipse contuli* "), knew nothing of any other reading.— Emphatic testimony on the subject is borne by Wotton in 1718 :—" There can be no doubt " (he says) " that this MS. always exhibited $\overline{\Theta C}$. Of this, *any one may easily convince himself who will be at the pains to examine the place with attention.*"[1]—Two years earlier,—(we have it on the testimony of Mr. John Creyk, of S. John's Coll., Cambridge,)—" the old line in the letter Θ was plainly to be seen." [2]—It was " much about the same time," also, (viz. about 1716) that Wetstein acknowledged to the Rev. John Kippax,—" who took it down in writing from his own mouth,— that though the middle stroke of the Θ has been evidently retouched, yet the fine stroke which was originally in the body of the Θ is discoverable at each end of the fuller stroke of the corrector."[3]—And Berriman himself, (who delivered a course of Lectures on the true reading of 1 Tim. iii. 16, in 1737–8,) attests emphatically that he had seen it also. " *If therefore* " (he adds) " *at any time hereafter the old line should become altogether undiscoverable, there will never be just cause to doubt but that the genuine, and original reading of the MS. was* $\overline{\Theta C}$: and that the new strokes, added at the top and in the middle by the corrector were not designed to corrupt and falsify, but to preserve and perpetuate the true reading, which was in danger of being lost by the decay of Time." [4]—Those memorable words (which I respectfully commend to your notice) were written in A.D. 1741. How *you* (A.D. 1882), after surveying all this

---

[1] *Clem. Rom.* ed. Wotton, p. 27.   [2] Berriman, pp. 154–5.

[3] *Ibid.* (*MS. Note.*) Berriman adds other important testimony, p. 156.

[4] *Dissertation,* p. 156.   Berriman refers to the fact that some one in recent times, with a view apparently to establish the actual reading of the place, has clumsily thickened the superior stroke with common black ink, and introduced a rude dot into the middle of the Θ. There has been no attempt at fraud. Such a line and such a dot could deceive no one.

accumulated and consistent testimony (borne A.D. 1628 to A.D. 1741) by eye-witnesses as competent to observe a fact of this kind as yourself ; and fully as deserving of credit, when they solemnly declare what they have seen :—how *you*, I say, after a survey of this evidence, can gravely sit down and inform the world that " *there is no sufficient evidence that there was ever a time when this reading was patent as the reading which came from the original scribe* " (p. 72) :—*this* passes my comprehension.—It shall only be added that Bengel, who was a very careful enquirer, had already cited the Codex Alexandrinus as a witness for Θεός in 1734 :[1]—and that Woide, the learned and conscientious editor of the Codex, declares that so late as 1765 he had seen traces of the Θ which twenty years later (viz. in 1785) were visible to him no longer.[2]

That Wetstein subsequently changed his mind, I am not unaware.   He was one of those miserable men whose visual organs return a false report to their possessor whenever they are shown a text which witnesses inconveniently to the GOD-head of JESUS CHRIST.[3]   I know too that Griesbach in 1785 announced himself of Wetstein's opinion.   It is suggestive

---

[1] "Quanquam lineola, quæ Θεός compendiose scriptum ab ὅς distinguitur, sublesta videtur nonnullis."—N. T. p. 710.

[2] Griesbach in 1785 makes the same report :—" Manibus hominum inepte curiosorum ea folii pars quæ dictum controversum continet, adeo detrita est, ut nemo mortalium hodie certi quidquam discernere possit . . . Non oculos tantum sed digitos etiam adhibuisse videntur, ut primitivam illius loci lectionem eruerent et velut exsculperent." (*Symb. Crit.* i. p. x.) The MS. was evidently in precisely the same state when the Rev. J. C. Velthusen (*Observations on Various Subjects*, pp. 74–87) inspected it in 1773.

[3] As C. F. Matthæi [N. T. m. xi. *Præfat.* pp. lii.–iii.] remarks :—" *cum de Divinitate* CHRISTI *agitur, ibi profecto sui dissimilior deprehenditur.*" Woide instances it as an example of the force of prejudice, that Wetstein "apparitionem lineolæ alii causæ adscripsisse, *quia eam abesse volebat.*" [*Præfat.* p. xxxi.]

however that ten years before, (N.T. ed. 1775,) he had rested
the fact *not* on the testimony borne by the MS. itself, but on
' *the consent of Versions, Copies, and Fathers* which exhibit the
Alexandrian Recension.'[1]—Since Griesbach's time, Davidson,
Tregelles, Tischendorf, Westcott and Hort, and Ellicott have
announced their opinion that Θ͞C was never written at 1 Tim.
iii. 16 : confessedly only because Θ͞C is to them invisible *one
hundred years after* Θ͞C *has disappeared from sight.*   The fact
remains for all *that*, that the original reading of A is attested
so amply, that no sincere lover of Tɩuth can ever hereafter
pretend to doubt it.   " Omnia testimonia," (my lord Bishop,)
" omnemque historicam veritatem in suspicionem adducere
non licet ; nec mirum est nos ea nunc non discernere, quæ,
antequam nos Codicem vidissemus, evanuerant."[2]

The sum of the matter, (as I pointed out to you on a
former occasion,[3]) is this,—That it is too late by 150 years to
contend on the negative side of this question.   Nay, a famous
living Critic (long may he live !) assures us that when his
eyes were 20 years younger (Feb. 7, 1861) he actually discerned, *still lingering*, a faint trace of the diameter of the Θ
which Berriman in 1741 had seen so plainly.   " I have
examined Codex A at least twenty times within as many
years " (wrote Prebendary Scrivener in 1874[4]), " and . . . .
seeing (as every one must) with my own eyes, I have always
felt convinced that it reads Θ͞C " . . . .   For *you* to assert, in
reply to all this mass of positive evidence, that the reading is
" indisputably " ОC,—and to contend that what makes this
indisputable, is the fact that behind part of the *theta* (Θ), [but
too high to mislead a skilful observer,] an *epsilon* stands on
the reverse side of the page ; — strikes me as bordering
inconveniently on the ridiculous.   If *this* be your notion of

---

[1] ' Patet, ut alia mittamus, e consensu Versionum,' &c. —ii. 149.
[2] Woide, *ibid.*   [3] *Supra*, p. 100.   [4] *Introduction*, p. 553.

what does constitute "sufficient evidence," well may the testimony of so many *testes oculati* seem to you to lack sufficiency. Your notions on these subjects are, I should think, peculiar to yourself. You even fail to see that your statement (in Scrivener's words) is "*not relevant to the point at issue.*"[1] The plain fact concerning cod. A is *this*:—That at 1 Tim. iii. 16, two delicate horizontal strokes in Θ͞C which were thoroughly patent in 1628, — which could be seen plainly down to 1737,—and which were discernible by an expert (Dr. Woide) so late as A.D. 1765,[2] — have for the last hundred years entirely disappeared ; which is precisely what Berriman (in 1741) predicted would be the case. Moreover, he solemnly warned men against drawing from this circumstance the mistaken inference which *you*, my lord Bishop, nevertheless *insist* on drawing, and representing as an "indisputable" fact.

I have treated so largely of the reading of the Codex Alexandrinus, not because I consider the testimony of a solitary copy, whether uncial or cursive, a matter of much importance,—certainly not the testimony of Codex A, which (in defiance of every other authority extant) exhibits "*the body of GOD*" in S. John xix. 40 :—but because *you* insist that A is a witness on your side : whereas it is demonstrable,

---

[1] *Introd.* p. 553.

[2] Any one desirous of understanding this question fully, should (besides Berriman's admirable *Dissertation*) read Woide's *Præfatio* to his edition of Codex A, pp. xxx. to xxxii. (§ 87).—"Erunt fortasse quidam" (he writes in conclusion) "qui suspicabuntur, nonnullos hanc lineolam diametralem in medio Θ vidisse, quoniam eam videre volebant. Nec negari potest præsumptarum opinionum esse vim permagnam. Sed idem, etiam Wetstenio, nec immerito, objici potest, eam apparitionem lineolæ alii causæ adscripsisse, quia eam abesse volebat. Et eruditissimis placere aliquando, quæ vitiosa sunt, scio : sed omnia testimonia, omnemque historicam veritatem in suspicionem adducere non licet : nec mirum est nos ea nunc non discernere, quæ, antequam nos Codicem vidissemus, evanuerant."

(and I claim to have demonstrated,) that you cannot honestly
do so; and (I trust) you will never do so any more.

[c] *Testimony of* Codices ℵ *and* c *concerning* 1 Tim. iii. 16.

That ℵ reads OC is admitted.—Not so Codex c, which the
excessive application of chemicals has rendered no longer
decipherable in this place. Tischendorf (of course) insists,
that the original reading was OC.[1] Wetstein and Griesbach
(just as we should expect,) avow the same opinion,—Woide,
Mill, Weber and Parquoi being just as confident that the
original reading was Θ̄C̄. As in the case of cod. A, it is too
late by full 100 years to re-open this question. Observable
it is that the witnesses yield contradictory evidence. Wetstein, writing 150 years ago, before the original writing had
become so greatly defaced,—(and Wetstein, inasmuch as he
collated the MS. for Bentley [1716], must have been
thoroughly familiar with its contents,)—only ' *thought* ' that
he read OC; ' because the delicate horizontal stroke which
makes Θ out of O,' was to him ' *not apparent*.'[2] Woide on the
contrary was convinced that Θ̄C̄ had been written by the first
hand : ' for ' (said he) ' though there *exists no vestige* of the
delicate stroke which out of O makes Θ, *the stroke written above
the letters is by the first hand*.' What however to Wetstein
and to Woide was not apparent, was visible enough to
Weber, Wetstein's contemporary. And Tischendorf, so late
as 1843, expressed his astonishment that the stroke in
question had hitherto escaped the eyes of every one; *having
been repeatedly seen by himself*.[3] He attributes it, (just as we

---

[1] *Prolegomena* to his ed. of Cod. c,—pp. 39–42.

[2] " Oꜱ habet codex c, ut puto; nam lineola illa tenuis, quæ ex O facit
Θ, non apparet." (*In loc.*) And so Griesbach, *Symb. Crit.* i. p. viii.
(1785).

[3] "Quotiescunque locum inspiciebam (inspexi autem per hoc biennium
sæpissime) mihi prorsus apparebat." "Quam [lineolam] miror hucusque
omnium oculos fugisse." [*Prolegg.* p. 41]. . . . Equidem miror sane.

should expect) to a corrector of the MS. ; partly, because of *its colour*, ('*subnigra*'); partly, because of *its inclining upwards to the right.* And yet, *who* sees not that an argument derived from *the colour* of a line which is already well-nigh invisible, must needs be in a high degree precarious ? while Scrivener aptly points out that the cross line in ϴ,—the ninth letter further on, (which has never been questioned,)— *also* 'ascends towards the right.' The hostile evidence collapses therefore.   In the meantime, what at least is certain is, that the subscribed musical notation indicates that *a thousand years ago, a word of two syllables* was read here. From a review of all of which, it is clear that the utmost which can be pretended is that some degree of uncertainty attaches to the testimony of cod. c.   Yet, *why* such a plea should be either set up or allowed, I really see not—except indeed by men who have made up their minds beforehand that OC *shall be* the reading of 1 Tim. iii. 16.   Let the sign of uncertainty however follow the notation of c for this text, if you will.   That cod. c is an indubitable witness for OC, I venture at least to think that no fair person will ever any more pretend.

[d] *Testimony of* CODICES F *and* G *of S. Paul, concerning*
1 Tim. iii. 16.

The next dispute is about the reading of the two IXth-century codices, F and G,—concerning which I propose to trouble you with a few words in addition to what has been already offered on this subject at pp. 100–1 : the rather, because you have yourself devoted one entire page of your pamphlet to the testimony yielded by these two codices ; and because you therein have recourse to what (if it proceeded from any one but a Bishop,) I should designate the *insolent* method of trying to put me down by authority,—instead of seeking to convince me of my error by producing some good

reasons for your opinion. You seem to think it enough to
hurl Wetstein, Griesbach, Lachmann, Tregelles, Tischendorf,
and (cruellest of all) my friend Scrivener, at my head. Permit
me to point out that this, *as an argument*, is the feeblest to
which a Critic can have recourse. He shouts so lustily for
help only because he is unable to take care of himself.

F and G then are confessedly independent copies of one
and the same archetype: and "both F and G" (you say)
"exhibit $\overline{OC}$."[1] Be it so. The question arises,—What does
the stroke above the OC signify? I venture to believe that
these two codices represent a copy which originally exhibited
$\overline{OC}$, but from which the diameter of the Θ had disappeared—
(as very often is the case in codex A)—through tract of time.
The effect of this would be that F and G are in reality
witnesses for Θεός. Not so, you say. *That* slanting stroke
represents the aspirate, and proves that these two codices are
witnesses for ὅς.[2] Let us look a little more closely into this
matter.

Here are two documents, of which it has been said that
they "were separately derived from some early codex, in
which there was probably no interval between the words."[3]
They were *not immediately* derived from such a codex, I
remark: it being quite incredible that two independent
copyists could have hit on the same extravagantly absurd
way of dividing the uncial letters.[4] The common archetype

---

[1] Page 75.

[2] Pages 64, 69, 71, 75.—Some have pointed out that opposite $\overline{OC}$ in F
—above $\overline{OC}$ in G,—is written 'quod.' Yes, but not '*qui*.' The Latin
version is independent of the Greek. In S. Mark xi. 8, above ΑΓΡѠΝ is
written '*arboribus* ;' and in 1 Tim. iv. 10, ΑΓѠΝΙΖΟΜΕΘΑ is translated
by F '*maledicimur*,'—by G, '*exprobramur vel maledicimur*.'

[3] *Introduction to* Cod. Augiensis, p. xxviij.

[4] E.g. Out of ΟΜΕΝΤΟΙΣΤΕΡΕΟΣ [2 Tim. ii. 19], they both make
Ο · μεν · το · ισ · τεραιος. For ὑγιαίνωσιν [Tit. i. 13], both write υγει ·

which both employed must have been the work of a late
Western scribe every bit as licentious and as unacquainted
with Greek as themselves.[1] *That* archetype however may
very well have been obtained from a primitive codex of the
kind first supposed, in which the words were written continuously, as in codex B. Such Manuscripts were furnished
with neither breathings nor accents: accordingly, "of the
ordinary breathings or accents there are no traces"[2] in either
F or G.

But then, cod. F occasionally,— G much oftener,—exhibits
a little straight stroke, nearly horizontal, over the initial
vowel of certain words. Some have supposed that this was
designed to represent the aspirate: but it is not so. The
proof is, that it is found *consistently* introduced over the same
vowels *in the interlinear Latin.* Thus, the Latin preposition
'a' *always* has the slanting stroke above it:[3] and the Latin
interjection 'o' is furnished with the same appendage,—
alike in the Gospels and in the Epistles.[4] This observation

ἐνώσειν :—for καινὴ κτίσις [2 Cor. v. 17] both give και · νηκτισις :—for
ἀνέγκλητοι ὄντες [1 Tim. iii. 10], both exhibit ανευ · κλητοιον · εχοντες
('nullum crimen habentes') :—for ὡς γάγγραινα νομὴν ἕξει [2 Tim. ii.
17], both exhibit ως · γανγρα · ινα · (F G) νομηνεξει (G, who writes above
the words '*sicut cancer ut serpat*').

[1] He must be held responsible for hΥΠΟΚΡΙϹΙ in place of ὑποκρίσει
[1 Tim. iv. 2]: ΑϹΤΙΖΟΜΕΝΟϹ instead of λογιζόμενος [2 Cor. v. 19]:
ΠΡΙΧΟΤΗΤΙ instead of πραότητι [2 Tim. ii. 25]. And he was the author
of ΓΕΡΜΑΝΕ in Phil. iv. 3: as well as of O δε πνευμα in 1 Tim. iv. 1.

But the scribes of F and G also were curiously innocent of Greek.
G suggests that γυναιξειν (in 1 Tim. ii. 10) may be '*infinitivus*'—(of course
from γυναίκω).

[2] *Introduction*, p. 155.

[3] Thirteen times between Rom. i. 7 and xiii. 1.

[4] E.g. Gal. iii. 1 ; 1 Cor. xv. 55 ; 2 Cor. vi. 11 (ὅς and ὅ). Those who
have Matthæi's reprint of G at hand are invited to refer to the last line of
fol. 91: (1 Tim. vi. 20) where Ὦ Τιμόθεε is exhibited thus :—O̅ ὧ
ΤΙΜΟΘΕΕ.

evacuates the supposed significance of the few instances
where ᾶ is written Ᾱ :[1] as well as of the much fewer places
where ὁ or ὃ are written Ō :[2] especially when account is taken
of the many hundred occasions, (often in rapid succession,)
when nothing at all is to be seen above the ' o.'[3] As for the
fact that ἵνα is always written ῙΝΑ (or ῙΝΑ),—let it only be
noted that besides ιδωμεν, ιχθυς, ισχυρος, &c., Ιακωβος,
Ιωαννης, Ιουδας, &c., (which are all distinguished in the
same way,)—*Latin words also beginning with an* 'I' are
similarly adorned,—and we become convinced that the little
stroke in question is to be explained on some entirely
different principle. At last, we discover (from the example
of ' sī,' ' sīc,' ' etsī,' ' servītus,' ' saeculīs,' ' idolīs,' &c.) that the
supposed sign of the rough breathing *is nothing else but
an ancient substitute for the modern dot over the* '*I.*'—We may
now return to the case actually before us.

It has been pointed out that the line above the oc in both
F and G " is not horizontal, but rises a little towards the
right." I beg to call attention to the fact that there are 38
instances of the slight super-imposed ' line ' here spoken of, in
the page of cod. F where the reading under discussion
appears : 7 in the Greek, 31 in the Latin. In the corresponding page of cod. G, the instances are 44 : 8 in the
Greek, 36 in the Latin.[4] These short horizontal strokes

---

[1] Col. ii. 22, 23 : iii. 2.

[2] As 1 Tim. iii. 1 : iv. 14 : vi. 15. Consider the practice of F in
1 Thess. i. 9 (Ō. ΠΟΙΑΝ) : in 2 Cor. viii. 11, 14 (Ō. ΠωC).

[3] Rarest of all are instances of this mark over the Latin ' e ' : but we
meet with ' spē ' (Col. i. 23) : ' sē ' (ii. 18) : rĕpēntes (2 Tim. iii. 6), &c.
So, in the Greek, ἡ or ῇ written ῌ are most unusual.—A few instances
are found of ' u ' with this appendage, as ' domūs' (1 Tim. v. 13) : ' spiritū '
(1 Cor. iv. 21), &c.

[4] This information is obtained from a photograph of the page procured from Dresden through the kindness of the librarian, Counsellor
Dr. Forstemann.

(they can hardly be called *lines*) generally — not by any means always—slant upwards; and *they are invariably the sign of contraction.*

The problem before us has in this way been divested of a needless encumbrance. The suspicion that the horizontal line above the word OC may possibly represent the aspirate, has been disposed of. It has been demonstrated that throughout these two codices a horizontal line slanting upwards, set over a vowel, is either—(1) The sign of contraction; or else—(2) A clerical peculiarity. In the place before us, then, *which* of the two is it?

The sign of contraction, I answer: seeing that whereas there are, in the page before us, 9 aspirated, and (including O̅C̅) 8 contracted Greek words, not one of those *nine* aspirated words has *any mark at all* above its initial letter; while every one of the *eight* contracted words is duly furnished with the symbol of contraction. I further submit that inasmuch as ὅς is *nowhere* else written O̅C̅ in either codex, it is unreasonable to assume that it is so written in this place. Now, that almost every codex in the world reads Θ̅C̅ in 1 Tim. iii. 16,—is a plain fact; and that O̅C̅ (in verse 16) *would be* Θεός if the delicate horizontal stroke which distinguishes Θ from O, were not away,—no one denies. Surely, therefore, the only thing which remains to be enquired after, is,—Are there *any other* such substitutions of one letter for another discoverable in these two codices? And it is notorious that instances of the phenomenon abound. The letters C, Є, O, Θ are confused throughout.[1] And what else are ΠЄΝΟΟΥΝΤЄC for πενθουντες (Matth. v. 4),—ЄΚΡΙΖШΟΗΤΙ for εκριζωθητι (Luc. xvii. 16),—ΚΑΤΑΒΗΟΙ for καταβηθι (xix. 6),—but

---

[1] See Rettig's *Prolegg.* pp. xxiv.-v.

instances of *the self-same mistake* which (as I contend) has
in this place turned Θ͞C into O͞C ?

My lord Bishop, I have submitted to all this painful
drudgery, not, you may be sure, without a sufficient reason.
*Never any more must we hear of 'breathings' in connexion with
codices* F *and* G.   The stroke above the OC in 1 Tim. iii. 16
has been proved to be *probably the sign of contraction.*   I
forbear, of course, to insist that the two codices are witnesses
on my side.   I require that you, in the same spirit of fairness,
will abstain from claiming them as certainly witnessing *on
yours.*   The Vth-century codex C, and the IXth-century
codex F–G must be regarded as equivocal in the testimony
they render, and are therefore not to be reckoned to either
of the contending parties.

These are many words about the two singularly corrupt
IXth-century documents, concerning which so much has
been written already.   But I sincerely desire,—(and so I
trust do you, as a Christian Bishop,)—to see the end of a
controversy which those only have any right to re-open (*pace
tuâ dixerim*) who have *something new to offer on the subject :*
and certain it is that the bearing of F and G on this matter
has never before been fully stated.   I dismiss those two
codices with the trite remark that they are, at all events, but
one codex : and that against them are to be set K L P,—*the
only uncials which remain ;* for D (of 'Paul') exhibits ὅ, and
the Vatican codex B no longer serves us.

[e] *Testimony of the* CURSIVE COPIES : *and specially of
    '* Paul 17,' '73 ' *and* ' 181,' *concerning* 1 Tim. iii. 16.

Next, for the cursive Copies.   You claim without enquiry,
—*and only because you find that men have claimed them before
you,*—Nos. 17, 73, 181, as witnesses for ὅς.   Will you permit
me to point out that no progress will ever be made in these

studies so long as "professed Critics" will persevere in the evil practice of transcribing one another's references, and thus appropriating one another's blunders?

About the reading of 'Paul 17,' (the notorious '33' of the Gospels,) there is indeed no doubt.—Mindful however of President Routh's advice to me always 'to verify my references,'—concerning 'Paul 73' I wrote a letter of enquiry to Upsala (July 28, 1879), and for all answer (Sept. 6th) received a beautiful tracing of what my correspondent called the '1 Thim. iii. 16 *paraphe.*' It proved to be an abridged exhibition of 21 lines of Œcumenius. I instantly wrote to enquire whether this was really all that the codex in question has to say to 1 Tim. iii. 16? but to this I received no reply. I presumed therefore that I had got to the bottom of the business. But in July 1882, I addressed a fresh enquiry to Dr. Belsheim of Christiania, and got his answer last October. By that time he had visited Upsala: had verified for me readings in other MSS., and reported that the reading here is ὅϛ. I instantly wrote to enquire whether he had seen the word with his own eyes? He replied that he desired to look further into *this* matter on some future occasion,—the MS. in question being (he says) a difficult one to handle. I am still awaiting his final report, which he promises to send me when next he visits Upsala. ('Aurivillius' says nothing about it.) Let 'Paul 73' in the meantime stand with a note of interrogation, or how you will.

About 'Paul 181,' (which Scholz describes as "vi. 36" in the Laurentian library at Florence,)I take leave to repeat (in a foot-note) what (in a letter to Dr. Scrivener) I explained in the 'Guardian' ten years ago.[1] In consequence however

---

[1] "You will perceive that I have now succeeded in identifying every Evangelium hitherto spoken of as existing in Florence, with the exception

of your discourteous remarks (which you will be gratified to find quoted at foot,[1]) I have written (not for the first time) to the learned custos of the Laurentian library on the subject; stating the entire case and reminding him of my pertinacity in 1871.   He replies,—"Scholz fallitur huic bibliothecæ tribuendo codicem sign. 'plut. vi. n. 36.' Nec est in præsenti, nec fuit antea, neque exstat in aliâ bibliothecâ apud nos."
. . . On a review of what goes before, I submit that one who has taken so much pains with the subject does not deserve to be flouted as I find myself flouted by the Bp. of Gloucester and Bristol,—who has not been at the pains to verify *one single point* in this entire controversy for himself.

Every other known copy of S. Paul's Epistles, (written in the cursive character,) I have ascertained (by laborious correspondence with the chiefs of foreign libraries) concurs in exhibiting Θεὸς ἐφανερώθη ἐν σαρκί.   The importance of this

---

of Evan 365 [Act. 145, Paul 181] (Laurent vi. 36), &c., which is said to 'contain also the Psalms.' I assure you no such Codex exists in the Laurentian Library; no, nor ever did exist there.   Dr. Anziani devoted full an hour to the enquiry, allowing me [for I was very incredulous] to see the process whereby he convinced himself that Scholz is in error.   It was just such an intelligent and exhaustive process as Coxe of the Bodleian, or dear old Dr. Bandinel before him, would have gone through under similar circumstances.   Pray strike that Codex off your list; and with it 'Acts 145' and 'Paul 181.' I need hardly say that Bandini's Catalogue knows nothing of it.   It annoys me to be obliged to add that I cannot even find out the history of Scholz's mistake."—*Guardian,* August 27, 1873.

[1] " *Whose* word on such matters is entitled to most credit,—the word of the Reviewer, or the word of the most famous manuscript collators of this century? . . . Those who have had occasion to seek in public libraries for manuscripts which are not famous for antiquity or beauty or completeness (*sic*), know that the answer '*non est inventus*' is no conclusive reason for believing that the object of their quest has not been seen and collated in former years by those who profess to have actually seen and collated it.   That 181 'is non-existent' must be considered unproven."—Bp. Ellicott's *Pamphlet*, p. 72.

testimony ought to be supremely evident to yourself who
contend so strenuously for the support of Paul 73 and 181.
But because, in my judgment, this practical unanimity of
the manuscripts is not only 'important' but *conclusive*, I
shall presently recur to it (viz. at pages 494-5,) more in detail.
For do but consider that these copies were one and all derived from yet older MSS. than themselves; and that the
remote originals of those older MSS. were perforce of higher
antiquity still, and were executed in every part of primitive
Christendom.   How is it credible that they should, one and
all, conspire to mislead?   I cannot in fact express better
than Dr. Berriman did 140 years ago, the logical result of
such a concord of the copies :—"From whence can it be
supposed that this general, I may say this universal consent
of the Greek MSS. should arise, but from hence,—That
Θεός is the genuine original reading of this Text?" (p. 325.)

In the meantime, you owe me a debt of gratitude : for, in
the course of an enquiry which I have endeavoured to make
exhaustive, I have discovered *three* specimens of the book
called "*Apostolus*," or "*Praxapostolus*" (i.e. Lections from
the Epistles and Acts) which also exhibit ὅς in this place.
One of these is Reg. 375 (our 'Apost. 12') in the French
collection, a *Western* codex, dated A.D. 1022.[1]   The story of
the discovery of the other two (to be numbered 'Praxapost.'
85, 86,) is interesting, and will enliven this dull page.

At Tusculum, near Rome,—(the locality which Cicero

---

[1] The learned Abbé Martin, who has obligingly inspected for me the
18 copies of the 'Praxapostolus' in the Paris library, reports as follows
concerning 'Apost. 12' (= Reg. 375),—'A very foul MS. of small value,
I believe: but a curious specimen of bad Occidental scholarship.   It was
copied for the monks of S. Denys, and exhibits many Latin words; having
been apparently revised on the Latin.   The lection is assigned to
Σαββάτῳ λ' (not λδ') in this codex.'

rendered illustrious, and where he loved to reside surrounded by his books,)—was founded early in the XIth century a Christian library which in process of time became exceedingly famous. It retains, in fact, its ancient reputation to this day. Nilus 'Rossanensis' it was, who, driven with his monks from Calabria by invading hordes, established in A.D. 1004 a monastery at Tusculum, to which either he, or his successors, gave the name of 'Crypta Ferrata.' It became the headquarters of the Basilian monks in the XVIIth century. Hither habitually resorted those illustrious men, Sirletus, Mabillon, Zacagni, Ciampini, Montfaucon,—and more lately Mai and Dom Pitra. To Signor Cozza-Luzi, the present learned and enlightened chief of the Vatican library, (who is himself 'Abbas Monachorum Basiliensium Cryptæ Ferratæ,') I am indebted for my copy of the Catalogue (now in process of publication[1]) of the extraordinary collection of MSS. belonging to the society over which he presides.

In consequence of the information which the Abbate Cozza-Luzi sent me, I put myself in communication with the learned librarian of the monastery, the 'Hieromonachus' D. Antonio Rocchi, (author of the Catalogue in question,) whom I cannot sufficiently thank for his courtesy and kindness. The sum of the matter is briefly this:—There are still preserved in the library of the Basilian monks of Crypta Ferrata,—(notwithstanding that many of its ancient treasures have found their way into other repositories,[2])—4 manuscripts of S. Paul's Epistles, which I number 290, –1, –2, –3 : and 7 copies of the book called 'Praxapostolus,' which I

---

[1] '*Codices Cryptenses seu Abbatiæ Cryptæ Ferratæ in Tusculano, digesti et illustrati cura et studio* D. Antonii Rocchi, Hieromonachi Basiliani Bibliothecæ custodis,'—*Tusculani*, fol. 1882.—I have received 424 pages (1 May, 1883).

[2] Not a few of the Basilian Codices have been transferred to the Vatican.

number 83, –4, –5, –6, –7, –8, –9. Of these eleven, 3 are defective hereabouts : 5 read Θεός : 2 (Praxapost.) exhibit ὅς ;
and 1 (Apost. 83) contains an only not unique reading, to be
mentioned at p. 478. Hieromonachus Rocchi furnishes me
with references besides to 3 Liturgical Codices out of a
total of 22, ('Αποστολοευαγγέλια), which also exhibit Θεός.[1]
I number them Apost. 106, 108, 110.

And now, we may proceed to consider the VERSIONS.

[f] *Testimony of the* VERSIONS *to the reading of* 1 Tim. iii. 16.

"Turning to the ancient Versions" (you assert) " we find
them almost unanimous against Θεός " (p. 65). But your
business, my lord Bishop, was to show that some of them
witness *in favour of* ὅς. If you cannot show that several
ancient Versions,—besides a fair proportion of ancient Fathers,
—are clearly on your side, your contention is unreasonable
as well as hopeless. What then do the VERSIONS say ?

(a) Now, it is allowed on all hands that the LATIN Version
was made from copies which must have exhibited μυστήριον
ὃ ἐφανερώθη. The agreement of the Latin copies is
absolute. The Latin Fathers also conspire in reading
' *mysterium quod:*' though some of them seem to have
regarded ' quod ' as a conjunction. Occasionally, (as by the
Translator of Origen,[2]) we even find ' quia' substituted *for*
' quod.' Estius conjectures that ' quod ' *is* a conjunction in
this place. But in fact the reasoning of the Latin Fathers is
observed invariably to proceed as if they had found nothing
else but "DEUS" in the text before them. They bravely
assume that the Eternal WORD, the second Person in the

---

[1] In an APPENDIX to the present volume, I will give fuller information. I am still (3rd May, 1883) awaiting replies to my˙ troublesome
interrogatories addressed to the heads of not a few continental libraries.

[2] Rufinus, namely (*fl.* A.D. 395). *Opp.* iv. 465.

Trinity, is *designated* by the expression '*magnum pietatis sacramentum.*'

(*b*) It is, I admit, a striking circumstance that such a mistake as this in the old Latin should have been retained in the VULGATE. But if you ever study this subject with attention, you will find that Jerome,—although no doubt he "professedly corrected the old Latin Version by the help of ancient Greek manuscripts," (p. 69,)—on many occasions retains readings which it is nevertheless demonstrable that he individually disapproved.   No certain inference therefore as to what Jerome *found* in ancient Greek MSS. can be safely drawn from the text of the Vulgate.

(*c*) Next, for the *Syriac* (PESCHITO) Version.   I beg to subjoin the view of the late loved and lamented P. E. Pusey, —the editor of Cyril, and who at the time of his death was engaged in re-editing the Peschito.   He says,—" In 1 Tim. iii. 16, the Syriac has '*qui manifestatus est.*'   The relative is indeterminate, but the verb is not.   In Syriac however μυστήριον is masculine; and thus, the natural way would be to take μυστήριον as the antecedent, and translate '*quod manifestatum est.*'   *No one would have thought of any other way of translating the Syriac*—but for the existence of the various reading ὅς in the Greek, and the *possibility* of its affecting the translation into Syriac.   But the Peschito is so really a translation into good Syriac, (not into word-for-word Syriac,) that if the translator had wanted to express the Greek ὅς, in so difficult a passage, *he would have turned it differently.*" [1] — The Peschito therefore yields the same testimony as the Latin; and may not be declared (as you declare it) to be indeterminate.   Still less may it be represented as witnessing to ὅς.

---

[1] MS. letter to myself, August 11, 1879.

(*d*) It follows to enquire concerning the rendering of 1 Tim. iii. 16 in the PHILOXENIAN, or rather the HARKLEIAN Version (VIIth cent.), concerning which I have had recourse to the learned Editor of that Version. He writes :—"There can be no doubt that the authors of this Version had either Θεός or Θεοῦ before them : while their marginal note shows that they were aware of the reading ὅς. They exhibit,— '*Great is the mystery of the goodness of the fear* (feminine) *of GOD, who-was-manifested* (masculine) *in the flesh.*' The marginal addition [oᴑ before ܠ܀ܙ] makes the reference to GOD all the plainer."[1]   See more below, at p. 489.

Now this introduction of the word Θεός into the text, however inartistic it may seem to you and to me, is a fatal circumstance to those who would contend on your side. It shows translators divided between two rival and conflicting readings : but determined to give prominence to the circumstance which constituted the greatness of the mystery : viz. GOD INCARNATE.   "May I suggest" (adds the witty scholar in his Post-script) "that there would be no mystery in 'a man being manifested in the flesh' ? "

The facts concerning the Harkleian Version being such, you will not be surprised to hear me say that I am at a loss to understand how, without a syllable expressive of doubt, you should claim this version (the 'Philoxenian' you call it— but it is rather the Harkleian), as a witness on your side,— a witness for ὅς.[2]   It not only witnesses *against* you, (for the Latin and the Peschito do *that*,) but, as I have shown you, it is a witness on *my* side.

(*e*) and (*f*). Next, for the Versions of LOWER and UPPER EGYPT.

---

[1] MS. letter from the Rev. Henry Deane, of S. John's College, Oxford.
[2] See above, page 429.

"We are content" (you say) to "refer our readers to Tischendorf and Tregelles, who unhesitatingly claim the Memphitic [or Coptic] and the Thebaic [or Sahidic] for ὅς."[1] But surely, in a matter of this kind, my lord Bishop—(I mean, when we are discussing some nicety of a language of which personally we know absolutely nothing,)—we may never " be content to refer our readers" to individuals who are every bit as ignorant of the matter as ourselves. Rather should we be at the pains to obtain for those whom we propose to instruct the deliberate verdict of those who have made the subject their special study. Dr. Malan (who must be heartily sick of me by this time), in reply to my repeated enquiries, assures me that in Coptic and in Sahidic alike, " the relative pronoun always takes the gender of the Greek antecedent. But, inasmuch as there is properly speaking no neuter in either language, the masculine does duty *for* the neuter; the gender of the definite article and relative pronoun being determined by the gender of the word referred to. Thus, in S. John xv. 26, the Coptic '*pi*' and '*phè*' respectively represent the definite article and the relative, alike in the expression ὁ Παράκλητος ὄν, and in the expression τὸ Πνεῦμα ὅ: and so throughout. In 1 Tim. iii. 16, therefore, '*pi mustèrion phè*,' must perforce be rendered, τὸ μυστήριον ὅ:—not, surely, ὁ μυστήριον ὅς. And yet, if *the relative* may be masculine, why not *the article* also? But in fact, we have no more right to render the Coptic (or the Sahidic) relative by ὅς in 1 Tim. iii. 16, than in any other similar passage where a neuter noun (e.g. πνεῦμα or σῶμα) has gone before. *In this particular case*, of course a pretence may be set up that the gender of the relative shall be regarded as an open question: but in strictness of grammar, it is far otherwise. No Coptic or Sahidic scholar, in fact, having to translate the Coptic or Sahidic back into Greek,

[1] Page 71. And so p. 65 and 69.

would ever dream of writing anything else but τὸ μυστήριον ὅ." [1] . . . . . And now I trust I have made it plain to you
that *you are mistaken* in your statement (p. 69),—that "῞Ος
is *supported by the two Egyptian Versions.*" It is supported
by *neither.* You have been shown that they both witness
against you. You will therefore not be astonished to hear
me again declare that I am at a loss to understand how you
can cite the ' Philoxenian, *Coptic and Sahidic,*' [2]—as witnesses
on your side. It is not in this way, my lord Bishop, that
GOD's Truth is to be established.

(*g*) As for the GOTHIC Version,—dissatisfied with the verdict of De Gabelentz and Loebe, [3] I addressed myself to
Dr. Ceriani of Milan, the learned and most helpful chief of
the Ambrosian Library : in which by the way is preserved *the
only known copy* of Ulphilas for 1 Tim. iii. 16.   He inclines
to the opinion that '*saei* ' is to be read,—the rather, because
Andreas Uppström, the recent editor of the codex, a diligent
and able scholar, has decided in favour of. that '*obscure*'
reading. [4]   The Gothic therefore must be considered to

---

[1] MS. letter to myself.   [2] See above, page 429.

[3] *Ulfilas. Veteris et Novi Test. Versionis Goth. fragmenta quæ super-
sunt,* &c. 4to. 1843.

[4] " "Si tamen Uppström '*obscurum*' dixit, non '*incertum,*' fides illi
adhiberi potest, quia diligentissime apices omnes investigabat; me enim
præsente in aula codicem tractabat."—(Private letter to myself.)
   Ceriani proceeds,—" Quæris quomodo componatur cum textu 1 Tim.
iii. 16, nota ⁵⁴ *Proleg.* Gabelentz Gothicam versionem legens Θεός. Putarem
ex loco Castillionæi in notis ad Philip. ii. 6, locutos fuisse doctos illos
Germanos, oblitos illius Routh præcepti ' *Let me recommend to you the
practice of always verifying your references, sir.* ' "
   The reader will be interested to be informed that Castiglione, the
former editor of the codex, was in favour of ' GOD ' in 1835, and of '*soei* '
(*quæ* [= ὅ], to agree with ' *runa,*' i.e. 'mystery,' which is feminine in
Gothic) in 1839. Gabelentz, in 1843, ventured to print ' *saei*' = ὅς.
" Et ' saei ' legit etiam diligentissimus Andreas Uppström nuperus codicis
Ambrosiani investigator et editor, in opere *Codicis Gothici Ambrosiani
sive Epist. Pauli,* &c. Holmiæ et Lipsiæ, 1868."

witness to the (more than) extraordinary combination ;—
μέγαΣ . . . μυστήριον . . . ͘ΟΣ. (See the footnote (⁴) p. 452.)

I obtain at the same time, the same verdict, and on the
same grounds, from that distinguished and obliging scholar,
Dr. John Belsheim of Christiania. "But" (he adds) "the
reading is a little dubious. H. F. Massmann, in the notes to
his edition,[1] at page 657, says,—'saei [qui] is altogether
obliterated.' "—In claiming the Gothic therefore as a witness
for ὅς, you will (I trust) agree with me that a single *scarcely
legible copy* of a Version is not altogether satisfactory testimony :—while certainly ' *magnus* est pietatis sacramentum,
qui manifestat*us* est in corpore '—is not a rendering of 1 Tim.
iii. 16 which you are prepared to accept.

(*h*) For the ÆTHIOPIC Version,—Dr. Hoerning, (of the
British Museum,) has at my request consulted six copies of
1 Timothy, and informs me that they present no variety of
text. *The antecedent, as well as the relative, is masculine in
all.* The Æthiopic must therefore be considered to favour
the reading μυστήριον· ὃ ἐφανερώθη, and to represent the
same Greek text which underlies the Latin and the Peschito
Versions. The Æthiopic therefore is against you.

(*i*) "The ARMENIAN Version," (writes Dr. Malan) "from
the very nature of the language, is indeterminate. There is
no grammatical distinction of genders in Armenian."

(*j*) The ARABIC Version, (so Dr. Ch. Rieu[2] informs me,)

---

[1] Stuttgard, 1857.

[2] Of the department of Oriental MSS. in the Brit. Mus., who derives
his text from "the three Museum MSS. which contain the Arabic Version
of the Epistles: viz. *Harl.* 5474 (dated A.D. 1332):—*Oriental* 1328 (Xth
cent.) :—*Arundel Orient.* 19 (dated A.D. 1616)."—Walton's Polyglott, he

exhibits,—" In *truth the mystery of this justice is great. It is that he*" (or "*it,*" for the Arabic has no distinction between masculine and neuter) "*was manifested in the body, and was justified in the spirit,*" &c.—This version therefore witnesses for neither ' who,' ' which,' nor ' GOD.'

(*k*) and (*l*). There only remain the GEORGIAN Version, which is of the VIth century,—and the SLAVONIC, which is of the IXth. Now, both of these (Dr. Malan informs me) *unequivocally witness to* Θεός.

Thus far then for the testimony yielded by ancient MANUSCRIPTS and VERSIONS of S. Paul's Epistles.

[g] *Review of the progress which has been hitherto made in the present Enquiry.*

Up to this point, you must admit that wondrous little sanction has been obtained for the reading for which *you* contend, (viz. μυστήριον · ὃς ἐφανερώθη,) as the true reading of 1 Tim. iii. 16. Undisturbed in your enjoyment of the testimony borne by Cod. א, you cannot but feel that such testimony is fully counterbalanced by the witness of Cod. A : and further, that the conjoined evidence of the HARKLEIAN, the GEORGIAN, and the SLAVONIC Versions outweighs the single evidence of the GOTHIC.

But what is to be said about the consent of the manuscripts of S. Paul's Epistles for reading Θεός in this place, *in the proportion of* 125 *to* 1 ? You must surely see that, (as I explained above at pp. 445–6,) such multitudinous testimony is absolutely decisive of the question before us. At

---

says, exhibits " a garbled version, quite distinct from the genuine Arabic : viz. ' *These glories commemorate them in the greatness of the mystery of fair piety. GOD appeared in the flesh,*' " &c.

p. 30 of your pamphlet, you announce it as a "lesson of
primary importance, often reiterated but often forgotten,
ponderari debere testes, non numerari."   You might have
added with advantage,—"*and oftenest of all, misunderstood.*"
For are you not aware that, generally speaking, 'Number'
constitutes 'Weight'?   If you have discovered some 'regia
via' which renders the general consent of COPIES,—the
general consent of VERSIONS, — the general consent of
FATHERS, a consideration of secondary importance, why do
you not at once communicate the precious secret to mankind, and thereby save us all a world of trouble?

You will perhaps propose to fall back on Hort's wild
theory of a '*Syrian Text,*'—executed by authority at Antioch
somewhere between A.D. 250 and A.D. 350.[1]   Be it so.   Let
that fable be argued upon as if it were a fact.   And what
follows?   That *at a period antecedent to the date of any existing copy* of the Epistle before us, the Church in her corporate
capacity declared Θεός (not ὅς) to be the true reading of
1 Tim. iii. 16.

Only one other head of Evidence (the PATRISTIC) remains
to be explored; after which, we shall be able to sum up,
and to conclude the present Dissertation.

[h]   *Testimony of the* FATHERS *concerning the true reading of*
   1 *Tim.* iii. 16 :—GREGORY OF NYSSA,—DIDYMUS,—THEO-
   DORET,—JOHN DAMASCENE,—CHRYSOSTOM,—GREGORY NAZ.,
   —SEVERUS OF ANTIOCH,—DIODORUS OF TARSUS.

It only remains to ascertain what the FATHERS have to
say on this subject.   And when we turn our eyes in this direction, we are encountered by a mass of evidence which effec-

---

[1] See above, pp. 271 to 294.

tually closes this discussion. You contended just now as
eagerly for the Vth-century Codex A, as if its witness were
a point of vital importance to you. But I am prepared to
show that GREGORY OF NYSSA (a full century before Codex A
was produced), in at least 22 places, knew of no other reading but Θεός.[1] Of his weighty testimony you appear to have
been wholly unaware in 1869, for you did not even mention
Gregory by name (see p. 429). Since however you now admit
that his evidence is unequivocally against you, I am willing
to hasten forward,—only supplying you (at foot) with the
means of verifying what I have stated above concerning
the testimony of this illustrious Father.

You are besides aware that DIDYMUS,[2] another illustrious
witness, is against you; and that he delivers unquestionable
testimony.

You are also aware that THEODORET,[3] in *four* places, is
certainly to be reckoned on the same side:

---

[1] i. 387 a : 551 a : 663 a *bis.*—ii. 430 a : 536 c : 581 c : 594 a, 595 b
(these two, of the 2nd pagination) : 693 d [= ii. 265, ed. 1615, from
which Tisch. quotes it. The place may be seen in full, *supra*, p. 101.]
—iii. 39 b *bis* : 67 a b.—*Ap. Galland.* vi. 518 c : 519 d : 520 b : 526 d :
532 a : 562 b : 566 d : 571 a. All but five of these places, I believe,
exhibit ὁ Θεός,—which seems to have been the reading of this Father.
The article is seldom seen in MSS. Only four instances of it,—(they will
be found distinctly specified below, page 493, *note* [1]),—are known to
exist. More places must have been overlooked.

Note, that Griesbach only mentions Gregory of Nyssa (whose name
Tregelles omits entirely) to remark that he is not to be cited for Θεός ;
seeing that, according to him, 1 Tim. iii. 16 is to be read thus :—τὸ
μυστήριον ἐν σαρκὶ ἐφανερώθη. Griesbach borrowed that quotation and
that blunder from Wetstein ; to be blindly followed in turn by Scholz
and Alford. And yet, the words in question are *not the words of Gregory
Nyss.* at all ; but of Apolinaris, against whom Gregory is writing,—as
Gregory himself explains. [*Antirrh. adv. Apol.* apud Galland. vi. 522 d.]

[2] *De Trin.* p. 83. The testimony is express.

[3] i. 92 : iii. 657.—iv. 19, 23.

And further, that John Damascene[1] *twice* adds his famous evidence to the rest,—and is also against you.

Chrysostom[2] again, whose testimony you called in question in 1869, you now admit is another of your opponents. I will not linger over his name therefore,—except to remark, that how you can witness a gathering host of ancient Fathers illustrious as these, without misgiving, passes my comprehension.   Chrysostom is *three* times a witness.

Next come two quotations from Gregory of Nazianzus, —which I observe you treat as "inconclusive."   I retain them all the same.[3]   You are reminded that this most rhetorical of Fathers is seldom more precise in quoting Scripture.

And to the same century which Gregory of Nazianzus adorned, is probably to be referred,—(it cannot possibly be later than A.D. 350, though it may be a vast deal more ancient,)—the title bestowed, in the way of summary, on that portion of S. Paul's first Epistle to Timothy which is contained between chap. iii. 16 and chap. iv. 7,—viz., Περὶ

---

[1] i. 313 :—ii. 263.

[2] i. 497 c d e.—viii. 85 e: 86 a.—xi. 605 f: 606 a b d e.—(The first of these places occurs in the Homily *de Beato Philogonio*, which Matthæi in the main [viz. from p. 497, line 20, to the end] edited from an independent source [*Lectt. Mosqq.* 1779]. Gallandius [xiv. *Append.* 141–4] reprints Matthæi's labours).—Concerning this place of Chrysostom (*vide suprà*, p. 101), Bp. Ellicott says (p. 66), —"The passage which he [the Quarterly Reviewer] does allege, deserves to be placed before our readers in full, as an illustration of the precarious character of patristic evidence.   If this passage attests the reading θεός in 1 Tim. iii. 16, does it not also attest the reading ὁ θεός in Heb. ii. 16, where no copyist or translator has introduced it?" . . .   I can but say, in reply,—'No, certainly not.'   May I be permitted to add, that it is to me simply unintelligible how Bp. Ellicott can show himself so *plane hospes* in this department of sacred Science as to be capable of gravely asking such a very foolish question?

[3] i. 215 a: 685 b.   The places may be seen quoted *suprà*, p. 101.

ΘΕΙ'ΑΣ ΣΑΡΚώσεως. We commonly speak of this as the seventh
of the 'Euthalian' κεφάλαια or chapters: but Euthalius himself
declares that those 18 titles were "devised by a certain very
wise and pious Father;" [1] and this particular title (Περὶ θείας
σαρκώσεως) is freely employed and discussed in Gregory of
Nyssa's treatise against Apolinaris,[2]—which latter had, in
fact, made it part of the title of his own heretical treatise.[3]
That the present is a very weighty attestation of the reading,
ΘΕΟ'Σ ἐφανερώθη ἐν ΣΑΡΚΙ' no one probably will deny: a
memorable proof moreover that Θεός [4] must have been universally read in 1 Tim. iii. 16 throughout the century which
witnessed the production of codices B and א.

SEVERUS, BP. OF ANTIOCH, you also consider a "not unambiguous" witness. I venture to point out to you that when
a Father of the Church, who has been already insisting on
the GODhead of CHRIST (καθ' ὃ γὰρ ὑπῆρχε Θεός,) goes on to
speak of Him as τὸν ἐν σαρκὶ φανερωθέντα Θεόν, there is
no 'ambiguity' whatever about the fact that he is quoting
from 1 Tim. iii. 16.[5]

And why are we only "perhaps" to add the testimony of
DIODORUS OF TARSUS; seeing that Diodorus adduces S. Paul's

---

[1] The place is quoted in Scrivener's Introduction, p. 59.

[2] Antirrheticus, ap. Galland. vi. 517-77.

[3] The full title was,—'Απόδειξις περὶ τῆς θείας σαρκώσεως τῆς καθ'
ὁμοίωσιν ἀνθρώπου. Ibid. 518 b, c : 519 a.

[4] Apolinaris did not deny that CHRIST was very GOD. His heresy (like
that of Arius) turned upon the nature of the conjunction of the Godhead
with the Manhood. Hear Theodoret :—A. Θεὸς Λόγος σαρκὶ ἐνωθεὶς
ἄνθρωπον ἀπετέλεσεν Θεόν. Ο. Τοῦτο οὖν λέγεις θείαν ἐμψυχίαν; A.
Καὶ πάνυ. Ο. 'Αντὶ ψυχῆς οὖν ὁ Λόγος; A. Ναί. Dial. vi. adv. Apol.
(Opp. v. 1080 = Athanas. ii. 525 d.)

[5] Cramer's Cat. in Actus, iii. 69. It is also met with in the Catena on
the Acts which J. C. Wolf published in his Anecdota Græca, iii. 137-8.
The place is quoted above, p. 102.

actual words (Θεὸς ἐφανερώθη ἐν σαρκί), and expressly says
that he finds them in *S. Paul's Epistle to Timothy?* [1] How—
may I be permitted to ask—would you have a quotation
made plainer?

[i] *Bp. Ellicott as a controversialist.   The case of* EUTHALIUS.

Forgive me, my lord Bishop, if I declare that the *animus*
you display in conducting the present critical disquisition
not only astonishes, but even shocks me. You seem to say,—
Non persuadebis, etiamsi persuaseris. The plainest testimony
you reckon doubtful, if it goes against you: an unsatisfactory
quotation, if it makes for your side, you roundly declare to
be "evidence" which "stands the test of examination." [2] . . .
"We have examined his references carefully" (you say).
"Gregory of Nyssa, Didymus of Alexandria, Theodoret and
John Damascene (*who died* severally about 394, 396, 457 and
756 A.D.) *seem* unquestionably to have read Θεός." [3] Excuse
me for telling you that this is not the language of a candid
enquirer after Truth. Your grudging admission of the *unequivocal* evidence borne by these four illustrious Fathers:—
your attempt to detract from the importance of their testimony by screwing down their date ' to the sticking place:'—
your assertion that the testimony of a fifth Father "*is not
unambiguous:*"—your insinuation that the emphatic witness
of a sixth may "*perhaps*" be inadmissible:—all this kind of
thing is not only quite unworthy of a Bishop when he turns
disputant, but effectually indisposes his opponent to receive
his argumentation with that respectful deference which else
would have been undoubtedly its due.

Need I remind you that men do not write their books when
they are *in articulo mortis?* Didymus *died* in A.D. 394, to be

---

[1] Cramer's *Cat. in Rom.* p. 124.   [2] P. 67.   [3] P. 65.

sure: but he was then 85 *years of age.* He was therefore born in A.D. 309, and is said to have flourished in 347. How old do you suppose were the sacred codices he had employed *till then ?* See you not that such testimony as his to the Text of Scripture must in fairness be held to belong to *the first quarter of the IVth century ?*—is more ancient in short (and infinitely more important) than that of any written codex with which we are acquainted ?

Pressed by my "cloud of witnesses," you seek to get rid of *them* by insulting *me.* "We pass over" (you say) "*names brought in to swell the number, such as Euthalius,—for whom no reference is given.*"[1] Do you then suspect me of the baseness,—nay, do you mean seriously to impute it to me,—of introducing 'names' 'to swell the number' of witnesses on my side? Do you mean further to insinuate that I prudently gave no reference in the case of 'Euthalius,' because I was unable to specify any place where his testimony is found? . . . I should really pause for an answer, but that a trifling circumstance solicits me, which, if it does not entertain the Bp. of Gloucester and Bristol, will certainly entertain every one else who takes the trouble to read these pages.

'Such as *Euthalius*'! You had evidently forgotten when you penned that offensive sentence, that EUTHALIUS is one of the few Fathers *adduced by yourself*[2] (but for whom you 'gave no reference,') in 1869,—when you were setting down the Patristic evidence in favour of Θεός. . . . This little incident is really in a high degree suggestive. Your practice has evidently been to appropriate Patristic references[3] without thought or verification,—prudently to abstain from dropping

---

[1] P. 65.   [2] See above, p. 429.
[3] Bentley, Scholz, Tischendorf, Alford and others adduce '*Euthalius.*'

a hint how you came by them,—but to use them like
dummies, for show. At the end of a few years, (naturally
enough,) you entirely forget the circumstance,—and proceed
vigorously to box the ears of the first unlucky Dean who
comes in your way, whom you suspect of having come by
his learning (such as it is) in the same slovenly manner.
Forgive me for declaring (while my ears are yet tingling)
that if you were even moderately acquainted with this department of Sacred Science, you would see at a glance that my
Patristic references are *never* obtained at second hand : for
the sufficient reason that elsewhere they are not to be met
with.   But waiving this, you have made it *luce clarius* to all
the world that so late as the year 1882, to *you* ' Euthalius '
was nothing else but ' a name.' And this really does astonish
me : for not only was he a famous Ecclesiastical personage,
(a Bishop like yourself,) but his work (the date of which is
A.D. 458,) is one with which no Author of a " *Critical* Commentary " on S. Paul's Epistles can afford to be unacquainted.
Pray read what Berriman has written concerning Euthalius
(pp. 217 to 222) in his admirable " *Dissertation on* 1 *Tim.* iii.
16." Turn also, if you please, to the *Bibliotheca* of Galland-
dius (vol. x. 197–323), and you will recognize the plain fact
that the *only* reason why, in the ' Quarterly Review,' " no
reference is given for Euthalius," is because the only reference
possible is—1 Tim. iii. 16.

[j] *The testimony of the letter ascribed to* Dionysius of
Alexandria. *Six other primitive witnesses to* 1 Tim. iii.
16, *specified.*

Then further, you absolutely take no notice of the remarkable testimony which I adduced (p. 101) from a famous Epistle
purporting to have been addressed by Dionysius of Alexandria (A.D. 264) to Paul of Samosata.   That the long and

interesting composition in question [1] was not actually the
work of the great Dionysius, is inferred—(whether rightly or
wrongly 1 am not concerned to enquire)—from the fact that
the Antiochian Fathers say expressly that Dionysius did not
deign to address Paul personally. But you are requested to
remember that the epistle must needs have been written by
somebody : [2] that it may safely be referred to the IIIrd century ; and that it certainly witnesses to Θεὸς ἐφανερώθη,[3]—
which is the only matter of any real importance to my argument. Its testimony is, in fact, as express and emphatic as
words can make it.

And here, let me call your attention to the circumstance
that there are at least SIX OTHER PRIMITIVE WITNESSES,
some of whom must needs have recognized the reading for
which I am here contending, (viz. Θεὸς ἐφανερώθη ἐν σαρκί,)
though not one of them quotes the place *in extenso,* nor indeed
refers to it in such a way as effectually to bar the door against
reasonable dispute. The present is in fact just the kind of
text which, from its undeniable grandeur, — its striking
rhythm,—and yet more its dogmatic importance,—was sure
to attract the attention of the earliest, no less than the latest
of the Fathers. Accordingly, the author of the Epistle *ad
Diognetum*[4] clearly refers to it early in the IInd century ;

---

[1] *Concilia,* i. 849–893. The place is quoted below in note ([3]).

[2] " Verum ex illis verbis illud tantum inferri debet false eam epistolam
Dionysio Alexandrino attribui: non autem scriptum non fuisse ab aliquo
ex Episcopis qui Synodis adversus Paulum Antiochenum celebratis in-
terfuerunt. Innumeris enim exemplis constat indubitatæ antiquitatis
Epistolas ex Scriptorum errore falsos titulos præferre."—(Pagi ad A.D. 264,
apud Mansi, *Concil.* i. 1039.)

[3] εἷς ἐστιν ὁ Χριστός, ὁ ὢν ἐν τῷ Πατρὶ συναΐδιος λόγος, ἐν αὐτοῦ
πρόσωπον, ἀόρατος Θεός, καὶ ὁρατὸς γενόμενος · ΘΕΟ῀Σ ΓΑ῀Ρ 'ΕΦΑΝΕΡΩ῀ΘΗ
'ΕΝ ΣΑΡΚΙ', γενόμενος ἐκ γυναικός, ὁ ἐκ Θεοῦ Πατρὸς γεννηθεὶς ἐκ γαστρὸς
πρὸ ἑωσφόρου.—*Concilia,* i. 853 a.

[4] Cap. xi.

though not in a way to be helpful to us in our present
enquiry. I cannot feel surprised at the circumstance.

The yet earlier references in the epistles of (1) Ignatius
(three in number) *are* helpful, and may not be overlooked.
They are as follows:—Θεοῦ ἀνθρωπίνως φανερουμένου :—ἐν
σαρκὶ γενόμενος Θεός:—εἷς Θεός ἐστιν ὁ φανερώσας ἑαυτὸν διὰ
Ἰησοῦ Χριστοῦ τοῦ υἱοῦ αὐτοῦ, ὅς ἐστιν αὐτοῦ Λόγος ἀΐδιος.[1]
It is to be wished, no doubt, that these references had been a
little more full and explicit : but the very early Fathers are
ever observed to quote Scripture thus partially,—allusively,
—elliptically.

(2) Barnabas has just such another allusive reference to
the words in dispute, which seems to show that he must have
read Θεὸς ἐφανερώθη ἐν σαρκί: viz. Ἰησοῦς .... ὁ υἱὸς τοῦ
Θεοῦ τύπῳ καὶ ἐν σαρκὶ φανερωθείς.[2]—(3) Hippolytus, on two
occasions, even more unequivocally refers to this reading.
Once, while engaged in proving that Christ is God, he
says:—Οὗτος προελθὼν εἰς κόσμον Θεὸς ἐν σώματι ἐφανερώθη :[3]—and again, in a very similar passage which Theodoret quotes from the same Father's lost work on the
Psalms:—Οὗτος ὁ προελθὼν εἰς τὸν κόσμον, Θεὸς καὶ ἄνθρωπος
ἐφανερώθη.[4]—(4) Gregory Thaumaturgus, (if it really be he,)
seems also to refer directly to this place when he says (in a
passage quoted by Photius[5]),—καὶ ἔστι Θεὸς ἀληθινὸς ὁ ἄσαρκος ἐν σαρκὶ φανερωθείς.—Further, (5) in the Apostolical
Constitutions, we meet with the expression,—Θεὸς Κύριος
ὁ ἐπιφανεὶς ἡμῖν ἐν σαρκί.[6]

---

[1] *Ad Ephes.* c. 19 : c. 7.   *Ad Magnes.* c. 8.   [2] Cap. xii.
[3] *Contra Hæresim Noeti*, c. xvii.   (Routh's *Opuscula*, i. 76.)   Read the
antecedent chapters.
[4] *Dialog.* ii. ' *Inconfusus.*'—*Opp.* iv. 132.
[5] Cod. 230,—p. 845, line 40.   [6] vii. 26, *ap. Galland.* iii. 182 a.

And when (6) BASIL THE GREAT [A.D. 377], writing to the
men of Sozopolis whose faith the Arians had assailed, remarks
that such teaching "subverts the saving Dispensation of our
LORD JESUS CHRIST;" and, blending Rom. xvi. 25, 26 with
"the great mystery" of 1 Tim. iii. 16,—(in order to afford
himself an opportunity of passing in review our SAVIOUR'S
work for His Church in ancient days,)—viz. "After all these,
at the end of the day, αὐτὸς ἐφανερώθη ἐν σαρκί, γενόμενος ἐκ
γυναικός:" [1]—who will deny that such an one probably found
neither ὅς nor ὅ, but Θεός, in the copy before him?

I have thought it due to the enquiry I have in hand to give
a distinct place to the foregoing evidence—such as it is—of
Ignatius, Barnabas, Hippolytus, Gregory Thaumaturgus, the
Apostolical Constitutions, and Basil. But I shall not *build*
upon such foundations. Let me go on with what is indisputable.

[k] *The testimony of* CYRIL OF ALEXANDRIA.

Next, for CYRIL OF ALEXANDRIA, whom you decline to
accept as a witness for Θεός. You are prepared, I trust, to
submit to the logic of *facts?*

In a treatise addressed to the Empresses Arcadia and
Marina, Cyril is undertaking to prove that our LORD is very
and eternal GOD.[2] His method is to establish several short
theses all tending to this one object, by citing from the
several books of the N. T., in turn, the principal texts which
make for his purpose. Presently, (viz. at page 117,) he
announces as his thesis, — "*Faith in* CHRIST *as* GOD;"
and when he comes to 1 Timothy, *he quotes* iii. 16 *at length;*

---

[1] iii. 401-2, *Epist.* 261 (=65). A quotation from Gal. iv. 4 follows.
[2] μαθήσεται γὰρ ὅτι φύσει μὲν καὶ ἀληθείᾳ Θεός ἐστιν ὁ Ἐμμανουήλ,
Θεοτόκος δὲ δι᾽ αὐτὸν καὶ ἡ τεκοῦσα παρθένος.—Vol. v. Part ii. 48 e.

reasons upon it, and points out that Θεὸς ἐν σαρκί is here
spoken of.[1] There can be no doubt about this quotation,
which exhibits no essential variety of reading;—a quotation
which Euthymius Zigabenus reproduces in his ' Panoplia,'—
and which C. F. Matthæi has with painful accuracy edited
from that source.[2]—Once more.   In a newly recovered treatise of Cyril, 1 Tim. iii. 16 is again *quoted at length with*
Θεός,—followed by the remark that " our Nature was justified, by God *manifested in Him*." [3]   I really see not how you
would have Cyril more distinctly recognize Θεὸς ἐφανερώθη
ἐν σαρκί as the reading of 1 Tim. iii. 16.[4]

You are requested to observe that in order to prevent cavil, I
forbear to build on two other famous places in Cyril's writings
where the evidence for reading Θεός is about balanced by a
corresponding amount of evidence which has been discovered
for reading ὅς.   Not but what the *context* renders it plain
that Θεός must have been Cyril's word on both occasions.
Of this let the reader himself be judge :—

(1) In a treatise, addressed to the Empresses Eudocia and
Pulcheria, Cyril quotes 1 Tim. iii. 16 *in extenso*.[5]   "If" (he
begins)—"the Word, being God, could be said to inhabit

---

[1] καὶ οὔτι που φαμὲν ὅτι καθ' ἡμᾶς ἄνθρωπος ἁπλῶς, ἀλλ' ὡς Θεὸς
ἐν σαρκὶ καὶ καθ' ἡμᾶς γεγονώς.—*Opp.* V. Part 2, p. 124 c d. (= *Concilia*,
iii. 221 c d.)

[2] N. T. vol. xi.   *Præfat.* p. xli.

[3] διὰ τοῦ ἐν αὐτῷ φανερωθέντος Θεοῦ.—*De Incarnatione Domini*, Mai,
Nov. PP. Bibliotheca, ii. 68.

[4] Earlier in the same Treatise, Cyril thus grandly paraphrases 1 Tim.
iii. 16:—τότε δὴ τότε τὸ μέγα καὶ ἄρρητον γίνεται τῆς οἰκονομίας μυστή-
ριον· αὐτὸς γὰρ ὁ Λόγος τοῦ Θεοῦ, ὁ δημιουργὸς ἁπάσης τῆς κτίσεως, ὁ
ἀχώρητος, ὁ ἀπερίγραπτος, ὁ ἀναλλοίωτος, ἡ πηγὴ τῆς ζωῆς, τὸ ἐκ τοῦ
φωτὸς φῶς, ἡ ζῶσα τοῦ Πατρὸς εἰκών, τὸ ἀπαύγασμα τῆς δόξης, ὁ χαρακ-
τὴρ τῆς ὑποστάσεως, τὴν ἀνθρωπείαν φύσιν ἀναλαμβάνει.—*Ibid.* p. 37.

[5] P. 153 d. (= *Concilia*, iii. 264 c d.)

Man's nature (ἐπανθρωπῆσαι) without yet ceasing to be GOD, but remained for ever what He was before,—then, great indeed is the mystery of Godliness." [1] He proceeds in the same strain at much length. [2] Next (2) the same place of Timothy is just as fully quoted in Cyril's *Explanatio xii. capitum*: where not only the Thesis, [3] but also the context constrains belief that Cyril wrote Θεός :—"What then means 'was manifested in the flesh'? It means that the Word of GOD the FATHER was made flesh ... In this way therefore we say that He was both GOD and Man .. Thus" (Cyril concludes) "is He GOD and LORD of all." [4]

But, as aforesaid, I do not propose to rest my case on either of these passages; but on those two other places concerning which there exists no variety of tradition as to the reading. Whether the passages in which the reading is *certain* ought not to be held to determine the reading of the passages concerning which the evidence is about evenly balanced;—whether in doubtful cases, the requirements of the context should not be allowed to turn the scale;—I forbear to enquire. I take my stand on what is clear and undeniable. On the other hand you are challenged to produce a single instance in Cyril of μυστήριον· ὃς ἐφανερώθη, where the reading is not equally

---

[1] *Ibid.* d e.

[2] εἰ μὲν γὰρ ὡς ἕνα τῶν καθ' ἡμᾶς, ἄνθρωπον ἁπλῶς, καὶ οὐχὶ δὴ μᾶλλον Θεὸν ἐνηνθρωπηκότα διεκήρυξαν οἱ μαθηταί κ.τ.λ. Presently,—μέγα γὰρ τότε τὸ τῆς εὐσεβείας ἐστὶ μυστήριον, πεφανέρωται γὰρ ἐν σαρκὶ Θεὸς ὢν ὁ Λόγος. p. 154 a b c.—In a subsequent page,—ὅ γε μὴν ἐνανθρωπήσας Θεός, καίτοι νομισθεὶς οὐδὲν ἕτερον εἶναι πλὴν ὅτι μόνον ἄνθρωπος ... ἐκηρύχθη ἐν ἔθνεσιν, ἐπιστεύθη ἐν κόσμῳ, τετίμηται δὲ καὶ ὡς Υἱὸς ἀληθῶς τοῦ Θεοῦ καὶ Πατρός ... Θεὸς εἶναι πεπιστευμένος.—*Ibid.* p. 170 d e.

[3] Ἀναθεματισμὸς β'.—Εἴ τις οὐχ ὁμολογεῖ σαρκὶ καθ' ὑπόστασιν ἡνῶσθαι τὸν ἐκ Θεοῦ Πατρὸς Λόγον, ἕνα τε εἶναι Χριστὸν μετὰ τῆς ἰδίας σαρκός, τὸν αὐτὸν δηλονότι Θεόν τε ὁμοῦ καὶ ἄνθρωπον, ἀνάθεμα ἔστω.—vi. 148 a.

[4] *Ibid.* b, c, down to 149 a. (= *Concilia*, iii. 815 b-e.)

balanced by μυστήριον· Θεός. And (as already explained) of
course it makes nothing for ὅς that Cyril should sometimes
say that 'the mystery' here spoken of is CHRIST who 'was
manifested in the flesh,' &c. A man with nothing else but
the A. V. of the 'Textus Receptus' before him might equally
well say *that*. See above, pages 427–8.

Not unaware am I of a certain brief Scholium[1] which the
Critics freely allege in proof that Cyril wrote ὅς (not Θεός),
and which *as they quote it*, (viz. so mutilated as effectually to
conceal its meaning,) certainly seems to be express in its testimony. But the thing is all a mistake. Rightly understood,
the Scholium in question renders no testimony at all ;—as I
proceed to explain. The only wonder is that such critics as
Bentley,[2] Wetstein,[3] Birch,[4] Tischendorf,[5] or even Tregelles,[6]
should not have seen this for themselves.

The author, (whether Photius, or some other,) is insisting
on our LORD's absolute exemption from sin, although for our
sakes He became very Man. In support of this, he quotes
Is. liii. 9, (or rather, 1 Pet. ii. 22)—"*Who did no sin, neither
was guile found in His mouth.*" "S. Cyril" (he proceeds) "in
the 12th ch. of his Scholia says,—'*Who was manifested in the
flesh, justified in the Spirit ;*' for He was in no way subject to
our infirmities," and so on. Now, every one must see at a glance
that it is entirely to misapprehend the matter to suppose
that it is any part of the Scholiast's object, in what precedes,
to invite attention to so irrelevant a circumstance as that
Cyril began his quotation of 1 Tim. iii. 16, with ὅς instead of

---

[1] Preserved by Œcumenius in his *Catena*, 1631, ii. 228.
[2] Ellis, p. 67.   [3] In loc.
[4] *Variæ Lect.* ii. 232. He enumerates ten MSS. in which he found it,
—but he only quotes down to ἐφανερώθη.
[5] In loc.   [6] P. 227 *note*.

Θεός.¹ As Waterland remarked to Berriman 150 years ago,²
the Scholiast's one object was to show how Cyril interpreted
the expression '*justified in the Spirit*.' Altogether misleading
is it to quote *only the first line*, beginning at ὅς and ending at
πνεύματι, as the Critics *invariably* do. The point to which in
this way prominence is exclusively given, was clearly, to the
Commentator, a matter of no concern at all. He quotes from
Cyril's '*Scholia de Incarnatione Unigeniti*,'³ in preference to any
other of Cyril's writings, for a vastly different reason.⁴ And
yet *this*—(viz. Cyril's supposed substitution of ὅς for Θεός)—
is, in the account of the Critics, the one thing which the
Scholiast was desirous of putting on record.

In the meanwhile, on referring to the place in Cyril, we
make an important discovery. The Greek of the Scholium
in question being lost, we depend for our knowledge of its
contents on the Latin translation of Marius Mercator, Cyril's
contemporary. And in that translation, no trace is discoverable of either ὅς or ὅ.⁵ The quotation from Timothy begins
abruptly at ἐφανερώθη. The Latin is as follows:—' Divinus
Paulus *magnum quidem* ait *esse mysterium pietatis*. Et vere ita
se res habet: *manifestatus est* enim *in carne*, cum sit DEUS
Verbum.' ⁶ The supposed hostile evidence from this quarter
proves therefore to be non-existent. I pass on.

---

¹ Pointed out long since by Matthæi, *N. T.* vol. xi. *Præfat.* p. xlviii.
Also in his ed. of 1807,—iii. 443-4. " Nec ideo laudatus est, ut doceret
Cyrillum loco θεός legisse ὅς, sed ideo, ne quis si Deum factum legeret
hominem, humanis peccatis etiam obnoxium esse crederet."

² See Berriman's *Dissertation*, p. 189.—(MS. note of the Author.)

³ Not from the 2nd article of his *Explanatio xii. capitum*, as Tischendorf supposes.

⁴ See how P. E. Pusey characterizes the ' Scholia,' in his *Preface* to
vol. vi. of his edition,—pp. xii. xiii.

⁵ Cyril's Greek, (to judge from Mercator's Latin,) must have run somewhat as follows :—Ὁ θεσπέσιος Παῦλος ὁμολογουμένως μέγα φησὶν εἶναι τὸ
τῆς εὐσεβείας μυστήριον. Καὶ ὄντως οὕτως ἔχει· ἐφανερώθη γὰρ ἐν σαρκί,
Θεὸς ὢν ὁ Λόγος.

⁶ *Opp.* vol. v. P. i. p. 785 d.—The original scholium (of which the extant

[1] *The argument* e silentio *considered.*

The argument *e silentio,* — (of all arguments the most precarious,) — has not been neglected. — 'But we cannot stop here,' you say:[1] 'Wetstein observed long ago that Cyril does not produce this text when he does produce Rom. ix. 5 in answer to the allegation which he quotes from Julian that S. Paul never employed the word Θεός of our LORD.'[2] Well but, neither does Gregory of Nyssa produce this text when he is writing a Treatise expressly to prove the GODhead of the SON and of the HOLY GHOST. '*Grave est,*'—says Tischendorf.[3] No, not '*grave*' at all, I answer: but whether '*grave*' or not, that *Gregory of Nyssa* read Θεός in this place, is at least certain. As for Wetstein, you have been reminded already, that '*ubi de Divinitate* CHRISTI *agitur, ibi profecto sui dissimilior deprehenditur.*'[4] Examine the place in Cyril Alex. for yourself, reading steadily on from p. 327 a to p. 333 b. Better still, read— paying special attention to his Scriptural proofs—Cyril's two Treatises '*De rectâ Fide.*'[5] But in fact attend to the method of Athanasius, of Basil, or of whomsoever else you will;[6] and you will speedily convince yourself that the argument *e silentio* is next to valueless on occasions like the present.

Greek proves to be only a garbled fragment, [see Pusey's ed. vi. p. 520,]) abounds in expressions which imply, (if they do not require,) that Θεός went before: e. g. '*quasi Deus homo factus:*'—'*erant ergo gentes in mundo sine Deo, cum absque Christo essent:*'—'*Deus enim erat incarnatus:*'—'*in humanitate tamen Deus remansit: Deus enim Verbum, carne assumptâ, non deposuit quod erat; intelligitur tamen idem Deus simul et homo,*' &c.

[1] P. 67.   [2] *Opp.* vi. 327.   [3] ii. 852.

[4] Matthæi, N. T. xi. *Præfat.* pp. lii.-iii.

[5] Vol. V. P. ii. pp. 55-180.

[6] 'How is the Godhead of Christ proved?' (asks Ussher in his *Body of Divinity,* ed. 1653, p. 161). And he adduces out of the N. T. only Jo. i. 1, xx. 28; Rom. ix. 5; 1 Jo. v. 20.—He *had* quoted 1 Tim. iii. 16 in p. 160 (with Rom. ix. 5) to prove the union of the two natures.

Certain of the Critics have jumped to the conclusion that the other Cyril cannot have been acquainted with S. Mark xvi. 19 (and therefore with the 'last Twelve Verses' of his Gospel), because when, in his Catechetical Lectures, he comes to the ' Resurrection,' ' Ascension,' and ' Session at the Right Hand,' —he does not quote S. Mark xvi. 19. And yet,—(as it has been elsewhere[1] fully shown, and in fact the reason is assigned by Cyril himself,)—this is only because, on the previous day, being Sunday, Cyril of Jerusalem had enlarged upon the Scriptural evidence for those august verities, (viz. S. Mark xvi. 19,—S. Luke xxiv. 51,—Acts i. 9) ; and therefore was unwilling to say over again before the same auditory what he had so recently delivered.

But indeed,—(the remark is worth making in passing,)— many of our modern Critics seem to forget that the heretics with whom Athanasius, Basil, the Gregories, &c., were chiefly in conflict, did not by any means deny the Godhead of our LORD. Arians and Apolinarians alike admitted that CHRIST *was* GOD. This, in fact, has been pointed out already. Very differently indeed would the ancient Fathers have expressed themselves, could they have imagined the calamitous use which, at the end of 1500 years, perverse wits would make of their writings,—the astonishing inferences they would propose to extract from their very silence. I may not go further into the subject in this place.

[m] *The story about* MACEDONIUS. *His testimony.*

It follows to say a few words concerning MACEDONIUS II., patriarch of Constantinople [A.D. 496–511], of whom it has been absurdly declared that he 'was *the inventor* of the reading for which I contend. I pointed out on a former occasion

---

[1] Burgon's *Last Twelve Verses*, &c., p. 195 and note. See Canon Cook on this subject,—pp. 146–7.

that it would follow from that very circumstance, (as far as it is true,) that Macedonius "*is a witness for* Θεός—*perforce.*" [1]

Instead of either assenting to this, (which is surely a self-evident proposition !),—or else disproving it,—you are at the pains to furbish up afresh, as if it were a novelty, the stale and stupid figment propagated by Liberatus of Carthage, that Macedonius was expelled from his see by the Emperor Anastasius for falsifying 1 Timothy iii. 16. This exploded fable you preface by announcing it as "*a remarkable fact,*" that "it was the *distinct belief of Latin writers* as early as the VIth century that the reading of this passage had been corrupted by the Greeks." [2]   How you get your "remarkable fact," out of your premiss,—"the distinct belief of Latin writers," out of the indistinct rumour ['*dicitur*'] vouched for by a single individual,—I see not.   But let that pass.

"The story shows" (you proceed) "that the Latins in the sixth century believed ὅς to be the reading of the older Greek manuscripts, and regarded Θεός as a false reading made out of it." (p. 69.)—My lord Bishop, I venture to declare that the story shows nothing of the sort.   The Latins in the VIth (and *every other*) century believed that—*not* ὅς, but—ὅ, was the right reading of the Greek in this place.   Their belief on this subject however has nothing whatever to do with the story before us.   Liberatus was not the spokesman of "the Latins of the VIth," (or any other bygone) "century:" but (as Bp. Pearson points out) a singularly ill-informed Archdeacon of Carthage; who, had he taken ever so little pains with the subject, would have become aware that for no such reason as he assigns was Macedonius [A.D. 511] thrust out of his bishopric. If, however, there were at least thus much of truth in the story, —namely, that one of the charges brought against Macedonius

---

[1] *Suprà*, p. 102.   [2] Pp. 68-9.

was his having corrupted Scripture, and notably his having altered ὅς into Θεός in 1 Tim. iii. 16 ; — surely, the most obvious of all inferences would be, that Θεός *was found in copies of S. Paul's epistles put forth at Constantinople by archiepiscopal authority between* A.D. 496 *and* A.D. 511. To say the least,— Macedonius, by his writings or by his discourses, certainly by his influence, *must have shown himself favourable to* Θεός (*not* ὅς) *ἐφανερώθη*. Else, with what show of reason could the charge have been brought against him ? "I suppose" (says our learned Dr. John Mill) "that the fable before us arose out of the fact that Macedonius, on hearing that in several MSS. of the Constantinopolitan Church the text of 1 Tim. iii. 16 (which witnesses expressly to the Godhead of CHRIST) had been depraved, was careful that those copies should be corrected in conformity with the best exemplars." [1]

But, in fact, I suspect you completely misunderstand the whole matter. You speak of "*the* story." But pray,— *Which* "story" do you mean ? "The story" which Liberatus told in the VIth century ? or the ingenious gloss which Hincmar, Abp. of Rheims, put upon it in the IXth ? You *mention* the first,—you *reason from* the second. Either will suit me equally well. But—*una la volta, per carità!*

Hincmar, (whom the critics generally follow,) relates that Macedonius turned ΟϹ into ΘΕΟϹ (i.e. ΘϹ).[2] *If Macedonius did, he preferred* Θεός *to* ὅς. . . . But the story which Liberatus promulgated is quite different.[3] Let him be heard :—

"At this time, Macedonius, bp. of CP., is said to have been deposed by the emperor Anastasius on a charge of having falsified the Gospels, and notably that saying of the Apostle,

---

[1] *Proleg. in N. T.,*—§ 1013.   [2] *Opp.* (ed. 1645) ii. 447.
[3] *Concilia,* v. 772 a. I quote from Garnier's ed. of the *Breviarium,* reprinted by Gallandius, xii. 1532.

'*Quia apparuit in carne, justificatus est in spiritu.*' He was charged with having turned the Greek monosyllable OC (i.e. '*qui*'), by the change of a single letter (ω for O) into ωC : i.e. '*ut esset Deus apparuit per carnem.*'"

Now, that this is a very lame story, all must see. In reciting the passage in Latin, Liberatus himself exhibits neither '*qui*,' nor '*quod*,' nor '*Deus*,'—but '*QUIA apparuit in carne.*' (The translator of Origen, by the way, does the same thing.[1]) And yet, Liberatus straightway adds (as the effect of the change) '*ut esset Deus apparuit per carnem :*' as if that were possible, unless '*Deus*' stood in the text already! Quite plain in the meantime is it, that, according to Liberatus, ὡς was the word which Macedonius introduced into 1 Tim. iii. 16. And it is worth observing that the scribe who rendered into Greek Pope Martin I.'s fifth Letter (written on the occasion of the Lateran Council A.D. 649),—having to translate the Pope's quotation from the Vulgate ('*quod manifestatus est*,')—exhibits ὡς ἐφανερώθη in this place.[2]

High time it becomes that I should offer it as my opinion that those Critics are right (Cornelius à Lapide [1614] and Cotelerius [1681]) who, reasoning from what Liberatus actually says, shrewdly infer that there must have existed codices in the time of Macedonius which exhibited OC ΘΕΟC in this place ; and that *this* must be the reading to which Liberatus refers.[3] *Such codices exist still.* One, is preserved in the library of the Basilian monks at Crypta Ferrata,

---

[1] iv. 465 c.   [2] *Concilia*, vi. 28 e [= iii. 645 c (ed. Harduin)].

[3] "Ex sequentibus colligo quædam exemplaria tempore Anastasii et Macedonii habuisse ὃς Θεός ; ut, mutatione factâ ὃς in ὡς, intelligeretur *ut esset Deus.*" (Cotelerii, *Eccl. Gr. Mon.* iii. 663)—"Q. d. Ut hic homo, qui dicitur Jesus, esset et dici posset Deus," &c. (Cornelius, *in loc.* He declares absolutely "olim legerunt . . . . ὃς Θεός.")—All this was noticed long since by Berriman, pp. 243–4.

already spoken of at pp. 446-8 : another, is at Paris.   I call
them respectively ' Apost. 83 ' and ' Paul 282.' [1]   This is new.

Enough of all this however.   Too much in fact.   I must
hasten on.   The entire fable, by whomsoever fabricated, has
been treated with well-merited contempt by a succession of
learned men ever since the days of Bp. Pearson.[2]   And although
during the last century several writers of the unbelieving
school (chiefly Socinians[3]) revived and embellished the silly
story, in order if possible to get rid of a text which witnesses
inconveniently to the GODHEAD of CHRIST, one would have
hoped that, in these enlightened days, a Christian Bishop of
the same Church which the learned, pious, and judicious John
Berriman adorned a century and a-half ago, would have been
ashamed to rekindle the ancient strife and to swell the Soci-

---

[1] ' Apost. 83,' is '*Crypta-Ferrat.* A. β. iv.' described in the APPENDIX.
I owe the information to the learned librarian of Crypta Ferrata, the
Hieromonachus A. Rocchi.   It is a pleasure to transcribe the letter which
conveyed information which the writer knew would be acceptable to me :—
" Clīne Rīne Domine.   Quod erat in votis, plures loci illius Paulini non
modo in nostris codd. lectiones, sed et in his ipsis variationes, adsequutus
es.   Modo ego operi meo finem imponam, descriptis prope sexcentis et
quinquaginta quinque vel codicibus vel MSS.   Tres autem, quos primum
nunc notatos tibi exhibeo, pertinent ad Liturgicorum ordinem.   Jam
felici omine tuas prosequere elucubrationes, cautus tantum ne studio et
labore nimio valetudinem tuam defatiges.   Vale.   De Tusculano, xi. kal.
Maias, an. R. S. MDCCCLXXXIII.   ANTONIUS ROCCHI, Hieromonachus
Basilianus."

For ' Paul 282,' (a bilingual MS. at Paris, known as ' Arménien 9,') I
am indebted to the Abbé Martin, who describes it in his *Introduction
à la Critique Textuelle du N. T.*, 1883,—pp. 660-1.   See APPENDIX.

[2] Prebendary Scrivener (p. 555) ably closes the list.   Any one desirous
of mastering the entire literature of the subject should study the Rev. John
Berriman's interesting and exhaustive *Dissertation*,—pp. 229-263.

[3] The reader is invited to read what Berriman, (who was engaged on his
' *Dissertation* ' while Bp. Butler was writing the ' Advertisement ' prefixed
to his ' *Analogy* ' [1736],) has written on this part of the subject,—pp.
120-9, 173-198, 231-240, 259-60, 262, &c.

nian chorus. I shall be satisfied if I have at least convinced you that Macedonius is a witness for Θεός in 1 Tim. iii. 16.

[n] *The testimony of an* ANONYMOUS *writer* (A.D 430),—*of* EPIPHANIUS (A.D. 787),—*of* THEODORUS STUDITA (A.D. 795 ?),—*of* SCHOLIA,—*of* ŒCUMENIUS,—*of* THEOPHYLACT,—*of* EUTHYMIUS.

The evidence of an ANONYMOUS Author who has been mistaken for Athanasius,—you pass by in silence. That this writer lived in the days when the Nestorian Controversy was raging,—namely, in the first half of the Vth century,—is at all events evident. He is therefore at least as ancient a witness for the text of Scripture as codex A itself : and Θεὸς ἐφανερώθη is clearly what he found written in this place.[1] Why do you make such a fuss about Cod. A, and yet ignore this contemporary witness ? We do not know *who wrote* the Epistle in question,—true. Neither do we know who wrote Codex A. What *then ?*

Another eminent witness for Θεός, whom also you do not condescend to notice, is EPIPHANIUS, DEACON OF CATANA in Sicily, — who represented Thomas, Abp. of Sardinia, at the 2nd Nicene Council, A.D. 787. A long discourse of this Ecclesiastic may be seen in the Acts of the Council, translated into Latin,—which makes his testimony so striking. But in fact his words are express,[2] and the more valuable because they come from a region of Western Christendom from which textual utterances are rare.

A far more conspicuous writer of nearly the same date, THEODORUS STUDITA of CP, [A.D. 759–826,] is also a witness

---

[1] Apud Athanasium, *Opp.* ii. 33 ; and see Garnier's introductory Note.

[2] ' Audi Paulum magnâ voce clamantem : *Deus manifestatus est in carne* [down to] *assumptus est in gloriâ.* O magni doctoris affatum! *Deus,* inquit, *manifestatus est in carne,*' &c.—*Concilia,* vii. p. 618 c

for Θεός.[1] How does it happen, my lord Bishop, that you
contend so eagerly for the testimony of codices F and G,
which are but *one* IXth-century witness after all,—and yet
entirely disregard living utterances like these, of known
men,—who belonged to known places,—and wrote at a
known time? Is it because they witness unequivocally
against you?

Several ancient SCHOLIASTS, expressing themselves diversely, deserve enumeration here, who are all witnesses for
Θεός exclusively.[2] Lastly,—

ŒCUMENIUS[3] (A.D. 990),—THEOPHYLACT[4] (A.D. 1077),—
EUTHYMIUS[5] (A.D. 1116), — close this enumeration. They
are all three clear witnesses for reading not ὅς but Θεός.

[o] *The testimony of* ECCLESIASTICAL TRADITION.

Nothing has been hitherto said concerning the Ecclesiastical usage with respect to this place of Scripture. 1 Tim.
iii. 16 occurs in a lection consisting of nine verses (1 Tim.
iii. 13–iv. 5), which used to be publicly read in almost all
the Churches of Eastern Christendom on the Saturday before
Epiphany.[6] It was also read, in not a few Churches, on the
34th Saturday of the year.[7] Unfortunately, the book which

---

[1] Theodori Studitæ, *Epistt.* lib. ii. 36, and 156. (Sirmondi's *Opera
Varia*, vol. v. pp. 349 e and 498 b,—Venet. 1728.)

[2] Paul 113, (Matthæi's a) contains two Scholia which witness to Θεὸς
ἐφανερώθη :—Paul 115, (Matthæi's d) also contains two Scholia.—Paul
118, (Matthæi's h).—Paul 123, (Matthæi's n). See Matthæi's N. T.
vol. xi. *Præfat.* pp. xlii.–iii.   [3] ii. 228 a.   [4] ii. 569 e : 570 a.

[5] *Panoplia*,—Tergobyst, 1710, fol. ρκγ´. p. 2, col. 1.

[6] Σαββάτῳ πρὸ τῶν φώτων.

[7] But in Apost. 12 (Reg. 375) it is the lection for the 30th (λ´) Saturday.—In Apost. 33 (Reg. 382), for the 31st (λα´).—In Apost. 26 (Reg.
320), the lection for the 34th Saturday begins at 1 Tim. vi. 11.—Apostt.
26 and 27 (Regg. 320–1) are said to have a peculiar order of lessons.

contains lections from S. Paul's Epistles, ('*Apostolus*' it is technically called,) is of comparatively rare occurrence,—is often found in a mutilated condition,—and (for this and other reasons) is, as often as not, without this particular lesson.[1] Thus, an analysis of 90 copies of the 'Apostolus' (No. 1 to 90), is attended by the following result:—10 are found to have been set down in error;[2] while 41 are declared—(sometimes, I fear, through the unskilfulness of those who profess to have examined them),—not to contain 1 Tim. iii. 16.[3] Of 7, I have not been able to obtain tidings.[4] Thus, there are but 32 copies of the book called 'Apostolus' available for our present purpose.

But of these thirty-two, *twenty-seven* exhibit Θεός.[5] You will be interested to hear that *one* rejoices in the unique

---

[1] For convenience, many codices are reckoned under this head (viz. of 'Apostolus') which are rather 'Απόστολο-εὐαγγέλια. Many again which are but fragmentary, or contain only a very few lessons from the Epistles : such are Apostt. 97 to 103. See the APPENDIX.

[2] No. 21, 28, 31 are said to be Gospel lessons ('Evstt.'). No. 29, 35 and 36 are Euchologia; "the two latter probably Melchite, for the codices exhibit some Arabic words" (Abbé Martin). No. 43 and 48 must be erased. No. 70 and 81 are identical with 52 (B. M. *Addit.* 32051).

[3] Viz. Apost. 1: 3: 6: 9 & 10 (which are Menologies with a few Gospel lections): 15: 16: 17: 19: 20: 24: 26: 27: 32: 37: 39: 44: 47: 50: 53: 55: 56: 59: 60: 61: 63: 64: 66: 67: 68: 71: 72: 73: 75: 76: 78: 79: 80: 87: 88: 90.

[4] Viz. Apost. 4 at Florence: 8 at Copenhagen: 40, 41, 42 at Rome: 54 at St. Petersburg: 74 in America.

[5] Viz. Apost. 2 and 52 (Addit. 32051) in the B. Mus., also 69 (Addit. 29714 verified by Dr. C. R. Gregory): 5 at Gottingen: 7 at the Propaganda (verified by Dr. Beyer): 11, 22, 23, 25, 30, 33 at Paris (verified by Abbé Martin): 13, 14, 18 at Moscow: 38, 49 in the Vatican (verified by Signor Cozza-Luzi): 45 at Glasgow (verified by Dr. Young): 46 at Milan (verified by Dr. Ceriani): 51 at Besançon (verified by M. Castan): 57 and 62 at Lambeth, also 65 B–C (all three verified by Scrivener): 58 at Ch. Ch., Oxford: 77 at Moscow: 82 at Messina (verified by Papas Matranga): 84 and 89 at Crypta Ferrata (verified by Hieromonachus Rocchi).

reading Θεοῦ :[1] while another Copy of the 'Apostolus' keeps
'Paul 282' in countenance by readi᷍ ͵ ὃς Θεός.[2] In other
words, 'GOD' is found in 29 copies out of 32: while 'who'
(ὅς) is observed to survive in only 3,—and they, Western
documents of suspicious character. Two of these were produced in one and the same Calabrian monastery; and they
still stand, side by side, in the library of Crypta Ferrata:[3]
being exclusively in sympathy with the very suspicious
Western document at Paris, already described at page 446.

ECCLESIASTICAL TRADITION is therefore clearly against you,
in respect of the reading of 1 Tim. iii. 16. How *you* estimate this head of Evidence, I know not. For my own part,
I hold it to be of superlative importance. It transports us
back, at once, to the primitive age; and is found to be
infinitely better deserving of attention than the witness of
any extant uncial documents which can be produced. And
why? For the plain reason that it must needs have been
once attested by *an indefinitely large number of codices more
ancient by far than any which we now possess.* In fact,
ECCLESIASTICAL TRADITION, when superadded to the testimony of Manuscripts and Fathers, becomes an overwhelming consideration.

And now we may at last proceed to sum up. Let me
gather out the result of the foregoing fifty pages; and remind

---

[1] Viz. Apost. 34 (Reg. 383), a XVth-century Codex. The Abbé Martin
assures me that this copy exhibits μυστήριον· | θὸ ἐφανερώθη. Note
however that the position of the point, as well as the accentuation, proves
that nothing else but θὶ̀ was intended. This is very instructive. What
if the same slip of the pen had been found in Cod. B?

[2] Viz. Apost. 83 (Crypta Ferrata, A. β. iv.)

[3] Viz. Praxapost. 85 and 86 (Crypta Ferrata, A. β. vii. which exhibits
μυστήριον· δσ ἐφα | νερώθη ἐν σαρκί· and A. β. viii., which exhibits μυστί-
ριον· δσ ἐ . . νερώθη | ἐν σαρκύ. [sic.]). Concerning these codices, see
above, pp. 446 to 448.

the reader briefly of the amount of external testimony producible in support of each of these rival readings :—ὅ,—ὅς,—
Θεός.

[I.] *Sum of the Evidence of* VERSIONS, COPIES, FATHERS, *in
favour of reading* μυστήριον · ὃ ἐφανερώθη *in* 1 Tim. iii. 16.

(*a*) The reading μυστήριον · ὃ ἐφανερώθη,—(which Wetstein strove hard to bring into favour, and which was highly
popular with the Socinian party down to the third quarter of
the last century,)—enjoys, as we have seen, (pp. 448–53,)
the weighty attestation of the Latin and of the Peschito,
—of the Coptic, of the Sahidic, and of the Æthiopic Versions.

No one may presume to speak slightingly of such evidence
as this. It is the oldest which can be produced for the
truth of anything in the inspired Text of the New Testament ; and it comes from the East as well as from the West.
Yet is it, in and by itself, clearly inadequate. Two characteristics of Truth are wanting to it,—two credentials,—
unfurnished with which, it cannot be so much as seriously
entertained. It demands *Variety* as well as *Largeness of
attestation.* It should be able to exhibit in support of its
claims the additional witness of COPIES and FATHERS. But,

(β) On the contrary, ὅ is found besides in *only one Greek
Manuscript,*—viz. the VIth-century codex Claromontanus, D.
And further,

(γ) *Two ancient writers* alone bear witness to this reading,
viz. GELASIUS OF CYZICUS,[1] whose date is A.D. 476 ;[2] and the
UNKNOWN AUTHOR of a homily of uncertain date in the

---

[1] *Concilia*, ii. 217 c (=ed. Hard. i. 418 b).

[2] He wrote a history of the Council of Nicæa, in which he introduces
the discussions of the several Bishops present,—all the product (as Cave
thinks) of his own brain.

Appendix to Chrysostom[1] .... It is scarcely intelligible
how, on such evidence, the Critics of the last century can
have persuaded themselves (with Grotius) that μυστήριον · ὃ
ἐφανερώθη is the true reading of 1 Timothy iii. 16. And yet,
in order to maintain this thesis, Sir Isaac Newton descended
from the starry sphere and tried his hand at Textual Criticism. Wetstein (1752) freely transferred the astronomer's
labours to his own pages, and thus gave renewed currency to
an opinion which the labours of the learned Berriman (1741)
had already *demonstrated* to be untenable.

Whether THEODORE OF MOPSUESTIA (in his work ' *de Incarnatione*') wrote ὅς or ὅ, must remain uncertain till a sight has
been obtained of his Greek together with its context. I find
that he quotes 1 Tim iii. 16 at least three times :—[1] Of the
first place, there is only a Latin translation, which begins
' QUOD *justificat*US *est in spiritu.*'[2]—[2] The second place
comes to us in Latin, Greek, and Syriac : but unsatisfac-
torily in all three :—(a) The Latin version introduces the
quotation thus,—' Consonantia et Apostolus dicit, *Et mani-
feste magnum est pietatis mysterium,* QUI[3] (or QUOD[4]) *manifestat*US (or TUM) *est in carne, justificat*US (or TUM) *est
in spiritu :*'— (b) The Greek, (for which we are indebted
to Leontius Byzantinus, A.D. 610,) reads, —Ὃς ἐφανερώθη ἐν σαρκί, ἐδικαιώθη ἐν πνεύματι[5]—divested of all

---

[1] viii. 214 b.

[2] Cited at the Council of CP. (A.D. 553). [*Concilia*, ed. Labbe et
Cossart, v. 447 b c=ed. Harduin, iii. 29 c and 82 e.]

[3] *Concilia*, Labbe, v. 449 a, and Harduin, iii. 84 d.   [4] Harduin, iii. 32 d.

[5] A Latin translation of the work of Leontius (*Contra Nestor. et
Eutych.*), wherein it is stated that the present place was found in *lib.* xiii.,
may be seen in Gallandius [xii. 660–99 : the passage under consideration
being given at p. 694 c d] : but Mai [*Script. Vett.* vi. 290–312], having
discovered in the Vatican the original text of the excerpts from Theod.
Mops., published (from the xiith book of Theod. *de Incarnatione*) the
Greek of the passage [vi. 308]. From this source, Migne [*Patr. Gr.* vol.
66, col. 988] seems to have obtained his quotation.

preface.[1] Those seven words, thus isolated from their context, are accordingly printed by Migne as *a heading* only:—
(c) The Syriac translation unmistakably reads, 'Et Apostolus dixit, *Vere sublime est hoc mysterium*, QUOD,'—omitting τῆς εὐσεβείας.[2]—[3] The third quotation, which is found only in Syriac,[3] begins,—'*For truly great is the-mystery of-the-fear-of* GOD, *who was manifested in-the-flesh and-was-justified in-the-spirit.*' This differs from the received text of the Peschito by substituting a different word for εὐσέβεια, and by employing the emphatic state 'the-flesh,' 'the-spirit' where the Peschito has the absolute state 'flesh,' 'spirit.' The two later clauses agree with the Harkleian or Philoxenian.[4]—I find it difficult from all this to know what precisely to do with Theodore's evidence. It has a truly oracular ambiguity; wavering between ὅ—ὅς—and even Θεός. You, I observe, (who are only acquainted with the second of the three places above cited, and but imperfectly with *that*,) do not hesitate to cut the knot by simply claiming the heretic's authority for the reading you advocate,—viz. ὅς. I have thought it due to my readers to tell

---

[1] Either as given by Mai, or as represented in the Latin translation of Leontius (obtained from a different codex) by Canisius [*Antiquæ Lectt.*, 1601, vol. iv.], from whose work Gallandius simply reprinted it in 1788.

[2] *Theodori Mops. Fragmenta Syriaca, vertit* Ed. Sachau, Lips. 1869, —p. 53.—I am indebted for much zealous help in respect of these Syriac quotations to the Rev. Thomas Randell of Oxford,—who, I venture to predict, will some day make his mark in these studies.

[3] *Ibid.* p. 64. The context of the place (which is derived from Lagarde's *Analecta Syriaca*, p. 102, top,) is as follows: "Deitas enim inhabitans hæc omnia gubernare incepit. Et in hac re etiam gratia Spiritus Sancti adjuvabat ad hunc effectum, ut beatus quoque Apostolus dixit: '*Vere grande . . . in spiritu;*' quoniam nos quoque auxilium Spiritûs accepturi sumus ad perfectionem justitiæ." A further reference to 1 Tim. iii. 16 at page 69, does not help us.

[4] I owe this, and more help than I can express in a foot-note, to my learned friend the Rev. Henry Deane, of S. John's.

2 I

them all that is known about the evidence furnished by Theodore of Mopsuestia. At all events, the utmost which can be advanced in favour of reading μυστήριον· ὅ in 1 Timothy iii. 16, has now been freely stated. I am therefore at liberty to pass on to the next opinion.

[II.] *Sum of the Evidence of* VERSIONS, COPIES, FATHERS *in favour of reading* μυστήριον· ὃς ἐφανερώθη *in* 1 Timothy iii. 16.

Remarkable it is how completely Griesbach succeeded in diverting the current of opinion with respect to the place before us, into a new channel. At first indeed (viz. in 1777) he retained Θεός in his Text, timidly printing ὅς in small type above it ; and remarking,—'*Judicium de hâc lectionis varietate lectoribus liberum relinquere placuit.*' But, at the end of thirty years (viz. in 1806), waxing bolder, Griesbach substituted ὃς for Θεός,—'*ut ipsi*' (as he says) '*nobis constaremus.*' Lachmann, Tischendorf, Tregelles, Westcott and Hort, and the Revisers, under your guidance, have followed him : which is to me unaccountable,—seeing that even less authority is producible for ὅς, than for ὅ, in this place. But let the evidence for μυστήριον· ὃς ἐφανερώθη ἐν σαρκί be briefly recapitulated :—

(*a*) It consists of *a single uncial copy*, viz. the corrupt cod. א,—(for, as was fully explained above,[1] codd. C and F-G yield uncertain testimony) : and *perhaps two cursive copies*, viz. Paul 17, (the notorious " 33 " of the Gospels,)—and a copy at Upsala (No. 73), which is held to require further verification.[2] To these, are to be added three other liturgical witnesses in the cursive character—being Western copies of the book called '*Apostolus*,' which have only recently come to

---

[1] Pages 437-43   [2] See above, p. 444.

light. Two of the codices in question are of Calabrian origin.[1] A few words more on this subject will be found above, at pages 477 and 478.

(β) *The only Version* which certainly witnesses in favour of ὅς, is the Gothic: which, (as explained at pp. 452–3) exhibits a hopelessly obscure construction, and rests on the evidence of a single copy in the Ambrosian library.

(γ) Of Patristic testimonies (to μυστήριον · ὃς ἐφανερώθη) *there exists not one.* That EPIPHANIUS [A.D. 360] *professing to transcribe* from an early treatise of his own, in which ἐφανερώθη stands *without a nominative*, should prefix ὅς— proves nothing, as I have fully explained elsewhere.[2]—The equivocal testimony rendered by THEODORE OF MOPSUESTIA [A.D. 390] is already before the reader.[3]

And this exhausts the evidence for a reading which came in,—and (I venture to predict) will go out,—with the present century. My only wonder is, how an exhibition of 1 Tim. iii. 16 so feebly attested,—so almost *without* attestation,—can have come to be seriously entertained by any. " Si,"—(as Griesbach remarks concerning 1 John v. 7)—" si tam pauci .... testes .... sufficerent ad demonstrandam lectionis cujusdam γνησιότητα, licet obstent tam multa tamque gravia et testimonia et argumenta; *nullum prorsus superesset in re criticâ veri falsique criterium, et textus Novi Testamenti universus plane incertus esset atque dubius.*"[4]

Yet *this* is the Reading which you, my lord Bishop, not only stiffly maintain, but which you insist is no longer so

---

[1] See above, pp. 446–8; also the *Appendix.*   [2] See pp. 426–8.
[3] See pp. 480–2.   [4] N. T. 1806 ii. *ad calcem*, p. [25].

much as "*open to reconsideration.*" You are, it seems, for
introducing the *clôture* into Textual debate. But in fact you
are for inflicting pains and penalties as well, on those who
have the misfortune to differ in opinion from yourself. You
discharge all the vials of the united sees of Gloucester and
Bristol on *me* for my presumption in daring to challenge the
verdict of "the Textual Criticism of the last fifty years,"—of
the Revisers,—and of yourself;—my folly, in venturing to
believe that the traditional reading of 1 Tim. iii. 16, (which
you admit is at least 1530 years old,) is the right reading
after all. You hold me up to public indignation. "He has
made" (you say) "an elaborate effort to shake conclusions
about which no professed Scholar has any doubt whatever; but
which an ordinary reader (and to such we address ourselves)
might regard as *still open to reconsideration.*"—"Moreover"
(you proceed) "this case is of great importance as an
example. It illustrates in a striking manner the complete
isolation of the Reviewer's position. If he is right, all other
Critics are wrong." [1]

Will you permit me, my lord Bishop, as an ordinary
writer, addressing (like yourself) "ordinary readers,"—respectfully to point out that you entirely mistake the problem in hand? The Greek Text of the N. T. is not to be
settled by MODERN OPINION, but by ANCIENT AUTHORITY.[2]
In this department of enquiry therefore, "*complete isolation*"
is his, and *his only*, who is forsaken by COPIES, VERSIONS,
FATHERS. The man who is able, on the contrary, to point to
an overwhelming company of Ancient Witnesses, and is
contented modestly to take up his station at their feet,—
such an one can afford to disregard "*The Textual Criticism
of the last fifty years,*" if it presumes to contradict *their* plain

---

[1] Page 76.   [2] See above, pp. 376–8.

decrees; can even afford to smile at the confidence of "professed Scholars" and "Critics," if they are so ill advised as to set themselves in battle array against that host of ancient men.

To say therefore of such an one, (as *you* now say of *me,*) "If he is right, all other Critics are wrong,"—is to present an irrelevant issue, and to perplex a plain question. The business of Textual Criticism (as you state at page 28 of your pamphlet) is nothing else but to ascertain "*the consentient testimony of the most ancient Authorities.*" The office of the Textual Critic is none other but to interpret rightly *the solemn verdict of Antiquity.* Do *I* then interpret that verdict rightly,—or do I not? The whole question resolves itself into *that!* If I do *not,*—pray show me wherein I have mistaken the facts of the case. But if I *do,*—why do you not come over instantly to my side? "*Since* he is right," (I shall expect to hear you say,) "it stands to reason that the 'professed Critics' whom he has been combating,—myself among the number,—must be wrong." .... I am, you see, loyally accepting the logical issue you have yourself raised. I do but seek to reconcile your dilemma with the actual facts of the problem.

And now, will you listen while I state the grounds on which I am convinced that your substitution of ὅς for Θεός in 1 Tim. iii. 16 is nothing else but a calamitous perversion of the Truth? May I be allowed at least to exhibit, in the same summary way as before, the evidence for reading in this place neither ὅ nor ὅς,—but Θεός?

[III.] *Sum of the Evidence of* Versions, Copies, Fathers, *in favour of reading* Θεὸς ἐφανερώθη *in* 1 Tim. iii. 16.

Entirely different,—in respect of variety, of quantity and

of quality,—from what has gone before, is the witness of Antiquity to the Received Text of 1 Timothy iii. 16 : viz. καὶ ὁμολογουμένως μέγα ἐστὶ τὸ τῆς εὐσεβείας μυστήριον· Θεὸς ἐφανερώθη ἐν σαρκί, κ.τ.λ. . . . . I proceed to rehearse it in outline, having already dwelt in detail upon so much of it as has been made the subject of controversy.[1] The reader is fully aware[2] that I do not propose to make argumentative use of the first six names in the ensuing enumeration. To those names, [enclosed within square brackets,] I forbear even to assign numbers ; not as entertaining doubt concerning the testimony they furnish, but as resolved to build exclusively on facts which are incontrovertible. Yet is it but reasonable that the whole of the Evidence for Θεὸς ἐφανερώθη should be placed before the reader : and *he* is in my judgment a wondrous unfair disputant who can attentively survey the evidence which I thus forego, without secretly acknowledging that its combined Weight is considerable ; while its Antiquity makes it a serious question whether it is not simply contrary to reason that it should be dispensed with in an enquiry like the present.

[(*a*) In the Ist century then,—it has been already shown (at page 463) that IGNATIUS (A.D. 90) probably recognized the reading before us in three places.]

[(*b*) The brief but significant testimony of BARNABAS will be found in the same page.]

[(*c*) In the IInd century,—HIPPOLYTUS [A.D. 190] (as was explained at page 463,) twice comes forward as a witness on the same side.]

[(*d*) In the IIIrd century,—GREGORY THAUMATURGUS, (if

---

[1] Viz. from p. 431 to p. 478.   [2] See above, pp. 462-4.

it be indeed he) has been already shown (at page 463) probably to testify to the reading Θεὸς ἐφανερώθη.]

[(e) To the same century is referred the work entitled
CONSTITUTIONES APOSTOLICÆ: which seems also to witness to
the same reading. See above, p. 463.]

[(f) BASIL THE GREAT also [A.D. 355], as will be found
explained at page 464, must be held to witness to Θεὸς
ἐφανερώθη in 1 Tim. iii. 16: though his testimony, like that
of the five names which go before, being open to cavil, is not
here insisted on.]—And now to get upon *terra firma*.

(1) To the IIIrd century then [A.D. 264 ?], belongs the
Epistle ascribed to DIONYSIUS OF ALEXANDRIA, (spoken of
above, at pages 461-2,) in which 1 Tim. iii. 16 is distinctly
quoted in the same way.

(2) In the next, (the IVth) century, unequivocal Patristic
witnesses to Θεὸς ἐφανερώθη abound. Foremost is DIDYMUS,
who presided over the Catechetical School of Alexandria,—
the teacher of Jerome and Rufinus. Born A.D. 309, and
becoming early famous, he clearly witnesses to what was the
reading of the first quarter of the IVth century. His testimony has been set forth at page 456.

(3) GREGORY, BISHOP OF NAZIANZUS [A.D. 355], a contemporary of Basil, in *two* places is found to bear similar
witness. See above page 457.

(4) DIODORUS, (or 'Theodorus' as Photius writes his
name,) the teacher of Chrysostom,—first of Antioch, afterwards the heretical BISHOP OF TARSUS in Cilicia,—is next to
be cited [A.D. 370]. His testimony is given above at pages
458-9.

(5) The next is perhaps our most illustrious witness,—viz. GREGORY, BISHOP OF NYSSA in Cappadocia [A.D. 370]. References to at least *twenty-two* places of his writings have been already given at page 456.

(6) Scarcely less important than the last-named Father, is CHRYSOSTOM [A.D. 380], first of· Antioch,—afterwards PATRIARCH OF CONSTANTINOPLE,—who in *three* places witnesses plainly to Θεὸς ἐφανερώθη. See above, page 457.

(7) And to this century, (not later certainly than the last half of it,) is to be referred the title of that κεφάλαιον, or chapter, of St. Paul's First Epistle to Timothy which contains chap. iii. 16,—(indeed, which *begins* with it,) viz. Περὶ θείας σαρκώσεως. Very eloquently does that title witness to the fact that Θεός was the established reading of the place under discussion, before either cod. B or cod. ℵ was produced. See above, pages 457–8.

(8) In the Vth century,—besides the CODEX ALEXANDRINUS (cod. A,) concerning which so much has been said already (page 431 to page 437),—we are able to appeal for the reading Θεὸς ἐφανερώθη, to,

(9) CYRIL, ARCHBISHOP OF ALEXANDRIA, [A.D. 410,] who in *at least two* places witnesses to it unequivocally. See above, pp. 464 to 470. So does,

(10) THEODORET, BISHOP OF CYRUS in Syria, [A.D. 420]: who, in at least *four* places, (see above, page 456) renders unequivocal and important witness on the same side.

(11) Next, the ANONYMOUS AUTHOR claims notice [A.D. 430], whose composition is found in the Appendix to the works of Athanasius. See above, page 475.

(12) You will be anxious to see your friend EUTHALIUS, BISHOP OF SULCA, duly recognized in this enumeration. He comes next. [A.D. 458.] The discussion concerning him will be found above, at page 459 to page 461.

(13) MACEDONIUS II., PATRIARCH OF CP. [A.D. 496] must of necessity be mentioned here, as I have very fully explained at page 470 to page 474.

(14) To the VIth century belongs the GEORGIAN Version, as already noted at page 454.

(15) And hither is to be referred the testimony of SEVERUS, BISHOP OF ANTIOCH [A.D. 512], which has been already particularly set down at page 458.

(16) To the VIIth century [A.D. 616] belongs the HARK-LEIAN (or PHILOXENIAN) Version; concerning which, see above, page 450.   "That Θεός was the reading of the manuscripts from which this Version was made, is put beyond reach of doubt by the fact that in twelve of the other places where εὐσέβεια occurs,[1] the words ‮ܩܘܝܡܐ ܕܕܚܠܬܐ‬ (' beauty-of-fear') are found *without* the addition of ‮ܐܠܗܐ‬ (' GOD'). It is noteworthy, that on the thirteenth occasion (1 Tim. ii. 2), where the Peschito reads '*fear of* GOD,' the Harkleian reads '*fear*' only.   On the other hand, the Harkleian margin of Acts iii. 12 expressly states that εὐσέβεια is the Greek equivalent of ‮ܩܘܝܡܐ ܕܕܚܠܬܐ‬ (' *beauty-of-fear* '). This effectually establishes the fact that the author of the Harkleian recension found Θεός in his Greek manuscript of 1 Tim. iii. 16." [2]

---

[1] Viz. Acts iii. 12; 1 Tim. iv. 7, 8; vi. 3, 5, 6; 2 Tim. iii. 5; Tit. i. 1; 2 Pet. i. 3, 6, 7; iii. 11.

[2] From the friend whose help is acknowledged at foot of pp. 450, 481.

(17) In the VIIIth century, JOHN DAMASCENE [A.D. 730] pre-eminently claims attention. He is *twice* a witness for Θεὸς ἐφανερώθη, as was explained at page 457.

(18) Next to be mentioned is EPIPHANIUS, DEACON OF CATANA; whose memorable testimony at the 2nd Nicene Council [A.D. 787] has been set down above, at page 475. And then,

(19) THEODORUS STUDITA of CP. [A.D. 790],—concerning whom, see above, at pages 475-6.

(20), (21) *and* (22). To the IXth century belong the three remaining uncial codices, which alike witness to Θεὸς ἐφανερώθη ἐν σαρκί:—viz. the 'COD. MOSQUENSIS' (K); the 'COD. ANGELICUS' (L); and the 'COD. PORPHYRIANUS' (P).

(23) The SLAVONIC VERSION belongs to the same century, and exhibits the same reading.

(24) Hither also may be referred several ancient SCHOLIA which all witness to Θεὸς ἐφανερώθη ἐν σαρκί, as I explained at page 476.

(25) To the Xth century belongs ŒCUMENIUS [A.D. 990], who is also a witness on the same side. See page 476.

(26) To the XIth century, THEOPHYLACT [A.D. 1077], who bears express testimony to the same reading. See page 476.

(27) To the XIIth century, EUTHYMIUS [A.D. 1116], who closes the list with his approving verdict. See page 476.

And thus we reach a period when there awaits us a mass of testimony which transports us back (*per saltum*) to the Church's palmiest days; testimony, which rightly under-

stood, is absolutely decisive of the point now under discussion.   I allude to the testimony of EVERY KNOWN COPY OF
S. PAUL'S EPISTLES except the three, or four, already specified,
viz. D of S. Paul; ℵ, 17, and perhaps 73.   A few words on
this last head of Evidence may not be without the grace of
novelty even to yourself.   They are supplementary to what
has already been offered on the same subject from page 443
to page 446.

The copies of S. Paul's Epistles (in cursive writing)
supposed to exist in European libraries,—not including
those in the monasteries of Greece and the Levant,[1]—amount
to at least 302.[2]   Out of this number, 2 are fabulous :[3]—
1 has been destroyed by fire :[4]—and 6 have strayed into
unknown localities.[5]   Add, that 37 (for various reasons) are
said not to contain the verse in question ;[6] while of 2, I

---

[1] Scholz enumerates 8 of these copies: Coxe, 15. But there must
exist a vast many more ; as, at M. Athos, in the convent of S. Catharine,
at Meteora, &c., &c.

[2] In explanation of this statement, the reader is invited to refer to the
APPENDIX at the end of the present volume. [Since the foregoing words
have been in print 1 have obtained from Rome tidings of about 34 more
copies of S. Paul's Epistles ; raising the present total to 336.   The
known copies of the book called ' *Apostolus* ' now amount to 127.]

[3] Viz. Paul 61 (see Scrivener's *Introduction*, 3rd ed. p. 251): and
Paul 181 (see above, at pp. 444–5).

[4] Viz. Paul 248, at Strasburg.

[5] Viz. Paul 8 (see Scrivener's *Introduction*): 15 (which is not in
the University library at Louvain): 50 and 51 (in Scrivener's *Introduction*): 209 and 210 (which, I find on repeated enquiry, are no longer
preserved in the Collegio Romano ; nor, since the suppression of the
Jesuits, is any one able to tell what has become of them).

[6] Viz. Paul 42: 53: 54: 58 (*Vat.* 165,—from Sig. Cozza-Luzi): 60 :
64: 66: 76: 82: 89: 118: 119: 124: 127: 146: 147: 148: 152: 160 :
161: 162: 163: 172: 187: 191: 202: 214: 225 (*Milan* N. 272 *sup.*,
—from Dr. Ceriani): 259: 263: 271: 275: 284 (*Modena* II. A. 13,—from
Sig. Cappilli [Acts, 195—see *Appendix*]): 286 (*Milan* E. 2 *inf.*—from
Dr. Ceriani [*see Appendix*]): 287 (*Milan* A. 241 *inf.*—from Dr. Ceriani

have been hitherto unsuccessful in obtaining any account :[1]—
and it will be seen that the sum of the available cursive
copies of S. Paul's Epistles is exactly 254.

Now, that 2 of these 254 cursive copies (viz. Paul 17
and 73)—exhibit ὅς,—you have been so eager (at pp. 71–2 of
your pamphlet) to establish, that I am unwilling to do more
than refer you back to pages 443,–4,–5, where a few words
have been already offered in reply.   Permit me, however, to
submit to your consideration, as a set-off against those *two
copies* of S. Paul's Epistles which read ὅς,—the following
two-hundred and fifty-two copies which read Θεός.[2]   To speak

---

[see *Appendix*]) : 293 (*Crypta Ferrata*, A. β. vi.—from the Hieromonachus
A. Rocchi [see *Appendix*]) : 302 (*Berlin, MS. Græc.* 8vo. No. 9.—from
Dr. C. de Boor [see *Appendix*]).

[1] Viz. Paul 254 (restored to CP., see Scrivener's *Introduction*) :
and Paul 261 (Muralt's 8 : Petrop. xi. 1. 2. 330).

[2] I found the reading of 150 copies of S. Paul's Epistles at 1 Tim.
iii. 16, ascertained ready to my hand,—chiefly the result of the labours
of Mill, Kuster, Walker, Berriman, Birch, Matthæi, Scholz, Reiche,
and Scrivener.   The following 102 I am enabled to contribute to the
number,—thanks to the many friendly helpers whose names follow :—
In the VATICAN (Abbate Cozza-Luzi, keeper of the library, whose
friendly forwardness and enlightened zeal I cannot sufficiently acknowledge. See the *Appendix*) No. 185, 186, 196, 204, 207, 294, 295,
296, 297.—PROPAGANDA (Dr. Beyer) No. 92.—CRYPTA FERRATA (the
Hieromonachus A. Rocchi. See the *Appendix*,) No. 290, 291, 292.—
VENICE (Sig. Veludo) No. 215.—MILAN (Dr. Ceriani, the most learned
and helpful of friends,) No. 173, 174, 175, 176, 223, 288, 289.—FERRARA,
(Sig. Gennari) No. 222.—MODENA (Sig. Cappilli) No. 285.—BOLOGNA
(Sig. Gardiani) No. 105.—TURIN (Sig. Gorresio) No. 165, 168.—FLORENCE
(Dr. Anziani) No. 182, 226, 239.—MESSINA (Papas Filippo Matranga.
See the *Appendix*,) No. 216, 283.—PALERMO (Sig. Penerino) No. 217.—
The ESCURIAL (S. Herbert Capper, Esq., of the British Legation. He
executed a difficult task with rare ability, at the instance of his Excellency,
Sir Robert Morier, who is requested to accept this expression of my
thanks,) No. 228, 229.—PARIS (M. Wescher, who is as obliging as he is
learned in this department,) No. 16, 65, 136, 142, 150, 151, 154, 155, 156,
157, 164.—(L'Abbé Martin. See the *Appendix*) No. 282. ARSENAL

with perfect accuracy,—4 of these (252) exhibit ὁ Θεὸς ἐφανερώθη ;[1]—1, ὃς Θεός ;[2]—and 247, Θεός absolutely. The numbers follow :—

1.	2.	3.	4.	5.	6.	7.	9.	10.	11.	12.
13.	14.	16.	18.	19.	20.	21.	22.	23.	24.	25.
26.	27.	28.	29.	30.	31.	32.	33.	34.	35.	36.
37.	38.	39.	40.	41.	43.	44.	45.	46.	47.	48.
49.	52.	55.	56.	57.	59.	62.	63.	65.	67.	68.
69.	70.	71.	72.	74.	75.	77.	78.	79.	80.	81.
83.	84.	85.	86.	87.	88.	90.	91.	92.	93.	94.
95.	96.	97.	98.	99.	100.	101.	102.	103.	104.	105.
106.	107.	108.	109.	110.	111.	112.	113.	114.	115.	116.
117.	120.	121.	122.	123.	125.	126.	128.	129.	130.	131.
132.	133.	134.	135.	136.	137.	138.	139.	140.	141.	142.
143.	144.	145.	149.	150.	151.	153.	154.	155.	156.	157.
158.	159.	164.	165.	166.	167.	168.	169.	170.	171.	173.
174.	175.	176.	177.	178.	179.	180.	182.	183.	184.	185.
186.	188.	189.	190.	192.	193.	194.	195.	196.	197.	198.
199.	200.	201.	203.	204.	205.	206.	207.	208.	211.	212.

(M. Thierry) No. 130.—S. Genevieve (M. Denis) No. 247.—Poictiers (M. Dartige) No. 276.—Berlin (Dr. C. de Boor) No. 220, 298, 299, 300, 301.—Dresden (Dr. Forstemann) No. 237.—Munich (Dr. Laubmann) No. 55, 125, 126, 128.—Gottingen (Dr. Lagarde) No. 243.—Wolfenbuttel (Dr. von Heinemann) No. 74, 241.—Basle (Mons. Sieber) No. 7.—Upsala (Dr. Belsheim) No. 273, 274.—Lincoping (the same) No. 272.—Zurich (Dr. Escher) No. 56.—Prebendary Scrivener verified for me l'aul 252 : 253 : 255 : 256 : 257 : 258 : 260 : 264 : 265 : 277.—Rev. T. Randell, has verified No. 13.—Alex. Peckover, Esq., No. 278.—Personally, I have inspected No. 24 : 34 : 62 : 63 : 224 : 227 : 234 : 235 : 236 : 240 : 242 : 249 : 250 : 251 : 262 : 266 : 267 : 268 : 269 : 270 : 279 : 280 : 281.

[1] Viz. Paul 37 (the *Codex Leicest.*, 69 of the Gospels) :—Paul 85 (Vat. 1136), observed by Abbate Cozza-Luzi :—Paul 93 (Naples 1. b. 12) which is 83 of the Acts,—noticed by Birch :—Paul 175 (Ambros. f. 125 *sup.*) at Milan ; as I learn from Dr. Ceriani. See above, p. 456 *note* (¹).

[2] Viz. Paul 282,—concerning which, see above, p. 474, note (¹).

213. 215. 216. 217. 218.[1] 219. 220. 221. 222. 223. 224.
226. 227. 228. 229. 230. 231. 232. 233. 234. 235. 236.
237. 238. 239. 240. 241. 242. 243. 244. 245. 246. 247.
249. 250. 251. 252. 253. 255. 256. 257. 258. 260. 262.
264. 265. 266. 267. 268. 269. 270. 272. 273. 274. 276.
277. 278. 279. 280. 281. 282.[2] 283. 285. 288. 289. 290.
291. 292. 294. 295. 296. 297. 298. 299. 300. 301.

Behold then the provision which THE AUTHOR of Scripture has made for the effectual conservation in its integrity of this portion of His written Word! Upwards of eighteen hundred years have run their course since the HOLY GHOST by His servant, Paul, rehearsed the ' mystery of Godliness ;' declaring *this* to be the great foundation-fact,—namely, that ' GOD WAS MANIFESTED IN THE FLESH.' And lo, out of *two hundred and fifty-four* copies of S. Paul's Epistles no less than *two hundred and fifty-two* are discovered to have preserved that expression. Such 'Consent' amounts to *Unanimity;* and, (as I explained at pp. 454-5,) unanimity in this subject-matter, is conclusive.

The copies of which we speak, (you are requested to observe,) were produced in every part of ancient Christendom,—being derived in every instance from copies older than themselves; which again were transcripts of copies older still. They have since found their way, without design or contrivance, into the libraries of every country of Europe,—where, for hundreds of years they have been jealously guarded. And,—(I repeat the question already hazarded at pp. 445-6, and now respectfully propose it to *you,* my

---

[1] The present locality of this codex (Evan. 421 = Acts 176 = Paul 218) is unknown. The only Greek codices in the public library of the 'Seminario' at Syracuse are an ' Evst.' and an ' Apost.' (which I number respectively 362 and 113). My authority for θεός in Paul 218, is Birch [*Proleg.* p. xcviii.], to whom Munter communicated his collations.

[2] For the ensuing codices, see the APPENDIX.

lord Bishop; requesting you at your convenience to favour
me publicly with an answer;)—For what conceivable reason
can this multitude of witnesses be supposed to have entered
into a wicked conspiracy to deceive mankind ?

True, that no miracle has guarded the sacred Text in this,
or in any other place. On the other hand, for the last 150
years, Unbelief has been carping resolutely at this grand
proclamation of the Divinity of CHRIST,—in order to prove
that not this, but some other thing, it must have been,
which the Apostle wrote. And yet (as I have fully shown)
the result of all the evidence procurable is to establish that
the Apostle must be held to have written no other thing
but *this.*

To the overwhelming evidence thus furnished by 252 out
of 254 cursive *Copies* of S. Paul's Epistles,—is to be added
the evidence supplied by the *Lectionaries.* It has been already
explained (viz. at pp. 477–8) that out of 32 copies of the
'Apostolus,' 29 concur in witnessing to Θεός. I have just
(May 7th) heard of another in the Vatican.[1] To these 30,
should be added the 3 Liturgical codices referfed to at pp.
448 and 474, *note* (¹). Now this is emphatically the voice
of *ancient Ecclesiastical Tradition.* The numerical result of
our entire enquiry, proves therefore to be briefly this :—

(I.) In 1 TIMOTHY iii. 16, the reading Θεὸς ἐφανερώθη ἐν
σαρκί, is witnessed to by 289 MANUSCRIPTS :[2]—by 3 VER-
SIONS :[3]—by upwards of 20 Greek FATHERS.[4]

---

[1] Vat. 2068 (Basil. 107),—which I number 'Apost. 115' (see APPENDIX.)

[2] Viz. by 4 uncials (A, K, L, P), + (247 Paul + 31 Apost. =) 278 cursive
manuscripts reading Θεός : + 4 (Paul) reading ὁ Θεός : + 2 (1 Paul, 1 Apost.)
reading ὃς Θεός : + 1 (Apost.) reading θὺ = 289. (See above, pp. 473–4 : 478.)

[3] The Harkleian (see pp. 450, 489): the Georgian, and the Slavonic
(p. 454).

[4] See above, pp. 487–490,—which is the summary of what will be
found more largely delivered from page 455 to page 476.

(II.) The reading ὅ (in place of Θεός) is supported by a single MS. (D) :—by 5 ancient VERSIONS :[1]—by 2 late Greek FATHERS.[2]

(III.) The reading ὅς (also in place of Θεός) is countenanced by 6 MANUSCRIPTS in all (א, Paul 17, 73 : Apost. 12, 85, 86) :— by *only one* VERSION for certain (viz. the Gothic [3]) :—*not for certain by a single Greek* FATHER.[4]

I will not repeat the remarks I made before on a general survey of the evidence in favour of ὅς ἐφανερώθη: but I must request you to refer back to those remarks, now that we have reached the end of the entire discussion. They extend from the middle of p. 483 to the bottom of p. 485.

The unhappy Logic which, on a survey of what goes before, can first persuade itself, and then seek to persuade others, that Θεός is a "*plain and clear error;*" and that there is "*decidedly preponderating evidence,*" in favour of reading ὅς in 1 Timothy iii. 16 ;—must needs be of a sort with which I neither have, nor desire to have, any acquaintance. I commend the case between you and myself to the judgment of Mankind; and trust you are able to await the common verdict with the same serene confidence as I am.

Will you excuse me if I venture, in the homely vernacular, to assure you that in your present contention you ' have not a leg to stand upon ' ? "Moreover" (to quote from your own pamphlet [p. 76],) "*this case is of great importance as an example.*" You made deliberate choice of it in order to convict me of error. I have accepted your challenge, you see. Let the present, by all means, be regarded by the public as

---

[1] See above, pp. 448–453: also p. 479.   [2] See above, pp. 479–480.
[3] See above, pp. 452–3.   [4] See above, pp. 482, 483.

a trial-place,—a test of our respective methods, yours and mine. I cheerfully abide the issue.

(p) Internal evidence *for reading* Θεὸς ἐφανερώθη *in* 1 Tim. iii. 16, *absolutely overwhelming.*

In all that precedes, I have abstained from pleading the *probabilities* of the case; and for a sufficient reason. Men's notions of what is ' probable ' are observed to differ so seriously. ' Facile intelligitur ' (says Wetstein) ' lectiones ὅς et Θεός esse interpretamenta pronominis ὅ : sed nec ὅ nec ὅς posse esse interpretamentum vocis Θεός.' Now, I should have thought that the exact reverse is as clear as the day. *What* more obvious than that Θ͞C, by exhibiting indistinctly either of its delicate horizontal strokes, (and they were often so traced as to be scarcely discernible,[1]) would become mistaken for ΟC ? What more natural again than that the masculine relative should be forced into agreement with its neuter antecedent? Why, *the thing has actually happened* at Coloss. i. 27; where ΄ΟΣ ἐστι Χριστός has been altered into ὅ, only because μυστήριον is the antecedent. But waiving this, the internal evidence in favour of Θεός must surely be admitted to be overwhelming, by all save one determined that the reading *shall be* ὅς or ὅ. I trust we are at least agreed that the maxim '*proclivi lectioni præstat ardua,*' does not enunciate so foolish a proposition as that in choosing between two or more conflicting readings, we are to prefer *that* one which has the feeblest external attestation,—provided it be but in itself almost unintelligible ?

And yet, in the present instance,—How (give me leave to ask) will you translate ? To those who acquiesce in the

---

[1] See above, page 436, and middle of page 439.

notion that the μέγα μυστήριον τῆς εὐσεβείας means our
SAVIOUR CHRIST Himself, (consider Coloss. i. 27,) it is obvious
to translate 'who:' yet how harsh, or rather how intolerable
is this! I should have thought that there could be no real
doubt that 'the mystery' here spoken of must needs be
that complex exhibition of Divine condescension which
the Apostle proceeds to rehearse in outline: and of which
the essence is that it was very and eternal GOD who was the
subject of the transaction. Those who see this, and yet
adopt the reading ὅς, are obliged to refer it to the remote
antecedent Θεός. You do not advocate this view: neither
do I. For reasons of their own, Alford [1] and Lightfoot [2] both
translate 'who.'

Tregelles (who always shows to least advantage when a
point of taste or scholarship is under discussion) proposes to
render:—

" He who was manifested in the flesh, (he who) was justified
in the spirit, (he who) was seen by angels, (he who) was
preached among Gentiles, (he who) was believed on in the
world, (he who) was received up in glory."[3]

I question if his motion will find a seconder. You yourself lay it down magisterially that ὅς "is not emphatic (' He
who,' &c.): nor, by a constructio ad sensum, is it the relative
to μυστήριον; but is a relative to an omitted though
easily recognized antecedent, viz. CHRIST." You add that it
is not improbable "that the words are quoted from some
known hymn, or probably from some familiar Confession of
Faith." Accordingly, in your Commentary you venture to
exhibit the words within inverted commas as a quotation:—
" And confessedly great is the mystery of godliness: ' who

---

[1] See his long and singular note.   [2] Fresh Revision, p. 27.
[3] Printed Text, p. 231.

was manifested in the flesh, justified in the spirit,'" &c.,[1]—
for which you are without warrant of any kind, and which
you have no right to do.   Westcott and Hort (the 'chartered
libertines') are even more licentious.   Acting on their own
suggestion that these clauses are 'a quotation from *an early
Christian hymn,*' they proceed to print the conclusion of
1 Tim. iii. 16 stichometrically, as if it were a *six-line stanza.*

This notwithstanding, the Revising body *have adopted* 'He
who,' as the rendering of ὅς; a mistaken rendering as it
seems to me, and (I am glad to learn) to yourself also.
Their translation is quite a curiosity in its way.   I proceed
to transcribe it :—

"He who was manifested in the flesh, justified in the spirit,
seen of angels, preached among the nations, believed on in the
world, received up in glory."

But this does not even pretend to be a sentence : nor do I
understand what the proposed construction is.   Any arrangement which results in making the six clauses last quoted
part of the subject, and 'great' the predicate of one long
proposition,—is unworthy.—Bentley's wild remedy testifies
far more eloquently to his distress than to his aptitude for
revising the text of Scripture.   He suggests,—"Christ *was
put to death* in the flesh, justified in the spirit, ... seen *by
Apostles.*"[2]—"According to the ancient view," (says the Rev.
T. S. Green,) "the sense would be : 'and confessedly great
is the mystery of godliness [in the person of him], who
[mystery notwithstanding] was manifested in the flesh,
&c.'"[3] ....   But, with submission, "the ancient view" was
not this.   The Latins,—calamitously shut up within the

---

[1] P. 226.

[2] '*Forte* μυστήριον · ὁ χς ἐθανατώθη ἐν σαρκί . . . ἐν πνεύματι, ὤφθη
ἀποστόλοις.'—Bentleii *Critica Sacra,* p. 67.

[3] *Developed Criticism,* p. 160.

limits of their '*pietatis sacramentum, quod,*'—are found to
have habitually broken away from that iron bondage, and to
have discoursed of our SAVIOUR CHRIST, as being Himself the
'sacramentum' spoken of. The 'sacramentum,' in their
view, was the incarnate WORD.[1]—Not so the Greek Fathers.
These all, without exception, understood S. Paul to say,—
what Ecclesiastical Tradition hath all down the ages faithfully
attested, and what to this hour the copies of his Epistles
prove that he actually wrote,—viz. "*And confessedly great is
the mystery of godliness :*—GOD *was manifested in the flesh,
justified in the spirit,*" and so on. Moreover this is the view
of the matter in which all the learning and all the piety
of the English Church has thankfully acquiesced for the last
350 years. It has commended itself to Andrewes and
Pearson, Bull and Hammond, Hall and Stillingfleet, Ussher
and Beveridge, Mill and Bengel, Waterland and Berriman.
The enumeration of names is easily brought down to our
own times. Dr. Henderson, (the learned non-conformist
commentator,) in 1830 published a volume with the following title :—

'The great mystery of godliness incontrovertible: or, Sir
Isaac Newton and the Socinians foiled in the attempt to prove a
corruption in the text 1 Tim. iii. 16 : containing a review of the

---

[1] Thus Augustine (viii. 828 f.) paraphrases,—'*In carne manifestatus
est* FILIUS DEI.'—And Marius Victorinus, A.D. 390 (ap. Galland. viii.
161),—'*Hoc enim est magnum sacramentum, quod* DEUS *exanimavit semet
ipsum cum esset in* DEI *formâ:*' '*fuit ergo antequam esset in carne, sed
manifestatum dixit in carne.*'—And Fulgentius, A.D. 513, thus expands
the text (ap. Galland. xi. 232) :—'*quia scilicet Verbum quod in principio
erat, et apud* DEUM *erat, et* DEUS *erat, id est* DEI *unigenitus Filius,* DEI
virtus et sapientia, per quem et in quo facta sunt omnia, ... *idem* DEUS
unigenitus,' &c. &c.—And Ferrandus, A.D. 356 (*ibid.* p. 356) :—'*ita pro
redemtione humani generis humanam naturam credimus suscepisse, ut ille
qui Trinitate perfecta* DEUS *unigenitus permanebat ac permanet, ipse ex
Maria fieret primogenitus in multis fratribus,*' &c.

,charges brought against the passage; an examination of the various readings; and a confirmation of that in the received text on principles of general and biblical criticism.'

And,—to turn one's eyes in quite a different direction,— ' Veruntamen,' wrote venerable President Routh, at the end of a life-long critical study of Holy Writ,—(and his days were prolonged till he reached his hundredth year,)—

' Veruntamen, quidquid ex sacri textûs historia, illud vero haud certum, critici collegerunt, me tamen interna cogunt argumenta præferre lectionem Θεός, quem quidem agnoscunt veteres interpretes, Theodoretus cæterique, duabus alteris ὅς et ὅ.'[1]

And here I bring my DISSERTATION on 1 TIM. iii. 16 to a close. It began at p. 424, and I little thought would extend to seventy-six pages. Let it be clearly understood that I rest my contention not at all on Internal, but entirely on External Evidence; although, to the best of my judgment, they are alike conclusive as to the matter in debate.—Having now incontrovertibly, as I believe, established ΘΕΟ'Σ as the best attested Reading of the place,—I shall conclude the present LETTER as speedily as I can.

(1) *" Composition of the Body which is responsible for the ' New Greek Text.' "*

There remains, I believe, but one head of discourse into which I have not yet followed you. I allude to your " few words about the composition of the body which is responsible for the ' New Greek Text,' "[2]—which extend from the latter part of p. 29 to the beginning of p. 32 of your pamphlet. " Among the sixteen most regular attendants at your meetings," (you say) " were to be found most of those persons who

---

[1] *MS. note in his interleaved copy of the N. T.* He adds, ' Hæc addenda posui Notis ad S. Hippolytum contra Noetum p. 93, vol. i. *Scriptor. Ecclesiast. Opusculorum.'* [2] Page 29.

were presumably best acquainted with the subject of Textual Criticism."[1] And with this insinuation that you had " all the talents " with you, you seek to put me down.

But (as you truly say) " the number of living Scholars in England who have connected their names with the study of the Textual Criticism of the New Testament is exceed-ingly small." [2] And, " of that exceedingly small number," you would be puzzled to name so much as *one*, besides the three-you proceed to specify (viz. Dr. Scrivener, Dr. Westcott, and Dr. Hort,)—who were members of the Revision company. On the other hand,—(to quote the words of the most learned of our living Prelates,)—" it is well known that there are *two opposite Schools* of Biblical Criticism among us, *with very different opinions as to the comparative value of our Manuscripts of the Greek Testament.*"[3] And in proof of his statement, the Bishop of Lincoln cites " on the one side "— *Drs. Westcott and Hort;* " and on the other "—*Dr. Scrivener.*

Now, let the account be read which Dr. Newth gives (and which you admit to be correct) of the extraordinary method by which the ' New Greek Text ' was " *settled*," [4] " for the most part at the First Revision,"[5]—and it becomes plain that it was not by any means the product of the independently-formed opinions of 16 experts, (as your words imply); but resulted from the aptitude of 13 of your body to be guided by the sober counsels of Dr. Scrivener on the one hand, or to be carried away by the eager advocacy of Dr. Hort, (supported as he ever was by his respected colleague Dr. Westcott,) on the other. As Canon Cook well puts it,—" The question really is, Were the members competent to form a correct judgment ?" [6] " In most cases," " a

[1] P. 29. [2] P. 30. [3] *Address*, on the Revised Version, p. 10.
[4] See above, pp. 37 to 39. [5] Bp. Ellicott's pamphlet, p. 34. [6] P. 231.

simple majority "[1] determined what the text should be. But *ponderari debent testes*, my lord Bishop, *non numerari*.[2] The vote of the joint Editors should have been reckoned practically as only *one* vote. And whenever Dr. Scrivener and they were irreconcilably opposed, the existing Traditional Text ought to have been let alone. All pretence that it was *plainly and clearly erroneous* was removed, when the only experts present were hopelessly divided in opinion. As for the rest of the Revising Body, inasmuch as they extemporized their opinions, they were scarcely qualified to vote at all. Certainly they were not entitled individually to an equal voice with Dr. Scrivener in determining what the text should be. Caprice or Prejudice, in short, it was, not Deliberation and Learning, which prevailed in the Jerusalem Chamber. A more unscientific,—to speak truly, a coarser and a clumsier way of manipulating the sacred Deposit, than that which you yourself invented, it would be impossible, in my judgment, to devise.

(2) *An Unitarian Revisionist intolerable.—The Westminster-Abbey Scandal.*

But this is not nearly all. You invite attention to the constituent elements of the Revising body, and congratulate yourself on its miscellaneous character as providing a guarantee that it has been impartial.

I frankly avow, my lord Bishop, that the challenge you thus deliberately offer, surprises me greatly. To have observed severe silence on this part of the subject, would have seemed to me your discreeter course. Moreover, had you not, in this marked way, invited attention to the component elements of the Revising body, I was prepared to give the subject the go-by. The *"New Greek Text,"* no less than the *"New*

---

[1] Fifth Rule of the Committee.   [2] Bp. Ellicott's pamphlet, p. 30.

English Version," must stand or fall on its own merits; and I have no wish to prejudice the discussion by importing into it foreign elements. Of this, you have had some proof already; for, (with the exception of what is offered above, in pages 6 and 7,) the subject has been, by your present correspondent, nowhere brought prominently forward.

Far be it from me, however, to decline the enquiry which you evidently court. And so, I candidly avow that it was in my account a serious breach of Church order that, on engaging in so solemn an undertaking as the Revision of the Authorized Version, a body of Divines professing to act under the authority of the Southern Convocation should spontaneously associate with themselves Ministers of various denominations,[1] — Baptists, Congregationalists, Wesleyan

---

[1] No fair person will mistake the spirit in which the next ensuing paragraphs (in the Text) are written. But I will add what shall effectually protect me from being misunderstood.

Against the respectability and personal worth of any member of the Revisionist body, let me not be supposed to breathe a syllable. All, (for aught I know to the contrary,) may be men of ability and attainment, as well as of high moral excellence. I will add that, in early life, I numbered several professing Unitarians among my friends. It were base in me to forget how wondrous kind I found them: how much I loved them: how fondly I cherish their memory.

Further. That in order to come at the truth of Scripture, we are bound to seek help at the hands of *any* who are able to render help,—*who* ever doubted? If a worshipper of the false prophet,—if a devotee of Buddha,—could contribute anything,—*who* would hesitate to sue to him for enlightenment? As for Abraham's descendants,—they are our very brethren.

But it is quite a different thing when Revisionists appointed by the Convocation of the Southern Province, co-opt Separatists and even Unitarians into their body, where they shall determine the sense of Scripture and vote upon its translation on equal terms. Surely, when the Lower House of Convocation accepted the 5th " Resolution " of the Upper House,—viz., that the Revising body "shall be at liberty to invite the co-operation of any eminent for scholarship, to whatever nation or religious

Methodists, Independents, and the like: and especially that a successor of the Apostles should have presided over the deliberations of this assemblage of Separatists. In my humble judgment, we shall in vain teach the sinfulness of Schism, if we show ourselves practically indifferent on the subject, and even set an example of irregularity to our flocks. My Divinity may appear unaccommodating and old-fashioned: but I am not prepared to unlearn the lessons long since got by heart in the school of Andrewes and Hooker, of Pearson and Bull, of Hammond and Sanderson, of Beveridge and Bramhall. I am much mistaken, moreover, if I may not claim the authority of a greater doctor than any of these,—I mean S. Paul,—for the fixed views I entertain on this head.

All this, however, is as nothing in comparison of the scandal occasioned by the co-optation into your body of

---

body they may belong;"—the Synod of Canterbury did not suppose that it was pledging itself to sanction *such* "co-operation" as is implied by actual *co-optation!*

It should be added that Bp. Wilberforce, (the actual framer of the 5th fundamental Resolution,) has himself informed us that "in framing it, it never occurred to him that it would apply to the admission of any member of the Socinian body." *Chronicle of Convocation* (Feb. 1871,) p. 4.

"I am aware," (says our learned and pious bishop of Lincoln,) "that the ancient Church did not scruple to avail herself of the translation of a renegade Jew, like Aquila; and of Ebionitish heretics, like Symmachus and Theodotion; and that St. Augustine profited by the expository rules of Tychonius the Donatist. But I very much doubt whether the ancient Church would have looked for a large outpouring of a blessing from God on a work of translating His Word, where the workmen were not all joined together in a spirit of Christian unity, and in the profession of the true Faith; and in which the opinions of the several translators were to be counted and not weighed; and where everything was to be decided by numerical majorities; and where the votes of an Arius or a Nestorius were to be reckoned as of equal value with those of an Athanasius or a Cyril." (*Address on the Revised Version,* 1881, pp. 38.)

Dr. G. Vance Smith, the Unitarian Minister of S. Saviour's Gate Chapel, York. That, while engaged in the work of interpreting the everlasting Gospel, you should have knowingly and by choice associated with yourselves one who, not only openly denies the eternal Godhead of our LORD, but in a recent publication is the avowed assailant of that fundamental doctrine of the Christian Religion, as well as of the Inspiration of Holy Scripture itself,[1]—filled me (and many besides myself) with astonishment and sorrow. You were respectfully memorialized on the subject;[2] but you treated the representations which reached you with scornful indifference.

Now therefore that you re-open the question, I will not scruple publicly to repeat that it seems to me nothing else but an insult to our Divine Master and a wrong to the Church, that the most precious part of our common Christian heritage, the pure Word of GOD, should day by day, week by week, month by month, year after year, have been thus handled; for the avowed purpose of producing a Translation which should supersede our Authorized Version. That the individual in question contributed aught to your deliberations has never been pretended. On the contrary. No secret has been made of the fact that he was, (as might have been anticipated from his published writings,) the most unprofitable member of the Revising body. Why then was he at first surreptitiously elected? and why was his election afterwards stiffly maintained? The one purpose achieved by his continued presence among you was that it might be thereby made to appear that the Church of England no

---

[1] *The Bible and Popular Theology*, by G. Vance Smith, 1871.

[2] *An Unitarian Reviser of our Authorized Version, intolerable: an earnest Remonstrance and Petition,*—addressed to yourself by your present correspondent:—Oxford, Parker, 1872, pp. 8.

longer insists on Belief in the eternal Godhead of our LORD,
as essential; but is prepared to surrender her claim to
definite and unequivocal dogmatic teaching in respect of
Faith in the Blessed TRINITY.

But even if this Unitarian had been an eminent Scholar,
my objection would remain in full force; for I hold, (and
surely so do you!), that the right Interpretation of GOD's
Word may not be attained without the guidance of the HOLY
SPIRIT, whose aid must first be invoked by faithful prayer.

In the meantime, this same person was invited to communicate with his fellow-Revisers in Westminster-Abbey,
and did accordingly, on the 22nd of June, 1870, receive the
Holy Communion, in Henry VII.'s Chapel, at the hands of
Dean Stanley: declaring, next day, that he received the
Sacrament on this occasion without 'joining in reciting
the Nicene Creed,' and without 'compromise,' (as he expressed it,) of his principles as an 'Unitarian.'[1] So conspicuous a sacrilege led to a public Protest signed by some
thousands of the Clergy.[2] It also resulted, in the next
ensuing Session of Convocation, in a Resolution whereby the
Upper House cleared itself of complicity in the scandal.[3] . . .

---

[1] See letter of 'One of the Revisionists, G. V. S.' in *the Times* of
July 11, 1870.

[2] *Protest against the Communion of an Unitarian in Westminster*
Abbey on June 22nd, 1870 :—Oxford, 1870, pp. 64.

[3] See the *Chronicle of Convocation* (Feb. 1871), pp. 3–28,—when a
Resolution was moved and carried by the Bp. (Wilberforce) of Winchester,—
".That it is the judgment of this House that no person who denies the
Godhead of our LORD JESUS CHRIST ought to be invited to join either
company to which is committed the Revision of the Authorized
Version of Holy Scripture: and that it is further the judgment of this
House that any such person now on either Company should cease to
act therewith.

" And that this Resolution be communicated to the Lower House,
and their concurrence requested :"—which was done. See p. 143.

How a good man like you can revive the memory of these many painful incidents without anguish, is to me unintelligible. That no blessing from Him, '*sine Quo nihil validum, nihil sanctum,*' could be expected to attend an undertaking commenced under such auspices,—was but too plain. The Revision was, a foredoomed thing—in the account of many besides myself—from the outset.

(3) *The probable Future of the Revision of* 1881.

Not unaware am I that it has nevertheless been once and again confidently predicted in public Addresses, Lectures, Pamphlets, that ultimate success is in store for the Revision of 1881. I cannot but regard it as a suspicious circumstance that these vaticinations have hitherto invariably proceeded from members of the Revising body.

It would ill become such an one as myself to pretend to skill in forecasting the future. But of *this* at least I feel certain :—that if, in an evil hour, (quod absit !), the Church of England shall ever be induced to commit herself to the adoption of the present Revision, she will by so doing expose herself to the ridicule of the rest of Christendom, as well as incur irreparable harm and loss. And such a proceeding on her part will be inexcusable, for she has been at least faithfully forewarned. Moreover, in the end, she will most certainly have to retrace her steps with sorrow and confusion.

Those persons evidently overlook the facts of the problem, who refer to what happened in the case of the Authorized Version when it originally appeared, some 270 years ago ; and argue that as the Revision of 1611 at first encountered opposition, which yet it ultimately overcame, so must it fare in the end with the present Revised Version also. Those who so reason forget that the cases are essentially dissimilar.

If the difference between the Authorized Version of 1611 and the Revision of 1881 were only this.—That the latter is characterized by a mechanical, unidiomatic, and even repulsive method of rendering; which was not only unattempted, but repudiated by the Authors of the earlier work;—there would have been something to urge on behalf of the later performance. The plea of zeal for GOD's Word,—a determination at all hazards to represent with even servile precision the *ipsissima verba* of Evangelists and Apostles,— *this* plea might have been plausibly put forward: and, to some extent, it must have been allowed,—although a grave diversity of opinion might reasonably have been entertained as to *what constitutes* ' accuracy ' and ' fidelity ' of translation.

But when once it has been made plain that *the underlying Greek* of the Revision of 1881 is an entirely new thing,—*is a manufactured article throughout*,—all must see that the contention has entirely changed its character. The question immediately arises, (and it is the *only* question which remains to be asked,)—Were then the Authors of this ' New Greek Text' *competent* to undertake so perilous an enterprise ? And when, in the words of the distinguished Chairman of the Revising body—(words quoted above, at page 369,) — " *To this question, we venture to answer very unhesitatingly in the negative,*"—What remains but, with blank astonishment, not unmingled with disgust, to close the volume ? Your own ingenuous admission,—(volunteered by yourself a few days before you and your allies "proceeded to the actual details of the Revision,") — that " *we have certainly not acquired sufficient Critical Judgment* for any body of Revisers hopefully to undertake such a work as this,"—is decisive on the subject.

The gravity of the issue thus raised, it is impossible to over-estimate. We find ourselves at once and entirely lifted out of the region originally proposed for investigation. It is no longer a question of the degree of skill which has been exhibited in translating the title-deeds of our heavenly inheritance out of Greek into English. Those title-deeds themselves have been empirically submitted to a process which, *rightly or wrongly,* seriously affects their integrity. Not only has a fringe of most unreasonable textual mistrust been tacked on to the margin of every inspired page, (as from S. Luke x. 41 to xi. 11) :—not only has many a grand doctrinal statement been evacuated of its authority, (as, by the shameful mis-statement found in the margin against S. John iii. 13,[1] and the vile Socinian gloss which disfigures the margin of Rom. ix. 5[2]) :—but we entirely miss many a solemn utterance of the Spirit,—as when we are assured that verses 44 and 46 of S. Mark ix. are omitted by *‘ the best ancient authorities,’* (whereas, on the contrary, the MSS. referred to are *the worst*). Let the thing complained of be illustrated by a few actual examples. Only five shall be subjoined. The words in the first column represent what *you* are pleased to designate as among “the most certain conclusions of modern Textual Criticism” (p. 78),—but what *I* assert to be nothing else but mutilated exhibitions of the inspired Text. The second column contains the indubitable Truth of Scripture,—the words which have been read by our Fathers’ Fathers for the last 500 years, and which we propose, (God helping us,) to hand on unimpaired to our Children, and to our Children’s Children, for many a century to come :—

Revised (1881).	Authorized (1611).
“ And come, follow me.”	“ And come, *take up the cross and* follow me.”[3]

---

[1] The Reader is invited to refer back to pp. 132–135.
[2] The Reader is requested to refer back to pp. 210–214.
[3] S. Mark x. 21.

" And they blindfolded him, and asked him, saying, Prophesy."

" And when they had blindfolded him, *they struck him on the face, and* asked him, saying, Prophesy." [1]

" And there was also a superscription over him, This is the King of the Jews."

" And a superscription also was *written* over him *in letters of Greek, and Latin, and Hebrew*, This is the King of the Jews."[2]

" And they gave him a piece of a broiled fish."

" And they gave him a piece of a broiled fish, *and of an honeycomb*."[3]

But the next (S. Luke ix. 54–6,) is a far more serious loss :—

" ' Lord, wilt thou that we bid fire to come down from heaven, and consume them ?' But he turned and rebuked them. And they went to another village."

" ' Lord, wilt thou that we command fire to come down from heaven, and consume them, *even as Elias did ?*' But he turned and rebuked them, *and said, ' Ye know not what manner of spirit ye are of. For the Son of man is not come to destroy men's lives, but to save them.'* And they went to another village."

The unlearned reader sees at a glance that the only difference of *Translation* here is the substitution of ' bid ' for ' command,'— which by the way, is not only uncalled for, but is a change *for the worse*.[4] On the other hand, how

---

[1] S. Luke xxii. 64.   [2] S. Luke xxiii. 38.   [3] S. Luke xxiv. 42.

[4] Εἰπεῖν is ' *to command*' in S. Matth. (and S. Luke) iv. 3: in S. Mark v. 43: viii. 7, and in many other places. On the other hand, the Revisers have thrust ' *command*' into S. Matth. xx. 21, where ' *grant*' had far better have been let alone: and have overlooked other places (as S. Matth. xxii. 24, S. James ii. 11), where ' *command*' might perhaps have been introduced with advantage. (I nothing doubt that when the Centurion of Capernaum said to our Lord μόνον εἰπὲ λόγῳ [Mtt. viii. 8 = Lu. vii. 7], he entreated Him ' only to give *the word of command*.')   [Over.

grievous an injury has been done by the mutilation of the
blessed record in respect of those $(3 + 5 + 7 + 4 + 24 =)$
forty-three (in English *fifty-seven*) undoubtedly inspired as
well as most precious words,—even "ordinary Readers" are
competent to discern.

I am saying that the systematic, and sometimes serious,—
always inexcusable,—liberties which have been taken with
the Greek Text by the Revisionists of 1881, constitute a
ground of offence against their work for which no pretext
was afforded by the Revision of 1611. To argue therefore
from what has been the fate of the one, to what is likely to
be the fate of the other, is illogical. The cases are not only
not parallel : they are even wholly dissimilar.

We all see, of course, that it was because Δός is rendered '*grant*' in
the (very nearly) parallel place to S. Matth. xx. 21 (viz. S. Mark x. 37),
that the Revisers thought it incumbent on them to represent Εἰπέ in the
earlier Gospel differently ; and so they bethought themselves of '*command*.' (Infelicitously enough, as I humbly think. '*Promise*' would
evidently have been a preferable substitute: the word in the original
(εἰπεῖν) being one of that large family of Greek verbs which vary their
shade of signification according to their context.) But it is plainly
impracticable to *level up* after this rigid fashion,—to translate in this
mechanical way. Far more is lost than is gained by this straining after
an impossible closeness of rendering. The spirit becomes inevitably
sacrificed to the letter. All this has been largely remarked upon above, at
pp. 187–206.

Take the case before us in illustration. S. James and S. John with
their Mother, have evidently agreed together to '*ask a favour*' of their
Lord (cf. Mtt. xx. 20, Mk. x. 35). The Mother begins Εἰπέ,—the sons
begin, Δός. Why are we to assume that the request is made by the
Mother in *a different spirit* from the sons ? Why are we to impose upon
her language the imperious sentiment which the very mention of
'*command*' unavoidably suggests to an English ear ?

A prior, and yet more fatal objection, remains in full force. The
Revisers, (I say it for the last time,) were clearly going beyond their
prescribed duty when they set about handling the Authorized Version
after this merciless fashion. Their business was to correct '*plain and
clear errors*,'—*not* to produce a 'New English Version.'

The cheapest copies of our Authorized Version at least exhibit the Word of GOD faithfully and helpfully. Could the same be said of a cheap edition of the work of the Revisionists,—destitute of headings to the Chapters, and containing no record of the extent to which the Sacred Text has undergone depravation throughout?

Let it be further recollected that the greatest Scholars and the most learned Divines of which our Church could boast, conducted the work of Revision in King James' days; and it will be acknowledged that the promiscuous assemblage which met in the Jerusalem Chamber cannot urge any corresponding claim on public attention. *Then*, the Bishops of Lincoln of 1611 were Revisers: the Vance Smiths stood without and found fault. But in the affair of 1881, Dr. Vance Smith revises, and ventilates heresy from within:[1] the Bp. of Lincoln stands outside, and is one of the severest Critics of the work.—Disappointed men are said to have been conspicuous among the few assailants of our 'Authorized Version,'—Scholars (as Hugh Broughton) who considered themselves unjustly overlooked and excluded. But on the present occasion, among the multitude of hostile voices, there is not a single instance known of a man excluded from the deliberations of the Jerusalem Chamber, who desired to share them.

---

[1] Take the following as a sample, which is one of the Author's proofs that the 'Results of the Revision' are 'unfavourable to Orthodoxy:'—"The only instance in the N. T. in which the religious worship or adoration of CHRIST was apparently implied, has been *altered* by the Revision: '*At* the name of JESUS every knee shall bow,' [Philipp. ii. 10] is now to be read '*in* the name.' Moreover, no alteration of text or of translation will be found anywhere to make up for this loss; as indeed it is well understood that the N. T. contains neither precept nor example which really sanctions the religious worship of JESUS CHRIST."—*Texts and Margins,*—p. 47.

To argue therefore concerning the prospects of the Revision of 1881 from the known history of our Authorized Version of 1611, is to argue concerning things essentially dissimilar. With every advance made in the knowledge of the subject, it may be confidently predicted that there will spring up increased distrust of the Revision of 1881, and an ever increasing aversion from it.

(4) *Review of the entire subject, and of the respective positions of Bp. Ellicott and myself.*

Here I lay down my pen,—glad to have completed what (because I have endeavoured to do my work *thoroughly*) has proved a very laborious task indeed. The present rejoinder to your Pamphlet covers all the ground you have yourself traversed, and will be found to have disposed of your entire contention.

I take leave to point out, in conclusion, that it places you individually in a somewhat embarrassing predicament. For you have now no alternative but to come forward and disprove my statements as well as refute my arguments : or to admit, by your silence, that you have sustained defeat in the cause of which you constituted yourself the champion. You constrained me to reduce you to this alternative when you stood forth on behalf of the Revising body, and saw fit to provoke me to a personal encounter.

But you must come provided with something vastly more formidable, remember, than denunciations,—which are but wind : and vague generalities,—which prove nothing and persuade nobody : and appeals to the authority of "Lachmann, Tischendorf, and Tregelles,"—which I disallow and disregard. You must produce a counter-array of well-ascertained facts ; and you must build thereupon irrefragable arguments. In other words, you must conduct your cause with learning and ability. Else, believe me, you will make the painful discovery that "the last error is worse than the first." You had better a thousand times, even now, ingenuously admit that you made a grievous mistake when you put yourself into the hands of those ingenious theorists, Drs. Westcott and Hort, and embraced their arbitrary decrees,—than persevere in your present downward course, only to sink deeper and deeper in the mire.

(5) *Anticipated effect of the present contention on the Text of* 1 Timothy iii. 16.

I like to believe, in the meantime, that this passage of arms has resulted in such a vindication[1] of the traditional Reading of 1 TIMOTHY iii. 16, as will effectually secure that famous place of Scripture against further molestation. *Faxit Deus!* ... In the margin of the Revision of 1881, I observe that you have ventured to state as follows,—

"The word GOD, in place of *He who*, rests on no sufficient ancient evidence."

In the words of your Unitarian ally, Dr. Vance Smith,—

"The old reading is pronounced untenable by the Revisers, as it has long been known to be by all careful students of the New Testament. ... It is in truth another example of the facility with which ancient copiers could introduce the word God into their manuscripts,—a reading which was the natural result of the growing tendency in early Christian times ... to look upon the humble Teacher as the incarnate Word, and therefore as ' God manifested in the flesh '" (p. 39).

Such remarks proceeding from such a quarter create no surprise. But, pray, my lord Bishop, of what were *you* thinking when you permitted yourself to make the serious

---

[1] *Supra*, p. 424 to p. 501.

2 L 2

mis-statement which stands in the margin? You must needs have meant thereby that,—' .he word *He who* in place of GOD, on the contrary, *does* rest on sufficient ancient evidence." I solemnly call upon you, in the Name of Him by whose Spirit Holy Scripture was given, to prove the truth of your marginal Note of which the foregoing 70 pages are a refutation.—You add,

"Some ancient authorities read *which*."

But why did you suppress the fact, which is undeniable, viz.: that a great many "*More* ancient authorities" read 'which' (ὅ), than read 'who' (ὅς)?

(6) *The nature of this contention explained.*

And yet, it was no isolated place which I was eager to establish, when at first I took up my pen. It was the general trustworthiness of the Traditional Text,—(the Text which you admit to be upwards of 1500 years old,)—which I aimed at illustrating: the essential rottenness of the foundation on which the Greek Text of the Revision of 1881 has been constructed by yourself and your fellow Revisers,—which I was determined to expose. I claim to have proved not only that your entire superstructure is tasteless and unlovely to a degree,—but also that you have reared it up on a foundation of sand. In no vaunting spirit, (GOD is my witness!), but out of sincere and sober zeal for the truth of Scripture I say it,—your work, whether you know it or not, has been so handled in the course of the present volume of 500 pages that its essential deformity must be apparent to every unprejudiced beholder. It can only be spoken of at this time of day as a shapeless ruin.

A ruin moreover it is which does not admit of being repaired or restored. And why? Because the mischief, which extends to every part of the edifice, takes its beginning, as already explained, in every part of the foundation.

And further, (to speak without a figure,) it cannot be too plainly stated that no compromise is possible between our respective methods,—yours and mine : between the NEW GERMAN system in its most aggravated and in fact intolerable form, to which you have incautiously and unconditionally given in your adhesion; and the OLD ENGLISH school of Textual Criticism, of which I humbly avow myself a disciple. Between the theory of Drs. Westcott and Hort (which you have made your own) and the method of your present Correspondent, there can be no compromise, because the two are antagonistic throughout. We have, in fact, nothing in common,—except certain documents; which *I* insist on interpreting by the humble Inductive process : while you and your friends insist on your right of deducing your estimate of them from certain antecedent imaginations of your own,—every one of which I disallow, and some of which I am able to disprove.

Such, my lord Bishop, is your baseless imagination— (1) That the traditional Greek Text (which, without authority, you style " *The Syrian text,*") is the result of a deliberate Recension made at Antioch, A.D. 250 and 350 :[1]—(2) That the Peschito, in like manner, is the result of a Recension made at Edessa or Nisibis about the same time :[2]—(3) That Cureton's is the Syriac ' Vetus,' and the Peschito the Syriac ' Vulgate :'[3] —(4) That the respective ancestries of our only two IVth-century Codices, B and ℵ, "diverged from a common parent extremely near the apostolic autographs:"[4] —(5) That this com-

---

[1] See above, pp. 272–275, pp. 278–281.   [2] See above, p. 275.
[3] See above, pp. 276–7.   [4] See above, pp. 303–305.

mon original enjoyed a "general immunity from substantive error;" and by consequence—(6) That B and ℵ provide "a safe criterion of genuineness," so that "no readings of ℵ B can be safely rejected absolutely."[1]—(7) Similar wild imaginations you cherish concerning C and D,—which, together with B and ℵ *you* assume to be among the most trustworthy guides in existence; whereas *I* have convinced myself, by laborious collation, that they are *the most corrupt of all.* We are thus diametrically opposed throughout. Finally,—(8) *You* assume that you possess a power of divination which enables you to dispense with laborious processes of Induction; while *I*, on the contrary, insist that the Truth of the Text of Scripture is to be elicited exclusively from the consentient testimony of the largest number of the best COPIES, FATHERS, VERSIONS.[2] There is, I am persuaded, no royal road to the attainment of Truth in this department of Knowledge. Only through the lowly portal of humility,—only by self-renouncing labour,—may we ever hope to reach the innermost shrine. *They* do but go astray themselves and hopelessly mislead others, who first *invent their facts,* and then proceed to build thereupon their premises.

Such builders are Drs. Westcott and Hort,—with whom (by your own avowal) you stand completely identified.[3] I repeat, (for I wish it to be distinctly understood and remembered,) that what I assert concerning those Critics is,—*not* that their superstructure rests upon an insecure foundation; but that it rests on *no foundation at all.* My complaint is,—*not* that they are *somewhat* and *frequently* mistaken; but that they are mistaken *entirely,* and that they are mistaken *throughout.* There is no possibility of approxima-

---

[1] See above, p. 304.   [2] See above, pp. 339-42; also pp. 422, 423.
[3] See above, pp. 391-7.

tion between *their* mere assumptions and the results of *my* humble and laborious method of dealing with the Text of Scripture. We shall only *then* be able to begin to reason together with the slightest prospect of coming to any agreement, when they have unconditionally abandoned all their preconceived imaginations, and unreservedly scattered every one of their postulates to the four winds.

(7) *Parting Counsels.*

Let me be allowed, in conclusion, to recommend to your attention and that of your friends,—(I.) " THE LAST TWELVE VERSES OF S. MARK'S GOSPEL : " — (II.) THE ANGELIC HYMN on the night of the Nativity :—(III.) The text of 1 TIMOTHY iii. 16,—these three,—(in respect of which up to this hour, you and I find ourselves to be hopelessly divided,) —as convenient *Test places.* When you are prepared frankly to admit,— (I.) That there is no reason whatever for doubting the genuineness of S. MARK xvi. 9–20 :[1]—(II.) That ἐν ἀνθρώποις εὐδοκία is unquestionably the Evangelical text of S. LUKE ii. 14 :[2]—and (III.) That Θεὸς ἐφανερώθη ἐν σαρκί is what the great Apostle must be held to have written in 1 TIMOTHY iii. 16,[3]—we shall be in good time to proceed to something else. *Until* this happy result has been attained, it is a mere waste of time to break up fresh ground, and to extend the area of our differences.

I cannot however disguise from you the fact that such an avowal on your part will amount to an admission that " the whole fabric of Textual Criticism which has been built up during the last fifty years by successive editors of the New Testament,"—Lachmann namely, Tischendorf, and Tregelles, —is worthless. Neither may the inevitable consequence

---

[1] See above, pp. 36–40: 47–9: 422–4.
[2] See above, pp. 41–7 : 420–2.   [3] See above, pp. 98–106 : 424–501.

of this admission be concealed : viz. that your own work as Revisionists has been, to speak plainly, one gigantic blunder, from end to end.

(8) *The subject dismissed.*

The issue of this prolonged contention I now commend, with deep humility, to ALMIGHTY GOD. The SPIRIT OF TRUTH will, (I know,) take good care of His own masterpiece,—the Written Word. May He have compassion on my ignorance, and graciously forgive me, if, (intending nothing less,) I shall prove to have anywhere erred in my strenuous endeavour to maintain the integrity of Scripture against the rashness of an impatient and unlearned generation.

But if, (as I humbly believe and confidently hope,) my conclusions are sound throughout, then may He enable men freely to recognize the Truth; and thus, effectually avert from our Church the supreme calamity with which, for a few months in 1881, it seemed threatened; namely, of having an utterly depraved Recension of the Greek Text of the New Testament thrust upon it, as the basis of a very questionable 'Revision' of the English.

My lord Bishop,—I have the honour to wish you respectfully farewell.

J. W. B.

DEANERY, CHICHESTER,
July, 1883.

THE GRASS WITHERETH : THE FLOWER FADETH :
BUT THE WORD OF OUR GOD SHALL STAND FOR EVER.

APPENDIX OF SACRED CODICES.

The inquiries into which I was led (January to June 1883) by my DISSERTATION in vindication of the Traditional Reading of 1 Tim. iii. 16, have resulted in my being made aware of the existence of a vast number of Sacred Codices which had eluded the vigilance of previous Critics.

I had already assisted my friend Prebendary Scrivener in greatly enlarging Scholz's list. We had in fact raised the enumeration of ' *Evangelia* ' to 621: of ' *Acts and Catholic Epistles* ' to 239 : of ' *Paul* ' to 281: of ' *Apocalypse* ' to 108 : of ' *Evangelistaria* ' to 299 : of the book called ' *Apostolus* ' to 81 :— making a total of 1629.—But at the end of a protracted and somewhat laborious correspondence with the custodians of not a few great Continental Libraries, I am able to state that our available ' *Evangelia* ' amount to at least 739 [1] : our ' *Acts and Cath. Epp.* ' to 261 : our ' *Paul* ' to 338 : our ' *Apoc.* ' to 122 : our ' *Evstt.* ' to 415 [2] : our copies of the ' *Apostolus* ' to 128 [3] : making a total of 2003. This shows an increase of *three hundred and seventy-four.*

My original intention had been to publish this enumeration of Sacred Codices in its entirety as an APPENDIX to the present volume : but finding that the third edition of Dr. Scrivener's ' Introduction ' would appear some months before my own pages could possibly see the light, I eagerly communicated my discoveries to my friend. I have indeed proposed to myself no

---

[1] Evan. 738 belongs to Oriel College, Oxford, [xii.], small 4to. of 130 foll. slightly *mut.* Evan. 739, Bodl. Greek Miscell. 323 [xiii.], 8vo. *membr.* foll. 183, *mut.* Brought from Ephesus, and obtained for the Bodleian in 1883.

[2] Evst. 415 belongs to Lieut. Bate, [xiii.], *chart.* foll. 219, mutilated throughout. He obtained it in 1878 from a Cyprus villager at Kikos, near Mount Trovodos (*i.e.* Olympus.) It came from a monastery on the mountain.

[3] Apost. 128 will be found described, for the first time, below, at p. 528.

other object throughout but the advancement of the study
of Textual Criticism : and it was reasonable to hope that by
means of his widely circulated volume, the great enlargement
which our previously ascertained stores have suddenly experienced would become more generally known to scholars. I
should of course still have it in my power to reproduce here the
same enumeration of Sacred Codices.

The great bulk however which the present volume has
acquired, induces me to limit myself in this place to some
account of those Codices which have been expressly announced
and discoursed about in my Text (as at pp. 474 and 492-5).
Some other occasion must be found for enlarging on the rest of
my budget.

It only remains to state that for most of my recent discoveries
I am indebted to the Abbate Cozza-Luzi, Prefect of the Vatican ;
who on being informed of the object of my solicitude, with
extraordinary liberality and consideration at once set three
competent young men to work in the principal libraries of
Rome. To him I am further indebted for my introduction to
the MS. treasures belonging to the Basilian monks of Crypta-
Ferrata, the ancient Tusculum.   Concerning the precious
library of that monastery so much has been offered already
(viz. at pp. 446-448, and again at pp. 473-4), as well as
concerning its learned chief, the Hieromonachus Antonio
Rocchi, that I must be content to refer my readers to those
earlier parts of the present volume. I cannot however sufficiently acknowledge the patient help which the librarian of
Crypta Ferrata has rendered me in the course of these re-
searches.

For my knowledge of the sacred Codices preserved at Messina,
I am indebted to the good offices and learning of Papas Filippo
Matranga.   In respect of those at Milan, my learned friend
Dr. Ceriani has (not for the first time) been my efficient helper.
M. Wescher has kindly assisted me at Paris ; and Dr. C. de
Boor at Berlin. It must suffice, for the rest, to refer to the
Notes at foot of pp. 491-2 and 477-8.

ADDITIONAL CODICES OF S. PAUL'S EPISTLES.

282. (= Act. 240. Apoc. 109). Paris, 'Arménien 9' (olim Reg. 2247). membr. foll. 323. This bilingual codex (Greek and Armenian) is described by the Abbé Martin in his *Introduction à la Critique Textuelle du N. T.* (1883), p. 660-1. See above, p. 474, note (1). An Italian version is added from the Cath. Epp. onwards. *Mut.* at beginning (Acts iv. 14) and end. (For its extraordinary reading at 1 Tim. iii. 16, see above, p. 473-4.)

283. (= Act. 241). Messina P K Z (i.e. 127) [xii.], *chart.* foll. 224. *Mut.* begins at Acts viii. 2,—ends at Hebr. viii. 2 ; also a leaf is lost between foll. 90 and 91. Has ὑποθθ. and Commentary of an unknown author.

284. (= Act. 195). Modena, ii. A. 13 [xiii. ?], *Mut.* at the end.

285. (= Act. 196), Modena, ii. c. 4 [xi. or xii.]. Sig. Ant. Cappelli (sub-librarian) sends me a tracing of 1 Tim. iii. 16.

286. Ambrosian library, E. 2, *inf.* the Catena of Nicetas. 'Textus particulatim præmittit Commentariis.'

287. Ambrosian A. 241, *inf.*, 'est Catena ejusdem auctoris ex initio, sed non complectitur totum opus.'

288. Ambrosian D. 541 *inf.* [x. or xi.] *membr.* Text and Catena on all S. Paul's Epp. 'Textus continuatus. Catena in marginibus.' It was brought from Thessaly.

289. Milan c. 295 *inf.* [x. or xi.] *membr.* with a Catena. 'Textus continuatus. Catena in marginibus.'

290. (= Evan. 622. Act. 242. Apoc. 110). Crypta Ferrata, A. α. i. [xiii. or xiv.] foll. 386 : *chart.* a beautiful codex of the entire N. T. described by Rocchi, p. 1-2. Menolog. *Mut.* 1 Nov. to 16 Dec.

291. (= Act. 243). Crypta Ferrata, A. β. i. [x.] foll. 139 : in two columns,—letters almost uncial. Particularly described by Rocchi, pp. 15, 16. Zacagni used this codex when writing about Euthalius. *Mut.*, beginning with the argument for 1 S. John and ending with 2 Tim.

†292. (= Act. 244). Crypta Ferrata, A. β. iii. [xi. or xii.]. *Membr.*, foll. 172. in 2 columns beautifully illuminated : described by Rocchi, p. 18–9. Zacagni employed this codex while treating of Euthalius. *Menolog.*

293. (= Act. 245). Crypta Ferrata, A. β. vi. [xi.], foll. 193. *Mut.* at the end, Described by Rocchi, p. 22–3.

294. (= Act. 246). Vat. 1208. Abbate Cozzi-Luzi confirms Berriman's account [p. 98–9] of the splendour of this codex. It is written in gold letters, and is said to have belonged to Carlotta, Queen of Jerusalem, Cyprus, and Armenia, who died at Rome A.D. 1487, and probably gave the book to Pope Innocent VIII., whose arms are printed at the beginning. It contains effigies of S. Luke, S. James, S. Peter, S. John, S. Jude, S. Paul.

295. (= Act 247). Palatino-Vat. 38 [xi.] *membr.* foll. 35. Berriman (p. 100) says it is of quarto size, and refers it to the ixth cent.

296. Barberini iv. 85 (olim 19), dated A.D. 1324. For my knowledge of this codex I am entirely indebted to Berriman, who says that it contains 'the arguments and marginal scholia written ' (p. 102).

297. Barberini, vi. 13 (*olim* 229), *membr.* [xi.] foll. 195: contains S. Paul's 14 Epp. This codex also was known to Berriman, who relates (p. 102), that it is furnished 'with the old marginal scholia.'

298. (= Act. 248), Berlin (Hamilton: N° 625 in the English printed catalogue, where it is erroneously described as a 'Lectionarium.') It contains Acts, Cath. Epp. and S. Paul,—as Dr. C. de Boor informs me.

299. (= Act. 249), Berlin, 4to. 40 [xiii.]: same contents as the preceding.

300. (= Act. 250), Berlin, 4to. 43 [xi.], same contents as the preceding, but commences with the Psalms.

301. (= Act. 251), Berlin, 4to. 57 [xiv.], *chart.* Same contents as Paul 298.

302. (= Evan. 642. Act. 252.) Berlin, 8vo. 9 [xi.], probably once contained all the N. T. It now begins with S. Luke xxiv. 53, and is *mut.* after 1 Thess.

303. Milan, N. 272 *inf.* "Excerpti loci."

304. (= Act. 253) Vat. 369 [xiv.] foll. 226, *chart.*

305. Vat. 549, *membr.* [xii.] foll. 380. S. Paul's Epistles, with Theophylact's Commentary.

306. Vat. 550, *membr.* [xii.] foll. 290; contains Romans with Comm. of Chrysostom.

307. Vat. 551, *membr.* [x.] foll. 283. A large codex, containing some of S. Paul's Epp. with Comm. of Chrysostom.

308. Vat. 552, *membr.* [xi.] foll. 155. Contains Hebrews with Comm. of Chrysostom.

309. Vat. 582, *membr.* [xiv.] foll. 146. S. Paul's Epistles with Comm. of Chrysostom.

310. Vat. 646 [xiv.], foll. 250: 'cum supplementis.' *Chart.* S. Paul's Epp. with Comm. of Theophylact and Euthymius. Pars I. et II.

311. (= Evan. 671). Vat. 647. *Chart.* foll. 338 [xv.]. S. Paul's Epistles and the Gospels, with Theophylact's Commentary.

312. Vat. 648, written A.D. 1232, at Jerusalem, by Simeon, 'qui et Saba dicitur:' foll. 338, *chart.* S. Paul's Epistles, with Comm. of Theophylact.

313. (= Act. 239). Vat. 652, *chart.* [xv.] foll. 105. The Acts and Epistles with Commentary. See the *Preface* to Theophylact, ed. 1758, vol. iii. p. v.–viii., also 'Acts 239' in Scrivener's 3rd. edit. (p. 263).

314. Vat. 692, *membr.* [xii.] foll. 93, *mut.* Corinthians, Galatians, Ephesians, with Commentary.

315. Vat. 1222, *chart.* [xvi.] foll. 437. S. Paul's Epp. with Theophylact's Comm.

316. (= Act. 255). Vat. 1654, *membr.* [x. or xi.], foll. 211. Acts and Epistles of S. Paul with Chrysostom's Comm.

317. Vat. 1656, *membr.* [xii.], foll. 182. Hebrews with Comm. of Chrysostom, *folio.*

318. Vat. 1659, *membr.* [xi.] foll. 444. S. Paul's Epp. with Comm. of Chrysostom.

319. Vat. 1971 (Basil 10) *membr.* [x.] foll. 247. 'Επιστολαὶ τῶν ἀποστόλων σὺν τοῖς τοῦ Εὐθαλίου.

320. Vat. 2055 (Basil 94), *membr.* [x.] foll. 292. S. Paul's Epp. with Comm. of Chrysostom.

321. Vat. 2065 (Basil 104), [x.] *membr.* foll. 358. Romans with Comm. of Chrysostom.

322. (= Act. 256) Vat. 2099 (Basil 138) *membr.* foll. 120 [x.]. Note that though numbered for the Acts, this code only contains ἐπιστολαὶ ιδ' καὶ καθολικαὶ, σὺν ταῖς σημειώσεσι λειτουργικαῖς περὶ τῶν ἡμερῶν ἐν αἷς λεκτέαι.

323. Vat. 2180 [xv.] foll. 294, *chart.* With Comm. of Theophylact.

324. Alexand. Vat. 4 [x.] foll. 256, *membr.* 'Optimæ notæ.' Romans with Comm. of Chrysostom, λογ. κβ'. 'Fuit monasterii dicti τοῦ Περιβλέπτου.'

325. (= Evan. 698. Apoc. 117). Alexand. Vat. 6. *chart.* foll. 336 [xvi.], a large codex. The Gospels with Comm. of Nicetas : S. Paul's Epp. with Comm. of Theophylact : Apocalypse with an anonymous Comm.

326. Vat. Ottob. 74 [xv.] foll. 291, *chart.* Romans with Theodoret's Comm.

327. Palatino-Vat. 10 [x.] *membr.* foll. 268. S. Paul's Epp. with a Patristic Commentary. 'Felkman adnotat.'

328. Palatino-Vat. 204 [x.] foll. 181, cum additamentis. With the interpretation of Œcumenius.

329. Palatino-Vat. 325 [x.] *membr.* foll. 163, *mut.* Inter alia adest εἰς ἐπιστ. πρὸς Τιμόθεον ὁμιλεῖαι τινες Χρυσοστόμου.

330. Palatino-Vat. 423 [xii.], partly *chart.* Codex miscell. habet ἐπιστολῶν πρὸς Κολασσαεῖς καὶ Θεσσαλονικεῖς περικοπὰς σὺν τῇ ἑρμηνείᾳ.

331. Angelic. T. 8, 6 [xii.] foll. 326. S. Paul's Epp. with Comm. of Chrysostom.

332. (= Act. 259). Barberini iii. 36 (*olim* 22): *membr.* foll. 328 [κι]. Inter alia ἐπιτομαὶ κεφαλ. τῶν Πράξεων καὶ ἐπιστολῶν τῶν ἁγ. ἀποστόλων.

333. (= Act. 260). Barberini iii. 10 (*olim* 259) *chart.* foll. 296 [xiv.]. Excerpta ἐκ Πράξ. (f. 152): 'Ιακώβου (f. 159): Πέτρου (f. 162): 'Ιωάνν. (f. 165): 'Ιούδ. (f. 166): πρὸς Ρωμ. (f. 167): πρὸς Κορ. (f. 179): πρὸς Κθλ. (fol. 189): πρὸς Θεσσ. (f. 193): πρὸς Τιμ. α' (def. infin.).

334. Barb. v. 38 (*olim* 30) [xi.] foll. 219, *mut.* Hebrews with Comm. of Chrysostom.

335. Vallicell. F. [xv.], *chart.* miscell. Inter alia, εἰς τὰς ἐπιστολὰς τῶν 'Αποστόλων ἐξηγήσεις τινες.

336. (= Act. 261), Casanatensis, G. 11, 6.—Note, that though numbered for ' Acts,' it contains only the Catholic Epp. and those of S. Paul with a Catena.

337. Ottob. 328. [All I know as yet of this and of the next codex is that θεός is read in both at 1 Tim. iii. 16].

338. Borg. F. vi. 16. [See note on the preceding.]

ADDITIONAL COPIES OF THE ' APOSTOLUS.'

82. Messina ΠΓ (i.e. 83) foll. 331, 8vo. Perfect.

83. Crypta Ferrata, A. β. iv. [x.] *membr.* foll. 139, Praxapostolus. Rocchi gives an interesting account of this codex, pp. 19-20. It seems to be an adaptation of the liturgical use of C P. to the requirements of the Basilian monks in the Calabrian Church. This particular codex is *mut.* in the beginning and at the end. (For its extraordinary reading at 1 Tim. iii. 16, see above, p. 473-4).

84. Crypta Ferrata, A. ¦β. v. [xi.], *membr.* foll. 245, a most beautiful codex. Rocchi describes it carefully, pp. 20–2. At the end of the Menology is some liturgical matter. 'Patet Menologium esse merum ἀπόγραφον alicujus Menologii CPtani, in usum. si velis, forte redacti Ecclesiae Rossanensis in Calabria.' A suggestive remark follows that from this source ' rituum rubricarumque magnum segetem colligi posse, nec non Commemorationem *Sanctorum* mirum sane numerum, quas in aliis Menologiis vix invenies.'

85. Crypta Ferrata A. β. vii. [xi.] *membr.* foll. 64, Praxapostolus. This codex and the next exhibit δς ἐφανερώθη in 1 Tim. iii. 16. The Menology is *mut.* after 17 Dec.

86 Crypta Ferrata A. β. viii. [xii. or xiii.] fragments of foll. 127. *membr.* Praxapostolus. (See the preceding.) Interestingly described by Rocchi, p. 23–4.

87. Crypta Ferrata A. β. ix. [xii.], foll. 104, *membr.* Praxapostolus. Interestingly described by Rocchi, p. 24–5. The Menology is unfortunately defective after 9th November.

88. Crypta Ferrata, A. β. x. [xiii. ?) *membr.* 16 fragmentary leaves. 'Vere lamentanda est quæ huic Eclogadio calamitas evenit' (says the learned Rocchi, p. 25), 'quoniam ex ejus residuis, multa Sanctorum nomina reperies quæ alibi frustra quæsieris.'

89. Crypta Ferrata A. β. xi. [xi.] *membr.* foll. 291, *mut.*, written in two columns. The Menology is defective after 12 June, and elsewhere. Described by Rocchi, p. 26.

90. (= Evst. 322) Crypta Ferrata, A. β. ii. [xi.] *membr.* foll. 259, with many excerpts from the Fathers, fully described by Rocchi, p. 17–8, fragmentary and imperfect.

91. (= Evst. 323) Crypta Ferrata, A. δ. ii. [x.] *membr.* foll. 155, a singularly full lectionary. Described by Rocchi, p. 38–40.

92. (= Evst. 325) Crypta Ferrata, A. δ. iv. [xiii.] *membr.* foll. 257, a beautiful and interesting codex, ' Calligrapho Joanne Rossanensi Hieromonacho Cryptæferratæ': fully described by Rocchi, p. 40–3. Like many other in the same collection, it is a palimpsest.

93. (= Evst. 327) Crypta Ferrata, A. δ. vi. [xiii.] *membr.* foll. 37, *mut.* at beginning and end, and otherwise much injured: described by Rocchi, p. 45–6.

94. (= Evst. 328) Crypta Ferrata, A. δ. ix. [xii.], *membr.* foll. 117, *mut.* at beginning and end.

95. (= Evst. 334) Crypta Ferrata, A. δ. xx. [xii.] *membr.* foll. 21, a mere fragment. (Rocchi, p. 51.)

96. (= Evst. 337) Crypta Ferrata, A. δ. xxiv. A collection of fragments. (Rocchi, p. 53.)

97. (= Evst. 339) Crypta Ferrata, Γ. β. ii. [xi.] *membr.* foll. 151, elaborately described by Rocchi, p. 244–9. This codex once belonged to Thomasius.

98. (= Evst. 340) Crypta Ferrata, Γ. β iii. [xiv.], *membr.* foll. 201. Goar used this codex: described by Rocchi, p. 249–51.

99. (= Evst. 341) Crypta Ferrata, Γ. β. vi. [xiii. or xiv.], *membr.* foll. 101 : described by Rocchi, p. 255–7.

100. (= Evst. 344) Crypta Ferrata, Γ. β. ix. [xvi.], *membr.* foll. 95, *mut.* at beginning and end, and much injured.

101. (= Evst. 346) Crypta Ferrata, Γ. β. xii. [xiv.], *membr.* foll. 98, *mut.* at beginning and end.

102. (= Evst. 347) Crypta Ferrata, Γ. β. xiii. [xiii.] *membr.* foll. 188: written by John of Rossano, Hieromonachus of Cryptaferrata, described by Rocchi, p. 265-7.

103. (= Evst. 349) Crypta Ferrata, Γ. β. xv. [xi. to xiv.] *membr.* foll. 41.— Described p. 268-9.

104. (= Evst. 350) Crypta 'Ferrata, Γ. β. xvii. [xvi.]. *Chart.* foll. 269. Described, p. 269-70.

105. (= Evst. 351), Crypta Ferrata, Γ. β. xviii. [xiv.] *chart.* foll. 54.

106. (= Evst. 352) Crypta Ferrata, Γ. β. xix. [xvi.] *chart,* foll. 195, described p. 271.

107. (= Evst. 353) Crypta Ferrata, Γ. β. xxiii. [xvii.], *membr.* foll. 75,—the work of Basilius Falasca, Hieromonachus, and head of the monastery, A.D. 1641,—described p. 273-4.

108. (= Evst. 354) Crypta Ferrata, Γ. β. xxiv. [xvi.] *chart.* foll. 302,—the work of Lucas Felix, head of the monastery; described, p. 274-5.

109. (= Evst. 356) Crypta Ferrata, Γ. β. xxxviii. [xvii.]. *chart.* foll. 91, the work of ' Romanus Vasselli '. and ' Michael Lodolinus.'

110. (= Evst. 357) Crypta Ferrata, Γ. β. xlii. [xvi.] *chart.* foll. 344.

111. (= Evst. 358) Crypta Ferrata, Δ. β. xxii. [xviii.] *chart.* foll. 77,— described foll. 365-6.

112. (= Evst. 312) Messina, *membr.* in 8vo. foll. 60 [xiii.],—' fragmentum parvi momenti.'

113. Syracuse (' Seminario') *chart.* foll. 219, *mut.* given by the Cav. Landolina.

114. (= Evan. 155) Alex. Vat.

115. [I have led Scrivener into error by assigning this number (Apost. 115) to ' Vat. 2068 (Basil 107).' See above, p. 495, note (1). I did not advert to the fact that ' Basil 107 ' had *already* been numbered ' Apost. 49.']

116. Vat. 368 (Praxapostolus) [xiii.] foll. 136, *membr.*

117. (= Evst. 381) Vat. 774 [xiii.], foll. 160, *membr.*

118. (= Evst. 387) Vat. 2012 (Basil 51), foll. 211 [xv.] *chart.*

119. Vat. 2116 (Basil 155) [xiii.] foll. 111.

120. Alexand. Vat. 11 (Praxapostolus), [xiv.] *membr.* foll. 169.

121. (= Evst. 395) Alexand. Vat. 59 [xii.] foll. 137.

122. Alexand. Vat. 70, A.D. 1544, foll. 18: " in fronte pronunciatio Græca Latinis literis descripta."

123. (= Evst. 400) Palatino-Vat. 241 [xv.] *chart.* foll. 149.

124. (= Evst. 410) Barb. iii. 129 (*olim* 234) *chart.* [xiv.] foll. 189.

125. Barb. iv. 11 (*olim* 193), A.D. 1566, *chart.* foll. 158, Praxapostolus.

126. Barb. iv. 60 (*olim* 116) [xi.] foll. 322, a fine codex with *menologium.* Praxapostolus.

127. Barb. iv. 84 (*olim* 117) [xiii.] foll. 185, with menologium. *Mut.*

128. Paris, *Reg. Greek*, 13, *membr.* [xiii. or xiv.], a huge folio of Liturgical Miscellanies, consisting of between 6 and 900 unnumbered leaves. (At the σαββ. πρὸ τῶν φώτων, line 11, θϛ̄ ἐφα.) Communicated by the Abbé Martin.

POSTSCRIPT (Nov. 1883.)

It will be found stated at p. 495 (line 10 from the bottom) that the Codices (of ' Paul ' and ' Apost.') which exhibit Θεὸς ἐφανερώθη amount in all to 289.

From this sum (for the reason already assigned above), *one* must be deducted, viz., ' Apost. 115.'

On the other hand, 8 copies of ' PAUL ' (communicated by the Abbate Cozza-Luzi) are to be added : viz. *Vat.* 646 (Paul 310): 647 (Paul 311): 1971 (Paul 319). *Palat. Vat.* 10 (Paul 327): 204 (Paul 328). *Casanat.* G. 11, 16 (Paul 336). *Ottob.* 328 (Paul 337). *Borg.* F. vi. 16 (Paul 338). So that no less than 260 out of 262 cursive copies of St. Paul's Epistle,—[not 252 out of 254, as stated in p. 495 (line 21 from the bottom)],—are found to witness to the Reading here contended for. The enumeration of Codices at page 494 is therefore to be continued as follows:—310, 311, 319, 327, 328, 336, 337, 338.

To the foregoing are also to be added 4 copies of the ' APOSTOLUS,' viz. *Vat.* 2116 (Apost. 119). *Palat. Vat.* 241 (Apost. 123). *Barb.* iv. 11 [*olim* 193] (Apost. 125). Paris, *Reg. Gr.* 13 (Apost. 128).

From all which, it appears that, (including copies of the ' Apostolus,') THE CODICES WHICH ARE KNOWN TO WITNESS TO ΘΕÒC 'ΕΦΑΝΕҺѠΘΗ IN 1 Tim. iii. 16, AMOUNT [289—1+8+4) TO EXACTLY THREE HUNDRED.

INDEX I.

of TEXTS OF SCRIPTURE,—*quoted, discussed, or only referred to in this volume.*—*Note, that an asterisk* (*) *distinguishes references to the Greek Text from references to the English Translation* (†).—*Where either the Reading of the Original, or the English Translation is largely discussed, the sign is doubled* (** *or* ††).

2 M

2 M 2

536   INDEX I.

INDEX II.

of FATHERS *referred to, or else quoted* (*), *in this volume. For the chief Editions employed, see the note at p.* 121.

INDEX III.

General Index of Persons, Places, *and* Subjects *referred to in this Volume. But* Scriptural References *are to be sought in* INDEX I.; *and* Patristic References, *in* INDEX II. 'New Codices' *will be found enumerated in the* APPENDIX.

APPENDIX

Westcott & Hort's Greek Text & Theory Refuted

~~~~~~

Summarized From
Dean Burgon's

𝕽𝖊𝖛𝖎𝖘𝖎𝖔𝖓 𝕽𝖊𝖛𝖎𝖘𝖊𝖉

~~~~~~

By Rev. D. A. Waite, Th.D., Ph.D.
Director, The Bible For Today, Inc.

the
BIBLE
FOR
TODAY

900 Park Avenue
Collingswood, NJ 08108
Phone: 856-854-4452
www.BibleForToday.org

B.F.T. #2695

[NOTE: This booklet is taken from a message delivered on Thursday evening, August 11, 1996, at the 18th Annual Meeting of the DEAN BURGON SOCIETY. The meetings were held at the Grace Baptist Church, Franklin, Massachusetts. The printed copy has been adapted for this purpose, though a few references to the occasion are included.]

Westcott & Hort's Greek Text And Theory Refuted

~~~~~~

Summarized From
Dean Burgon's

𝕽𝖊𝖛𝖎𝖘𝖎𝖔𝖓 𝕽𝖊𝖛𝖎𝖘𝖊𝖉

By Rev. D. A. Waite, Th.D., Ph.D.
President of THE DEAN BURGON SOCIETY, and
Director of THE BIBLE FOR TODAY, INCORPORATED
900 Park Avenue, Collingswood, NJ 08108
Phone: 856-854-4452; FAX: 856-854-2464;
Orders: 1-800-JOHN 10:9; E-Mail: BFT@BibleForToday.org

I
INTRODUCTORY REMARKS

A. The Purpose of This Booklet. As the title indicates, it is the purpose and intention of this booklet to deal with the false and erroneous Greek New Testament Greek text and theory promulgated by what Dean Burgon refers to as "two irresponsible scholars of the University of Cambridge." These "irresponsible scholars" are none other than Bishop Brooke Foss Westcott and Professor Fenton John Anthony Hort. Their "invention" of the new Revised Greek Text that surfaced in 1881. It is strange indeed that very few people saw as clearly as Dean John William Burgon, their fellow Anglican clergyman, that Westcott and Hort were indeed "irresponsible scholars."

Instead, there has been, from that day to this, a stampede of pastors, teachers, "scholars," lay people, students and others who have followed their false lead into serious error. From the quotations taken from Dean Burgon's *Revision Revised*, it is hoped that the reader will turn from the errors of Westcott and Hort and enter into the truth and acceptance of the Traditional Greek text. It is also hoped that the it is hoped that the reader will turn from the errors of Westcott and Hort and enter into the truth and acceptance of the Traditional Greek text. It is also hoped that the reader will purchase and read *The Revision Revised* in its entirety. It is available as **B.F.T. #611** for a GIFT of **$25.00 + $3.00** for postage and handling. It is the new hardback edition published by the Dean Burgon Society.

B. The Relationship Between the Westcott and Hort Greek Text and the Modern So-Called "Eclectic" or "Critical" Text. Many of those who despise the Textus Receptus today and are powerful advocates of the false Revised Greek texts of Nestle-Aland or the United Bible Society have attempted to distance themselves from the Westcott and Hort Greek Text of 1881. In reality, with some minor changes, they are virtually identical. This fact is what makes this present booklet and the entire *Revision Revised* so powerful and so necessary. Here are some quotes from various writers about modern New Testament Greek **texts** and **theories** compared with the Greek **text** and **theories** of Westcott and Hort, showing the similarity between the two in both areas.

1. Seven Testimonies By Writers from 1914 through 1990 Stating the Similarity between the Westcott and Hort Text and Theory and that of the Current Greek Texts.

a. 1914--The Testimony of Herman Hoskier.

"The **text** printed by **Westcott and Hort** has been accepted as `the **true text**,' and grammars, works on the synoptic problem, works on higher criticism, and others have been grounded on this **text**." [Herman C. Hoskier, *Codex B and Its Allies--a Study and an Indictment*, (1914), Vol I, p. 468]

b. 1964--The Testimony of J. H. Greenlee.

"The textual **theories** of **W-H [Westcott & Hort]** underlies virtually all subsequent work in NT textual criticism." [J. H. Greenlee, *Introduction to New Testament Textual Criticism*, (1964), p. 78]

c. 1979--The Testimony of D. A. Carson.

"The **theories** of **Westcott and Hort** . . . [are] almost universally accepted today. . . . Subsequent textual critical work [since 1881] accepted the **theories** of **Westcott and Hort**. The vast majority of evangelical scholars hold that the basic textual **theories** of **Westcott and Hort** were right and the church stands greatly in their debt." [D. A. Carson, *The King James Version Debate*, (1979), p. 75]

d. 1980--The Testimony of Wilbur N. Pickering.

"The two most popular manual editions of the **text** today, Nestles-Aland and U.B.S. (United Bible Society) really vary little from the **W-H [Westcott & Hort] text**." [Dr. Wilbur N. Pickering, *The Identity of the New Testament Text*, (1980), pp. 42]

e. 1987--The Testimony of John R. Kohlenberger.

"**Westcott and Hort** . . . all subsequent versions from the Revised Version (1881) to those of the present . . . have adopted their basic

approach . . . [and] accepted the **Westcott and Hort** [Greek] **text.**"
[John R. Kohlenberger, *Words About the Word*, (1987) p. 42]

    f. 1990--The Testimony of Philip W. Comfort.
"But textual critics have not been able to advance beyond **Hort** in formalizing a **theory** . . . this has troubled certain textual scholars. " [Philip W. Comfort, *Early Manuscripts and Modern Translations of the New Testament*, (1990), p. 21]

    g. 1990--The Testimony of Bruce Metzger. In 1990, Dr. Kirk D. DiVietro, a Baptist Pastor who was then in New Jersey, wrote to Dr. Bruce Metzger about how he and the other members of the Nestle-Aland and United Bible Societies Committee began their work on their New Testament Greek Texts. Dr. Metzger replied to him as follows::

    "We took as our base at the beginning the **text of Westcott and Hort** (1881) and introduced changes as seemed necessary on the basis of MSS evidence."

This documentation is found in Metzger's own handwriting in **B.F.T. #2490-P**, p. 272 in *The Dean Burgon Society (1978--1994) Messages From the 16th Annual Meeting, August, 1994.*

    2. The Conclusion and Importance to be Drawn from these Seven Testimonies. Have you ever wondered just WHY the basic Greek text of Westcott and Hort dated in 1881 is virtually identical with the basic Greek text of the present critical editions? The simple reason is that they are derived from the same basic, corrupt Greek manuscripts, namely "B" (Vatican) and "Aleph" (Sinai) and a few others that followed them.

    Do you remember the axiom we were taught in high school plane geometry class: "Things equal to the same thing are equal to each other"? This applies in this case as well. The conclusion drawn from this is that when we attack the text and theory of Westcott and Hort, we are at the same time attacking the text and theory behind the Nestle-Aland Greek text, the United Bible Society text, and others that go along with them. What is said against Westcott and Hort's text in these quotes can also be said against the texts of Nestle-Aland and the United Bible Society!

    C. The History of Burgon's *Revision Revised*. *The Revision Revised*, by Dean John William Burgon, was originally published in 1883. In 1973, I read a condensed version of it in *True or False?* edited by Dr. David Otis Fuller. The first complete and unedited copy I read was the Conservative Classics edition which was published in Paradise, Pennsylvania. This edition has long since gone out of print. THE BIBLE FOR TODAY, INCORPORATED, has been publishing a xerox copy of this book for many years in order to make it available for those who wanted to read it. Jay Green published portions of Dean Burgon's books in his book *Unholy Hands on God's Holy Word*. Since Dean Burgon's various books do not have their original page numbers, and are not organized in their original order, it is difficult to see if every word has been included.

D. The New Dean Burgon Society Hardback Edition. In view of the continued need for *The Revision Revised,* the Executive Committee of the Dean Burgon Society voted to make hardback copies (with the original page numbers) again available for the many who want to read it. An important fact to remember about *The Revision Revised* is that it was still unanswered even after two full years after it was published. It is still unanswered to this day!

E. The Method Used in this Booklet. Though *The Revision Revised* has almost 600 pages, in this brief booklet, I will only allude to about fifty quotations that summarize the argument of the book. It is important that we see why Dean Burgon's book, *The Revision Revised*, is such a valuable tool for people to read and understand. It is hoped that these fifty quotations will whet the appetite for this solid documentation so that the reader might be anxious to read every page of the book itself!!

F. Outline of the book. *The Revision Revised* consists of three major ARTICLES. Each of the ARTICLES appeared first in a periodical in England called *The Quarterly Review.* In **ARTICLE I** Dean Burgon evaluated the new Greek text of Westcott and Hort (pages 1-110). In **ARTICLE II** he enumerated the defects of the English Revised Version (ERV) and the superiority of the King James Bible (pages 111-232). In **ARTICLE III** Dean Burgon refuted Westcott and Hort's new textual theory and its serious defects (pp. 233-366). These three ARTICLES are followed by a LETTER TO BISHOP ELLICOTT in reply to his pamphlet, various APPENDICES and the INDEX (pages 367-549).

G. Background. In 1995, at the DEAN BURGON SOCIETY, I spoke about *Dean Burgon's CONFIDENCE in the King James Bible.* Quotations were taken from **ARTICLE II** of *The Revision Revised* in which the English Revised Version (ERV) and the King James Bible (AV) were compared. The Authorized (King James) Version was found by Dean Burgon to be far superior in every way to any other version of his day. By extension, similar arguments might be made against the false versions of our own day. This is available in a printed booklet form as **B.F.T. #2591 (36 pages)** for a GIFT of **$3.00 + $2.00** postage and handling.

H. The Refutation of Westcott and Hort's Greek Text and Theory. At this time, I would like to summarize some of the highlights, main arguments, and quotations from Dean Burgon's PREFACE, from his **ARTICLE I,** and from his **ARTICLE III** as found in his book, *The Revision Revised.* As mentioned before, **ARTICLE I** dealt with Westcott and Hort's false New Testament Greek text (pages 1-110). **ARTICLE III** condemned in strong, yet clear language, Westcott and Hort's false **theory** behind their New Testament Greek text (pages 233-366).

II
Quotations From Dean Burgon's
PREFACE--Setting the Stage
(pages iv-xxxii)

A. Dr. Frederick Scrivener Backed Dean Burgon's Attack on Westcott and Hort's New Testament Greek Text. Dr. Frederick H. A. Scrivener was an Anglican clergyman who was a contemporary of both Westcott and Hort and Dean Burgon. Dr. Scrivener was one of the greatest and most exacting scholars of his day in the field of textual criticism. He was quoted by Dean Burgon in his PREFACE.

    1. Westcott and Hort's Greek Text Was Based on "Ingenious Conjecture." Dr. Scrivener wrote:

"There is little hope for the stability of their **[that is, Westcott & Hort's]** imposing structure, if its foundations have been laid on the sandy ground of ingenious conjecture. And, since barely the smallest vestige of historical evidence has ever been alleged in support of the views of these accomplished editors, their teaching must either be received as intuitively true, or dismissed from our consideration as precarious and even visionary." [Dr. F. H. A. Scrivener's *Plain Introduction*, 1883, p. 531, quoted by Dean John W. Burgon, *Revision Revised*, p. iv].

    2. Dr. Hort's Greek Textual System Was "Destitute of Historical Foundation." Dr. Scrivener again wrote:

"Dr. Hort's System is entirely destitute of historical foundation. . . We are compelled to repeat as emphatically as ever our strong conviction that the Hypothesis to whose proof he has devoted so many laborious years, is destitute not only of historical foundation, but of all probability, revealing from the internal goodness of the Text which its adoption would force upon us." [Dr. F. H. A. Scrivener's *Plain Introduction*, 1883, pp. 537, 542, quoted by Dean John W. Burgon, *Revision Revised*, p. iv].

B. Dean Burgon's Sage Comments of an Introductory Nature.

    1. Dean Burgon's One Object in *The Revision Revised*. He wrote:

"My one object has been to defeat the mischievous attempt which was made in 1881 to thrust upon this Church **[the Anglican Church]** and Realm **[London and the whole British Commonwealth]** a Revision of the Sacred Text, which--recommended though it be by eminent names--I am thoroughly convinced, and am able to prove, is untrustworthy from beginning to end." [Dean John W. Burgon, *Revision Revised*, p. v].

2. "Poisoning the River of Life."   Dean Burgon wrote:

"It is, however, the systematic depravation of the underlying Greek which does so grievously offend me: for this is nothing else but a poisoning of the River of Life at its sacred source. Our Revisers (with the best and purest intentions, no doubt,) stand convicted of having deliberately rejected the words of Inspiration in every page, and of having substituted for them fabricated Readings which the Church has long since refused to acknowledge, or else has rejected with abhorrence, and which only survive at this time in a little handful of documents of the most depraved type." [Dean John W. Burgon, *Revision Revised*, pp. vi-vii].

He is referring to "B" and "Aleph," the Vatican and Sinai manuscripts.

3. A Time for Hitting His Opponents "Hard." Dean Burgon was often charged with hitting his opponents "rather hard." This was his response:

"If, therefore, any do complain that I have sometimes hit my opponents rather hard, I take leave to point out that `to everything there is a season, and a time to every purpose under the sun'; `a time to embrace, and a time to be far from embracing'; a time for speaking smoothly, and a time for speaking sharply. And that when the Words of Inspiration are seriously imperilled, as now they are, it is scarcely possible for one who is determined effectually to preserve the Deposit in its integrity, to hit either too straight or too hard." [Dean John W. Burgon, *Revision Revised*, pp. vii-viii].

4. This book Was Unanswered After Two Years while Dean Burgon Was Still Alive, And Is Still Unanswered. Dean Burgon wrote:

"Two full years have elapsed since the first of these Essays was published; and my Criticism--for the best of reasons--remains to this hour unanswered. The public has been assured indeed, (in the course of some hysterical remarks by Canon Farrar), that `the "Quarterly Reviewer" can be refuted as fully as he desires as soon as any scholar has the leisure to answer him.'  The `Quarterly Reviewer' can afford to wait,--if the Revisers can. But they are reminded that it is no answer to one who has demolished their master's `Theory,' for the pupils to keep on reproducing fragments of it; and by their mistakes and exaggerations, to make both themselves and him, ridiculous." [Dean John W. Burgon, *Revision Revised*, p. xv].

5. Inventing Facts and "Oracular Decrees." Dean Burgon wrote:

"In this department of sacred Science, men have been going on too long inventing their facts, and delivering themselves of oracular decrees, on the sole responsibility of their own inner consciousness. There is great convenience in such a method certainly,--a charming simplicity which is in a high degree attractive to flesh and blood. It dispenses with proof. It furnishes no evidence. **[that is, Westcott and Hort's text and theory]** It asserts when it ought to argue. It reiterates when it is called upon to explain. `I am sir Oracle.' . . . This,--which I venture to style the *unscientific* method,--reached its culminating point when Professors Westcott and Hort recently put forth their Recension of the Greek Text."

"Their work is indeed quite a psychological curiosity. Incomprehensible to me is it how two able men of disciplined understandings can have seriously put forth the volume which they call `INTRODUCTION-- APPENDIX.' It is the very *Reductio ad absurdum* of the uncritical method of the last fifty years. And it is especially in opposition to this new method of theirs that I so strenuously insist that *the consentient voice of Catholic Antiquity* is to be diligently inquired after and submissively listened to; for that *this*, in the end, will prove our *only* safe guide." [Dean John W. Burgon, *Revision Revised*, pp. xxv-xxvi].

   6. **"Catholic Antiquity" Defined as Universal Antiquity.** Dean Burgon defined what he meant by "Catholic antiquity." He did not mean "Roman Catholic antiquity," but "universal antiquity." He wrote:

"The method I persistently advocate in every case of a supposed doubtful Reading. (I say it for the last time, and request that I may be no more misrepresented.) is, that *an appeal shall be unreservedly made to Catholic Antiquity*; and that the combined verdict of Manuscripts, Versions, Fathers, shall be regarded as decisive." [Dean John W. Burgon, *Revision Revised*, pp. xxvii].

That is what Dean Burgon appeals to, Westcott and Hort do not.

   7. **Dean Burgon Longed to Teach the Bible.** Dean Burgon would rather engage in Bible interpretation than needing to battle for the Words of God. He wrote:

"But I more than long,--I fairly *ache* to have done with Controversy, and to be free to devote myself to the work of Interpretation. My apology for bestowing so large a portion of my time on Textual Criticism, is David's when he was reproached by his brethren for appearing on the field of battle,--`Is there not a cause?'" [Dean John W. Burgon, *Revision Revised*, pp. xxix].

Many of us would love to be able to "have done with controversy," but the battle for the Words of God is there. I think we chose a good name for our society--The Dean Burgon Society. As Dean Burgon did, we certainly have a cause, don't we!

   8. **Westcott and Hort as "Irresponsible Scholars."** Dean Burgon characterized Westcott and Hort as two "irresponsible scholars." He wrote:

"But instead of all this, a Revision of the *English Authorised Version* having been sanctioned by the Convocation of the Southern Province in 1871, the opportunity was eagerly snatched at by two irresponsible scholars of the University of Cambridge **[He is talking about Westcott and Hort]** for obtaining the general sanction of the Revising body, and thus indirectly of Convocation, for a private venture of their own,--their own privately devised Revision of the *Greek Text*. On that Greek Text of theirs, (which

I hold to be the most depraved which has ever appeared in print), with some slight modifications, our Authorised English Version has been silently revised: silently, I say, for in the margin of the English no record is preserved of the underlying Textual changes which have been introduced by the Revisionists." [Dean John W. Burgon, *Revision Revised*, pp. xxx].

Though Westcott and Hort's Greek text is *"the most depraved which has ever appeared in print,"* this is virtually the same text used by the new versions and perversions of today.

9. Why Dean Burgon Descended into "the Arena of Controversy."
Dean Burgon wrote:

"If all this does not constitute a valid reason for descending into the arena of controversy, it would in my judgment be impossible to indicate an occasion when the Christian soldier *is* called upon to do so:--the rather because certain of these who, from their rank and station in the Church, ought to be the champions of the Truth, are at this time found to be among its most vigorous assailants." [Dean John W. Burgon, *Revision Revised*, pp. xxxi-xxxii].

Notice what he said about some of the preachers of his day. We have this today do we not? Some claim to be "champions," and "Fundamentalists," yet they are assailants of the truth. When the Words of God are at stake, we must, at times, contend with even our own Christian brethren. If our brethren are wrong on the Words of God, and don't want to preserve the Words of our Lord Jesus Christ, then we must stand up as David did and ask: "Is there not a cause?" We of course should also expose those who are in error who are not "brethren." In so doing, we will no doubt get into trouble from both of these groups.

III
ARTICLE I: THE NEW GREEK TEXT--
Refuted by Dean John William Burgon
(pages 1-110)

A. The Importance of Dean Burgon's ARTICLE I on THE NEW GREEK TEXT. In Dean Burgon's ARTICLE I on THE NEW GREEK TEXT, he totally destroyed the erroneous New Testament Greek Text that was foisted upon an unsuspecting people in 1881 by Westcott and Hort. Sad to say, this false Greek text was, in the main, the basis for the English Revised Version (ERV). I have cited above, in **Section I** (pages 2-3), seven critical scholars in the 20th century (from 1914 to 1990) who have proclaimed that this false Greek text is STILL the primary basis for the modern Greek texts of Nestle-Aland and the United Bible Society! When Dean Burgon destroyed Westcott and Hort's Greek text, he also destroyed the present Greek texts that form the basis of the modern New Testament versions and perversions. These Westcott and Hort-type Greek texts are used, not only in the apostate schools, colleges, and seminaries, and the New Evangelical schools, colleges, and seminaries, but, sadly, also in entirely too many so-called "Fundamentalist" schools, colleges and seminaries!

I would urge you to pay close attention to the quotations from this section of Dean Burgon's masterful book, *The Revision Revised*.

B. Important Quotations from Dean Burgon's ARTICLE I: THE NEW GREEK TEXT (pages 1-110)

   1. God's Threefold Means of Preservation of His Written Words.

      a. God's Preservation Means #1: MANUSCRIPT COPIES. Dean Burgon wrote of the manuscript COPIES:

"(1) The provision, then, which the Divine Author of Scripture is found to have made for the preservation of His written Word, is of a peculiarly varied and highly complex description, First--By causing that a vast multiplication of Copies should be required all down the ages,--beginning at the earliest period, and continuing in an ever-increasing ratio until the actual invention of Printing,--He provided the most effectual security imaginable against fraud. True, that millions of the copies so produced have long since perished; but it is nevertheless a plain fact that there survive of the Gospels alone upwards of one thousand copies in the present day." [Dean John W. Burgon, *Revision Revised*, pp. 8-9].

b. God's Preservation Means #2: ANCIENT NEW TESTAMENT VERSIONS. On the subject of the VERSIONS, Dean Burgon wrote:

"(2) Next, VERSIONS. The necessity of translating the Scriptures into divers languages for the use of different branches of the early Church, procured that many an authentic record has been preserved for the New Testament as it existed in the first few centuries of the Christian era. Thus, the Peschito Syriac and the Old Latin version are believed to have been executed in the IInd century **[Early versions show the text that the translators had in their hands and were using.]**. . . . The two Egyptian translations are referred to the IIIrd and IVth. The Vulgate (or revised Latin) and the Gothic are also claimed for the IVth; the Armenian and possibly the Aethiopic, belong to the Vth." [Dean John W. Burgon, *Revision Revised*, p. 9].

c. God's Preservation Means #3: Quotations From CHURCH FATHERS. Here's what Dean Burgon wrote on the value of "patristic" quotations, or references to the Bible by the Church Fathers:

"(3) Lastly, the requirements of assailants and apologists alike, the business of Commentators, the needs of controversialists and teachers in every age, have resulted in a vast accumulation of additional evidence, of which it is scarcely possible to over-estimate the importance. For in this way it has come to pass that every famous Doctor of the Church in turn has quoted more or less largely from the sacred writings, and thus has borne testimony to the contents of the codices with which he was individually familiar. PATRISTIC CITATIONS." [Dean John W. Burgon, *Revision Revised*, p. 9]

These "Church Fathers" were leaders in the early churches who either quoted the New Testament directly, or made references to certain verses. What text did they have in their hands when they referred to these verses? This evidence is very important. Dean Burgon made an index of over 86,000 quotations from these Church Fathers showing the text of Scripture they used. This is a third mighty safeguard of the integrity of the deposit of the Words of God.

2. The Value of "Lectionaries." Dean Burgon wrote:

"In truth, the security which the Text of the New Testament enjoys is altogether unique and extraordinary. To specify the single consideration, which has never yet attracted nearly the amount of attention it deserves. Lectionaries abound which establish the Text which has been publicly read in the churches of the East, from *at least* A.D. 400 until the time of the invention of printing." [Dean John W. Burgon, *Revision Revised*, p. 11]

"Lectionaries" were portions of the New Testament that were read on certain feast days such as Christmas, Easter, and so on. We have at least 2,143 of these Greek Lectionaries preserved for us today. This evidence is very important.

3. The Blind Superstitious Reverence for "B," "Aleph," and Others. Dean Burgon wrote:

"Singular to relate, the first, second, fourth and fifth of these codices (B, Aleph, C, D) but especially B and Aleph have within the last twenty years established a tyrannical ascendency over the imagination of the Critics which can only be fitly spoken of as a blind superstition. It matters nothing that all four ["B", "Aleph", "C", and "D"] are discovered on careful scrutiny to differ essentially, not only from ninety-nine out of a hundred of the whole body of extant MSS, besides, but even *from one another.*" [Dean John W. Burgon, *Revision Revised*, pp. 11-12].

Yet these same manuscripts, by "blind superstition" are used as the very foundations of the versions and perversions of our day. Even the ones that Bible-believing Christians are using such as: the New International Version, the New American Standard Version, the New King James Version in the footnotes, the New Berkeley, and others.

4. The Similarities Between "B" (Vatican) and "Aleph" (Sinai) Manuscripts. Dean Burgon wrote:

"Between the first two (B and Aleph) there subsists an amount of sinister resemblance, which proves that they must have been derived at no very remote period from the same corrupt original. . . . It is in fact *easier to find two consecutive verses in which these two MSS differ the one from the other, than two consecutive verses in which they entirely agree.*" [Dean John W. Burgon, *Revision Revised*, p. 12]

5. The Unreliability of "Aleph" the Sinai Manuscript. Dean Burgon wrote:

"Next to "D," the most untrustworthy codex is Aleph, which bears on its front a memorable note of the evil repute under which it has always laboured:--viz. it is found that at least ten revisers between the IVth and the XIIth centuries busied themselves with the task of correcting its many and extraordinary perversions of the truth of Scripture." [Dean John W. Burgon, *Revision Revised*, p. 13].

6. The Depravity of Manuscripts "Aleph," "B," and "D." Dean Burgon wrote:

"We venture to assure him, without a particle of hesitation, that "Aleph," "B," "D" are *three of the most scandalously corrupt copies extant:*--exhibit *the most shamefully mutilated* texts which are anywhere to be met with:--have become, by whatever process (for their history is wholly unknown), the depositories of the largest amount of *fabricated readings* ancient *blunders,* and *intentional perversions of Truth,*--which are discoverable in any known copies of the Word of God." [Dean John W. Burgon, *Revision Revised*, p. 16].

Dean Burgon knew what these old ancient Uncials were. They were depraved, and mutilated. Yet these are respected, revered, and put on a pedestal today.

7. The Worst Corruptions of the New Testament Came Within the First 100 Years After They Were Made. Dean Burgon wrote:

"`It is no less true to fact than paradoxical in sound,' writes the most learned of the Revisionist body **[that is, Dr. Frederick H. A. Scrivener]**, `that the worst corruptions to which the New Testament has ever been subjected, originated within a hundred years after it was composed: that Irenaeus (A.D. 150), and the African Fathers, and the whole Western, with a portion of the Syrian Church, used far inferior manuscripts to those employed by Stunica, or Erasmus, or Stephens thirteen centuries later, when moulding the Textus Receptus.'" [Dean John W. Burgon, *Revision Revised*, p. 30].

What he is saying is that the corruptions in the Greek texts at the time of Irenaeu the African Church, the Western Church, and the early days of "B", and "Aleph were far worse than and inferior to the texts used to develop the Textus Receptu

8. Dean Burgon Defended the Traditional Greek Text Against th False Westcott and Hort Type of Text in the Following Thirty Passage
Though Dean Burgon defended the traditional text throughout the book, here is section which takes examples one after another in rapid succession. Withor comment, these thirty passages are listed here with the pages in *The Revisio Revised* where they are taken up in detail:

1. Mark 2:1-12 (pp. 30-34)
2. Luke 11:2-4 (pp. 34-36)
3. Mark 16:9-20 (pp. 36-40)
4. Luke 2:14 (pp. 41-51)
5. Acts 27:37 (pp. 51-53)
6. Acts 18:7 (pp. 53-54)
7. Matthew 11:23 & Luke 10:15 (pp. 54-56)
8. Mark 11:3 (pp. 56-58)
9. Mark 11:8 (pp. 58-61)
10. Luke 23:45 (pp. 61-66)
11. Mark 6:20 (pp. 66-70)
12. Mark 9:24 (pp. 70-71)
13. Matthew 14:30 (p. 71)
14. Mark 15:39 (pp. 71-72)
15. Luke 23;42 (p. 72)
16. John 14:4 (pp. 72-73)
17. Luke 6:1 (pp. 73-75)
18. Luke 22:19-20--32 words (pp. 75-79)
19. Luke 22:43-44--26 words (pp. 79-83)
20. Luke 23:34--12 words (pp.82-85)
21. Luke 23:38--7 words (pp. 85-88)
22. Luke 24:1,3,6,9,12--37 words (pp. 88-90)
23. Luke 24:40,42,51-53--23 words (pp. 90-91)
24. Matthew 27:21 (pp. 91-92)
25. Matthew 28:11 (pp. 92-93)

26.   Luke 9:55-56 (p. 93)
27.   Luke 24:41 (p. 93)
28.   Luke 6:1 (pp. 93-98)
29.   1 Timothy 3:16 ("God was manifest in the
       flesh") (pp. 98-106, and pp. 424- 491)
30.   2 Peter 2:22 (p. 106)

9. Dean Burgon's Conclusion About the False Type of Greek Text Adopted by Westcott and Hort. Dean Burgon wrote:

"It has been the ruin of the present undertaking--as far as the Sacred Text is concerned--that the majority of the Revisionist body have been misled throughout by the oracular decrees and impetuous advocacy of Drs. Westcott and Hort, who, with the purest intentions and most laudable industry, have constructed a Text demonstrably more remote from the Evangelic verity than any which has ever yet seen the light." [Dean John W. Burgon, *Revision Revised*, p. 110].

Did Dean Burgon name names? Yes, he did. He names Westcott and Hort. Did he name names within his own denominational framework? Yes, he did. Both of these men were Anglicans, that is, members of the clergy of the Church of England. Dean Burgon was a fundamental, conservative Anglican. Westcott and Hort, on the other hand, were apostate and heretical unbelievers. This is shown in both of my booklets: *The Theological Heresies of Westcott and Hort* [**B.F.T. #595** for a GIFT of **$3.00**], and *Bishop Westcott's Clever Denial of the Bodily Resurrection of Christ* [**B.F.T. #1131** for a GIFT of **$4.00**]. The latter booklet shows clearly that Westcott denied the bodily resurrection of Christ.

Westcott and Hort have to be named and exposed, not only in textual matters, but also in doctrinal matters. Dr. Stewart Custer of Bob Jones University, in his booklet, *The Truth About the King James Controversy*, on page 26, stated of Westcott and Hort: ". . . these men have written in their mature years book after book defending the **CONSERVATIVE** interpretation of Scripture, . . ." *The Theological Heresies of Westcott and Hort* shows clearly that these men have written books that do **NOT** defend "the **CONSERVATIVE** interpretation of Scripture." There are about 125 quotations from five of their books to prove this point.

Using the term, "**conservative,**" to refer to such a man as Westcott who clearly denied the bodily resurrection of the Lord Jesus Christ, would require a complete redefinition of what is meant by the word, "**conservative.**" I don't want any part of that kind of "**conservativism,**" do you? Dean Burgon named names politely and gently. We can be gentlemen and, where appropriate, still name names in the same manner.

IV
ARTICLE III--WESTCOTT & HORT'S NEW TEXTUAL THEORY--
Refuted by Dean Burgon (pages 233-366)

A. The Importance of Dean Burgon's ARTICLE III Which Refuted Westcott and Hort's NEW TEXTUAL THEORY. In 1881, Westcott and Hort and the other members of the translation committee of the English Revised Version (ERV) published their very inferior work. At about the same time Westcott and Hort published an *Introduction to the Greek New Testament*. This amazingly misleading book has been answered fully by Dean Burgon in his ARTICLE III. The BIBLE FOR TODAY has re-printed this *Introduction* for those who wish to see their false theory for themselves. It is **BFT #1303 (540 pp.)** which is available for a gift of **$25.00**.

This false **THEORY** behind the false Revised Greek text is as important as the Greek text itself. Not only is the same basic false Greek **text** in use today by the various versions and perversions, but also the same basic false **THEORY** supporting this text is in use today by the same versions and perversions!!

B. Important Quotations from Dean Burgon's ARTICLE III: WESTCOTT AND HORT'S NEW TEXTUAL THEORY (pages 233-366).

1. Dean Burgon's Massive Evidence in Favor of the Reading "GOD Was Manifest in the Flesh" in 1 Timothy 3:16. Dean Burgon shows strong and irrefutable proof for the correctness of **"GOD WAS MANIFEST IN THE FLESH."**

Evidence for *THEOS* ("God")

N.T. Greek Manuscripts (Lectionaries & Copies) =	289
Ancient N.T. Versions =	3
Greek Church Fathers =	c. 20

There is an abundance of evidence for this reading as contained in the King James Bible. *Theos* or "God" is without any doubt the original and proper reading.

Evidence for *HO* ("which")

N.T. Greek Manuscripts = ... 1

Ancient N.T. Versions = ... 5

Greek Church Fathers = ... 2

---

his evidence for *ho*, or "which," is extremely scanty. It has no opportunity to
ucceed as the original and proper reading.

Evidence for *HOS* ("who")

N.T. Greek Manuscripts = ... 6

Ancient N.T. Versions = ... 1

Greek Church Fathers = ... 0

[Dean John W. Burgon, *Revision Revised*, pp. 486-496].

---

gain, this is not sufficient evidence to favor *hos*, or "who." It is unreasonable to
ave the modern versions favoring it, yet they do.

"GOD was manifest in the flesh" is the correct reading in the King James
;ible. Though it is entirely in error, *HOS* is what is used in the new versions and
erversions of our day. Here are a few of them:

"HE WHO was manifested in the flesh"--the American Standard Version.

"HE was manifested in the flesh"--the Revised Standard Version.

"HE WHO was revealed in the flesh"--New American Standard Version.

"HE appeared in a body"--the New International Version.

"HE was shown to us in a human body"--the New Century Version.

"HE was revealed in flesh"--the New Revised Standard Version.

---

2. The Error of "Alternative Readings." Dean Burgon wrote:
"What are found in the margin are therefore `alternative readings'--in the
opinion of these self-constituted representatives of the Church and of the
Sects. It becomes evident that by this ill-advised proceeding, our Revisionists would convert every Englishman's copy of the New Testament into a
one-sided Introduction to the Critical difficulties of the Greek Text; a
labyrinth, out of which they have not been at the pains to supply him with
a single hint as to how he may find his way. . . . What else must be the
result of all this but general uncertainty, confusion, distress? A hazy mis-

trust of all Scripture has been insinuated into the hearts and minds of countless millions, who in this way have been *forced* to become doubters,-- yea, doubters in the Truth of Revelation itself." [Dean John W. Burgon, *Revision Revised*, pp. 236-237].

Dean Burgon is opposed to alternative readings. These are what abound in the footnotes of the study edition of the New King James Version. The reader doesn't know which to believe, the words of the text or the words of the footnotes! This results in a *"hazy mistrust of all Scripture"*!

3. The False Textual Theory of the German Lachmann. Dean Burgon wrote:

"Lachmann's ruling principle then, was exclusive reliance on a very few ancient authorities--*because* they are `ancient.' He constructed his text on three or four--not infrequently on *one or two*--Greek codices. Of the Greek Fathers, he relied on Origen. Of the oldest Versions, he cared only for the Latin. To the Syrian . . . he paid no attention. We venture to think his method *irrational*." [Dean John W. Burgon, *Revision Revised*, pp. 242-43].

4. The False Textual Theory of the Frenchman Tregelles. Dean Burgon wrote:

"Tregelles adopted the same strange method. He resorted to a very few out of the entire mass of `ancient Authorities' for the construction of his Text. His proceeding is exactly that of a man, who--in order that he may the better explore a comparatively unknown region--begins by putting out both his eyes; and resolutely refuses the help of the natives to show him the way. *Why* he rejected the testimony of *every Father of the IVth century except Eusebius,*--it were unprofitable to enquire." [Dean John W. Burgon, *Revision Revised*, p. 243].

Dean Burgon's humor and picturesque figures of speech add to his clear logic of argumentation.

5. The False Textual Theory of German Tischendorf (1831 A.D.). Tischendorf was the man that found the Sinai manuscript in the wastebasket on Mt. Sinai. The monks were getting ready to burn it and Tischendorf was getting ready to buy it. Which one, do you think, had the correct appreciation of the value of the Sinai manuscript? I think it was the monks! Dean Burgon wrote:

"Tischendorf, the last and by far the ablest of the three, knew better than to reject `eighty-nine ninetieth' of the extant witnesses. He had recourse to the ingenious expedient of *adducing* all the available evidence, but *adopting* just as little of it as he chose; and he *chose* to adopt those readings only, which are vouched for by the same little band of authorities whose partial testimony had already proved fatal to the decrees of Lachmann and Tregelles." [Dean John W. Burgon, *Revision Revised*, p. 243].

6. The False Textual Theories of Lachmann, Tregelles, and Tischendorf Summarized. Dean Burgon wrote:

"Enough has been said to show--(the only point we are bent on establishing)--that the one distinctive tenet of the three most famous Critics since 1831 has been a superstitious reverence for whatever is found in the *same little handful of early,*--but *not* the earliest,--*nor yet of necessity the purest,*--documents." [Dean John W. Burgon, *Revision Revised*, p. 244].

He is talking now about Westcott and Hort's almost exclusive use of "B" and "Aleph." Notice he calls it "superstitious reverence." This is tantamount to worship, is it not?

7. **The Errors of the Last Three False Textual Theories.** Dean Burgon wrote:

"'Strange,' we venture to exclaim, (addressing the living representatives of the school of Lachmann, and Tregelles, and Tischendorf):--'Strange, that you should not perceive that you are the dupes of a fallacy which is even transparent. You *talk* of "Antiquity." But you must know very well that you actually *mean* something different. You fasten upon three, or perhaps four,--on two, or perhaps three,--on *one, or perhaps two,*--documents of the IVth or Vth century. But then, confessedly, these are one, two, three, or four *specimens only* of Antiquity,--not "Antiquity" itself. And what if they should even prove to be *unfair samples* of Antiquity? . . .'" [Dean John W. Burgon, *Revision Revised*, p. 244].

8. **The Errors in Dr. Hort's False New Testament Textual Theory.** Dean Burgon wrote:

". . . Dr. Hort informs us that Lachmann's Text of 1831 was 'the first founded on documentary authority.' . . . On *what* then, pray, does the learned Professor imagine that the Texts of Erasmus (1516) and of Stunica (1522) were founded: His statement is incorrect. The actual difference between Lachmann's Text and those of the earlier Editors is that *his* 'documentary authority' is partial, narrow, self-contradictory; and is proved to be untrustworthy by a free appeal to Antiquity."

"*Their* documentary authority, derived from independent sources,-- though partial and narrow as that on which Lachmann relied,--exhibits (*under the good Providence of God,*) a Traditional Text, the general purity of which is demonstrated by all the evidence which 350 years of subsequent research have succeeded in accumulating; and which is confessedly the Text of A.D. 375." [Dean John W. Burgon, *Revision Revised*, p. 250].

What he is trying to say is that the opposite of the Westcott and Hort text is a traditional text which has been the text of A.D. 375. This is, of course, what Westcott and Hort have agreed, but they have a false theory to explain it.

9. **The Errors in Both "Intrinsic Probability" and "Transcriptional Probability."** The page references are to Westcott and Hort's *Introduction to the Greek New Testament*. Dean Burgon wrote:

"The dissertation on 'Intrinsic' and 'Transcriptional Probability' which follows (pp. 20-30)--being *unsupported by one single instance or illustration,*--

we pass by. It ignores throughout the fact, that the most serious corruptions of MSS are due *not* to `Scribes'` or `Copyists,'` . . . but to the persons who employed them . . . . We venture to declare that inasmuch as one expert's notions of what is `transcriptionally probable,'` prove to be the diametrical reverse of another expert's notions, the supposed evidence to be derived from this source may, with advantage, be neglected altogether. Let the study of *Documentary Evidence* be allowed to take its place. Notions of `Probability'` are the very pest of these departments of Science which admit of an appeal to *Fact.*" [Dean John W. Burgon, *Revision Revised*, pp. 251-52].

"Intrinsic probability" refers to what the original might have been. With their mind the textual critics try to figure out what might have been there in the original text "Transcriptional probability" refers to what changes the scribe might have made to the document. Both forms of "probability" are evil and pure guesswork!

10.   The Errors in the Alleged "Genealogical Evidence" in the Greek Manuscripts. Dean Burgon wrote:

"High time however is it to declare that, in strictness, all this talk about `Genealogical evidence'` when applied to Manuscripts is *moonshine.* . . .But then, it happens, unfortunately, that we are unacquainted with *one single instance* of a known MS copied from another known MS. And perforce all talk about `Genealogical evidence,'` where *no single step in the descent* can be produced,--in other words, *where no Genealogical evidence exists,*--is absurd." [Dean John W. Burgon, *Revision Revised*, pp. 255-56].

Genealogy in documents refers to those that are clearly related, one to the other just like a relation might exist between a father, a son, a grandson and so on. Yet that is one of the errors that Westcott and Hort made up. It is this false genealogy argument which is used by the so-called Majority Greek text for John 7:53--8:11 and the entire book of Revelation.

11.   The Errors of the So-Called "Genealogical Evidence" Illustrated Dean Burgon wrote:

"The living inhabitants of a village, congregated in the churchyard where the bodies of their forgotten progenitors for 1000 years repose without memorials of any kind, **[In other words, there are no gravestones in this cemetery.]**--is a faint image of the relation which subsists between extant copies of the Gospels and the sources from which they were derived." [Dean John W. Burgon, *Revision Revised*, p. 256].

12.   The False Argument of "Conflation" Answered. The following eight verses are the only ones offered as alleged examples of "conflation" in Westcott and Hort's *Introduction*: (1) Mark 6:33; (2) Mark 8:26; (3) Mark 9:38; (4) Mark 9:49; (5) Luke 9:10; (6) Luke 11:54; (7) Luke 12:18; (8) Luke 24:53. Dean Burgon shows clearly that the above ##1, 2, 5, 6, & 7 don't even exhibit the phenomenon. Dean Burgon wrote:

"The interpretation put upon them by Drs. Westcott and Hort, is purely arbitrary: a baseless imagination,--a dream and nothing more." [Dean John W. Burgon, *Revision Revised*, pp. 258-262].

Here is what Westcott and Hort mean by conflation. You might take a car and a van someplace. In writing about this, you might have one manuscript that reads "car" and another manuscript that reads "van." Then you have a manuscript that combines the two of them and reads "car and van." Westcott and Hort alleged that this is what the Textus Receptus did in the preceding eight examples. They said there were two parts to some texts, one part from "B" and "Aleph" their "true" text, and another part from some other manuscript. They claimed that the Textus Receptus took both parts and added them together. This is what Westcott and Hort called "conflation." If "conflation" were true to fact, wouldn't they be able to produce more than eight examples of it? Yet Westcott and Hort couldn't find any more than eight, and only three have any possible hope of being proper examples.

13.   **The False So-Called "Syrian Text Recension" of 250 and 350 A.D. Refuted.** Westcott and Hort wrote:

"The Syrian Text **[our Textus Receptus]** must in fact be the result of a 'Recension,' . . . performed deliberately by Editors, and not merely by Scribes." (*Introduction*, p. 133).

Dean Burgon answered them as follows:

"But *why* 'must' it? Instead of '*must in fact*,' we are disposed to read '*may-in fiction*.' The learned Critic can but mean that, on comparing the Text of Fathers of the IVth century with the Text of cod. B, it becomes to himself self-evident that *one of the two* has been fabricated. Granted. Then,--Why should not *the solitary Codex* be the offending party? . . . *why* (we ask) should *codex B* be upheld 'contra mundum'?" **[Against the whole world]** [Dean John W. Burgon, *Revision Revised*, pp. 272-73].

It is Codex "B" (the Vatican manuscript) versus the text of the Church Fathers of the 4th century. Both can't be right. One of the two must be fabricated. Can you guess which one Dean Burgon believes to be "fabricated"?

14.   **The False Alleged "Syrian Text Recension of 250 and 350 A.D. Only A Guess.** Dean Burgon wrote:

"Apart however from the gross intrinsic improbability of the supposed Recension,--the utter absence of one particle of evidence, traditional or otherwise, that it ever did take place, must be laid to be fatal to the hypothesis that it *did*. It is simply incredible that an incident of such magnitude and interest would leave no trace of itself in history. As a conjecture--(and it only professes to be a conjecture)--Dr. Hort's notion of how the Text of the Fathers of the IIIrd, IVth, and Vth centuries,--which, as he truly remarks, is in the main identical with our own *Received Text*,-- came into being, must be unconditionally abandoned." [Dean John W. Burgon, *Revision Revised*, pp. 293-94].

A "recension" of the Greek New Testament Text would mean that this text was fabricated by editors. The editor would throw out all the other contrary texts, and come up with just one text. There is not a scrap of history that tells anything about this event. This is a false theory, but they had to account for the fact that the Textus Receptus-type manuscripts have over 99% of the manuscript evidence behind it. Westcott and Hort had to say that someone made an editorial recension or revision of the New Testament. They then said that all of the Textus Receptus-type manuscripts were carbon copies of that original recension or revision. This is their false, flawed, and unhistorical hypothesis to account for 99% of the evidence.

   15.   The Importance of Refuting the False "Recension Theory" of Westcott and Hort. Dean Burgon wrote:

   "We have been so full on the subject of this imaginary `Antiochian' or `Syrian text,' not (the reader may be sure) without sufficient reason. Scant satisfaction truly is there in scattering to the winds an airy tissue which its ingenious authors have been industriously weaving for 30 years; But it is clear that with this hypothesis of a `Syrian' text,--the immediate source and actual prototype of the commonly received Text of the N.T.,--*stands or falls their entire Textual theory.* Reject it, and the entire fabric is observed to collapse, and subside into a shapeless ruin. And with it, of necessity, goes the `New Greek Text,'--and therefore the `*New English Version*' of our Revisionists, which in the main has been founded on it." [Dean John W. Burgon, *Revision Revised*, p. 294].

Westcott and Hort's whole house of cards will fall if their hypothesis falls. It does fall because there is no historical record that shows that anybody ever destroyed the many thousands of New Testament documents and edited the text down to just one document, a recension. This is absolutely false to history and cannot be proven to be true by any facts. The **theory** falls, the **text** falls, the English **translation** falls!

   16.   Westcott and Hort's Admission that the Textus Receptus Is the Greek Text Found Abundantly in the "Fourth Century." Many Westcott and Hort supporters claim that the text of our Textus Receptus kind of manuscripts is of a more recent date thatn "B" and "Aleph." Westcott and Hort admitted:

   "The fundamental text of the late extant Greek MSS generally is, beyond all question, identical with (what Dr. Hort chooses to call) the dominant Antiochian or Graeco-Syrian text of the second half of the IVth century . . . The Antiochian (and other) Fathers, and the bulk of extant MSS, written from about three or four, to ten or eleven centuries later, must have had, in the greater number of extant variations, a common original *either contemporary with, or older than, our oldest extant MSS.*" [Westcott & Hort, *Introduction to the Greek N.T.*, p. 92. quoted by Dean John W. Burgon, *Revision Revised*, p. 295].

Westcott and Hort admitted forthrightly that the Textus Receptus text is a 4th century text. They explained this fact by its being the result of a rescension/revision made in 250 A.D. and again in 350 A.D. Again, Westcott and Hort did not attempt to prove this, nor could they. It is merely a false hypothesis.

   17.   Dean Burgon Agrees Wholeheartedly with Westcott and Hort's

Admission that the Textus Receptus Was the Dominant Text of the Fourth Century A.D., But for Different Reasons. Dean Burgon wrote:

"So far then, happily, we are entirely agreed. The only question is--How is this resemblance to be accounted for? *Not*, we answer,--not, certainly, by putting forward so violent and improbable--as *irrational* a conjecture as that, first, about A.D. 250,--and then again about A.D. 350,--an authoritative standard Text was fabricated at Antioch; of which all other known MSS. (except a very little handful) are nothing else but transcripts; but rather, by loyally recognizing, in the practical identity of the Text exhibited by 99 out of 100 of our extant MSS, the probable general fidelity of those *many manuscripts to the inspired exemplars themselves from which remotely they are confessedly descended.*"

"And surely, if it be allowable to assume (with Dr. Hort) that for 1532 years, (viz. from A.D. 350 to A.D. 1882) the *Antiochian* standard has been faithfully retained and transmitted,--it will be impossible to assign any valid reason why the inspired Original itself, the *Apostolic* standard, should not have been as faithfully transmitted and retained from the Apostolic age to the Antiochian (*i.e.* say, from A.D. 90 to A.D. 250-350)--i.e. throughout an interval of less than 250 years, or *one-sixth* of the period." [Dean John W. Burgon, *Revision Revised*, pp. 295-96].

Dean Burgon is saying clearly that God has preserved His Words.

18.   More Explanation of the False "Recension" Theory of the Greek New Testament. Dean Burgon wrote:

"Drs. Westcott and Hort assume that this `Antiochian text'--found in the later cursives and the Fathers of the latter half of the IVth century--must be an *artificial*, an *arbitrarily invented* standard; a text *fabricated* between A.D. 250 and A.D. 350. And if they may but be so fortunate as to persuade the world to adopt their hypothesis, then all will be easy; for they will have reduced the supposed `consent of Fathers' to the reproduction of one and the same single `primary documentary witness': . . ."

"*Upset* the hypothesis on the other hand, and all is reversed in a moment. Every attesting Father is perceived to be a dated MS. and an independent authority; and the combined evidence of several of these becomes simply unmanageable. In like manner, `the approximate consent of the cursives' . . . is perceived to be equivalent *not* to `A PRIMARY DOCUMENTARY WITNESS,'--*not to* `ONE ANTIOCHIAN ORIGINAL,'--but to be tantamount to the articulate speech of *many* witnesses *of high character*, coming to us *from every quarter* of primitive Christendom." [Dean John W. Burgon, *Revision Revised*, pp. 296-97].

19.   The Vatican ("B") Manuscript Described. Dean Burgon wrote: "Behold then the altar at which Copies, Fathers, Versions, are all to be ruthlessly sacrificed,--the tribunal from which there shall be absolutely no appeal,--the Oracle which is to silence every doubt, resolve every riddle, smooth away every difficulty. All has been stated, where the name has been pronounced of--codex B." [Dean John W. Burgon, *Revision Revised*, p. 301].

Again, Dean Burgon uses the element of humor as he paints the picture of this false "altar" of "B" and "Aleph" worshiped by Westcott and Hort and their followers.

20.   The Fallacy of Worshiping the "B" (Vatican) Greek Manuscript.
Dean Burgon wrote:

"And then, by an unscrupulous use of the process of Reiteration, accompanied by a boundless exercise of the imaginative faculty, we have reached the goal to which all that went before has been steadily tending; viz. the absolute supremacy of codices B and Aleph above all other codices,--and when they differ, then of codex B. And yet, the `immunity from substantive error' of a lost Codex of *imaginary* date and *unknown* history cannot but be a pure imagination,--(a mistaken one, as we shall presently show,)-- of these respected Critics: while their proposed practical inference from it,--(viz. to regard two remote and confessedly depraved Copies of that original, as `*a safe criterion of genuineness,*')-- this, at all events, is the reverse of logical. In the meantime, the presumed proximity of the Text of Aleph and B to the Apostolic age is henceforth discoursed of as if it were no longer a matter of conjecture." [Dean John W. Burgon, *Revision Revised*, p. 304].

21.   An Explanation of Why the Vatican ("B) and the Sinai ("Aleph") Greek Manuscripts Survived for so Long. Dean Burgon wrote:

"Lastly,--We suspect that these two Manuscripts are indebted for their preservation, *solely to their ascertained evil character*; which has occasioned that the one eventually found its way, four centuries ago, to a forgotten shelf in the Vatican library; while the other, after exercising the ingenuity of several generations of critical Correctors, eventually (viz. in A.D. 1844) got deposited in the waste-paper basket of the Convent at the foot of Mount Sinai. Had B and Aleph been copies of average purity, they must long since have shared the inevitable fate of books which are freely *used* and highly prized; namely, they would have fallen into decadence and disappeared from sight." [Dean John W. Burgon, *Revision Revised*, p.319]

This is a powerful argument. Dean Burgon here explains why it is that "B" and "Aleph" were still in existence after so many centuries.

22.   Previous Veneration of the Vatican ("B") and the Sinai ("Aleph") Greek Manuscripts. Dean Burgon wrote:

"Since 1881, Editors have vied with one another in the fulsomeness of the homage they have paid to these `two false Witnesses,'--for such B and Aleph *are*, as the concurrent testimony of Copies, Fathers and Versions abundantly prove. Even superstitious reverence has been claimed for these two codices; and Drs. Westcott and Hort are so far in advance of their predecessors in the servility of their blind adulation; that they must be allowed to have easily won the race." [Dean John W. Burgon, *Revision Re-*

vised, pp. 319-20]

Westcott and Hort have won the race for being the leading "worshipers" of both
"B" and "Aleph."

23.   **The Preference for "B" (Vatican) and "Aleph" (Sinai) Is A
Superstition."** Dean Burgon wrote:

"B Aleph C . . . But when I find them hopelessly at *variance among themselves*: above all, when I find (1) *all other Manuscripts* of whatever date,--(2)
the *most ancient Versions*,--and (3) *the whole body of the primitive Fathers*,
decidedly opposed to them,--I am (to speak plainly) at a loss to understand
how any man of sound understanding acquainted with all the facts of the
case and accustomed to exact reasoning, can hesitate to regard the unsupported (or the *slenderly* supported) testimony of one or other of them as
simply worthless. The craven homage which the foremost of the three
[that is, manuscript "B"] habitually receives at the hands of Drs.
Westcott and Hort. I can only describe as a weak superstition. It is
something more than unreasonable. It becomes even ridiculous." [Dean
John W. Burgon, *Revision Revised*, p. 325]

24.   **The Illogical Nature of Concluding a Universal from a Very Few
Particulars.** Dean Burgon disagreed that Westcott and Hort could take a very
small number of particular examples of Antiquity and conclude a UNIVERSAL
about ALL Antiquity. He wrote:

"To make them **[that is, manuscripts "B" and "Aleph"]** the basis of
an induction is preposterous. It is not allowable to infer the universal from
the particular. If the bones of Goliath were to be discovered to-morrow,
would you propose as an induction therefrom that it was the fashion to
wear four-and-twenty fingers and toes on one's hands and feet in the days
of the giant of Gath?" [Dean John W. Burgon, *Revision Revised*, pp. 329-
30]

In logic, "induction" is the process whereby you take many particulars and then
arrive at a generalization or a universal drawn from those many particulars. From
just one, two, or a few specimens, you cannot come to any valid generalization,
universal, or conclusion.

25.   **Dean Burgon's Firsthand Manuscript Comparisons of "B,"
"Aleph," "C," and "D."** Dean Burgon wrote:

"On first seriously applying ourselves to these studies, many years ago, we
found it wondrous difficult to divest ourselves of prepossessions very like
your own. Turn which way we would, we were encountered by the same
confident terminology: **[We hear similar sentiments today!]**--'the
best documents,' **[this is a reference to "B" and "Aleph" of course]**--
'primary manuscripts,'--'first-rate authorities,'--'primitive evidence,'--
'ancient readings,'--and so forth: and we found that thereby cod. A or B,--
cod. C or D--*were invariably and exclusively meant"*

"It was not until we had laboriously collated these documents (including

Aleph) for ourselves that we became aware of their true character. Long before coming to the end of our task (and it occupied us, off and on, for eight years) we had become convinced that the supposed `best documents' and `first-rate authorities' are in reality among *the worst:--. . .* A diligent inspection of a vast number of later Copies scattered throughout the principal libraries of Europe, and the exact Collation of a few, further convinced us that the deference generally claimed for B, Aieph, C, D is nothing else but a weak superstition and a vulgar error:--that the date of a MS. is not of its essence, but is a mere accident of the problem." [Dean John W. Burgon, *Revision Revised*, p. 337]

26.   Dean Burgon's Best and Only Method of Seeking Proper New Testament Greek Readings. Dean Burgon wrote:

"We deem this laborious method the only true method, in our present state of imperfect knowledge: the method, namely, of *adopting that Reading which has the fullest, the widest, and the most varied attestation. Antiquity and Respectability of Witnesses,* are thus secured. How men can persuade themselves that 19 Copies out of every 20 may be safely disregarded, if they be but written in minuscule characters,--we fail to understand. To ourselves it seems simply an irrational proceeding. . . . As for building up a Text, (as Drs. Westcott and Hort have done) with special superstitious deference to *a single codex,*--we deem it about as reasonable as would be the attempt to build up a pyramid from its apex; in the expectation that it would stand firm on its extremity, and remain horizontal for ever." [Dean John W. Burgon, *Revision Revised*, p. 342]

27.   The Peculiar Mind-Set of the Westcott and Hort Followers—Even Those of Today. Dean Burgon wrote:

"Phantoms of the imagination **[That's where they begin.]** henceforth usurp the place of substantial forms. Interminable doubt,--wretched misbelief,--childish credulity,--judicial blindness,--are the inevitable sequel and penalty. The mind that has long allowed itself in a systematic trifling with Evidence, is observed to fall the easiest prey to Imposture. It has doubted what is *demonstrably* true: has rejected what is *indubitably* Divine. Henceforth, it is observed to mistake its own fantastic creations for historical facts; to believe things which rest on insufficient evidence, or on no evidence at all." [Dean John W. Burgon, *Revision Revised*, p. 350]

When you begin the descent down the slippery slope of phantomizing, rationalizing, and spiritualizing, this is where Dean Burgon stated it ends up. This is where Westcott and Hort ended up. This is where their modern day followers have ended up or will end up before long! It is a frightening prospect!

28.   For Dean Burgon, There Can Be No Compromise in the Battle for the Words of God. Dean Burgon wrote:

"Compromise of any sort between the two conflicting parties, is impossible also; for they simply contradict one another. Codd. B and Aleph are either among the purest of manuscripts,--or else they are among the very foulest.

The Text of Drs. Westcott and Hort is either the very best which has ever appeared,--or else it is the very worst; the nearest to the sacred Autographs,--or the furthest from them."

"There is no room for *both* opinions; and there cannot exist any middle ground. The question will have to be fought out; and it must be fought out fairly. It may not be magisterially settled; but must be advocated, on either side, by the old logical method. . . . The combatants may be sure that, in consequence of all that has happened, the public will be no longer indifferent spectators of the fray; for the issue concerns the inner life of the whole community,--touches men's heart of hearts. . . . GOD'S TRUTH will be, as it has been throughout, the one object of all our striving." [Dean John W. Burgon, *Revision Revised*, pp. 365-66]

a. Compromise not possible. Some people might ask if this is going to divide the church and separate us. Maybe it has come to that. Certainly, for Dean Burgon, there can be no compromise. Was Dean Burgon a fighter? Yes he was. He was a fighter for the right and for the very Words of God. Shouldn't we of the Dean Burgon Society, get Dean Burgon's spirit and also be fighters? Should we not be fighters for the right and for the very Words of God? Yes, yes we should.

b. The Question Will Have To Be "Fought Out." Was young David a fighter? Yes he was. Did David want to fight? No. Did he come out to fight? No, he just came out to bring his brothers some food when that giant, Goliath, came after him. We have Goliaths coming after us. Our precious Textus Receptus, the Masoretic Text, and our King James Bible are all under attack today. Yes, we do have Goliaths coming after us.

c. The Battle Must Be Fought "Fairly." There is nothing in my constitution that wants to be unfair. I want to fight only with truth. That's the only basis on which we can fight. I want to be kind, but I want to be firm. I believe Dean Burgon's writings follow this path. The battle cannot be decided by some judge who can declare one side or the other as the winner.

d. The "Public" Will Not Be "Indifferent Spectators." As Dean Burgon predicted, the "public" has indeed become interested in the battle for their Bible. This is important. The "public" was aroused in his day, and it is being aroused today. As Dean Burgon reminded us, "GOD'S TRUTH" must be the object of our striving in the Dean Burgon Society.

Consider some of the books that have been written to alert the general public concerning this problem. Dr. David Otis Fuller's books--*Which Bible, True or False,* and *Counterfeit or Genuine*--greatly assisted in this project. D. A. Carson wrote against Dr. Fuller's position

My own book, *Defending the King James Bible,* has made an impact as well. Mrs. Riplinger's book, *New Age Bible Versions,* which stands for the Textus Receptus and the King James Bible, has sold over 100,000 copies The BIBLE FOR TODAY has reprinted some 900 titles in defense of the Masoretic Hebrew, the Textus Receptus, and the King James Bible in an effort to make available the facts in this area. James White's recent book opposes these positions.

In 1995, the Dean Burgon Society reprinted, in perfect binding, their 400-page edition of Dean Burgon's book, *The Last Twelve Verses of Mark.* In December, 1996, the DEAN BURGON SOCIETY published Dean Burgon's book, *The Revision Revised.* This is a 640-page hardback edition. The DEAN BURGON SOCIETY, at its annual meetings, has also contributed much information on this theme throughout its present eighteen years of existence. These messages are all centered on the main theme, "IN DEFENSE OF TRADITIONAL BIBLE TEXTS." The messages are available as audio cassettes, video cassettes, and in writing in the DBS MESSAGE BOOKS.

Many other writers for the side of the Masoretic Text, the Textus Receptus, and the King James Bible position have contributed to this "public" educational mission, including, but not limited to the following: Rev. David Cloud of the Way of Life Ministries; Dr. Jack Moorman, missionary in Great Britain; Dr. Edward Hills; Mr. Everett Fowler; Mr. Cecil Carter; Dr. Bob Barnett; Pastor Bob Steward; D. A. Waite, Jr.; and many others.

V
CONCLUSION

A. *The Revision Revised* **Can Be Used to Combat Current False Greek Texts.** There is no one book that exposes Westcott and Hort's false Greek text and false Greek theory behind that text any more thoroughly and convincingly than *The Revision Revised.* Dean Burgon defends the traditional text of the New Testament. He also shows clearly the defects in both manuscript "B" (Vatican) and manuscript "Aleph" (Sinai). It is very important to see the arguments contained in this historic volume. Virtually the same Greek text of Westcott and Hort (1881) has been used for almost all of the modern versions and perversions. As proof of this, you can turn back to pages 2-3 for seven quotes that tie the Westcott and Hort's Greek text to that of Nestle-Aland and the United Bible Society. Therefore, *The Revision Revised* forms a strong basis for a refutation of the false Greek texts and theories rampant today which form the basis for the modern English versions.

B. **Why Westcott and Hort's Text Is So Similar to Current Greek Texts.** It is very easy to understand why the 1881 Greek Text of Westcott and Hort is almost the same as that of the modern revised Greek Texts such as Nestle-Aland, United Bible Society and others. Both groups (Westcott and Hort and modern textual revisers) draw largely, if not exclusively, on the false readings of manuscripts "B" (Vatican) and "Aleph" (Sinai). It is axiomatic that "things equal to the same thing are equal to each other."

C. **The Excellence of** *The Revision Revised.* This present book, *The Revision Revised,* is another of Dean John William Burgon's masterpieces. It contains, as do all of his books, overwhelming evidence from manuscripts, lectionaries, ancient versions, and church fathers showing clearly three deficiencies: (1) The **deficient Greek Text** of Westcott and Hort; (2) The **deficient English translation** based upon it; and (3) The **deficient theory** underlying the Greek text. His arguments are powerful and convincing!

D. *The Revision Revised* **Can Be Used to Combat Current False Modern Versions.** In the way Dean Burgon repudiates the English Revised Version of 1881 and **defends the Authorized King James Bible,** this book will also form a strong basis for defending the King James Bible against the modern versions such as the ASV, RSV, NASV, NIV, TEV, NIV, NRSV, CEV, the footnotes in the study edition of the NKJV, and many others.

INDEX

About the Author

The author of this booklet, Dr. D. A. Waite, received a B.A. (Bachelor of Arts) in classical Greek and Latin from the University of Michigan in 1948, a Th.M. (Master of Theology), with high honors, in New Testament Greek Literature and Exegesis from Dallas Theological Seminary in 1952, an M.A. (Master of Arts) in Speech from Southern Methodist University in 1953, a Th.D. (Doctor of Theology), with honors, in Bible Exposition from Dallas Theological Seminary in 1955, and a Ph.D. in Speech from Purdue University in 1961. He holds both New Jersey and Pennsylvania teacher certificates in Greek and Language Arts.

He has been a teacher in the areas of Greek, Hebrew, Bible, Speech, and English for over thirty-five years in nine schools, including one junior high, one senior high, three Bible institutes, two colleges, two universities, and one seminary. He served his country as a Navy Chaplain for five years on active duty; pastored two churches; was Chairman and Director of the Radio and Audio-Film Commission of the American Council of Christian Churches; since 1971, has been Founder, President, and Director of THE BIBLE FOR TODAY; since 1978, has been President of the DEAN BURGON SOCIETY; has produced over 700 other studies, booklets, cassettes, or VCR's on various topics; and is heard on both a five-minute daily and thirty-minute weekly radio program IN DEFENSE OF TRADITIONAL BIBLE TEXTS, presently on 25 stations. Dr. and Mrs. Waite have been married since 1948; they have four sons, one daughter, and, at present, eight grandchildren.

Order Blank

Name:_____

Address:_____

City & State:_____Zip:_____

Credit Card #:_____Expires:_____

[ ] **Enclosed is $_____.** Send _____copy(ies) of *Westcott &*
   Hort's Greek Text & Theory Refuted by Burgon's Revision
   Revised **(39 pages) each for a GIFT of $3.00 + $2.00 P&H**
   Ask for quantity prices on this new booklet!
[ ] Send the **"DBS Articles of Faith & Organization"** (N.C.)
[ ] Send **Brochure #1: "900 Titles Defending KJB/TR"** (N.C.)
[ ] Send information on **DBS pamphlets** on KJB & T.R. (N.C.)
[ ] **Send *The Revision Revised* by Dean Burgon ($25 + $3)**
   A hardback book c. 640 pages in length. Due out 12/96.
[ ] **Send *The Last 12 Verses of Mark* by Dean Burgon ($15+$3)**
   A perfect bound paperback book c. 400 pages in length.
[ ] Send *The Traditional Text* by Dean Burgon ($15 + $3)
[ ] Send *The Causes of Corruption* by Dean Burgon ($14 + $3)
[ ] Send *Inspiration and Interpretation*, Dean Burgon ($25+$3)
[ ] Send *Defending the King James Bible* by Dr. Waite ($12 + $3)
[ ] Send *Guide to Textual Criticism* by Edward Miller ($7 + $3)
[ ] Send *Heresies of Westcott & Hort* by Dr.D.A. Waite ($3+$2)
[ ] Send *Westcott's Denial of Resurrection*, Dr. Waite ($4+$2)
[ ] Send *Four Reasons for Defending KJB* by Dr. Waite ($2+$2)
[ ] Send *Vindicating Mark 16:9-20* by Dr. D. A. Waite ($3 + $2)
[ ] Send *Dean Burgon's Confidence in KJB* by Dr. Waite ($3+$2)
[ ] Send *Readability of A.V. (KJB)* by D. A. Waite, Jr. ($5 + $3)

Send or Call Orders to:
THE BIBLE FOR TODAY
900 Park Ave., Collingswood, NJ 08108
Phone: 856-854-4452; FAX:--2464; Orders: 1-800 JOHN 10:9
E-Mail Orders: BFT@BibleForToday,org Credit Card OK

the
BIBLE
FOR
TODAY

900 Park Avenue
Collingswood, NJ 08108
Phone: 856-854-4452
www.BibleForToday.org

B.F.T. #2695

SEND GIFT SUBSCRIPTIONS!
All gifts to Dean Burgon Society are tax deductible!

THE DEAN BURGON SOCIETY
Box 354, Collingswood, New Jersey 08108, U.S.A. • Phone (609) 854-4452

MEMBERSHIP FORM

I have a copy of the **"Articles of Faith, Operation, and Organization"** of **The Dean Burgon Society, Incorporated.** After reading these **"Articles,"** I wish to state, by my signature below, that I believe in and accept such **"Articles."** I understand that my "Membership" is for one year and that I must renew my "Membership" at that time in order to remain a "Member" in good standing of the Society.

( ) I wish to become a member of **The Dean Burgon Society** for the first time.
( ) I wish to **renew** my membership subscription which has expired as of:_____

SIGNED _____

DATE _____

I enclose   **Attention: The Dean Burgon Society**
                 Box 354, Collingswood, New Jersey 08108
*Membership Donation ($7.00/year) $ _____
*Life Membership Donation ($50.00) $ _____
*Additional Donation to the Society $ _____
               TOTAL $ _____

Please PRINT in CAPITAL LETTERS your name and address below:

NAME_____

ADDRESS _____

CITY_____STATE_____ ZIP _____

Although I am not a member of **The Dean Burgon Society,** I do wish to sub-scribe to the **newsletter** by making a gift of $3.50 to the Society.

NAME_____

ADDRESS _____

CITY_____STATE_____ ZIP _____

*I understand that, included in my first **$3.50 gift** accompanying any donatioin or order — regardless of the amount of the order or donation — is my year's subscription to **The Dean Burgon Society NEWSLETTER.**

Canada and All Foreign Subscriptions $7.00 Yearly

Order Blank (p.1)

Name:_____

Address:_____

City & State:_____Zip:_____

Credit Card #:_____Expires:_____

[ ] **Enclosed is $_____. Send _____copy(ies) of *The Revision Revised* (640 pages) each for a GIFT of $25 +$5)**
Ask for quantity prices on this new book!

[ ] Send *The Last 12 Verses of Mark* by Dean Burgon **($15+$4)**
A perfect bound paperback book c. 400 pages in length.

[ ] Send *The Traditional Text* by Dean Burgon **($16 + $4)**
A hardback book, 384 pages.

[ ] Send *The Causes of Corruption* by Dean Burgon **($15 + $4)**
A hardback book, 360 pages.

[ ] Send *Inspiration and Interpretation*, Dean Burgon **($25+$5)**
A hardback book, 610 pages.

[ ] Send *Forever Settled*, by Dr. Jack Moorman **($20+$4)**
A hardback book, 300 pages.

[ ] Send *Defending the King James Bible* by Dr. D. A. Waite,
A hardback book, 352 pages, ($12+$4)

[ ] Send *Defined King James Bible*, large print **($40+$6)**; medium
print **($35+$4) Genuine leather, uncommon words defined**
accurately in the footnotes.. Case prices upon request.

[ ] Send *Scrivener's Annotated Greek New Testament* ($35+$4
hardback) ($45+$4 genuine leather).

[ ] Send the **"DBS Articles of Faith & Organization"** (N.C.)
[ ] Send **Brochure #1: "1000 Titles Defending KJB/TR"** (N.C.)

Send or Call Orders to:
THE BIBLE FOR TODAY
900 Park Ave., Collingswood, NJ 08108
Phone: 856-854-4452; FAX:--2464; Orders: 1-800 JOHN 10:9
E-Mail Orders: DBS@DeanBurgonSociety.org
www.DeanBurgonSociety.org

Order Blank (p.2)

Name:_____

Address:_____

City & State:_____Zip:_____

*Credit Card #:*_____*Expires:*_____

Other Books on the King James Bible

[ ] Send *Westcott & Hort's Greek Text & Theory Refuted by Burgon's Revision Revised--Summarized* by Dr. D. A. Waite **($3.00 + $2.00)**

[ ] Send *Defending the King James Bible* by Dr. Waite **($12 + $3)**

[ ] Send *Guide to Textual Criticism* by Edward Miller **($7 + $3)**

[ ] Send *Heresies of Westcott & Hort* by Dr. D.A. Waite **($3+$2)**

[ ] Send *Westcott's Denial of Resurrection*, Dr. Waite **($4+$2)**

[ ] Send *Four Reasons for Defending KJB* by Dr. Waite **($2+$2)**

[ ] Send *Vindicating Mark 16:9-20* by Dr. D. A. Waite **($3 + $2)**

[ ] Send *Dean Burgon's Confidence in KJB* by Dr. Waite **($3+$2)**

[ ] Send *Readability of A.V. (KJB)* by D. A. Waite, Jr. **($5 + $3)**

Send or Call Orders to:
THE BIBLE FOR TODAY
900 Park Ave., Collingswood, NJ 08108
Phone: 856-854-4452; FAX:--2464; Orders: 1-800 JOHN 10:9
E-Mail Orders: DBS@DeanBurgonSociety.org
www.DeanBurgonSociety.org

CPSIA information can be obtained at www.ICGtesting.com
Printed in the USA
BVOW040435200112

280985BV00007B/20/P